AMERICAN GOVERNMENT
Readings and Cases

AMERICAN GOVERNMENT
Readings and Cases

THIRD EDITION

PETER WOLL Brandeis University

 Little, Brown and Company Boston

LIBRARY OF CONGRESS CATALOG CARD NO. 69-19149

THIRD PRINTING

Printed simultaneously in Canada by
Little, Brown & Company (Canada) Limited

PRINTED IN THE UNITED STATES OF AMERICA

5-19-72

THIS BOOK IS DEDICATED TO

John W. Woll
AND
Ruth C. Woll

Preface

This book is designed to supplement standard textbooks in the introductory college course in American government. It provides readings, with explanatory notes, to stimulate student interest in the major areas generally covered.

In making the selections for this and the earlier editions, I have placed strong emphasis upon those materials used for the core parts of the American government course: the general nature of political analysis and political systems; the nature and origins of constitutional theory and practice; the relationship between the national government and the states; the organization and functions of political parties, the role of elections, and the nature of electoral behavior; interest groups; the responsibilities, powers, and limitations of the President; the structure and functions of Congress, and the environment of congressional decision making; the judicial process; the structure, functions, and role of the bureaucracy; and finally, selected policy outputs of the political system, including civil liberties and civil rights, electoral reapportionment, the economic role of government, urban problems, and foreign policy.

The book offers readings from current research, and cases in politics and constitutional law. New selections in this edition reflect the increasing emphasis being placed upon the nature of political analysis and the characteristics of political systems. Other areas receiving increased attention include the bureaucracy and, in the policy field, urban problems.

Another innovation in this edition is the numbering of each selection, making it easy to adapt the book to any course plan. At the same time, the sequence of selections has its own logic, progressing from political analysis and a theoretical discussion of political systems, to a consideration of the context of the American system, the channels of participation, the structures of government, and finally the policy outputs of the system.

The author has been helped immeasurably in the preparation of this and previous editions by the thoughtful comments of many. I would particularly like to thank James Prothro, Allan Sindler, Frank Sorauf, and Nelson Polsby for their assistance with the third edition. Also the comments of A. Lee Fritschler, F. Lee Harrell, M. Glenn Abernathy, Merrill Jacobs, Parris Glendening, J. S. Moon, Charles Pyles, Gottlieb Baer, Herbert Stephens, Frederick Zuercher, Gary London, William Brigman, Glenn Morgan, Paul Willis, and Thomas Laughlin have been a great help. The general development of the book has been aided by George Brasington, Bernard C. Cohen, I. Ridgway Davis, Earl F. Kohler, Robert L. Peabody, Robert L. Peterson, John H. Schaar, Karl M. Schmidt, and Robert G. Thompson.

Finally, I am especially indebted to my wife, Mary, as well as to Bob and Cindy Woll, who have always given the kind of generous support that makes possible the undertaking and completion of projects such as this one.

P.W.

Contents

ix

CHAPTER TWELVE

AMERICAN GOVERNMENT
Readings and Cases

PART I

INTRODUCTION

CHAPTER ONE

The Study of Government

All governments are a product of the societies within which they function, and societies are in turn profoundly affected by the actions of their governments. The links between governments and their societies are highly complex, always changing, often obscured, and present in virtually every facet of human existence. Consequently, it is a formidable challenge to attempt to understand the significance of government and the governmental process.

While almost everything can be considered relevant to the study of government, it would be unmanageable to approach the subject with such an undefined and wide-ranging perspective. On the other hand, it would be unrealistic and misleading simply to focus upon the formal structure of government: the constitutions, laws and regulations, offices and institutions, procedures, and official actions. A multitude of informal forces that we customarily include within the term "politics" cannot be ignored. Indeed, they have more to do with the nature and impact of the governmental process than do the formal arrangements prescribing the official operations and actions of government. The following selection by Harold Lasswell develops a frame of reference that should help students as they embark upon their study of the American political process.

1   HAROLD LASSWELL

POLITICS: WHO GETS WHAT, WHEN, HOW

When you have been away from an American town for a while and ask what has happened in politics you are told who has been

From the postscript to Harold Lasswell, *Politics: Who Gets What, When, How.* Postscript © 1958 by Meridian Books, Inc., pp. 181–87, 207, 208. Reprinted by permission of the publisher.

elected to what office, or appointed to which job. It will not be hard to discover whose political star is rising or falling, and who is working with or against whom. Jones, it appears, has broken with Smith and run against him in the last election. Smith, we are told, alienated the Negro vote on the school issue, and lost trade union support by his stand when the municipal employees struck. We may hear that Jones now has the support of the State Democratic machine, and has a good chance for the Governorship. Smith has strong friends in Washington and rumor says that he will soon be taken care of with a Federal job. And so on and on.

Now is this what politics is about? If so we may very well ask why anybody bothers to study the subject. Any well-informed journalist, lobbyist, interest group representative, or lawyer would seem to know all there is to know; and besides, he keeps up to date.

The same question can be raised about business. If you want to know what has been happening find a business acquaintance or a business reporter and ask him. He can summarize which stocks have been going up or down, which firms have been expanding or shrinking, and who is now on the list of richest men or women. Is there any point to studying economics when such information is readily at hand?

If we are in a question raising mood skepticism may extend to every other sphere of social life. Take churches, for example. It is possible to find an individual who is informed about changes in the number of churches and in their membership, and who can say which clergymen have become more or less popular as public personalities.

Or take educational institutions. We can learn who holds top administrative posts in the colleges, high schools, grade schools and vocational schools of the region. Information is available about number of students and trends in the level of excellence in mathematics, the sciences, and other subjects of examination.

Consider such agencies of public enlightenment as radio-TV, newspapers, magazines and books. We can quickly identify the most important publishers and station owners, and the best known commentators. Regular readers or viewers will report whether there has been a change in the amount of space or time spent on civic affairs.

If we ask about family life we may be told that the Hills section is full of broken homes, and of neighborhood quarrels. On the other hand certain new districts are said to be full of congenial people who like to do things together.

Congeniality may be closely connected with the social acceptability of an area. The persons in the Hills section, for instance, were once among the most respected elements of the community. But families of social prestige, we are told, have moved out. We may learn in fact that top-drawer families have moved outside the city limits.

We may hear a great deal about the state of safety, health and comfort during recent times. New traffic systems have cut down the accident rate. Better alarm systems are credited with having reduced burglaries and other crimes. New hospitals have become available; and many long standing nuisances, like loud factory whistles, smoke and open garbage dumps, have disappeared.

As our information begins to catch up with events in the community our questions about government and politics take on a different character. Instead of asking about individual careers we begin to inquire about the role government has played in connection with the changes that have been going on throughout the entire community.

Consider business, for instance. We are asking to what extent the bonding authority of the municipality has been used to obtain the capital necessary to install an airport, to relocate freight and passenger terminals, to clear new industrial districts. Or churches. Has the planning authority of the city been used to make strategic sites available to churches in all the communities that have developed around the new shopping service centers? Educational institutions. Of the total amount of money that goes into education at every level (and for every professional, occupational and artistic skill) how much has been raised by government? (Local? State? National?) Think of the media of public enlightenment. Has the government channel of action been used to establish radio-TV stations in order to break up a private monopoly? And to encourage further diversity by encouraging independent or competing services to come into the locality? Consider family and neighborhood life. Has the government been alert enough to arrest the disintegration of residential neighborhoods by using its planning authority to give protection against non-residential encroachments? And to make sites available for community facilities needed for a constructive common life? Are governmental authorities awake to the challenge of "upgrading" socially disrespected groups by the use of residential building and neighborhood development projects? Has the government been effectively employed to take the initiatives required to cut down accidents, disease, physical violence, and public nuisances?

To raise such questions is to bring into the open the need of a more comprehensive picture of government and politics than can come from casual interviewing and reading. A map of public affairs is required that is carefully researched and systematically organized. Obviously the preparation of such a map is beyond the professional duty of a city councilman or a newspaper editor. Hence we are brought to the professional student of government, the political scientist. It is his special task to provide a comprehensive account of what governments are doing. This implies that he must go far beyond the limits of one city or county. If the significance of local trends is to be grasped it must be seen in the perspective of the region and the nation; and some important points will appear when the national picture is supplemented with information about trends in Canada and other nations whose tradition is predominantly English. We also share many historic and contemporary traits and interests with the peoples of Western Europe; and the years are gradually bringing us into closer contact with the new nations of the world.

We depend upon specialized students of government to hold mirrors up to the government and politics of any locality. One mirror is statewide or regional; another is sectional or national; another is continental, or hemispherical, or oceanic (e.g., the Atlantic, the Pacific). It may be a traditional area with many cultural characteristics in common (the English-speaking peoples), a major bloc in world politics (the Soviet world), or the world as a whole.

It is quite impossible to examine phenomena of such range, interest and practicality without raising a host of questions. A basic issue is the effect of relying exclusively upon the channel of government to carry out a given social activity; or of leaving the matter almost entirely to private initiatives, or of striking a balance at a point between. Assuming that some activities are to be within the province of government many problems of organization appear. How centralized shall the organization be (internationally, nationally, regionally, locally)? At any "horizontal" level, like the metropolitan district, how concentrated shall the top decisions be (in one organ? two or more co-ordinate organs)? In regard to the decisions taken at any level how active shall the electorate (with what qualifications) be?

Even this abbreviated list is enough to remind the informed reader of scores of issues that relate to the organization of government at every level. Such questions are the professional stock in trade of scholars who variously describe themselves as specialists on comparative government, public administration, and public law.

Most of the problems mentioned deal directly with the "structure" of government; and we have implied that the expert who contributes to their solution is a student of "government." This usage is unobjectionable provided that it is not assumed to imply that the expert limits his study to the organized details of official agencies. We believe that no important conclusion can be reached that does not rest upon a wider basis of knowledge than the structural details of government agencies.

THE CONTEXTUAL APPROACH

The fundamental importance of the contextual requirement can be recognized if, for instance, we refresh our memories about some facts of municipal government. I refer to the mode of apportioning a city council. In the city government of the United States during the nineteenth century the prestige of the Federal Constitution was such that cities fashioned themselves in the image of Federal systems. City legislatures were often split into two chambers; and councillors were chosen from territorial constituencies (wards). Because corruption became rampant in city government the tendency has been to repudiate both "bicameralism" and wards. Even professional students of government not infrequently assume that local legislatures, when elected by districts, are predestined to corruption. It is possible to show that such an assertion is false. English municipalities were relatively free of corruption at the time American cities were brimming with bribery and favoritism; and English councils were chosen by ward. An explanation might be that the people who went into city government in England, or who kept watch on local affairs, made different demands upon government and upon themselves in relation to government than their opposite numbers in America. Interviews with knowledgeable persons would, in all probability, quickly confirm this hypothesis.

Studies that give attention to the context in which formal structures of government operate are often called studies of "politics" rather than "government." This distinction is not only vague; it has created confusion by using two words ("government," "politics") to cover the same frame of reference. In the present discussion we use the term "politics" as the global word, leaving "government" free to receive a more specialized meaning. The important point, however, is not to standardize the term but to underscore the point that, irrespective of terms, no detail of governmental organization can be fully understood apart from its relationship to the context of which it is part. This is the contextual principle (or, synonymously, the configurative principle) of politics.

FIVE KEY QUESTIONS

It becomes apparent, as we have seen in connection with our initial allusions to city affairs, that five questions are pertinent to every political situation:

What goal values are to be sought?
What are the trends in the realization of values?
What factors condition trends?
What projections characterize the probable course of future developments?
What policy alternatives will bring the greatest net realization of values?

Goals. The first question is the traditional problem of political philosophy.

Trends. The second suggests the special task of political and social history.

Conditions. The third is the scientific question. It calls for the systematic statement of theory and the use of empirical methods of gathering and processing data.

Projections. The projecting of future lines of political change is less commonly cultivated as a systematic intellectual task than the others — and this, despite the fact that all decisions depend upon assumptions about the future.

Alternatives. Students of politics are expected to have something pertinent to offer about the probable effects of adopting one form of government or another, or one policy or another relating to power. . . .

THE SCIENTIFIC FRAME OF REFERENCE

. . . The scientific mode of thinking proceeds by formulating a theoretical model of how selected factors condition one another, and confronts the theory with observable "reality." The most comprehensive theories seek to explain the conditions under which one outcome is preferred over another and is in fact achieved. It is essential to distinguish between subjective events of "preference" and outcomes actually "achieved," since objectives are often pursued and remain unattained. The factors contributing to this disparity must be included in a comprehensive explanation of decision. . . .

It is to be noticed that participants [in the political process] are not only isolated individuals acting on their own, but groups of individuals acting together in varying degree as presure groups, parties, government organs and the like. Theories of decision must also account for the demands and expectations made in the name of collectivities.

The political process can be analyzed with all its complexity if the value-institution analysis is fully applied. We think of politics in terms of *participants* (with identifications, demands, expectations; with control over base values) interacting in *arenas* (situations in which decision outcomes are expected) employing *strategies* to maximize value indulgences over deprivations by influencing *decision outcomes* and hence *effects.*

Lasswell's article makes it clear that the study of government must take into account a variety of environmental factors. It is impossible to understand the governmental process merely by examining the formal aspects of political institutions; rather, the context within which government functions must be analyzed to find those forces that determine the sources, uses, distribution, and effects of political power. One of the most fruitful ways to analyze government is to think of it as part of a broad *political system*, the components of which interconnect to produce varying results. A political system is more than a series of formal governmental institutions. All countries of the world have political systems that can be categorized by the nature of their component parts, some of which are the demands made upon the system, the supports given to it, the nature of the governmental structures through which the demands pass (including the character and distribution of formal authority), and finally the "outputs" of the system — the public policy that is developed and applied.

A political system is very different from other social systems, such as business organizations, clubs, fraternities, labor unions, agricultural groups, and all *private* groups. Like a political system, each of these private or semi-private organizations is a social system, possessing differing demands and governing structures; but in a political system, unlike other social systems, the outputs have a compulsory effect and are binding upon all members of the community. Political outputs derive their legitimacy from the fact that they are based upon the sovereignty of the state or, in democratic countries, of the people. The concept of sovereignty justifies and indeed necessitates making the decisions of government, arrived at through the interplay of the components of the political system, binding upon the citizenry. In addition to its formal authority, the state possesses a monopoly of force, and therefore can enforce its decisions. No private organization has this ability. Private organizations can enforce decisions only within the boundaries of the private group, which makes their decisions less compelling than those of a political system. Moreover, it is much easier to withdraw from a private system than from the jurisdiction of a government. The attributes of a political system are examined in the next selection.

2   DAVID EASTON

AN APPROACH TO THE ANALYSIS
OF POLITICAL SYSTEMS

I. SOME ATTRIBUTES OF POLITICAL SYSTEMS

In an earlier work I have argued for the need to develop general, empirically oriented theory as the most economical way in the long run to understand political life. Here I propose to indicate a point of view that, at the least, might serve as a springboard for discussion of alternative approaches and, at most, as a small step in the direction of a general political theory. I wish to stress that what I have to say is a mere orientation to the problem of theory; outside of economics and perhaps psychology, it would be presumptuous to call very much in social science "theory," in the strict sense of the term.

Furthermore, I shall offer only a Gestalt of my point of view, so that it will be possible to evaluate, in the light of the whole, those parts that I do stress. In doing this, I know I run the definite risk that the meaning and implications of this point of view may be only superficially communicated; but it is a risk I shall have to undertake since I do not know how to avoid it sensibly.

The study of politics is concerned with understanding how authoritative decisions are made and executed for a society. We can try to understand political life by viewing each of its aspects piecemeal. We can examine the operation of such institutions as political parties, interest groups, government, and voting; we can study the nature and consequences of such political practices as manipulation, propaganda, and violence; we can seek to reveal the structure within which these practices occur. By combining the results we can obtain a rough picture of what happens in any self-contained political unit.

In combining these results, however, there is already implicit the notion that each part of the larger political canvas does not stand alone but is related to each other part; or, to put it positively, that the operation of no one part can be fully understood without reference to the way in which the whole itself operates. I have suggested in my book,

From David Easton, "An Approach to the Analysis of Political Systems," *World Politics*, Vol. IX (April 1957). The framework outlined in this article has since its publication been elaborated in two books: *A Framework for the Analysis of Political Systems* (Prentice-Hall, 1965) and *A Systems Analysis of Political Life* (John Wiley & Sons, 1965). Reprinted by permission of the author and the publisher.

The Political System,[1] that it is valuable to adopt this implicit assumption as an articulate premise for research and to view political life as a system of interrelated activities. These activities derive their relatedness or systemic ties from the fact that they all more or less influence the way in which authoritative decisions are formulated and executed for a society.

Once we begin to speak of political life as a system of activity, certain consequences follow for the way in which we can undertake to analyze the working of a system. The very idea of a system suggests that we can separate political life from the rest of social activity, at least for analytical purposes, and examine it as though for the moment it were a self-contained entity surrounded by, but clearly distinguishable from, the environment or setting in which it operates. In much the same way, astronomers consider the solar system a complex of events isolated for certain purposes from the rest of the universe.

Furthermore, if we hold the system of political actions as a unit before our mind's eye, as it were, we can see that what keeps the system going are inputs of various kinds. These inputs are converted by the processes of the system into outputs and these, in turn, have consequences both for the system and for the environment in which the system exists. The formula here is very simple but, as I hope to show, also very illuminating: inputs — political system or processes — outputs. These relationships are shown diagrammatically in Figure 1. This diagram represents a very primitive "model" — to dignify it with a fashionable name — for approaching the study of political life.

FIGURE ONE

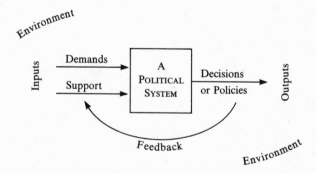

Political systems have certain properties because they are systems. To present an over-all view of the whole approach, let me identify the major attributes, say a little about each, and then treat one of these properties at somewhat greater length, even though still inadequately.

[1] New York, 1953.

1. *Properties of Identification.* To distinguish a political system from other social systems, we must be able to identify it by describing its fundamental units and establishing the boundaries that demarcate it from units outside the system.

a. Units of a Political System. The units are the elements of which we say a system is composed. In the case of a political system, they are political actions. Normally it is useful to look at these as they structure themselves in political roles and political groups.

b. Boundaries. Some of the most significant questions with regard to the operation of political systems can be answered only if we bear in mind the obvious fact that a system does not exist in a vacuum. It is always immersed in a specific setting or environment. The way in which a system works will be in part a function of its response to the total social, biological, and physical environment.

The special problem with which we are confronted is how to distinguish systematically between a political system and its setting. Does it even make sense to say that a political system has a boundary dividing it from its setting? If so, how are we to identify the line of demarcation?

Without pausing to argue the matter, I would suggest that it is useful to conceive of a political system as having a boundary in the same sense as a physical system. The boundary of a political system is defined by all those actions more or less directly related to the making of binding decisions for a society; every social action that does not partake of this characteristic will be excluded from the system and thereby will automatically be viewed as an external variable in the environment.

2. *Inputs and Outputs.* Presumably, if we select political systems for special study, we do so because we believe that they have characteristically important consequences for society, namely, authoritative decisions. These consequences I shall call the outputs. If we judged that political systems did not have important outputs for society, we would probably not be interested in them.

Unless a system is approaching a state of entropy — and we can assume that this is not true of most political systems — it must have continuing inputs to keep it going. Without inputs the system can do no work; without outputs we cannot identify the work done by the system. The specific research tasks in this connection would be to identify the inputs and the forces that shape and change them, to trace the processes through which they are transformed into outputs, to describe the general conditions under which such processes can be maintained, and to establish the relationship between outputs and succeeding inputs of the system.

From this point of view, much light can be shed on the working of a political system if we take into account the fact that much of what happens within a system has its birth in the efforts of the members of the system to cope with the changing environment. We can appreciate this point if we consider a familiar biological system such as the human organism. It is subject to constant stress from its surroundings to which it must adapt in one way or another if it is not to be completely destroyed. In part, of course, the way in which the body works represents responses to needs that are generated by the very organization of its anatomy and functions; but in large part, in order to understand both the structure and the working of the body, we must also be very sensitive to the inputs from the environment.

In the same way, the behavior of every political system is to some degree imposed upon it by the kind of system it is, that is, by its own structure and internal needs. But its behavior also reflects the strains occasioned by the specific setting within which the system operates. It may be argued that most of the significant changes within a political system have their origin in shifts among the external variables. Since I shall be devoting the bulk of this article to examining some of the problems related to the exchange between political systems and their environments, I shall move on to a rapid description of other properties of political systems.

3. *Differentiation within a System.* As we shall see in a moment, from the environment come both energy to activate a system and information with regard to which the system uses this energy. In this way a system is able to do work. It has some sort of output that is different from the input that enters from the environment. We can take it as a useful hypothesis that if a political system is to perform some work for anything but a limited interval of time, a minimal amount of differentiation in its structure must occur. In fact, empirically it is impossible to find a significant political system in which the same units all perform the same activities at the same time. The members of a system engage in at least some minimal division of labor that provides a structure within which action takes place.

4. *Integration of a System.* This fact of differentiation opens up a major area of inquiry with regard to political systems. Structural differentiation sets in motion forces that are potentially disintegrative in their results for the system. If two or more units are performing different kinds of activity at the same time, how are these activities to be brought into the minimal degree of articulation necessary if the members of the system are not to end up in utter disorganization with regard to the production of the outputs of interest to us? We can hypothesize that if a structured system is to maintain itself, it must provide mechanisms whereby its members are integrated or induced to cooperate in some minimal degree so that they can make authoritative decisions.

II. Inputs: Demands

Now that I have mentioned some major attributes of political systems that I suggest require special attention if we are to develop a generalized approach, I want to consider in greater detail the way in which an examination of inputs and outputs will shed some light on the working of these systems.

Among inputs of a political system there are two basic kinds: demands and support. These inputs give a political system its dynamic character. They furnish it both with the raw material or information that the system is called upon to process and with the energy to keep it going.

The reason why a political system emerges in a society at all — that is, why men engage in political activity — is that demands are being made by persons or groups in the society that cannot all be fully satisfied. In all societies one fact dominates political life: scarcity prevails with regard to most of the valued things. Some of the claims for these relatively scarce things never find their way into the political system but are satisfied through the private negotiations of or settlements by the persons involved. Demands for prestige may find satisfaction through the status relations of society; claims for wealth are met in part through the economic system; aspirations for power find expression in educational, fraternal, labor, and similar private organizations. Only where wants require some special organized effort on the part of society to settle them authoritatively may we say that they have become inputs of the political system.

Systematic research would require us to address ourselves to several key questions with regard to these demands.

1. How do demands arise and assume their particular character in a society? In answer to this question, we can point out that demands have their birth in two sectors of experience: either in the environment of a system or within the system itself. We shall call these the external and internal demands, respectively.

Let us look at the external demands first. I find it useful to see the environment not as an undifferentiated mass of events but rather as systems clearly distinguishable from one another and from the political system. In the environment we have such systems as the ecology, economy, culture, personality, social structure, and demography. Each of these constitutes a major set of variables in the setting that helps to shape the kind of demands entering a political system. For purposes of illustrating what I mean, I shall say a few words about culture.

The members of every society act within the framework of an ongoing culture that shapes their general goals, specific objectives, and the procedures that the members feel ought to be used. Every culture derives part of its unique quality from the fact that it emphasizes one or more special aspects of behavior and this strategic emphasis serves to differentiate it from other cultures with respect to the demands that it generates. As far as the mass of the people is concerned, some cultures, such as our own, are weighted heavily on the side of economic wants, success, privacy, leisure activity, and rational efficiency. Others, such as that of the Fox Indians, strive toward the maintenance of harmony, even if in the process the goals of efficiency and rationality may be sacrificed. Still others, such as the Kachins of highland Burma, stress the pursuit of power and prestige. The culture embodies the standards of value in a society and thereby marks out areas of potential conflict, if the valued things are in short supply relative to demand. The typical demands that will find their way into the political process will concern the matters in conflict that are labeled important by the culture. For this reason we cannot hope to understand the nature of the demands presenting themselves for political settlement unless we are ready to explore systematically and intensively their connection with the culture. And what I have said about culture applies, with suitable modifications, to other parts of the setting of a political system.

But not all demands originate or have their major locus in the environment. Important types stem from situations occurring within a political system itself. Typically, in every on-going system, demands may emerge for alterations in the political relationships of the members themselves, as the result of dissatisfaction stemming from these relationships. For example, in a political system based upon representation, in which equal representation is an important political norm, demands may arise for equalizing representation between urban and rural voting districts. Similarly, demands for changes in the process of recruitment of formal political leaders, for modifications of the way in which constitutions are amended, and the like may all be internally inspired demands.

I find it useful and necessary to distinguish these from external demands because they are, strictly speaking, not inputs of the system but something that we can call "withinputs," if we can tolerate a cumbersome neologism, and because their consequences for the character of a political system are more direct than in the case of external demands. Furthermore, if we were not aware of this difference in classes of demands, we might search in vain for an explanation of the emergence of a given set of internal demands if we turned only to the environment.

2. How are demands transformed into issues? What determines whether a demand becomes a matter for serious political discussion or remains something to be resolved privately among the members of

society? The occurrence of a demand, whether internal or external, does not thereby automatically convert it into a political *issue*. Many demands die at birth or linger on with the support of an insignificant fraction of the society and are never raised to the level of possible political decision. Others become issues, an issue being a demand that the members of a political system are prepared to deal with as a significant item for discussion through the recognized channels in the system.

The distinction between demands and issues raises a number of questions about which we need data if we are to understand the processes through which claims typically become transformed into issues. For example, we would need to know something about the relationship between a demand and the location of its initiators or supporters in the power structures of the society, the importance of secrecy as compared with publicity in presenting demands, the matter of timing of demands, the possession of political skills or know-how, access to channels of communication, the attitudes and states of mind of possible publics, and the images held by the initiators of demands with regard to the way in which things get done in the particular political system. Answers to matters such as these would possibly yield a conversion index reflecting the probability of a set of demands being converted into live political issues.

If we assume that political science is primarily concerned with the way in which authoritative decisions are made for a society, demands require special attention as a major type of input of political systems. I have suggested that demands influence the behavior of a system in a number of ways. They constitute a significant part of the material upon which the system operates. They are also one of the sources of change in political systems, since as the environment fluctuates it generates new types of demand-inputs for the system. Accordingly, without this attention to the origin and determinants of demands we would be at a loss to be able to treat rigorously not only the operation of a system at a moment of time but also its change over a specified interval. Both the statics and historical dynamics of a political system depend upon a detailed understanding of demands, particularly of the impact of the setting on them.

III. INPUTS: SUPPORT

Inputs of demands alone are not enough to keep a political system operating. They are only the raw material out of which finished products called decisions are manufactured. Energy in the form of actions or orientations promoting and resisting a political system, the demands arising in it, and the decisions issuing from it must also be put into the system to keep it running. This input I shall call support. Without support, demands could not be satisfied or conflicts in goals composed. If demands are to be acted upon, the members of a system undertaking to pilot the demands through to their transformation into binding decisions and those who seek to influence the relevant processes in any way must be able to count on support from others in the system. Just how much support, from how many and which members of a political system, are separate and important questions that I shall touch on shortly.

What do we mean by support? We can say that A supports B either when A acts on behalf of or when he orients himself favorably toward B's goals, interests, and actions. Supportive behavior may thus be of two kinds. It may consist of actions promoting the goals, interests, and actions of another person. We may vote for a political candidate, or defend a decision by the highest court of the land. In these cases, support manifests itself through overt action.

On the other hand, supportive behavior may involve not external observable acts, but those internal forms of behavior we call orientations or states of mind. As I use the phrase, a supportive state of mind is a deep-seated set of attitudes or predispositions, or a readiness to act on behalf of some other person. It exists when we say that a man is loyal to his party, attached to democracy, or infused with patriotism. What such phrases as these have in common is the fact that they refer to a state of feelings on the part of a person. No overt action is involved at this level of description, although the implication is that the individual will pursue a course of action consistent with his attitudes. Where the anticipated action does not flow from our perception of the state of mind, we assume that we have not penetrated deeply enough into the true feelings of the person but have merely skimmed off his surface attitudes.

Supportive states of mind are vital inputs for the operation and maintenance of a political system. For example, it is often said that the struggle in the international sphere concerns mastery over men's minds. To a certain extent this is true. If the members of a political system are deeply attached to a system or its ideals, the likelihood of their participating in either domestic or foreign politics in such a way as to undermine the system is reduced by a large factor. Presumably, even in the face of considerable provocation, ingrained supportive feelings of loyalty may be expected to prevail.

We shall need to identify the typical mechanisms through which supportive attitudes are inculcated and continuously reinforced within a political system. But our prior task is to specify and examine the political objects in relation to which support is extended.

1. *The Domain of Support.* Support is fed into the political system in relation to three objects: the community, the regime, and the government. There must be convergence of attitude and opinion

as well as some willingness to act with regard to each of these objects. Let us examine each in turn.

a. The Political Community. No political system can continue to operate unless its members are willing to support the existence of a group that seeks to settle differences or promote decisions through peaceful action in common. The point is so obvious — being dealt with usually under the heading of the growth of national unity — that it may well be overlooked; and yet it is a premise upon which the continuation of any political system depends. To refer to this phenomenon we can speak of the political community. At this level of support we are not concerned with whether a government exists or whether there is loyalty to a constitutional order. For the moment we only ask whether the members of the group that we are examining are sufficiently oriented toward each other to want to contribute their collective energies toward pacific settlement of their varying demands.

The American Civil War is a concrete illustration of the cessation of input of support for the political community. The war itself was definitive evidence that the members of the American political system could no longer contribute to the existence of a state of affairs in which peaceful solution of conflicting demands was the rule. Matters had come to the point where it was no longer a question of whether the South would support one or another alternative government, or whether it could envision its demands being satisfied through the normal constitutional procedures. The issue turned on whether there was sufficient mutual identification among the members of the system for them to be able to work together as a political community. Thus in any political system, to the extent that there is an in-group or we-group feeling and to the extent that the members of the system identify one another as part of this unit and exclude others according to some commonly accepted criteria, such as territoriality, kinship, or citizenship, we shall say that they are putting in support for the political community.

b. The Regime. Support for a second major part of a political system helps to supply the energy to keep the system running. This aspect of the system I shall call the regime. It consists of all those arrangements that regulate the way in which the demands put into the system are settled and the way in which decisions are put into effect. They are the so-called rules of the game, in the light of which actions by members of the system are legitimated and accepted by the bulk of the members as authoritative. Unless there is a minimum convergence of attitudes in support of these fundamental rules — the constitutional principles, as we call them in Western society — there would be insufficient harmony in the actions of the members of a system to meet the problems generated by their support of a political community. The fact of trying to settle demands in common means that there must be known principles governing the way in which resolutions of differences of claims are to take place.

c. The Government. If a political system is going to be able to handle the conflicting demands put into it, not only must the members of the system be prepared to support the settlement of these conflicts in common and possess some consensus with regard to the rules governing the mode of settlement; they must also be ready to support a government as it undertakes the concrete tasks involved in negotiating such settlements. When we come to the outputs of a system, we shall see the rewards that are available to a government for mobilizing support. At this point, I just wish to draw attention to this need on the part of a government for support if it is going to be able to make decisions with regard to demands. Of course, a government may elicit support in many ways: through persuasion, consent, or manipulation. It may also impose unsupported settlements of demands through threats of force. But it is a familiar axiom of political science that a government based upon force alone is not long for this world; it must buttress its position by inducing a favorable state of mind in its subjects through fair or foul means.

The fact that support directed to a political system can be broken down conceptually into three elements — support for the community, regime, and government — does not mean, of course, that in the concrete case support for each of these three objects is independent. In fact we might and normally do find all three kinds of support very closely intertwined, so that the presence of one is a function of the presence of one or both of the other types.

For example, withdrawal of support from the government of Louis XVI in effect also meant that members of the French monarchical system were challenging at least the regime; as it turned out in the ensuing revolution and civil war, there was even doubt whether the members of the system would continue to support a unified political community. In this case, what was initially opposition to the ruling sovereign — that is, to the government — quickly turned out to signify a lack of sufficient support for the regime and ultimately, to some extent, for the political community. But this is not always so and fortunately, from the point of view of social order, it is not typically the case. We are accustomed to calling for a change of government without thereby suggesting dissatisfaction with the regime or community. And at times, although this is less frequently true, the community shows sufficient intention to continue as a cooperating group to be able to accept a challenge to the regime. From 1832 to the 1880's England underwent a serious modification in its regime, introducing the basic elements of a system of popular democracy, without serious diminution of input of support at the community level. It is always a matter for empirical enquiry to discover the degree to which support at any one level is dependent upon support at the others.

This very brief discussion of support points up one major fact. If a system is to absorb a variety of demands and negotiate some sort of settlement among them, it is not enough for the members of the system to support only their own demands and the particular government that will undertake to promote these demands. For the demands to be processed into outputs it is equally essential that the members of the system stand ready to support the existence of a political community and some stable rules of common action that we call the regime.

2. *Quantity and Scope of Support.* How much support needs to be put into a system and how many of its members need to contribute such support if the system is to be able to do the job of converting demands to decisions? No ready answer can be offered. The actual situation in each case would determine the amount and scope required. We can, however, visualize a number of situations that will be helpful in directing our attention to possible generalizations.

Under certain circumstances very few members need to support a system at any level. The members might be dull and apathetic, indifferent to the general operations of the system, its progress or decisions. In a loosely connected system such as India has had, this might well be the state of mind of by far the largest segment of the membership. Either in fact they have not been affected by national decisions or they have not perceived that they were so affected. They may have little sense of identification with the present regime and government and yet, with regard to the input of demands, the system may be able to act on the basis of the support offered by the known 3 per cent of the Western-oriented politicians and intellectuals who are politically active. In other words, we can have a small minority putting in quantitatively sufficient supportive energy to keep the system going. However, we can venture the hypothesis that where members of a system are putting in numerous demands, there is a strong probability that they will actively offer support or hostility at one of the three levels of the system, depending upon the degree to which these demands are being met through appropriate decisions.

Alternatively, we may find that all the members of a system are putting in support, but the amount may be so low as to place one or all aspects of the system in jeopardy. Modern France is perhaps a classic illustration. The input of support at the level of the political community is probably adequate for the maintenance of France as a national political unit. But for a variety of historical and contemporary reasons, there is considerable doubt as to whether the members of the French political system are putting in anything but a low order of support to the regime or any particular government. This low amount of support, even though spread over a relatively large segment of the population, leaves the French political system on somewhat less secure foundations than is the case with India. There support is less widespread but more active — that is, quantitatively greater — on the part of a minority. As this illustration indicates, the amount of support is not necessarily proportional to its scope.

It may seem from the above discussion as though the members of a political system either put in support or withhold it — that is, demonstrate hostility or apathy. In fact, members may and normally do simultaneously engage in supportive and hostile behavior. What we must be interested in is the net balance of support.

IV. MECHANISMS OF SUPPORT

To this point I have suggested that no political system can yield the important outputs we call authoritative decisions unless, in addition to demands, support finds its way into the system. I have discussed the possible object to which support may be directed, and some problems with regard to the domain, quantity, and scope of support. We are now ready to turn to the main question raised by our attention to support as a crucial input: how do systems typically manage to maintain a steady flow of support? Without it a system will not absorb sufficient energy from its members to be able to convert demands to decisions.

In theory, there might be an infinite variety of means through which members could be induced to support a system; in practice, certain well-established classes of mechanisms are used. Research in this area needs to be directed to exploring the precise way in which a particular system utilizes these mechanisms and to refining our understanding of the way in which they contribute to the making of authoritative policy.

A society generates support for a political system in two ways: through outputs that meet the demands of the members of society; and through the processes of politicization. Let us look at outputs first.

1. *Outputs as a Mechanism of Support.* An output of a political system, it will be recalled, is a political decision or policy. One of the major ways of strengthening the ties of the members to their system is through providing decisions that tend to satisfy the day-to-day demands of these members. Fundamentally this is the truth that lies in the aphorism that one can fool some of the people some of the time but not all of them all of the time. Without some minimal satisfaction of demands, the ardor of all but the most fanatical patriot is sure to cool. The outputs, consisting of political decisions, constitute a body of specific inducements for the members of a system to support that system.

Inducements of this kind may be positive or negative. Where negative, they threaten the members of the system with various kinds of sanctions ranging from a small monetary fine to physical detention, ostracism, or loss of life, as in our own system with regard to the case of legally defined treason. In every system support stems in part from fear of sanctions or compulsion; in autocratic systems the proportion of coerced support is at a maximum. For want of space I shall confine myself to those cases where positive incentives loom largest.

Since the specific outputs of a system are policy decisions, it is upon the government that the final responsibility falls for matching or balancing outputs of decisions against input of demand. But it is clear that to obtain the support of the members of a system through positive incentives, a government need not meet all the demands of even its most influential and ardent supporters. Most governments, or groups such as political parties that seek to control governments, succeed in building up a reserve of support. This reserve will carry the government along even though it offends its followers, so long as over the extended short run these followers perceive the particular government as one that is in general favorable to their interests. One form that this reserve support takes in Western society is that of party loyalty, since the party is the typical instrument in a mass industrialized society for mobilizing and maintaining support for a government. However, continuous lack of specific rewards through policy decisions ultimately leads to the danger that even the deepest party loyalty may be shaken.

For example, labor has continued to support the Democratic Party even though much of the legislation promoted by members of that party has not served to meet labor's demands. In some measure, large sections of labor may continue to vote and campaign vigorously on behalf of the Democratic Party because they have no realistic alternative other than to support this party; but in addition the Democrats have built up in recent years, especially during the Roosevelt era, a considerable body of good will. It would take repeated neglect of labor's demands on the part of the Democratic Party to undermine the strong urban working-class support directed toward it and the government that the party dominates from time to time.

Thus a system need not meet *all the demands* of its members so long as it has stored up a reserve of support over the years. Nor need it satisfy even *some of the demands* of all its members. Just whose demands a system must seek to meet, how much of their demands, at what time, and under what conditions are questions for special research. We can say in advance that at least the demands of the most influential members require satisfaction. But this tells us little unless we know how to discover the influentials in a political system and how new sets of members rise to positions of influence.

The critical significance of the decisions of governments for the support of the other two aspects of a system — namely, the political community and the regime — is clear from what I have said above. Not all withdrawal of support from a government has consequences for the success or failure of a regime or community. But persistent inability of a government to produce satisfactory outputs for the members of a system may well lead to demands for changing of the regime or for dissolution of the political community. It is for this reason that the input-output balance is a vital mechanism in the life of a political system.

2. *Politicization as a Mechanism of Support.* It would be wrong to consider that the level of support available to a system is a function exclusively of the outputs in the form of either sanctions or rewards. If we did so conclude, we could scarcely account for the maintenance of numerous political systems in which satisfaction of demands has been manifestly low, in which public coercion is limited, and yet which have endured for epochs. Alternately, it might be difficult to explain how political systems could endure and yet manage to flout or thwart urgent demands, failing thereby to render sufficient *quid pro quo* for the input of support. The fact is that whatever reserve of support has been accumulated through past decisions is increased and reinforced by a complicated method for steadily manufacturing support through what I shall call the process of politicization. It is an awkward term, but nevertheless an appropriately descriptive one.

As each person grows up in a society, through a network of rewards and punishments the other members of society communicate to and instill in him the various institutionalized goals and norms of that society. This is well known in social research as the process of socialization. Through its operation a person learns to play his various social roles. Part of these goals and norms relate to what the society considers desirable in political life. The ways in which these political patterns are learned by the members of society constitute what I call the process of politicization. Through it a person learns to play his political roles, which include the absorption of the proper political attitudes.

Let us examine a little more closely something of what happens during the process of politicization. As members of a society mature, they must absorb the various orientations toward political matters that one is expected to have in that society. If the expectations of the members of society with regard to the way each should behave in specific political situations diverged beyond a certain range, it would be impossible to get common action with regard to the making of binding decisions. It is essential for the viability of an orderly political system that the members of the system have some common basic expectations with regard to the standards that are to be used in making political evaluations, to the way people will feel about various political matters, and to the way members of the system will perceive and interpret political phenomena.

The mechanism through which this learning takes place is of considerable significance in understanding how a political system generates and accumulates a strong reserve of support. Although we cannot pursue the details, we can mention a few of the relevant dimensions. In the first place, of course, the learning or politicization process does not stop at any particular period for the individual; it starts with the child and, in the light of our knowledge of learning, may have its deepest impact through the teen age. The study of the political experiences of and the influences operating on the child and the adolescent emerges as an important and neglected area of research.

In the second place, the actual process of politicization at its most general level brings into operation a complex network of rewards and punishments. For adopting the correct political attitudes and performing the right political acts, for conforming to the generally accepted interpretations of political goals, and for undertaking the institutionalized obligations of a member of the given system, we are variously rewarded or punished. For conforming we are made to feel worthy, wanted, and respected and often obtain material advantages such as wealth, influence, improved opportunities. For deviating beyond the permissible range, we are made to feel unworthy, rejected, dishonored, and often suffer material losses.

This does not mean that the pattern of rewards and punishments is by any means always effective; if it were, we would never have changed from the Stone Age. A measure of non-conformity may at certain stages in the life history of a political system itself become a respected norm. Even where this is not the case, the most seductive rewards and the severest punishments will never succeed in preventing some of the members of a system from pursuing what they consider to be their inextinguishable interests and from seeking, with varying degrees of success, to change the goals and norms of the system. This is one of the important sources of political change closely associated with changes in the inputs of demands that are due to a changing environment. But we cannot pursue this crucial matter of the nature of political change, as it would lead us off in a new direction.

In the third place, the means used for communicating the goals and norms to others tend to be repetitive in all societies. The various political myths, doctrines, and philosophies transmit to each generation a particular interpretation of the goals and norms. The decisive links in this chain of transmission are parents, siblings, peers, teachers, organizations, and social leaders, as well as physical symbols such as flags or totems, ceremonies, and rituals freighted with political meaning.

These processes through which attachments to a political system become built into the maturing member of a society I have lumped together under the rubric of politicization. They illustrate the way in which members of a system learn what is expected of them in political life and how they ought to do what is expected of them. In this way they acquire knowledge about their political roles and a desire to perform them. In stable systems the support that accrues through these means adds to the reservoir of support being accumulated on a day-to-day basis through the outputs of decisions. The support obtained through politicization tends to be relatively — although, as we have seen, not wholly — independent of the vagaries of day-to-day outputs.

When the basic political attachments become deeply rooted or institutionalized, we say that the system has become accepted as legitimate. Politicization therefore effectively sums up the way in which legitimacy is created and transmitted in a political system. And it is an empirical observation that in those instances where political systems have survived the longest, support has been nourished by an ingrained belief in the legitimacy of the relevant governments and regimes.

What I am suggesting here is that support resting on a sense of the legitimacy of a government and regime provides a necessary reserve if the system is to weather those frequent storms when the more obvious outputs of the system seem to impose greater hardships than rewards. Answers to questions concerning the formation, maintenance, transmission, and change of standards of legitimacy will contribute generously to an understanding of the way in which support is sufficiently institutionalized so that a system may regularly and without excessive expenditure of effort transform inputs of demand into outputs of decisions.

That there is a need for general theory in the study of political life is apparent. The only question is how best to proceed. There is no one royal road that can be said to be either the correct one or the best. It is only a matter of what appears at the given level of available knowledge to be the most useful. At this stage it appears that system theory, with its sensitivity to the input-output exchange between a system and its setting offers a fruitful approach. It is an economical way of organizing presently disconnected political data and promises interesting dividends.

PART II

THE SETTING OF THE
AMERICAN SYSTEM

CHAPTER TWO

Constitutional Government

The most accurate and helpful way to characterize our political system is to call it a constitutional democracy. The term implies a system in which the government is regulated by laws which control and limit the exercise of political power. In a constitutional democracy people participate in government on a limited basis. A distinction should be made between an unlimited democratic government and a constitutional democracy. In the former, the "people" govern through the operation of a principle such as majority rule without legal restraint; in the latter, majority rule is curtailed and checked through various legal devices. A constitutional system is one in which the formal authority of government is restrained. The checks upon government in a constitutional society customarily include a division or fragmentation of authority which prevents government from controlling all sectors of human life.

Ideological Foundations: Philosophies of Constitutional Democracy

The Western political heritage has emphasized the importance of democracy and the rule of law. As early as Aristotle's *Politics,* the viability of democracy, provided there are sufficient checks upon unlimited popular rule, has been stressed.

The American constitutional tradition reflects the beliefs of many political philosophers. One of the most dominating figures is John Locke. It is not suggested that Locke was read by most of the colonists, but only that his ideas invariably found their way into many writings of eighteenth-century America, most importantly the Declaration of Independence. In a letter to Henry Lee in 1825, Thomas Jefferson wrote:

"When forced . . . to resort to arms for redress, an appeal to the tribunal of the world was deemed proper for our justification. This was the object of the Declaration of Independence. Not to find out new principles, or new arguments, never before thought of, not merely to say things which had never been said before; but to place before mankind the common sense of the subject, in terms so plain and firm as to command their assent, and to justify ourselves in the independent stand we are compelled to take. Neither aiming at originality of principle or sentiment, nor yet copied from any particular and previous writing, it was intended to be an expression of the American mind, and to give to that expression the proper tone and spirit called for by the occasion. All its authority rests then on the harmonizing sentiments of the day, whether expressed in conversation, in letters, printed essays, or in the elementary books of public right [such] as Aristotle, Cicero, Locke, Sidney, etc. . . ."

In May of 1790, Jefferson wrote: "Locke's little book on government is perfect as far as it goes." Although Jefferson's admiration of Locke was perhaps greater than that of many other colonists, his views did reflect a mood of eighteenth-century America. Locke's *Second Treatise, Of Civil Government* attempted to trace the reasons why men enter into political societies in the first place. The eighteenth century, no less than the twentieth, was an era characterized by attempts to be "scientific" in political formulations. Locke's *Second Treatise,* first published in 1690, reflected the scientific emphasis that was to prevail so widely beginning in the eighteenth century. To Locke, natural law was objectively valid, and therefore once ascertained, governments based upon it would have a superior claim to legitimacy. Locke is notable for his discussions of natural law, from which he derived the "best" form of government. In reading Locke, one should observe how much importance he placed upon property rights, and the right of the people to dissolve government once it no longer met their legitimate expectations.

3   JOHN LOCKE

SECOND TREATISE, OF CIVIL GOVERNMENT

OF THE STATE OF NATURE

To understand political power aright, and derive it from its original, we must consider what estate all men are naturally in, and that is, a state of perfect freedom to order their actions, and dispose of their possessions and persons as they think fit, within the bounds of the law of Nature, without asking leave or depending upon the will of any other man.

A state also of equality, wherein all the power and jurisdiction is reciprocal, no one having more than another, there being nothing more evident than that creatures of the same species and rank, promiscuously born to all the same advantages of Nature, and the use of the same faculties, should also be equal one amongst another, without subordination or subjection, unless the lord and master of them all should, by any manifest declaration of his will, set one above another, and confer on him, by an evident and clear appointment, an undoubted right to dominion and sovereignty. . . .

But though this be a state of liberty, yet it is not a state of license; though man in that state have an uncontrollable liberty to dispose of his person or possessions, yet he has not liberty to destroy himself, or so much as any creature in his possession, but where some nobler use than its bare preservation calls for it. The state of Nature has a law of Nature to govern it, which obliges every one, and reason, which is that law, teaches all mankind who will but consult it, that being all equal and independent, no one ought to harm another in his life, health, liberty or possessions . . . And, being furnished with like faculties, sharing all in one community of Nature, there cannot be supposed any such subordination among us that may authorize us to destroy one another, as if we were made for one another's uses, as the inferior ranks of creatures are for ours. Every one as he is bound to preserve himself, and not to quit his station wilfully, so by the like reason, when his own preservation comes not in competition, ought he as much as he can to preserve the rest of mankind, and not unless it be to do justice on an offender, take away or impair the life, or what tends to the preservation of the life, the liberty, health, limb, or goods of another.

And that all men may be restrained from invading others' rights, and from doing hurt to one another, and the law of Nature be observed, which willeth the peace and preservation of all mankind, the execution of the law of Nature is in that state put into every man's hands, whereby every one has a right to punish the transgressors of that law to such a degree as may hinder its violation. For the law of Nature would, as all other laws that concern men in this world, be in vain if there were nobody that in the state of Nature had a power to execute that law, and thereby preserve the innocent and restrain offenders; and if any one in the state of Nature may punish another for any evil he has done, every one may do so. For in that state of perfect equality, where naturally there is no superiority or jurisdiction of one over another, what any may do in prosecution of that law, every one must needs have a right to do.

And thus, in the state of Nature, one man comes by a power over another, but yet no absolute or arbitrary power to use a criminal, when he has got him in his hands, according to the passionate heats or boundless extravagancy of his own will, but only to retribute to him so far as calm reason and conscience dictate, what is proportionate to his transgression, which is so much as may serve for reparation and restraint. . . .

Every offence that can be committed in the state of Nature may, in the state of Nature, be also punished equally, and as far forth, as it may, in a commonwealth. For-though it would be beside my present purpose to enter here into the particulars of the law of nature, or its measures of punishment, yet it is certain there is such a law, and that too as intelligible and plain to a rational creature and a studier of that law as the positive laws of commonwealths, nay, possibly plainer; as much as reason is easier to be understood than the fancies and intricate contrivances of men, following contrary and hidden interests put into words. . . .

Of the Ends of Political Society and Government

If man in the state of Nature be so free as has been said, if he be absolute lord of his own person and possessions, equal to the greatest and subject to nobody, why will he part with his freedom, this empire, and subject himself to the dominion and control of any other power? To which it is obvious to answer, that though in the state of Nature he hath such a right, yet the enjoyment of it is very uncertain and constantly exposed to the invasion of others; for all being kings as much as he, every man his equal, and the greater part no strict observers of equity and justice, the enjoyment of the property he has in this state is very unsafe, very insecure. This makes him willing to quit this condition which, however free, is full of fears and continual dangers; and it is not without reason that he seeks out and is willing to join in society with others who are already united, or have a mind to unite for the mutual preservation of their lives, liberties and estates, which I call by the general name — property.

The great and chief end, therefore, of men uniting into commonwealths, and putting themselves under government, is the preservation of their property; to which in the state of Nature there are many things wanting.

Firstly, there wants an established, settled, known law, received and allowed by common consent to be the standard of right and wrong, and the common measure to decide all controversies between them. For though the law of Nature be plain and intelligible to all rational creatures, yet men, being biased by their interest, as well as ignorant for want of study of it, are not apt to allow of it as a law binding to them in the application of it to their particular cases.

Secondly, in the state of Nature there wants a known and indifferent judge, with authority to determine all differences according to the established law. For every one in that state being both judge and executioner of the law of Nature, men being partial to themselves, passion and revenge is very apt to carry them too far, and with too much heat in their own cases, as well as negligence and unconcernedness, make them too remiss in other men's.

Thirdly, in the state of Nature there often wants power to back and support the sentence when right, and to give it due execution. They who by any injustice offended will seldom fail where they are able by force to make good their injustice. Such resistance many times makes the punishment dangerous, and frequently destructive to those who attempt it.

Thus mankind, notwithstanding all the privileges of the state of Nature, being but in an ill condition while they remain in it are quickly driven into society. Hence it comes to pass, that we seldom find any number of men live any time together in this state. The inconveniencies that they are therein exposed to by the irregular and uncertain exercise of the power every man has of punishing the transgressions of others, make them take sanctuary under the established laws of government, and therein seek the preservation of their property. It is this makes them so willingly give up every one his single power of punishing to be exercised by such alone as shall be appointed to it amongst them, and by such rules as the community, or those authorised by them to that purpose, shall agree on. And in this we have the original right and rise of both the legislative and executive power as well as of the governments and societies themselves.

For in the state of Nature to omit the liberty he has of innocent delights, a man has two powers. The first is to do whatsoever he thinks fit for the preservation of himself and others within the permission of the law of Nature; by which law, common to them all, he and all the rest of mankind are one community, make up one society distinct from all other creatures, and were it not for the corruption and viciousness of degenerate men, there would be no need of any other, no necessity that men should separate from this great and natural community, and associate into lesser combinations. The other power a man has in the state of Nature is the power to punish the crimes committed against that law. Both these he gives up when he joins in a private, if I may so call it, or particular political society, and incorporates into any commonwealth separate from the rest of mankind.

The first power — viz., of doing whatsoever he thought fit for the preservation of himself and the rest of mankind, he gives up to be regulated by laws made by the society, so far forth as the preservation of himself and the rest of that society shall require; which laws of the society in many things confine the liberty he had by the law of Nature.

Secondly, the power of punishing he wholly gives up, and engages his natural force, which he might before employ in the execution of the law of Nature, by his own single authority, as he thought fit, to assist the executive power of the society as the law thereof shall require. For being now in a new state, wherein he is to enjoy many conveniences from the labor, assistance, and society of others in the same community, as well as protection from its whole strength, he is to part also with as much of his natural liberty, in providing for himself, as the good, prosperity, and safety of the society shall require, which is not only necessary but just, since the other members of the society do the like.

But though men when they enter into society give up the equality, liberty, and executive power they had in the state of Nature into the hands of the society, to be so far disposed of by the legislative as the good of the society shall require, yet it being only with an intention in every one the better to preserve himself, his liberty and property (for no rational creature can be supposed to change his condition with an intention to be worse), the power of the society or legislative constituted by them can never be supposed to extend farther than the common against those three defects above mentioned that made the state of Nature so unsafe and uneasy. And so, whoever has the legislative or supreme power of any commonwealth, is bound to govern by established standing laws, promulgated and known to the people, and not by extemporary decrees, by indifferent and upright judges, who are to decide controversies by those laws; and to employ the force of the community at home only in the execution of such laws, or abroad to prevent or redress foreign injuries and secure the community from inroads and invasion. And all this to be directed to no other end but the peace, safety, and public good of the people. . . .

Of the Extent of the Legislative Power

The great end of men's entering into society being the enjoyment of their properties in peace and safety, and the great instrument and means of that being the laws established in that society, the first and fundamental positive law of all commonwealths is the establishing of the legislative power, as the first and fundamental natural law, which is to govern even the legislative itself, is the preservation of the society and (as far as will consist with the public good) of every person in it. This legislative is not only the supreme power of the commonwealth, but sacred and unalterable in the hands where the community have once placed it. Nor can any edict of anybody else, in what form soever conceived, or by what power soever backed, have the force and obligation of a law which has not its sanction from that legislative which the public has chosen and appointed; for without this the law could not have that which is absolutely necessary to its being a law, the consent of the society, over whom nobody can have a power to make laws but by their own consent and by authority received from them. . . .

These are the bounds which the trust that is put in them by the society and the law of God and Nature have set to the legislative power of every commonwealth, in all forms of government. First: They are to govern by promulgated established laws, not to be varied in particular cases, but to have one rule for rich and poor, for the favorite at Court, and the countryman at plough. Secondly: These laws also ought to be designed for no other end ultimately but the good of the people. Thirdly: They must not raise taxes on the property of the people without the consent of the people given by themselves or their deputies. And this properly concerns only such governments where the legislative is always in being, or at least where the people have not reserved any part of the legislative to deputies, to be from time to time chosen by themselves. Fourthly: Legislative neither must nor can transfer the power of making laws to anybody else, or place it anywhere but where the people have. . . .

Of the Dissolution of Government

The constitution of the legislative [authority] is the first and fundamental act of society, whereby provision is made for the continuation of their union under the direction of persons and bonds of laws, made by persons authorised thereunto, by the consent and appointment of the people, without which no one man, or number of men, amongst them can have authority of making laws that shall be binding to the rest. When any one, or more, shall take upon them to make laws whom the people have not appointed so to do, they make laws without authority, which the people are not therefore bound to obey; by which means they come again to be out of subjection, and may constitute to themselves a new legislative, as they think best, being in full liberty to resist the force of those who, without authority, would impose anything upon them. . . .

Whosoever uses force without right — as every one does in society who does it without law — puts himself into a state of war with those against whom he so uses it, and in that state all former ties are cancelled, all other rights cease, and every one has a right to defend himself, and to resist the aggressor. . . .

Here it is like the common question will be made: Who shall be judge whether the prince or legislative act contrary to their trust?

This, perhaps, ill-affected and factious men may spread amongst the people, when the prince only makes use of his due prerogative. To this I reply, The people shall be judge; for who shall be judge whether his trustee or deputy acts well and according to the trust reposed in him, but he who deputes him and must, by having deputed him, have still a power to discard him when he fails in his trust? If this be reasonable in particular cases of private men, why should it be otherwise in that of the greatest moment, where the welfare of millions is concerned and also where the evil, if not prevented, is greater, and the redress very difficult, dear, and dangerous? . . .

To conclude. The power that every individual gave the society when he entered into it can never revert to the individuals again, as long as the society lasts, but will always remain in the community; because without this there can be no community — no commonwealth, which is contrary to the original agreement; so also when the society hath placed the legislative in any assembly of men, to continue in them and their successors, with direction and authority for providing such successors, the legislative can never revert to the people whilst that government lasts; because, having provided a legislative with power to continue for ever, they have given up their political power to the legislative, and cannot resume it. But if they have set limits to the duration of their legislative, and made this supreme power in any person or assembly only temporary; or else when, by the miscarriages of those in authority, it is forfeited; upon the forfeiture of their rulers, or at the determination of the time set, it reverts to the society, and the people have a right to act as supreme, and continue the legislative in themselves or place it in a new form, or new hands, as they think good.

The influence of John Locke goes far beyond his impact on the thinking of the founding fathers of the United States, such as Thomas Jefferson. Some scholars (among them, Louis Hartz, *The Liberal Tradition in America*) have interpreted the American political tradition in terms of the pervasive attachment to the ideas and values set forth in the writings of Locke. There is little question that American political life has been uniquely characterized by widespread adherence to the fundamental principles about the relations among men, society, and government expressed in Locke's writings.

It is not just that we have representative government, with institutions similar in structure and function to those of the constitutional democracy described in Locke's *Second Treatise*, but that through the years we have probably maintained, more than any other society, a widespread agreement about the fundamental human values cherished by Locke. His emphasis upon the sanctity of private property has been paramount in the American political tradition from the very beginning. Moreover, Locke's views on the nature of man are shared by most Americans. All our governmental institutions, processes, and traditions rest upon principles such as the primacy of the individual, man's inborn ability to exercise reason in order to discern truth and higher principles of order and justice, and a political and social equality among men in which no man shall count for more than another in determining the actions of government and their application. We may not have always practiced these ideals, but we have been *theoretically* committed to them.

The following selection analyzes the sources of Locke's ideas and also points out other important political theories bearing upon the development of constitutional government in the United States.

4   EDWARD S. CORWIN

THE "HIGHER LAW" BACKGROUND OF AMERICAN CONSTITUTIONAL LAW

The conveyance of natural law ideas into American constitutional theory was the work pre-eminently — though by no means exclusively — of John Locke's *Second Treatise on Civil Government,* which appeared in 1690 as an apology for the Glorious Revolution. The outstanding feature of Locke's treatment of natural law is the almost complete dissolution which this concept undergoes through his handling into the natural rights of the individual; or — to employ Locke's own phrase, borrowed from the debates between Stuart adherents and Parliamentarians — into the rights of "life, liberty, and estate." The dissolving agency by which Locke brings this transformation about is the doctrine of the Social Compact, with its corollary notion of a State of Nature. Indeed, it is hardly an exaggeration to say that the only residuum which remains in the Lockian crucible from the original Ciceronian concept is the sanction which is

From Edward S. Corwin, *The "Higher Law" Background of American Constitutional Law* (Cornell University Press, 1955), pp. 61–89. First published in 42 *Harvard Law Review* 149, 365 (1928). Copyright 1928 by The Harvard Law Review Association.

claimed from natural law for the social compact, and at one point, he dispenses even with this. It thus becomes of interest to inquire whence Locke derived his intense preoccupation with rights, as well as the form in which he chose to express them.

A recent effort has been made to refer Locke's system to Calvinistic premises; but if it is meant that the outstanding features of Locke's political thinking are traceable to Calvin himself, the thesis falls of its own weight. Calvin knows nothing of the social compact — he rests civil authority on the basis of divine right. Far from being an apologist for revolution, he in general teaches non-resistance. The doctrine of the sovereignty of God which looms so large in his pages bears not the faintest analogy to anything in Locke; and the doctrine of election with its undemocratic implications is entirely antithetical to Lockian optimism. The founder of the Geneva theocracy, who burned Servetus at the stake, and the author of the *Letters on Toleration* have little in common.

It is evident that certain important distinctions have been overlooked. The entire Protestant movement with its emphasis on the priesthood of the individual believer was permeated with individualistic implications; but before these could come to effective political expression, they had to be released from the very medievalism which Calvinism seems at the outset to have been principally bent on restoring. Fortunately for its ultimate reputation in the history of political thought, Calvinism found itself much more frequently than not in the position of a religious minority subject to persecution. Its adherents were consequently forced either to adopt Calvin's own teaching of non-resistance, or to develop a type of political theory that countenanced resistance, and many of them took the latter route. That is to say, because of the actual situation of Calvinism, certain Calvinists developed doctrines of political liberalism, as for that matter did also certain Catholic writers of the same era. As Dr. Figgis has put it, "Political liberty is the residuary legatee of ecclesiastical animosities."

Nor is this to disparage Locke's indebtedness to such forerunners, which was indeed immense. For taking up the thread of later medieval political thought at the point where it had been broken off by Machiavelli and Bodin, to say nothing of Luther and Calvin, they at once revived the postulates of popular sovereignty which underlay Roman law and institutions and supplemented these by principles adapted from the matured Roman law of private contract. Yet, this concession made, it still remains true that the contact of Locke's system with the writers alluded to is indirect, and through a question which they left unsolved rather than through those they purported to answer. Sixteenth century liberalism rested its case largely on the notion of an original compact between governors and governed, between rulers and the people. The question inevitably emerged: Who are "the people," and how did they become an entity capable of contracting?

Locke's own answer to these questions springs from a threefold rootage. Its primary source was English legal tradition as illustrated in Fortescue and Coke, the entire emphasis of which has always been on rights of the individual rather than on rights of the people considered in the mass. The latter, indeed, was sufficiently provided for in Parliament. A second source was English Independency, which was in turn the direct outgrowth of Luther's doctrine of the priesthood of the individual. For in a period in which religious and political controversy were so closely involved with each other as in seventeenth century England, ideas developed in the one forum were easily and inevitably transferred to the other. Finally, Locke himself would have been the first to own his indebtedness to Grotius and Pufendorf and so ultimately to Cicero; while his citations of "the judicious Hooker," a still earlier apostle of the Ciceronian revival, outnumber those to any other writer. The first and last of these sources need only to be cataloged. The second, however, demands some further comment.

The leader of the extreme sect of the Independents, called the Levellers, was John Lilburne, a veritable ragamuffin, in whose writings the concern of his highly respectable successor, Locke, for "property" is replaced by demands for the "natural rights" of freedom of conscience and expression, and to political equality — demands which even in the deepest dungeons he seems never to have lacked pen and ink to indite. The political *chef d'oeuvre* of Independency was the famous Agreement of the People of 1647, which was an effort to give concrete realization to the principle of the Social Compact.

In America the filiation of Independency with the Social Compact philosophy can be traced at a still earlier date in connection with the Pilgrim foundation of Plymouth. The expedition comprised John Robinson's Scrooby congregation, of which a contemporary critic wrote: "Do we not know the beginnings of his Church? that there was first one stood up and made a covenant, and then another, and these two joyned together, and so a third, and these became a church, say they." And the procedure which, under the sanction of God, was effective to produce a church, could also be availed of under the same sanction to produce a commonwealth, as was shown in the famous Mayflower Compact:

> In the name of God, Amen. We whose names are underwritten, the loyall subjects of our dread soveraigne lord, King James . . . doe by these presents solemnly and mutualy in the presence of God, and one of another, covenant and combine ourrselves togeather into a civill body politick, for our better ordering and preservation . . . and by vertue hearof to enacte, constitute, and frame such just and equall lawes,

> ordinances, acts, constitutions, and offices, from time to time, as shall be thought most meete and convenient for the general good of the Colonie, unto which we promise all due submission and obedience.

Thus, more than two generations before Locke's *Second Treatise,* a social compact was conceived as supplying the second permanent government within what is now the United States. Whereas with Locke the ultimate basis of authority is supplied by natural law, here it is supplied by God. We shall observe presently how the rapprochement between the two positions was effected by eighteenth century Deism.

A generation later, though still more than a generation before the appearance of Locke's *Treatise,* we find another Independent, Thomas Hooker of Connecticut, proffering the theory of contract as explanatory of all human association.

> Every spiritual or ecclesiastical corporation receives its being from a spiritual combination . . . there is no man constrained to enter into such a condition, unless he will; and he that will enter, must also willingly bind and engage himself to each member of that society to promote the good of the whole, or else a member actually he is not.

Though Hooker is here speaking of "ecclesiastical corporations," the Fundamental Orders of Connecticut of 1639, whereby the inhabitants of the three towns did "assotiate and conjoyne" themselves "to be as one Publike State or Commonwelth," embodies his political application of the same thought. Nor is this the only significance of the Fundamental Orders. Taken along with the Agreement of the People a decade later, it shows the powerful, ineluctable necessity felt by those who held the compact theory for placing governmental institutions on a documentary basis.

One other predecessor of Locke must be mentioned before turning more particularly to the *Second Treatise,* Thomas Hobbes, author of the *Leviathan.* It is usual to contrast these two writers, but they also have much in common, and in relation to American constitutional theory, their contributions are often complementary rather than contradictory. For if Locke shares with Coke the paternity of American constitutional limitations, Hobbes's emphasis upon the *salus populi* is a definite forerunner of the modern doctrine of the police power, as well as a clear prophecy of legal tendency even in a constitutional state when conditions of emergency menace public order. Hobbes is at the outset as thoroughly individualistic as Locke, and the prosecution by the individual of his own interest is as much his objective as it is Locke's. Both Hobbes and Locke also agree in dispensing with the governmental contract; but whereas a sovereign law-making body is the direct outcome of the social compact with Hobbes, with Locke it is the corporate majority, which then determines the form of government.

Where Hobbes and Locke part company is in their view of the state of nature, that is to say, in their view of human nature when not subjected to political control. Hobbes, a timid man who had been called upon to witness stern events, pictures the state of nature as one of "force and fraud," in which "every man is to every man a wolf." Locke, who was perhaps of a more robust type, and at any rate wrote amid happier surroundings, depicts the state of nature as in the main an era of "peace, good will, mutual assistance, and preservation," in which the "free, sovereign" individual is already in possession of all valuable rights, though from defect of "executive power" he is not always able to make them good or to determine them accurately in relation to the like rights of his fellows. And from this difference flow all the others. With Hobbes a dissolution of government is substantially a dissolution of society; with Locke it is not, society having existed before government. With Hobbes natural law and civil law are coextensive; that is to say, "when a commonwealth is once settled, then are they [natural laws] actually laws, and not before." With Locke, natural law approximates to positive law from the first, while even after the establishment of government, popular interpretation of natural law is the ultimate test of the validity of civil law. Thus Hobbes becomes, more or less in spite of himself, the founder of the Positive School of Jurisprudence, which traces all rights to government and regards them simply as implements of public policy. Locke, on the other hand, regards government as creative of no rights, but as strictly fiduciary in character, and as designed to make more secure and more readily available rights which antedate it and which would survive it.

The two features of the *Second Treatise* which have impressed themselves most definitely upon American constitutional law are the limitations which it lays down for legislative power and its emphasis on the property right. The legislature is the supreme organ of Locke's commonwealth, and it is upon this supremacy that he depends in the main for the safeguarding of the rights of the individual. But for this very reason legislative supremacy is supremacy within the law, not a power above the law. In fact, the word "sovereign" is never used by Locke in its descriptive sense except in reference to the "free, sovereign" individual in the state of nature. In detail, the limitations which Locke specifies to legislative power are the following: First, it is not arbitrary power. Not even the majority which determines the form of the government can vest its agent with arbitrary power, for the reason that the majority right itself originates in a delegation by free sovereign individuals who had "in the state of nature no arbitrary power over the life, liberty, or possessions" of others, or even over their own. In this caveat against "arbitrary power," Locke definitely anticipates the modern latitudinarian concept of due process of law.

"Secondly, the legislative . . . cannot assume to itself a power to rule by extemporary, arbitrary decrees, but is bound to dispense justice and decide the rights of the subject by promulgated standing laws, and known authorised judges"; nor may it vary the law in particular cases, but there must be one rule for rich and poor, for favorite and the ploughman. In this pregnant passage, Locke foreshadows some of the most fundamental propositions of American constitutional law: *Law must be general; it must afford equal protection to all; it may not validly operate retroactively; it must be enforced through the courts — legislative power does not include judicial power.*

Thirdly, as also follows from its fiduciary character, the legislature "cannot transfer the power of making laws to any other hands: for it being but a delegated power from the people, they who have it cannot pass it over to others." More briefly, *legislative power cannot be delegated.*

Finally, *legislative power is not the ultimate power of the commonwealth,* for "the community perpetually retains a supreme power of saving themselves from the attempts and designs of anybody, even their legislators, whenever they shall be so foolish or so wicked as to lay and carry on designs against the liberties and properties of the subject." So while legislative supremacy is the normal sanction of the rights of men, it is not the final sanction. The identical power which was exerted against James II would in like case be equally available against Parliament itself.

Locke's bias in favor of property is best shown in the fifth chapter of the *Treatise,* where he brings the labor theory of value to the defense of inequality of possessions, and endeavors to show that the latter is harmonious with the social compact. His course of reasoning is as follows: All value, or almost all, is due to labor; and as there were different degrees of industry, so there were apt to be different degrees of possession. Yet most property, in those early days, was highly perishable, whence arose a natural limit to the accumulation of wealth, to wit, that no man must hoard up more than he could make use of, since that would be to waste nature's bounty. Nevertheless, "the exceeding of his just property" lay, Locke is careful to insist, not "in the largeness of his possession, but the perishing of anything uselessly in it." Accordingly, when mankind, by affixing value to gold, silver, and other imperishable but intrinsically valueless things for which perishable commodities might be traded, made exchanges possible, it thereby, as by deliberate consent, ratified unequal possessions; and the later social compact did not disturb this covenant.

So, having transmuted the law of nature into the rights of men, Locke next converts these into the rights of ownership. The final result is to base his commonwealth upon the balanced and antithetical concepts of the rule of the majority and the security of property. Nor, thanks to the labor theory of value, is this the merely static conception that at first consideration it might seem to be. Taken up a century later by Adam Smith, the labor theory became the cornerstone of the doctrine of *laissez faire*. It thus assisted to adapt a political theory conceived in the interest of a quiescent landed aristocracy to the uses of an aggressive industrial plutocracy. By the same token, it also assisted to adapt a theory conceived for a wealthy and civilized community to the exactly opposed conditions of life in a new and undeveloped country. In a frontier society engrossed in the conquest of nature and provided with but meagre stimulation to artistic and intellectual achievement, the inevitable index of success was accumulation, and accumulation did, in fact, represent social service. What is more, the singular affinity which Calvinistic New England early discovered for Lockian rationalism is in some measure explicable on like grounds. The central pillar of Calvinism was the doctrine of election. It goes without saying that all who believed this dogma also believed themselves among the elect; yet of this what better, what more objective evidence than material success? Locke himself, it may be added, was a notable preacher of the gospel of industry and thrift.

Two other features of Locke's thought deserve brief comment. The first is his insistence upon the "public good" as the object of legislation and of governmental action in general. It should not be supposed that this in any way contradicts the main trend of his thought. Rather he is laying down yet another limitation on legislative freedom of action. That the public good might not always be compatible with the preservation of rights, and especially with the rights of property, never once occurs to him. A century later the possibility did occur to Adam Smith, and was waived aside by his "harmony of interests" theory. Also the dimensions which Locke assigns to executive prerogative are, in view both of the immediate occasion for which he wrote and of his "constitutionalism," not a little astonishing. On this matter he writes:

> Where the legislative and executive power are in distinct hands (as they are in all moderated monarchies and well-framed governments), there the good of the society requires, that several things should be left to the discretion of him that has the executive power: for the legislators not being able to foresee, and provide by laws, for all that may be useful to the community, the executor of the laws, having the power in his hands, has by the common law of nature a right to make use of it for the good of the society, in many cases, where the municipal law has given no direction, till the legislative can conveniently be assembled to provide for it;

> Many things there are, which the law can by no means provide for; and
> those must necessarily be left to the discretion of him that has the
> executive power in his hands, to be ordered by him as the public good
> and advantage shall require: nay, it is fit that the laws themselves should
> in some cases give way to the executive power, or rather to the funda-
> mental law of nature and government — viz., That as much as may be,
> all the members of the society are to be preserved.

Extrication from the trammels of a too rigid constitutionalism
through a broad view of executive power is a device by no means
unknown to American constitutional law and theory.

Locke's contribution is best estimated in relation to Coke's. Locke's
version of natural law not only rescues Coke's version of the English
constitution from a localized *patois,* restating it in the universal
tongue of the age, it also supplements it in important respects. Coke's
endeavor was to put forward the historical procedure of the common
law as a permanent restraint on power, and especially on the power of
the English crown. Locke, in the limitations which he imposes on legislative power, is looking rather to the security of the substantive rights
of the individual — those rights which are implied in the basic
arrangements of society at all times and in all places. While Coke rescued the notion of fundamental law from what must sooner or later
have proved a fatal nebulosity, yet he did so at the expense of
archaism. Locke, on the other hand, in cutting loose in great measure
from the historical method of reasoning, opened the way to the larger
issues with which American constitutional law has been called upon to
grapple in its latest maturity. Without the Lockian or some similar
background, judicial review must have atrophied by 1890 in the very
field in which it is today most active; nor is this to forget his emphasis
on the property right. Locke's weakness is on the institutional side.
While he contributed to the *doctrine* of judicial review, it was without
intention; nor does he reveal any perception of the importance of giving imperative written form to the constitutional principles which he
formulated. The hardfisted Coke, writing with a civil war ahead of
him instead of behind him, was more prescient.

The influence of higher law doctrine associated with the names of
Coke [whose decisions and ideas suggested that all branches of government are bound by a higher law, which should be interpreted and upheld by the common law courts against parliamentary or executive en-
croachment] and Locke was at its height in England during the period
when the American colonies were being most actively settled, which
means that Coke had, to begin with, the advantage since he was first
on the ground. The presence of Coke's doctrines in the colonies during the latter two-thirds of the seventeenth century is widely evidenced

by the repeated efforts of colonial legislatures to secure for their constituencies the benefits of *Magna Carta* and particularly of the twenty-ninth chapter thereof [which pledged: "No freeman shall be taken or imprisoned or disseised or exiled or in any way destroyed . . . except by the lawful judgment of his peers and by the law of the land."]. Because of the menace they were thought to spell for the prerogative, the majority of such measures incurred the royal veto. In point of fact, since the "law of the land" clause of chapter twenty-nine was interpretable as contemplating only law which was enacted by the colonial legislature, the menace went even further. Clothed with this construction, chapter twenty-nine afforded affirmation not only of rights of the individual, but also of local legislative autonomy. The frequently provoked discussion of such matters, moreover, served to fix terminology for the future moulding of thought. *Magna Carta* became a generic term for all documents of constitutional significance, and thereby a symbol and reminder of principles binding on government.

But more specific evidence of Coke's influence also occurs during this period. One such instance is furnished by the opinion of a Massachusetts magistrate in 1657 holding void a tax by the town of Ipswich for the purpose of presenting the local minister with a dwelling house. Such a tax, said the magistrate, "to take from Peter and give it to Paul," is against fundamental law. "If noe kinge or Parliament can justly enact or cause that one man's estate, in whole or in part, may be taken from him and given to another without his owne consent, then surely the major part of a towne or other inferior powers cannot doe it." An opinion of the attorney general of the Barbados, rendered sometime during the reign of Anne, which held void a paper money act because it authorized summary process against debtors, is of like import. The entire argument is based on chapter twenty-nine of *Magna Carta* and "common right, or reason." Evidence of the persistence of the dictum in *Bonham's Case* also crops up outside New England now and then, even before its notable revival by Otis in his argument in the *Writs of Assistance Case*. As late as 1759 we find a New York man referring quite incidentally to "a Judicial power of declaring them [laws] void." The allusion is inexplicable unless it was to Coke's "dictum."

If the seventeenth century was Coke's, the early half of the eighteenth was Locke's, especially in New England. After the Glorious Revolution the migration to America of important English elements ceased. Immediate touch with political developments in the mother country was thus lost. The colonies were fain henceforth to be content for the most part with the stock of political ideas already on hand; and in fact these met their own necessities, which grew chiefly out of the quarrels between the governors and the assemblies, extremely well. And along with this comparative isolation from new currents of thought in the mother country went the general intellectual poverty of frontier life itself. There were few books, fewer newspapers, and little travel. But one source of intellectual stimulation for the adult there was, one point of contact with the world of ideas, and that was the sermon. Through their election sermons in particular and through controversial pamphlets, the New England clergy taught their flocks political theory, and almost always this was an elaboration upon the stock of ideas which had come from seventeenth century England. . . .

After the Bible, Locke was the principal authority relied on by the preachers to bolster up their political teachings, although Coke, Pufendorf, Sydney, and later on some others were also cited. The substance of the doctrine of these discourses is, except at two points, that of the *Second Treatise*. Natural rights and the social compact, government bounded by law and incapable of imparting legality to measures contrary to law, and the right of resistance to illegal measures all fall into their proper place. One frequent point of deviation from the Lockian model is the retention of the idea of a compact between governed and governors; that notion fitted in too well with the effort to utilize the colonial charters as muniments of local liberty to be discarded. The other point of deviation from Locke is more apparent than real, for all these concepts are backed up by religious sanction. Yet to the modern reader the difference between the Puritan God of the eighteenth century and Locke's natural law often seems little more than nominal. "The Voice of Nature is the Voice of God," asserts one preacher; "reason and the voice of God are one," is the language of another; "Christ confirms the law of nature," is the teaching of a third. The point of view is thoroughly deistic; reason has usurped the place of revelation, and without affront to piety.

Nor should it be imagined that all this teaching and preaching on political topics took place *in vacuo* — in deliberate preparation, as it were, for a great emergency as yet descried only by the most perspicacious. Much of it was evoked by warm and bitter controversy among the New England congregations themselves. One such controversy was that which arose in the second decade of the eighteenth century over the question whether the congregations should submit themselves to the governance of a synod. Even more heated was the quarrel which was produced by the great awakening consequent on the preaching of George Whitefield in 1740. Whitefield's doctrine was distinctly and disturbingly equalitarian. A spirit of criticism of superiors by inferiors, of elders by juniors ensued from it; while, at the same time the intellectual superiority of the clergy was menaced by the sudden appearance of a great crop of popular exhorters. Men turned again to

Locke, Sydney, and others, but this time in order to discover the sanctions of authority rather than its limitations. Still some years later the outbreak of the French and Indian Wars inspired a series of sermons extolling English liberty and contrasting the balanced constitution of England with French tyranny, sermons in which the name of Montesquieu was now joined with that of Locke.

This kind of preaching was not confined to New England, nor even to dissenting clergymen. Patrick Henry from his eleventh to his twenty-second year listened to an Anglican preacher who taught that the British constitution was but the "voluntary compact of sovereign and subject." Henry's own words later were "government is a conditional compact between king and people . . . violation of the covenant by either party discharges the other from obligation"; and more than half of the signers of the Declaration of Independence were members of the Church of England. It is also an important circumstance that the famous Parson's Cause, in which Henry participated as the champion of local liberty, was pending in Virginia from 1752 to 1758, helping to bring the people of Virginia during the period face to face with fundamental constitutional questions. "On a small scale, the whole episode illustrates the clash of political theories which lay back of the American Revolution." And meantime the first generation of the American bar was coming to maturity — students of Coke, and equipped to bring his doctrines to the support of Locke should the need arise.

The opening gun of the controversy leading to the Revolution was Otis' argument in 1761 in the *Writs of Assistance Case,* which, through Bacon's and Viner's *Abridgments,* goes straight back to *Bonham's Case.* Adams' summary of it reads: "As to acts of Parliament. An act against the Constitution is void: an Act against natural Equity is void: and if an Act of Parliament should be made, in the very words of the petition, it would be void. The Executive Courts must pass such Acts into disuse. — 8 Rep. 118 from Viner." "Then and there," exclaims Adams, "the child Independence was born." Today he must have added that then and there American constitutional law was born, for Otis' contention goes far beyond Coke's: an ordinary court may traverse the specifically enacted will of Parliament, and its condemnation is final.

The suggestion that the local courts might be thus pitted against a usurping Parliament in defence of "British rights," served to bring the idea of judicial review to the very threshold of the first American constitutions, albeit it was destined to wait there unattended for some years. Adams himself in a plea before the Governor and Council of Massachusetts, turned Otis' argument against the Stamp Act, while a Virginia county court actually declared that measure void. "The judges were unanimously of the opinion," a report of the case reads, "that the law did not bind, affect, or concern the inhabitants of Virginia 'inasmuch as they conceived the said act to be unconstitutional.'" As late as 1776, Chief Justice William Cushing of Massachusetts, who was later one of Washington's first appointees to the Supreme Court of the United States, was congratulated by Adams for telling a jury of the nullity of acts of Parliament.

Nor did the controversy with Great Britain long rest purely on Coke's doctrines. Otis himself, declares Adams, "was also a great master of the law of nature and nations. He had read Pufendorf, Grotius, Barbeyrac, Burlamaqui, Vattel, Heineccius. . . . It was a maxim which he inculcated in his pupils . . . that a lawyer ought never to be without a volume of natural or public law, or moral philosophy, on his table or in his pocket." Otis' own pamphlet, *The Rights of the British Colonies Asserted and Proved,* none the less was almost altogether of Lockian provenience. The colonists were entitled to "as ample rights, liberties, and privileges as the subjects of the mother country are and in some respects to more. . . . Should the charter privileges of the Colonists be disregarded or revoked, there are natural, inherent, and inseparable rights as men and citizens that would remain." And Adams argues the year following in his dissertation on *The Canon and the Feudal Law* for

> Rights antecedent to all earthly government — Rights that cannot be repealed or restrained by human laws — Rights derived from the great Legislator of the universe. . . . British liberties are not the grants of princes or parliaments, but original rights, conditions of original contracts . . . coeval with government. . . . Many of our rights are inherent and essential, agreed on as maxims, and established as preliminaries, even before a parliament existed.

But it is the Massachusetts Circular Letter of 1768 that perfects the blend of Coke and Locke, while it also reformulates in striking terms, borrowed perhaps from Vattel, the medieval notion of authority as intrinsically conditioned. The outstanding paragraph of the letter is the following:

> The House have humbly represented to the ministry, their own sentiments, that his Majesty's high court of Parliament is the supreme legislative power over the whole empire; that in all free states the constitution is fixed, and as the supreme legislative derives its power and authority from the constitution, it cannot overleap the bounds of it, without destroying its own foundation; that the constitution ascertains and limits both sovereignty and allegiance, and, therefore, his Majesty's American subjects, who acknowledge themselves bound by the ties of allegiance, have an equitable claim to the full enjoyment of the fundamental rules of the British constitution; that it is an essential,

unalterable right, in nature, engrafted into the British constitution, as a fundamental law, and ever held sacred and irrevocable by the subjects within the realm, that what a man has honestly acquired is absolutely his own, which he may freely give, but cannot be taken from him without his consent; that the American subjects may, therefore, exclusive of any consideration of charter rights, with a decent firmness, adopted to the character of free men and subjects, assert this natural and constitutional right.

Notwithstanding all this, as late as the first Continental Congress there were still those who opposed any reliance whatsoever on natural rights. One of "the two points which we laboured most" John Adams records in his *Diary* was "whether we should recur to the law of nature, as well as to the British constitution, and our American charters and grants. Mr. Galloway and Mr. Duane were for excluding the law of nature. I was strenuous for retaining and insisting on it, as a recourse to which we might be driven by Parliament much sooner than we were aware." The "Declaration and Resolves" of the Congress proves that Adams carried the day. The opening resolution asserts "that the inhabitants of the American colonies in North America," by the immutable laws of nature, the principles of the British constitution, and the several charters or compacts "are entitled to life, liberty, and property."

Nor did the corollary notion of a single community claiming common rights on the score of a common humanity, escape American spokesmen. It was in this same first Continental Congress that Patrick Henry made his famous deliverance:

> Government is dissolved. . . . Where are your landmarks, your boundaries of Colonies? We are in a state of nature, sir. . . . The distinctions between Virginians, Pennsylvanians, New Yorkers, and New Englanders, are no more. I am not a Virginian, but an American.

And the less casual evidence of everyday speech is to like effect: "the people of these United Colonies," "your whole people," "the people of America," "the liberties of Americans," "the rights of Americans," "American rights," "Americans." The constant recurrence of such phrases in contemporary documents bespeaks the conscious identity of Americans everywhere in possession of the rights of men. Natural rights were already on the way to becoming national rights.

At the same time it is necessary to recognize that the American Revolution was also a contest for local autonomy as well as one for individual liberty. The two motives were in fact less competitive than complementary. The logical deduction from the course of political history in the colonies, especially in the later decades of it, was that the best protection of the rights of the individual was to be found in the maintenance of the hardwon prerogatives of the colonial legislatures against the royal governors; in other words, of what they locally termed their "Constitutions." The final form of the American argument against British pretensions was, therefore, by no means a happy idea suggested by the stress of contention, but was soundly based on autochthonous institutional developments. As stated by Jefferson in his *Summary View,* published in 1774, it comprised the thesis that Parliament had no power whatsoever to legislate for the colonies, whether in harmony with the rights of men or no; that the colonies were mutually independent communities, equal partners in the British Empire with England herself; that each part had its own parliament which was the supreme law-making power within its territorial limits; that each was connected with the Empire only through the person of a common monarch, who was "no more than the chief officer of the people, appointed by the laws . . . to assist in working the great machine of government erected for their use." The Declaration of Independence, two years later from the same hand, proceeds on the same theory. It is addressed not to Parliament but to the king, since it was with the king alone that the bond about to be severed had subsisted; in it the American doctrine of the relation of government to individual rights finds its classic expression; these rights are vindicated by the assertion of the independence of the thirteen states.

From the destructive phase of the Revolution we turn to its constructive phase. This time it was Virginia who led the way. The Virginia constitution of 1776 is preceded by a "Declaration of rights made by the representatives of the good people of Virginia . . . which rights do appertain to them and their posterity, as the basis and foundation of government." In this document, antedating the Declaration of Independence by a month, are enumerated at length those rights which Americans, having laid claim to them first as British subjects and later as men, now intended as citizens to secure through governments of their own erection. For the first time in the history of the world the principles of revolution are made the basis of settled political institutions.

What was the nature of these governments? Again the Virginia constitution of 1776 may serve as a model. Here the horn of the legislative department is mightily exalted, that of the executive correspondingly depressed. The early Virginia governors were chosen by the legislature annually and were assisted by a council of state also chosen by the legislature, and if that body so desired, from the legislature. The governor was without the veto power, or any other participation in the work of law-making, and his salary was entirely at the mercy of the assembly. The judges were in somewhat better case, holding their offices "during good behavior," yet they too were the legislature's appointees, and judicial review is nowhere hinted. Finally, both judges and governors were subject to impeachment, which as still defined by English precedents, amounted to a practically unrestricted inquest of office. The underlying asumption of the instrument, gatherable from its various provisions, is that the rights of the individual have nothing to fear from majority rule exercised through legislative assemblies chosen for brief terms by a restricted, though on the whole democratic, electorate. In short, as in both Coke and Locke, the maintenance of higher law is intrusted to legislative supremacy, though qualified by annual elections. Fortunately or unfortunately, in 1776 the influence of Coke and Locke was no longer the predominant one that it had been. In the very process of controversy with the British Parliament, a new point of view had been brought to American attention, the ultimate consequences of which were as yet unforeseeable.

Lord Acton has described the American Revolution as a contest between two ideas of legislative power. Even as late as the debate on the Declaratory Act of 1766, the American invocation of a constitution setting metes and bounds to Parliament did not fail of a certain response among the English themselves. Burke, it is true, brushed aside all questions of prescriptive rights and based his advocacy of the American cause on expediency only; but Camden, who possessed the greatest legal reputation of the age, quoted both Coke and Locke in support of the proposition that Parliament's power was not an unlimited one; while Chatham, taking halfway ground, pretended to discover a fundamental distinction between the power of taxation and that of legislation, qualifying the former by the necessity of representation. Camden and Chatham were, none the less, illustrious exceptions. The direction which the great weight of professional opinion was now taking was shown when Mansfield, who a few years earlier had as solicitor general quoted the dictum in *Bonham's Case* with approval, arose in the House of Lords to support the Declaratory Act. The passage of that measure by an overwhelming majority committed Parliament substantially to Milton's conclusion of a century earlier that "Parliament was above all positive law, whether civil or common."

The vehicle of the new doctrine to America was Blackstone's *Commentaries,* of which, before the Revolution, nearly 2500 copies had been sold on this side of the Atlantic, while the spread of his influence in the later days of the pre-Revolutionary controversy is testified to by Jefferson in his reference to that "young brood of lawyers" who, seduced by the "honeyed Mansfieldism of Blackstone, . . . began to slide into Toryism." Nor is Blackstone's appeal to men of all parties difficult to understand. Eloquent, suave, undismayed in the presence of the palpable contradictions in his pages, adept in insinuating new points of view without unnecessarily disturbing old ones, he is the very exemplar and model of legalistic and judicial obscurantism.

While still a student, Blackstone had published an essay on *The Absolute Rights of British Subjects,* and chapter one of book one of his greater work bears a like caption. Here he appears at first glance to underwrite the whole of Locke's philosophy, but a closer examination discloses important divergences. "Natural liberty" he defines as "the power of acting as one thinks fit, without any restraint or control, unless by the law of nature." It is "inherent in us by birth," and is that gift of God which corresponds with "the faculty of free will." Yet every man, he continues, "when he enters into society, gives up a part of his natural liberty as the price of so valuable a purchase," receiving in return "civil liberty," which is natural liberty "so far restrained by human laws (and no farther) as is necessary and expedient for the general advantage of the public." The divergence which this phraseology marks from the strictly Lockian position is twofold. Locke also, as we saw above, suggests public utility as one requirement of allowable restraints upon liberty, but by no means the sole requirement; nor is the law-making power with him, as with Blackstone, the final arbiter of the issue.

The divergence becomes even more evident when the latter turns to consider the positive basis of British liberties in *Magna Carta* and "the corroborating statutes." His language in this connection is peculiarly complacent. The rights declared in these documents, he asserts, comprise nothing less than

> either that residuum of natural liberty, which is not required by the laws of society to be sacrificed to public convenience, or else those civil privileges, which society hath engaged to provide in lieu of the natural liberties so given up by individuals. These, therefore, were formerly, either by inheritance or purchase, the rights of all mankind; but, in most other countries of the world, being now more or less debased and destroyed, they at present may be said to remain, in a peculiar and emphatical manner, the rights of the people of England.

Yet when he comes to trace the limits of the "rights and liberties" so grandiloquently characterized, his invariable reference is simply to the state of the law in his own day — never to any more exalted standard.

And so by phraseology drawn from Locke and Coke themselves, he paves the way to the entirely opposed position of Hobbes and Mansfield. In elaboration of this position he lays down the following propositions: First, "there is and must be in all of them [states] a supreme, irresistible, absolute, uncontrolled authority . . ."; secondly, this authority is the "natural, inherent right that belongs to the sovereignty of the state . . . of making and enforcing laws"; thirdly, to the law-making power "all other powers of the state" must conform "in the execution of their several functions or else the Constitution is at an end"; and, finally, the law-making power in Great Britain is Parliament, in which, therefore, the sovereignty resides. It follows, of course, that neither judicial disallowance of acts of Parliament nor yet the right of revolution has either legal or constitutional basis. To be sure, "Acts of Parliament that are impossible to be performed are of no validity"; yet this is so only in a truistic sense, for "there is no court that has power to defeat the intent of the legislature, when couched in . . . evident and express words." As to the right of revolution — "So long . . . as the English Constitution lasts, we may venture to affirm that the power of Parliament is absolute and without control."

Nor does Blackstone at the end, despite his previous equivocations, flinch from the conclusion that the whole legal fabric of the realm was, by his view, at Parliament's disposal. Thus he writes:

> It hath sovereign and uncontrollable authority in the making, confirming, enlarging, restraining, abrogating, repealing, reviving, and expounding of laws . . . this being the place where that absolute, despotic power which must in all governments reside somewhere, is entrusted by the Constitution of these kingdoms. All mischiefs and grievances, operations and remedies that transcend the ordinary course of the laws, are within the reach of this extraordinary tribunal. . . . It can, in short, do everything that is not naturally impossible, and therefore some have not scrupled to call its power by a figure rather too bold, the omnipotence of Parliament. True it is, that what the Parliament doth no authority upon earth can undo.

This absolute doctrine was summed up by De Lolme a little later in the oft-quoted aphorism that "Parliament can do anything except make a man a woman or a woman a man."

Thus was the notion of legislative sovereignty added to the stock of American political ideas. Its essential contradiction of the elements of theory which had been contributed by earlier thinkers is manifest. What Coke and Locke give us is, for the most part, cautions and safeguards against power; in Blackstone, on the other hand, as in Hobbes, we find the claims of power exalted. This occurred, moreover, at a moment when, as it happened, not merely the actual structure of government in the United States, but this strong trend of thought among the American people afforded the thesis of legislative sovereignty every promise of easy lodgement.

The formula laid down by the Declaration of Independence regarding the right of revolution is a most conservative one. The right is not to be exercised for "light and transient causes," but only to arrest a settled and deliberate course of tyranny. Yet within a twelve-month

of the Declaration we find one Benjamin Hichborn of Boston
proclaiming the following doctrine:

> I define civil liberty to be not a "government by laws," made agreeable
> to charters, bills of rights or compacts, but a power existing in the
> people at large, at any time, for any cause, or for no cause, but their own
> sovereign pleasure, to alter or annihilate both the mode and essence of
> any former government, and adopt a new one in its stead.

Ultimately the doctrine of popular sovereignty thus voiced was to be
turned against both legislative sovereignty and at a critical moment
against state particularism. But at the outset it aided both these ideas,
because the state was conceived to stand nearer to the people than the
Continental Congress, and because, within the state, the legislature
was conceived to stand nearer to the people than the other departments. Thus legislative sovereignty, a derivative from the notion of
popular sovereignty . . . from Justinian . . . was recruited afresh from
the parent stream, with the result that all the varied rights of man were
threatened with submergence in a single right, that of belonging to a
popular majority, or more accurately, of being represented by a legislative majority.

   Why, then, did not legislative sovereignty finally establish itself in
our constitutional system? To answer at this point solely in terms of
institutions, the reason is twofold. In the first place, in the American
written Constitution, higher law at last attained a form which made
possible the attribution to it of an entirely new sort of validity, the
validity of a *statute emanating from the sovereign people.* Once the
binding force of higher law was transferred to this new basis, the
notion of the sovereignty of the ordinary legislative organ disappeared
automatically, since that cannot be a *sovereign* law-making body
which is subordinate to another law-making body. But in the second
place, even statutory form could hardly have saved the higher law as *a
recourse for individuals* had it not been backed up by *judicial review.*
Invested with statutory form and implemented by judicial review,
higher law, as with renewed youth, entered upon one of the great periods of its history, and juristically the most fruitful one since the days
of Justinian.

The Constitutional Framework

The framers of the Constitution were guided by a rich political
tradition. The delegates to the Constitutional Convention were
pragmatic politicians with conflicting interests and motivations.
In attempting to assess motives, historians are confronted with

an almost impossible task. Indeed it can be argued that it is not the motives that count but only the results of the actions that were taken. In this regard the Constitution was a conservative document that carefully provided for indirect rather than direct democracy. But with respect to the times in which it was drafted, the Constitution can be viewed in a different fashion. This is the argument presented in the selection by John P. Roche.

3   JOHN P. ROCHE

THE FOUNDING FATHERS:
A REFORM CAUCUS IN ACTION

Over the last century and a half, the work of the Constitutional Convention and the motives of the Founding Fathers have been analyzed under a number of different ideological auspices. To one generation of historians, the hand of God was moving in the assembly; under a later dispensation, the dialectic (at various levels of philosophical sophistication) replaced the Deity: "relationships of production" moved into the niche previously reserved for Love of Country. Thus in counterpart to the Zeitgeist, the Framers have undergone miraculous metamorphoses: at one time acclaimed as liberals and bold social engineers, today they appear in the guise of sound Burkean conservatives, men who in our time would subscribe to *Fortune,* look to Walter Lippmann for political theory, and chuckle patronizingly at the antics of Barry Goldwater. The implicit assumption is that if James Madison were among us, he would be President of the Ford Foundation, while Alexander Hamilton would chair the Committee for Economic Development.

The "Fathers" have thus been admitted to our best circles; the revolutionary ferocity which confiscated all Tory property in reach and populated New Brunswick with outlaws has been converted by the "Miltown School" of American historians into a benign dedication to "consensus" and "prescriptive rights." The Daughters of the American Revolution have, through the ministrations of Professors Boorstin, Hartz, and Rossiter, at last found ancestors worthy of their descendants. It is not my purpose here to argue that the "Fathers" were, in fact, radical revolutionaries; that proposition has been brilliantly demonstrated by Robert R. Palmer in his *Age of the Democratic Revolution.* My concern is with the further position that not only were they revolutionaries, but also they were democrats. Indeed, in my view,

From *The American Political Science Review* (December 1961). Reprinted by permission of The American Political Science Association and the author.

there is one fundamental truth about the Founding Fathers that *every* generation of Zeitgeisters has done its best to obscure: they were first and foremost superb democratic politicians. I suspect that in a contemporary setting, James Madison would be Speaker of the House of Representatives and Hamilton would be the *eminence grise* dominating (*pace* Theodore Sorensen or Sherman Adams) the Executive Office of the President. They were, with their colleagues, *political men* — not metaphysicians, disembodied conservatives or Agents of History — and as recent research into the nature of American politics in the 1780s confirms, they were committed (perhaps willy-nilly) to working within the democratic framework, within a universe of public approval. Charles Beard *and* the filiopietists to the contrary notwithstanding, the Philadelphia Convention was not a College of Cardinals or a council of Platonic guardians working within a manipulative, predemocratic framework; it was a *nationalist* reform caucus which had to operate with great delicacy and skill in a political cosmos full of enemies to achieve the one definitive goal — popular approbation.

Perhaps the time has come, to borrow Walton Hamilton's fine phrase, to raise the Framers from immortality to mortality, to give them credit for their magnificent demonstration of the art of democratic politics. The point must be reemphasized; they *made* history and did it within the limits of consensus. There was nothing inevitable about the future in 1787; the *Zeitgeist*, that fine Hegelian technique of begging causal questions, could only be discerned in retrospect. What they did was to hammer out a pragmatic compromise which would both bolster the "National interest" and be acceptable to the people. What inspiration they got came from their collective experience as professional politicians in a democratic society. As John Dickinson put it to his fellow delegates on August 13, "Experience must be our guide. Reason may mislead us."

In this context, let us examine the problems they confronted and the solutions they evolved. The Convention has been described picturesquely as a counter-revolutionary junta and the Constitution as a *coup d'état,* but this has been accomplished by withdrawing the whole history of the movement for constitutional reform from its true context. No doubt the goals of the constitutional elite were "subversive" to the existing political order, but it is overlooked that their subversion could only have succeeded if the people of the United States endorsed it by regularized procedures. Indubitably they were "plotting" to establish a much stronger central government than existed under the Articles, but only in the sense in which one could argue equally well that John F. Kennedy was, from 1956 to 1960, "plotting" to become President. In short, on the fundamental *procedural* level, the Constitutionalists had to work according to the prevailing rules of the game.

Whether they liked it or not is a topic for spiritualists — and is irrelevant: one may be quite certain that had Washington agreed to play the de Gaulle (as the Cincinnati once urged), Hamilton would willingly have held his horse, but such fertile speculation in no way alters the actual context in which events took place.

I

When the Constitutionalists went forth to subvert the Confederation, they utilized the mechanisms of political legitimacy. And the roadblocks which confronted them were formidable. At the same time, they were endowed with certain potent political assets. The history of the United States from 1786 to 1790 was largely one of a masterful employment of political expertise by the Constitutionalists as against bumbling, erratic behavior by the opponents of reform. Effectively, the Constitutionalists had to induce the states, by democratic techniques of coercion, to emasculate themselves. To be specific, if New York had refused to join the new Union, the project was doomed; yet before New York was safely in, the reluctant state legislature had *sua sponte* to take the following steps: (1) agree to send delegates to the Philadelphia Convention; (2) provide maintenance for these delegates (these were distinct stages: New Hampshire was early in naming delegates, but did not provide for their maintenance until July); (3) set up the special *ad hoc* convention to decide on ratification; and (4) concede to the decision of the *ad hoc* convention that New York should participate. New York admittedly was a tricky state, with a strong interest in a *status quo* which permitted her to exploit New Jersey and Connecticut, but the same legal hurdles existed in every state. And at the risk of becoming boring, it must be reiterated that the *only* weapon in the Constitutionalist arsenal was an effective mobilization of public opinion.

The group which undertook this struggle was an interesting amalgam of a few dedicated nationalists with the self-interested spokesmen of various parochial bailiwicks. The Georgians, for example, wanted a strong central authority to provide military protection for their huge, under-populated state against the Creek Confederacy; Jerseymen and Connecticuters wanted to escape from economic bondage to New York; the Virginians hoped to establish a system which would give that great state its rightful place in the councils of the republic. The dominant figures in the politics of these states therefore cooperated in the call for the Convention. In other states, the thrust towards national reform was taken up by opposition groups who added the "national interest" to their weapons system; in Pennsylvania, for instance, the group fighting to revise the Constitution of 1776 came out four-square behind the Constitutionalists, and in New York, Hamilton and the

Schuyler *ambiance* took the same tack against George Clinton. There was, of course, a large element of personality in the affair: there is reason to suspect that Patrick Henry's opposition to the Convention and the Constitution was founded on his conviction that Jefferson was behind both, and a close study of local politics elsewhere would surely reveal that others supported the Constitution for the simple (and politically quite sufficient) reason that the "wrong" people were against it.

To say this is not to suggest that the Constitution rested on a foundation of impure or base motives. It is rather to argue that in politics there are no immaculate conceptions, and that in the drive for a stronger general government, motives of all sorts played a part. Few men in the history of mankind have espoused a view of the "common good" or "public interest" that militated against their private status; even Plato with all his reverence for disembodied reason managed to put philosophers on top of the pile. Thus it is not surprising that a number of diversified private interests joined to push the nationalist public interest; what would have been surprising was the absence of such a pragmatic united front. And the fact remains that, however motivated, these men did demonstrate a willingness to compromise their parochial interests in behalf of an ideal which took shape before their eyes and under their ministrations.

As Stanley Elkins and Eric McKitrick have suggested in a perceptive essay [76 *Pol. Science Quarterly* 181 (1961)], what distinguished the leaders of the Constitutionalist caucus from their enemies was a "Continental" approach to political, economic and military issues. To the extent that they shared an institutional base of operations, it was the Continental Congress (thirty-nine of the delegates to the Federal Convention had served in Congress), and this was hardly a locale which inspired respect for the state governments. Robert de Jouvenal observed French politics half a century ago and noted that a revolutionary Deputy had more in common with a non-revolutionary Deputy than he had with a revolutionary non-Deputy; similarly one can surmise that membership in the Congress under the Articles of Confederation worked to establish a continental frame of reference, that a Congressman from Pennsylvania and one from South Carolina would share a universe of discourse which provided them with a conceptual common denominator *vis à vis* their respective state legislatures. This was particularly true with respect to external affairs: the average state legislator was probably about as concerned with foreign policy then as he is today, but Congressmen were constantly forced to take the broad view of American prestige, were compelled to listen to the reports of Secretary John Jay and to the dispatches and pleas from their frustrated envoys in Britain, France and Spain. From considerations such as these, a "Continental" ideology developed which seems to have demanded a revision of our domestic institutions primarily on the ground that only by invigorating our general government could we assume our rightful place in the international arena. Indeed, an argument with great force — particularly since Washington was its incarnation — urged that our very survival in the Hobbesian jungle of world politics depended upon a reordering and strengthening of our national sovereignty.

The great achievement of the Constitutionalists was their ultimate success in convincing the elected representatives of a majority of the white male population that change was imperative. A small group of political leaders with a Continental vision and essentially a consciousness of the United States' *international* impotence, provided the matrix of the movement. To their standard other leaders rallied with their own parallel ambitions. Their great assets were (1) the presence in their caucus of the one authentic American "father figure," George Washington, whose prestige was enormous; (2) the energy and talent of their leadership (in which one must include the towering intellectuals of the time, John Adams and Thomas Jefferson, despite their absence abroad), and their communications "network," which was far superior to anything on the opposition side; (3) the preemptive skill which made "their" issue The Issue and kept the locally oriented opposition permanently on the defensive; and (4) the subjective consideration that these men were spokesmen of a new and compelling credo: *American* nationalism, that ill-defined but nonetheless potent sense of collective purpose that emerged from the American Revolution.

Despite great institutional handicaps, the Constitutionalists managed in the mid-1780s to mount an offensive which gained momentum as years went by. Their greatest problem was lethargy, and paradoxically, the number of barriers in their path may have proved an advantage in the long run. Beginning with the initial battle to get the Constitutional Convention called and delegates appointed, they could never relax, never let up the pressure. In practical terms, this meant that the local "organizations" created by the Constitutionalists were perpetually in movement building up their cadres for the next fight. (The word organization has to be used with great caution: a political organization in the United States — as in contemporary England — generally consisted of a magnate and his following, or a coalition of magnates. This did not necessarily mean that it was "undemocratic" or "aristocratic," in the Aristotelian sense of the word: while a few magnates such as the Livingstons could draft their followings, most exercised their leadership without coercion on the basis of popular endorsement. The absence of organized opposition did not imply the impossibility of competition any more than low public participation in elections necessarily indicated an undemocratic suffrage.)

The Constitutionalists got the jump on the "opposition" (a collective noun: oppositions would be more correct) at the outset with the demand for a Convention. Their opponents were caught in an old political trap: they were not being asked to approve any specific program of reform, but only to endorse a meeting to discuss and recommend needed reforms. If they took a hard line at the first stage, they were put in the position of glorifying the *status quo* and of denying the need for *any* changes. Moreover, the Constitutionalists could go to the people with a persuasive argument for "fair play" — "How can you condemn reform before you know precisely what is involved?" Since the state legislatures obviously would have the final say on any proposals that might emerge from the Convention, the Constitutionalists were merely reasonable men asking for a chance. Besides, since they did not make any concrete proposals at that stage, they were in a position to capitalize on every sort of generalized discontent with the Confederation.

Perhaps because of their poor intelligence system, perhaps because of over-confidence generated by the failure of all previous efforts to alter the Articles, the opposition awoke too late to the dangers that confronted them in 1787. Not only did the Constitutionalists manage to get every state but Rhode Island (where politics was enlivened by a party system reminiscent of the "Blues" and the "Greens" in the Byzantine Empire) to appoint delegates to Philadelphia, but when the results were in, it appeared that they dominated the delegations. Given the apathy of the opposition, this was a natural phenomenon: in an ideologically nonpolarized political atmosphere those who get appointed to a special committee are likely to be the men who supported the movement for its creation. Even George Clinton, who seems to have been the first opposition leader to awake to the possibility of trouble, could not prevent the New York legislature from appointing Alexander Hamilton — though he did have the foresight to send two of his henchmen to dominate the delegation. Incidentally, much has been made of the fact that the delegates to Philadelphia were not elected by the people; some have adduced this fact as evidence of the "undemocratic" character of the gathering. But put in the context of the time, this argument is wholly specious: the central government under the Articles was considered a creature of the component states and in all the states but Rhode Island, Connecticut and New Hampshire, members of the national Congress were chosen by the state legislatures. This was not a consequence of elitism or fear of the mob; it was a logical extension of states' rights doctrine to guarantee that the national institution did not end-run the state legislatures and make direct contact with the people.

II

With delegations safely named, the focus shifted to Philadelphia. While waiting for a quorum to assemble, James Madison got busy and drafted the so-called Randolph or Virginia Plan with the aid of the Virginia delegation. This was a political master-stroke. Its consequence was that once business got underway, the framework of discussion was established on Madison's terms. There was no interminable argument over agenda; instead the delegates took the Virginia Resolutions — "just for purposes of discussion" — as their point of departure. And along with Madison's proposals, many of which were buried in the course of the summer, went his major premise: a new start on a Constitution rather than piecemeal amendment. This was not necessarily revolutionary — a little exegesis could demonstrate that a new Constitution might be formulated as "amendments" to the Articles of Confederation — but Madison's proposal that this "lump sum" amendment go into effect after approval by nine states (the Articles required unanimous state approval for any amendment) was thoroughly subversive.

Standard treatments of the Convention divide the delegates into "nationalists" and "states'-righters" with various improvised shadings ("moderate nationalists," etc.), but these are *a posteriori* categories which obfuscate more than they clarify. What is striking to one who analyzes the Convention as a case-study in democratic politics is the lack of clear-cut ideological divisions in the Convention. Indeed, I submit that the evidence — Madison's *Notes,* the correspondence of the delegates, and debates on ratification — indicates that this was a remarkably homogeneous body on the ideological level. Yates and Lansing, Clinton's two chaperones for Hamilton, left in disgust on July 10. (Is there anything more tedious than sitting through endless disputes on matters one deems fundamentally misconceived? It takes an iron will to spend a hot summer as an ideological *agent provocateur.*) Luther Martin, Maryland's bibulous narcissist, left on September 4 in a huff when he discovered that others did not share his self-esteem; others went home for personal reasons. But the hard core of delegates accepted a grinding regimen throughout the attrition of a Philadelphia summer precisely because they shared the Constitutionalist goal.

Basic differences of opinion emerged, of course, but these were not ideological; they were *structural.* If the so-called "states'-rights" group had not accepted the fundamental purposes of the Convention, they could simply have pulled out and by doing so have aborted the whole enterprise. Instead of bolting, they returned day after day to argue and to compromise. An interesting symbol of this basic homogeneity was the initial agreement on secrecy: these professional politicians did not want to become prisoners of publicity; they wanted to retain that freedom of maneuver which is only possible when men are not forced to take public stands in the preliminary stages of negotiation. There was no legal means of binding the tongues of the delegates: at any stage in the game a delegate with basic principled objections to the emerging project could have taken the stump (as Luther Martin did after his exit) and denounced the convention to the skies. Yet Madison did not even inform Thomas Jefferson in Paris of the course of the deliberations and available correspondence indicates that the delegates generally observed the injunction. Secrecy is certainly uncharacteristic of any assembly marked by strong ideological polarization. This was noted at the time: the *New York Daily Advertiser,* August 14, 1787, commented that the "profound secrecy hitherto observed by the Convention [we consider] a happy omen, as it demonstrates that the spirit of party on any great and essential point cannot have arisen to any height."

Commentators on the Constitution who have read *The Federalist* in lieu of reading the actual debates have credited the Fathers with the invention of a sublime concept called "Federalism." Unfortunately *The Federalist* is probative evidence for only one proposition: that Hamilton and Madison were inspired propagandists with a genius for retrospective symmetry. Federalism, as the theory is generally defined, was an improvisation which was later promoted into a political theory. Experts on "federalism" should take to heart the advice of David Hume, who warned in his *Of the Rise and Progress of the Arts and Sciences* that "there is no subject in which we must proceed with more caution than in [history], lest we assign causes which never existed and reduce what is merely contingent to stable and universal principles." In any event, the final balance in the Constitution between the states and the nation must have come as a great disappointment to Madison, while Hamilton's unitary views are too well known to need elucidation.

It is indeed astonishing how those who have glibly designated James Madison the "father" of Federalism have overlooked the solid body of fact which indicates that he shared Hamilton's quest for a unitary central government. To be specific, they have avoided examining the clear import of the Madison-Virginia Plan, and have disregarded Madison's dogged inch-by-inch retreat from the bastions of centralization. The Virginia Plan envisioned a unitary national government effectively freed from and dominant over the states. The lower house of the national legislature was to be elected directly by the people of the states with membership proportional to population. The upper house was to be selected by the lower and the two chambers would elect the executive and choose the judges. The national government would be thus cut completely loose from the states.

The structure of the general government was freed from state control in a truly radical fashion, but the scope of the authority of the national sovereign as Madison initially formulated it was breathtaking — it was a formulation worthy of the Sage of Malmesbury himself. The national legislature was to be empowered to disallow the acts of state legislatures, and the central government was vested, in addition to the powers of the nation under the Articles of Confederation, with plenary authority wherever "the separate States are incompetent or in which the harmony of the United States may be interrupted by the exercise of individual legislation." Finally, just to lock the door against state intrusion, the national Congress was to be given the power to use military force on recalcitrant states. This was Madison's "model" of an ideal national government, though it later received little publicity in *The Federalist*.

The interesting thing was the reaction of the Convention to this militant program for a strong autonomous central government. Some delegates were startled, some obviously leery of so comprehensive a project of reform, but nobody set off any fireworks and nobody walked out. Moreover, in the two weeks that followed, the Virginia Plan received substantial endorsement *en principe;* the initial temper of the gathering can be deduced from the approval "without debate or dissent," on May 31, of the Sixth Resolution which granted Congress the authority to disallow state legislation "contravening *in its opinion* the Articles of Union." Indeed, an amendment was included to bar states from contravening national treaties.

The Virginia Plan may therefore be considered, in ideological terms, as the delegates' Utopia, but as the discussions continued and became more specific, many of those present began to have second thoughts. After all, they were not residents of Utopia or guardians in Plato's Republic who could simply impose a philosophical ideal on subordinate strata of the population. They were practical politicians in a democratic society, and no matter what their private dreams might be, they had to take home an acceptable package and defend it — and their own political futures — against predictable attack. On June 14 the breaking point between dream and reality took place. Apparently realizing that under the Virginia Plan, Massachusetts, Virginia and Pennsylvania could virtually dominate the national government — and probably appreciating that to sell this program to "the folks back home" would be impossible — the delegates from the small states dug in their heels and demanded time for a consideration of alternatives. One gets a graphic sense of the inner politics from John Dickinson's reproach to Madison: "You see the consequences of pushing things too far. Some of the members from the small States wish for two branches in the General Legislature and are friends to a good National Government; but we would sooner submit to a foreign power than . . . be deprived of an equality of suffrage in both branches of the Legislature, and thereby be thrown under the domination of the large States."

The bare outline of the *Journal* entry for Tuesday, June 14, is suggestive to anyone with extensive experience in deliberative bodies. "It was moved by Mr. Patterson [*sic,* Paterson's name was one of those consistently misspelled by Madison and everybody else] seconded by Mr. Randolph that the further consideration of the report from the Committee of the whole House [endorsing the Virginia Plan] be postponed til tomorrow and before the question for postponement was taken. It was moved by Mr. Randolph seconded by Mr. Patterson that the House adjourn." The House adjourned by obvious prearrangement of the two principals: since the preceding Saturday when Brearley and Paterson of New Jersey had announced their fundamental discontent with the representational features of the Virginia Plan, the informal pressure had certainly been building up to slow down the steamroller. Doubtless there were extended arguments at the Indian Queen between Madison and Paterson, the latter insisting that events were moving rapidly towards a probably disastrous conclusion, towards a political suicide pact. Now the process of accommodation was put into action smoothly — and wisely, given the character and strength of the doubters. Madison had the votes, but this was one of those situations where the enforcement of mechanical majoritarianism could easily have destroyed the objectives of the majority: the Constitutionalists were in quest of a qualitative as well as a quantitative consensus. This was hardly from deference to local Quaker custom; it was a political imperative if they were to attain ratification.

III

According to the standard script, at this point the "states'-rights" group intervened in force behind the New Jersey Plan, which has been characteristically portrayed as a reversion to the *status quo* under the Articles of Confederation with but minor modifications. A careful examination of the evidence indicates that only in a marginal sense is this an accurate description. It is true that the New Jersey Plan put the states back into the institutional picture, but one could argue that to do so was a recognition of political reality rather than an affirmation of states'-rights. A serious case can be made that the advocates of the New Jersey Plan, far from being ideological addicts of states'-rights, intended to substitute for the Virginia Plan a system which would both retain strong national power and have a chance of adoption in the states. The leading spokesman for the project asserted quite clearly that his views were based more on counsels of expediency than on principle; said Paterson on June 16: "I came here not to speak my own sentiments, but the sentiments of those who sent me. Our object is not such a Governmt. as may be best in itself, but such a one as our Constituents have authorized us to prepare, and as they will approve." This is Madison's version; in Yates' transcription, there is a crucial sentence following the remarks above: "I believe that a little practical virtue is to be preferred to the finest theoretical principles, which cannot be carried into effect." In his preliminary speech on June 9, Paterson had stated "to the public mind we must accommodate ourselves," and in his notes for this and his later effort as well, the emphasis is the same. The *structure* of government under the Articles should be retained:

> 2. Because it accords with the Sentiments of the People
>   [Proof:] 1. Coms. [Commissions from state legislatures defining the jurisdiction of the delegates]
>   2. News-papers — Political Barometer. Jersey never would have sent Delegates under the first [Virginia] Plan —
>   Not here to sport Opinions of my own. Wt. [What] can be done. A little practicable Virtue preferrable to Theory.

This was a defense of political acumen, not of states'-rights. In fact, Paterson's notes of his speech can easily be construed as an argument for attaining the substantive objectives of the Virginia Plan by a sound political route, *i.e.,* pouring the new wine in the old bottles. With a shrewd eye, Paterson queried:

> Will the Operation, and Force of the [central] Govt. depend upon the mode of Representn. — No — it will depend upon the Quantum of Power lodged in the leg. ex. and judy. Departments — Give [the existing] Congress the same Powers that you intend to give the two Branches, [under the Virginia Plan] and I apprehend they will act with as much Propriety and more Energy. . . .

In other words, the advocates of the New Jersey Plan concentrated their fire on what they held to be the *political liabilities* of the Virginia Plan — which were matters of institutional structure — rather than on the proposed scope of national authority. Indeed, the Supremacy Clause of the Constitution first saw the light of day in Paterson's Sixth Resolution; the New Jersey Plan contemplated the use of military force to secure compliance with national law; and finally Paterson made clear his view that under either the Virginia or the New Jersey systems, the general government would " . . . act on individuals and not on states." From the states'-rights viewpoint, this was heresy: the fundament of that doctrine was the proposition that any central government had as its constituents the states, not the people, and could only reach the people through the agency of the state government.

Paterson then reopened the agenda of the Convention, but he did so within a distinctly nationalist framework. Paterson's position was one of favoring a strong central government in principle, but opposing one which in fact *put the big states in the saddle.* (The Virginia Plan, for all its abstract merits, did very well by Virginia.) As evidence for this speculation, there is a curious and intriguing proposal among Paterson's preliminary drafts of the New Jersey Plan:

> Whereas it is necessary in Order to form the People of the U.S. of America in to a Nation, that the States should be consolidated, by which means all the Citizens thereof will become equally intitled to and will equally participate in the same Privileges and Rights . . . it is therefore resolved, that all the Lands contained within the Limits of each state individually, and of the U.S. generally be considered as constituting one Body or Mass, and be divided into thirteen or more integral parts.
>
> Resolved, That such Divisions or integral Parts shall be styled Districts.

This makes it sound as though Paterson was prepared to accept a strong unified central government along the lines of the Virginia Plan if the existing states were eliminated. He may have gotten the idea from his New Jersey colleague Judge David Brearley, who on June 9 had commented that the only remedy to the dilemma over representation was "that a map of the U.S. be spread out, that all the existing boundaries be erased, and that a new partition of the whole be made into 13 equal parts." According to Yates, Brearley added at this point, "then a government on the present [Virginia Plan] system will be just."

This proposition was never pushed — it was patently unrealistic — but one can appreciate its purpose: it would have separated the men from the boys in the large-state delegations. How attached would the Virginians have been to their reform principles if Virginia were to disappear as a component geographical unit (the largest) for representational purposes? Up to this point, the Virginians had been in the happy position of supporting high ideals with that inner confidence born of knowledge that the "public interest" they endorsed would nourish their private interest. Worse, they had shown little willingness to compromise. Now the delegates from the small states announced that they were unprepared to be offered up as sacrificial victims to a "national interest" which reflected Virginia's parochial ambition. Caustic Charles Pinckney was not far off when he remarked sardonically that "the whole [conflict] comes to this": "Give N. Jersey an equal vote, and she will dismiss her scruples, and concur in the Natil.

system." What he rather unfairly did not add was that the Jersey delegates were not free agents who could adhere to their private convictions; they had to take back, sponsor and risk their reputations on the reforms approved by the Convention — and in New Jersey, not in Virginia.

Paterson spoke on Saturday, and one can surmise that over the weekend there was a good deal of consultation, argument, and caucusing among the delegates. One member at least prepared a full length address: on Monday Alexander Hamilton, previously mute, rose and delivered a six-hour oration. It was a remarkably apolitical speech; the gist of his position was that *both* the Virginia and New Jersey Plans were inadequately centralist, and he detailed a reform program which was reminiscent of the Protectorate under the Cromwellian *Instrument of Government* of 1653. It has been suggested that Hamilton did this in the best political tradition to emphasize the moderate character of the Virginia Plan, to give the cautious delegates something *really* to worry about; but this interpretation seems somehow too clever. Particularly since the sentiments Hamilton expressed happened to be completely consistent with those he privately — and sometimes publicly — expressed throughout his life. He wanted, to take a striking phrase from a letter to George Washington, a "strong well mounted government"; in essence, the Hamilton Plan contemplated an elected life monarch, virtually free of public control, on the Hobbesian ground that only in this fashion could strength and stability be achieved. The other alternatives, he argued, would put policy-making at the mercy of the passions of the mob; only if the sovereign was beyond the reach of selfish influence would it be possible to have government in the interests of the whole community.

From all accounts, this was a masterful and compelling speech, but (aside from furnishing John Lansing and Luther Martin with ammunition for later use against the Constitution) it made little impact. Hamilton was simply transmitting on a different wave-length from the rest of the delegates; the latter adjourned after his great effort, admired his rhetoric, and then returned to business. It was rather as if they had taken a day off to attend the opera. Hamilton, never a particularly patient man or much of a negotiator, stayed for another ten days and then left, in considerable disgust, for New York. Although he came back to Philadelphia sporadically and attended the last two weeks of the Convention, Hamilton played no part in the laborious task of hammering out the Constitution. His day came later when he led the New York Constitutionalists into the savage imbroglio over ratification — an arena in which his unmatched talent for dirty political infighting may well have won the day. For instance, in the New York Ratifying Convention, Lansing threw back into Hamilton's teeth the sentiments the latter had expressed in his June 18 oration in the Convention. However, having since retreated to the fine defensive positions immortalized in *The Federalist,* the Colonel flatly denied that he had ever been an enemy of the states, or had believed that conflict between states and nation was inexorable! As Madison's authoritative *Notes* did not appear until 1840, and there had been no press coverage, there was no way to verify his assertions, so in the words of the reporter, "a warm personal altercation between [Lansing and Hamilton] engrossed the remainder of the day [June 28, 1788]."

IV

On Tuesday morning, June 19, the vacation was over. James Madison led off with a long, carefully reasoned speech analyzing the New Jersey Plan which, while intellectually vigorous in its criticisms, was quite conciliatory in mood. "The great difficulty," he observed, "lies in the affair of Representation; and if this could be adjusted, all others would be surmountable." (As events were to demonstrate, this diagnosis was correct.) When he finished, a vote was taken on whether to continue with the Virginia Plan as the nucleus for a new constitution: seven states voted "Yes"; New York, New Jersey, and Delaware voted "No"; and Maryland, whose position often depended on which delegates happened to be on the floor, divided. Paterson, it seems, lost decisively; yet in a fundamental sense he and his allies had achieved their purpose: from that day onward, it could never be forgotten that the state governments loomed ominously in the background and that no verbal incantations could exorcise their power. Moreover, nobody bolted the convention: Paterson and his colleagues took their defeat in stride and set to work to modify the Virginia Plan, particularly with respect to its provisions on representation in the national legislature. Indeed, they won an immediate rhetorical bonus; when Oliver Ellsworth of Connecticut rose to move that the word "national" be expunged from the Third Virginia Resolution ("Resolved that a *national* Government ought to be established consisting of a *supreme* Legislative, Executive and Judiciary"), Randolph agreed and the motion passed unanimously. The process of compromise had begun.

For the next two weeks, the delegates circled around the problem of legislative representation. The Connecticut delegation appears to have evolved a possible compromise quite early in the debates, but the Virginians and particularly Madison (unaware that he would later be acclaimed as the prophet of "federalism") fought obdurately against providing for equal representation of states in the second chamber. There was a good deal of acrimony and at one point Benjamin Franklin — of all people — proposed the institution of a daily prayer; practical politicians in the gathering, however, were meditating more on the merits of a good committee than on the utility of Divine intervention. On July 2, the ice began to break when through a number of fortuitous events — and one that seems deliberate — the majority against equality of representation was converted into a dead tie. The Convention had reached the stage where it was "ripe" for a solution (presumably all the therapeutic speeches had been made), and the South Carolinians proposed a committee. Madison and James Wilson wanted none of it, but with only Pennsylvania dissenting, the body voted to establish a working party on the problem of representation.

The members of this committee, one from each state, were elected by the delegates — and a very interesting committee it was. Despite the fact that the Virginia Plan had held majority support up to that date, neither Madison nor Randolph was selected (Mason was the Virginian) and Baldwin of Georgia, whose shift in position had resulted in the tie, was chosen. From the composition, it was clear that this was not to be a "fighting" committee: the emphasis in membership was on what might be described as "second-level political entrepreneurs." On the basis of the discussions up to that time, only Luther Martin of Maryland could be described as a "bitter-ender." Admittedly, some divination enters into this sort of analysis, but one does get a sense of the mood of the delegates from these choices — including the interesting selection of Benjamin Franklin, despite his age and intellectual wobbliness, over the brilliant and incisive Wilson or the sharp, polemical Gouverneur Morris, to represent Pennsylvania. His passion for conciliation was more valuable at this juncture than Wilson's logical genius, or Morris' acerbic wit.

There is a common rumor that the Framers divided their time between philosophical discussions of government and reading the classics in political theory. Perhaps this is as good a time as any to note that their concerns were highly practical, that they spent little time canvassing abstractions. A number of them had some acquaintance with the history of political theory (probably gained from reading John Adams' monumental compilation *A Defense of the Constitutions of Government,* the first volume of which appeared in 1786), and it was a poor rhetorician indeed who could not cite Locke, Montesquieu, or Harrington *in support* of a desired goal. Yet up to this point in the deliberations, no one had expounded a defense of states'-rights or the "separation of powers" on anything resembling a theoretical basis. It should be reiterated that the Madison model had no room either for the states or for the "separation of powers": effectively *all* governmental power was vested in the national legislature. The merits of Montesquieu did not turn up until *The Federalist;* and although a perverse argument could be made that Madison's ideal was truly in the tradition of John Locke's *Second Treatise of Government,* the Locke whom the American rebels treated as an honorary president was a pluralistic defender of vested rights, not of parliamentary supremacy.

It would be tedious to continue a blow-by-blow analysis of the work of the delegates; the critical fight was over representation of the states and once the Connecticut Compromise was adopted on July 17, the Convention was over the hump. Madison, James Wilson, and Gouverneur Morris of New York (who was there representing Pennsylvania!) fought the compromise all the way in a last-ditch effort to get a unitary state with parliamentary supremacy. But their allies deserted them and they demonstrated after their defeat the essentially opportunist character of their objections — using "opportunist" here in a nonpejorative sense, to indicate a willingness to swallow their objections and get on with the business. Moreover, once the compromise had carried (by five states to four, with one state divided), its advocates threw themselves vigorously into the job of strengthening the general government's substantive powers — as might have been predicted, indeed, from Paterson's early statements. It nourishes an increased respect for Madison's devotion to the art of politics, to realize that this dogged fighter could sit down six months later and prepare essays for *The Federalist* in contradiction to his basic convictions about the true course the Convention should have taken.

V

Two tricky issues will serve to illustrate the later process of accommodation. The first was the institutional position of the Executive. Madison argued for an executive chosen by the National Legislature and on May 29 this had been adopted with a provision that after his seven-year term was concluded, the chief magistrate should not be eligible for re-election. In late July this was reopened and for a week the matter was argued from several different points of view. A good deal of desultory speech-making ensued, but the gist of the problem was the opposition from two sources to election by the legislature. One group felt that the states should have a hand in the process; another small but influential circle urged direct election by the people. There were a number of proposals: election by the people, election by state governers, by electors chosen by state legislatures, by the National Legislature (James Wilson, perhaps ironically, proposed at one point that an Electoral College be chosen by lot from the National Legislature!), and there was some resemblance to three-dimensional chess in the dispute because of the presence of two other variables, length of tenure and reeligibility. Finally, after opening, reopening, and re-reopening the debate, the thorny problem was consigned to a committee for absolution.

The Brearley Committee on Postponed Matters was a superb aggregation of talent and its compromise on the Executive was a masterpiece of political improvisation. (The Electoral College, its creation, however, had little in its favor as an *institution* — as the delegates well appreciated.) The point of departure for all discussion about the presidency in the Convention was that in immediate terms, the problem was non-existent; in other words, everybody present knew that under any system devised, George Washington would be President. Thus they were dealing in the future tense and to a body of working politicians the merits of the Brearley proposal were obvious: everybody got a piece of cake. (Or to put it more academically, each viewpoint could leave the Convention and argue to its constitutents that it had *really* won the day.) First, the state legislatures had the right to determine the mode of selection of the electors; second, the small states received a bonus in the Electoral College in the form of a guaranteed minimum of three votes while the big states got acceptance of the principle of proportional power; third, if the state legislatures agreed (as six did in the first presidential election), the people could be involved directly in the choice of electors; and finally, if no candidate received a majority in the College, the right of decision passed to the National Legislature with each state exercising equal strength. (In the Brearley recommendation, the election went to the Senate, but a motion from the floor substituted the House; this was accepted on the ground that the Senate already had enough authority over the executive in its treaty and appointment powers.)

This compromise was almost too good to be true, and the Framers snapped it up with little debate or controversy. No one seemed to think well of the College as an *institution;* indeed, what evidence there is suggests that there was an assumption that once Washington had finished his tenure as President, the electors would cease to produce majorities and the chief executive would usually be chosen in the House. George Mason observed casually that the selection would be made in the House nineteen times in twenty and no one seriously disputed this point. The vital aspect of the Electoral College was that it got the Convention over the hurdle and protected everybody's interests. The future was left to cope with the problem of what to do with this Rube Goldberg mechanism.

In short, the Framers did not in their wisdom endow the United States with a College of Cardinals — the Electoral College was neither an exercise in applied Platonism nor an experiment in indirect government based on elitist distrust of the masses. It was merely a jerry-rigged improvisation which has subsequently been endowed with a high theoretical content. When an elector from Oklahoma in 1960 refused to cast his vote for Nixon (naming Byrd and Goldwater instead) on the ground that the Founding Fathers intended him to exercise his great independent wisdom, he was indulging in historical fantasy. If one were to indulge in counter-fantasy, he would be tempted to suggest that the Fathers would be startled to find the College still in operation — and perhaps even dismayed at their descendants' lack of judgment or inventiveness.

The second issue on which some substantial practical bargaining took place was slavery. The morality of slavery was, by design, not at issue; but in its other concrete aspects, slavery colored the arguments over taxation, commerce, and representation. The "Three-Fifths Compromise," that three-fifths of the slaves would be counted both for representation and for purposes of direct taxation (which was drawn from the past — it was a formula of Madison's utilized by Congress in 1783 to establish the basis of state contributions to the Confederation treasury) had allayed some Northern fears about Southern over-representation (no one then foresaw the trivial role that direct taxation would play in later federal financial policy), but doubts still remained. The Southerners, on the other hand, were afraid that Congressional control over commerce would lead to the exclusion of slaves or to their excessive taxation as imports. Moreover, the Southerners were disturbed over "navigation acts," i.e., tariffs, or special legislation providing, for example, that exports be carried only in American ships; as a section depending upon exports, they wanted protection from the potential voracity of their commercial brethren of the Eastern states. To achieve this end, Mason and others urged that the Constitution include a proviso that navigation and commercial laws should require a two-thirds vote in Congress.

These problems came to a head in late August and, as usual, were handed to a committee in the hope that, in Gouverneur Morris' words, "these things may form a bargain among the Northern and Southern states." The Committee reported its measures of reconciliation on August 25, and on August 29 the package was wrapped up and delivered. What occurred can best be described in George Mason's dour version (he anticipated Calhoun in his conviction that permitting navigation acts to pass by majority vote would put the South in economic bondage to the North — it was mainly on this ground that he refused to sign the Constitution):

> The Constitution as agreed to till a fortnight before the Convention rose was such a one as he would have set his hand and heart to. . . . [Until that time] The 3 New England States were constantly with us in all questions . . . so that it was these three States with the 5 Southern ones against Pennsylvania, Jersey and Delaware. With respect to the importation of slaves, [decision-making] was left to Congress. This disturbed the two Southernmost States who knew that Congress would

immediately suppress the importation of slaves. Those two States there-fore struck up a bargain with the three New England States. If they would join to admit slaves for some years, the two Southern-most States would join in changing the clause which required the ⅔ of the Legisla-ture in any vote [on navigation acts]. It was done.

On the floor of the Convention there was a virtual love-feast on this happy occasion. Charles Pinckney of South Carolina attempted to overturn the committee's decision, when the compromise was reported to the Convention, by insisting that the South needed protection from the imperialism of the Northern states. But his Southern colleagues were not prepared to rock the boat and General C. C. Pinckney arose to spread oil on the suddenly ruffled waters; he admitted that:

> It was in the true interest of the S [outhern] States to have no regulation of commerce; but considering the loss brought on the commerce of the Eastern States by the Revolution, their liberal conduct towards the views of South Carolina [on the regulation of the slave trade] and the interests the weak Southn. States had in being united with the strong Eastern states, he thought it proper that no fetters should be imposed on the power of making commercial regulations; *and that his constituents, though prejudiced against the Eastern States, would be reconciled to this liberality*. He had himself prejudices agst the Eastern States before he came here, but would acknowledge that he had found them as liberal and candid as any men whatever. (Italics added.)

Pierce Butler took the same tack, essentially arguing that he was not too happy about the possible consequences, but that a deal was a deal. Many Southern leaders were later — in the wake of the "Tariff of Abominations" — to rue this day of reconciliation; Calhoun's *Disqui-sition on Government* was little more than an extension of the argu-ment in the Convention against permitting a congressional majority to enact navigation acts.

VI

Drawing on their vast collective political experience, utilizing every weapon in the politician's arsenal, looking constantly over their shoulders at their constituents, the delegates put together a Constitution. It was a makeshift affair; some sticky issues (for example, the qualification of voters) they ducked entirely; others they mastered with that ancient instrument of political sagacity, studied ambiguity (for example, citizenship), and some they just overlooked. In this last category, I suspect, fell the matter of the power of the federal courts to determine the constitutionality of acts of Congress. When the judicial article was formulated (Article III of the Constitution), deliberations were still in the stage where the legislature was endowed with broad power under the Randolph formulation, authority which by its own terms was scarcely amenable to judicial review. In essence, courts could hardly determine when "the separate States are incompetent or . . . the harmony of the United States may be interrupted"; the National Legislature, as critics pointed out, was free to define its own jurisdiction. Later the definition of legislative authority was changed into the form we know, a series of stipulated powers, *but the delegates never seriously reexamined the jurisdiction of the judiciary under this new limited formulation*. All arguments on the intention of the Framers in this matter are thus deductive and *a posteriori*, though some obviously make more sense than others.

The Framers were busy and distinguished men, anxious to get back to their families, their positions, and their constituents, not members of the French Academy devoting a lifetime to a dictionary. They were trying to do an important job, and do it in such a fashion that their handiwork would be acceptable to very diverse constituencies. No one was rhapsodic about the final document, but it was a beginning, a move in the right direction, and one they had reason to believe the people would endorse. In addition, since they had modified the impossible amendment provisions of the Articles (the requirement of unanimity which could always be frustrated by "Rogues Island") to one demanding approval by only three-quarters of the states, they seemed confident that gaps in the fabric which experience would reveal could be rewoven without undue difficulty.

So with a neat phrase introduced by Benjamin Franklin (but devised by Gouverneur Morris) which made their decision sound unanimous, and an inspired benediction by the Old Doctor urging doubters to doubt their own infallibility, the Constitution was accepted and signed. Curiously, Edmund Randolph, who had played so vital a role throughout, refused to sign, as did his fellow Virginian George Mason and Elbridge Gerry of Massachusetts. Randolph's behavior was eccentric, to say the least — his excuses for refusing his signature have a factitious ring even at this late date; the best explanation seems to be that he was afraid that the Constitution would prove to be a liability in Virginia politics, where Patrick Henry was burning up the countryside with impassioned denunciations. Presumably, Randolph wanted to check the temper of the populace before he risked his reputation, and perhaps his job, in a fight with both Henry and Richard Henry Lee. Events lend some justification to this speculation: after much temporizing and use of the conditional subjunctive tense, Randolph endorsed ratification in Virginia and ended up getting the best of both worlds.

Madison, despite his reservations about the Constitution, was the campaign manager in ratification. His first task was to get the Congress in New York to light its own funeral pyre by approving the

"amendments" to the Articles and sending them on to the state legislatures. Above all, momentum had to be maintained. The anti-
Constitutionalists, now thoroughly alarmed and no novices in politics,
realized that their best tactic was attrition rather than direct opposition. Thus they settled on a position expressing qualified approval but
calling for a second Convention to remedy various defects (the one
with the most demagogic appeal was the lack of a Bill of Rights). Madison knew that to accede to this demand would be equivalent to losing
the battle, nor would he agree to conditional approval (despite waver-
ing even by Hamilton). This was an all-or-nothing proposition:
national salvation or national impotence with no intermediate positions possible. Unable to get congressional approval, he settled for second best: a unanimous resolution of Congress transmitting the Constitution to the states for whatever action they saw fit to take. The
opponents then moved from New York and the Congress, where they
had attempted to attach amendments and conditions, to the states for
the final battle.

At first the campaign for ratification went beautifully: within eight
months after the delegates set their names to the document, eight
states had ratified. Only in Massachusetts had the result been close
(187-168). Theoretically, a ratification by one more state convention
would set the new government in motion, but in fact until Virginia
and New York acceded to the new Union, the latter was a fiction. New
Hampshire was the next to ratify; Rhode Island was involved in its
characteristic political convulsions (the Legislature there sent the Constitution out to the towns for decision by popular vote and it got lost
among a series of local issues); North Carolina's convention did not
meet until July and then postponed a final decision. This is hardly the
place for an extensive analysis of the conventions of New York and Virginia. Suffice it to say that the Constitutionalists clearly outmaneu-
vered their opponents, forced them into impossible political positions,
and won both states narrowly. The Virginia Convention could serve as
a classic study in effective floor management: Patrick Henry had to be
contained, and a reading of the debates discloses a standard two-stage
technique. Henry would give a four- or five-hour speech denouncing
some section of the Constitution on every conceivable ground (the federal district, he averred at one point, would become a haven for con-
victs escaping from state authority!); when Henry subsided, "Mr. Lee
of Westmoreland" would rise and literally poleaxe him with sardonic
invective (when Henry complained about the militia power, "Light-
horse Harry" really punched below the belt: observing that while the
former Governor had been sitting in Richmond during the Revolution, *he* had been out in the trenches with the troops and thus felt better qualified to discuss military affairs). Then the gentlemanly Consti-

tutionalists (Madison, Pendleton and Marshall) would pick up the matters at issue and examine them in the light of reason.

Indeed, modern Americans who tend to think of James Madison as a rather desiccated character should spend some time with this transcript. Probably Madison put on his most spectacular demonstration of nimble rhetoric in what might be called "The Battle of the Absent Authorities." Patrick Henry in the course of one of his harangues alleged that Jefferson was known to be opposed to Virginia's approving the Constitution. This was clever: Henry hated Jefferson, but was prepared to use any weapon that came to hand. Madison's riposte was superb: First, he said that with all due respect to the great reputation of Jefferson, he was not in the country and therefore could not formulate an adequate judgment; second, no one should utilize the reputation of an outsider — the Virginia Convention was there to think for itself; third, if there were to be recourse to outsiders, the opinions of George Washington should certainly be taken into consideration; and finally, he knew from privileged personal communications from Jefferson that in fact the latter *strongly favored* the Constitution. To devise an assault route into this rhetorical fortress was literally impossible.

VII

The fight was over; all that remained now was to establish the new frame of government in the spirit of its framers. And who were better qualified for this task than the Framers themselves? Thus victory for the Constitution meant simultaneous victory for the Constitutionalists; the anti-Constitutionalists either capitulated or vanished into limbo — soon Patrick Henry would be offered a seat on the Supreme Court and Luther Martin would be known as the Federalist "bull-dog." And irony of ironies, Alexander Hamilton and James Madison would shortly accumulate a reputation as the formulators of what is often alleged to be our political theory, the concept of "federalism." Also, on the other side of the ledger, the arguments would soon appear over what the Framers "really meant"; while these disputes have assumed the proportions of a big scholarly business in the last century, they began almost before the ink on the Constitution was dry. One of the best early ones featured Hamilton versus Madison on the scope of presidential power, and other Framers characteristically assumed positions in this and other disputes on the basis of their political convictions.

Probably our greatest difficulty is that we know so much more about what the Framers *should have meant* than they themselves did. We are intimately acquainted with the problems that their Constitution should have been designed to master; in short, we have read the mystery story backwards. If we are to get the right "feel" for their time and their circumstances, we must in Maitland's phrase, "think ourselves back into a twilight." Obviously, no one can pretend completely to escape from the solipsistic web of his own environment, but if the effort is made, it is possible to appreciate the past roughly on its own terms. The first step in this process is to abandon the academic premise that because we can ask a question, there must be an answer.

Thus we can ask what the Framers meant when they gave Congress the power to regulate interstate and foreign commerce, and we emerge, reluctantly perhaps, with the reply that they may not have known what they meant, that there may not have been any semantic consensus. The Convention was not a seminar in analytic philosophy or linguistic analysis. Commerce was *commerce* — and if different interpretations of the word arose, later generations could worry about the problem of definition. The delegates were in a hurry to get a new government established; when definitional arguments arose, they characteristically took refuge in ambiguity. If different men voted for the same proposition for varying reasons, that was politics (and still is); if later generations were unsettled by this lack of precision, that would be their problem.

There was a good deal of definitional pluralism with respect to the problems the delegates did discuss, but when we move to the question of extrapolated intentions, we enter the realm of spiritualism. When men in our time, for instance, launch into elaborate talmudic exegesis to demonstrate that federal aid to parochial schools is (or is not) in accord with the intentions of the men who established the Republic and endorsed the Bill of Rights, they are engaging in historical Extra-Sensory Perception. (If one were to join this E. S. P. contingent for a minute, he might suggest that the hard-boiled politicians who wrote the Constitution and Bill of Rights would chuckle scornfully at such an invocation of authority: obviously a politician would chart his course on the intentions of the living, not of the dead, and count the number of Catholics in his constituency.)

The Constitution, then, was not an apotheosis of "constitutionalism," a triumph of architectonic genius; it was a patch-work sewn together under the pressure of both time and events by a group of extremely talented democratic politicians. They refused to attempt the establishment of a strong, centralized sovereignty on the principle of legislative supremacy for the excellent reason that the people would not accept it. They risked their political fortunes by opposing the established doctrines of state sovereignty because they were convinced that the existing system was leading to national impotence and probably foreign domination. For two years, they worked to get a convention established. For over three months, in what must have seemed to the faithful participants an endless process of give-and-take, they reasoned, cajoled, threatened, and bargained amongst themselves. The result was a Constitution which the people, in fact, by democratic processes, did accept, and a new and far better national government was established.

Beginning with the inspired propaganda of Hamilton, Madison and Jay, the ideological build-up got under way. *The Federalist* had little impact on the ratification of the Constitution, except perhaps in New York, but this volume had enormous influence on the image of the Constitution in the minds of future generations, particularly on historians and political scientists who have an innate fondness for theoretical symmetry. Yet, while the shades of Locke and Montesquieu *may* have been hovering in the background, and the delegates *may* have been unconscious instruments of a transcendent *telos,* the careful observer of the day-to-day work of the Convention finds no overarching principles. The "separation of powers" to him seems to be a by-product of suspicion, and "federalism" he views as a *pis aller,* as the farthest point the delegates felt they could go in the destruction of state power without themselves inviting repudiation.

To conclude, the Constitution was neither a victory for abstract theory nor a great practical success. Well over half a million men had to die on the battlefields of the Civil War before certain constitutional principles could be defined — a baleful consideration which is somehow overlooked in our customary tributes to the farsighted genius of the Framers and to the supposed American talent for "constitutionalism." The Constitution was, however, a vivid demonstration of effective democratic political action, and of the forging of a national elite which literally persuaded its countrymen to hoist themselves by their own boot straps. American pro-consuls would be wise not to translate the Constitution into Japanese, or Swahili, or treat it as a work of semi-Divine origin; but when students of comparative politics examine the process of nation-building in countries newly freed from colonial rule, they may find the American experience instructive as a classic example of the potentialities of a democratic elite.

Hamilton noted in *Federalist 1,* "It seems to have been reserved to the people of this country, to decide by their conduct and example, the important question, whether societies of men are really capable or not, of establishing good government from reflection and choice, or whether they are forever destined to depend, for their political constitutions, on accident and force." The framers of our Constitution attempted to structure the government in such a way that it would meet the needs and aspirations of the people and at the same time check the arbi-

trary exercise of political power. The doctrine of the separation
of powers was designed to prevent any one group from gaining
control of the national governmental apparatus. The selections
reprinted here from *The Federalist,* which was written between
October, 1787 and August, 1788, outline the theory and mechanism of the separation of powers.

6   ALEXANDER HAMILTON

FEDERALIST 1

I propose, in a series of papers to discuss the following
interesting particulars . . . The utility of the UNION to your political
prosperity . . . The insufficiency of the present confederation to preserve that Union . . . The necessity of a government, at least equally
energetic with the one proposed, to the attainment of this object . . .
The conformity of the proposed constitution to the true principles of
republican government . . . Its analogy to your own state constitution
. . . and lastly, The additional security, which its adoption will afford
to the preservation of that species of government, to liberty, and to
property.

7   JAMES MADISON

FEDERALIST 47

I proceed to examine the particular structure of this
government, and the distribution of this mass of power among its constituent parts.

One of the principal objections inculcated by the more respectable
adversaries to the constitution, is its supposed violation of the political
maxim, that the legislative, executive, and judiciary departments,
ought to be separate and distinct. In the structure of the federal government, no regard, it is said, seems to have been paid to this essential
precaution in favor of liberty. The several departments of power are
distributed and blended in such a manner, as at once to destroy all
symmetry and beauty of form; and to expose some of the essential parts
of the edifice to the danger of being crushed by the disproportionate
weight of other parts.

No political truth is certainly of greater intrinsic value, or is
stamped with the authority of more enlightened patrons of liberty,
than that on which the objection is founded. The accumulation of all
powers, legislative, executive, and judiciary, in the same hands, whether of one, a few, or many, and whether hereditary, self-appointed, or

elective, may justly be pronounced the very definition of tyranny. Were the federal constitution, therefore, really chargeable with this accumulation of power, or with a mixture of powers, having a dangerous tendency to such an accumulation, no further arguments would be necessary to inspire a universal reprobation of the system. I persuade myself, however, that it will be made apparent to every one, that the charge cannot be supported, and that the maxim on which it relies has been totally misconceived and misapplied.

The oracle who is always consulted and cited on this subject, is the celebrated Montesquieu. If he be not the author of this invaluable precept in the science of politics, he has the merit of at least displaying and recommending it most effectually to the attention of mankind. . . .

From . . . facts, by which Montesquieu was guided, it may clearly be inferred, that in saying, "there can be no liberty, where the legislative and executive powers are united in the same person, or body of magistrates"; or "if the power of judging, be not separated from the legislative and executive powers," he did not mean that these departments ought to have no *partial agency* in, or no *control* over, the acts of each other. His meaning . . . can amount to no more than this, that where the *whole* power of one department is exercised by the same hands which possess the *whole* power of another department, the fundamental principles of a free constitution are subverted. . . .

If we look into the constitutions of the several states, we find, that notwithstanding the emphatical, and, in some instances, the unqualified terms in which this axiom has been laid down, there is not a single instance in which the several departments of power have been kept absolutely separate and distinct. . . .

The constitution of Massachusetts has observed a sufficient, though less pointed caution, in expressing this fundamental article of liberty. It declares, "that the legislative department shall never exercise the executive and judicial powers, or either of them: the executive shall never exercise the legislative and judicial powers, or either of them: the judicial shall never exercise the legislative and executive powers, or either of them." This declaration corresponds precisely with the doctrine of Montesquieu. . . . It goes no farther than to prohibit any one of the entire departments from exercising the powers of another department. In the very constitution to which it is prefixed, a partial mixture of powers has been admitted. . . .

FEDERALIST 48

. . . I shall undertake in the next place to show, that unless these departments be so far connected and blended, as to give to each a constitutional control over the others, the degree of separation which the maxim requires, as essential to a free government, can never in practice be duly maintained.

It is agreed on all sides, that the powers properly belonging to one of the departments ought not to be directly and completely administered by either of the other departments. It is equally evident, that neither of them ought to possess, directly or indirectly, an overruling influence over the others in the administration of their respective powers. It will not be denied, that power is of an encroaching nature, and that it ought to be effectually restrained from passing the limits assigned to it. After discriminating, therefore, in theory, the several classes of power, as they may in their nature be legislative, executive, or judiciary; the next, and most difficult task, is to provide some practical security for each, against the invasion of the others. What this security ought to be, is the great problem to be solved.

Will it be sufficient to mark, with precision, the boundaries of these departments, in the constitution of the government, and to trust to these parchment barriers against the encroaching spirit of power? This is the security which appears to have been principally relied on by the compilers of most American constitutions. But experience assures us, that the efficacy of the provision has been greatly overrated; and that some more adequate defense is indispensably necessary for the more feeble, against the more powerful members of the government. The legislative department is everywhere extending the sphere of its activity, and drawing all power into its impetuous vortex. . . .

In a government where numerous and extensive prerogatives are placed in the hands of an hereditary monarch, the executive department is very justly regarded as the source of danger, and watched with all the jealousy which a zeal for liberty ought to inspire. In a democracy, where a multitude of people exercise in person the legislative functions, and are continually exposed, by their incapacity for regular deliberation and concerted measures, to the ambitious intrigues of their executive magistrates, tyranny may well be apprehended on some favorable emergency, to start up in the same quarter. But in a representative republic, where the executive magistracy is carefully limited, both in the extent and the duration of its power; and where the legislative is exercised by an assembly, which is inspired by a supposed influence over the people, with an intrepid confidence in its own strength; which is sufficiently numerous to feel all the passions which actuate a multitude; yet not so numerous as to be incapable of pursuing the objects of its passions, by means which reason prescribes; it is against the enterprising ambition of this department, that the people ought to indulge all their jealousy and exhaust all their precautions.

The legislative department derives a superiority in our governments from other circumstances. Its constitutional powers being at once more extensive, and less susceptible of precise limits, it can, with the greater facility, mask, under complicated and indirect measures, the encroachment which it makes on the co-ordinate departments. It is not infrequently a question of real nicety in legislative bodies, whether the operation of a particular measure will, or will not extend beyond the legislative sphere. On the other side, the executive power being restrained within a narrower compass, and being more simple in its nature; and the judiciary being described by landmarks, still less uncertain, projects of usurpation by either of these departments would immediately betray and defeat themselves. Nor is this all: as the legislative department alone has access to the pockets of the people, and has in some constitutions full discretion, and in all a prevailing influence over the pecuniary rewards of those who fill the other departments; a dependence is thus created in the latter, which gives still greater facility to encroachments of the former. . . .

FEDERALIST 51

To what expedient then shall we finally resort, for maintaining in practice the necessary partition of power among the several departments, as laid down in the constitution? The only answer that can be given is, that as all these exterior provisions are found to be inadequate, the defect must be supplied, by so contriving the interior structure of the government, as that its several constituent parts may, by their mutual relations, be the means of keeping each other in their proper places. . . .

In order to lay a due foundation for that separate and distinct exercise of the different powers of government, which, to a certain extent, is admitted on all hands to be essential to the preservation of liberty, it is evident that each department should have a will of its own; and consequently should be so constituted, that the members of each should have as little agency as possible in the appointment of the members of the others. . . .

It is equally evident, that the members of each department should be as little dependent as possible on those of the others, for the emoluments annexed to their offices. Were the executive magistrate, or the judges, not independent of the legislature in this particular, their independence in every other, would be merely nominal.

But the great security against a gradual concentration of the several powers in the same department, consists in giving to those who administer each department, the necessary constitutional means, and personal motives, to resist encroachments of the others. The provision for defense must in this, as in all other cases, be made commensurate to the danger of attack. Ambition must be made to counteract ambition. The interest of the man must be connected with the constitutional rights of the place. It may be a reflection on human nature, that such devices should be necessary to control the abuses of government. But what is government itself, but the greatest of all reflections on human nature? If men were angels, no government would be necessary. If angels were to govern men, neither external nor internal controls on government would be necessary. In framing a government, which is to be administered by men over men, the great difficulty lies in this: You must first enable the government to control the governed; and in the next place, oblige it to control itself. A dependence on the people is, no doubt, the primary control on the government; but experience has taught mankind the necessity of auxiliary precautions.

This policy of supplying by opposite and rival interests, the defect of better motives, might be traced through the whole system of human affairs, private as well as public. We see it particularly displayed in all the subordinate distributions of power; where the constant aim is, to divide and arrange the several offices in such a manner, as that each may be a check on the other; that the private interest of every individual, may be a sentinel over the public rights. These inventions of prudence cannot be less requisite to the distribution of the supreme powers of the state.

But it is not possible to give to each department an equal power of self-defense. In republican government, the legislative authority necessarily predominates. The remedy for this inconvenience is, to divide the legislature into different branches; and to render them by different modes of election, and different principles of action, as little connected with each other, as the nature of their common functions, and their common dependence on the society will admit. It may even be necessary to guard against dangerous encroachments, by still further precautions. As the weight of the legislative authority requires that it should be thus divided, the weakness of the executive may require, on the other hand, that it should be fortified. An absolute negative on the legislature, appears, at first view, to be the natural defense with which the executive magistrate should be armed. But perhaps it would be neither altogether safe, nor alone sufficient. On ordinary occasions, it might not be exerted with the requisite firmness; and on extraordinary occasions, it might be perfidiously abused. May not this defect of an absolute negative be supplied by some qualified connection between this weaker department, and the weaker branch of the stronger department, by which the latter may be led to support the constitutional rights of the former, without being too much detached from the rights of its own department?

CHAPTER THREE

Federalism

American government utilizes a "federal" form in order to secure certain political and economic objectives. This chapter identifies both the traditional and modern goals of American federalism from the writings of important theorists who have examined general and specific problems in national-state relationships. The validity of federalism is also analyzed.

Constitutional Background

No subject attracted greater attention or was more carefully analyzed at the time of the framing of the Constitution than federalism. *The Federalist* devoted a great deal of space to proving the advantages of a federal form of government relative to a confederacy, since the Constitution was going to take some of the power traditionally within the jurisdiction of state governments and give it to a newly constituted national government. Once again it is necessary to return to the Constitution and *The Federalist* to ascertain the basis for the establishment of a federal system of government, in which state governments as well as the national government receive independent constitutional grants of authority in defined areas.

8   ALEXANDER HAMILTON

FEDERALIST 16

The . . . death of the confederacy . . . is what we now seem to be on the point of experiencing, if the federal system be not speedily renovated in a more substantial form. It is not probable, considering the genius of this country, that the complying states would often be inclined to support the authority of the union, by engaging in a war against the non-complying states. They would always be more ready to pursue the milder course of putting themselves upon an equal footing with the delinquent members, by an imitation of their example. And the guilt of all would thus become the security of all. Our past experience has exhibited the operation of this spirit in its full light. There would, in fact, be an insuperable difficulty in ascertaining when force would with propriety be employed. In the article of pecuniary contribution, which would be the most usual source of delinquency, it would often be impossible to decide whether it had proceeded from disinclination, or inability. The pretense of the latter would always be at hand. And the case must be very flagrant in which its fallacy could be detected with sufficient certainty to justify the harsh expedient of compulsion. It is easy to see that this problem alone, as often as it should occur, would open a wide field to the majority that happened to prevail in the national council, for the exercise of factious views, of partiality, and of oppression.

It seems to require no pains to prove that the states ought not to prefer a national constitution, which could only be kept in motion by the instrumentality of a large army, continually on foot to execute the ordinary requisitions or decrees of the government. And yet this is the plain alternative involved by those who wish to deny it the power of extending its operations to individuals. Such a scheme, if practicable at all, would instantly degenerate into a military despotism; but it will be found in every light impracticable. The resources of the union would not be equal to the maintenance of any army considerable enough to confine the larger states within the limits of their duty; nor would the means ever be furnished of forming such an army in the first instance. Whoever considers the populousness and strength of several of these states singly at the present juncture, and looks forward to what they will become, even at the distance of half a century, will at once dismiss as idle and visionary any scheme which aims at regulating their movements by laws, to operate upon them in their collective capacities, and to be executed by a coercion applicable to them in the same capacities. A project of this kind is little less romantic than the monster-taming spirit attributed to the fabulous heroes and demigods of antiquity. . . .

The result of these observations to an intelligent mind must clearly be this, that if it be possible at any rate to construct a federal government capable of regulating the common concerns, and preserving the general tranquillity, it must be founded, as to the objects committed to its case, upon the reverse of the principle contended for by the opponents of the proposed constitution [i.e., a confederacy]. It must carry its agency to the persons of the citizens. It must stand in need of no intermediate legislations; but must itself be empowered to employ the arm of the ordinary magistrate to execute its own resolutions. The majesty of the national authority must be manifested through the medium of the courts of justice. The government of the union, like that of each state, must be able to address itself immediately to the hopes and fears of individuals; and to attract to its support, those passions which have the strongest influence upon the human heart. It must, in short, possess all the means, and have a right to resort to all the methods, of executing the powers with which it is entrusted, that are possessed and exercised by the governments of the particular states.

To this reasoning it may perhaps be objected, that if any state should be disaffected to the authority of the union, it could at any time obstruct the execution of its laws, and bring the matter to the same issue of force, with the necessity of which the opposite scheme is reproached.

The plausibility of this objection will vanish the moment we advert to the essential difference between a mere NON-COMPLIANCE and a DIRECT and ACTIVE RESISTANCE. If the interposition of the state legislatures be necessary to give effect to a measure of the union [as in a confederacy], they have only NOT TO ACT, or TO ACT EVASIVELY, and the measure is defeated. This neglect of duty may be disguised under affected but unsubstantial provisions so as not to appear, and of course not to excite any alarm in the people for the safety of the constitution. The state leaders may even make a merit of their surreptitious invasions of it, on the ground of some temporary convenience, exemption, or advantage.

But if the execution of the laws of the national government should not require the intervention of the state legislatures; if they were to pass into immediate operation upon the citizens themselves, the particular governments could not interrupt their progress without an open and violent exertion of an unconstitutional power. No omission, nor evasions, would answer the end. They would be obliged to act, and in such a manner, as would leave no doubt that they had encroached on the national rights. An experiment of this nature would always be hazardous in the face of a constitution in any degree competent to its own defense, and of a people enlightened enough to distinguish between a legal exercise and an illegal usurpation of authority. The success of it would require not merely a factious majority in the legislature, but the concurrence of the courts of justice, and of the body of the people. . . .

FEDERALIST 17

An objection, of a nature different from that which has been stated and answered in my last address, may, perhaps, be urged against the principle of legislation for the individual citizens of America. It may be said, that it would tend to render the government of the union too powerful, and to enable it to absorb those residuary authorities, which it might be judged proper to leave with the states for local purposes. Allowing the utmost latitude to the love of power, which any reasonable man can require, I confess I am at a loss to discover what temptation the persons entrusted with the administration of the general government could ever feel to divest the states of the authorities of that description. The regulation of the mere domestic police of a state, appears to me to hold out slender allurements to ambition. Commerce, finance, negotiation, and war, seem to comprehend all the objects which have charms for minds governed by that passion; and all the powers necessary to those objects, ought, in the first instance, to be lodged in the national depository. The administration of private justice between the citizens of the same state; the supervision of agriculture, and of other concerns of a similar nature; all those things, in short, which are proper to be provided for by local legislation, can never be desirable cares of a general jurisdiction. It is therefore improbable, that there should exist a disposition in the federal councils, to usurp the powers with which they are connected; because the attempt to exercise them would be as troublesome as it would be nugatory; and the possession of them, for that reason, would contribute nothing to the dignity, to the importance, or to the splendor, of the national government.

But let it be admitted, for argument's sake, that mere wantonness, and lust of domination, would be sufficient to beget that disposition; still, it may be safely affirmed, that the sense of the constituent body of the national representatives, or in other words, of the people of the several states, would control the indulgence of so extravagant an appetite. It will always be far more easy for the state governments to encroach upon the national authorities, than for the national government to encroach upon the state authorities. The proof of this proposition turns upon the greater degree of influence which the state governments, if they administer their affairs with uprightness and prudence, will generally possess over the people; a circumstance which at the same time teaches us, that there is an inherent and intrinsic weakness in all federal constitutions; and that too much pains cannot be taken in their organization, to give them all the force which is compatible with the principles of liberty.

The superiority of influence in favor of the particular governments, would result partly from the diffusive construction of the national government; but chiefly from the nature of the objects to which the attention of the state administrations would be directed.

It is a known fact in human nature, that its affections are commonly weak in proportion to the distance of diffusiveness of the object. Upon the same principle that a man is more attached to his family than to his neighborhood, to his neighborhood than to the community at large, the people of each state would be apt to feel a stronger bias towards their local governments, than towards the government of the union, unless the force of that principle should be destroyed by a much better administration of the latter.

This strong propensity of the human heart, would find powerful auxiliaries in the objects of state regulation.

The variety of more minute interests, which will necessarily fall under the superintendence of the local administrations, and which will form so many rivulets of influence, running through every part of the society, cannot be particularized, without involving a detail too tedious and uninteresting to compensate for the instruction it might afford.

There is one transcendent advantage belonging to the province of the state governments, which alone suffices to place the matter in a clear and satisfactory light — I mean the ordinary administration of criminal and civil justice. This, of all others, is the most powerful, most universal and most attractive source of popular obedience and attachment. It is this, which, being the immediate and visible guardian of life and property; having its benefits and its terrors in constant activity before the public eye; regulating all those personal interests, and familiar concerns, to which the sensibility of individuals is more immediately awake; contributes, more than any other circumstance, to impress upon the minds of the people affection, esteem, and reverence towards the government. This great cement of society, which will diffuse itself almost wholly through the channels of the particular governments, independent of all other causes of influence, would insure them so decided an empire over their respective citizens, as to render them at all times a complete counterpoise, and not infrequently dangerous rivals to the power of the union.

Tracing the historical development of national-state relationships, one finds that there has been constant strife over the determination of the boundaries of national power in relation to the reserved powers of the states. The Civil War did not settle once and for all the difficult question of national versus state power. The Supreme Court has played an important role in the development of the federal system, and some of its most historic opinions have upheld national power at the expense of the states. In the early period of the Court, Chief Justice John Marshall in *McCulloch* v. *Maryland,* 4 Wheaton 316 (1819), stated two doctrines that have had a profound effect upon the federal system: (1) the doctrine of implied powers; (2) the doctrine of the supremacy of national law. The former enables Congress to expand its power into numerous areas affecting states directly. By utilizing the commerce clause, for example, Congress may now regulate what is essentially *intrastate* commerce, for the Court has held that this is implied in the original clause giving Congress the power to regulate commerce among the several states. The immediate issues in *McCulloch* v. *Maryland* were, first, whether or not Congress had the power to incorporate, or charter, a national bank; second, if Congress did have such a power, although nowhere stated in the Constitution, did the existence of such a bank prevent state action that would interfere in its operation?

9

McCULLOCH v. MARYLAND

4 Wheaton 316 (1819)

Mr. Chief Justice Marshall delivered the opinion of the Court, saying in part:

In the case now to be determined, the defendant, a sovereign State, denies the obligation of a law enacted by the legislature of the Union; and the plaintiff, on his part, contests the validity of an Act which has been passed by the legislature of that State. The Constitution of our country, in its most interesting and vital parts, is to be considered; the conflicting powers of the government of the Union and of its members, as marked in that Constitution, are to be discussed; and an opinion given, which may essentially influence the great operations of the government. . . .

If any one proposition could command the universal assent of mankind, we might expect it would be this: that the government of the Union, though limited in its powers, is supreme within its sphere of action. This would seem to result necessarily from its nature. It is the government of all; its powers are delegated by all; it represents all, and acts for all. Though any one State may be willing to control its operations, no State is willing to allow others to control them. The nation, on those subjects on which it can act, must necessarily bind its component parts. But this question is not left to mere reason: the people have, in express terms, decided it, by saying, "this Constitution, and the laws of the United States, which shall be made in pursuance thereof," "shall be the supreme law of the land," and by requiring that the members of the State legislatures, and the officers of the executive and judicial departments of the States, shall take the oath of fidelity to it. . . .

A constitution, to contain an accurate detail of all the subdivisions of which its great powers will admit, and of all the means by which they may be carried into execution, would partake of the prolixity of a legal code, and could scarcely be embraced by the human mind. It would probably never be understood by the public. Its nature, therefore, requires that only its great outlines should be marked, its important objects designated, and the minor ingredients which compose those objects be deduced from the nature of the objects themselves. That this idea was entertained by the framers of the American Constitution, is not only to be inferred from the nature of the instrument, but from the language. . . .

Although, among the enumerated powers of government, we do not find the word "bank," or "incorporation," we find the great powers to lay and collect taxes; to borrow money; to regulate commerce; to declare and conduct a war; and to raise and support armies and navies. The sword and the purse, all the external relations, and no inconsiderable portion of the industry of the nation, are entrusted to its government. It can never be pretended that these vast powers draw after them others of inferior importance, merely because they are inferior. Such an idea can never be advanced. But it may, with great reason, be contended, that a government, entrusted with such ample powers, on the due execution of which the happiness and prosperity of the nation so vitally depends, must also be entrusted with ample means for their execution. The power being given, it is the interest of the nation to facilitate its execution. It can never be their interest, and cannot be presumed to have been their intention, to clog and embarrass its execution by withholding the most appropriate means. Throughout this vast republic, from the St. Croix to the Gulf of Mexico, from the Atlantic to the Pacific, revenue is to be collected and expended, armies are to be marched and supported. The exigencies of the nation may require, that the treasure raised in the North should be transported to the South, that raised in the East conveyed to the West, or that this order should be reversed. Is that construction of the Constitution to be preferred which would render these operations difficult, hazardous, and expensive? Can we adopt that construction (unless the words imperiously require it) which would impute to the framers of that instrument, when granting these powers for the public good, the intention of impeding their exercise by withholding a choice of means? If, indeed, such be the mandate of the Constitution, we have only to obey; but that instrument does not profess to enumerate the means by which the powers it confers may be executed; nor does it prohibit the creation of a corporation, if the existence of such a being be essential to the beneficial exercise of those powers. It is, then, the subject of fair inquiry, how far such means may be employed. . . .

We admit, as all must admit, that the powers of the government are limited, and that its limits are not to be transcended. But we think the sound construction of the Constitution must allow to the national legislature that discretion, with respect to the means by which the powers it confers are to be carried into execution, which will enable that body to perform the high duties assigned to it, in the manner most beneficial to the people. Let the end be legitimate, let it be within the scope of the Constitution, and all means which are appropriate, which are plainly adapted to that end, which are not prohibited, but consist with the letter and spirit of the Constitution, are constitutional. . . .

It being the opinion of the court that the act incorporating the bank is constitutional; and that the power of establishing a branch in the State of Maryland might be properly exercised by the bank itself, we proceed to inquire:

Whether the State of Maryland may, without violating the Constitution, tax that branch? . . .

That the power of taxation is one of vital importance; that it is retained by the States; that it is not abridged by the grant of a similar power to the government of the Union; that it is to be concurrently exercised by the two governments: are truths which have never been denied. But, such is the paramount character of the Constitution, that its capacity to withdraw any subject from the action of even this power, is admitted. The States are expressly forbidden to lay any duties on imports or exports, except what may be absolutely necessary for executing their inspection laws. If the obligation of this prohibition must be conceded — if it may restrain a State from the exercise of its taxing power on imports and exports; the same paramount character would seem to restrain, as it certainly may restrain, a State from such other exercise of this power, as is in its nature incompatible with, and repugnant to, the constitutional laws of the Union. A law, absolutely repugnant to another, as entirely repeals that other as if express terms of repeal were used.

On this ground the counsel for the bank place its claim to be exempted from the power of a State to tax its operations. There is no express provision for the case, but the claim has been sustained on a principle which so entirely pervades the Constitution, is so intermixed with the materials which compose it, so interwoven with its web, so blended with its texture, as to be incapable of being separated from it, without rending it into shreds.

This great principle is, that the Constitution and the laws made in pursuance thereof are supreme; that they control the Constitution and laws of the respective States, and cannot be controlled by them. From this, which may be almost termed an axiom, other propositions are deduced as corollaries, on the truth or error of which, and on their application to this case, the cause has been supposed to depend. These are, 1. That a power to create implies a power to preserve. 2. That a power to destroy, if wielded by a different hand, is hostile to, and incompatible with, these powers to create and preserve. 3. That where this repugnancy exists, that authority which is supreme must control, not yield to that over which it is supreme. . . .

If we apply the principle for which the State of Maryland contends, to the Constitution generally, we shall find it capable of changing totally the character of that instrument. We shall find it capable of arresting all the measures of the government, and of prostrating it at the foot of the States. The American people have declared their Constitution, and the laws made in pursuance thereof, to be supreme; but this principle would transfer the supremacy, in fact, to the States. . . .

The court has bestowed on this subject its most deliberate consideration. The result is a conviction that the States have no power, by taxation or otherwise, to retard, impede, burden, or in any manner control, the operations of the constitutional laws enacted by Congress to carry into execution the powers vested in the general government. That is, we think, the unavoidable consequence of that supremacy which the Constitution has declared. . . .

Constitutional doctrine regarding the power of the national government to regulate commerce among the states to promote general prosperity has been clarified in a series of Supreme Court cases. At issue is the interpretation of the power to "regulate commerce with foreign nations, and among the several States," granted to Congress in Article 1. Some of these cases have emphasized the role of the national government as umpire, enforcing certain rules of the game within which the free enterprise system functions; others have emphasized the positive role of the government in regulating the economy.

A key case supporting the supremacy of the national government in commercial regulation is *Gibbons* v. *Ogden,* 9 Wheaton 1 (1824). The New York legislature, in 1798, granted Robert R. Livingston the exclusive privilege to navigate by steam the rivers and other waters of the state, provided he could build a boat which would travel at four miles an hour against the current of the Hudson River. A two-year time limitation was imposed, and the conditions were not met; however, New York renewed its grant for two years in 1803 and again in 1807. In 1807 Robert Fulton, who now held the exclusive license with

Livingston, completed and put into operation a steamboat which met the legislative conditions. The New York legislature now provided that a five-year extension of their monopoly would be given to Livingston and Fulton for each new steamboat they placed into operation on New York waters. The monopoly could not exceed thirty years, but during that period anyone wishing to navigate New York waters by steam had first to obtain a license from Livingston and Fulton, who were given the power to confiscate unlicensed boats. New Jersey and Connecticut passed retaliatory laws, the former authorizing confiscation of any New York ship for each ship confiscated by Livingston and Fulton, the latter prohibiting boats licensed in New York from entering Connecticut waters. Ohio also passed retaliatory legislation. Open commercial warfare seemed a possibility among the states of the union.

In 1793 Congress passed an act providing for the licensing of vessels engaged in the coasting trade, and Gibbons obtained under this statute a license to operate boats between New York and New Jersey. Ogden was engaged in a similar operation under an exclusive license issued by Livingston and Fulton, and thus sought to enjoin Gibbons from further operation. The New York court upheld the exclusive grants given to Livingston and Fulton, and Gibbons appealed to the Supreme Court. Chief Justice Marshall, in the following opinion, makes it quite clear that (1) states cannot interfere with a power granted to Congress by passing conflicting state legislation, and (2) the commerce power includes anything affecting "commerce among the states" and thus may include *intrastate* as well as interstate commerce. In this way the foundation was laid for broad national control over commercial activity.

10

GIBBONS v. OGDEN

9 Wheaton 1 (1824)

Mr. Chief Justice Marshall delivered the opinion of the Court, saying in part:

The appellant contends that this decree [of the New York court enjoining Gibbons from further operation because of the exclusive nature of the New York law granting a monopoly to Fulton and Livingston] is erroneous, because the laws which purport to give the exclusive privilege it sustains, are repugnant to the Constitution and laws of the United States.

They are said to be repugnant —

1. To that clause in the Constitution which authorizes Congress to regulate commerce.

2. To that which authorizes Congress to promote the progress of science and useful arts. . . .

As preliminary to the very able discussions of the Constitution which we have heard from the bar, and as having some influence on its construction, reference has been made to the political situation of these States, anterior to its formation. It has been said that they were sovereign, were completely independent, and were connected with each other only by a league. This is true. But, when these allied sovereigns converted their league into a government, when they converted their congress of ambassadors, deputed to deliberate on their common concerns, and to recommend measures of general utility, into a legislature, empowered to enact laws on the most interesting subjects, the whole character in which the States appear underwent a change, the extent of which must be determined by a fair consideration of the instrument by which that change was effected.

This instrument contains an enumeration of powers expressly granted by the people to their government. It has been said that these powers ought to be construed strictly. But why ought they to be so construed? Is there one sentence in the Constitution which gives countenance to this rule? In the last of the enumerated powers, that which grants, expressly, the means for carrying all others into execution, Congress is authorized "to make all laws which shall be necessary and proper" for the purpose. But this limitation on the means which may be used, is not extended to the powers which are conferred; nor is there one sentence in the Constitution, which has been pointed out by the gentlemen of the bar, or which we have been able to discern, that prescribes this rule. We do not, therefore, think ourselves justified in adopting it. . . . If, from the imperfections of human language, there should be serious doubts respecting the extent of any given power, it is a well settled rule that the objects for which it was given, especially when those objects are expressed in the instrument itself, should have great influence in the construction. . . . We know of no rule for construing the extent of such powers, other than is given by the language of the instrument which confers them, taken in connection with the purposes for which they were conferred.

The words are: "Congress shall have power to regulate commerce with foreign nations, and among the several States, and with the Indian tribes."

The subject to be regulated is commerce; and our Constitution being, as was aptly said at the bar, one of enumeration, and not of definition, to ascertain the extent of the power, it becomes necessary to settle the meaning of the word. The counsel for the appellee would limit it to traffic, to buying and selling, or the interchange of commodities, and do not admit that it comprehends navigation. This would restrict a general term, applicable to many objects, to one of its significations. Commerce, undoubtedly, is traffic, but it is something more: it is intercourse. It describes the commercial intercourse between nations, and parts of nations, in all its branches, and is regulated by prescribing rules for carrying on that intercourse. The mind can scarcely conceive a system for regulating commerce between nations, which shall exclude all laws concerning navigation, which shall be silent on the admission of the vessels of the one nation into the ports of the other, and be confined to prescribing rules for the conduct of individuals, in the actual employment of buying and selling, or of barter.

If commerce does not include navigation, the government of the Union has no direct power over that subject, and can make no law prescribing what shall constitute American vessels, or requiring that they shall be navigated by American seamen. Yet this power has been exercised from the commencement of the government, has been exercised with the consent of all, and has been understood by all to be a commercial regulation. . . .

The word used in the Constitution, then, comprehends, and has been always understood to comprehend, navigation, within its meaning; and a power to regulate navigation is as expressly granted as if that term had been added to the word "commerce."

To what commerce does this power extend? The Constitution informs us, to commerce "with foreign nations, and among the several States, and with the Indian tribes."

It has, we believe, been universally admitted that these words comprehend every species of commercial intercourse between the United States and foreign nations. No sort of trade can be carried on between this country and any other, to which this power does not extend. It has been truly said that commerce, as the word is used in the Constitution, is a unit, every part of which is indicated by the term.

If this be the admitted meaning of the word, in its application to foreign nations, it must carry the same meaning throughout the sentence, and remain a unit, unless there be some plain intelligible cause which alters it.

The subject to which the power is next applied, is to commerce "among the several States." The word "among" means intermingled with. A thing which is among others, is intermingled with them. Commerce among the States, cannot stop at the external boundary line of each State, but may be introduced into the interior.

It is not intended to say that these words comprehend that commerce which is completely internal, which is carried on between man and man in a State, or between different parts of the same State, and which does not extend to or affect other States. Such a power would be inconvenient, and is certainly unnecessary.

Comprehensive as the word "among" is, it may very properly be restricted to that commerce which concerns more States than one. The phrase is not one which would probably have been selected to indicate the completely interior traffic of a State. . . . The completely internal commerce of a State, then, may be considered as reserved for the State itself.

But, in regulating commerce with foreign nations, the power of Congress does not stop at the jurisdictional lines of the several States. It would be a very useless power if it could not pass those lines. The commerce of the United States with foreign nations is that of the whole United States. Every district has a right to participate in it. The deep streams which penetrate our country in every direction pass through the interior of almost every State in the Union, and furnish the means of exercising this right. If Congress has the power to regulate it, that power must be exercised whenever the subject exists. If it exists within the States, if a foreign voyage may commence or terminate at a port within a State, then the power of Congress may be exercised within a State.

This principle is, if possible, still more clear when applied to commerce "among the several States." They either join each other, in which case they are separated by a mathematical line, or they are remote from each other, in which case other States lie between them. What is commerce "among" them; and how is it to be conducted? Can a trading expedition between two adjoining States commence and terminate outside of each? And if the trading intercourse be between two States remote from each other, must it not commence in one, terminate in the other, and probably pass through a third? Commerce among the States must, of necessity, be commerce with the States. In the regulation of trade with the Indian tribes, the action of the law, especially when the Constitution was made, was chiefly within a State. The power of Congress, then, whatever it may be, must be exercised within the territorial jurisdiction of the several States. . . .

We are now arrived at the inquiry, what is this power?

It is the power to regulate; that is, to prescribe the rule by which commerce is to be governed. This power, like all others vested in Congress, is complete in itself, may be exercised to its utmost extent, and acknowledges no limitations other than are prescribed in the Constitution. These are expressed in plain terms, and do not affect the questions which arise in this case, or which have been discussed at the bar. . . .

The power of Congress, then, comprehends navigation within the limits of every State in the Union, so far as that navigation may be, in any manner, connected with "commerce with foreign nations, or among the several States, or with the Indian tribes." It may, of consequence, pass the jurisdictional line of New York, and act upon the very waters to which the prohibition now under consideration applies.

But it has been urged with great earnestness that, although the power of Congress to regulate commerce with foreign nations, and among the several States, be coextensive with the subject itself, and have no other limits than are prescribed in the Constitution, yet the States may severally exercise the same power, within their respective jurisdictions. In support of this argument, it is said that they possessed it as an inseparable attribute of sovereignty, before the formation of the Constitution, and still retain it, except so far as they have surrendered it by that instrument; that this principle results from the nature of the government, and is secured by the Tenth Amendment; that an affirmative grant of power is not exclusive, unless in its own nature it be such that the continued exercise of it by the former possessor is inconsistent with the grant, and that this is not of that description.

The appellant, conceding these postulates, except the last, contends that full power to regulate a particular subject, implies the whole power, and leaves no *residuum;* that a grant of the whole is incompatible with the existence of a right in another to any part of it. . . .

. . . The sole question is, can a State regulate commerce with foreign nations and among the States, while Congress is regulating it? . . .

In our complex system, presenting the rare and difficult scheme of one general government, whose action extends over the whole, but which possesses only certain enumerated powers; and of numerous State governments, which retain and exercise all powers not delegated to the Union, contests respecting power must arise. Were it even otherwise, the measures taken by the respective governments to execute their acknowledged powers, would often be of the same description, and might, sometimes, interfere. This, however, does not prove that the one is exercising, or has a right to exercise, the powers of the other. . . .

It has been contended, by the counsel for the appellant, that, as the word to "regulate" implies in its nature full power over the thing to be regulated, it excludes, necessarily, the action of all others that would perform the same operation on the same thing. That regulation is designed for the entire result, applying to those parts which remain as they were, as well as to those which are altered. It produces a uniform whole, which is as much disturbed and deranged by changing what the regulating power designs to leave untouched, as that on which it has operated.

There is great force in this argument, and the Court is not satisfied that it has been refuted.

Since, however, in exercising the power of regulating their own purely internal affairs, whether of trading or police, the States may sometimes enact laws, the validity of which depends on their interfering with, and being contrary to, an act of Congress passed in pursuance of the Constitution, the Court will enter upon the inquiry, whether the laws of New York, as expounded by the highest tribunal of that State, have, in their application to this case, come into collision with an act of Congress, and deprived a citizen of a right to which that act entitles him. Should the collision exist, it will be immaterial whether those laws were passed in virtue of a concurrent power "to regulate commerce with foreign nations, or among the several States," or, in virtue of a power to regulate their domestic trade and police. In one case and the other, the acts of New York must yield to the law of Congress; and the decision sustaining the privilege they confer, against a right given by a law of the Union, must be erroneous.

This opinion has been frequently expressed in this Court, and is founded as well on the nature of the government as on the words of the Constitution. In argument, however, it has been contended that, if a law passed by a State, in the exercise of its acknowledged sovereignty, comes into conflict with a law passed by Congress in pursuance of the Constitution, they affect the subject, and each other, like equal opposing powers.

But the framers of our Constitution foresaw this state of things, and provided for it by declaring the supremacy not only of itself, but of the laws made in pursuance of it. The nullity of any act, inconsistent with the Constitution, is produced by the declaration that the Constitution is the supreme law. The appropriate application of that part of the clause which confers the same supremacy on laws and treaties, is to such acts of the State legislatures as do not transcend their powers, but, though enacted in the execution of acknowledged State powers, interfere with, or are contrary to the laws of Congress, made in pursuance of the Constitution, or some treaty made under the authority of the United States. In every such case, the act of Congress, or the treaty, is supreme; and the law of the State, though enacted in the exercise of powers not controverted, must yield to it. . . .

. . . The real and sole question seems to be, whether a steam machine, in actual use, deprives a vessel of the privileges conferred by a license. . . .

But all inquiry into this subject seems to the Court to be put completely at rest, by the act . . . entitled "An act for the enrolling and licensing of steam-boats." . . .

This act demonstrates the opinion of Congress, that steam-boats may be enrolled and licensed, in common with vessels using sails. They are, of course, entitled to the same privileges, and can no more be restrained from navigating waters, and entering ports which are free to such vessels, than if they were wafted on their voyage by the winds, instead of being propelled by the agency of fire. The one element may be as legitimately used as the other, for every commercial purpose authorized by the laws of the Union; and the act of a State inhibiting the use of either to any vessel having a license under the act of Congress, comes, we think, in direct collision with that act.

As this decides the cause, it is unnecessary to enter in an examination of that part of the Constitution which empowers Congress to promote the progress of science and the useful arts. . . .

Congress has used its constitutional power to regulate "commerce among the several States" to justify broad regulatory programs. In *Champion* v. *Ames*, 188 U.S. 321 (1903), the Court stated that Congress could bar transportation of objectionable articles in interstate commerce. This was in reference to an 1895 lottery law prohibiting lottery tickets from being sent through the channels of interstate commerce. After this decision Congress prohibited transportation of numerous other "objectionable" articles in interstate commerce; e.g., impure food and drugs, uninspected meat, and fabrics, stolen automobiles, kidnapped persons, and women for immoral purposes. In this way a national police power was developed similar to that of the states in intent; i.e., the power to protect the health, welfare, and morals of the community, initially within the "reserved" powers of the states.

In 1916 Congress attempted to regulate child labor conditions within states by preventing the transportation in interstate commerce of goods produced by children under conditions which violated the standards of the Child Labor Act of 1916. Although the initial attempt was declared unconstitutional in *Hammer* v. *Dagenhart*, 247 U.S. 251 (1918), the device of regulation through controlling the transportation of goods in interstate commerce is now an accepted constitutional practice. Furthermore, the regulatory power of Congress extends to all economic areas — production, distribution, etc. — which in any way have an effect upon interstate commerce. Thus labor disputes that burden or obstruct interstate commerce are controlled under the Wagner Labor Relations Act of 1935 and the Taft-Hartley Act of 1947. The radio and television industry, because it uses the channels of interstate commerce, is regulated by the Federal Communications Act of 1934. The same is true of banks, securities dealers and exchanges, railroads, telephone companies, petroleum firms and natural gas companies, trucking firms, etc. The list of industries subject to national regulation through the commerce clause could be extended indefinitely. Marshall's decision in *Gibbons* v. *Ogden* set the stage for extensive national regulation through its broad and flexible interpretation of the commerce clause.

Both *McCulloch* v. *Maryland* and *Gibbons* v. *Ogden* clearly held that the states cannot take action that will impinge upon the legitimate authority of Congress. These opinions reflected judicial acceptance of the fact that when the federal government acts, it generally pre-empts the field. But this does not mean that the states can never legislate concurrently with the national government. It depends upon the circumstances. For example, in *Pennsylvania* v. *Nelson,* 350 U.S. 497 (1956), the Supreme Court found that the Smith Act superseded a Pennsylvania sedition statute under which Nelson had been convicted. The Pennsylvania law, like the Smith Act, made it a crime to advocate the violent overthrow of the government of the United States or the government of Pennsylvania. The Supreme Court found that the Smith Act, in combination with a number of other federal subversive control statutes such as the Internal Security Act of 1950 and the Communist Control Act of 1954, proscribed advocacy to overthrow any government, whether federal, state, or local. On the basis of the aggregate of federal statutes in the sedition field, the Court concluded, "Congress had intended to occupy the field of sedition. Taken as a whole, they [the statutes] evince a Congressional plan which makes it reasonable to determine that no room has been left for the states to supplement it. Therefore, a state's sedition statute is superseded regardless of whether it purports to supplement the federal law. . . . " Although the *Nelson* case apparently nullified more than forty state sedition statutes, the issue has not been finally resolved. Several cases since the *Nelson* decision reflect a judicial hesitancy to prevent state and local authorities from enforcing statutes controlling subversive activities. (See *Beilan* v. *Board of Education,* 357 U.S. 399 [1958], and *Lerner* v. *Casey,* 357 U.S. 468 [1958].) The real problems that arise concerning the doctrine of national supremacy do not develop where there is clear state defiance of a federal law or a federal court order, for in these situations the enforcement of the principle of the supremacy of the Constitution and of national law can easily and clearly be carried out. Thus in *Cooper* v. *Aaron,* 358 U.S. 1 (1958), a federal district court order to proceed with integration at Central High School in Little Rock was upheld by the Supreme Court in face of the defiance of the Governor of Arkansas. The supremacy of the national government was clear, and the opinion of the Court was not ambiguous.

A recent example of the problem of concurrent jurisdiction arose in the case of *Colorado Anti-Discrimination Commission* v. *Continental Air Lines,* 372 U.S. 714 (1963). This case involved the constitutionality of the Colorado Anti-Discrimination Act, which made it an unfair employment practice to refuse to hire qualified individuals because of race, creed, color, national origin, or ancestry. Under the Act a commission was established to investigate complaints. Marlon D. Green, a Negro, applied for a job as a pilot with Continental Air Lines, a small interstate carrier whose route passes through Colorado. He was refused a position, and he filed a complaint with the Anti-Discrimination Commission, claiming that the only reason he was not hired was because he was a Negro. The Commission held extensive hearings to determine the validity of his charge, and finally upheld it. Continental Air Lines was ordered to cease and desist from this particular discrimination and from any other discriminatory practices. The Commission directed the air line to enroll the applicant for its first opening in its pilot training school.

The validity of the Commission's cease and desist order was immediately attacked by Continental, which secured a judgment vacating the order from a lower State District Court. On appeal, the Supreme Court of Colorado affirmed the judgment. Both state courts held that the Colorado statute placed an undue burden upon interstate commerce, which was within the exclusive jurisdiction of the national government. However, the Supreme Court found that the Colorado statute merely extended, rather than conflicted with, the federal laws dealing with the same subject.

The Nature of Federalism Today

The problems involved in determining the constitutional division of authority between the federal and the state governments reflect the more formal aspects of our federal system. Contemporary federalism must be viewed not only in this way but also in relation to the broader political and economic dimensions of the division of powers between the national and state levels of government. Also, as the following selection points out, there are many factors in addition to federalism that decentralize the American political system. All kinds of interest groups, including state and local governments, have numerous access points at the national level through which they can influence policy making. Our decentralized political parties, a major cause of disunity, are controlled more by state organizations than by the national leaders. Federalism has not caused the disunity in the

American system, although it has contributed to it. What kind of balance should exist between the federal and state levels in the exercise of governmental functions? In essence, this is part of a broader problem of centralization versus decentralization in government. The next selection deals with the many facets of this problem.

11   MORTON GRODZINS

THE FEDERAL SYSTEM

Federalism is a device for dividing decisions and functions of government. As the constitutional fathers well understood, the federal structure is a means, not an end. The pages that follow are therefore not concerned with an exposition of American federalism as a formal, legal set of relationships. The focus, rather, is on the purpose of federalism, that is to say, on the distribution of power between central and peripheral units of government.

I. The Sharing of Functions

The American form of government is often, but erroneously, symbolized by a three-layer cake. A far more accurate image is the rainbow or marble cake, characterized by an inseparable mingling of differently colored ingredients, the colors appearing in vertical and diagonal strands and unexpected whirls. As colors are mixed in the marble cake, so functions are mixed in the American federal system. Consider the health officer, styled "sanitarian," of a rural county in a border state. He embodies the whole idea of the marble cake of government.

The sanitarian is appointed by the state under merit standards established by the federal government. His base salary comes jointly from state and federal funds, the county provides him with an office and office amenities and pays a portion of his expenses, and the largest city in the county also contributes to his salary and office by virtue of his appointment as a city plumbing inspector. It is impossible from moment to moment to tell under which governmental hat the sanitar-

From Morton Grodzins, "The Federal System," *Goals for Americans,* pp. 265–82. © 1960 by The American Assembly, Columbia University, New York City. Reprinted by permission of Prentice-Hall, Inc., Englewood Cliffs, New Jersey.

ian operates. His work of inspecting the purity of food is carried out under federal standards; but he is enforcing state laws when inspecting commodities that have not been in interstate commerce; and somewhat perversely he also acts under state authority when inspecting milk coming into the county from producing areas across the state border. He is a federal officer when impounding impure drugs shipped from a neighboring state; a federal-state officer when distributing typhoid immunization serum; a state officer when enforcing standards of industrial hygiene; a state-local officer when inspecting the city's water supply; and (to complete the circle) a local officer when insisting that the city butchers adopt more hygienic methods of handling their garbage. But he cannot and does not think of himself as acting in these separate capacities. All business in the county that concerns public health and sanitation he considers his business. Paid largely from federal funds, he does not find it strange to attend meetings of the city council to give expert advice on matters ranging from rotten apples to rabies control. He is even deputized as a member of both the city and county police forces.

The sanitarian is an extreme case, but he accurately represents an important aspect of the whole range of governmental activities in the United States. Functions are not neatly parceled out among the many governments. They are shared functions. It is difficult to find any governmental activity which does not involve all three of the so-called "levels" of the federal system. In the most local of local functions — law enforcement or education, for example — the federal and state governments play important roles. In what, *a priori,* may be considered the purest central government activities — the conduct of foreign affairs, for example — the state and local governments have considerable responsibilities, directly and indirectly.

The federal grant programs are only the most obvious example of shared functions. They also most clearly exhibit how sharing serves to disperse governmental powers. The grants utilize the greater wealth-gathering abilities of the central government and establish nationwide standards, yet they are "in aid" of functions carried out under state law, with considerable state and local discretion. The national supervision of such programs is largely a process of mutual accommodation. Leading state and local officials, acting through their professional organizations, are in considerable part responsible for the very standards that national officers try to persuade all state and local officers to accept.

Even in the absence of joint financing, federal-state-local collaboration is the characteristic mode of action. Federal expertise is available to aid in the building of a local jail (which may later be used to house federal prisoners), to improve a local water purification system, to step up building inspections, to provide standards for state and local personnel in protecting housewives against dishonest butchers' scales, to prevent gas explosions, or to produce a land use plan. States and localities, on the other hand, take important formal responsibilities in the development of national programs for atomic energy, civil defense, the regulation of commerce, and the protection of purity in foods and drugs; local political weight is always a factor in the operation of even a post office or a military establishment. From abattoirs and accounting through zoning and zoo administration, any governmental activity is almost certain to involve the influence, if not the formal administration, of all three planes of the federal system.

II. Attempts to Unwind the Federal System

Within the past dozen years there have been four major attempts to reform or reorganize the federal system: the first (1947–49) and second (1953–55) Hoover Commissions on Executive Organization; the Kestnbaum Commission on Intergovernmental Relations (1953–55); and the Joint Federal-State Action Committee (1957–59). All four of these groups have aimed to minimize federal activities. None of them has recognized the sharing of functions as the characteristic way American governments do things. Even when making recommendations for joint action, these official commissions take the view (as expressed in the Kestnbaum report) that "the main tradition of American federalism [is] the tradition of separateness." All four have, in varying degrees, worked to separate functions and tax sources.

The history of the Joint Federal-State Action Committee is especially instructive. The committee was established at the suggestion of President Eisenhower, who charged it, first of all, "to designate functions which the States are ready and willing to assume and finance that are now performed or financed wholly or in part by the Federal Government." He also gave the committee the task of recommending "Federal and State revenue adjustments required to enable the States to assume such functions."[1]

The committee subsequently established seemed most favorably situated to accomplish the task of functional separation. It was composed

[1] The President's third suggestion was that the committee "identify functions and responsibilities likely to require state or federal attention in the future and . . . recommend the level of state effort, or federal effort, or both, that will be needed to assure effective action." The committee initially devoted little attention to this problem. Upon discovering the difficulty of making separatist recommendations, i.e., for turning over federal functions and taxes to the states, it developed a series of proposals looking to greater effectiveness in intergovernmental collaboration. The committee was succeeded by a legislatively based, 26-member Advisory Commission on Intergovernmental Relations, established September 29, 1959.

of distinguished and able men, including among its personnel three leading members of the President's cabinet, the director of the Bureau of the Budget, and ten state governors. It had the full support of the President at every point, and it worked hard and conscientiously. Excellent staff studies were supplied by the Bureau of the Budget, the White House, the Treasury Department, and, from the state side, the Council of State Governments. It had available to it a large mass of research data, including the sixteen recently completed volumes of the Kestnbaum Commission. There existed no disagreements on party lines within the committee and, of course, no constitutional impediments to its mission. The President, his cabinet members, and all the governors (with one possible exception) on the committee completely agreed on the desirability of decentralization-via-separation-of-functions-and-taxes. They were unanimous in wanting to justify the committee's name and to produce action, not just another report.

The committee worked for more than two years. It found exactly two programs to recommend for transfer from federal to state hands. One was the federal grant program for vocational education (including practical-nurse training and aid to fishery trades); the other was federal grants for municipal waste treatment plants. The programs together cost the federal government less than $80 million in 1957, slightly more than two per cent of the total federal grants for that year. To allow the states to pay for these programs, the committee recommended that they be allowed a credit against the federal tax on local telephone calls. Calculations showed that this offset device, plus an equalizing factor, would give every state at least 40 per cent more from the tax than it received from the federal government in vocational education and sewage disposal grants. Some states were "equalized" to receive twice as much.

The recommendations were modest enough, and the generous financing feature seemed calculated to gain state support. The President recommended to Congress that all points of the program be legislated. None of them was, none has been since, and none is likely to be.

III. A Point of History

The American federal system has never been a system of separated governmental activities. There has never been a time when it was possible to put neat labels on discrete "federal," "state," and "local" functions. Even before the Constitution, a statute of 1785, reinforced by the Northwest Ordinance of 1787, gave grants-in-land to the states for public schools. Thus the national government was a prime force in making possible what is now taken to be the most local function of all, primary and secondary education. More important, the nation, before it was fully organized, established by this action a first principle of American federalism: the national government would use its superior resources to initiate and support national programs, principally administered by the states and localities.

The essential unity of state and federal financial systems was again recognized in the earliest constitutional days with the assumption by the federal government of the Revolutionary War debts of the states. Other points of federal-state collaboration during the Federalist period concerned the militia, law enforcement, court practices, the administration of elections, public health measures, pilot laws, and many other matters.

The nineteenth century is widely believed to have been the preeminent period of duality in the American system. Lord Bryce at the end of the century described (in *The American Commonwealth*) the federal and state governments as "distinct and separate in their action." The system, he said, was "like a great factory wherein two sets of machinery are at work, their revolving wheels apparently intermixed, their bands crossing one another, yet each set doing its own work without touching or hampering the other." Great works may contain gross errors. Bryce was wrong. The nineteenth century, like the early days of the republic, was a period principally characterized by intergovernmental collaboration.

Decisions of the Supreme Court are often cited as evidence of nineteenth century duality. In the early part of the century the Court, heavily weighted with Federalists, was intent upon enlarging the sphere of national authority; in the later years (and to the 1930's) its actions were in the direction of paring down national powers and indeed all governmental authority. Decisions referred to "areas of exclusive competence" exercised by the federal government and the states; to their powers being "separated and distinct"; and to neither being able "to intrude within the jurisdiction of the other."

Judicial rhetoric is not always consistent with judicial action, and the Court did not always adhere to separatist doctrine. Indeed, its rhetoric sometimes indicated a positive view of cooperation. In any case, the Court was rarely, if ever, directly confronted with the issue of cooperation vs. separation as such. Rather it was concerned with defining permissible areas of action for the central government and the states; or with saying with respect to a point at issue whether any government could take action. The Marshall Court contributed to intergovernmental cooperation by the very act of permitting federal operations where they had not existed before. Furthermore, even Marshall was willing to allow interstate commerce to be affected by the states in their use of the police power. Later courts also upheld state laws that had an impact on interstate commerce, just as they approved the expansion of the national commerce power, as in statutes providing for the control of telegraphic communication or prohibiting the interstate transportation of lotteries, impure foods and drugs, and prostitutes. Similar room for cooperation was found outside the commerce field, notably in the Court's refusal to interfere with federal grants in land or cash to the states. Although research to clinch the point has not been completed, it is probably true that the Supreme Court from 1800 to 1936 allowed far more federal-state collaboration than it blocked.

Political behavior and administrative action of the nineteenth century provide positive evidence that, throughout the entire era of so-called dual federalism, the many governments in the American federal system continued the close administrative and fiscal collaboration of the earlier period. Governmental activities were not extensive. But relative to what governments did, intergovernmental cooperation during the last century was comparable with that existing today.

Occasional presidential vetoes (from Madison to Buchanan) of cash and land grants are evidence of constitutional and ideological apprehensions about the extensive expansion of federal activities which produced widespread intergovernmental collaboration. In perspective, however, the vetoes are a more important evidence of the continuous search, not least by state officials, for ways and means to involve the central government in a wide variety of joint programs. The search was successful.

Grants-in-land and grants-in-services from the national government were of first importance in virtually all the principal functions undertaken by the states and their local subsidiaries. Land grants were made to the states for, among other purposes, elementary schools, colleges, and special educational institutions; roads, canals, rivers, harbors, and railroads; reclamation of desert and swamp lands; and veterans' welfare. In fact whatever was at the focus of state attention became the recipient of national grants. (Then, as today, national grants established state emphasis as well as followed it.) If Connecticut wished to establish a program for the care and education of the deaf and dumb, federal money in the form of a land grant was found to aid that program. If higher education relating to agriculture became a pressing need, Congress could dip into the public domain and make appropriate grants to states. If the need for swamp drainage and flood control appeared, the federal government could supply both grants-in-land and, from the Army's Corps of Engineers, the services of the only trained engineers then available.

Aid also went in the other direction. The federal government, theoretically in exclusive control of the Indian population, relied continuously (and not always wisely) on the experience and resources of state and local governments. State militias were an all-important ingredient in the nation's armed forces. State governments became unofficial but real partners in federal programs for homesteading, reclamation, tree culture, law enforcement, inland waterways, the nation's internal communications system (including highway and railroad routes), and veterans' aid of various sorts. Administrative contacts were voluminous, and the whole process of interaction was lubricated, then as today, by constituent-conscious members of Congress.

The essential continuity of the collaborative system is best demonstrated by the history of the grants. The land grant tended to become a cash grant based on the calculated disposable value of the land, and the cash grant tended to become an annual grant based upon the national government's superior tax powers. In 1887, only three years before the frontier was officially closed, thus signalizing the end of the disposable public domain, Congress enacted the first continuing cash grants.

A long, extensive, and continuous experience is therefore the foundation of the present system of shared functions characteristic of the American federal system, what we have called the marble cake of government. It is a misjudgment of our history and our present situation to believe that a neat separation of governmental functions could take place without drastic alterations in our society and system of government.

IV. DYNAMICS OF SHARING: THE POLITICS OF THE FEDERAL SYSTEM

Many causes contribute to dispersed power in the federal system. One is the simple historical fact that the states existed before the nation. A second is in the form of creed, the traditional opinion of Americans that expresses distrust of centralized power and places great value in the strength and vitality of local units of government. Another is pride in locality and state, nurtured by the nation's size and by variations of regional and state history. Still a fourth cause of decentralization is the sheer wealth of the nation. It allows all groups, including state and local governments, to partake of the central government's largesse, supplies room for experimentation and even waste, and makes unnecessary the tight organization of political power that must follow when the support of one program necessarily means the deprivation of another.

In one important respect, the Constitution no longer operates to impede centralized government. The Supreme Court since 1937 has given Congress a relatively free hand. The federal government can build substantive programs in many areas on the taxation and commerce powers. Limitations of such central programs based on the argument, "it's unconstitutional," are no longer possible as long as Congress (in the Court's view) acts reasonably in the interest of the whole nation. The Court is unlikely to reverse this permissive view in the foreseeable future.

Nevertheless, some constitutional restraints on centralization continue to operate. The strong constitutional position of the states — for example, the assignment of two senators to each state, the role given the states in administering even national elections, and the relatively few limitations on their law-making powers — establish the geographical units as natural centers of administrative and political strength. Many clauses of the Constitution are not subject to the same latitude of interpretation as the commerce and tax clauses. The simple, clearly stated, unambiguous phrases — for example, the President "shall hold his office during the term of four years" — are subject to change only through the formal amendment process. Similar provisions exist with respect to the terms of senators and congressmen and the amendment process. All of them have the effect of retarding or restraining centralizing action of the federal government. The fixed terms of the President and members of Congress, for example, greatly impede the development of nation-wide, disciplined political parties that almost certainly would have to precede continuous large-scale expansion of federal functions.

The constitutional restraints on the expansion of national authority are less important and less direct today than they were in 1879 or in 1936. But to say that they are less important is not to say that they are unimportant.

The nation's politics reflect these decentralizing causes and add some of their own. The political parties of the United States are unique. They seldom perform the function that parties traditionally perform in other countries, the function of gathering together diverse strands of power and welding them into one. Except during the period of nominating and electing a president and for the essential but nonsubstantive business of organizing the houses of Congress, the American parties rarely coalesce power at all. Characteristically they do the reverse, serving as a canopy under which special and local interests are represented with little regard for anything that can be called a party program. National leaders are elected on a party ticket, but in Congress they must seek cross-party support if their leadership is to be effective. It is a rare president during rare periods who can produce legislation without facing the defection of substantial numbers of his own party. (Wilson could do this in the first session of the sixty-third Congress; but Franklin D. Roosevelt could not, even during the famous hundred days of 1933.) Presidents whose parties form the majority of the congressional houses must still count heavily on support from the other party.

The parties provide the pivot on which the entire governmental system swings. Party operations, first of all, produce in legislation the basic division of functions between the federal government, on the one hand, and state and local governments, on the other. The Supreme Court's permissiveness with respect to the expansion of national powers has not in fact produced any considerable extension of exclusive federal functions. The body of federal law in all fields has remained, in the words of Henry M. Hart, Jr., and Herbert Wechsler, "interstitial in its nature," limited in objective and resting upon the principal body of legal relationships defined by state law. It is difficult to find any area of federal legislation that is not significantly affected by state law.

In areas of new or enlarged federal activity, legislation characteristically provides important roles for state and local governments. This is as true of Democratic as of Republican administrations and true even of functions for which arguments of efficiency would produce exclusive federal responsibility. Thus the unemployment compensation program of the New Deal and the airport program of President Truman's administration both provided important responsibilities for state governments. In both cases attempts to eliminate state participation were defeated by a cross-party coalition of pro-state votes and influence. A large fraction of the Senate is usually made up of ex-governors, and the membership of both houses is composed of men who know that their re-election depends less upon national leaders or national party organization than upon support from their home constituencies. State and local officials are key members of these constituencies, often central figures in selecting candidates and in turning out the vote. Under such circumstances, national legislation taking state and local views heavily into account is inevitable.

Second, the undisciplined parties affect the character of the federal system as a result of senatorial and congressional interference in federal administrative programs on behalf of local interests. Many aspects of the legislative involvement in administrative affairs are formalized. The Legislative Reorganization Act of 1946, to take only one example, provided that each of the standing committees "shall exercise continuous watchfulness" over administration of laws within its jurisdiction. But the formal system of controls, extensive as it is, does not compare in importance with the informal and extralegal network of relationships in producing continuous legislative involvement in administrative affairs.

Senators and congressmen spend a major fraction of their time representing problems of their constituents before administrative agencies. An even larger fraction of congressional staff time is devoted to the same task. The total magnitude of such "case work" operations is great. In one five-month period of 1943 the Office of Price Administration received a weekly average of 842 letters from members of Congress. If phone calls and personal contacts are added, each member of Congress on the average presented the OPA with a problem involving one of his constituents twice a day in each five-day work week. Data for less vulnerable agencies during less intensive periods are also impressive. In 1958, to take only one example, the Department of Agriculture estimated (and under-estimated) that it received an average of 159 congressional letters per working day. Special congressional liaison staffs have been created to service this mass of business, though all higher officials meet it in one form or another. The Air Force in 1958 had, under the command of a major general, 137 people (55 officers and 82 civilians) working in its liaison office.

The widespread, consistent, and in many ways unpredictable character of legislative interference in administrative affairs has many consequences for the tone and character of American administrative behavior. From the perspective of this paper, the important consequence is the comprehensive, day-to-day, even hour-by-hour, impact of local views on national programs. No point of substance or procedure is immune from congressional scrutiny. A substantial portion of the entire weight of this impact is on behalf of the state and local governments. It is a weight that can alter procedures for screening immigration applications, divert the course of a national highway, change the tone of an international negotiation, and amend a social security law to accommodate local practices or fulfill local desires.

The party system compels administrators to take a political role. This is a third way in which the parties function to decentralize the American system. The administrator must play politics for the same reason that the politician is able to play in administration: the parties are without program and without discipline.

In response to the unprotected position in which the party situation places him, the administrator is forced to seek support where he can find it. One ever-present task is to nurse the Congress of the United States, that crucial constituency which ultimately controls his agency's budget and program. From the administrator's view, a sympathetic consideration of congressional requests (if not downright submission to them) is the surest way to build the political support without which the administrative job could not continue. Even the completely task-oriented administrator must be sensitive to the need for congressional support and to the relationship between case work requests, on one side, and budgetary and legislative support, on the other. "You do a good job handling the personal problems and requests of a Congress-man," a White House officer said, "and you have an easier time convincing him to back your program." Thus there is an important link between the nursing of congressional requests, requests that largely concern local matters, and the most comprehensive national programs. The administrator must accommodate to the former as a price of gaining support for the latter.

One result of administrative politics is that the administrative agency may become the captive of the nation-wide interest group it serves or presumably regulates. In such cases no government may come out with effective authority: the winners are the interest groups themselves. But in a very large number of cases, states and localities also win influence. The politics of administration is a process of making peace with legislators who for the most part consider themselves the guardians of local interests. The political role of administrators therefore contributes to the power of states and localities in national programs.

Finally, the way the party system operates gives American politics their over-all distinctive tone. The lack of party discipline produces an openness in the system that allows individuals, groups, and institutions (including state and local governments) to attempt to influence national policy at every step of the legislative-administrative process. This is the "multiple-crack" attribute of the American government. "Crack" has two meanings. It means not only many fissures or access points; it also means, less statically, opportunities for wallops or smacks at government.

If the parties were more disciplined, the result would not be a cessation of the process by which individuals and groups impinge themselves upon the central government. But the present state of the parties clearly allows for a far greater operation of the multiple crack than would be possible under the conditions of centralized party control. American interest groups exploit literally uncountable access points in the legislative-administrative process. If legislative lobbying, from committee stages to the conference committee, does not produce results, a cabinet secretary is called. His immediate associates are petitioned. Bureau chiefs and their aides are hit. Field officers are put under pressure. Campaigns are instituted by which friends of the agency apply a secondary influence on behalf of the interested party. A conference with the President may be urged.

To these multiple points for bringing influence must be added the multiple voices of the influencers. Consider, for example, those in a small town who wish to have a federal action taken. The easy merging of public and private interest at the local level means that the influence attempt is made in the name of the whole community, thus removing it from political partisanship. The Rotary Club as well as the City Council, the Chamber of Commerce and the mayor, eminent citizens and political bosses — all are readily enlisted. If a conference in a senator's office will expedite matters, someone on the local scene can be found to make such a conference possible and effective. If technical information is needed, technicians will supply it. State or national professional organizations of local officials, individual congressmen and senators, and not infrequently whole state delegations will make the local cause their own. Federal field officers, who service localities, often assume local views. So may elected and appointed state officers. Friendships are exploited, and political mortgages called due. Under these circumstances, national policies are molded by local action.

In summary, then, the party system functions to devolve power. The American parties, unlike any other, are highly responsive when directives move from the bottom to the top, highly unresponsive from top to bottom. Congressmen and senators can rarely ignore concerted demands from their home constituencies; but no party leader can expect the same kind of response from those below, whether he be a President asking for congressional support or a congressman seeking aid from local or state leaders.

Any tightening of the party apparatus would have the effect of strengthening the central government. The four characteristics of the system, discussed above, would become less important. If control from the top were strictly applied, these hallmarks of American decentralization might entirely disappear. To be specific, if disciplined and program-oriented parties were achieved: (1) It would make far less likely legislation that takes heavily into account the desires and prejudices of the highly decentralized power groups and institutions of the country, including the state and local governments. (2) It would to a large extent prevent legislators, individually and collectively, from intruding themselves on behalf of non-national interests in national administrative programs. (3) It would put an end to the administrator's search for his own political support, a search that often results in fostering state, local, and other non-national powers. (4) It would dampen the process by which individuals and groups, including state and local political leaders, take advantage of multiple cracks to steer national legislation and administration in ways congenial to them and the institutions they represent.

Alterations of this sort could only accompany basic changes in the organization and style of politics which, in turn, presuppose fundamental changes at the parties' social base. The sharing of functions is, in fact, the sharing of power. To end this sharing process would mean the destruction of whatever measure of decentralization exists in the United States today.

V. GOALS FOR THE SYSTEM OF SHARING

The Goal of Understanding. Our structure of government is complex, and the politics operating that structure are mildly chaotic. Circumstances are ever-changing. Old institutions mask intricate procedures. The nation's history can be read with alternative glosses, and what is nearest at hand may be furthest from comprehension. Simply to understand the federal system is therefore a difficult task. Yet without understanding there is little possibility of producing desired changes in the system. Social structures and processes are relatively impervious to purposeful change. They also exhibit intricate interrelationships so that change induced at point "A" often produces unanticipated results at point "Z." Changes introduced into an imperfectly understood system are as likely to produce reverse consequences as the desired ones.

This is counsel of neither futility nor conservatism for those who seek to make our government a better servant of the people. It is only to say that the first goal for those setting goals with respect to the federal system is that of understanding it.

Two Kinds of Decentralization. The recent major efforts to reform the federal system have in large part been aimed at separating functions and tax sources, at dividing them between the federal government and the states. All of these attempts have failed. We can now add that their success would be undesirable.

It is easy to specify the conditions under which an ordered separation of functions could take place. What is principally needed is a majority political party, under firm leadership, in control of both Presidency and Congress, and, ideally but not necessarily, also in control of a number of states. The political discontinuities, or the absence of party links, (1) between the governors and their state legislatures, (2) between the President and the governors, and (3) between the President and Congress clearly account for both the picayune recommendations of the Federal-State Action Committee and for the failure of even those recommendations in Congress. If the President had been in control of Congress (that is, consistently able to direct a majority of House and Senate votes), this alone would have made possible some genuine separation and devolution of functions. The failure to decentralize by order is a measure of the decentralization of power in the political parties.

Stated positively, party centralization must precede governmental decentralization by order. But this is a slender reed on which to hang decentralization. It implies the power to centralize. A majority party powerful enough to bring about ordered decentralization is far more likely to choose in favor of ordered centralization. And a society that produced centralized national parties would, by that very fact, be a society prepared to accept centralized government.

Decentralization by order must be contrasted with the different kind of decentralization that exists today in the United States. It may be called the decentralization of mild chaos. It exists because of the existence of dispersed power centers. This form of decentralization is less visible and less neat. It rests on no discretion of central authorities. It produces at times specific acts that many citizens may consider undesirable or evil. But power sometimes wielded even for evil ends may be desirable power. To those who find value in the dispersion of power, decentralization by mild chaos is infinitely more desirable than decentralization by order. The preservation of mild chaos is an important goal for the American federal system.

Oiling the Squeak Points. In a governmental system of genuinely shared responsibilities, disagreements inevitably occur. Opinions clash over proximate ends, particular ways of doing things become the subject of public debate, innovations are contested. These are not basic defects in the system. Rather, they are the system's energy-reflecting life blood. There can be no permanent "solutions" short of changing the system itself by elevating one partner to absolute supremacy. What can be done is to attempt to produce conditions in which conflict will not fester but be turned to constructive solutions of particular problems.

A long list of specific points of difficulty in the federal system can be easily identified. No adequate congressional or administrative mechanism exists to review the patchwork of grants in terms of national needs. There is no procedure by which to judge, for example, whether the national government is justified in spending so much more for highways than for education. The working force in some states is inadequate for the effective performance of some nation-wide programs, while honest and not-so-honest graft frustrates efficiency in others. Some federal aid programs distort state budgets, and some are so closely supervised as to impede state action in meeting local needs. Grants are given for programs too narrowly defined, and over-all programs at the state level consequently suffer. Administrative, accounting and auditing difficulties are the consequence of the multiplicity of grant programs. City officials complain that the states are intrusive fifth wheels in housing, urban redevelopment, and airport building programs.

Some differences are so basic that only a demonstration of strength on one side or another can solve them. School desegregation illustrates such an issue. It also illustrates the correct solution (although not the most desirable method of reaching it): in policy conflicts of fundamental importance, touching the nature of democracy itself, the view of the whole nation must prevail. Such basic ends, however, are rarely at issue, and sides are rarely taken with such passion that loggerheads are reached. Modes of settlement can usually be found to lubricate the squeak points of the system.

A pressing and permanent state problem, general in its impact, is the difficulty of raising sufficient revenue without putting local industries at a competitive disadvantage or without an expansion of sales taxes that press hardest on the least wealthy. A possible way of meeting this problem is to establish a state-levied income tax that could be used as an offset for federal taxes. The maximum level of the tax which could be offset would be fixed by federal law. When levied by a state, the state collection would be deducted from federal taxes. But if a state did not levy the tax, the federal government would. An additional fraction of the total tax imposed by the states would be collected directly by the federal government and used as an equalization fund, that is, distributed among the less wealthy states. Such a tax would almost certainly be imposed by all states since not to levy it would give neither political advantage to its public leaders nor financial advantage to its citizens. The net effect would be an increase in the total personal and corporate income tax.

The offset has great promise for strengthening state governments. It would help produce a more economic distribution of industry. It would have obvious financial advantages for the vast majority of states. Since a large fraction of all state income is used to aid political subdivisions, the local governments would also profit, though not equally as long as cities are under-represented in state legislatures. On the other hand, such a scheme will appear disadvantageous to some low-tax states which profit from the in-migration of industry (though it would by no means end all state-by-state tax differentials). It will probably excite the opposition of those concerned over governmental centralization, and they will not be assuaged by methods that suggest themselves for making both state and central governments bear the psychological impact of the tax. Although the offset would probably produce an across-the-board tax increase, wealthier persons, who are affected more by an income tax than by other levies, can be expected to join forces with those whose fear is centralization. (This is a common alliance and, in the nature of things, the philosophical issue rather than financial advantage is kept foremost.)

Those opposing such a tax would gain additional ammunition from the certain knowledge that federal participation in the scheme would lead to some federal standards governing the use of the funds. Yet the political strength of the states would keep these from becoming onerous. Indeed, inauguration of the tax offset as a means of providing funds to the states might be an occasion for dropping some of the specifications for existing federal grants. One federal standard, however, might be possible because of the greater representation of urban areas in the constituency of Congress and the President than in the constituency of state legislatures: Congress might make a state's participation in the offset scheme dependent upon a periodic reapportionment of state legislatures.

The income tax offset is only one of many ideas that can be generated to meet serious problems of closely meshed governments. The fate of all such schemes ultimately rests, as it should, with the politics of a free people. But much can be done if the primary technical effort of those concerned with improving the federal system were directed not at separating its interrelated parts but at making them work together more effectively. Temporary commissions are relatively inefficient in this effort, though they may be useful for making general assessments and for generating new ideas. The professional organizations of government workers do part of the job of continuously scrutinizing programs and ways and means of improving them. A permanent staff, established in the President's office and working closely with state and local officials, could also perform a useful and perhaps important role.

The Strength of the Parts. Whatever governmental "strength" or "vitality" may be, it does not consist of independent decision-making in legislation and administration. Federal-state interpenetration here is extensive. Indeed, a judgment of the relative domestic strength of the two planes must take heavily into account the influence of one on the other's decisions. In such an analysis the strength of the states (and localities) does not weigh lightly. The nature of the nation's politics makes federal functions more vulnerable to state influence than state offices are to federal influence. Many states, as the Kestnbaum Commission noted, live with "self-imposed constitutional limitations" that make it difficult for them to "perform all of the services that their citizens require." If this has the result of adding to federal responsibilities, the states' importance in shaping and administering federal programs eliminates much of the sting.

The geography of state boundaries, as well as many aspects of state internal organization, are the products of history and cannot be justified on any grounds of rational efficiency. Who, today, would create major governmental subdivisions the size of Maryland, Delaware, New Jersey, or Rhode Island? Who would write into Oklahoma's fundamental law an absolute state debt limit of $500,000? Who would design (to cite only the most extreme cases) Georgia's and Florida's gross under-representation of urban areas in both houses of the legislature?

A complete catalogue of state political and administrative horrors would fill a sizeable volume. Yet exhortations to erase them have roughly the same effect as similar exhortations to erase sin. Some of the worst inanities — for example, the boundaries of the states, themselves — are fixed in the national constitution and defy alteration for all foreseeable time. Others, such as urban under-representation in state legislatures, serve the over-represented groups, including some urban ones, and the effective political organization of the deprived groups must precede reform.

Despite deficiencies of politics and organizations that are unchangeable or slowly changing, it is an error to look at the states as static anachronisms. Some of them — New York, Minnesota, and California, to take three examples spanning the country — have administrative organizations that compare favorably in many ways with the national establishment. Many more in recent years have moved rapidly towards integrated administrative departments, state-wide budgeting, and central leadership. The others have models-in-existence to follow, and active professional organizations (led by the Council of State Governments) promoting their development. Slow as this change may be, the states move in the direction of greater internal effectiveness.

The pace toward more effective performance at the state level is likely to increase. Urban leaders, who generally feel themselves disadvantaged in state affairs, and suburban and rural spokesmen, who are most concerned about national centralization, have a common interest in this task. The urban dwellers want greater equality in state affairs, including a more equitable share of state financial aid; non-urban dwellers are concerned that city dissatisfactions should not be met by exclusive federal, or federal-local, programs. Antagonistic, rather than amiable, cooperation may be the consequence. But it is a cooperation that can be turned to politically effective measures for a desirable upgrading of state institutions.

If one looks closely, there is scant evidence for the fear of the federal octopus, the fear that expansion of central programs and influence threatens to reduce the states and localities to compliant administrative arms of the central government. In fact, state and local governments are touching a larger proportion of the people in more ways than ever before; and they are spending a higher fraction of the total national product than ever before. Federal programs have increased, rather than diminished, the importance of the governors; stimulated professionalism in state agencies; increased citizen interest and participation in government; and, generally, enlarged and made more effective the scope of state action.[2] It may no longer be true in any significant sense that the states and localities are "closer" than the federal government to the people. It is true that the smaller governments remain active and powerful members of the federal system.

[2] See the valuable report, *The Impact of Federal Grants-in-Aid on the Structure and Functions of State and Local Governments*, submitted to the Commission on Intergovernmental Relations by the Governmental Affairs Institute (Washington, 1955).

Central Leadership: The Need for Balance. The chaos of party processes makes difficult the task of presidential leadership. It deprives the President of ready-made congressional majorities. It may produce, as in the chairmen of legislative committees, power-holders relatively hidden from public scrutiny and relatively protected from presidential direction. It allows the growth of administrative agencies which sometimes escape control by central officials. These are prices paid for a wide dispersion of political power. The cost is tolerable because the total results of dispersed power are themselves desirable and because, where clear national supremacy is essential, in foreign policy and military affairs, it is easiest to secure.

Moreover, in the balance of strength between the central and peripheral governments, the central government has on its side the whole secular drift towards the concentration of power. It has on its side technical developments that make central decisions easy and sometimes mandatory. It has on its side potent purse powers, the result of superior tax-gathering resources. It has potentially on its side the national leadership capacities of the presidential office. The last factor is the controlling one, and national strength in the federal system has shifted with the leadership desires and capacities of the chief executive. As these have varied, so there has been an almost rhythmic pattern: periods of central strength put to use alternating with periods of central strength dormant.

Following a high point of federal influence during the early and middle years of the New Deal, the post-war years have been, in the weighing of central-peripheral strength, a period of light federal activity. Excepting the Supreme Court's action in favor of school desegregation, national influence by design or default has not been strong in domestic affairs. The danger now is that the central government is doing too little rather than too much. National deficiencies in education and health require the renewed attention of the national government. Steepening population and urbanization trend lines have produced metropolitan area problems that can be effectively attacked only with the aid of federal resources. New definitions of old programs in housing and urban redevelopment, and new programs to deal with air pollution, water supply, and mass transportation are necessary. The federal government's essential role in the federal system is that of organizing, and helping to finance, such national-wide programs.

The American federal system exhibits many evidences of the dispersion of power not only because of formal federalism but more importantly because our politics reflect and reinforce the nation's diversities-within-unity. Those who value the virtues of decentralization, which writ large are virtues of freedom, need not scruple at recognizing the defects of those virtues. The defects are principally the danger that parochial and private interests may not coincide with, or give way to, the nation's interest. The necessary cure for these defects is effective national leadership.

The centrifugal force of domestic politics needs to be balanced by the centripetal force of strong presidential leadership. Simultaneous strength at center and periphery exhibits the American system at its best, if also at its noisiest. The interests of both find effective spokesmen. States and localities (and private interest groups) do not lose their influence opportunities, but national policy becomes more than the simple consequence of successful, momentary concentrations of non-national pressures: it is guided by national leaders.

PART III

POLITICAL PARTIES AND INTEREST GROUPS

CHAPTER FOUR

Political Parties and the Electorate

The political process involves the sources, distribution, and use of power in the state. All the institutions and processes of government relate to this area. This chapter will discuss the role of political parties and the electoral system in determining and controlling political power.

Constitutional Background

Political parties and interest groups have developed outside of the original constitutional framework to channel political power in the community, and for this reason they deserve special consideration from students of American government. The Constitution was designed to structure power relationships in such a way that the arbitrary exercise of political power by any one group or individual would be prevented. One of the most important concepts held by the framers of the Constitution was that faction, i.e., parties and interest groups, is inherently dangerous to political freedom and stable government. This is evident from *Federalist 10*.

12   JAMES MADISON

FEDERALIST 10

Among the numerous advantages promised by a well constructed Union, none deserves to be more accurately developed than its tendency to break and control the violence of faction. The friend of popular governments, never finds himself so much alarmed for their character and fate, as when he contemplates their propensity to this dangerous vice. He will not fail, therefore, to set a due value on any plan which, without violating the principles to which he is attached, provides a proper cure for it. The instability, injustice, and confusion, introduced into the public councils, have, in truth, been the mortal diseases under which popular governments have everywhere perished; as they continue to be the favorite and fruitful topics from which the adversaries to liberty derive their most specious declamations. The valuable improvements made by the American constitutions on the popular models, both ancient and modern, cannot certainly be too much admired; but it would be an unwarrantable partiality, to contend that they have as effectually obviated the danger on this side, as was wished and expected. Complaints are everywhere heard from our most considerate and virtuous citizens, equally the friends of public and private faith, and of public and personal liberty, that our governments are too unstable; that the public good is disregarded in the conflicts of rival parties; and that measures are too often decided, not according to the rules of justice, and the rights of the minor party, but by the superior force of an interested and overbearing majority. However anxiously we may wish that these complaints had no foundation, the evidence of known facts will not permit us to deny that they are in some degree true. It will be found, indeed, on a candid review of our situation, that some of the distresses under which we labor, have been erroneously charged on the operation of our governments; but it will be found, at the same time, that other causes will not alone account for many of our heaviest misfortunes; and, particularly, for that prevailing and increasing distrust of public engagements, and alarm for private rights, which are echoed from one end of the continent to the other. These must be chiefly, if not wholly, effects of the unsteadiness and injustice, with which a factious spirit has tainted our public administrations.

By a faction, I understand a number of citizens, whether amounting to a majority or minority of the whole, who are united and actuated by some common impulse of passion, or of interest, adverse to the rights of other citizens, or to the permanent and aggregate interest of the community.

There are two methods of curing the mischiefs of faction: The one, by removing its causes; the other, by controlling its effects.

There are again two methods of removing the causes of faction: the one, by destroying the liberty which is essential to its existence; the other, by giving to every citizen the same opinions, the same passions, and the same interests.

It could never be more truly said, that of the first remedy, that it was worse than the disease. Liberty is to faction what air is to fire, an aliment, without which it instantly expires. But it could not be a less folly to abolish liberty, which is essential to political life because it nourishes faction, than it would be to wish the annihilation of air, which is essential to animal life, because it imparts to fire its destructive agency.

The second expedient is as impracticable, as the first would be unwise. As long as the reason of man continues fallible, and he is at liberty to exercise it, different opinions will be formed. As long as the connection subsists between his reason and his self-love, his opinions and his passions will have a reciprocal influence on each other; and the former will be objects to which the latter will attach themselves. The diversity in the faculties of men, from which the rights of property originate, is not less an insuperable obstacle to a uniformity of interests. The protection of those faculties is the first object of government. From the protection of different and unequal faculties of acquiring property, the possession of different degrees and kinds of property immediately results; and from the influence of these on the sentiments and views of the respective proprietors, ensues a division of the society into different interests and parties.

The latent causes of faction are thus sown in the nature of man; and we see them everywhere brought into different degrees of activity, according to the different circumstances of civil society. A zeal for different opinions concerning religion, concerning government, and many other points, as well of speculation as of practice; an attachment to different leaders, ambitiously contending for pre-eminence and power; or to persons of other descriptions, whose fortunes have been interesting to the human passions, have, in turn, divided mankind into parties, inflamed them with mutual animosity, and rendered them much more disposed to vex and oppress each other, than to co-operate for their common good. So strong is this propensity of mankind, to fall into mutual animosities, that where no substantial occasion presents itself, the most frivolous and fanciful distinctions have been sufficient to kindle their unfriendly passions, and excite their most violent conflicts. But the most common and durable source of factions has been the various and unequal distribution of property. Those who hold, and those who are without property, have ever formed distinct interests in society. Those who are creditors, and those who are debtors, fall under a like discrimination. A landed interest, a manufacturing interest, a mercantile interest, a moneyed interest, with many lesser interests, grow up of necessity in civilized nations, and divide them into different classes, actuated by different sentiments and views. The regulation of these various and interfering interests forms the principal task of modern legislation, and involves the spirit of party and faction in the necessary and ordinary operations of government.

No man is allowed to be a judge in his own cause; because his interest will certainly bias his judgment, and, not improbably, corrupt his integrity. With equal, nay, with greater reason, a body of men are unfit to be both judges and parties at the same time; yet what are many of the most important acts of legislation, but so many judicial determinations, not indeed concerning the rights of single persons, but concerning the rights of large bodies of citizens? And what are the different classes of legislators, but advocates and parties to the causes which they determine? Is a law proposed concerning private debts? It is a question to which the creditors are parties on one side, and the debtors on the other. Justice ought to hold the balance between them. Yet the parties are, and must be, themselves the judges; and the most numerous party, or, in other words, the most powerful faction, must be expected to prevail. Shall domestic manufactures be encouraged, and in what degree, by restrictions on foreign manufactures? are questions which would be differently decided by the landed and the manufacturing classes; and probably by neither with a sole regard to justice and the public good. . . .

It is in vain to say, that enlightened statesmen will be able to adjust these clashing interests, and render them all subservient to the public good. Enlightened statesmen will not always be at the helm; nor, in many cases, can such an adjustment be made at all, without taking into view indirect and remote considerations, which will rarely prevail over the immediate interest which one party may find in disregarding the rights of another, or the good of the whole.

The inference to which we are brought is, that the *causes* of faction cannot be removed; and that relief is only to be sought in the means of controlling its *effects*.

If a faction consists of less than a majority, relief is supplied by the republican principle, which enables the majority to defeat its sinister views, by regular vote. It may clog the administration, it may convulse the society; but it will be unable to execute and mask its violence under the forms of the constitution. When a majority is included in a faction, the form of popular government, on the other hand, enables it to sacrifice to its ruling passion or interest, both the public good and the rights of other citizens. To secure the public good, and private rights, against the danger of such a faction, and at the same time to preserve the spirit and the form of popular government, is then the great object to which our inquiries are directed. Let me add, that it is the great desideratum, by which alone this form of government can be rescued from the opprobrium under which it has so long labored, and be recommended to the esteem and adoption of mankind.

By what means is this object attainable? Evidently by one of two only. Either the existence of the same passion or interest in a majority, at the same time must be prevented; or the majority, having such coexistent passion or interest, must be rendered, by their number and local situation, unable to concert and carry into effect schemes of oppression. If the impulse and the opportunity be suffered to coincide, we well know, that neither moral nor religious motives can be relied on as an adequate control. They are not found to be such on the injustice and violence of individuals, and lose their efficacy in proportion to the number combined together; that is, in proportion as their efficacy becomes needful.

From this view of the subject, it may be concluded, that a pure democracy, by which I mean a society consisting of a small number of citizens, who assemble and administer the government in person, can admit of no cure from the mischiefs of faction. A common passion or interest will, in almost every case, be felt by a majority of the whole; a communication and concert, results from the form of government itself; and there is nothing to check the inducements to sacrifice the weaker party, or an obnoxious individual. Hence it is, that such democracies have ever been spectacles of turbulence and contention; have ever been found incompatible with personal security, or the rights of property; and have, in general, been as short in their lives, as they have been violent in their deaths. Theoretic politicians, who have patronized this species of government, have erroneously supposed that by reducing mankind to a perfect equality in their political rights, they would, at the same time, be perfectly equalized and assimilated in their possessions, their opinions, and their passions.

A republic, by which I mean a government in which the scheme of representation takes place, opens a different prospect, and promises the cure for which we are seeking. Let us examine the points in which it varies from pure democracy, and we shall comprehend both the nature of the cure and the efficacy which it must derive from the union.

The two great points of difference, between a democracy and a republic, are, first, the delegation of the government, in the latter, to a small number of citizens elected by the rest; secondly, the greater number of citizens, and greater sphere of country, over which the latter may be extended.

The effect of the first difference is, on the one hand, to refine and enlarge the public views, by passing them through the medium of a chosen body of citizens, whose wisdom may best discern the true interest of their country, and whose patriotism and love of justice, will be least likely to sacrifice it to temporary or partial considerations. Under such a regulation, it may well happen, that the public voice, pronounced by the representatives of the people, will be more consonant to the public good, than if pronounced by the people themselves, convened for the purpose. On the other hand, the effect may be inverted. Men of factious tempers, of local prejudices, or of sinister designs, may by intrigue, by corruption, or by other means, first obtain the suffrages, and then betray the interests of the people. The question resulting is, whether small or extensive republics are most favorable to the election of proper guardians of the public weal; and it is clearly decided in favor of the latter by two obvious considerations.

In the first place, it is to be remarked, that however small the republic may be, the representatives must be raised to a certain number, in order to guard against the cabals of a few; and that however large it may be, they must be limited to a certain number, in order to guard against the confusion of a multitude. Hence, the number of representatives in the two cases not being in proportion to that of the constituents, and being proportionally greatest in the small republic, it follows that if the proportion of fit characters be not less in the large than in the small republic, the former will present a greater option, and consequently a greater probability of a fit choice.

In the next place, as each representative will be chosen by a greater number of citizens in the large than in the small republic, it will be more difficult for unworthy candidates to practice with success the vicious arts, by which elections are too often carried; and the suffrages of the people being more free, will be more likely to center in men who possess the most attractive merit, and the most diffusive and established characters. . . .

The other point of difference is, the greater number of citizens, and extent of territory, which may be brought within the compass of republican, than of democratic government; and it is this circumstance principally which renders factious combinations less to be dreaded in the former, than in the latter. The smaller the society, the fewer probably will be the distinct parties and interests composing it; the fewer the distinct parties and interests, the more frequently will a majority be found of the same party; and the smaller the number of individuals composing a majority, and the smaller the compass within which they are placed, the more easily will they concert and execute their plans of oppression. Extend the sphere, and you take in a greater variety of parties and interests; you make it less probable that a majority of the whole will have a common motive to invade the rights of other citizens; or if such a common motive exists, it will be more difficult for all who feel it to discover their own strength, and to act in unison with each other. . . .

Hence, it clearly appears, that the same advantage, which a republic has over a democracy, in controlling the effects of faction, is enjoyed by a large over a small republic — is enjoyed by the union over the states composing it. Does this advantage consist in the substitution of representatives, whose enlightened views and virtuous sentiments render them superior to local prejudices, and to schemes of injustice? It will not be denied, that the representation of the union will be most likely to possess these requisite endowments. Does it consist in the greater security afforded by a greater variety of parties, against the event of any one party being able to outnumber and oppress the rest? In an equal degree does the increased variety of parties, comprised within the union, increase this security? Does it, in fine, consist in the greater obstacles opposed to the concert and accomplishment of the secret wishes of an unjust and interested majority? Here, again, the extent of the union gives it the most palpable advantage.

The influence of factious leaders may kindle a flame within their particular states, but will be unable to spread a general conflagration through the other states; a religious sect may degenerate into a political faction in a part of the confederacy; but the variety of sects dispersed over the entire fact of it, must secure the national councils against any danger from that source; a rage for paper money, for an abolition of debts, for an equal division of property, or for any other improper or wicked project, will be less apt to pervade the whole body of the union, than a particular member of it; in the same proportion as such a malady is more likely to taint a particular county or district, than an entire state.

In the extent and proper structure of the union, therefore, we behold a republican remedy for the diseases most incident to republican government. And according to the degree of pleasure and pride we feel in being republicans, ought to be our zeal in cherishing the spirit, and supporting the character of Federalists.

The following selection is taken from E. E. Schattschneider's well-known treatise, *Party Government*. In this material he examines both the implications of *Federalist 10* and counterarguments to the propositions stated by Madison, with regard to political parties and interest groups.

13   E. E. SCHATTSCHNEIDER

PARTY GOVERNMENT

The Convention at Philadelphia produced a constitution with a dual attitude: it was proparty in one sense and antiparty in another. The authors of the Constitution refused to suppress the parties by destroying the fundamental liberties in which parties originate. They or their immediate successors accepted amendments that guaranteed civil rights and thus established a system of party tolerance, i.e.,

From E. E. Schattschneider, *Party Government*, pp. 7–8, 32–34. Copyright © 1942, by E. E. Schattschneider. Quoted with the permission of Holt, Rinehart and Winston, Inc., publishers.

the right to agitate and to organize. This is the proparty aspect of the system. On the other hand, the authors of the Constitution set up an elaborate division and balance of powers within an intricate governmental structure designed to make parties ineffective. It was hoped that the parties would lose and exhaust themselves in futile attempts to fight their way through the labyrinthine framework of the government, much as an attacking army is expected to spend itself against the defensive works of a fortress. This is the antiparty part of the constitutional scheme. To quote Madison, the "great object" of the Constitution was "to preserve the public good and private rights against the danger of such a faction [party] and at the same time to preserve the spirit and form of popular government."

In Madison's mind the difference between an autocracy and a free republic seems to have been largely a matter of the precise point at which parties are stopped by the government. In an autocracy parties are controlled (suppressed) at the source; in a republic parties are tolerated but are invited to strangle themselves in the machinery of government. The result in either case is much the same, sooner or later the government checks the parties but *never do the parties control the government*. Madison was perfectly definite and unmistakable in his disapproval of party government as distinguished from party tolerance. In the opinion of Madison, parties were intrinsically bad, and the sole issue for discussion was the means by which bad parties might be prevented from becoming dangerous. What never seems to have occurred to the authors of the Constitution, however, is that parties might be *used* as beneficent instruments of popular government. It is at this point that the distinction between the modern and the antique attitude is made.

The offspring of this combination of ideas was a constitutional system having conflicting tendencies. The Constitution made the rise of parties inevitable yet was incompatible with party government. This scheme, in spite of its subtlety, involved a miscalculation. Political parties refused to be content with the role assigned to them. The vigor and enterprise of the parties have therefore made American political history the story of the unhappy marriage of the parties and the Constitution, a remarkable variation of the case of the irresistible force and the immovable object, which in this instance have been compelled to live together in a permanent partnership. . . .

The Raw Materials of Politics

People who write about interests sometimes seem to assume that all interests are special and exclusive, setting up as a result of this assumption a dichotomy in which the interests on the one side are perpetually opposed to the public welfare on the other side. But there are common interests as well as special interests, and common interests resemble special interests in that they are apt to influence political behavior. The raw materials of politics are not all antisocial. Alongside of Madison's statement that differences in wealth are the most durable causes of faction there should be placed a corollary that the common possessions of the people are the most durable cause of unity. To assume that people have merely conflicting interests and nothing else is to invent a political nightmare that has only a superficial relation to reality. The body of agreement underlying the conflicts of a modern society ought to be sufficient to sustain the social order provided only that the common interests supporting this unity are mobilized. Moreover, not all differences of interests are durable causes of conflict. Nothing is apt to be more perishable than a political issue. In the democratic process, the nation moves from controversy to agreement to forgetfulness; politics is not a futile exercise like football, forever played back and forth over the same ground. The government creates and destroys interests at every turn.

There are, in addition, powerful factors inhibiting the unlimited pursuit of special aims by any organized minority. To assume that minorities will stop at nothing to get what they want is to postulate a degree of unanimity and concentration within these groups that does not often exist in real life. If every individual were capable of having only one interest to the exclusion of all others, it might be possible to form dangerous unions of monomaniacs who would go to great extremes to attain their objectives. In fact, however, people have many interests leading to a dispersion of drives certain to destroy some of the unanimity and concentration of any group. How many interests can an individual have? Enough to make it extremely unlikely that any two individuals will have the same combination of interests. Anyone who has ever tried to promote an association of people having some special interest in common will realize, first, that there are marked differences of enthusiasm within the group and, second, that interests compete with interests for the attention and enthusiasm of every individual. Every organized special interest consists of a group of busy, distracted individuals held together by the efforts of a handful of specialists and enthusiasts who sacrifice other matters in order to concentrate on one. The notion of resolute and unanimous minorities on the point of violence is largely the invention of paid lobbyists and press agents.

The result of the fact that every individual is torn by the diversity of his own interests, the fact that he is a member of many groups, is *the law of the imperfect political mobilization of interests*. That is, it has never been possible to mobilize any interest 100 per cent. . . .

It is only another way of saying the same thing to state that conflicts of interests are not cumulative. If it were true that the dividing line in every conflict (or in all major conflicts) split the community identically in each case so that individuals who are opposed on one issue would be opposed to each other on all other issues also, while individuals who joined hands on one occasion would find themselves on the same side on all issues, always opposed to the same combination of antagonists, the cleavage created by the cumulative effect of these divisions would be fatal. But actually conflicts are not cumulative in this way. In real life the divisions are not so clearly marked, and the alignment of people according to interests requires an enormous shuffling back and forth from one side to the other, tending to dissipate the tensions created.

In view of the fact, therefore, (1) that there are many interests, including a great body of common interests, (2) that the government pursues a multiplicity of policies and creates and destroys interests in the process, (3) that each individual is capable of having many interests, (4) that interests cannot be mobilized perfectly, and (5) that conflicts among interests are not cumulative, it seems reasonable to suppose that the government is not the captive of blind forces from which there is no escape. There is nothing wrong about the raw materials of politics.

The Functions of Political Parties

The preceding material provides a useful introduction both to parties and interest groups. It is indicative, in part, of the constitutional and political frame of reference within which these institutions should be examined.

Clinton Rossiter, a distinguished commentator on the American scene, discusses below the functions of American political parties. It will become evident to the student that, although the Constitution was framed in an atmosphere of distrust of parties, they are an integral part of the democratic process.

14   CLINTON ROSSITER

THE FUNCTIONS OF AMERICAN PARTIES

Parties, it could be argued, exist primarily to serve the interests of the men who lead or support them. They are justified by

From Clinton Rossiter, *Parties and Politics in America*, pp. 38–50. Copyright © 1960, by Cornell University. Reprinted with the permission of the author and the publisher, Cornell University Press.

their fruits, by which I mean the fruits that are showered on the leaders in the form of power and on the supporters in the form of favors. This, however, is a crude and narrow view of the role of parties in our society; for whatever they may have been in their beginnings, parties are now public institutions rather than private preserves. They stand closer to Congress and the courts than they do, say, to the American Legion or General Motors or the A.F.L.-C.I.O. on the spectrum of social organization that runs from the very private to the totally official. They are justified by their functions, by which I mean functions that are performed as services to the entire nation. We tolerate and even celebrate their existence because they do things for us in the public realm that would otherwise be done poorly or not at all.

Let us turn now to look at our parties in this light. Let us describe the political and social functions of any party in any democracy, and see how well our particular parties have performed each of these functions in our peculiar democracy. Let us see, too, if there are any special "characteristically American" functions that they have been called upon to perform or, more accurately, have performed without knowing it. . . .

The primary function of a political party in a democracy such as ours is to control and direct the struggle for power. From this function all others derive naturally. I trust that no apologies need be made for calling attention to the fact that the political process in a free country is essentially a conflict, limited and regularized but nonetheless relentless, among groups of men who have contradictory interests and more or less mutually exclusive hopes of securing them. . . .

It is one of the aspirations of democracy to bring this struggle as much as possible into the open. It is the great purpose of political parties, the handmaidens of democracy, to bring the struggle under control: to institutionalize it with organization, to channel it through nominations and elections, to publicize it by means of platforms and appeals, above all to stabilize it in the form of that traditional quadrille in which the Ins and the Outs change places from time to time on a signal from the voters. The parties did not create the struggle for power; it would go on merrily without them. It would go on, however, much less purposefully and effectively and openly, and we might well be more grateful to our own parties for their modest efforts to bring under benevolent control the eternal conflict of interests described by Madison in *The Federalist,* no. 10. . . .

The first of what we might call the subsidiary functions of a party in a democracy (subsidiary, that is, to the great, inclusive function we have just noted) is to act as an immense personnel agency. Constitutions make frugal provision for the election or appointment of persons to high office, but they extend no aid at all to those persons in and out of government who must act as recruiters. Statutes and ordinances bloom in profusion to create the rules and rewards of a civil service, but they offer no guaranty that the men on top of the permanent bureaucracy will be like-minded enough to give it a sense of cohesion or alert enough to the needs of the public to give it a sense of direction.

This is exactly where parties enter the picture decisively and why, all things considered, we could hardly do without them. Willingly and indeed eagerly they set up and operate the machinery that places men and women in public office, and they do it at four key points: *nominations,* for they are organized to do the preliminary sifting of aspirants to elective office, or, if necessary, to go out and recruit them actively; *campaigns,* for they make known to the voting public the credentials and promises of the narrowed list of candidates; *elections,* for they can provide (in bulk and at small cost) the swarm of citizens needed to man the polls and count the votes; and *appointments,* for they are no less eager to assist in the selective process than they are in the elective process. Indeed, they can come up even more quickly with a reasonably qualified candidate for appointment as Secretary of State or district attorney or recorder of deeds than with an equally qualified candidate for election as President or assemblyman or county coroner. . . .

How would we ever get through the process of electing a Congress if the parties did not take over the primaries and elections? How would the President ever find candidates for several thousand offices a year if his party's informal patronage machinery were not quick with suggestions? How would we go about filling the 750,000 (give or take 100,000) elective offices in the United States if we were a strictly non-partisan people? If we do not get as many first-rate men as we should in Congress and the administration, in state legislatures and school boards, the blame must be laid at the doors of the people with their antipolitical mores and not of the politicians with their vulgar methods. The latter, after all, stay in business by pleasing the former, and up to now they seem to have pleased us well enough. . . .

Parties can also serve as important sources of public policy. They have no monopoly of this function, to be sure, nor should they in the kind of pluralistic society we identify with democracy. The great and small policies by which we live emerged first as special pleadings of an infinite variety of groups and persons, and we should be happy to live in a society in which organizations like N.A.M. or N.A.A.C.P. and men like Walter Lippmann or Bernard Baruch come up constantly with new proposals for our consideration. Yet the parties — and in this instance I include third parties — are perhaps best fitted of all agencies to convert formless hopes or frustrations into proposals that can be understood, debated, and, if found appealing, approved by the people.

Because they are the only truly national, multi-interest, broadly based organizations active in our society (the only ones, indeed, that we can permit to be active), they are uniquely situated to originate policies themselves or to broaden the special pleadings of other men and groups. Their policies, moreover, are likely to be a little more realistic than those that emerge from the paid researches of interest groups, for any one policy must be fitted with dozens of others into a full program for governing the nation.

Thanks to the fuzzy nature of our political system, the major parties have not been especially effective in performing this function. In the words of the Committee on Political Parties of the American Political Science Association, "the American two-party system has shown little propensity for evolving original or creative ideas about public policy; it has even been rather sluggish in responding to such ideas in the public interest." The platforms of the parties, which are presumably the most eloquent statements they can make of their current intentions, have never been noted for originality or clarity. One cannot fail to be impressed by some of the reports of the Democratic Advisory Council or by the Report of the Republican Committee on Program and Progress, *Decisions for a Better America,* issued in September 1959, yet one is struck by the scarcity of concrete proposals in all these reports and bound to wonder if the members of these committees really speak with the voice of authority. Yet the remembrance of Wilson's New Freedom and Roosevelt's New Deal should be enough to convince us that parties can originate policies, and that their policies, unlike those of most interest groups, can cut a broad swath through American life. . . .

The point at which our parties may indeed have failed us in this matter of policies is not in originating or formulating or advertising them, but in converting them into the hard coin of purposeful law and skillful administration. Before we go into that problem, however, we must take note of the function that makes it possible and even mandatory for parties in a democracy to put their policies into effect: the organization and operation of government. Within every true party there exists . . . a governmental party, a hard core of office-holders whose duty to the community goes beyond mere electioneering or even formulating policies. If this party has been victorious in the most recent election, it is expected to organize the legislative and executive branches and to run them with the aid of the appeals and disciplines of party loyalty. . . . A political organization unwilling to govern is not, by any definition, a party. . . .

If we have few complaints about the technical competence with which our majority parties organize and operate the agencies of government, we have many, probably more than any other people in the democratic world, about the skill and dedication they bring to the process of making their own policies the policies of city or state or nation; and that, as I have already indicated, is one of the basic functions of a party in a democracy: to make concrete promises to the electorate and then, if invited by the electorate to govern, to make good on those promises. . . . If parties are not expected or encouraged to make good on their reasonable promises, then other groups less open in operation and accountable in fact — blocs and interest groups and loose coalitions of lobby-ridden legislators — will assume the authority to make public policy.

The last of what we might call the political functions of parties in a democracy is one that a party does not choose happily yet must accept willingly if the burden is thrust upon it. This is the delicate function, so necessary to democracy and so incomprehensible to autocracy, of "loyal opposition." . . . They must oppose the proposals of the majority, develop alternative proposals for the electorate to consider at the next election, and keep a close watch on those who are executing the laws under the direction of the majority party. . . .

American parties have had perhaps more success in opposition than in governing, which is a revealing commentary on the nature of our political system. In fact, it often seems that American politicians are happier out of power than in it. Like the great Constitution under which we live serenely, our political instinct seems to prefer restraint to power and delay to action. . . .

To this list of the political functions of parties in a democracy we can add three others that might more accurately be described as social, since in performing them parties serve men in their roles as social rather than political animals. First, parties are important agencies in the educational process. The citizens of a free country must be instructed in the practices of democracy and kept informed on the issues of their times, not merely to become more forceful agents of public opinion and more skillful voters, but also to live more satisfying lives. Once they have finished the last stage of their formal education, they must rely on a battery of informal instruments ranging from Sunday afternoon television to word of mouth. Political parties are at best crude instruments of adult education, yet they can do much to compel study and discussion of important problems. . . .

Next, the parties serve a useful social purpose in acting as buffers and adjusters between individuals and society, especially as the latter intrudes into the lives of ordinary persons in the shape of impersonal political authority. . . .

. . . [T]he parties are still important dispensers of those aids, favors, and immunities (for example, from prosecution of father for peddling without a license or son for breaking windows) that make it possible for men and women to live reasonably confident lives in a harsh environment. If poor Negroes in Atlantic City no longer need to be given coal, they do need help in obtaining unemployment compensation with which to buy coal. The more penetrating and complicated the power of government becomes, the more demand there is for skilled "adjusters," who might as well be politicians as priests or social workers. There is, of course, a seamy side to this function; politicians contribute more than their fair share to the corruptions and injustices of American life, in the country as well as in the city. Yet the fact that a function is performed corruptly is no decisive argument against its being performed in the first place. . . . The lives of millions of Americans would have been much harder to bear if the parties had not done their work as agencies of social welfare.

Finally, parties serve a symbolic function — or should we start from the other direction and call it psychological? — by providing an object, large and friendly and often exciting, to which men can extend allegiance. Graham Wallas, in his memorable study of *Human Nature in Politics,* was perhaps the first observer to isolate and examine this function. Having taken note of the multitude of voters and of the physical inability of any one voter to deal with more than a few men and ideas, he went on: "Something is required simpler and more permanent, something which can be loved and trusted, and which can be recognized at successive elections as being the same thing that was loved and trusted before; and a party is such a thing." . . .

> The following selection outlines a model of party government in a democracy. The carefully constructed model is based upon certain premises about the nature of political behavior, some of which can be challenged on the basis of information presented in later selections dealing with political parties and the electorate. But the attempt that the author makes to unite economic and political theory is intriguing and brilliant. Many of the insights are very useful in helping to understand the nature of political action in a democracy.

15   ANTHONY DOWNS

AN ECONOMIC THEORY
OF POLITICAL ACTION
IN A DEMOCRACY

I

In spite of the tremendous importance of government decisions in every phase of economic life, economic theorists have never successfully integrated government with private decision-makers in a single general equilibrium theory. Instead they have treated government action as an exogenous variable, determined by political considerations that lie outside the purview of economics. This view is really a carry-over from the classical premise that the private sector is a self-regulating mechanism and that any government action beyond maintenance of law and order is "interference" with it rather than an intrinsic part of it.

However, in at least two fields of economic theory, the centrality of government action has forced economists to formulate rules that indicate how government "should" make decisions. Thus in the field of public finance, Hugh Dalton states:

> As a result of [the] operations of public finance, changes take place in the amount and in the nature of the wealth which is produced, and in the distribution of that wealth among individuals and classes. Are these changes in their aggregate effects socially advantageous? If so the operations are justified; if not, not. The best system of public finance is that which secures the maximum social advantage from the operations which it conducts.

A similar attempt to differentiate the operations "proper" to government from those "proper" to private agents has been made by Harvey W. Peck, who writes: "If public operation of an enterprise will produce a greater net social utility, the services rendered by this enterprise should belong in the category of public goods." In addition, several welfare economists have posited general principles to guide government action in the economy. For example, Abba P. Lerner indirectly states such a rule when he says: "If it is desired to maximize the total satisfaction in a society, the rational procedure is to divide income on an equalitarian basis."

Admittedly, this list of examples is not very long, primarily because overt statements of a decision rule to guide government action are extremely rare in economic theory. However, it does not unduly distort reality to state that most welfare economists and many public finance theorists implicitly assume that the "proper" function of government is to maximize social welfare. Insofar as they face the problem of government decision-making at all, they nearly all subscribe to some approximation of this normative rule.

The use of this rule has led to two major difficulties. First, it is not clear what is meant by "social welfare," nor is there any agreement about how to "maximize" it. In fact, a long controversy about the nature of social welfare in the "new welfare economics" led to Kenneth Arrow's conclusion that no rational method of maximizing social welfare can possibly be found unless strong restrictions are placed on the preference orderings of the individuals in society.

The complexities of this problem have diverted attention from the second difficulty raised by the view that government's function is to maximize social welfare. Even if social welfare could be defined, and methods of maximizing it could be agreed upon, what reason is there to believe that the men who run the government would be motivated to maximize it? To state that they "should" do so does not mean that they will. As Schumpeter, one of the few economists who have faced this problem, has pointed out:

> It does not follow that the social meaning of a type of activity will necessarily provide the motive power, hence the explanation of the latter. If it does not, a theory that contents itself with an analysis of the social end or need to be served cannot be accepted as an adequate account of the activities that serve it.

Schumpeter here illuminates a crucial objection to most attempts to deal with government in economic theory: they do not really treat the government as part of the division of labor. Every agent in the division of labor has both a private motive and a social function. For example, the social function of a coal-miner is removing coal from the ground, since this activity provides utility for others. But he is motivated to carry out this function by his desire to earn income, not by any desire to benefit others. Similarly, every other agent in the division of labor carries out his social function primarily as a means of attaining his own private ends: the enjoyment of income, prestige, or power. Much of economic theory consists in essence of proving that men thus pursuing their own ends may nevertheless carry out their social functions with great efficiency, at least under certain conditions.

In light of this reasoning, any attempt to construct a theory of government action without discussing the motives of those who run the government must be regarded as inconsistent with the main body of economic analysis. Every such attempt fails to face the fact that governments are concrete institutions run by men, because it deals with them on a purely normative level. As a result, these attempts can never lead to an integration of government with other decision-makers in a general equilibrium theory. Such integration demands a positive approach that explains how the governors are led to act by their own selfish motives. In the following sections, I present a model of government decision-making based on this approach.

II

In building this model, I shall use the following definitions:

1. *Government* is that agency in the division of labor which has the power to coerce all other agents in society; it is the locus of "ultimate" power in a given area.

2. A *democracy* is a political system that exhibits the following characteristics:

a. Two or more parties compete in periodic elections for control of the governing apparatus.

b. The party (or coalition of parties) winning a majority of votes gains control of the governing apparatus until the next election.

c. Losing parties never attempt to prevent the winners from taking office, nor do winners use the powers of office to vitiate the ability of losers to compete in the next election.

d. All sane, law-abiding adults who are governed are citizens, and every citizen has one and only one vote in each election.

Though these definitions are both somewhat ambiguous, they will suffice for present purposes.

Next I set forth the following axioms:

1. Each political party is a team of men who seek office solely in order to enjoy the income, prestige, and power that go with running the governing apparatus.

2. The winning party (or coalition) has complete control over the government's actions until the next election. There are no votes of confidence between elections either by a legislature or by the electorate, so the governing party cannot be ousted before the next election. Nor are any of its orders resisted or sabotaged by an intransigent bureaucracy.

3. Government's economic powers are unlimited. It can nationalize

everything, hand everything to private interests, or strike any balance between these extremes.

4. The only limit on government's powers is that the incumbent party cannot in any way restrict the political freedom of opposition parties or of individual citizens, unless they seek to overthrow it by force.

5. Every agent in the model — whether an individual, a party or a private coalition — behaves rationally at all times; that is, it proceeds toward its goals with a minimal use of scarce resources and undertakes only those actions for which marginal return exceeds marginal cost.

From these definitions and axioms springs my central hypothesis: political parties in a democracy formulate policy strictly as a means of gaining votes. They do not seek to gain office in order to carry out certain preconceived policies or to serve any particular interest groups; rather they formulate policies and serve interest groups in order to gain office. Thus their social function — which is to formulate and carry out policies when in power as the government — is accomplished as a by-product of their private motive — which is to attain the income, power, and prestige of being in office.

This hypothesis implies that, in a democracy, the government always acts so as to maximize the number of votes it will receive. In effect, it is an entrepreneur selling policies for votes instead of products for money. Furthermore, it must compete for votes with other parties, just as two or more oligopolists compete for sales in a market. Whether or not such a government maximizes social welfare (assuming this process can be defined) depends upon how the competitive struggle for power influences its behavior. We cannot assume a priori that this behavior is socially optimal any more than we can assume a priori that a given firm produces the socially optimal output.

I shall examine the nature of government decision-making in two contexts: (1) in a world in which there is perfect knowledge and information is costless and (2) in a world in which knowledge is imperfect and information is costly.

III

The analysis of government decision-making in a perfectly informed world is intended only to highlight the basic relationship between a democratic government and its citizens. This relationship can be stated in the following set of propositions:

1. The actions of the government are a function of the way it expects voters to vote and of the strategies of its opposition.

2. The government expects voters to vote according to (a) changes

in their utility incomes from government activity and (*b*) the strategies of opposition parties.

3. Voters actually vote according to (*a*) changes in their utility incomes from government activity and (*b*) the alternatives offered by the opposition.

4. Voters' utility incomes from government activity depend on the actions taken by government during the election period.

5. The strategies of opposition parties depend on their views of the voters' utility incomes from government activity and on the actions taken by the government in power.

These propositions actually form a set of five equations containing five unknowns: expected votes, actual votes, opposition strategies, government actions, and individual utility incomes from government activity. Thus the political structure of a democracy can be viewed in terms of a set of simultaneous equations similar to those often used to analyze an economic structure.

Because the citizens of our model democracy are rational, each of them views elections strictly as means of selecting the government most beneficial to him. Each citizen estimates the utility income from government action he expects each party would provide him if it were in power in the forthcoming election period, that is, he first estimates the utility income Party A would provide him, then the income Party B would provide, and so on. He votes for whatever party he believes would provide him with the highest utility income from government action. The primary factor influencing his estimate of each party's future performance is not its campaign promises about the future but its performance during the period just ending. Thus his voting decision is based on a comparison of the utility income he actually received during this period from the actions of the incumbent party and those he believes he would have received had each of the opposition parties been in power (I assume that each opposition party has taken a verbal stand on every issue dealt with concretely by the incumbents). This procedure allows him to found his decision on facts rather than on conjectures. Of course, since he is helping to choose a future government, he modifies his analysis of each party's past performance according to his estimate of probable changes in its behavior. Nevertheless, the current record of the incumbents remains the central item in his evaluation.

The government also makes decisions rationally, but its behavior is not so easy to analyze, because it is engaged in political warfare with its opponents. Each party resembles a player in an *N*-person game or an oligopolist engaged in cut-throat competition. However, the conjectural variation problem is somewhat simplified, because the incumbent party must always commit itself on each issue before the opposition parties do. Since it is in power, it must act whenever the occasion for a decision arises, if failure to respond is counted as a form of action. But the opposition, which is not responsible for the government, can wait until the pressure of events has forced the governing party to commit itself. Thus opposition parties have a strategic advantage — which incidentally makes the analysis of interparty warfare simpler than it would be if all parties revealed their strategies simultaneously.

However, I shall not explore party strategies in a perfectly informed world, because nearly all the conclusions that could be drawn are inapplicable to the imperfectly informed world in which we are primarily interested. Only one point should be stressed: in a world where perfect knowledge prevails, the government gives the preferences of each citizen exactly the same weight as those of every other citizen. This does not mean that its policies favor all citizens equally, since strategic considerations may lead it to ignore some citizens and to woo others ardently or to favor some with one policy and others with another. But it never deliberately eschews the vote of Citizen A to gain that of Citizen B. Since each citizen has one and only one vote, it cannot gain by trading A's vote for B's, *ceteris paribus*. In short, the equality of franchise is successful as a device for distributing political power equally among citizens.

IV

Lack of complete information on which to base decisions is a condition so basic to human life that it influences the structure of almost every social institution. In politics especially, its effects are profound. For this reason, I devote the rest of my analysis to the impact of imperfect knowledge upon political action in a democracy.

In this model, imperfect knowledge means (1) that parties do not always know exactly what citizens want; (2) that citizens do not always know what the government or its opposition has done, is doing, or should be doing to serve their interests; and (3) that the information needed to overcome both types of ignorance is costly — in other words, that scarce resources must be used to procure and assimilate it. Although these conditions have many effects upon the operation of government in the model, I concentrate on only three: persuasion, ideologies, and rational ignorance.

V

As long as we retain the assumption of perfect knowledge, no citizen can possibly influence another's vote. Each knows what would benefit him most, what the government is doing, and what other parties would do if they were in power. Therefore, the citizen's political taste structure, which I assume to be fixed, leads him directly to an unambiguous decision about how he should vote. If he remains rational, no persuasion can change his mind.

But, as soon as ignorance appears, the clear path from taste structure to voting decision becomes obscured by lack of knowledge. Though some voters want a specific party to win because its policies are clearly the most beneficial to them, others are highly uncertain about which party they prefer. They are not sure just what is happening to them or what would happen to them if another party were in power. They need more facts to establish a clear preference. By providing these facts, persuaders can become effective.

Persuaders are not interested per se in helping people who are uncertain become less so; they want to produce a decision that aids their cause. Therefore, they provide only those facts which are favorable to whatever group they are supporting. Thus, even if we assume that no erroneous or false data exist, some men are able to influence others by presenting them with a biased selection of facts.

This possibility has several extraordinarily important consequences for the operation of government. First, it means that some men are more important than others politically, because they can influence more votes than they themselves cast. Since it takes scarce resources to provide information to hesitant citizens, men who command such resources are able to wield more than proportional political influence, *ceteris paribus*. The government, being rational, cannot overlook this fact in designing policy. As a result, equality of franchise no longer assures net equality of influence over government action. In fact, it is irrational for a democratic government to treat its citizens with equal deference in a world in which knowledge is imperfect.

Second, the government is itself ignorant of what its citizens want it to do. Therefore it must send out representatives (1) to sound out the electorate and discover their desires and (2) to persuade them it should be re-elected. In other words, lack of information converts democratic government into representative government, because it forces the central planning board of the governing party to rely upon agents scattered throughout the electorate. Such reliance amounts to a decentralization of government power from the planning board to the agents.[1] The central board continues to decentralize its power until the marginal vote-gain from greater conformity to popular desires is equal to the marginal vote-loss caused by reduced ability to co-ordinate its actions.

This reasoning implies that a democratic government in a rational world will always be run on a quasi-representative, quasi-decentralized

[1] Decentralization may be geographical or by social groups, depending upon the way society is divided into homogeneous parts.

basis, no matter what its formal constitutional structure, as long as communication between the voters and the governors is less than perfect. Another powerful force working in the same direction is the division of labor. To be efficient, a nation must develop specialists in discovering, transmitting, and analyzing popular opinion, just as it develops specialists in everything else. These specialists are the representatives. They exercise more power, and the central planning board exercises less, the less efficient communication facilities are in society.

The third consequence of imperfect knowledge and the resulting need for persuasion is really a combination of the first two. Because some voters can be influenced, specialists in influencing them appear. And, because government needs intermediaries between it and the people, some of these influencers pose as "representatives" of the citizenry. On one hand, they attempt to convince the government that the policies they stand for — which are of direct benefit to themselves — are both good for and desired by a large portion of the electorate. On the other hand, they try to convince the electorate that these policies are in fact desirable. Thus one of their methods of getting government to believe that public opinion supports them is to create favorable opinion through persuasion. Though a rational government will discount their claims, it cannot ignore them altogether. It must give the influencers more than proportional weight in forming policy, because they may have succeeded in creating favorable opinions in the silent mass of voters and because their vociferousness indicates a high intensity of desire. Clearly, people with an intense interest in some policy are more likely to base their votes upon it alone than are those who count it as just another issue; hence government must pay more attention to the former than the latter. To do otherwise would be irrational.

Finally, imperfect knowledge makes the governing party susceptible to bribery. In order to persuade voters that its policies are good for them, it needs scarce resources, such as television time, money for propaganda, and pay for precinct captains. One way to get such resources is to sell policy favors to those who can pay for them, either by campaign contributions, favorable editorial policies, or direct influence over others. Such favor buyers need not even pose as representatives of the people. They merely exchange their political help for policy favors — a transaction eminently rational for both themselves and the government.

Essentially, inequality of political influence is a necessary result of imperfect information, given an unequal distribution of wealth and income in society. When knowledge is imperfect, effective political action requires the use of economic resources to meet the cost of information. Therefore, those who command such resources are able to swing more than their proportional weight politically. This outcome is not the result of irrationality or dishonesty. On the contrary, lobbying in a democracy is a highly rational response to the lack of perfect information, as is government's submission to the demands of lobbyists. To suppose otherwise is to ignore the existence of information costs — that is, to theorize about a mythical world instead of the real one. Imperfect knowledge allows the unequal distributions of income, position, and influence — which are all inevitable in any economy marked by an extensive division of labor — to share sovereignty in a realm where only the equal distribution of votes is supposed to reign.

VI

Since the parties in this model have no interest per se in creating any particular type of society, the universal prevalence of ideologies in democratic politics appears to contradict my hypothesis. But this appearance is false. In fact, not only the existence of ideologies, but also many of their particular characteristics, may be deduced from the premise that parties seek office solely for the income, power, and prestige that accompany it.[2] Again, imperfect knowledge is the key factor.

In a complex society the cost in time alone of comparing all the ways in which the policies of competing parties differ is staggering. Furthermore, citizens do not always have enough information to appraise the differences of which they are aware. Nor do they know in advance what problems the government is likely to face in the coming election period.

Under these conditions many a voter finds party ideologies useful because they remove the necessity for relating every issue to his own conception of "the good society." Ideologies help him focus attention on the differences between parties; therefore, they can be used as samples of all the differentiating stands. Furthermore, if the voter discovers a correlation between each party's ideology and its policies, he can rationally vote by comparing ideologies rather than policies. In both cases he can drastically reduce his outlay on political information by informing himself only about ideologies instead of about a wide range of issues.

Thus lack of information creates a demand for ideologies in the electorate. Since political parties are eager to seize any method of gaining votes available to them, they respond by creating a supply. Each party invents an ideology in order to attract the votes of those citizens who wish to cut costs by voting ideologically.[3]

[2] I define "ideologies" as verbal images of "the good society" and of the chief policies to be used in creating it.

[3] In reality, party ideologies probably stem originally from the interests of those

This reasoning does not mean that parties can change ideologies as though they were disguises, putting on whatever costume suits the situation. Once a party has placed its ideology "on the market," it cannot suddenly abandon or radically alter that ideology without convincing the voters that it is unreliable. Since voters are rational, they refuse to support unreliable parties; hence no party can afford to acquire a reputation for dishonesty. Furthermore, there must be some persistent correlation between each party's ideology and its subsequent actions; otherwise voters will eventually eschew ideological voting as irrational. Finally, parties cannot adopt identical ideologies, because they must create enough product differentiation to make their output distinguishable from that of their rivals, so as to entice voters to the polls. However, just as in the product market, any markedly successful ideology is soon imitated, and differentiation takes place on more subtle levels.

Analysis of political ideologies can be carried even further by means of a spatial analogy for political action. To construct this analogy, I borrow and elaborate upon an apparatus first used by Harold Hotelling in his famous article "Stability in Competition."[4] My version of Hotelling's spatial market consists of a linear scale running from zero to one hundred in the usual left-to-right fashion. To render it politically meaningful, I make the following assumptions:

1. The political parties in any society can be ordered from left to right in a manner agreed upon by all voters.

2. Each voter's preferences are single-peaked at some point on the scale and slope monotonically downward on either side of the peak (unless it lies at one extreme of the scale).

3. The frequency distribution of voters along the scale is variable from society to society but fixed in any one society.

4. Once placed on the political scale, a party can move ideologically either to the left or to the right up to but not beyond the nearest party toward which it is moving.[5]

5. In a two-party system, if either party moves away from the extreme nearest it toward the other party, extremist voters at its end of the scale may abstain because they see no significant difference between the choices offered them.

---

persons who found each party. But, once a political party is created, it takes on an existence of its own and eventually becomes relatively independent of any particular interest group. When such autonomy prevails, my analysis of ideologies is fully applicable.

[4] *Economic Journal,* XXXIX (1929), 41–57.

[5] It cannot go beyond the adjacent parties, because such "leaping" would indicate ideological unreliability and would cause its rejection by the electorate.

Under these conditions Hotelling's conclusion that the parties in a two-party system inevitably converge on the center does not necessarily hold true. If voters are distributed along the scale as shown in Figure 1, then Hotelling is right. Assuming that Party A starts at position 25

FIGURE ONE

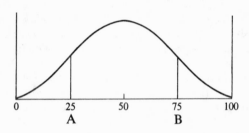

and Party B at 75, both move toward 50, since each can gain more votes in the center than it loses at the extremes because of abstention. But, if the distribution is like that shown in Figure 2, the two parties diverge toward the extremes rather than converge on the center. Each gains more votes by moving toward a radical position than it loses in the center.

This reasoning implies that stable government in a two-party democracy requires a distribution of voters roughly approximating a normal curve. When such a distribution exists, the two parties come to resemble each other closely. Thus, when one replaces the other in office, no drastic policy changes occur, and most voters are located relatively close to the incumbent's position no matter which party is in power. But when the electorate is polarized, as in Figure 2, a change in

FIGURE TWO

parties causes a radical alteration in policy. And, regardless of which party is in office, half the electorate always feels that the other half is imposing policies upon it that are strongly repugnant to it. In this situation, if one party keeps getting re-elected, the disgruntled supporters of the other party will probably revolt; whereas if the two parties alternate in office, social chaos occurs, because government policy keeps changing from one extreme to the other. Thus democracy does not lead to effective, stable government when the electorate is polarized. Either the distribution must change or democracy will be replaced by tyranny in which one extreme imposes its will upon the other.

Hotelling's original model was limited to the two-firm (or two-party) case, because, when three firms existed, the two outside ones converged on the middle one, which then leaped to the outside to avoid strangulation. Since this process repeated itself endlessly, no stable equilibrium emerged. But, in my model, such leaping is impossible, because each party has to maintain continuity in its ideology. Hence this model can be applied to multiparty systems without resulting in disequilibrium.

Multiparty systems are most likely to exist when the distribution of voters is multimodal, as shown in Figure 3. A separate party forms at

FIGURE THREE

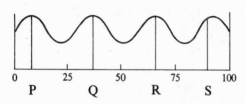

each mode, and each party is motivated to stay at its mode and to differentiate itself as completely as possible from its neighbors. If it moves to the left so as to gain votes, it loses just as many votes to the party on its right (or loses them because of abstention if it is an extremist party at the right end of the scale), and vice versa. Thus its optimal course is to stay where it is and keep other parties from approaching it. In a multiparty system, therefore, we find conditions exactly opposite to those in a viable two-party system. Whereas in the former each party links itself to a definite ideological position and stresses its differences from other parties, in the latter both parties move toward the political center so as to resemble each other as closely as possible.

This conclusion implies that voters in multiparty systems have a wider range of choice than voters in two-party systems and that each choice in this range is more definitely linked to some ideological position. Thus it appears that the electorate exercises a more significant function in a multiparty system than in a two-party system, because only in the former does it make much difference which party gets elected.

However, appearances are deceiving in politics, because in fact the government in a multiparty system is likely to have a less definite, less coherent, and less integrated program than the government in a two-party system. This paradoxical outcome arises from the necessity in most multiparty systems of forming coalition governments. Since voters are scattered among several modes, only rarely does one party obtain the support of a majority of those voting. Yet, in most democracies, the government cannot function without at least the indirect support of a majority of voters. Even in systems in which the legislature selects the government, a majority of its members must support the coalition chosen to govern before the coalition can take office. If we assume that representation in the legislature is "fair" — that each member represents the same number of citizens — then even a coalition government must receive the indirect support of a majority in order to govern.

Such support can be maintained only if the government implements at least some policies that appeal to — are ideologically near — each cluster of voters whose support it needs. If a majority of voters are massed in one relatively narrow band on the left-right scale, then the government can choose all its policies from within this band. Hence its policies will form a fairly cohesive set embodying the ideological viewpoint associated with that area of the scale. This outcome is typical of a two-party system.

But in a multiparty system there are many modes scattered across the whole scale. Therefore, in order to appeal to a majority of voters, the government must be a coalition of parties and must include in its policy-set some policies espoused by each party in the coalition. In this manner it "pays off" voters at each cluster in return for their support. However, the result is that its program contains policies reflecting a wide variety of ideological viewpoints, so that no real cohesion or integration about any one Weltanschauung is possible. This outcome necessarily occurs whenever the distribution of voters along the scale is so scattered that only a very wide band can encompass a majority.

Consequently, a multiparty system offers voters an ostensible choice between definite, well-integrated policy-sets in each election, but only rarely does one of these sets actually govern. Usually a coalition governs, and its policies are likely to be less definite and less well integrated than those of the government in a two-party system. This is true even though voters in the latter are offered only two relatively unintegrated alternatives which closely resemble each other. No wonder politics often seems confusing.

Whether a political system has two or more parties depends on the distribution of voters along the scale and on the electoral rules governing the system. To demonstrate this dual dependence, I use the concept of "political equilibrium." A state of political equilibrium exists when no new parties can successfully be formed and when no existing party is motivated to move away from its present position.

The limit to the number of new parties that can be formed successfully springs from my definition of success as ability to gain the income, power, and prestige that go with office; that is, as ability to get elected. If the constitution calls for the election of a legislature by proportional representation and the subsequent formation of a government by the legislature, then many parties can be formed, because any given party can get at least some of its members elected by winning the support of only a small proportion of the citizens. Once elected, these members have a chance to share in the fruits of office by joining a coalition government. Hence it follows from my hypothesis about party motivation that many parties are likely to exist in a proportional representation system. Their number is limited only by the number of seats in the legislature and by the necessity of formulating ideologies sufficiently different from those of existing parties to attract votes away from them.[6] New parties continue to form until the distribution of voters is "saturated" — until there is not enough ideological "room" between existing parties to support others significantly different from them.

In an electoral system in which a plurality is necessary for victory, the limit on successful party formation is much more stringent. Since the only way to insure a plurality against all opponents is to win a majority of votes, small parties tend to combine until two giants are left, each of which has a reasonable chance of capturing a majority in any given election. Where these two parties are located on the ideological scale depends upon the distribution of voters, as explained before.

Actually, the policy position and stability of the government in a democracy are relatively independent of the number of parties; they follow primarily from the nature of the distribution of voters along the left-right scale.[7] If a majority of voters are massed within a narrow range of that scale, democratic government is likely to be stable and effective, no matter how many parties exist. As noted earlier, the government can formulate a policy-set which appeals to a majority of voters and yet does not contain policies embodying widely disparate points of view. But, if the government can win the support of a majority only by adopting a scattering of policies chosen from a broad range of viewpoints, these policies tend to cancel each other out, and the government's net ability to solve social problems is low. Thus the distribution of voters — which is itself a variable in the long run — determines whether or not democracy leads to effective government.

[6] The number of sufficiently different parties a system can support depends upon the shape of the distribution of voters along the scale.

[7] However, because the preferences of rising generations are influenced by the alternatives offered them, the number of parties is one of the factors that determine the shape of the distribution of voters.

VII

When information is costly, no decision-maker can afford to know everything that might possibly bear on his decision before he makes it. He must select only a few data from the vast supply in existence and base his decision solely upon them. This is true even if he can procure data without paying for them, since merely assimilating them requires time and is therefore costly.

The amount of information it is rational for a decision-maker to acquire is determined by the following economic axiom: It is always rational to perform any act if its marginal return is larger than its marginal cost. The marginal cost of a "bit" of information is the return foregone by devoting scarce resources — particularly time — to getting and using it. The marginal return from a "bit" is the increase in utility income received because the information enabled the decision-maker to improve his decision. In an imperfectly informed world, neither the precise cost nor the precise return is usually known in advance; but decision-makers can nevertheless employ the rule just stated by looking at expected costs and expected returns.

This reasoning is as applicable to politics as it is to economics. Insofar as the average citizen is concerned, there are two political decisions that require information. The first is deciding which party to vote for; the second is deciding on what policies to exercise direct influence on government policy formation (that is, how to lobby). Let us examine the voting decision first.

Before we do so, it is necessary to recognize that in every society a stream of "free" information is continuously disseminated to all citizens. Though such "free" data take time to assimilate, this time is not directly chargeable to any particular type of decision-making, since it is a necessary cost of living in society. For example, conversation with business associates, small talk with friends, reading the newspaper in a barber shop, and listening to the radio while driving to work are all sources of information which the average man encounters without any particular effort to do so. Therefore, we may consider them part of the "free" information stream and exclude them from the problem of how much information a decision-maker should obtain specifically to improve his decisions.

The marginal return on information acquired for voting purposes is measured by the expected gain from voting "correctly" instead of "incorrectly." In other words, it is the gain in utility a voter believes he will receive if he supports the party which would really provide him with the highest utility income instead of supporting some other party. However, unless his vote actually decides the election, it does not cause the "right" party to be elected instead of a "wrong" party;

whether or not the "right" party wins does not depend on how he votes. Therefore, voting "correctly" produces no gain in utility whatsoever; he might as well have voted "incorrectly."

This situation results from the insignificance of any one voter in a large electorate. Since the cost of voting is very low, hundreds, thousands, or even millions of citizens can afford to vote. Therefore, the probability that any one citizen's vote will be decisive is very small indeed. It is not zero, and it can even be significant if he thinks the election will be very close; but, under most circumstances, it is so negligible that it renders the return from voting "correctly" infinitesimal. This is true no matter how tremendous a loss in utility income the voter would experience if the "wrong" party were elected. And if that loss is itself small — as it may be when parties resemble each other closely or in local elections — then the incentive to become well informed is practically nonexistent.

Therefore, we reach the startling conclusion that it is irrational for most citizens to acquire political information for purposes of voting. As long as each person considers the behavior of others as given, it is simply not worthwhile for him to acquire information so as to vote "correctly" himself. The probability that his vote will determine which party governs is so low that even a trivial cost of procuring information outweighs its return. Hence ignorance of politics is not a result of unpatriotic apathy; rather it is a highly rational response to the facts of political life in a large democracy.

This conclusion does not mean that every citizen who is well informed about politics is irrational. A rational man can become well informed for four reasons: (1) he may enjoy being well informed for its own sake, so that information as such provides him with utility; (2) he may believe the election is going to be so close that the probability of his casting the decisive vote is relatively high; (3) he may need information to influence the votes of others so that he can alter the outcome of the election or persuade government to assign his preferences more weight than those of others; or (4) he may need information to influence the formation of government policy as a lobbyist. Nevertheless, since the odds are that no election will be close enough to render decisive the vote of any one person, or the votes of all those he can persuade to agree with him, the rational course of action for most citizens is to remain politically uninformed. Insofar as voting is concerned, any attempt to acquire information beyond that furnished by the stream of "free" data is for them a sheer waste of resources.

The disparity between this conclusion and the traditional conception of good citizenship in a democracy is indeed striking. How can we explain it? The answer is that the benefits which a majority of citizens would derive from living in a society with a well-informed electorate are indivisible in nature. When most members of the electorate know what policies best serve their interests, the government is forced to follow those policies in order to avoid defeat (assuming that there is a consensus among the informed). This explains why the proponents of democracy think citizens should be well informed. But the benefits of these policies accrue to each member of the majority they serve, regardless of whether he has helped bring them about. In other words, the individual receives these benefits whether or not he is well informed, so long as most people are well informed and his interests are similar to those of the majority. On the other hand, when no one else is well informed, he cannot produce these benefits by becoming well informed himself, since a collective effort is necessary to achieve them.

Thus, when benefits are indivisible, each individual is always motivated to evade his share of the cost of producing them. If he assumes that the behavior of others is given, whether or not he receives any benefits does not depend on his own efforts. But the cost he pays does depend on his efforts; hence the most rational course for him is to minimize that cost — in this case, to remain politically ignorant. Since every individual reasons in the same way, no one bears any costs, and no benefits are produced.

The usual way of escaping this dilemma is for all individuals to agree to be coerced by a central agency. Then each is forced to pay his share of the costs, but he knows all others are likewise forced to pay. Thus everyone is better off than he would be if no costs were borne, because everyone receives benefits which (I here assume) more than offset his share of the costs. This is a basic rationale for using coercion to collect revenues for national defense and for many other government operations that yield indivisible benefits.

But this solution is not feasible in the case of political information. The government cannot coerce everyone to be well informed, because "well-informedness" is hard to measure, because there is no agreed-upon rule for deciding how much information of what kinds each citizen "should" have, and because the resulting interference in personal affairs would cause a loss of utility that would probably outweigh the gains to be had from a well-informed electorate. The most any democratic government has done to remedy this situation is to compel young people in schools to take courses in civics, government, and history.

Consequently, it is rational for every individual to minimize his investment in political information, in spite of the fact that most citizens might benefit substantially if the whole electorate were well informed. As a result, democratic political systems are bound to operate at less than maximum efficiency. Government does not serve the interests of the majority as well as it would if they were well informed, but they never become well informed. It is collectively rational, but individually irrational, for them to do so; and, in the absence of any mechanism to insure collective action, individual rationality prevails.

VIII

When we apply the economic concept of rationality to the second political use of information, lobbying, the results are similarly incompatible with the traditional view of democracy. In order to be an effective lobbyist, a citizen must persuade the governing party that the policies he wants either are already desired by a large number of other citizens or are sufficiently beneficial to the rest of the electorate so that it will, at worst, not resent the enactment of these policies. To be persuasive, the would-be lobbyist must be extremely well informed about each policy area in which he wishes to exert influence. He must be able to design a policy that benefits him more than any other would, to counter any arguments advanced by opposing lobbyists, and to formulate or recognize compromises acceptable to him. Therefore, being a lobbyist requires much more information than voting, since even well-informed voters need only compare alternatives formulated by others.

For this reason, the cost of acquiring enough information to lobby effectively is relatively high. A lobbyist must be an expert in the policy areas in which he tries to exert influence. Since few men can afford the time or money necessary to become expert in more than one or two policy areas (or to hire those already expert), most citizens must specialize in a very few areas. Such behavior is rational even though policies in many areas affect them to some extent. Conversely, only a few specialists will actively exert pressure on the government in any one policy area. As a result, each need not heavily discount his own impact because of the large number of other persons influencing the decision, as he does in regard to voting. On the contrary, for those few lobbyists who specialize in any given area, the potential return from political information may be very high — precisely because they are so few.

The men who can best afford to become lobbyists in any policy area are those whose incomes stem from that area. This is true because nearly every citizen derives all his income from one or two sources; hence any government policy affecting those sources is of vital interest to him. In contrast, each man spends his income in a great many policy areas, so that a change in any one of them is not too significant to him. Therefore, men are much more likely to exert direct influence on government policy formation in their roles as producers than in their roles as consumers. In consequence, a democratic government is usually biased in favor of producer interests and against consumer interests, even though the consumers of any given product usually outnumber its producers. Tariff legislation provides a notorious example of this bias.

It should be stressed that such systematic exploitation of consumers by producers acting through government policy is not a result of foolish apathy on the part of consumers. In fact, just the opposite is true. Government's anticonsumer bias occurs because consumers rationally seek to acquire only that information which provides a return larger than its cost. The saving a consumer could make by becoming informed about how government policy affects any one product he purchases simply does not recompense him for the cost of informing himself — particularly since his personal influence on government policy would probably be slight. Since this is true of almost every product he buys, he adopts a course of rational ignorance, thereby exposing himself to extensive exploitation. Yet it would be irrational for him to act otherwise. In other words, lobbying is effective in a democracy *because* all the agents concerned — the exploiters, the exploited, and the government — behave rationally.

IX

Clearly, rational behavior in a democracy is not what most normative theorists assume it to be. Political theorists in particular have often created models of how the citizens of a democracy ought to behave without taking into account the economics of political action. Consequently, much of the evidence frequently cited to prove that democratic politics are dominated by irrational (non-logical) forces in fact demonstrates that citizens respond rationally (efficiently) to the exigencies of life in an imperfectly informed world.[8] Apathy among citizens toward elections, ignorance of the issues, the tendency of parties in a two-party system to resemble each other, and the anticonsumer bias of government action can all be explained logically as efficient reactions to imperfect information in a large democracy. Any normative theory that regards them as signs of unintelligent behavior in politics has failed to face the fact that information is costly in the real world. Thus political theory has suffered because it has not taken into account certain economic realities.

[8] In this sentence the word "irrational" is not the opposite of the word "rational," as the synonyms in parentheses show. Admittedly, such dual usage may cause confusion. However, I have employed the word "rational" instead of its synonym "efficient" throughout this article because I want to emphasize the fact that an intelligent citizen always carries out any act whose marginal return exceeds its marginal cost. In contrast, he does not always make use of logical thinking, because, under some conditions, the marginal return from thinking logically is smaller than its marginal cost. In other words, it is sometimes rational (efficient) to act irrationally (nonlogically), in which case an intelligent man eschews rationality in the traditional sense so as to achieve it in the economic sense. This is really what is meant by the sentence in the text to which this footnote is attached.

On the other hand, economic theory has suffered because it has not taken into account the political realities of government decision-making. Economists have been content to discuss government action as though governments were run by perfect altruists whose only motive was to maximize social welfare. As a result, economists have been unable to incorporate government into the rest of economic theory, which is based on the premise that all men act primarily out of self-interest. Furthermore, they have falsely concluded that government decision-making in all societies should follow identical principles, because its goal is always the maximization of social welfare. If my hypothesis is true, the goal of government is attaining the income, power, and prestige that go with office. Since methods of reaching this goal are vastly different in democratic, totalitarian, and aristocratic states, no single theory can be advanced to explain government decision-making in all societies. Nor can any theory of government decision-making be divorced from politics. The way every government actually makes decisions depends upon the nature of the fundamental power relation between the governors and the governed in its society; that is, upon the society's political constitution. Therefore, a different theory of political action must be formulated for each different type of constitution.

I conclude that a truly useful theory of government action in a democracy — or in any other type of society — must be both economic and political in nature. In this article I have attempted to outline such a theory. If nothing else, the attempt demonstrates how much economists and political scientists must depend on each other to analyze government decision-making, which is the most important economic and political force in the world today.

Democrats and Republicans: Are They Different?

One often hears that the American party system presents no meaningful choice to the electorate because of the lack of significant differences between the two major parties. Admittedly, there are many similarities between the presidential wings of the two parties and also between the leadership of the congressional Republicans and their Democratic counterparts. But which party occupies the White House does seem to make a difference, despite the fact that the presidential candidates of the two parties often agree on many important issues of public policy, particularly in foreign affairs. The next selection presents the results of a systematic study designed to determine the nature and extent of divergence in attitudes among the leaders and the followers of the Democrats and Republicans.

16   HERBERT MC CLOSKY, PAUL J. HOFFMANN,
     AND ROSEMARY O'HARA

ISSUE CONFLICT AND CONSENSUS AMONG PARTY LEADERS AND FOLLOWERS

American political parties are often regarded as "brokerage" organizations, weak in principle, devoid of ideology, and inclined to differ chiefly over unimportant questions. In contrast to the "ideological" parties of Europe — which supposedly appeal to their followers through sharply defined, coherent, and logically related doctrines — the American parties are thought to fit their convictions to the changing demands of the political contest. According to this view, each set of American party leaders is satisfied to play Tweedledee to the other's Tweedledum.

I. Pressures Toward Uniformity and Cleavage

Although these "conclusions" are mainly derived from *a priori* analysis or from casual observations of "anecdotal" data (little systematic effort having been made so far to verify or refute them), they are often taken as confirmed — largely, one imagines, because they are compatible with certain conspicuous features of American politics. Among these features is the entrenchment of a two-party system which, by affording both parties a genuine opportunity to win elections, tempts them to appeal to as many diverse elements in the electorate as are needed to put together a majority. Since both parties want to attract support from the centrist and moderate segments of the electorate, their views on basic issues will, it is thought, tend to converge. Like giant business enterprises competing for the same market, they will be led to offer commodities that are in many respects identical. It is one thing for a small party in a multi-party system to preserve its ideological purity, quite another for a mass party in a two-party system to do so. The one has little hope of becoming a majority, and can most easily survive by remaining identified with the narrow audience from which it draws its chief supporters; the other can succeed only by accommodating the conflicting claims of many diverse groups — only, in short, by blunting ideological distinctions.

From *The American Political Science Review* (June 1960). Reprinted by permission of The American Political Science Association and the authors.

Constraints against enlarging intellectual differences also spring from the loosely confederated nature of the American party system, and from each national party's need to adjust its policies to the competing interests of the locality, the state, and the nation. Many party units are more concerned with local than with national elections, and prefer not to be handicapped by clear-cut national programs. Every ambitious politician, moreover, hopes to achieve a *modus vivendi* tailored to the particular and often idiosyncratic complex of forces prevailing in his constituency, an objective rarely compatible with doctrinal purity. Often, too, local politics are largely non-partisan or are partisan in ways that scarcely affect the great national issues around which ideologies might be expected to form. The development and enforcement of a sharply delineated ideology are also hindered by the absence in either party of a firmly established, authoritative, and continuing organizational center empowered to decide questions of doctrine and discipline. Party affiliation is loosely defined, responsibility is weak or non-existent, and organs for indoctrinating or communicating with party members are at best rudimentary.

Cultural and historical differences may also contribute to the weaker ideological emphasis among American, as compared with European, parties. Many of the great historical cleavages that have divided European nations for centuries — monarchism *vs.* republicanism; clericalism *vs.* anticlericalism; democracy *vs.* autocracy, etc. — have never taken root in this country. Apart from the slavery (and subsequently the race) issue, the United States has not experienced the intense class or caste conflict often found abroad, and contests of the capitalism *vs.* socialism variety have never achieved an important role in American politics. In addition, never having known a titled nobility, we have largely been freed from the conflicts found elsewhere between the classes of inherited and acquired privilege.

Consider, too, the progress made in the United States toward neutralizing the forces which ordinarily lead to sharp social, and hence intellectual and political, differentiation. The class and status structure of American society has attained a rate of mobility equalling or exceeding that of any other long established society. Popular education, and other facilities for the creation of common attitudes, have been developed on a scale unequalled elsewhere. Improvements in transportation and communication, and rapid shifts in population and industry have weakened even sectionalism as a source of political cleavage. Rural-urban differences prevailing, for example, between a French peasant proprietor and a Parisian *boulevardier*. In short, a great many Americans have been subjected in their public lives to identical stimuli — a condition unlikely to generate strong, competing ideologies.

The research reported here was designed not to refute these observations but to test the accuracy of the claim that they are sufficient to prevent differences in outlook from taking root in the American party system. We believed that the homogenizing tendencies referred to are strongly offset by contrary influences, and that voters are preponderantly led to support the party whose opinions they share. We further thought that the competition for office, though giving rise to similarities between the parties, also impels them to diverge from each other in order to sharpen their respective appeals. For this and other reasons, we expected to find that the leaders of the two parties, instead of ignoring differences alleged to exist within the electorate, would differ on issues more sharply than their followers would. We believed further that even in a brokerage system the parties would serve as independent reference groups, developing norms, values, and self-images to which their supporters could readily respond. Their influence, we felt, would frequently exceed that of ethnic, occupational, residential and other reference groups. In sum, we preceeded on the belief that the parties are not simply spokesmen for other interest groups, but are in their own right agencies for formulating, transmitting, and anchoring political opinions, that they attract adherents who in general share those opinions, and that through a feedback process of mutual reinforcement between the organization and its typical supporters, the parties develop integrated and stable political tendencies. Other hypotheses will be specified as we present and analyze our findings.

II. Procedures

The questions considered in this paper were part of a large field study made in 1957–1958 on the nature, sources, and correlates of political affiliation, activity, and belief in the American party system (hereafter referred to as the PAB study). Pilot studies on Minnesota samples had led us to suspect that many "settled" notions about party affiliation and belief in America would not stand up under careful empirical scrutiny; further, we felt that little progress would be made in the exploration of this subject until a comprehensive portrait of party membership in America has been drawn. Accordingly, a nationwide study was launched to acquire a detailed description of party leaders and supporters, gathering data on their backgrounds, political experiences, personality characteristics, values, motivations, social and political attitudes, outlooks on key issues, and related matters.

For our samples of party "leaders" we turned to the Democratic and Republican national conventions, largely because they are the leading and most representative of the party organs, their delegates coming from every part of the United States and from every level of party and government activity. Our samples ranged from governors, senators, and national committeemen at the one end to precinct workers and local officials at the other. In the absence of comprehensive information about the characteristics of the party elites in America, no one can say how closely the convention delegates mirror the total party leadership. We felt it fair to assume, nevertheless, that the delegates represented as faithful a cross section of American party leadership as could be had without an extraordinary expenditure of money and labor. Using convention delegates as our universe of leaders also held some obvious advantages for research, since the composition of this universe (by name, address, party, state, sex, place of residence, and party or public office) can usually be ascertained from the convention calls. Of the 6,848 delegates and alternates available to be sampled, 3,193 actually participated; 3,020 (1,788 Democrats and 1,232 Republicans) completed and returned questionnaires that were usable in all respects. The proportion of returns was roughly equivalent for both sets of party leaders.

The rank and file sample, which we wanted both for its intrinsic value and for its utility as a control group, was obtained by special arrangement with the American Institute of Public Opinion. In January 1958, Gallup interviewers personally distributed our questionnaire to 2,917 adult voters in two successive national cross-section surveys. Some 1,610 questionnaires were filled out and returned, of which 1,484 were completely usable. This sample closely matched the national population on such characteristics as sex, age, region, size of city, and party affiliation, and, though it somewhat oversampled the upper educational levels, we considered it sufficiently large and representative for most of our purposes. Of the 1,484 respondents, 821 were Democratic supporters (629 "pure" Democrats, plus 192 whom we classified as "independent" Democrats) and 623 were Republican supporters (479 "pure" Republicans, plus 144 "independent" Republicans). Forty respondents could not be identified as adherents of either party. . . .

The questions most relevant for the present article were those which asked each respondent to express his attitudes toward twenty-four important national issues, and to state whether he believed support for each issue should be "increased," "decreased," or "remain as is." The list of issues and the responses of each sample will be found in Tables II-A through II-E, where for convenience of analysis, the issues have been grouped under five broad headings: Public Ownership, Government Regulation of the Economy, Equalitarianism and Human Welfare, Tax Policy and Foreign Policy.

In tabulating the results, we first scored each individual on each issue and then computed aggregate scores for all the members of a given sample. To begin with, percentages were used to show the proportion who favored increasing, decreasing, or retaining the existing level of support on each issue. But as it was clumsy to handle three figures for each issue, we constructed a single index or "ratio of support" which would simultaneously take account of all three scores. The index was built by assigning a weight of 1.0 to each "increase" response in the sample, of 0 to each "decrease" response, and of .50 to each "remain as is" (or "same") response. Thus the ratio-of-support score shown for any given sample is in effect a mean score with a possible range of 0 to 1.0, in which support for an issue increases as the scores approach 1.0 and decreases as they approach 0. In general, the scores can be taken to approximate the following over-all positions: .0 to .25 — strongly wish to reduce support; .26 to .45 — wish to reduce support; .46 to .55 — satisfied with the *status quo;* .56 to .75 — wish to increase support; and .76 to 1.00 — strongly wish to increase support. Note that the differences in degree suggested by these categories refer

TABLE ONE

Average Differences in the Ratio-of-Support Scores among Party Leaders and Followers for Five Categories of Issues

Category of Issues	Democratic leaders vs. Republican leaders	Democratic followers vs. Republican followers	Democratic leaders vs. Democratic followers	Republican leaders vs. Republican followers	Democratic leaders vs. Republican followers	Republican leaders vs. Democratic followers
a. Public Ownership of Resources	.28	.04	.06	.18	.10	.22
b. Government Regulation of the Economy	.22	.06	.08	.10	.12	.16
c. Equalitarianism, Human Welfare	.22	.05	.08	.21	.06	.25
d. Tax Policy	.20	.06	.06	.20	.04	.26
e. Foreign Policy	.15	.02	.05	.08	.07	.10
	—	—	—	—	—	—
Average Differences in Ratio Scores for All Categories	.21	.04	.07	.15	.08	.20

Sample Sizes: Democratic Leaders, 1,788; Republican Leaders, 1,232; Democratic Followers, 821; Republican Followers, 623.

not to the *strength of feeling* exhibited by individuals toward an issue but rather to the *numbers of people* in a sample who hold points of view favoring or opposing that issue. . . .

One may wonder about the value of opinions stated on a questionnaire compared with the worth of views formally expressed by an organization or implicit in the actions of its leaders. Advantages can be cited on both sides. The beliefs expressed in official party statements or in legislative roll calls, it might be claimed, represent the *operating* beliefs of the organization by virtue of having been tested in the marketplace or in the competition of legislative struggle. Positions taken on issues on which a party stakes its future may be more valid evidence of what the party truly believes than are the opinions expressed by individual members under conditions of maximum safety. On the other hand, the responses to the issue and attitude questions in the PAB study represent the anonymous private opinions of party leaders and followers, uncomplicated by any need to make political capital, to proselytize, to conciliate critics, or to find grounds for embarrassing the opposition at the next election. Hence they may for some purposes represent the most accurate possible reflection of the "actual" state of party opinion. The controversy over the value of the two approaches is to some extent spurious, however, for they offer different perspectives on the same thing. In addition, considerable correspondence exists between the party positions evident in congressional roll calls and the privately expressed opinions of the party leaders in our study.

III. Findings: Comparisons Between Leaders

No more conclusive findings emerge from our study of party issues than those growing out of the comparisons between the two sets of party leaders. Despite the brokerage tendency of the American parties, their active members are obviously separated by large and important differences. The differences, moreover, conform with the popular image in which the Democratic party is seen as the more "progressive" or "radical," the Republican as the more "moderate" or "conservative" of the two. In addition, the disagreements are remarkably consistent, a function not of chance but of systematic points of view, whereby the responses to any one of the issues could reasonably have been predicted from knowledge of the responses to the other issues.

Examination of Tables II-A-E . . . shows that the leaders differ significantly on 23 of the 24 issues listed and that they are separated on 15 of these issues by .18 or more ratio points — in short, by differences that are in absolute magnitude very large. The two samples are further apart in their attitudes toward public ownership and are especially divided on the question of government ownership of natural

TABLE TWO-A

Comparison of Party Leaders and Followers on "Public Ownership" Issues, by Percentages and Ratios of Support

Issues	Leaders		Followers	
	Dem. N=1,788	Repub. N=1,232	Dem. N=821	Repub. N=623
		(%s down)		
Public Ownership of Natural Resources				
% favoring: Increase	57.5	12.9	35.3	31.1
Decrease	18.6	51.9	15.0	19.9
Same, n.c.[a]	23.8	35.2	49.7	49.0
Support Ratio	.69	.30	.60	.56
Public Control of Atomic Energy				
% favoring: Increase	73.2	45.0	64.2	59.4
Decrease	7.2	15.3	7.1	10.0
Same, n.c.[a]	19.6	39.7	28.7	30.6
Support Ratio	.83	.65	.79	.75
Mean Support Ratios for the Public Ownership Category	.76	.48	.70	.66

[a] n.c. = no code.

resources, the Democrats strongly favoring it, the Republicans just as strongly wanting it cut back. The difference of .39 in the ratio scores is the largest for any of the issues tested. In percentages, the differences are 58 per cent (D) vs. 13 per cent (R) in favor of increasing support, and 19 per cent (D) vs. 52 per cent (R) in favor of decreasing support. Both parties preponderantly support public control and development of atomic energy, but the Democrats do so more uniformly.

V. O. Key, among others, has observed that the Republican party is especially responsive to the "financial and manufacturing community," reflecting the view that government should intervene as little as possible to burden or restrain prevailing business interests. The validity of this observation is evident throughout all our data, and is most clearly seen in the responses to the issues listed under Government Regulation of the Economy, Equalitarianism and Human Welfare, Tax Policy. Democratic leaders are far more eager than Republican leaders to strengthen enforcement of anti-monopoly laws and to increase regulation of public utilities and business. Indeed, the soli-

Comparison of Party Leaders and Followers on
"Government Regulation of the Economy" Issues,
by Percentages and Ratios of Support

Issues	Leaders		Followers	
	Dem. N=1,788	Repub. N=1,232	Dem. N=821	Repub. N=623
		(%s down)		
Level of Farm Price Supports				
% favoring: Increase	43.4	6.7	39.0	23.0
Decrease	28.1	67.4	27.6	40.3
Same, n.c.	28.5	25.8	33.4	36.7
Support Ratio	.58	.20	.56	.41
Government Regulation of Business				
% favoring: Increase	20.2	0.6	18.6	7.4
Decrease	38.5	84.1	33.4	46.2
Same, n.c.	41.3	15.3	48.0	46.4
Support Ratio	.41	.08	.43	.31
Regulation of Public Utilities				
% favoring: Increase	59.0	17.9	39.3	26.0
Decrease	6.4	17.6	11.1	12.0
Same, n.c.	34.6	64.5	49.6	62.0
Support Ratio	.76	.50	.64	.57
Enforcement of Anti-Monopoly Laws				
% favoring: Increase	78.0	44.9	53.2	51.0
Decrease	2.9	9.0	7.9	6.6
Same, n.c.	19.1	46.1	38.9	42.4
Support Ratio	.88	.68	.73	.72
Regulation of Trade Unions				
% favoring: Increase	59.3	86.4	46.6	57.8
Decrease	12.4	4.5	8.9	10.6
Same, n.c.	28.3	9.2	44.5	31.6
Support Ratio	.73	.91	.69	.74

TABLE TWO-B *(cont.)*

Comparison of Party Leaders and Followers on
"Government Regulation of the Economy" Issues,
by Percentages and Ratios of Support

Issues	Leaders		Followers	
	Dem.	*Repub.*	*Dem.*	*Repub.*
	N=1,788	*N=1,232*	*N=821*	*N=623*
		(%s down)		
Level of Tariffs				
% favoring: Increase	13.0	19.2	16.6	15.2
Decrease	43.0	26.3	25.3	21.3
Same, n.c.	43.9	54.5	58.1	63.4
Support Ratio	.35	.46	.46	.47
Restrictions on Credit				
% favoring: Increase	24.8	20.6	26.1	25.7
Decrease	39.3	20.6	22.2	23.8
Same, n.c.	35.9	58.8	51.8	50.5
Support Ratio	.43	.50	.52	.51
Mean Support Ratios for "Government Regulation of the Economy" Category	.59	.48	.58	.53

darity of Republican opposition to the regulation of business is rather
overwhelming: 84 per cent want to decrease such regulation and fewer
than .01 per cent say they want to increase it. Although the Democrats,
on balance, also feel that government controls on business should not
be expanded further, the differences between the two samples on this
issue are nevertheless substantial.

The two sets of leaders are also far apart on the farm issue, the Democrats preferring slightly to increase farm supports, the Republicans
wanting strongly to reduce them. The Republican ratio score of .20 on
this issue is among the lowest in the entire set of scores. The magnitude
of these scores somewhat surprised us, for while opposition to agricultural subsidies is consistent with Republican dislike for state intervention, we had expected the leaders to conform more closely to the familiar image of the Republican as the more "rural" of the two parties. It
appears, however, that the party's connection with business is far more
compelling than its association with agriculture. The Republican
desire to reduce government expenditures and to promote independence from "government handouts" prevails on the farm question as

TABLE   TWO-C

Comparison of Party Leaders and Followers on
"Equalitarian and Human Welfare" Issues,
by Percentages and Ratios of Support

Issues	Leaders		Followers	
	Dem. N=1,788	Repub. N=1,232	Dem. N=821	Repub. N=623
		(%s down)		
Federal Aid to Education				
% favoring: Increase	66.2	22.3	74.9	64.8
Decrease	13.4	43.2	5.6	8.3
Same, n.c.	20.4	34.5	19.5	26.8
Support Ratio	.76	.40	.85	.78
Slum Clearance and Public Housing				
% favoring: Increase	78.4	40.1	79.5	72.5
Decrease	5.6	21.6	5.8	7.9
Same, n.c.	16.0	38.3	14.6	19.6
Support Ratio	.86	.59	.87	.82
Social Security Benefits				
% favoring: Increase	60.0	22.5	69.4	57.0
Decrease	3.9	13.1	3.0	3.8
Same, n.c.	36.1	64.4	27.5	39.2
Support Ratio	.78	.55	.83	.77
Minimum Wages				
% favoring: Increase	50.0	15.5	59.0	43.5
Decrease	4.7	12.5	2.9	5.0
Same, n.c.	45.2	72.0	38.1	51.5
Support Ratio	.73	.52	.78	.69
Enforcement of Integration				
% favoring: Increase	43.8	25.5	41.9	40.8
Decrease	26.6	31.7	27.4	23.6
Same, n.c.	29.5	42.8	30.7	35.6
Support Ratio	.59	.47	.57	.59
Immigration into United States				
% favoring: Increase	36.1	18.4	10.4	8.0
Decrease	27.0	29.9	52.0	44.6
Same, n.c.	36.9	51.7	37.6	47.4
Support Ratio	.54	.44	.29	.32
Mean Support Ratios for "Equalitarian and Human Welfare" Category	.71	.50	.70	.66

TABLE TWO-D

Comparison of Party Leaders and Followers on "Tax Policy" Issues, by Percentages and Ratios of Support

Issues	Leaders		Followers	
	Dem. N=1,788	Repub. N=1,232	Dem. N=821	Repub. N=623
		(%s down)		
Corporate Income Tax				
% favoring: Increase	32.3	4.0	32.0	23.3
Decrease	23.3	61.5	20.5	25.7
Same, n.c.	44.4	34.5	47.5	51.0
Support Ratio	.54	.21	.56	.49
Tax on Large Incomes				
% favoring: Increase	27.0	5.4	46.6	34.7
Decrease	23.1	56.9	13.8	21.7
Same, n.c.	49.9	37.7	39.6	43.6
Support Ratio	.52	.24	.66	.56
Tax on Business				
% favoring: Increase	12.6	1.0	24.6	15.9
Decrease	38.3	71.1	24.1	32.6
Same, n.c.	49.1	27.8	51.3	51.5
Support Ratio	.37	.15	.50	.42
Tax on Middle Incomes				
% favoring: Increase	2.7	0.8	4.5	3.0
Decrease	50.2	63.9	49.3	44.3
Same, n.c.	47.1	35.3	46.2	52.6
Support Ratio	.26	.18	.28	.29
Tax on Small Incomes				
% favoring: Increase	1.4	2.9	1.6	2.1
Decrease	79.2	65.0	77.5	69.6
Same, n.c.	19.4	32.1	20.9	28.3
Support Ratio	.11	.19	.12	.16
Mean Support Ratios for "Tax Policy" Category	.36	.19	.42	.38

Comparison of Party Leaders and Followers on
"Foreign Policy" Issues, by Percentages and
Ratios of Support

Issues	Leaders		Followers	
	Dem. N=1,788	Repub. N=1,232	Dem. N=821	Repub. N=623
		(%s down)		
Reliance on the United Nations				
% favoring: Increase	48.9	24.4	34.7	33.4
Decrease	17.6	34.8	17.3	19.3
Same, n.c.	33.5	40.7	48.0	47.3
Support Ratio	.66	.45	.59	.57
American Participation in Military Alliances				
% favoring: Increase	41.5	22.7	39.1	32.3
Decrease	17.6	25.7	14.0	15.4
Same, n.c.	40.9	51.6	46.9	52.3
Support Ratio	.62	.48	.62	.58
Foreign Aid				
% favoring: Increase	17.8	7.6	10.1	10.1
Decrease	51.0	61.7	58.6	57.3
Same, n.c.	31.1	30.7	31.3	32.6
Support Ratio	.33	.23	.26	.26
Defense Spending				
% favoring: Increase	20.7	13.6	50.5	45.7
Decrease	34.4	33.6	16.4	15.4
Same, n.c.	44.8	52.8	33.0	38.8
Support Ratio	.43	.40	.67	.65
Mean Support Ratios for "Foreign Policy" Category (excl. Defense Spending)	.54	.39	.49	.47

it does on other issues, while the Democratic preference for a more
regulated economy in which government intervenes to reduce economic risk and to stabilize prosperity is equally evident on the other

side. Party attitudes on this issue appear to be determined as much by ideological tendencies as by deliberate calculation of the political advantages to be gained by favoring or opposing subsidies to farmers.

Having implied that agricultural policies partly result from principle, we must note that on three other issues in this category (trade unions, credit, and tariffs), principle seems to be overweighed by old-fashioned economic considerations. In spite of their distaste for government interference in economic affairs, the Republicans almost unanimously favor greater regulation of trade unions and they are more strongly disposed than the Democrats toward government intervention to restrict credit and to raise tariffs. Of course, party cleavages over the credit and tariff issues have a long history, which may by now have endowed them with ideological force beyond immediate economic considerations. The preponderant Democratic preference for greater regulation of trade unions is doubtless a response to recent "exposures" of corrupt labor practices, though it may also signify that the party's perspective toward the trade unions is shifting somewhat.

The closer Republican identification with business, free enterprise, and economic conservatism in general, and the friendlier Democratic attitude toward labor and toward government regulation of the economy, are easily observed in the data from other parts of our questionnaire. Republican leaders score very much higher than Democratic leaders on, for example, such scales as economic conservatism, independence of government, and business attitudes. On a question asking respondents to indicate the groups from which they would be most and least likely to take advice, 41 per cent of the Democratic leaders but only 3.8 per cent of the Republican leaders list trade unions as groups from which they would seek advice. Trade unions are scored in the "least likely" category by 25 per cent of the Democrats and 63 per cent of the Republicans. Similarly, more than 94 per cent of the Republican leaders, but 56 per cent of the Democratic leaders, name trade unions as groups that have "too much power." These differences, it should be noted, cannot be accounted for by reference to the greater number of trade union members among the Democratic party leadership, for in the 1956 conventions only 14 per cent of the Democrats belonged to trade unions, and while an even smaller percentage (4 per cent) of the Republicans were trade unionists, this disparity is hardly great enough to explain the large differences in outlook. The key to the explanation has to be sought in the symbolic and reference group identifications of the two parties, and in their underlying values.

Nowhere do we see this more clearly than in the responses to the Equalitarian and Human Welfare issues. The mean difference in the ratio scores for the category as a whole is .22, a very large difference and one that results from differences in the expected direction on all six issues that make up the category. On four of these issues — federal aid to education, slum clearance and public housing, social security, and minimum wages — the leaders of the two parties are widely separated, the differences in their ratio scores ranging from .36 to .21. The percentages showing the proportions who favor increased support for these issues are even more striking. In every instance the Democratic percentages are considerably higher: 66 *vs.* 22 per cent (education); 78 *vs.* 40 per cent (slum clearance and housing); 60 *vs.* 23 per cent (social security); and 50 *vs.* 16 per cent (minimum wages). The Democratic leaders also are better disposed than the Republican leaders toward immigration: twice as many of them (36 per cent *vs.* 18 per cent) favor a change in policy to permit more immigrants to enter. The over-all inclination of both party élites, however, is to accept the present levels of immigration, the Democratic ratio score falling slightly above, and the Republican slightly below, the midpoint.

More surprising are the differences on the segregation issue, for, despite strong Southern influence, the Democratic leaders express significantly more support for enforcing integration than the Republicans do. Moreover, the difference between the two parties rises from .12 for the national samples as a whole to a difference of .18 when the southern leaders are excluded. . . .

Examination of the actual magnitude of the ratio scores in this category reveals that the Republicans want not so much to abrogate existing social welfare or equalitarian measures as to keep them from being broadened. The Democrats, by comparison, are shown to be the party of social equality and reform, more willing than their opponents to employ legislation for the benefit of the underprivileged. . . .

The self-images and reference group identifications of the two parties also should be noted in this connection. For example, many more Democratic than Republican leaders call themselves liberal and state that they would be most likely to take advice from liberal reform organizations, the Farmers' Union, and (as we have seen) from the trade unions; only a small number consider themselves conservative or would seek advice from conservative reform organizations, the National Association of Manufacturers, or the Farm Bureau Federation. The Republicans have in almost all instances the reverse identifications: only a handful regard themselves as liberal or would seek counsel from liberal organizations, while more than 42 per cent call themselves conservative and would look to the NAM or to conservative reform organizations for advice. Almost two-thirds of the Republicans (compared with 29 per cent of the Democrats) regard the Chamber of Commerce as an important source of advice. Businessmen are listed as having "too much power" by 42 per cent of the Democrats but by only 9 per cent of the Republicans. The Democrats are also significantly more inclined than the Republicans to consider Catholics, Jews, and the foreign born as having "too little power." While self-descriptions and reference group identifications often correspond poorly with actual beliefs — among the general population they scarcely correspond at all, in fact — we are dealing, in the case of the leaders, with a politically informed and highly articulate set of people who have little difficulty connecting the beliefs they hold and the groups that promote or obstruct those beliefs.

Our fourth category, Tax Policy, divides the parties almost as severely as do the other categories. The mean difference for the category as a whole is .20, and it would doubtless have been larger but for the universal unpopularity of proposals to increase taxes on small and middle income groups. Table II-d shows that the differences between the parties on the tax issues follow the patterns previously observed and that tax policy is for the Democrats a device for redistributing income and promoting social equality. Neither party, however, is keen about raising taxes for *any* group: even the Democrats have little enthusiasm for new taxes on upper income groups or on business and corporate enterprises. The Republican leaders are overwhelmingly opposed to increased taxes for *any* group, rich *or* poor. This can be seen in their low ratio scores on the tax issues, which range from only .15 to .24. But while they are far more eager than the Democratic leaders to cut taxes on corporate and private wealth, they are less willing to reduce taxes on the lower income groups. These differences, it should be remarked, are not primarily a function of differences in the income of the two samples. Although there are more people with high incomes among the Republican leaders, the disproportion between the two samples is not nearly great enough to account for the dissimilarities in their tax views.

Of the five categories considered, Foreign Policy shows the smallest average difference, but even on these issues the divergence between Democratic and Republican leader attitudes is significant. Except for defense spending the Democrats turn out to be more internationalist than the Republicans, as evidenced in their greater commitment to the United Nations and to American participation in international military alliances like NATO. Twice as many Democrats as Republicans want the United States to rely more heavily upon such organizations, while many more Republicans want to reduce our international involvements. Both parties are predominantly in favor of cutting back foreign aid — a somewhat surprising finding in light of Democratic public pronouncements on this subject — but more Republicans feel strongly on the subject. Our data thus furnish little support for the claim that the parties hold the same views on foreign policy or that their seeming differences are merely a response to the demands of political competition.

Nevertheless, it would be incorrect to conclude that one party believes in internationalism and the other in isolationism. The differences are far too small to warrant any such inference. Traces of isolationism, to be sure, remain stronger in the Republican party than in the Democratic party — an observation buttressed by the finding that twice as many Republicans as Democrats score high on the isolationism scale. The pattern of Republican responses on both the issue and scale items signifies, however, that the leaders of that party generally accept the degree of "internationalism" now in effect, but shrink from extending it further. Consider too, the similarities in the leaders' scores on defense spending, for despite their greater leaning toward isolationism, the Republicans are no more inclined than the Democrats to leave the country defenseless. . . .

IV. Comparisons Between Followers

So far we have addressed ourselves to the differences between Democratic and Republican *leaders*. In each of the tables presented, however, data are included from which the two sets of party *followers* may also be compared.

The observation most clearly warranted from these data is that the rank and file members of the two parties are far less divided than their leaders. Not only do they diverge significantly on fewer issues — seven as compared with 23 for the leader samples — but the magnitudes of the differences in their ratio scores are substantially smaller for every one of the 24 issues. . . .

. . . Even on business attitudes, independence of government, and economic conservatism, the differences are small and barely significant. No differences were found on such scales as tolerance, faith in democracy, procedural rights, conservatism-liberalism (classical), . . . and isolationism. The average Democrat is slightly more willing than the average Republican to label himself a liberal or to seek advice from liberal organizations; the contrary is true when it comes to adopting conservative identifications. Only in the differential trust they express toward business and labor are the two sets of followers widely separated.

These findings give little support to the claim that the "natural divisions" of the electorate are being smothered by party leaders. Not only do the leaders disagree more sharply than their respective followers, but the level of consensus among the electorate (with or without regard to party) is fairly high. . . . Of course, voters may divide more sharply on issues at election time, since campaigns intensify party feeling and may also intensify opinions on issues. . . . But even the party-linked differences found among voters during elections may largely be echoes of the opinions announced by the candidates — transient sentiments developed for the occasion and quickly forgotten.

V. LEADER CONFLICT AND FOLLOWER CONSENSUS: EXPLANATIONS

Considering the nature of the differences between the leader and follower samples, the interesting question is not why the parties fail to represent the "natural division" in the electorate (for that question rests on an unwarranted assumption) but why the party élites disagree at all, and why they divide so much more sharply than their followers.

Despite the great pressures toward uniformity we have noted in American society, many forces also divide the population culturally, economically, and politically. The United States is, after all, a miscellany of ethnic and religious strains set down in a geographically large and diverse country. Many of these groups brought old conflicts and ideologies with them, and some have tried to act out in the new world the hopes and frustrations nurtured in the old. Then, too, despite rapid social mobility, social classes have by no means been eliminated. No special political insight is needed to perceive that the two parties characteristically draw from different strata of the society, the Republicans from the managerial, proprietary, and to some extent professional classes, the Democrats from labor, minorities, low income groups, and a large proportion of the intellectuals. Partly because the leaders of the two parties tend to overrespond to the modal values of the groups with which they are principally identified, they gradually grow further apart on the key questions which separate their respective supporters. The Republican emphasis on business ideology is both a cause and a consequence of its managerial and proprietary support; the greater Democratic emphasis on social justice, and on economic and social levelling, is both the occasion and the product of the support the party enjoys among intellectuals and the lower strata. These interrelationships are strengthened, moreover, by the tendency for a party's dominant supporters to gain a disproportionate number of positions in its leadership ranks.

The differences which typically separate Democratic from Republican leaders seem also to reflect a deep-seated ideological cleavage often found among Western parties. One side of this cleavage is marked by a strong belief in the power of collective action to promote social justice, equality, humanitarianism, and economic planning, while preserving freedom; the other is distinguished by faith in the wisdom of the natural competitive process and in the supreme virtue of individualism, "character," self-reliance, frugality, and independence from government. To this cleavage is added another frequent source of political division, namely, a difference in attitude toward change between "radicals" and "moderates," between those who prefer to move quickly or slowly, to reform or to conserve. These differences in social philosophy and posture do not always coincide with the divisions in the social structure, and their elements do not, in all contexts, combine in the same way. But, however crudely, the American parties do tend to embody these competing points of view and to serve as reference groups for those who hold them.

Party cleavage in America was no doubt intensified by the advent of the New Deal, and by its immense electoral and intellectual success. Not only did it weld into a firm alliance the diverse forces that were to be crucial to all subsequent Democratic majorities, but it also made explicit the doctrines of the "welfare state" with which the party was henceforth to be inseparably identified. Because of the novelty of its program and its apparently radical threat to the familiar patterns of American political and economic life, it probably deepened the fervor of its Republican adversaries and drove into the opposition the staunchest defenders of business ideology. The conflict was further sharpened by the decline of leftwing politics after the war, and by the transfer of loyalties of former and potential radicals to the Democratic party. Once launched, the cleavage has been sustained by the tendency for each party to attract into its active ranks a disproportionate number of voters who recognize and share its point of view.

Why, however, are the leaders so much more sharply divided than their followers? The reasons are not hard to understand and are consistent with several of the hypotheses that underlie the present study.

(1) Consider, to begin with, that the leaders come from the more articulate segments of society and, on the average, are politically more aware than their followers and far better informed about issues. For them, political issues and opinions are the everyday currency of party competition, not esoteric matters that surpass understanding. With their greater awareness and responsibility, and their greater need to defend their party's stands, they have more interest in developing a consistent set of attitudes — perhaps even an ideology. The followers of each party, often ignorant of the issues and their consequences, find it difficult to distinguish their beliefs from those of the opposition and have little reason to be concerned with the consistency of their attitudes. Furthermore, the American parties make only a feeble effort to educate the rank and file politically, and since no central source exists for the authoritative pronouncement of party policy, the followers often do not know what their leaders believe or on what issues the par-

ties chiefly divide. In short, if we mean by ideology a coherent body of informed social doctrine, it is possessed mainly by the articulate leadership, rarely by the masses.

(2) Differences in the degree of partisan involvement parallel the differences in knowledge and have similar consequences. The leaders, of course, have more party spirit than the followers and, as the election studies make plain, the stronger the partisanship, the larger the differences on issues. The leaders are more highly motivated not only to belong to a party appropriate to their beliefs, but to accept its doctrines and to learn how it differs from the opposition party. Since politics is more salient for leaders than for followers, they develop a greater stake in the outcome of the political contest and are more eager to discover the intellectual grounds by which they hope to make victory possible. Through a process of circular reinforcement, those for whom politics is most important are likely to become the most zealous participants, succeeding to the posts that deal in the formation of opinion. Ideology serves the instrumental purpose, in addition, of justifying the heavy investment that party leaders make in political activity. While politics offers many rewards, it also makes great demands on the time, money, and energies of its practitioners — sacrifices which they can more easily justify if they believe they are serving worthwhile social goals. The followers, in contrast, are intellectually far less involved, have less personal stake in the outcome of the competition, have little need to be concerned with the "correctness" of their views on public questions, and have even less reason to learn in precisely what ways their opinions differ from their opponents'. Hence, the party élites recruit members from a population stratified in some measure by ideology, while the rank and file renews itself by more random recruitment and is thus more likely to mirror the opinions of a cross section of the population.

(3) Part of the explanation for the greater consensus among followers than leaders resides in the nature and size of the two types of groups. Whereas the leader groups are comparatively small and selective, each of the follower groups number in the millions and, by their very size and unwieldiness, are predisposed to duplicate the characteristics of the population as a whole. Even if the Republicans draw disproportionately from the business-managerial classes and the Democrats from the trade union movement, neither interest group has enough influence to shape distinctively the aggregate opinions of so large a mass of supporters. Size also affects the nature and frequency of interaction within the two types of groups. Because they comprise a smaller, more selectively chosen, organized, and articulate élite, the leaders are apt to associate with people of their own political persuasion more frequently and consistently than the followers do. They are

not only less cross-pressured than the rank and file but they are also subjected to strong party group efforts to induce them to conform. Because their political values are continually renewed through frequent communication with people of like opinions, and because they acquire intense reference group identifications, they develop an extraordinary ability to resist the force of the opposition's arguments. While the followers, too, are thrown together and shielded to some extent, they are likely to mingle more freely with people of hostile political persuasions, to receive fewer partisan communications, and to hold views that are only intermittently and inconsistently reinforced. Since, by comparison with the leaders, they possess little interest in or information about politics, they can more easily embrace "deviant" attitudes without discomfort and without challenge from their associates. Nor are they likely to be strongly rewarded for troubling to have "correct" opinions. The followers, in short, are less often and less effectively indoctrinated than their leaders. The group processes described here would function even more powerfully in small, sectarian, tightly organized parties of the European type, but they are also present in the American party system, where they yield similar though less potent consequences.

(4) Political competition itself operates to divide the leaders more than the followers. If the parties are impelled to present a common face to the electorate, they are also strongly influenced to distinguish themselves from each other. For one thing, they have a more heightened sense of the "national interest" than the followers do, even if they do not all conceive it in the same way. For another, they hope to improve their chances at the polls by offering the electorate a recognizable and attractive commodity. In addition, they seek emotional gratification in the heightened sense of brotherhood brought on by the struggle against an "outgroup" whose claim to office seems always, somehow, to border upon usurpation. As with many ingroup-outgroup distinctions, the participants search for moral grounds to justify their antagonisms toward each other, and ideologies help to furnish such grounds. Among the followers, on the other hand, these needs exist, if at all, in much weaker form. . . .

VI. The Homogeneity of Support for Leaders and Followers

So far we have only considered conflict and agreement *between* groups. We should now turn to the question of consensus *within* groups. To what extent is each of our samples united on fundamental issues?

In order to assess homogeneity of opinion within party groups, standard deviation scores were computed on each issue for each of the four samples. The higher the standard deviation, of course, the greater the disagreement. The range of possible sigma scores is from 0 (signifying that every member of the sample has selected the same response) to .500 (signifying that all responses are equally divided between the "increase" and "decrease" alternatives). If we assume that the three alternative responses had been randomly (and therefore equally) selected, the standard deviations for the four samples would fall by chance alone around .410. Scores at or above this level may be taken to denote extreme dispersion among the members of a sample while scores in the neighborhood of .300 or below suggest that unanimity within the sample is fairly high. By these somewhat arbitrary criteria we can observe immediately (Table IV) that consensus within groups is greater on most issues than we would expect by chance alone, but that it is extremely high in only a few instances. Although the Republican leaders appear on the average to be the most united and the Democratic leaders the least united of the four groups, the difference between their homogeneity scores (.340 vs. .310) is too small to be taken as conclusive. The grounds are somewhat better for rejecting the belief that leaders are more homogeneous in their outlooks than their followers, since the hypothesis holds only for one party and not for the other.

While generalizations about the relative unity of the four samples seem risky, we can speak more confidently about the rank order of agreement *within* samples. In Table IV we have ranked the issues according to the degree of consensus exhibited toward them by the members of each of the four party groups. There we see that the leaders of the Republican party are most united on the issues that stem from its connections with business — government regulation of business, taxes (especially on business), regulation of trade unions, and minimum wages. The Democratic leaders are most united on those issues which bear upon the support the party receives from the lower and middle income groups — taxes on small and middle incomes, anti-monopoly, slum clearance, social security, and minimum wages. The Republican leaders divide most severely on federal aid to education, slum clearance, U.N. support, segregation, and public control of atomic energy and natural resources; the Democratic leaders are most divided on farm prices, segregation, credit restrictions, immigration, and the natural resources issue. Among the followers the patterns of unity and division are very similar, as attested by the high correlation of .83 between the rank orders of their homogeneity scores. Both Republican and Democratic followers exhibit great cohesion, for example, on taxes on small and middle incomes, social security, slum clearance, and minimum wages. Both divide rather sharply on segregation, farm price supports, defense spending, U.N. support, and taxes on large incomes. The two sets of followers, in short, are alike not only

Consensus within Party Groups: Rank Order of
Homogeneity of Support on Twenty-four Issues

rage nk der[a]	Issue	Democratic leaders Rank order	Sigma	Republican leaders Rank order	Sigma	Democratic followers Rank order	Sigma	Republican followers Rank order	Sigma
	Tax on Small Incomes	1	.220	6	.270	1	.224	1	.250
	Tax on Middle Incomes	3	.276	4	.248	6	.292	2	.278
	Social Security Benefits	5	.282	8	.296	2	.266	3	.286
	Minimum Wages	6	.292	5	.268	4	.276	4	.294
	Enforcement of Anti-Monopoly	2	.246	13	.321	8	.324	7	.314
	Regulation of Public Utilities	8	.307	10	.300	10	.336	5.5	.310
	Slum Clearance	4	.276	23	.386	3	.274	5.5	.310
	Regulation of Trade Unions	12	.356	3	.240	9	.331	15	.345
	Government Regulation of Business	17	.376	1	.192	20	.363	8	.315
	Tax on Business	9	.338	2	.236	19	.362	16	.348
	Level of Tariffs	10	.350	16	.344	11	.338	9	.316
	Public Control of Atomic Energy	7	.302	20	.362	7	.312	13	.340
	Federal Aid to Education	13	.360	24	.394	5	.283	11	.322
	Foreign Aid	19	.383	12	.317	12.5	.340	12	.340
	Tax on Large Incomes	11	.356	9	.298	17	.358	22	.379
	American Participation in Military Alliances, NATO	14	.370	18	.351	14	.350	14	.344
	Immigration into U.S.	21	.399	17	.345	12.5	.340	10	.318
	Corporate Income Tax	16	.375	7	.284	21	.371	17	.361
	Restrictions on Credit	22	.400	14	.324	16	.358	18	.362
	Defense Spending	15	.371	15	.334	22	.380	21	.366
	Public Ownership of Natural Resources	20	.393	19	.354	15	.352	19	.362
	Reliance on U.N.	18	.380	22	.384	18	.359	20	.365
	Level of Farm Supports	24	.421	11	.306	23	.414	23	.397
	Enforce Integration	23	.416	21	.382	24	.418	24	.399

e range of sigma scores is from .192 to .421, out of a possible range of .000 (most united) to .500
ast united). Hence, the lower the rank order the greater the unity on the issue named.

in their opinions on issues but in the degree of unanimity they exhibit toward them. . . .

VII. Summary and Conclusions

The research described in this paper — an outgrowth of a nationwide inquiry into the nature and sources of political affiliation, activity, and belief — was principally designed to test a number of hypotheses about the relation of ideology to party membership. Responses from large samples of Democratic and Republican leaders and followers were compared on twenty-four key issues and on a number of attitude questions and scales. Statistical operations were carried out to assess conflict and consensus among party groups and to estimate the size and significance of differences. From the data yielded by this inquiry, the following inferences seem most warranted:

1. Although it has received wide currency, especially among Europeans, the belief that the two American parties are identical in principle and doctrine has little foundation in fact. Examination of the opinions of Democratic and Republican leaders shows them to be distinct communities of co-believers who diverge sharply on many important issues. Their disagreements, furthermore, conform to an image familiar to many observers and are generally consistent with differences turned up by studies of Congressional roll calls. The unpopularity of many of the positions held by Republican leaders suggests also that the parties submit to the demands of their constituents less slavishly than is commonly supposed.

2. Republican and Democratic leaders stand furthest apart on the issues that grow out of their group identification and support — out of the managerial, proprietary, and high-status connections of the one, and the labor, minority, low-status, and intellectual connections of the other. The opinions of each party élite are linked less by chance than by membership in a common ideological domain. Democratic leaders typically display the stronger urge to elevate the lowborn, the uneducated, the deprived minorities, and the poor in general; they are also more disposed to employ the nation's collective power to advance humanitarian and social welfare goals (e.g., social security, immigration, racial integration, a higher minimum wage, and public education). They are more critical of wealth and big business and more eager to bring them under regulation. Theirs is the greater faith in the wisdom of using legislation for redistributing the national product and for furnishing social services on a wide scale. Of the two groups of leaders, the Democrats are the more "progressively" oriented toward social reform and experimentation. The Republican leaders, while not uniformly differentiated from their opponents, subscribe in greater measure to the symbols and practices of individualism, *laissez-faire,*

and national independence. They prefer to overcome humanity's misfortunes by relying upon personal effort, private incentives, frugality, hard work, responsibility, self-denial (for both men and government), and the strengthening rather than the diminution of the economic and status distinctions that are the "natural" rewards of the differences in human character and fortunes. Were it not for the hackneyed nature of the designation and the danger of forcing traits into a mold they fit only imperfectly, we might be tempted to describe the Republicans as the chief upholders of what Max Weber has called the "Protestant Ethic." Not that the Democrats are insensible to the "virtues" of the Protestant-capitalistic ethos, but they embrace them less firmly and uniformly. The differences between the two élites have probably been intensified by the rise of the New Deal and by the shift of former radicals into the Democratic party following the decline of socialist and other left-wing movements during and after the war.

3. Whereas the leaders of the two parties diverge strongly, their followers differ only moderately in their attitudes toward issues. The hypothesis that party beliefs unite adherents and bring them into the party ranks may hold for the more active members of a mass party but not for its rank and file supporters. Republican followers, in fact, disagree far more with their own leaders than with the leaders of the Democratic party. Little support was found for the belief that deep cleavages exist among the electorate but are ignored by the leaders. One might, indeed, more accurately assert the contrary, to wit: that the natural cleavages between the leaders are largely ignored by the voters. However, we cannot presently conclude that ideology exerts no influence over the habits of party support, for the followers do differ significantly and in the predicted directions on some issues. Furthermore, we do not know how many followers may previously have been led by doctrinal considerations to shift their party allegiances.

4. Except for their desire to ingratiate themselves with as many voters as possible, the leaders of the two parties have more reason than their followers to hold sharply opposing views on the important political questions of the day. Compared with the great mass of supporters, they are articulate, informed, highly partisan, and involved; they comprise a smaller and more tightly knit group which is closer to the well-springs of party opinion, more accessible for indoctrination, more easily rewarded or punished for conformity or deviation, and far more affected, politically and psychologically, by engagement in the party struggle for office. If the leaders of the two parties are not always candid about their disagreements, the reason may well be that they sense the great measure of consensus to be found among the electorate.

5. Finding that party leaders hold contrary beliefs does not prove that they *act* upon those beliefs or that the two parties are, in practice, governed by different outlooks. In a subsequent paper we shall con-

sider these questions more directly by comparing platform and other official party pronouncements with the private opinions revealed in this study. Until further inquiries are conducted, however, it seems reasonable to assume that the views held privately by party leaders can never be entirely suppressed but are bound to crop out in hundreds of large and small ways — in campaign speeches, discussions at party meetings, private communications to friends and sympathizers, statements to the press by party officials and candidates, legislative debates, and public discussions on innumerable national, state, and local questions. If, in other words, the opinions of party leaders are as we have described them, there is every chance that they are expressed and acted upon to some extent. Whether this makes our parties "ideological" depends, of course, on how narrowly we define that term. Some may prefer to reserve that designation for parties that are more obviously preoccupied with doctrine, more intent upon the achievement of a systematic political program, and more willing to enforce a common set of beliefs upon their members and spokesmen.

6. The parties are internally united on some issues, divided on others. In general, Republican leaders achieve greatest homogeneity on issues that grow out of their party's identification with business, Democratic leaders on issues that reflect their connection with liberal and lower-income groups. We find no support for the hypothesis that the parties achieve greatest internal consensus on the issues which principally divide them from their opponents.

In a sequel to this paper we shall offer data on the demographic correlates of issue support, which show that most of the differences presented here exist independently of factors like education, occupation, age, religion, and sectionalism. Controlling for these influences furnishes much additional information and many new insights but does not upset our present conclusions in any important respect. Thus, the parties must be considered not merely as spokesmen for other interest groups but as reference groups in their own right, helping to formulate, to sustain, and to speak for a recognizable point of view.

Voting Behavior: Rational or Irrational?

Parties are supposed to bridge the gap between the people and their government. Theoretically they are the primary vehicles for translating the wishes of the electorate into public policy, sharing this role with interest groups and other governmental instrumentalities in varying degrees. If parties are to perform this aspect of their job properly, the party system must be conducive to securing meaningful debate and action. Party organization and procedure profoundly affect the ability of parties to act in a democratically responsible manner. It should also be pointed out, however, that the electorate has a responsibility in the political process — the responsibility to act rationally, debate the issues of importance, and record a vote for one party or the other at election time. These, at least, are electoral norms traditionally discussed. But does the electorate act in this manner? Is it desirable to have 100 per cent electoral participation considering the characteristics of voting behavior? What are the determinants of electoral behavior? These questions will be discussed in the readings that follow.

17   BERNARD R. BERELSON, PAUL F. LAZARSFELD,
      AND WILLIAM N. MC PHEE

DEMOCRATIC PRACTICE AND DEMOCRATIC THEORY

REQUIREMENTS FOR THE INDIVIDUAL

Perhaps the main impact of realistic research on contemporary politics has been to temper some of the requirements set by our traditional normative theory for the typical citizen. "Out of all this literature of political observation and analysis, which is relatively new," says Max Beloff, "there has come to exist a picture in our minds of the political scene which differs very considerably from that familiar to us from the classical texts of democratic politics."

Experienced observers have long known, of course, that the individual voter was not all that the theory of democracy requires of him. As Bryce put it:

> How little solidity and substance there is in the political or social beliefs of nineteen persons out of every twenty. These beliefs, when examined, mostly resolve themselves into two or three prejudices and aversions, two or three prepossessions for a particular party or section of a party, two or three phrases or catch-words suggesting or embodying arguments which the man who repeats them has not analyzed.

While our data [from the Elmira study] do not support such an extreme statement, they do reveal that certain requirements commonly

From Bernard R. Berelson, Paul F. Lazarsfeld, and William N. McPhee, *Voting*, Chap. 14. Reprinted by permission of the University of Chicago Press. Copyright © 1954 by the University of Chicago.

assumed for the successful operation of democracy are not met by the behavior of the "average" citizen. The requirements, and our conclusions concerning them, are quickly reviewed.

Interest, Discussion, Motivation. The democratic citizen is expected to be interested and to participate in political affairs. His interest and participation can take such various forms as reading and listening to campaign materials, working for the candidate or the party, arguing politics, donating money, and voting. In Elmira the majority of the people vote, but in general they do not give evidence of sustained interest. Many vote without real involvement in the election, and even the party workers are not typically motivated by ideological concerns or plain civic duty.

If there is one characteristic for a democratic system (besides the ballot itself) that is theoretically required, it is the capacity for and the practice of discussion. "It is as true of the large as of the small society," says Lindsay, "that its health depends on the mutual understanding which discussion makes possible; and that discussion is the only possible instrument of its democratic government." How much participation in political discussion there is in the community, what it is, and among whom — these questions have been given answers . . . earlier. . . . In this instance there was little true discussion between the candidates, little in the newspaper commentary, little between the voters and the official party representatives, some within the electorate. On the grass-roots level there was more talk than debate, and, at least inferentially, the talk had important effects upon voting, in reinforcing or activating the partisans if not in converting the opposition.

An assumption underlying the theory of democracy is that the citizenry has a strong motivation for participation in political life. But it is a curious quality of voting behavior that for large numbers of people motivation is weak if not almost absent. It is assumed that this motivation would gain its strength from the citizen's perception of the difference that alternative decisions made to him. Now when a person buys something or makes other decisions of daily life, there are direct and immediate consequences for him. But for the bulk of the American people the voting decision is not followed by any direct, immediate, visible personal consequences. Most voters, organized or unorganized, are not in a position to foresee the distant and indirect consequences for themselves, let alone the society. The ballot is cast, and for most people that is the end of it. If their side is defeated, "it doesn't really matter."

Knowledge. The democratic citizen is expected to be well informed about political affairs. He is supposed to know what the issues are, what their history is, what the relevant facts are, what alternatives are proposed, what the party stands for, what the likely conse-

quences are. By such standards the voter falls short. Even when he has
the motivation, he finds it difficult to make decisions on the basis of
full information when the subject is relatively simple and proximate;
how can he do so when it is complex and remote? The citizen is not
highly informed on details of the campaign, nor does he avoid a certain misperception of the political situation when it is to his psychological advantage to do so. The electorate's perception of what goes on
in the campaign is colored by emotional feeling toward one or the
other issue, candidate, party, or social group.

 Principle. The democratic citizen is supposed to cast his
vote on the basis of principle — not fortuitously or frivolously or
impulsively or habitually, but with reference to standards not only of
his own interest but of the common good as well. Here, again, if this
requirement is pushed at all strongly, it becomes an impossible
demand on the democratic electorate.

Many voters vote not for principle in the usual sense but "for" a
group to which they are attached — their group. The Catholic vote or
the hereditary vote is explainable less as principle than as a traditional
social allegiance. The ordinary voter, bewildered by the complexity of
modern political problems, unable to determine clearly what the
consequences are of alternative lines of action, remote from the arena,
and incapable of bringing information to bear on principle, votes the
way trusted people around him are voting. . . .

On the issues of the campaign there is a considerable amount of
"don't know" — sometimes reflecting genuine indecision, more often
meaning "don't care." Among those with opinions the partisans *agree*
on most issues, criteria, expectations, and rules of the game. The supporters of the different sides disagree on only a few issues. Nor, for that
matter, do the candidates themselves always join the issue sharply and
clearly. The partisans do not agree overwhelmingly with their own
party's position, or, rather, only the small minority of highly partisan
do; the rest take a rather moderate position on the political consideration involved in an election.

 Rationality. The democratic citizen is expected to exercise rational judgment in coming to his voting decision. He is expected
to have arrived at his principles by reason and to have considered
rationally the implications and alleged consequences of the alternative
proposals of the contending parties. Political theorists and commentators have always exclaimed over the seeming contrast here between
requirement and fulfillment. . . . The upshot of this is that the usual
analogy between the voting "decision" and the more or less carefully
calculated decisions of consumers or businessmen or courts, incidentally, may be quite incorrect. For many voters political preferences may
better be considered analogous to cultural tastes — in music, litera-

ture, recreational activities, dress, ethics, speech, social behavior. Consider the parallels between political preferences and general cultural tastes. Both have their origin in ethnic, sectional, class, and family traditions. Both exhibit stability and resistance to change for individuals but flexibility and adjustment over generations for the society as a whole. Both seem to be matters of sentiment and disposition rather than "reasoned preferences." While both are responsive to changed conditions and unusual stimuli, they are relatively invulnerable to direct argumentation and vulnerable to indirect social influences. Both are characterized more by faith than by conviction and by wishful expectation rather than careful prediction or consequences. The preference for one party rather than another must be highly similar to the preference for one kind of literature or music rather than another, and the choice of the same political party every four years may be parallel to the choice of the same old standards of conduct in new social situations. In short, it appears that a sense of fitness is a more striking feature of political preference than reason and calculation.

Requirements for the System

If the democratic system depended solely on the qualifications of the individual voter, then it seems remarkable that democracies have survived through the centuries. After examining the detailed data on how individuals misperceive political reality or respond to irrelevant social influences, one wonders how a democracy ever solves its political problems. But when one considers the data in a broader perspective — how huge segments of the society adapt to political conditions affecting them or how the political system adjusts itself to changing conditions over long periods of time — he cannot fail to be impressed with the total result. Where the rational citizen seems to abdicate, nevertheless angels seem to tread. . . .

That is the paradox. *Individual voters* today seem unable to satisfy the requirements for a democratic system of government outlined by political theorists. But the *system of democracy* does meet certain requirements for a going political organization. The individual members may not meet all the standards, but the whole nevertheless survives and grows. This suggests that where the classic theory is defective is in its concentration on the *individual citizen*. What are under-valued are certain collective properties that reside in the electorate as a whole and in the political and social system in which it functions.

The political philosophy we have inherited, then, has given more consideration to the virtues of the typical citizen of the democracy than to the working of the *system* as a whole. Moreover, when it dealt with the system, it mainly considered the single constitutive institutions of the system, not those general features necessary if the institutions are to work as required. For example, the rule of law, representative government, periodic elections, the party system, and the several freedoms of discussion, press, association, and assembly have all been examined by political philosophers seeking to clarify and to justify the idea of political democracy. But liberal democracy is more than a political system in which individual voters and political institutions operate. For political democracy to survive, other features are required: the intensity of conflict must be limited, the rate of change must be restrained, stability in the social and economic structure must be maintained, a pluralistic social organization must exist, and a basic consensus must bind together the contending parties.

Such features of the system of political democracy belong neither to the constitutive institutions nor to the individual voter. It might be said that they form the atmosphere or the environment in which both operate. In any case, such features have not been carefully considered by political philosophers, and it is on these broader properties of the democratic political system that more reflection and study by political theory is called for. In the most tentative fashion let us explore the values of the political system, as they involve the electorate, in the light of the foregoing considerations.

Underlying the paradox is an assumption that the population is homogeneous socially and should be homogeneous politically: that everybody is about the same in relevant social characteristics; that, if something is a political virtue (like interest in the election), then everyone should have it; that there is such a thing as "the" typical citizen on whom uniform requirements can be imposed. The tendency of classic democratic literature to work with an image of "the" voter was never justified. For, as we will attempt to illustrate here, some of the most important requirements that democratic values impose on a system require a voting population that is not homogeneous but heterogeneous in its political qualities.

The need for heterogeneity arises from the contradictory functions we expect our voting system to serve. We expect the political system to adjust itself and our affairs to changing conditions; yet we demand too that it display a high degree of stability. We expect the contending interests and parties to pursue their ends vigorously and the voters to care; yet, after the election is over, we expect reconciliation. We expect the voting outcome to serve what is best for the community; yet we do not want disinterested voting unattached to the purposes and interests of different segments of that community. We want voters to express their own free and self-determined choices; yet, for the good of the community, we would like voters to avail themselves of the best information and guidance available from the groups and leaders around them. We expect a high degree of rationality to prevail in the decision; but were all irrationality and mythology absent, and all ends pursued by the most coldly rational selection of political means, it is doubtful if the system would hold together.

In short, our electoral system calls for apparently incompatible properties — which, although they cannot all reside in each individual voter, can (and do) reside in a heterogeneous electorate. What seems to be required of the electorate as a whole is a *distribution* of qualities along important dimensions. We need some people who are active in a certain respect, others in the middle, and still others passive. The contradictory things we want from the total require that the parts be different. This can be illustrated by taking up a number of important dimensions by which an electorate might be characterized.

Involvement and Indifference. How could a mass democracy work if all the people were deeply involved in politics? Lack of interest by some people is not without its benefits, too. True, the highly interested voters vote more, and know more about the campaign, and read and listen more, and participate more; however, they are also less open to persuasion and less likely to change. Extreme interest goes with extreme partisanship and might culminate in rigid fanaticism that could destroy democratic processes if generalized throughout the community. Low affect toward the election — not caring much — underlies the resolution of many political problems; votes can be resolved into a two-party split instead of fragmented into many parties (the splinter parties of the left, for example, splinter because their advocates are *too* interested in politics). Low interest provides maneuvering room for political shifts necessary for a complex society in a period of rapid change. Compromise might be based upon sophisticated awareness of costs and returns — perhaps impossible to demand of a mass society — but it is more often induced by indifference. Some people are and should be highly interested in politics, but not everyone is or needs to be. Only the doctrinaire would deprecate the moderate indifference that facilitates compromise.

Hence, an important balance between action motivated by strong sentiments and action with little passion behind it is obtained by heterogeneity within the electorate. Balance of this sort is, in practice, met by a distribution of voters rather than by a homogeneous collection of "ideal" citizens.

Stability and Flexibility. A similar dimension along which an electorate might be characterized is stability-flexibility. The need for change and adaptation is clear, and the need for stability ought equally to be (especially from observation of current democratic practice in, say, certain Latin-American countries). . . . [I]t may be that the very people who are most sensitive to changing social conditions are those most susceptible to political change. For, in either case, the people exposed to membership in overlapping strata, those whose former life-patterns are being broken up, those who are moving about socially or physically, those who are forming new families and new friendships — it is they who are open to adjustments of attitudes and tastes. They may be the least partisan and the least interested voters, but they perform a valuable function for the entire system. Here again is an instance in which an individual "inadequacy" provides a positive service for society: The campaign can be a reaffirming force for the settled majority and a creative force for the unsettled minority. There is stability on both sides and flexibility in the middle.

Progress and Conservation. Closely related to the question of stability is the question of past versus future orientation of the system. In America a progressive outlook is highly valued, but, at the same time, so is a conservative one. Here a balance between the two is easily found in the party system and in the distribution of voters themselves from extreme conservatives to extreme liberals. But a balance between the two is also achieved by a distribution of political dispositions through time. There are periods of great political agitation (*i.e.,* campaigns) alternating with periods of political dormancy. Paradoxically, the former — the campaign period — is likely to be an instrument of conservatism, often even of historical regression. . . .

Again, then, a balance (between preservation of the past and receptivity to the future) seems to be required of a democratic electorate. The heterogeneous electorate in itself provides a balance between liberalism and conservatism; and so does the sequence of political events from periods of drifting change to abrupt rallies back to the loyalties of earlier years.

Consensus and Cleavage. . . . [T]here are required *social* consensus and cleavage — in effect pluralism — in politics. Such pluralism makes for enough consensus to hold the system together and enough cleavage to make it move. Too much consensus would be deadening and restrictive of liberty; too much cleavage would be destructive of the society as a whole. . . . Thus again a requirement we might place on an electoral system — balance between total political war between segments of the society and total political indifference to group interests of that society — translates into varied requirements for different individuals. With respect to group or bloc voting, as with other aspects of political behavior, it is perhaps not unfortunate that "some do and some do not."

Individualism and Collectivism. Lord Bryce pointed out the difficulties in a theory of democracy that assumes that each citizen must himself be capable of voting intelligently:

> Orthodox democratic theory assumes that every citizen has, or ought to have, thought out for himself certain opinions, *i.e.,* ought to have a definite view, defensible by argument, of what the country needs, of what principles ought to be applied in governing it, of the man to whose hands the government ought to be entrusted. There are persons who talk, though certainly very few who act, as if they believed this theory, which may be compared to the theory of some ultra-Protestants that every good Christian has or ought to have . . . worked out for himself from the Bible a system of theology.

In the first place, however, the information available to the individual voter is not limited to that directly possessed by him. True, the individual casts his own personal ballot. But, as we have tried to indicate . . . , that is perhaps the most individualized action he takes in an election. His vote is formed in the midst of his fellows in a sort of group decision — if, indeed, it may be called a decision at all — and the total information and knowledge possessed in the group's present and past generations can be made available for the group's choice. Here is where opinion-leading relationships, for example, play an active role.

Second, and probably more important, the individual voter may not have a great deal of detailed information, but he usually has picked up the crucial *general* information as part of his social learning itself. He may not know the parties' positions on the tariff, or who is for reciprocal trade treaties, or what are the differences on Asiatic policy, or how the parties split on civil rights, or how many security risks were exposed by whom. But he cannot live in an American community without knowing broadly where the parties stand. He has learned that the Republicans are more conservative and the Democrats more liberal — and he can locate his own sentiments and cast his vote accordingly. After all, he must vote for one or the other party, and, if he knows the big thing about the parties, he does not need to know all the little things. The basic role a party plays as an institution in American life is more important to his voting than a particular stand on a particular issue.

It would be unthinkable to try to maintain our present economic style of life without a complex system of delegating to others what we are not competent to do ourselves, without accepting and giving training to each other about what each is expected to do, without accepting our dependence on others in many spheres and taking responsibility for their dependence on us in some spheres. And, like it or not, to maintain our present political style of life, we may have to accept much the same interdependence with others in collective behavior. We have learned slowly in economic life that it is useful not to have everyone a butcher or a baker, any more than it is useful to have no one skilled in such activities. The same kind of division of labor — as

repugnant as it may be in some respects to our individualistic tradition — is serving us well today in mass politics. There is an implicit
division of political labor within the electorate.

18 V. O. KEY, JR.

THE VOICE OF THE
PEOPLE: AN ECHO

In his reflective moments even the most experienced politician senses a nagging curiosity about why people vote as they do. His
power and his position depend upon the outcome of the mysterious
rites we perform as opposing candidates harangue the multitudes who
finally march to the polls to prolong the rule of their champion, to
thrust him, ungratefully, back into the void of private life, or to raise
to eminence a new tribune of the people. What kinds of appeals enable
a candidate to win the favor of the great god, The People? What circumstances move voters to shift their preferences in this direction or
that? What clever propaganda tactic or slogan led to this result? What
mannerism of oratory or style of rhetoric produced another outcome?
What band of electors rallied to this candidate to save the day for him?
What policy of state attracted the devotion of another bloc of voters? What action repelled a third sector of the electorate?

The victorious candidate may claim with assurance that he has the
answers to all such questions. He may regard his success as vindication
of his beliefs about why voters vote as they do. And he may regard the
swing of the vote to him as indubitably a response to the campaign
positions he took, as an indication of the acuteness of his intuitive estimates of the mood of the people, and as a ringing manifestation of the
esteem in which he is held by a discriminating public. This narcissism
assumes its most repulsive form among election winners who have
championed intolerance, who have stirred the passions and hatreds of
people, or who have advocated causes known by decent men to be outrageous or dangerous in their long-run consequences. No functionary
is more repugnant or more arrogant than the unjust man who asserts,
with a color of truth, that he speaks from a pedestal of popular approbation.

It thus can be a mischievous error to assume, because a candidate
wins, that a majority of the electorate shares his views on public ques-

Reprinted by permission of the publishers from V. O. Key, Jr., *The Responsible
Electorate* (Cambridge, Mass.: The Belknap Press of Harvard University Press),
Chap. 1, pp. 1–8. Copyright 1966, by the President and Fellows of Harvard College.

tions, approves his past actions, or has specific expectations about his future conduct. Nor does victory establish that the candidate's campaign strategy, his image, his television style, or his fearless stand against cancer and polio turned the trick. The election returns establish only that the winner attracted a majority of the votes — assuming the existence of a modicum of rectitude in election administration. They tell us precious little about why the plurality was his.

For a glaringly obvious reason, electoral victory cannot be regarded as necessarily a popular ratification of a candidate's outlook. The voice of the people is but an echo. The output of an echo chamber bears an inevitable and invariable relation to the input. As candidates and parties clamor for attention and vie for popular support, the people's verdict can be no more than a selective reflection from among the alternatives and outlooks presented to them. Even the most discriminating popular judgment can reflect only ambiguity, uncertainty, or even foolishness if those are the qualities of the input into the echo chamber. A candidate may win despite his tactics and appeals rather than because of them. If the people can choose only from among rascals, they are certain to choose a rascal.

Scholars, though they have less at stake than do politicians, also have an abiding curiosity about why voters act as they do. In the past quarter of a century they have vastly enlarged their capacity to check the hunches born of their curiosities. The invention of the sample survey — the most widely known example of which is the Gallup poll — enabled them to make fairly trustworthy estimates of the characteristics and behaviors of large human populations. This method of mass observation revolutionized the study of politics — as well as the management of political campaigns. The new technique permitted large-scale tests to check the validity of old psychological and sociological theories of human behavior. These tests led to new hunches and new theories about voting behavior, which could, in turn, be checked and which thereby contributed to the extraordinary ferment in the social sciences during recent decades.

The studies of electoral behavior by survey methods cumulate into an imposing body of knowledge which conveys a vivid impression of the variety and subtlety of factors that enter into individual voting decisions. In their first stages in the 1930's the new electoral studies chiefly lent precision and verification to the working maxims of practicing politicians and to some of the crude theories of political speculators. Thus, sample surveys established that people did, indeed, appear to vote their pocketbooks. Yet the demonstration created its embarrassments because it also established that exceptions to the rule were numerous. Not all factory workers, for example, voted alike. How was the behavior of the deviants from "group interest" to be explained?

Refinement after refinement of theory and analysis added complexity to the original simple explanation. By introducing a bit of psychological theory it could be demonstrated that factory workers with optimistic expectations tended less to be governed by pocketbook considerations than did those whose outlook was gloomy. When a little social psychology was stirred into the analysis, it could be established that identifications formed early in life, such as attachments to political parties, also reinforced or resisted the pull of the interest of the moment. A sociologist, bringing to play the conceptual tools of his trade, then could show that those factory workers who associate intimately with like-minded persons on the average vote with greater solidarity than do social isolates. Inquiries conducted with great ingenuity along many such lines have enormously broadened our knowledge of the factors associated with the responses of people to the stimuli presented to them by political campaigns.[1]

Yet, by and large, the picture of the voter that emerges from a combination of the folklore of practical politics and the findings of the new electoral studies is not a pretty one. It is not a portrait of citizens moving to considered decision as they play their solemn role of making and unmaking governments. The older tradition from practical politics may regard the voter as an erratic and irrational fellow susceptible to manipulation by skilled humbugs. One need not live through many campaigns to observe politicians, even successful politicians, who act as though they regarded the people as manageable fools. Nor does a heroic conception of the voter emerge from the new analyses of electoral behavior. They can be added up to a conception of voting not as a civic decision but as an almost purely deterministic act. Given knowledge of certain characteristics of a voter — his occupation, his residence, his religion, his national origin, and perhaps certain of his attitudes — one can predict with a high probability the direction of his vote. The actions of persons are made to appear to be only predictable and automatic responses to campaign stimuli.

Most findings of the analysts of voting never travel beyond the circle of the technicians; the popularizers, though, give wide currency to the most bizarre — and most dubious — theories of electoral behavior. Public-relations experts share in the process of dissemination as they

[1] The principal books are: Paul F. Lazarsfeld, Bernard Berelson, and Hazel Gaudet, *The People's Choice* (New York: Duell, Sloan and Pearce, 1944); Angus Campbell, Gerald Gurin, and Warren E. Miller, *The Voter Decides* (Evanston, Ill.: Row, Peterson, 1954); Bernard R. Berelson, Paul F. Lazarsfeld, and William N. McPhee, *Voting* (Chicago: University of Chicago Press, 1954); Angus Campbell, Philip E. Converse, Warren E. Miller, and Donald E. Stokes, *The American Voter* (New York: Wiley, 1960). The periodical literature is almost limitless. The footnotes in Robert E. Lane's *Political Life* (Glencoe, Ill.: Free Press, 1959) constitute a handy guide to most of it.

sell their services to politicians (and succeed in establishing that politicians are sometimes as gullible as businessmen). Reporters pick up the latest psychological secret from campaign managers and spread it through a larger public. Thus, at one time a goodly proportion of the literate population must have placed some store in the theory that the electorate was a pushover for a candidate who projected an appropriate "father image." At another stage, the "sincere" candidate supposedly had an overwhelming advantage. And even so kindly a gentleman as General Eisenhower was said to have an especial attractiveness to those of authoritarian personality within the electorate.

Conceptions and theories of the way voters behave do not raise solely arcane problems to be disputed among the democratic and antidemocratic theorists or questions to be settled by the elegant techniques of the analysts of electoral behavior. Rather, they touch upon profound issues at the heart of the problem of the nature and workability of systems of popular government. Obviously the perceptions of the behavior of the electorate held by political leaders, agitators, and activists condition, if they do not fix, the types of appeals politicians employ as they seek popular support. These perceptions — or theories — affect the nature of the input to the echo chamber, if we may revert to our earlier figure, and thereby control its output. They may govern, too, the kinds of actions that governments take as they look forward to the next election. If politicians perceive the electorate as responsive to father images, they will give it father images. If they see voters as most certainly responsive to nonsense, they will give them nonsense. If they see voters as susceptible to delusion, they will delude them. If they see an electorate receptive to the cold, hard realities, they will give it the cold, hard realities.

In short, theories of how voters behave acquire importance not because of their effects on voters, who may proceed blithely unaware of them. They gain significance because of their effects, both potentially and in reality, on candidates and other political leaders. If leaders believe the route to victory is by projection of images and cultivation of styles rather than by advocacy of policies to cope with the problems of the country, they will project images and cultivate styles to the neglect of the substance of politics. They will abdicate their prime function in a democratic system, which amounts, in essence, to the assumption of the risk of trying to persuade us to lift ourselves by our bootstraps.

Among the literary experts on politics there are those who contend that, because of the development of tricks for the manipulation of the masses, practices of political leadership in the management of voters have moved far toward the conversion of election campaigns into obscene parodies of the models set up by democratic idealists. They

point to the good old days when politicians were deep thinkers, eloquent orators, and farsighted statesmen. Such estimates of the course
of change in social institutions must be regarded with reserve. They
may be only manifestations of the inverted optimism of aged and melancholy men who, estopped from hope for the future, see in the past a
satisfaction of their yearning for greatness in our political life.

Whatever the trends may have been, the perceptions that leadership
elements of democracies hold of the modes of response of the electorate
must always be a matter of fundamental significance. Those perceptions determine the nature of the voice of the people, for they determine the character of the input into the echo chamber. While the output may be governed by the nature of the input, over the longer run
the properties of the echo chamber may themselves be altered. Fed a
steady diet of buncombe, the people may come to expect and to respond with highest predictability to buncombe. And those leaders
most skilled in the propagation of buncombe may gain lasting advantage in the recurring struggles for popular favor.

The perverse and unorthodox argument of this little book [*The
Responsible Electorate*] is that voters are not fools. To be sure, many
individual voters act in odd ways indeed; yet in the large the electorate
behaves about as rationally and responsibly as we should expect, given
the clarity of the alternatives presented to it and the character of the
information available to it. In American presidential campaigns of
recent decades the portrait of the American electorate that develops
from the data is not one of an electorate straitjacketed by social determinants or moved by subconscious urges triggered by devilishly skillful propagandists. It is rather one of an electorate moved by concern
about central and relevant questions of public policy, of governmental
performance, and of executive personality. Propositions so uncompro-
misingly stated inevitably represent overstatements. Yet to the extent
that they can be shown to resemble the reality, they are propositions of
basic importance for both the theory and the practice of democracy.

To check the validity of this broad interpretation of the behavior of
voters, attention will center on the movements of voters across party
lines as they reacted to the issues, events, and candidates of presidential campaigns between 1936 and 1960. Some Democratic voters of one
election turned Republican at the next; others stood pat. Some
Republicans of one presidential season voted Democratic four years
later; others remained loyal Republicans. What motivated these shifts,
sometimes large and sometimes small, in voter affection? How did the
standpatters differ from the switchers? What led them to stand firmly
by their party preference of four years earlier? Were these actions governed by images, moods, and other irrelevancies; or were they expressions of judgments about the sorts of questions that, hopefully, voters

will weigh as they responsibly cast their ballots? On these matters evidence is available that is impressive in volume, if not always so complete or so precisely relevant as hindsight would wish. If one perseveres through the analysis of this extensive body of information, the proposition that the voter is not so irrational a fellow after all may become credible.

Functions and Types of Elections

Most people transmit their political desires to government through elections. Elections are a critical part of the democratic process, and the existence of *free* elections is a major difference between democracies and totalitarian or authoritarian forms of government. Because elections reflect popular attitudes toward governmental parties, policies, and personalities, it is useful to attempt to classify different types of elections on the basis of changes and trends that take place within the electorate. Every election is not the same. For example, the election of 1932 and the resulting Democratic landslide were profoundly different from the election of 1960, in which Kennedy won by less than 1 per cent of the popular vote.

Members of the Survey Research Center at the University of Michigan as well as V. O. Key, Jr., have developed a typology of elections that is useful in analyzing the electoral system. The most prevalent type of election can be classified as a "maintaining election," "one in which the pattern of partisan attachments prevailing in the preceding period persists and is the primary influence on the forces governing the vote."[1] Most elections fall into the maintaining category, a fact significant for the political system because such elections result in political continuity and reflect a lack of serious upheavals within the electorate and government. Maintaining elections result in the continuation of the majority political party.

At certain times in American history, what V. O. Key, Jr., has called "critical elections" take place. This type of election, which is discussed in the reading below, results in permanent realignment of the electorate. Critical elections reflect basic changes in political attitudes.

Apart from maintaining and critical elections, a third type, in which only temporary shifts take place within the electorate, can be called "deviating elections." For example, the Eisenhower victories of 1952 and 1956 were deviating elections for several reasons, including the personality of Eisenhower and the fact that voters could register their choice for President without

[1] Angus Campbell, Philip E. Converse, Warren E. Miller, and Donald E. Stokes, *The American Voter* (New York: John Wiley & Sons, 1960), Chap 19.

changing their basic partisan loyalties at congressional and state levels. Deviating elections, with reference to the office of President, are probable when popular figures are running for the office.

In "reinstating elections," a final category that can be added to a typology of elections, there is a return to normal voting patterns. Reinstating elections take place after deviating elections as a result of the demise of the temporary forces that caused the transitory shift in partisan choice. The election of 1960, in which most of the Democratic majority in the electorate returned to the fold and voted for John F. Kennedy,[2] has been classified as a reinstating election.

19   V. O. KEY, JR.

A THEORY OF CRITICAL ELECTIONS

Perhaps the basic differentiating characteristic of democratic orders consists in the expression of effective choice by the mass of the people in elections. The electorate occupies, at least in the mystique of such orders, the position of the principal organ of governance; it acts through elections. An election itself is a formal act of collective decision that occurs in a stream of connected antecedent and subsequent behavior. Among democratic orders elections, so broadly defined, differ enormously in their nature, their meaning, and their consequences. Even within a single nation the reality of election differs greatly from time to time. A systematic comparative approach, with a focus on variations in the nature of elections would doubtless be fruitful in advancing understanding of the democratic governing process. In behavior antecedent to voting, elections differ in the proportions of the electorate psychologically involved, in the intensity of attitudes associated with campaign cleavages, in the nature of expectations about the consequences of the voting, in the impact of objective events relevant to individual political choice, in individual sense of effective connection with community decision, and in other ways. These and other antecedent variations affect the act of voting itself as well as subsequent behavior. An understanding of elections and, in turn, of the

[2] See Philip E. Converse, Angus Campbell, Warren E. Miller, and Donald E. Stokes, "Stability and Change in 1960: A Reinstating Election," *The American Political Science Review*, Vol. 55 (June 1961), pp. 269–80.

From *The Journal of Politics*, Vol. 17, No. 1 (February 1955). Reprinted by permission of the publisher.

democratic process as a whole must rest partially on broad differentiations of the complexes of behavior that we call elections.

While this is not the occasion to develop a comprehensive typology of elections, the foregoing remarks provide an orientation for an attempt to formulate a concept of one type of election — based on American experience — which might be built into a more general theory of elections. Even the most fleeting inspection of American elections suggests the existence of a category of elections in which voters are, at least from impressionistic evidence, unusually deeply concerned, in which the extent of electoral involvement is relatively quite high, and in which the decisive results of the voting reveal a sharp alteration of the pre-existing cleavage within the electorate. Moreover, and perhaps this is the truly differentiating characteristic of this sort of election, the realignment made manifest in the voting in such elections seems to persist for several succeeding elections. All these characteristics cumulate to the conception of an election type in which the depth and intensity of electoral involvement are high, in which more or less profound readjustments occur in the relations of power within the community, and in which new and durable electoral groupings are formed. These comments suppose, of course, the existence of other types of complexes of behavior centering about formal elections, the systematic isolation and identification of which, fortunately, are not essential for the present discussion.

I

The presidential election of 1928 in the New England states provides a specific case of the type of critical election that has been described in general terms. In that year Alfred E. Smith, the Democratic Presidential candidate, made gains in all the New England states. The rise in Democratic strength was especially notable in Massachusetts and Rhode Island. When one probes below the surface of the gross election figures it becomes apparent that a sharp and durable realignment also occurred within the electorate, a fact reflective of the activation by the Democratic candidate of low-income, Catholic, urban voters of recent immigrant stock. In New England, at least, the Roosevelt revolution of 1932 was in large measure an Al Smith revolution of 1928, a characterization less applicable to the remainder of the country.

The intensity and extent of electoral concern before the voting of 1928 can only be surmised, but the durability of the realignment formed at the election can be determined by simple analyses of election statistics. An illustration of the new division thrust through the electorate by the campaign of 1928 is provided by the graphs in Figure A, which show the Democratic percentages of the presidential vote

from 1916 through 1952 for the city of Somerville and the town of Ashfield in Massachusetts. Somerville, adjacent to Boston, had a population in 1930 of 104,000 of which 28 per cent was foreign born and 41
per cent was of foreign-born or mixed parentage. Roman Catholics
constituted a large proportion of its relatively low-income population.
Ashfield, a farming community in western Massachusetts with a 1930
population of 860, was predominantly native born (8.6 per cent foreign born), chiefly rural-farm (66 per cent), and principally Protestant.

The impressiveness of the differential impact of the election of 1928
on Somerville and Ashfield may be read from the graphs in Figure A.
From 1920 the Democratic percentage in Somerville ascended steep-
ly while the Democrats in Ashfield, few in 1920, became even less
numerous in 1928. Inspection of the graphs also suggests that the great
reshuffling of voters that occurred in 1928 was perhaps the final and
decisive stage in a process that had been under way for some time.
That antecedent process involved a relatively heavy support in 1924
for La Follette in those towns in which Smith was subsequently to find
special favor. Hence, in Figure A, as in all the other charts, the 1924
figure is the percentage of the total accounted for by the votes of both
the Democratic and Progressive candidates rather than the Democratic percentage of the two-party vote. This usage conveys a minimum
impression of the size of the 1924–1928 Democratic gain but probably
depicts the nature of the 1920–1928 trend.

FIGURE A
　　　Democratic Percentages of Major-Party Presidential
　　　Vote, Somerville and Ashfield, Massachusetts, 1916–1952

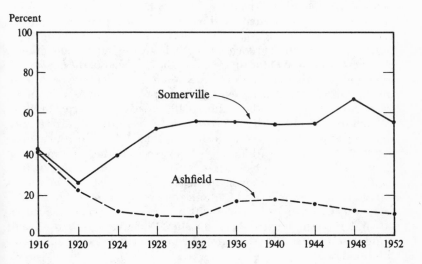

For present purposes, the voting behavior of the two communities shown in Figure A after 1928 is of central relevance. The differences established between them in 1928 persisted even through 1952, although the two series fluctuated slightly in response to the particular influences of individual campaigns. The nature of the process of maintenance of the cleavage is, of course, not manifest from these data. Conceivably the impress of the events of 1928 on individual attitudes and loyalties formed partisan attachments of lasting nature. Yet it is doubtful that the new crystallization of 1928 projected itself through a quarter of a century solely from the momentum given it by such factors. More probably subsequent events operated to re-enforce and to maintain the 1928 cleavage. Whatever the mechanism of its maintenance, the durability of the realignment is impressive.

Somerville and Ashfield may be regarded more or less as samples of major population groups within the electorate of Massachusetts. Since no sample survey data are available for 1928, about the only analysis feasible in inspection of election returns for geographic units contrasting in their population composition. Lest it be supposed, however, that the good citizens of Somerville and Ashfield were aberrants simply unlike the remainder of the people of the Commonwealth, examination of a large number of towns and cities is in order. In the interest of both compression and comprehensibility, a mass of data is telescoped into Figure B. The graphs in that figure compare over the period 1916–1952 the voting behavior of the 29 Massachusetts towns and cities having the sharpest Democratic increases, 1920–1928, with that of the 30 towns and cities having the most marked Democratic loss, 1920–1928. In other words, the figure averages out a great many Ashfields and Somervilles. The data of Figure B confirm the expectation that the pattern exhibited by the pair of voting units in Figure A represented only a single case of a much more general phenomenon. Yet by virtue of the coverage of the data in the figure, one gains a stronger impression of the difference in the character of the election of 1928 and the other elections recorded there. The cleavage confirmed by the 1928 returns persisted. At subsequent elections the voters shifted to and fro within the outlines of the broad division fixed in 1928.

Examination of the characteristics of the two groups of cities and towns of Figure B — those with the most marked Democratic gains, 1920–1928, and those with the widest movement in the opposite direction — reveals the expected sorts of differences. Urban, industrial, foreignborn, Catholic areas made up the bulk of the first group of towns, although an occasional rural Catholic community increased its Democratic vote markedly. The towns with a contrary movement tended to be rural, Protestant, native-born. The new Democratic vote correlated quite closely with a 1930 vote on state enforcement of the national prohibition law.

FIGURE B

Persistence of Electoral Cleavage of 1928 in
Massachusetts: Mean Democratic Percentage of
Presidential Vote in Towns with Sharpest Democratic
Gains, 1920–1928, and in Towns of Widest
Democratic Losses, 1920–1928

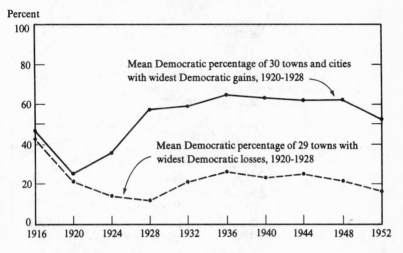

Melancholy experience with the eccentricities of data, be they quantitative or otherwise, suggests the prudence of a check on the interpretation of 1928. Would the same method applied to any other election yield a similar result, *i.e.,* the appearance of a more or less durable realignment? Perhaps there can be no doubt that the impact of the events of any election on many individuals forms lasting party loyalties; yet not often is the number so affected so great as to create a sharp realignment. On the other hand, some elections are characterized by a large-scale transfer of party affection that is quite short-term, a different sort of phenomenon from that which occurs in elections marked by broad and durable shifts in party strength. The difference is illustrated by the data on the election of 1932 in New Hampshire in Figure C. The voting records of the twenty-five towns with the widest Democratic gains from 1928 to 1932 are there traced from 1916 to 1952. Observe that Democratic strength in these towns shot up in 1932 but fairly quickly resumed about the same position in relation to other towns that it had occupied in 1928. It is also evident from the graph that this group of towns had on the whole been especially strongly repelled by the Democratic appeal of 1928. Probably the depression drove an appreciable number of hardened Republicans of these towns to vote for a change in 1932, but they gradually found their way back

FIGURE C

Impact of Election of 1932 in New Hampshire:
Mean Democratic Percentage of Presidential Vote of
Towns with Sharpest Democratic Gain, 1928–1932,
Compared with Mean Vote of Towns at Opposite
Extreme of 1928–1932 Change

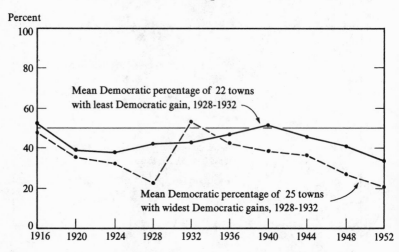

to the party of their fathers. In any case, the figure reflects a type of
behavior differing markedly from that of 1928. To the extent that
1932 resembled 1928 in the recrystallization of party lines, the proportions of new Democrats did not differ significantly among the groups
of towns examined. In fact, what probably happened to a considerable
extent in New England was that the 1928 election broke the electorate into two new groups that would have been formed in 1932 had
there been no realignment in 1928.

The Massachusetts material has served both to explain the method
of analysis and to present the case of a single state. Examinations of the
election of 1928 in other New England states indicate that in each a
pattern prevailed similar to that of Massachusetts. The total effect of
the realignment differed, of course, from state to state. In Massachusetts and Rhode Island the number of people affected by the upheaval
of 1928 was sufficient to form a new majority coalition. In Maine, New
Hampshire, and Vermont the same sort of reshuffling of electors
occurred, but the proportions affected were not sufficient to overturn
the Republican combination, although the basis was laid in Maine
and New Hampshire for later limited Democratic successes. To under-
pin these remarks the materials on Connecticut, Maine, New Hamp-

shire, and Rhode Island are presented in Figure D. The data on Vermont, excluded for lack of space, form a pattern similar to that emerging from the analysis of the other states.

In the interpretation of all these 1928 analyses certain limitations of the technique need to be kept in mind. The data and the technique most clearly reveal a shift when voters of different areas move in opposite directions. From 1928 to 1936 apparently a good deal of Democratic growth occurred in virtually all geographic units, a shift not shown up sharply by the technique. Hence, the discussion may fail adequately to indicate the place of 1928 as the crucial stage in a process of electoral change that began before and concluded after that year.

II

One of the difficulties with an ideal type is that no single actual case fits exactly its specifications. Moreover, in any system of categorization the greater the number of differentiating criteria for classes, the more nearly one tends to create a separate class for each instance. If taxonomic systems are to be of analytical utility, they must almost inevitably group together instances that are unlike at least in peripheral characteristics irrelevant to the purpose of the system. All of which serves to warn that an election is about to be classified as critical even though in some respects the behavior involved differed from that of the 1928 polling.

Central to our concept of critical elections is a realignment within the electorate both sharp and durable. With respect to these basic criteria the election of 1896 falls within the same category as that of 1928, although it differed in other respects. The persistence of the new division of 1896 was perhaps not so notable as that of 1928; yet the Democratic defeat was so demoralizing and so thorough that the party could make little headway in regrouping its forces until 1916. Perhaps the significant feature of the 1896 contest was that, at least in New England, it did not form a new division in which partisan lines became more nearly congruent with lines separating classes, religions, or other such social groups. Instead, the Republicans succeeded in drawing new support, in about the same degree, from all sorts of economic and social classes. The result was an electoral coalition formidable in its mass but which required both good fortune and skill in political management for its maintenance, given its latent internal contradictions.

If the 1896 election is described in our terms as a complex of behavior preceding and following the formal voting, an account of the action must include the panic of 1893. Bank failures, railroad receiverships, unemployment, strikes, Democratic championship of deflation and of the gold standard, and related matters created the setting for a

FIGURE D

Realignment of 1928 in Connecticut, Maine, New Hampshire, and Rhode Island

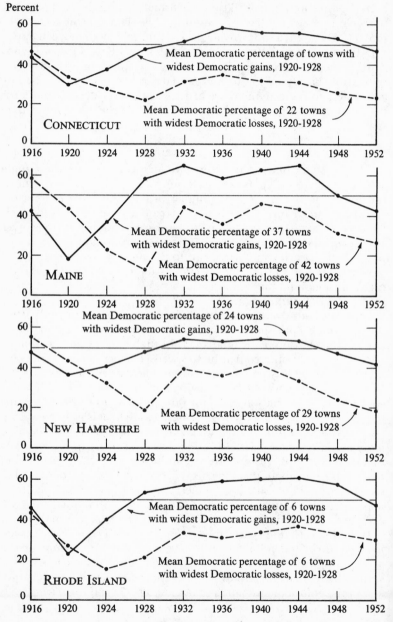

Percent

CONNECTICUT

Mean Democratic percentage of towns with widest Democratic gains, 1920-1928

Mean Democratic percentage of 22 towns with widest Democratic losses, 1920-1928

1916 1920 1924 1928 1932 1936 1940 1944 1948 1952

MAINE

Mean Democratic percentage of 37 towns with widest Democratic gains, 1920-1928

Mean Democratic percentage of 42 towns with widest Democratic losses, 1920-1928

1916 1920 1924 1928 1932 1936 1940 1944 1948 1952

NEW HAMPSHIRE

Mean Democratic percentage of 24 towns with widest Democratic gains, 1920-1928

Mean Democratic percentage of 29 towns with widest Democratic losses, 1920-1928

1916 1920 1924 1928 1932 1936 1940 1944 1948 1952

RHODE ISLAND

Mean Democratic percentage of 6 towns with widest Democratic gains, 1920-1928

Mean Democratic percentage of 6 towns with widest Democratic losses, 1920-1928

1916 1920 1924 1928 1932 1936 1940 1944 1948 1952

Democratic setback in 1894. Only one of the eight New England Democratic Representatives survived the elections of 1894. The two 1892 Democratic governors fell by the wayside and in all the states the Democratic share of the gubernatorial vote fell sharply in 1894. The luckless William Jennings Bryan and the free-silver heresy perhaps did not contribute as much as is generally supposed to the 1892–1896 decline in New England Democratic strength; New England Democrats moved in large numbers over to the Republican ranks in 1894.

The character of the 1892–1896 electoral shift is suggested by the data of Figure E, which presents an analysis of Connecticut and New Hampshire made by the technique used earlier in examining the election of 1928. The graphs make plain that in these states (and the other New England states show the same pattern) the rout of 1896 produced a basic realignment that persisted at least until 1916. The graphs in

FIGURE E

Realignment of 1896 in Connecticut and New Hampshire

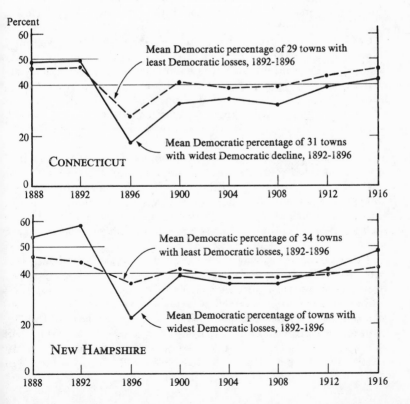

Percent

Mean Democratic percentage of 29 towns with least Democratic losses, 1892-1896

Mean Democratic percentage of 31 towns with widest Democratic decline, 1892-1896

CONNECTICUT

Mean Democratic percentage of 34 towns with least Democratic losses, 1892-1896

Mean Democratic percentage of towns with widest Democratic losses, 1892-1896

NEW HAMPSHIRE

Figure E also make equally plain that the 1892–1896 realignment differed radically from that of 1928 in certain respects. In 1896 the net movement in all sorts of geographic units was toward the Republicans; towns differed not in the direction of their movement but only in the extent. Moreover, the persistence of the realignment of 1896 was about the same in those towns with the least Democratic loss from 1892 to 1896 as it was in those with the most marked decline in Democratic strength. Hence, the graphs differ from those on 1928 which took the form of opening scissors. Instead, the 1896 realignment appears as a parallel movement of both groups to a lower plateau of Democratic strength.

If the election of 1896 had had a notable differential impact on geographically segregated social groups, the graphs in Figure E of towns at the extremes of the greatest and least 1892–96 change would have taken the form of opening scissors as they did in 1928. While the election of 1896 is often pictured as a last-ditch fight between the haves and the have-nots, that understanding of the contest was, at least in New England, evidently restricted to planes of leadership and oratory. It did not extend to the voting actions of the electorate. These observations merit some buttressing, although the inference emerges clearly enough from Figure E.

Unfortunately the census authorities have ignored the opportunity to advance demographic inquiry by publishing data of consequence about New England towns. Not much information is available on the characteristics of the populations of these small geographic areas. Nevertheless, size of total population alone is a fair separator of towns according to politically significant characteristics. Classification of towns according to that criterion groups them roughly according to industrialization and probably generally also according to religion and national origin. Hence, with size of population of towns and cities as a basis, Table 1 contrasts the elections of 1896 and 1928 for different types of towns. Observe from the table that the mean shift between 1892 and 1896 was about the same for varying size groups of towns. Contrast this lack of association between size and political movement with the radically different 1920–28 pattern which also appears in the table.

Table 1 makes clear that in 1896 the industrial cities, in their aggregate vote at least, moved toward the Republicans in about the same degree as did the rural farming communities. Some of the misinterpretations of the election of 1896 flow from a focus on that election in isolation rather than in comparison with the preceding election. In 1896, even in New England cities, the Democrats tended to be strongest in the poor, working-class, immigrant sections. Yet the same relation had existed, in a sharper form, in 1892. In 1896 the Republicans gained in

TABLE ONE

Contrasts between Elections of 1896 and 1928 in
Massachusetts: Shifts in Democratic Strength, 1892–1896 and
1920–1928, in Relation to Population Size of Towns

Population size group	Mean Democratic percentage		Mean change	Mean Democratic percentage		Mean change
	1892	1896	1892–96	1920	1928	1920–28
1–999	34.0	14.7	−19.3	16.5	18.6	+2.1
2000–2999	38.8	18.3	−20.5	21.0	33.1	+12.1
10,000–14,999	46.7	26.9	−19.8	25.8	43.7	+17.9
50,000+	47.7	30.1	−17.6	29.5	55.7	+26.2

the working-class wards, just as they did in the silk-stocking wards,
over their 1892 vote. They were able to place the blame for unemployment upon the Democrats and to propagate successfully the doctrine
that the Republican Party was the party of prosperity and the "full
dinner pail." On the whole, the effect apparently was to reduce the
degree of coincidence of class affiliation and partisan inclination. Nor
was the election of 1896, in New England at least, a matter of heightened tension between city and country. Both city and country voters
shifted in the same direction. Neither urban employers nor industrial
workers could generate much enthusiasm for inflation and free trade;
rather they joined in common cause. Instead of a sharpening of class
cleavages within New England the voting apparently reflected more a
sectional antagonism and anxiety, shared by all classes, expressed in
opposition to the dangers supposed to be threatening from the West.

Other contrasts between the patterns of electoral behavior of 1896
and 1928 could be cited but in terms of sharpness and durability of
realignment both elections were of roughly the same type, at least in
New England. In these respects they seem to differ from most other
elections over a period of a half century, although it may well be that
each round at the ballot boxes involves realignment within the electorate similar in kind but radically different in extent.

III

The discussion points toward the analytical utility of a
system for the differentiation of elections. A concept of critical elections has been developed to cover a type of election in which there
occurs a sharp and durable electoral realignment between parties,
although the techniques employed do not yield any information of
consequences about the mechanisms for the maintenance of a new
alignment, once it is formed. Obviously any sort of system for the gross

characterization of elections presents difficulties in application. The actual election rarely presents in pure form a case fitting completely any particular concept. Especially in a large and diverse electorate a single polling may encompass radically varying types of behavior among different categories of voters; yet a dominant characteristic often makes itself apparent. Despite such difficulties, the attempt to move toward a better understanding of elections in the terms here employed could provide a means for better integrating the study of electoral behavior with the analysis of political systems. In truth, a considerable proportion of the study of electoral behavior has only a tenuous relation to politics.

The sorts of questions here raised, when applied sufficiently broadly on a comparative basis and carried far enough, could lead to a consideration of basic problems of the nature of democratic orders. A question occurs, for example, about the character of the consequences for the political system of the temporal frequency of critical elections. What are the consequences for public administration, for the legislative process, for the operation of the economy of frequent serious upheavals within the electorate? What are the correlates of that pattern of behavior? And, for those disposed to raise such questions, what underlying changes might alter the situation? Or, when viewed from the contrary position, what consequences flow from an electorate which is disposed, in effect, to remain largely quiescent over considerable periods? Does a state of moving equilibrium reflect a pervasive satisfaction with the course of public policy? An indifference about matters political? In any case, what are the consequences for the public order? Further, what are the consequences when an electorate builds up habits and attachments, or faces situations, that make it impossible for it to render a decisive and clear-cut popular verdict that promises not to be upset by caprice at the next round of polling? What are the consequences of a situation that creates recurring, evenly balanced an electorate or what conditions permit sharp and decisive changes in the power structure from time to time? Such directions of speculation are suggested by a single criterion for the differentiation of elections. Further development of an electoral typology would probably point to useful speculation in a variety of directions.

CHAPTER FIVE

Interest Groups and Their Demands

Interest groups are vital cogs in the wheel of the democratic process. Although *Federalist 10* suggests that one of the major purposes of the separation of powers system is to break and control the "evil effects" of faction, modern political theorists take a much more sanguine view of the role that political interest groups as well as parties play in government. No longer are interest groups defined as being opposed to the "public interest." They are vital channels through which particular publics participate in the governmental process. This chapter will examine the origin and nature of contemporary interest group theory, and illustrate the way in which interest groups function.

Interest Groups and Constitutional Government: The Theory of Concurrent Majority

It is very useful to discuss the operation of interest groups within the framework of what can best be described as a concurrent majority system. In contemporary usage the phrase "concurrent majority" means a system in which major government policy decisions must be approved by the dominant interest groups directly affected. The word "concurrent" suggests that each group involved must give its consent before policy can be enacted. Thus a concurrent majority is a majority of each group considered separately. If we take as an example an area such as agricultural policy, in which three or four major private interest groups can be identified, we can say that the concurrent majority is reached when each group affected gives its approval before agricultural policy is passed. The extent to which such a system of concurrent majority is actually functioning is a matter that has not been fully clarified by empirical research. Nevertheless, it does seem tenable to conclude that in many major areas of public policy, it is necessary at least to achieve a concurrent majority of the *major* or *dominant* interests affected.

The *theory* of concurrent majority originated with John C. Calhoun. Calhoun, born in 1781, had a distinguished career in public service at both the national and state levels. The idea of concurrent majority evolved from the concept of state nullification of federal law. Under this states' rights doctrine, states would be able to veto any national action. The purpose of this procedure was theoretically to protect states in a minority from encroachment by a national majority that could act through Congress, the President, and even the Supreme Court. Those who favored this procedure had little faith in the separation of powers doctrine as an effective device to prevent the arbitrary exercise of national power. At the end of his career Calhoun decided to incorporate his earlier views on state nullification into a more substantial theoretical treatise in political science; thus he wrote his famous *Disquisition on Government* in the decade between 1840 and 1850. He attempted to develop a general theory of constitutional (limited) government, the primary mechanism of which would be the ability of the major interest groups (states in Calhoun's time) to veto legislation adverse to their interests. Students should overlook some of the theoretical inconsistencies in Calhoun and concentrate upon the basic justification he advances for substituting his system of concurrent majority for the separation of powers device. Under the latter, group interests are not necessarily taken into account, for national laws can be passed on the basis of a numerical majority. And even though this majority may reflect the interests of some groups, it will not necessarily reflect the interests of all groups affected. Thus Calhoun is arguing that a system in which the major interest groups can dominate the policy process is really more in accord with constitutional democracy than the system established in our Constitution and supported in *Federalist 10*.

20 JOHN C. CALHOUN

A DISQUISITION ON GOVERNMENT

. . . What I propose is . . . to explain on what principles government must be formed in order to resist by its own interior structure — or to use a single term, *organism* — the tendency to abuse of power. This structure . . . is what is meant by constitution, in its strict and more usual sense; and it is this which distinguishes what are called "constitutional" governments from "absolute." . . .

How government, then, must be constructed in order to counteract, through its organism, this tendency on the part of those who make and execute the laws to oppress those subject to their operation is the next question which claims attention.

There is but one way in which this can possibly be done, and that is by such an organism as will furnish the ruled with the means of resisting successfully this tendency on the part of the rulers to oppression and abuse. Power can only be resisted by power — and tendency by tendency. Those who exercise power and those subject to its exercise — the rulers and the ruled — stand in antagonistic relations to each other. The same constitution of our nature which leads rulers to oppress the ruled — regardless of the object for which government is ordained — will, with equal strength, lead the ruled to resist when possessed of the means of making peaceable and effective resistance. Such an organism, then, as will furnish the means by which resistance may be systematically and peaceably made on the part of the ruled to oppression and abuse of power on the part of the rulers is the first and indispensable step toward *forming* a constitutional government. And as this can only be effected by or through the right of suffrage — the right on the part of the ruled to choose their rulers at proper intervals and to hold them thereby responsible for their conduct — the responsibility of the rulers to the ruled, through the right of suffrage, is the indispensable and primary principle in the foundation of a constitutional government. When this right is properly guarded, and the people sufficiently enlightened to understand their own rights and the interests of the community and duly to appreciate the motives and conduct of those appointed to make and execute the laws, it is all-sufficient to give to those who elect effective control over those they have elected.

I call the right of suffrage the indispensable and primary principle, for it would be a great and dangerous mistake to suppose, as many do, that it is, of itself, sufficient to form constitutional governments. To this erroneous opinion may be traced one of the causes why so few attempts to form constitutional governments have succeeded, and why of the few which have, so small a number have had durable existence. It has led not only to mistakes in the attempts to form such governments, but to their overthrow when they have, by some good fortune, been correctly formed. So far from being, of itself, sufficient — however well guarded it might be and however enlightened the people — it would, unaided by other provisions, leave the government as absolute as it would be in the hands of irresponsible rulers; and with a tendency, at least as strong, toward oppression and abuse of its power, as I shall next proceed to explain.

. . . The right of suffrage . . . transfers, in reality, the actual control over the government from those who make and execute the laws to the body of the community and thereby places the powers of the government as fully in the mass of the community as they would be if they, in fact, had assembled, made, and executed the laws themselves without the intervention of representatives or agents. The more perfectly it does this, the more perfectly it accomplishes its ends; but in doing so, it only changes the seat of authority without counteracting, in the least, the tendency of the government to oppression and abuse of its powers.

If the whole community had the same interests so that the interests of each and every portion would be so affected by the action of the government that the laws which oppressed or impoverished one portion would necessarily oppress and impoverish all others — or the reverse — then the right of suffrage, of itself, would be all-sufficient to counteract the tendency of the government to oppression and abuse of its powers, and, of course, would form, of itself, a perfect constitutional government. . . .

But such is not the case. On the contrary, nothing is more difficult than to equalize the action of the government in reference to the various and diversified interests of the community; and nothing more easy than to pervert its powers into instruments to aggrandize and enrich one or more interests by oppressing and impoverishing the others. . . . The more extensive and populous the country, the more diversified the condition and pursuits of its population; and the richer, more luxurious, and dissimilar the people, the more difficult is it to equalize the action of the government, and the more easy for one portion of the community to pervert its powers to oppress and plunder the other.

Such being the case, it necessarily results that the right of suffrage, by placing the control of the government in the community, must, from the same constitution of our nature which makes government necessary to preserve society, lead to conflict among its different interests — each striving to obtain possession of its powers as the means of protecting itself against the others or of advancing its respective interests regardless of the interests of others. For this purpose, a struggle will take place between the various interests to obtain a majority in order to control the government. If no one interest be strong enough, of itself, to obtain it, a combination will be formed between those whose interests are most alike — each conceding something to the others until a sufficient number is obtained to make a majority. The process may be slow and much time may be required before a compact, organized majority can be thus formed, but formed it will be in time, even without preconcert or design, by the sure workings of that principle or constitution of our nature in which government itself originates. When once formed, the community will be divided into two great parties — a major and minor — between which there will be incessant struggles on the one side to retain, and on the other to obtain the majority and, thereby, the control of the government and the advantages it confers. . . .

Nor is it less certain . . . that the dominant majority . . . would have the same tendency to oppression and abuse of power which, without the right of suffrage, irresponsible rulers would have. No reason, indeed, can be assigned why the latter would abuse their power, which would not apply, with equal force, to the former. The dominant majority, for the time, would in reality, through the right of suffrage, be the rulers — the controlling, governing, and irresponsible power; and those who make and execute the laws would, for the time, be in reality but *their* representatives and agents.

Nor would the fact that the former would constitute a majority of the community counteract a tendency originating in the constitution of man and which, as such, cannot depend on the number by whom the powers of the government may be wielded. . . . Be it which it may, the minority, for the time, will be as much the governed or subject portion as are the people in an aristocracy or the subjects in a monarchy. The only difference in this respect is that in the government of a majority the minority may become the majority, and the majority the minority, through the right of suffrage, and thereby change their relative positions without the intervention of force and revolution. But the duration or uncertainty of the tenure by which power is held cannot, of itself, counteract the tendency inherent in government to oppression and abuse of power. On the contrary, the very uncertainty of the tenure, combined with the violent party warfare which must ever precede a change of parties under such governments, would rather tend to increase than diminish the tendency to oppression.

As, then, the right of suffrage, without some other provision, cannot counteract this tendency of government, the next question for consideration is, What is that other provision? . . .

From what has been said, it is manifest that this provision must be of a character calculated to prevent any one interest or combination of interests from using the powers of government to aggrandize itself at the expense of the others. . . . There is but one certain mode in which this result can be secured, and that is by the adoption of some restriction or limitation which shall so effectually prevent any one interest or combination of interests from obtaining the exclusive control of the government as to render hopeless all attempts directed to that end. There is, again, but one mode in which this can be effected, and that is by taking the sense of each interest or portion of the community which may be unequally and injuriously affected by the action of the government separately, through its own majority or in some other way by which its voice may be fairly expressed, and to require the consent of each interest either to put or to keep the government in action. This, too, can be accomplished only . . . by dividing and distributing the powers of government, giv[ing] to each division or interest, through its appropriate organ, either a concurrent voice in making and executing the laws or a veto on their execution. It is only by such an organism that the assent of each can be made necessary to put the government in motion, or the power made effectual to arrest its action when put in motion; and it is only by the one or the other that the different interests, orders, classes, or portions into which the community may be divided can be protected, and all conflict and struggle between them prevented — by rendering it impossible to put or to keep it in action without the concurrent consent of all.

Such an organism as this, combined with the right of suffrage, constitutes, in fact, the elements of constitutional government. The one, by rendering those who make and execute the laws responsible to those on whom they operate, prevents the rulers from oppressing the ruled; and the other, by making it impossible for any one interest or combination of interests, or class, or order, or portion of the community to obtain exclusive control, prevents any one of them from oppressing the other. It is clear that oppression and abuse of power must come, if at all, from the one or the other quarter. . . . It follows that the two, suffrage and proper organism combined, are sufficient to counteract the tendency of government to oppression and abuse of power and to restrict it to the fulfillment of the great ends for which it is ordained.

In coming to this conclusion I have assumed the organism to be perfect and the different interests, portions, or classes of the community to be sufficiently enlightened to understand its character and object, and to exercise, with due intelligence, the right of suffrage. . . . Where the organism is perfect, every interest will be truly and fully represented, and of course the whole community must be so. It may be difficult, or even impossible, to make a perfect organism — but, although this be true, yet even when, instead of the sense of each and of all, *it takes that of a few great and prominent interests only,* it would still, in a great measure, if not altogether, fulfill the end intended by a constitution. For in such case it would require so large a portion of the community, compared with the whole, to concur or acquiesce in the action of the government that the number to be plundered would be too few and the number to be aggrandized too many to afford adequate notices to oppression and the abuse of its powers. . . .

It results, from what has been said, that there are two different modes in which the sense of the community may be taken: one, simply by the right of suffrage, unaided; the other, by the right through a proper organism. Each collects the sense of the majority. But one regards numbers only and considers the whole community as a unit having but one common interest throughout, and collects the sense of the greater number of the whole as that of the community. The other, on the contrary, regards interests as well as numbers — considering the community as made up of different and conflicting interests, as far as the action of the government is concerned — and takes the sense of each through its majority or appropriate organ, and the united sense of all as the sense of the entire community. The former of these I shall call the numerical or absolute majority, and the latter, the concurrent or constitutional majority. . . .

The Nature and Functions of Interest Groups

> What is an "interest group"? The typical picture painted of interest or "Pressure" groups presents an evil-minded, crooked-nosed lobbyist attempting to corner a congressman to get him to vote for some "selfish" proposal which is, of course, against the "public interest." Lobbyists and interest groups are generally considered to be bad, working for their own ends against a higher national purpose.
>
> The following selection, taken from David Truman's *The Governmental Process* (1951), contains (1) a definition of the term "interest group" and (2) a brief outline of a frame of reference within which the operations of interest groups should be considered. A fairly articulate interest group theory of the governmental process is sketched by Truman. It will become evident to the student of American government that interest groups, like political parties, form an integral part of our political system. Further, interest group theory suggests an entirely new way of looking at government.

21   DAVID TRUMAN

THE GOVERNMENTAL PROCESS

INTEREST GROUPS

Interest group refers to any group that, on the basis of one or more shared attitudes, makes certain claims upon other groups in the society for the establishment, maintenance, or enhancement of forms of behavior that are implied by the shared attitudes. . . . [F]rom interaction in groups arise certain common habits of response, which may be called norms, or shared attitudes. These afford the participants frames of reference for interpreting and evaluating events and behaviors. In this respect all groups are interest groups because they are shared-attitude groups. In some groups at various points in time, however, a second kind of common response emerges, in addition to the frame of reference. These are shared attitudes toward what is needed or wanted in a given situation, as demands or claims upon other groups in the society. The term "interest group" will be reserved here for those groups that exhibit both aspects of the shared attitudes. . . .

Definition of the interest group in this fashion . . . permits the identification of various potential as well as existing interest groups. That is, it invites examination of an interest whether or not it is found at the moment as one of the characteristics of a particular organized group. Although no group that makes claims upon other groups in the society will be found without an interest or interests, it is possible to examine interests that are not at a particular point in time the basis of interactions among individuals, but that may become such. . . .

GROUPS AND GOVERNMENT:
DIFFICULTIES IN A GROUP INTERPRETATION OF POLITICS

Since we are engaged in an effort to develop a conception of the political process in the United States that will account adequately for the role of groups, particularly interest groups, it will be appropriate to take account of some of the factors that have been regarded as obstacles to such a conception and that have caused such groups to be neglected in many explanations of the dynamics of government. Perhaps the most important practical reason for this neglect is that the significance of groups has only fairly recently been forced

From David Truman, *The Governmental Process.* Reprinted by permission of Alfred A. Knopf, Inc. Copyright © 1952, by Regents of U. of Michigan.

to the attention of political scientists by the tremendous growth in the number of formally organized groups in the United States within the last few decades. It is difficult and unnecessary to attempt to date the beginning of such attention, but Herring in 1929, in his ground-breaking book, *Group Representation Before Congress,* testified to the novelty of the observations he reported when he stated: "There has developed in this government an extra-legal machinery of as integral and of as influential a nature as the system of party government that has long been an essential part of the government. . . ." Some implications of this development are not wholly compatible with some of the proverbial notions about representative government held by specialists as well as laymen. . . . This apparent incompatibility has obstructed the inclusion of group behaviors in an objective description of the governmental process.

More specifically, it is usually argued that any attempt at the interpretation of politics in terms of group patterns inevitably "leaves something out" or "destroys something essential" about the processes of "our" government. On closer examination, we find this argument suggesting that two "things" are certain to be ignored: the individual, and a sort of totally inclusive unity designated by such terms as "society" and "the state."

The argument that the individual is ignored in any interpretation of politics as based upon groups seems to assume a differentiation or conflict between "the individual" and some such collectivity as the group. . . .

Such assumptions need not present any difficulties in the development of a group interpretation of politics, because they are essentially unwarranted. They simply do not square with . . . evidence concerning group affiliations and individual behavior. . . . We do not, in fact, find individuals otherwise than in groups; complete isolation in space and time is so rare as to be an almost hypothetical situation. It is equally demonstrable that the characteristics of any interest group, including the activities by which we identify it, are governed by the attitudes and the circumstances that gave rise to the interactions of which it consists. There are variable factors, and, although the role played by a particular individual may be quite different in a lynch mob from that of the same individual in a meeting of the church deacons, the attitudes and behaviors involved in both are as much a part of his personality as is his treatment of his family. "The individual" and "the group" are at most merely convenient ways of classifying behavior, two ways of approaching the same phenomena, not different things.

The persistence among nonspecialists of the notion of an inherent conflict between "the individual" and "the group" or "society" is understandable in view of the doctrines of individualism that have underlain various political and economic conflicts over the past three centuries. The notion persists also because it harmonizes with a view of the isolated and independent individual as the "cause" of complicated human events. The personification of events, quite apart from any ethical considerations, is a kind of shorthand convenient in everyday speech and, like supernatural explanations of natural phenomena, has a comforting simplicity. Explanations that take into account multiple causes, including group affiliations, are difficult. The "explanation" of a national complex like the Soviet Union wholly in terms of a Stalin or the "description" of the intricacies of the American government entirely in terms of a Roosevelt is quick and easy. . . .

The second major difficulty allegedly inherent in any attempt at a group interpretation of the political process is that such an explanation inevitably must ignore some greater unity designated as society or the state. . . .

Many of those who place particular emphasis upon this difficulty assume explicitly or implicitly that there is an interest of the nation as a whole, universally and invariably held and standing apart from and superior to those of the various groups included within it. This assumption is close to the popular dogmas of democratic government based on the familiar notion that if only people are free and have access to "the facts," they will all want the same thing in any political situation. It is no derogation of democratic preferences to state that such an assertion flies in the face of all that we know of the behavior of men in a complex society. Were it in fact true, not only the interest group but even the political party should properly be viewed as an abnormality. The differing experiences and perceptions of men not only encourage individuality but also . . . inevitably result in differing attitudes and conflicting group affiliations. "There are," says Bentley in his discussion of this error of the social whole, "always some parts of the nation to be found arrayed against other parts." [From *The Process of Government* (1908).] Even in war, when a totally inclusive interest should be apparent if it is ever going to be, we always find pacifists, conscientious objectors, spies, and subversives, who reflect interests opposed to those of "the nation as a whole."

There is a political significance in assertions of a totally inclusive interest within a nation. Particularly in times of crisis, such as an international war, such claims are a tremendously useful promotional device by means of which a particularly extensive group or league of groups tries to reduce or eliminate opposing interests. Such is the pain attendant upon not "belonging" to one's "own" group that if a normal person can be convinced that he is the lone dissenter to an otherwise universally accepted agreement, he usually will conform. This pressure accounts at least in part for the number of prewar pacifists who, when the United States entered World War II, accepted the draft or volunteered. Assertion of an inclusive "national" or "public interest" is an effective device in many less critical situations as well. In themselves, these claims are part of the data of politics. However, they do not describe any actual or possible political situation within a complex modern nation. In developing a group interpretation of politics, therefore, we do not need to account for a totally inclusive interest, because one does not exist.

Denying the existence of an interest of the nation as a whole does not completely dispose of the difficulty raised by those who insist that a group interpretation must omit "the state." We cannot deny the obvious fact that we are examining a going political system that is supported or at least accepted by a large proportion of the society. We cannot account for such a system by adding up in some fashion the National Association of Manufacturers, the Congress of Industrial Organizations, the American Farm Bureau Federation, the American Legion, and other groups that come to mind when "lobbies" and "pressure groups" are mentioned. Even if the political parties are added to the list, the result could properly be designated as "a view which seems hardly compatible with the relative stability of the political system. . . ." Were such the exclusive ingredients of the political process in the United States, the entire system would have torn itself apart long since.

If these various organized interest groups more or less consistently reconcile their differences, adjust, and accept compromises, we must acknowledge that we are dealing with a system that is not accounted for by the "sum" of the organized interest groups in the society. We must go farther to explain the operation of such ideals or traditions as constitutionalism, civil liberties, representative responsibility, and the like. These are not, however, a sort of disembodied metaphysical influence, like Mr. Justice Holmes's "brooding omnipresence." We know of the existence of such factors only from the behavior and the habitual interactions of men. If they exist in this fashion, they are interests. We can account for their operation and for the system by recognizing such interests as representing what . . . we called potential interest groups in the "becoming" stage of activity. "It is certainly true," as Bentley has made clear, "that we must accept a . . . group of this kind as an interest group itself." It makes no difference that we cannot find the home office and the executive secretary of such a group. Organization in this formal sense, as we have seen, represents merely a stage or degree of interaction that may or may not be significant at any particular point in time. Its absence does not mean that these interests do not exist, that the familiar "pressure groups" do not operate as if such potential groups were organized and active, or that these interests may not move from the potential to the organized stage of activity.

It thus appears that the two major difficulties supposedly obstacles to a group interpretation of the political process are not insuperable. We can employ the fact of individuality and we can account for the existence of the state without doing violence to the evidence available from the observed behaviors of men and groups. . . .

INTEREST GROUPS AND THE NATURE OF THE STATE

Men, wherever they are observed, are creatures participating in those established patterns of interaction that we call groups. Excepting perhaps the most casual and transitory, these continuing interactions, like all such interpersonal relationships, involve power. This power is exhibited in two closely interdependent ways. In the first place, the group exerts power over its members; an individual's group affiliations largely determine his attitudes, values, and the frames of reference in terms of which he interprets his experiences. For a measure of conformity to the norms of the group is the price of acceptance within it. . . . In the second place, the group, if it is or becomes an interest group, which any group in a society may be, exerts power over other groups in the society when it successfully imposes claims upon them.

Many interest groups, probably an increasing proportion in the United States, are politicized. That is, either from the outset or from time to time in the course of their development they make their claims through or upon the institutions of government. Both the forms and functions of government in turn are a reflection of the activities and claims of such groups. . . .

The institutions of government are centers of interest-based power; their connections with interest groups may be latent or overt and their activities range in political character from the routinized and widely accepted to the unstable and highly controversial. In order to make claims, political interest groups will seek access to the key points of decision within these institutions. Such points are scattered throughout the structure, including not only the formally established branches of government but also the political parties in their various forms and the relationships between governmental units and other interest groups.

The extent to which a group achieves effective access to the institutions of government is the resultant of a complex of interdependent factors. For the sake of simplicity these may be classified in three somewhat overlapping categories: (1) factors relating to a group's strategic position in the society; (2) factors associated with the internal characteristics of the group; and (3) factors peculiar to the governmental institutions themselves. In the first category are: the group's status or prestige in the society, affecting the ease with which it commands deference from those outside its bounds; the standing it and its activities have when measured against the widely held but largely unorganized interests or "rules of the game"; the extent to which government officials are formally or informally "members" of the group; and the usefulness of the group as a source of technical and political knowledge. The second category includes: the degree and appropriateness of the group's organization; the degree of cohesion it can achieve in a given situation, especially in the light of competing group demands upon its membership; the skills of the leadership; and the group's resources in numbers and money. In the third category are: the operating structure of the government institutions, since such established features involve relatively fixed advantages and handicaps; and the effects of the group life of particular units or branches of the government. . . .

A characteristic feature of the governmental system in the United States is that it contains a multiplicity of points of access. The federal system establishes decentralized and more or less independent centers of power, vantage points from which to secure privileged access to the national government. Both a sign and a cause of the strength of the constituent units in the federal scheme is the peculiar character of our party system, which has strengthened parochial relationships, especially those of national legislators. National parties, and to a lesser degree those in the States, tend to be poorly cohesive leagues of locally based organizations rather than unified and inclusive structures. Staggered terms for executive officials and various types of legislators accentuate differences in the effective electorates that participate in choosing these officers. Each of these different, often opposite, localized patterns (constituencies) is a channel of independent access to the larger party aggregation and to the formal government. Thus, especially at the national level, the party is an electing-device and only in limited measure an integrated means of policy determination. Within the Congress, furthermore, controls are diffused among committee chairmen and other leaders in both chambers. The variety of these points of access is further supported by relationships stemming from the constitutional doctrine of separation of powers, from related checks and balances, and at the State and local level from the common practice of choosing an array of executive officials by popular election. At the Federal level the formal simplicity of the executive branch has been complicated by a Supreme Court decision that has placed a number of administrative agencies beyond the removal power of the president. The position of these units, however, differs only in degree from that of many that are constitutionally within the executive branch. In consequence of alternative lines of access available through the legislature and the executive and of divided channels for the control of administrative policy, many nominally executive agencies are at various times virtually independent of the chief executive.

. . . Within limits, therefore, organized interest groups, gravitating toward responsive points of decision, may play one segment of the structure against another as circumstances and strategic considerations permit. The total pattern of government over a period of time thus presents a protean complex of crisscrossing relationships that change in strength and direction with alternations in the power and standing of interests, organized and unorganized.

From Truman's definition *any* group, organized or unorganized, which has a shared attitude toward goals and methods for achieving them should be classified as an "interest group." Truman is essentially saying that, since people generally function as members of groups, it is more useful and accurate for the political observer to view the governmental process as the interaction of political interest groups. If one accepts the sociologist's assumption that men act and interact only as members of groups, then it is imperative that the governmental process be viewed as one of interest group interaction.

Within the framework of Truman's definition it is possible to identify both *public* and *private* interest groups. In the political process governmental groups sometimes act as interest groups in the same sense as private organizations. In many public policies, governmental groups may have more at stake than private organizations. Thus administrative agencies, for example, may "lobby" as vigorously as their private counterparts to advance their own interests.

The discussion by V. O. Key, Jr., concentrates upon private pressure groups and the extent to which they are links between public opinion and government. One of the most interesting conclusions of Key is that the elites of interest groups are not able to influence the attitudes of their members to anywhere near the degree commonly thought possible. Pressure group participation in government more often than not reflects highly limited participation by the active elements of the groups. Public policy is often hammered out by very small numbers of individuals both in the government and the private sphere. Political leaders can never stray too far beyond the boundaries of consent, but these are often very broad.

22 V. O. KEY, JR.

PRESSURE GROUPS

Pressure groups occupy a prominent place in analyses of American politics. In a regime characterized by official deference to public opinion and by adherence to the doctrine of freedom of association, private organizations may be regarded as links that connect the citizen and government. They are differentiated in both composition and function from political parties. Ordinarily they concern themselves with only a narrow range of policies, those related to the peculiar interests of the group membership. Their aim is primarily to influence the content of public policy rather than the results of elections. Those groups with a mass membership, though, may oppose or support particular candidates; in that case they are treated as groups with power to affect election results and, thereby, with the capacity to pressure party leaders, legislators, and others in official position to act in accord with their wishes. . . .

Puzzles of Pressure Politics

. . . [There are] a series of puzzles as we seek to describe the role of pressure groups as links between opinion and government. Clearly the model of the lobbyist who speaks for a united following, determined in its aims and prepared to reward its friends and punish its enemies at the polls, does not often fit reality. Nor is it probable that the unassisted effort of pressure organizations to mold public opinion in support of their position has a large effect upon mass opinion. Yet legislators listen respectfully to the representations of the spokesmen of private groups, which in turn spend millions of dollars every year in propagandizing the public. Leaders of private groups articulate the concerns of substantial numbers of persons, even though they may not have succeeded in indoctrinating completely the members of their own groups. All this activity must have some functional significance in the political system. The problem is to identify its functions in a manner that seems to make sense. In this endeavor a distinction of utility is that made . . . between mass-membership organizations and nonmass organizations, which far outnumber the former.

From V. O. Key, Jr., *Public Opinion and American Democracy*, pp. 500, 524–31. Reprinted by permission of Alfred A. Knoph, Inc. Copyright © 1961, by V. O. Key, Jr.

Representation of Mass-Membership Groups. Only the spokesmen for mass-membership organizations can give the appearance of representing voters in sufficient numbers to impress (or intimidate) government. The influence of nonmass groups, which often have only a few hundred or a few thousand members, must rest upon something other than the threat of electoral retribution. As has been seen, the reality of the behavior of members of mass organizations is that in the short run they are not manipulable in large numbers by their leaders. Their party identification anchors many of them to a partisan position, and over the longer run they seem to be moved from party to party in presidential elections by the influences that affect all types and classes of people.

The spokesmen of mass-membership groups also labor under the handicap that they may be made to appear to be unrepresentative of the opinions of their members. When the president of an organization announces to a congressional committee that he speaks for several million people, the odds are that a substantial proportion of his members can be shown to have no opinion or even to express views contrary to those voiced by their spokesmen. This divergency is often explained as a wicked betrayal of the membership or as a deliberate departure from the mass mandate. Yet it is not unlikely that another type of explanation more often fits the facts. Opinions, as we have seen in many contexts, do not fall into blacks and whites. It may be the nature of mass groups that attachment to the positions voiced by the peak spokesmen varies with attachment to and involvement in the group. At the leadership level the group position is voiced in its purest and most uncompromising form. A substantial layer of group activists subscribes to the official line, but among those with less involvement the faith wins less general acceptance. At the periphery of the group, though, the departure from the official line may be more a matter of indifference than of dissent. Leadership policy is often pictured as the consequence of interaction between leadership and group membership, which may be only partially true. Leaders may be more accurately regarded as dedicated souls who bid for group support of their position. Almost invariably they receive something less than universal acquiescence. This may be especially true in mass organizations in which political endeavor is to a degree a side issue — as, for example, in trade unions and farm organizations. As one traces attitudes and opinions across the strata of group membership, the clarity of position and the extremeness of position become more marked at the level of high involvement and activism.

If it is more or less the nature of mass organizations to encompass a spectrum of opinion rather than a single hue, much of the discussion of the representativeness of group leadership may be beside the point.

However that may be, circumstances surrounding the leadership elements of mass organizations place them, in their work of influencing
government, in a position not entirely dissimilar to that of leaders of
nonmass groups. They must rely in large measure on means not unlike
those that must be employed by groups with only the smallest membership. The world of pressure politics becomes more a politics among
the activists than a politics that involves many people. Yet politics
among the activists occurs in a context of concern about public opinion, a concern that colors the mode of action if not invariably its substance.

    Arenas of Decision and Norms of Action. The maneuvers
of pressure-group politics thus come ordinarily to occur among those
highly involved and immediately concerned about public policy; the
connection of these maneuvers with public opinion and even with the
opinions of mass-membership organizations tends to be tenuous.
Many questions of policy are fought out within vaguely bounded arenas in which the activists concerned are clustered. A major factor in
the determination of the balance of forces within each arena is party
control of the relevant governmental apparatus. Included among the
participants in each issue-cluster of activists are the spokesmen for the
pressure groups concerned, the members of the House and Senate committees with jurisdiction, and the officials of the administrative
departments and agencies concerned. In the alliances of pressure politics those between administrative agencies and private groups are
often extremely significant in the determination of courses of action.
The cluster of concerned activists may include highly interested persons, firms, and organizations scattered over the country, though the
boundaries delimiting those concerned vary from question to question, from arena to arena. In short, pressure politics among the activists takes something of the form that it would take if there were no elections or no concern about the nature of public opinion; that is, those
immediately concerned make themselves heard in the process of decision.

    In the give and take among the activists, norms and values with
foundations in public opinion are conditioning factors. The broad
values of the society determine to a degree who will be heard, who can
play the game. Those who claim to speak for groups that advocate
causes outside the range of consensus may be given short shrift. Some
groups advocating perfectly respectable causes may be heard with less
deference than others. Subtle standards define what David Truman
calls "access" to the decisionmakers. To some extent this is a party matter: an AFL-CIO delegation does not expect to be heard with much
sympathy by a committee dominated by right-wing Republicans. The
reality of access, too, may provide an index to the tacit standards in

definition of those interests regarded as having a legitimate concern about public policy. The spokesmen of groups both large and small are often heard with respect, not because they wield power, but because they are perceived as the representatives of interests entitled to be heard and to be accorded consideration as a matter of right.

Within the range of the permissible, the process of politics among the activists is governed to some extent by the expectation that all entitled to play the game shall get a fair deal (or at least a fair hearing before their noses are rubbed in the dirt). Doubtless these practices parallel a fairly widespread set of attitudes within the population generally. Probably those attitudes could be characterized as a disposition to let every group — big business and labor unions as well — have its say, but that such groups should not be permitted to dominate the government. In the implementation of these attitudes the legalism of American legislators plays a role. Frequently congressional committeemen regard themselves as engaged in a judicial role of hearing the evidence and of arriving at decisions based on some sort of standards of equity.

Rituals of the Activists. The maneuvers of group spokesmen, be they spokesmen for mass or nonmass organizations, are often accompanied by rituals in obeisance to the doctrine that public opinion governs. The belief often seems to be that congressmen will be impressed by a demonstration that public opinion demands the proposed line of action or inaction. Hence, groups organize publicity campaigns and turn up sheaves of editorials in support of their position. They stimulate people to write or to wire their congressmen; if the labor of stimulation is too arduous, they begin to sign to telegrams names chosen at random from the telephone directory. They solicit the endorsement of other organizations for their position. They lobby the American Legion and the General Federation of Women's Clubs for allies willing to permit their names to be used. On occasion they buy the support of individuals who happen to hold official positions in other organizations. They form fraudulent organizations with impressive letterheads to advance the cause. They attempt to anticipate and to soften the opposition of organizations that might be opposed to their position. Groups of similar ideological orientation tend to "run" together or to form constellations in confederation for mutual advantage.

All these maneuvers we have labelled "rituals"; that is, they are on the order of the dance of the rainmakers. That may be too brutal a characterization, for sometimes these campaigns have their effects — just as rain sometimes follows the rainmakers' dance. Yet the data make it fairly clear that most of these campaigns do not affect the opinion of many people and even clearer that they have small effect by way of punitive or approbative feedback in the vote. Their function in the political process is difficult to divine. The fact that organizations engage in these practices, though, is in itself a tribute to the importance of public opinion. To some extent, too, these opinion campaigns are not so much directed to mass opinion as to other activists who do not speak for many people either but have access to the arena of decision-making and perhaps have a viewpoint entitled to consideration. In another direction widespread publicity, by its creation of the illusion of mass support, may legitimize a position taken by a legislator. If a legislator votes for a measure that seems to arouse diverse support, his vote is not so likely to appear to be a concession to a special interest.

Barnums among the Businessmen. An additional explanation that apparently accounts for a good deal of group activity is simply that businessmen (who finance most of the campaigns of public education by pressure groups) are soft touches for publicity men. The advertising and public-relations men have demonstrated that they can sell goods; they proceed on the assumption that the business of obtaining changes in public policy is analogous to selling soap. They succeed in separating businessmen from large sums of money to propagate causes, often in a manner that sooner or later produces a boomerang effect.

Professional bureaucrats of the continuing and well-established organizations practice restraint in their public-relations campaigns. They need to gain the confidence of congressmen and other officials with whom they also need to be able to speak the next time they meet. The fly-by-night organization or the business group that falls into the clutches of an unscrupulous public-relations firm is more likely to indulge in the fantastic public relations and pressure campaign. Thus the National Tax Equality Association raised some $600,000 to finance a campaign against the tax exemptions of cooperatives, the most important of which are farm coops. Contributions came from concerns as scattered as the Central Power & Light Co., of Corpus Christi, Texas; Fairmont Foods Co., of Omaha, Nebraska; Central Hudson Gas and Electric Corporation, of Poughkeepsie, New York; and the Rheem Manufacturing Co., of San Francisco. The late Representative Reed, of New York, who was not one to attack business lightly, declared:

> Mr. Speaker, an unscrupulous racket, known as the National Tax Equality Association, has been in operation for some time, directing its vicious propaganda against the farm co-operatives. To get contributions from businessmen, this racketeering organization has propagandized businessmen with false statements to the effect that if farm co-operatives were taxed and not exempted the revenue to the government would mount annually to over $800,000,000. [The treasury esti-

mate was in the neighborhood of $20,000,000.] This is, of course, absolutely false and nothing more nor less than getting money under false pretenses. . . . This outfit of racketeers known as the Tax Equality Association has led honest businessmen to believe that their contributions were deductible from gross income as ordinary and necessary business expense with reference to their Federal income-tax return.

The Tax Equality Association provided its subscribers with the following form letter to send to their Congressmen:

Dear Mr. Congressman: You raised my income taxes. Now I hear you are going to do it again. But you still let billions in business and profits escape. How come you raise my taxes, but let co-ops, mutuals, and other profit-making corporations get off scot free, or nearly so? I want a straight answer — and I want these businesses fully taxed before you increase my or anyone else's income taxes again.

Letters so phrased are not well designed to produce favorable congressional response. The ineptness of this sort of campaign creates no little curiosity about the political judgment of solvent businessmen who put their money or their corporation's money into the support of obviously stupidly managed endeavors.

Autonomous Actors or Links? This review of the activities of pressure groups may raise doubts about the validity of the conception of these groups as links between public opinion and government. The reality seems to be that the conception applies with greater accuracy to some groups than to others. Certainly group spokesmen may represent a shade of opinion to government even though not all their own members share the views they express. Yet to a considerable degree the work of the spokesmen of private groups, both large and small, proceeds without extensive involvement of either the membership or a wider public. Their operations as they seek to influence legislation and administration, though, occur in a milieu of concern about opinion, either actual or latent. That concern also disposes decision-makers to attend to shades of opinion and preference relevant to decision though not necessarily of great electoral strength — a disposition of no mean importance in the promotion of the equitable treatment of people in a democratic order. The chances are that the effects of organized groups on public opinion occur mainly over the long run rather than in short-run maneuvers concerned with particular congressional votes. Moreover, group success may be governed more by the general balance of partisan strength than by the results of group endeavors to win friends in the mass public. An industry reputed to be led by swindlers may not expect the most cordial reception from legislative committees, especially at times when the balance of strength is not friendly to any kind of business. If the industry can modify its public image, a task that requires time, its position as it maneuvers on particulars (about which few of the public can ever know anything) may be less unhappy. That modification may be better attained by performance than by propaganda.

Case Studies in Pressure Group Politics

Administrative agencies often are the focal point of government policy making, and therefore pressure groups concentrate upon the bureaucracy in order to achieve their objectives. Public policy often emerges from administrative agency — pressure group interaction, for together such an alliance of public and private interest is very difficult to overcome. The following selection illustrates the way in which such a combination of interests has developed in the defense policy field, causing concern to proponents of greater presidential and congressional control independent of the Pentagon and private contractors' interests.

23

THE "MILITARY LOBBY": ITS IMPACT ON CONGRESS AND THE NATION

What led President Eisenhower, on the eve of his retirement, to warn the Nation of "unwarranted influence" by what he called "the military-industrial complex"?

What is this complex, what is the nature and extent of its influence, and how is it exercised?

What dangers — if any — are implicit in the situation described by the former President?

These were the principal questions raised by the President's parting words (for text, see below). In an attempt to answer them, *Congressional Quarterly* culled the record of Presidential press conferences, Congressional hearings, and other public documents. In addition, extensive off-the-record interviews were conducted with Members of

From the *Congressional Quarterly*, March 24, 1961. Copyright © 1961 by the Congressional Quarterly Service. Reprinted by permission. This article appeared in the *Congressional Record*, March 27, 1961, pp. 4557 ff.

Congress, representatives of defense contractors, former Government officials, and other persons with pertinent information. Results of this survey of fact and opinion are summarized on the following pages.

EISENHOWER'S WARNING

In his final address to the Nation on January 17, President Eisenhower noted that the United States has been compelled to "create a permanent armaments industry of vast proportions" and to maintain a defense establishment employing 3.5 million persons and spending huge sums. He continued as follows:

> This conjunction of an immense military establishment and a large arms industry is new in American experience. The total influence — economic, political, even spiritual — is felt in every city, every State house, every office of the Federal government. We recognize the imperative need for this development. Yet we must not fail to comprehend its grave implications. Our toil, resources and livelihood are all involved; so is the very structure of our society.
>
> In the councils of government, we must guard against the acquisition of unwarranted influence, whether sought or unsought, by the military-industrial complex. The potential for the disastrous rise of misplaced power exists and will persist. We must never let the weight of this combination endanger our liberties or democratic processes. We should take nothing for granted. Only an alert and knowledgeable citizenry can compel the proper meshing of the huge industrial and military machinery of defense with our peaceful methods and goals, so that security and liberty may prosper together.

EISENHOWER'S VIEWS

The President's warning of January 17 was his first public reference to a "military-industrial complex." But the concept was in the making for 8 years, during which the President had touched on most of the major components of his final declaration. These were the principal elements of his thinking, as seen by his associates and partially reflected in the record:

National survival, he stated in 1953 and repeatedly thereafter, rested on "security with solvency." To achieve this required maximum effort to counter the inherent tendency of Federal expenditures in general, and defense spending in particular, to rise. The key to success lay in "balance" — not, as he said April 25, 1958, during his battle with Congress over reorganization, in "overindulging sentimental attachments to outmoded military machines and concepts," nor, as he put it January 27, 1960, in heeding the "noisy trumpeting about dazzling military schemes or untrustworthy programs."

Ranged against this view, the President realized, was a host of special interests — the armed services and their civilian allies in business and in Congress. Beginning in 1953, when he cut the Air Force budget by $5 billion, the services had repeatedly carried their fight for more funds to Congress and the press. (More than one Member had called him to say that they were changing their votes in response to local pressures generated by the Pentagon.) "Obviously political and financial considerations" rather than "strict military needs" were influencing the situation, he said June 3, 1959. If such forces were allowed to prevail, he said March 11, 1959, "everybody with any sense knows that we are finally going to a garrison state."

Revered by the Nation as its chief military hero, and respected as its Commander in Chief, the President was confident of his ability to "put need above pressure-group inducement, before local argument, before every kind of any pressure except that that America needs," as he put it February 11, 1960. The star-studded brass of the Pentagon awed him not a bit; "there are too many of these generals who have all sorts of ideas," he said February 3, 1960. Knowing how they "operated," however, he feared that his successor — whether Nixon or Kennedy — would be unable to withstand their pressures.

This, according to a close associate, was what impelled the President to speak out as he prepared to leave office. Deeply committed to the goal of disarmament, he was sensitive to the counterinfluence of the "military-industrial complex." The extent of his concern was indicated when, at his final press conference, January 18, he described the impact of widespread advertising by missile manufacturers as "almost an insidious penetration of our own minds that the only thing this country is engaged in is weaponry and missiles." This, he said, was something "we just can't afford."

BACKGROUND

Defense spending reached its postwar low of $11.1 billion in fiscal 1948. By 1953, the cold war and a hot war in Korea had boosted spending to its postwar high of $43.7 billion. President Eisenhower cut that to $35.5 billion in 1955; thereafter, defense outlays climbed each year, to reach a projected $42.9 billion in fiscal 1962. At no time during his 8 years in office did military spending amount to less than one-half of the Federal budget or less than 8 per cent of the Nation's gross national product. All told, the armed services spent $313 billion during the 8 years, fiscal 1954–61; when the costs of military aid, atomic energy, and stockpiling are added, that total mounts to $354 billion.

There is no yardstick by which to measure with precision the economic impact of these expenditures, but there is no question that it has been considerable. According to a 1960 study by the Defense Procurement Subcommittee of the Joint Economic Committee, there were

38 million procurement transactions with a dollar volume of $228 billion from 1950 through 1959. Few areas of the economy were untouched by these purchases of goods and services.

The largest portion of defense spending, however, is allocated to the development, production, and deployment of major weapons systems. In fiscal 1960, when military prime contract awards of $10,000 or more totaled $21 billion, $15.4 billion or 73.4 per cent of the total went to 100 companies (or their subsidiaries) of which 65 were engaged primarily in "research, development, test or production of aircraft, missiles, or electronics." . . .

Despite the heavy concentration of prime contract awards among a small number of companies (in 1960 five companies accounted for 25 per cent of the dollar volume, 21 companies for 50 per cent), extensive subcontracting helps to spread procurement expenditures, employment and profits throughout the country — although not as evenly as some States would like it. In addition, some 1.5 million members of the armed services and almost 1 million civilian employees of the Defense Department are spread throughout the 50 States, with payrolls that totaled $11.4 billion in fiscal 1960. Another $650 million was paid to more than 1 million members of the National Guard and other Reserve groups. . . .

A further indication of the extent of defense-related activities is the wide distribution of facilities. From lists furnished by the military services, Atomic Energy Commission, and National Aeronautics and Space Administration, CQ determined the location of 738 separate installations by Congressional district. According to this list, there are one or more installations in 282 of the country's 437 districts. . . .

Taken together, these data suggest the sweeping extent of the defense establishment and its economic impact, and provide the background against which to examine the concept of a "military-industrial complex."

HÉBERT PROBE

In mid-1959, the House Armed Services Special Investigations Subcommittee, headed by Representative F. Edward Hébert, Democrat of Louisiana, questioned 75 witnesses over 25 days regarding the employment of retired officers by defense industries. The public, and Hébert as the hearings began, was alarmed by reports "about the alleged conduct of some military men who depart the ranks of defense for lush places on the payrolls of defense contractors." As it turned out, no real evidence of misconduct was produced. But the hearings shed considerable light on the ramifications of military-industrial relations.

Retired Officers. More than 1,400 retired officers in the rank of major or higher — including 261 of general or flag rank — were found to be employed by the top 100 defense contractors. The company employing the largest number (187, including 27 retired generals and admirals) was General Dynamics Corp., headed by former Secretary of the Army Frank Pace, which also received the biggest defense orders of any company in 1960. Duties of these officers, according to the testimony of their employers, encompassed a wide range of technical, management, and "representation" functions. But in no case, it appeared, was the officer involved in "selling" or the negotiation of defense contracts.

"Influence." With little variation, retired officers told the Hébert subcommittee that they were "has-beens" without influence upon the decisions of their former colleagues still on active duty. None had experienced "pressure" of this kind while still in the service; if any retired officers had asked him for a favor, "I would throw them out on their ear," said Lt. Gen. C. S. Irvine (retired), director of planning for Avco Corp. No one, however, took issue with the statement of Vice Adm. H. G. Rickover that the former jobs of retired officers often were filled "by people who are their dear friends, or even by people whom they have been influential in appointing, and naturally they will be listened to."

Illustrative of this point was the testimony of Adm. William M. Fechteler, retired, former Chief of Naval Operations and a consultant to General Electric Atomic Products Division. He told of arranging appointments for a GE vice president: "I took him in to see Mr. Gates, the Secretary of the Navy. I took him in to see Admiral Burke. He had not met Admiral Burke before. And then I made appointments with him with the Chief of the Bureau of Ships. But I did not accompany him there, because those are materiel bureaus which make contracts. And I studiously avoid even being in the room when anybody talks about a contract."

Entertainment. Two instances of entertainment by defense contractors came before the Hébert subcommittee. George Bunker, chairman of the Martin Co., acknowledged that his firm had entertained at least 26 active-duty officers at a weekend retreat in the Bahamas. Bunker denied there was any impropriety involved, saying "a man could neither operate nor compete effectively unless he had a close personal relationship." But spokesmen for the Secretaries of the three services agreed that such chumminess "doesn't look well" and could not be condoned.

The second case concerned an invitation to a "small off-the-record party" to discuss the plans and problems of the Air Research and Development Command with its newly promoted chief, Lt. Gen. Bernard S. Schriever. The invitation, sent to Representative Hébert and nine other Members of Congress (all but two of whom were members of the Armed Services or Appropriations Committees), was issued by three Air Force contractors: Aerojet-General President Dan A. Kimball (onetime Secretary of the Navy), General Dynamics' Pace, and Martin's Bunker. All three men defended the propriety of the proposed party (which was called off because of the "publicity") as being in Pace's words, "a means of advancing the interests of the United States of America."

Advertising. Shortly before the Hébert hearings began, a major controversy developed in and out of Congress over the respective merits of two competing antiaircraft missile systems — the Army's Nike-Hercules and the Air Force's Bomarc. Advertisements extolling the virtues of the two systems were inserted in Washington, D.C., newspapers by their prime contractors — Western Electric Co. and Boeing Airplane Co., respectively — while the issue was before Congress. Questioned by the Hébert subcommittee about the timing and purpose of the ads, spokesmen for the companies insisted that they were parts of long-term "information" programs.

However, Boeing's Harold Mansfield acknowledged that his company was fighting against a "campaign" of "misinformation" about the Bomarc, while Western Electric's W. M. Reynolds said the Nike ads had been suggested to the company by the Army. Both companies also acknowledged discussing proposed cutbacks in the Nike and Bomarc programs with Members of Congress from areas where employment would be affected. Said Mansfield: "Many of the most important decisions in the defense of our country are not made by military technicians. They are made in the Congress of the United States. And the Bomarc-Nike decision is one such decision."

Associations. Also questioned by the Hébert subcommittee were representatives of six organizations engaged in promoting the mutual interests of the armed services and their contractors in national security matters. All headquartered in Washington, they are the —

Association of the U.S. Army, with about 63,000 members (including military personnel on active duty) and 1958 income of $290,000, of which $143,000 was revenue from advertising in *Army* magazine. One of its aims: "To foster public understanding and support of the U.S. Army." Executive vice president: Lt. Gen. W. L. Weible, USA (retired). Among those on its advisory board: Donald Douglas, Jr., president of Douglas Aircraft Co.; Frank Pace, chairman of General Dynamics Corp.; Senators John J. Sparkman, Democrat, of Alabama, and Strom Thurmond, Democrat, of South Carolina.

Navy League, with about 38,000 members (no active duty personnel) and 1958 income of $179,000 plus $32,000 from advertising in *Navy — The Magazine of Sea Power.* Self-description: "The civilian arm of the Navy." President: Frank Gard Jameson. Among those on its advisory council: Dan Kimball, president of Aerojet-General and former Secretary of the Navy; Adm. Robert B. Carney (retired), chairman of Bath Iron Works Shipbuilding Corp., and former Chief of Naval Operations.

Air Force Association, with about 60,000 members (including about 30,000 Air Force personnel) and 1958 income of $1.2 million, including $527,000 from advertising in *Air Force and Space Digest.* Its aim: "To support the achievement of such airpower as is necessary" for national security. Executive director: James H. Straubel. Among its directors: 14 employees of defense contractors, including Lt. Gen. James H. Doolittle, USAF (retired) of Space Technology Laboratories.

American Ordnance Association, formerly the Army Ordnance Association, with about 42,000 members and 1958 income of $474,000, of which subscriptions and advertisements in the magazine *Ordnance* furnished $253,000. Its aim: "Armament preparedness." Executive vice president: Col. Leo A. Codd, USAR (retired).

Aerospace Industries Association, formerly the Aircraft Industries Association, a trade association with 79 member companies and 1958 income of $1.4 million in dues ranging up to $75,000 per member. Its aim: To promote the manufacture and sale of "aircraft and astronautical vehicles of every nature and description." President: Gen. Orval R. Cook, USAF (retired).

National Security Industrial Association, formerly the Navy Industrial Association, with 502 member companies and 1958 income $238,000, mostly from dues. Its aim: "To establish a close working relationship between industrial concerns" and national security agencies. Executive director: Capt. R. N. McFarlane, USN (retired).

According to the testimony of their representatives, none of these groups had anything to do with procurement; all were ignorant of any "pressure" in behalf of one or another manufacturer. The three service groups acknowledged their interest in building up grassroots support for the respective branches of the Armed Forces; they also maintained that they were fully independent of the services they represented, although the testimony showed that, for the most part, Army, Navy, and Air Force doctrines and weapon systems received enthusiastic support in their respective publications.

All of the groups insisted that their primary function was to inform and educate. Only the Aerospace Industries Association has registered under the lobby law, but General Cook said "we believe we do not operate according to the classic definition of a lobbyist. . . . We don't even dream of buying any influence of any kind." Asked whether the best interests of the industry would be served by an increase or decrease in defense spending, Cook said: "From a selfish point of view, the best interest of the industry would be served by an increase, of course, but from a patriotic and national point of view, it might not be."

Peter J. Schenck, then president of the Air Force Association and an official of Raytheon Corp., described the basis for close military-industrial relations as follows: "The day is past when the military requirements for a major weapons system is set up by the military and passed on to industry to build the hardware. Today it is more likely that the military requirement is the result of joint participation of military and industrial personnel, and it is not unusual for industry's contribution to be a key factor. Indeed there are highly placed military men who sincerely feel that industry currently is setting the pace in the research and development of new weapons systems."

Conclusion. In its report filed January 18, 1960, the Hébert subcommittee said it was "impressed by several obvious inconsistencies in testimony" relating to the influence enjoyed by retired officers in the employment of defense contractors. Said the report: "The better grade and more expensive influence is a very subtle thing when being successfully applied. . . . The 'coincidence' of contract and personal contacts with firms represented by retired officers and retired civilian officials sometimes raises serious doubts as to the complete objectivity of some of these decisions." The subcommittee proposed, among other steps, a much tighter law regarding "sales" to the Government by retired personnel; the House later passed a watered-down version of the proposal. (1959 Almanac, p. 727; 1960 Almanac, p. 279.)

Role of Congress

Charged with the responsibility of appropriating more than $40 billion each year for defense — and in the process deciding how to meet the conflicting claims of competing services for a larger share of the pie — Congress is up to its ears in the military-industrial issue. Collectively, the record shows, the Members strive to sift fact from fancy, and to point up and root out instances of waste and duplication in the defense program. The record also shows that, individually, the Members are zealous in representing the interests of their districts and States. Here are some examples:

"Fair Share." Documenting his case with facts and figures, Representative Hechler, Democrat, of West Virginia, told the House of June 1, 1959: "I am firmly against the kind of logrolling which would subject our defense program to narrowly sectional or selfish pulling and hauling. But I am getting pretty hot under the collar about the way my State of West Virginia is shortchanged in Army,

Navy, and Air Force installations. I am going to stand up on my hind legs and roar until West Virginia gets the fair treatment she deserves." (Hechler plans to resume his campaign shortly.)

In the same vein, Members of the New York delegation, led by Senators Kenneth B. Keating, Republican, and Jacob K. Javits, Republican, have long complained about the overconcentration of prime contract awards placed with California firms. Asking only for a "fair share," they want defense procurement officials to consider "the strategic and economic desirability of allocating purchases to different geographic areas" of the country. . . .

Installations. The opening, expansion, cutback, or closing of any military installation is of vital interest to the Member whose area is affected. In recent years, with reductions in the size of the Army and other changes in the composition of defense forces, there have been more closings than openings, and the affected Members have been quick to take issue. Some recent instances: Senator Albert Gore, Democrat, of Tennessee, said February 15 that he had written Secretary of the Air Force Eugene M. Zuckert about reports that Stewart Air Force Base at Smyrna, Tenn., might be closed, and had been assured that "as of now no change is contemplated which should cause any concern."

Senator Olin D. Johnston, Democrat, of South Carolina, after calling on President Kennedy February 20, said he had been assured that careful consideration would be given to the future of Fort Jackson at Columbia, S.C., and Donaldson Air Force Base at Greenville, S.C.

Representative Samuel S. Stratton, Democrat, of New York, said March 3 that he had wired Secretary Zuckert about reports of a plan to transfer certain operations from Griffiss Air Force Base at Rome, N.Y. Said Stratton: "It is fantastic to learn that one more defense department is considering recommendations which would have the effect of increasing unemployment in upstate New York, already hard hit by layoffs."

Representative Emanuel Celler, Democrat, of New York, said March 6 that Secretary of Defense Robert S. McNamara had assured him he had no knowledge "of any plans or proposals to shut down the operations" at the Brooklyn Navy Yard.

Procurement. Decisions to begin, accelerate, reduce, or stop production of various weapons and weapon systems are also of major interest to Members in whose districts or States the manufacturers involved are located. Here are examples of Representatives at work:

When the House Appropriations Committee chopped the Air Force's 1959 request for the Bomarc by $162.7 million, Representative Don Magnuson, Democrat, of Washington, charged that few Members were aware of "the incredible lengths to which the adherents of the Nike defense system have gone in their attempt to discredit the Bomarc. . . . Of course, this is Army inspired." (Contractor for Bomarc was Boeing Airplane Co., headquartered in Seattle, Wash.)

Also in 1959, Representative John R. Foley, Democrat, of Maryland, offered an amendment to the defense bill to add $10 million to Air Force funds to buy 10 F–27 transports from the Fairchild Aircraft Co. of Hagerstown, Md., in Foley's district. This failed, but the Senate obliged with $11 million. When House conferees refused to go along, Senator J. Glenn Beall, Republican, of Maryland, begged the Senate to insist, saying that, of the $4 billion to be spent on aircraft, "all we ask for Fairchild is $11 million."

Recent reports that the Pentagon was thinking of cutting back the B–70 program led Representative Edgar W. Hiestand, Republican, of California, to write Secretary McNamara February 27 to assure him of "the strong congressional support for this valued program." North American Aviation, Inc., prime contractor for the B–70, is located in Hiestand's district.

Reserves. The well-known solicitude shown by Congress for the National Guard and other Reserve forces reflects to some degree a widespread local interest in the payrolls, armories, and other benefits involved, as well as effective work by the National Guard Association and the Reserve Officers Association. Among the 40 Reserve officers in Congress are . . . [four] generals: Howard W. Cannon, Democrat, of Nevada, brigadier general, USAFR; Strom Thurmond, Democrat, of South Carolina, major general, USAR; and Representatives James Roosevelt, Democrat, of California, brigadier general, USMCR; and Robert L. F. Sikes, Democrat, of Florida, brigadier general, USAR; Cannon and Thurmond are members of the Armed Services Committee; Sikes, of the Defense Appropriations Subcommittee. . . .

President Eisenhower made no headway whatsoever in his 3-year campaign to reduce National Guard and Army Reserve manpower levels to "conform to the changing character and missions" of the active forces; Congress responded with a mandatory floor of 400,000 for the Guard, and funds to maintain both the Guard and the Reserve at full strength. These actions, said the President in his final budget message, "are unnecessarily costing the American people over $80 million annually and have been too long based on other than strictly military needs." Even at the lower strengths he again proposed, the Reserves would cost "well over $1 billion in 1962," he said.

Summing up the cumulative impact of these varied expressions of Congressional interest, Representative Jamie L. Whitten, Democrat, of Mississippi, a member of the House Appropriations Defense Sub-

committee, testified as follows Jan. 29, 1960, before the Joint Economic
Committee's Defense Procurement Subcommittee:

> I am convinced defense is only one of the factors that enter into our
> determinations for defense spending. The others are pump priming,
> spreading the immediate benefits of defense spending, taking care of all
> services, giving all defense contractors a fair share, spreading the mili-
> tary bases to include all sections, etc. There is no State in the Union and
> hardly a district in a State which doesn't have defense spending, con-
> tracting, or a defense establishment. We see the effect in public and
> Congressional insistence on continuing contracts, or operating military
> bases, though the need has expired.

CASE OF THE ZEUS

The confluence of service, contractor, and Congressional
pressures is illustrated by the current revival of a campaign to launch
production of the Army's Nike-Zeus anti-missile system, although final
tests are more than a year away. Congress added $137 million to the
budget in 1958 to start production, but the President refused to spend
it; in his final budget, providing about $287 million for further devel-
opment of Nike-Zeus, he said, "funds should not be committed to
production until development tests are satisfactorily completed." Subsequently, these things happened.

On February 1 the magazine *Army* appeared with seven articles
lauding the Nike-Zeus — four of them by Army commanders on active
duty. Also in the issue: full-page advertisements by Western Electric
Co., prime contractor for Nike-Zeus, and 8 of its major subcontractors,
together with a map showing how much of the $410 million contract
was being spent in each of 37 States (but $111 million in California,
$110 million in New Jersey). The general message: It's time to start
production.

On February 2, Senator Thurmond told the Senate that "we must
start production of the Nike-Zeus now." Extolling the "experienced
Army-industry team" that developed the system, he argued that "by
spending money now to provide a capability for the production of
components in quantity, we will save money in the long run." Rising
to support his arguments were Senators B. Everett Jordan, Democrat,
of North Carolina, and Frank Carlson, Republican, of Kansas.
(*Army's* map showed spending of $36 million in North Carolina and
$8.5 million in Kansas.)

On February 7, Representative George P. Miller, Democrat, of California, urged every Member of the House to "read the current issue of
Army magazine" and to "support immediate action for limited component production of the Nike-Zeus system." Miller, a member of the Science and Astronautics Committee, said this could be done "with the
addition of less than $175 million to the present Army budget."

On February 13, Representative Daniel J. Flood, Democrat, of Pennsylvania, gave the House substantially the same speech delivered February 2 by Senator Thurmond, and also concluded that "we must start production of the Nike-Zeus now." Flood appended an article on the subject published by the Sperry Rand Corp., a subcontractor for Nike-Zeus. (*Army's* figure for spending in Pennsylvania: $10 million.)

On February 23, Representative John W. McCormack, Democrat, of Massachusetts, House majority leader, asked every Member to read Flood's "prescient address" of February 13. McCormack's conclusion: "Close the gap in our military posture; muzzle the mad-dog missile threat of the Soviet Union; loose the Zeus through America's magnificent production lines now." (*Army's* figure for Massachusetts: $1.5 million.)

On March 6, the press reported that President Kennedy was expected to approve a Defense Department compromise plan calling for an additional $100 million to $200 million to start tooling up. Eventual costs were estimated at from $5 billion to $20 billion.

Extent of Influence

Proponents of the Nike-Zeus, it should be noted, base their case squarely on the national interest — the touchstone of debate, pro and con, concerning the merits of every proposal made in the name of defense. It is never clear, however, where the national interest begins and self-interest leaves off.

All of the persons questioned by CQ agreed that an element of self-interest pervades relationships among the services, their contractors and Members of Congress. There was no consensus, however, regarding the extent to which decisions affecting the national interest are influenced by the self-interest of persons and organizations involved. Here is the gist of these views.

The Services. Locked in competition for larger shares of a defense budget that has not kept pace with the soaring costs of new weapon systems, the services toil constantly to "sell" their particular doctrines, programs, and requirements to the public, industry, and Congress. Recent examples: television programs on the Navy's Polaris and "The New Marine," an Army-Industry Liaison Seminar in New Orleans, an Air Force tour of Strategic Air Command headquarters in Omaha for 35 new Members of Congress.

The services are especially careful of their relations with Congress, particularly with members of the Armed Services and Appropriations Committees. When a senior member of the House Armed Services Committee complained of rumors that a Marine Corps installation might be removed from his district, the Commandant came in person to assure him that no change would be made "so long as I am in the job." A junior committee member, on learning that an unsolicited

Army training center was to be located in his district, concluded that "someone" in the Pentagon was looking out for his interests.

There is some truth, all agree, in Representative Whitten's statement to the Defense Procurement Subcommittee that "you can look at some of our key people in the key places in Congress and go see how many military establishments are in their districts." One oft-cited example: the state of Georgia, home of the chairmen of both Senate and House Armed Services Committees. (To the proposal that a new Air Force installation be placed in Georgia, one brave General is credited with replying that "one more base would sink the State.")

But Congressmen accustomed to the prevalence of "logrolling" in many other areas see nothing sinister in this situation. The services are generally credited with being "correct" in their dealings with Members; none of those questioned by CQ complained of "pressure" by the services.

The Contractors. For many of the major defense contractors, their only client of any importance is the U.S. Government and the bulk of their business is obtained through negotiated contracts with one or more of the armed services. It is a highly competitive field, by all accounts, in which a considerable premium is placed on "good personal relations" with the client. Even those companies doing business exclusively with one service will be found supporting all three service sounding-boards: the Air Force Association, Navy League, and Association of the U.S. Army. Entertainment practices vary widely throughout the industry, but no one denies that personal friendships play an important part in shaping working relationships between client and vendor. Two episodes serve to illustrate the point.

In one "competition" for a new weapon system, Navy technicians decided to throw out one proposal on grounds it was based on faulty data. Warned by a Navy friend of the impending decision, the contractor promptly went to the admiral in charge and persuaded him to order a 30-day delay to permit all bidders to submit additional data. (The well-informed contractor failed to win in the end, however.)

An Air Force "competition" for a new missile ended with a top-level decision to award the contract to Company A. Learning of this, the president of Company B went straight to the Secretary and persuaded him to order a complete review of the decision. Result: the contract went to Company B.

Sometimes helped and sometimes hurt by such manifestations of "influence," contractors generally accept it as "part of the game," recognizing that to some degree the outcome reflects a tendency on the part of all three services to take care of companies with whom they have been doing business for some time, before admitting any "outsiders." (Some companies have nevertheless managed to secure important prime contracts from all three services.)

Defense contractors vary in their attitudes toward relations with Congress. Small, new companies, trying to gain a foothold in the defense business, are quick to seek the aid of their Congressmen; established contractors recognize that such intercession may backfire, especially in an attempt to reverse an essentially technical decision by the services. As the Hébert hearings demonstrated, however, contractors are not at all reluctant to solicit the aid of interested Members when (as in the Nike-Bomarc dispute) it is in the mutual interest of all concerned.

Congress. As the elected representatives of their States and districts, Members of Congress take a keen political interest in the economic impact of defense activities in their areas, and are the first to admit it. But few believe that such considerations exert any significant influence over the course of defense spending or the shape of national strategy. The major complaint of some Members is their lack of influence!

Certain members of the Armed Services Committees admit seeking the assignment because of large military installations and defense industries in their states or districts. Others consider themselves fortunate that they do not have such activities — and the local pressures that go along with them — in their own areas. Recognizing that changing military requirements may produce a "boom and bust" effect on any given community, they try to dissuade local enthusiasts who clamor for a new installation.

Outsiders detect a Navy bias in the makeup of the House Armed Services Committee and to a lesser extent, the Senate Armed Services Committee. (Of the former's 37 members, 25 come from coastal states.) Committee members acknowledge that some of their colleagues reflect a service point of view (10 members of the House Committee are active reservists) and that the Navy's position is amply represented; they also contend, however, that there is a minimum of service-oriented partisanship in the work of the Committees.

As for dealings with contractors, most Members express doubt concerning both the desirability and feasibility of intervening in procurement decisions. One Senator who did go to bat for one of his constituents (to no avail) found himself under fire from a competitor in the same state. His conclusion: it doesn't pay to get involved.

Pros and Cons

Does the evidence support President Eisenhower's warning against "the acquisition of unwarranted influence, whether sought or unsought, by the military-industrial complex"? The answer varies with the individual.

"There is no question that the services and their contractors have an interest in maintaining a high degree of tension in the country," says a senior member of the House Defense Appropriations Subcommittee. But he foresees no threat to the democratic process, although admitting the need to guard against overly intimate relations between soldier, salesman, and legislator.

"There is a real danger that we may go the way of prewar Japan and Germany," says one member of the House Armed Services Committee, who objects to the presence of reserve officers on the Committee and sees the appointment of industrialists to top Defense Department posts as a bad practice.

"I don't know what Eisenhower was talking about," says a former Defense Department official. Strong civilian control over the military services can be maintained, he believes, by the selection of a sufficient number of able Presidential appointees, regardless of their industrial background.

"The trouble is that national security has become popular — and the record of Congressional appropriations proves it," says a former Eisenhower associate. He sees the military-industrial complex as a "floating power" largely free of any restraint.

Several of those questioned by CQ ascribed the President's concern to over-preoccupation with the budget. Believing that the nation needs and can afford an even larger defense effort, they were inclined to dismiss his warning as misdirected. This point of view was reflected in *Air Force* magazine, which characterized reaction to the President's statement as a "flap" and deplored the "small wave of learned essays rehashing all of the irresponsible charges and insinuations that have been bandied around in Congressional hearings for the past few years." The great danger, it concluded, was that "an exercise of misdirected caution . . . could menace national security."

The first moves of the Kennedy administration suggest little sympathy with the Eisenhower viewpoint. Orders have been placed for large numbers of additional transport planes. Steps have been taken to speed up defense purchases and "spread the business" in the interests of stimulating the lagging economy. Other proposals under consideration would add substantially to defense spending in the future.

At the same time, the new administration stands pledged to seek an agreement with the Soviets on banning nuclear tests and to pursue the goal of arms control. As yet, the chances of achieving either appear to be so remote as to preclude serious consideration of the possible opposition to any agreement by a "military-industrial complex." It may be worth noting, however, that the American Ordnance Assn. is calling for the "immediate resumption . . . of nuclear tests for both small and large weapons," and that *Ordnance* magazine argues that until the Communist "goal of world dominion . . . is abandoned, there can be no lessening of our armament preparedness."

The kind of amalgamation of interests that has created the "military-industrial complex" is not unique. "How the Farmers Get What They Want" presents additional empirical evidence to support the view that a concurrent majority system often operates in contemporary American politics. That is, major public policy is not usually made without the consent of the dominant private interest groups concerned, whose views are more often than not directly represented in the administrative agency that is responsible for making policy in their area.

25   THEODORE LOWI

HOW THE FARMERS GET WHAT THEY WANT

In his Farm Message of January 31 [1964], President Johnson proposed that Congress establish a bipartisan commission to investigate the concentration of power in the food industry. In the same message the President called for new legislation to strengthen farmer co-operatives, to encourage their expansion through merger and acquisition, and to provide them with further exemptions from the anti-trust laws.

This was the beginning of the "Johnson round" in agriculture. It is part of a familiar pattern. An attack on the food industry's market power, coupled with proposals for expanded and stronger farm co-operatives, is obviously not an attack on concentration itself. Rather it is an attack on the intervention of nonagricultural groups into strictly agricultural affairs.

That agricultural affairs should be handled strictly within the agricultural community is a basic political principle established before the turn of the century and maintained since then without serious re-examination. As a result, agriculture has been neither public nor private enterprise. It is a system of self-government in which each leading farm interest controls a segment of agriculture through a delegation of national sovereignty. Agriculture has emerged as a largely self-governing federal estate within the Federal structure of the United States.

President Johnson recognized these facts within three weeks of his

From *The Reporter,* May 21, 1964. Reprinted by permission of the author and *The Reporter.* Copyright 1964 by The Reporter Magazine Company.

accession when he summoned a conference of agricultural leaders to formulate a program by which agriculture should be served and regulated. The most recent concession to agriculture's self-government was the wheat-cotton bill. Because cotton supports were too high, the cotton interests wrote a bill providing for a subsidy of six to eight cents a pound to mills in order to keep them competitive with foreign cotton and domestic rayon without touching the price supports. On the other hand, wheat supports were too low because wheat farmers last year in referendum overwhelmingly rejected President Kennedy's plan to provide some Federal regulation along with supports. The wheat section of the new act calls for a program whereby wheat farmers may voluntarily comply with acreage reduction for subsidies of up to seventy cents a bushel but without the Federal supply regulations. The press called this a major legislative victory for Mr. Johnson, but the credit is not his. That the press could see this as a victory for anyone but organized cotton and wheat is a testimonial to the total acceptance by President, press, and public of the principle that private agricultural interests alone govern agriculture and should do so.

The reasons for agriculture's self-government are deep-rooted, and the lessons to be drawn are important to the future of American politics. For a century agriculture has been out of step with American economic development. Occasional fat years have only created unreal expectations, to be undercut by the more typical lean years.

Quite early, farmers discovered the value of politics as a counterweight to industry's growth and concentration. Land-grant and homesteading acts were followed by governmental services in research and education. Continuing distress led to bolder demands. First there were efforts to effect a redistribution of wealth in favor of agriculture. As a debtor class, farmers saw inflation as the solution, and Bryan was their spokesman for cheaper money and cheaper credit. The monopolies, the railroads, the grain merchants and other processors, the banks, and the brokers were to be deprived of power over the market by dissolution or by severe restraints. Next, farmers sought solutions by emulating the business system: the co-operative to restrain domestic trade and international dumping over high tariff walls to restrain international trade. Yet all these mechanisms either were not enacted or did not live up to expectations.

With the coming of the New Deal and with its help, organized agriculture turned to self-regulation. The system created during the 1930's has endured to this day, and with only a few marginal additions and alterations is accepted almost unanimously by farm leaders. Self-regulation might have taken several forms, the most likely one being a national system of farm-leader representation within a farmers' NRA. Instead, a more complicated system of highly decentralized and highly autonomous subgovernments developed, largely for Constitutional reasons. Agriculture was the most "local" of the manufacturing groups the Federal government was trying to reach. The appearance if not the reality of decentralizing Federal programs through farmer-elected local committees helped avoid strains on the interstate commerce clause of the Constitution. But this avoidance of Constitutional troubles created very special political difficulties.

The Local Committees

The Federal Extension Service shows how the system works. It is "co-operative" in that it shares the job of farm improvement with the states, the land-grant colleges, the county governments, and the local associations of farmers. The county agent is actually employed by the local associations. In the formative years, the aid of local chambers of commerce was enlisted, the local association being the "farm bureau" of the chamber. In order to co-ordinate local activities and to make more effective claims for additional outside assistance, these farm bureaus were organized into state farm bureau federations. The American Farm Bureau Federation, formed at the Agriculture College of Cornell University in 1919, was used as a further step toward amalgamation. To this day there is a close relationship between the farm bureaus, the land-grant colleges, and the Extension Service. This transformation of an administrative arrangement into a political system has been repeated in nearly all the agricultural programs during recent decades. The Extension Service exercises few controls from the top. There are cries of "Federal encroachment" at the mere suggestion in Washington that the Department of Agriculture should increase its supervision of the extension programs or co-ordinate them with other Federal activities.

As the financial stakes have grown larger, the pattern of local self-government remains the same. Price support — the "parity program" — is run by the thousands of farmer-elected county committees that function alongside but quite independently of the other local committees. Acreage allotments to bring supply down and prices up are apportioned among the states by the Agricultural Stabilization and Conservation Service. State committees of farmers apportion the allotment among the counties. The farmer-elected county Stabilization and Conservation Committees receive the county allotment.

These committees made the original acreage allotments among individual farmers back in the 1930's; today, they make new allotments, work out adjustments and review complaints regarding allotments, determine whether quotas have been complied with, inspect and approve storage facilities; and perform as the court of original jurisdiction on violations of price-support rules and on eligibility for parity payments. The committees are also vitally important in the campaigns for the two-thirds vote required to fix high price supports. Congress determines the general level of supports, and the Secretary of Agriculture proclaims the national acreage quotas for adjusting the supply to the guaranteed price. But the locally elected committees stand between the farmer and Washington.

Most other agricultural programs have evolved similarly. Each is independent of the others, and any conflicts or overlapping mandates have been treated as nonexistent or beyond the jurisdiction of any one agency. The Soil Conservation Service operates through its independent soil-conservation districts, of which there were 2,936 in 1963, involving ninety-six per cent of the nation's farms. Each district's farmer-elected committee is considered a unit of local government. The Farmer Co-operative Service operates through the member-elected boards of directors of the farm co-ops. In agricultural credit, local self-government is found in even greater complexity. The Farm Credit Administration exists outside the Department of Agriculture and is made up of not one but three separate bodies politic, a triangular system mostly farmer-owned and totally farmer-controlled.

Ten Systems and Politics

The ten principal self-governing systems in agriculture, in fiscal 1962 disposed of $5.6 billion of the total of $6.7 billion in expenditures passing through the Department of Agriculture. During the calendar year 1962, $5.8 billion in loans was handled similarly. This combined amount represents a large portion of the total of Federal activity outside national defense.

Each of the ten systems has become a powerful political instrumentality. The self-governing local units become one important force in a system that administers a program and maintains the autonomy of that program against political forces emanating from other agricultural programs, from antagonistic farm and nonfarm interests, from Congress, from the Secretary of Agriculture, and from the President. To many a farmer, the local outpost of one or another of these systems *is* the government.

The politics within each system is built upon a triangular trading pattern involving the central agency, a Congressional committee or subcommittee, and the local district farmer committees (usually federated in some national or regional organization). Each side of the triangle complements and supports the other two.

The Extension Service, for example, is one side of the triangle completed by the long-tenure "farm bureau" members of the Agriculture Committees in Congress and, at the local level, the American Farm Bureau Federation with its local committees. Further group support is provided by two intimately related groups, the Association of Land Grant Colleges and Universities and the National Association of County Agricultural Agents.

Another such triangle unites the Soil Conservation Service, the Agriculture subcommittee of the House Appropriations Committee, and the local districts organized in the energetic National Association of Soil Conservation Districts. Further support comes from the Soil Conservation Society of America (mainly professionals) and the former Friends of the Land, now the Izaak Walton League of America.

Probably the most complex of the systems embraces the parity program. It connects the Agricultural Stabilization and Conservation Service with the eight (formerly ten) commodity subcommittees of the House Agriculture Committee and the dozens of separately organized groups representing the various commodities. (Examples: National Cotton Council, American Wool Growers Association, American Cranberry Growers Association.) These groups and congressmen draw support from the local price-support committees wherever a particular commodity is grown.

The Farmer Had His Way

These systems have a vigorous capacity to maintain themselves and to resist encroachment. They have such institutional legitimacy that they have become practically insulated from the three central sources of democratic political responsibility. Thus, within the Executive branch, they are autonomous. Secretaries of Agriculture have tried and failed to consolidate or even to co-ordinate related programs. Within Congress, they are sufficiently powerful to be able to exercise an effective veto or create a stalemate. And they are almost totally removed from the view, not to mention the control, of the general public. (Throughout the 1950's, Victor Anfuso of Brooklyn was the only member of the House Agriculture Committee from a non-farm constituency.)

Important cases illustrate their power:

In 1947, Secretary of Agriculture Clinton P. Anderson proposed a consolidation of all soil-conservation, price-support, and FHA programs into one committee system with a direct line from the committees to the Secretary. Bills were prepared providing for consolidation within the price-support committees. Contrary bills provided for consolidation under soil conservation districts. The result: stalemate. In 1948, a leading farm senator proposed consolidation of the programs under the local associations of the Extension Service. Immediately a House farm leader introduced a contrary bill. The result: continuing stalemate.

In Waco, Texas, on October 14, 1952, Presidential candidate Eisenhower said: "I would like to see in every county all Federal farm agencies under the same roof." Pursuant to this promise, Secretary Ezra Taft Benson issued a series of orders during early 1953 attempting to bring about consolidation of local units as well as unification at the top. Finally, amid cries of "sneak attack" and "agricrat," Benson proclaimed that "any work on the further consolidation of county and state offices . . . shall be suspended."

From the very beginning, Secretary Benson sought to abandon rigid price supports and bring actual supports closer to market prices. In 1954, as he was beginning to succeed, Congress enacted a "commodity set-aside" by which $2.5 billion of surplus commodities already held by the government were declared to be a "frozen reserve" for national defense. Since the Secretary's power to cut price supports depends heavily upon the amount of government-owned surplus carried over from previous years, the commodity set-aside was a way of freezing parity as well as reserves. Benson eventually succeeded in reducing supports on the few commodities over which he had authority. But thanks to the set-aside, Congress, between fiscal 1952 and 1957, helped increase the value of commodities held by the government from $1.1 billion to $5.3 billion. What appeared, therefore, to be a real Republican policy shift amounted to no more than giving back with one hand what had been taken away by the other.

President Eisenhower's first budget sought to abolish farm home-building and improvement loans by eliminating the budgetary request and by further requesting that the 1949 authorization law be allowed to expire. Congress overrode his request in 1953 and each succeeding year, and the President answered Congress with a year-by-year refusal to implement the farm housing program. In 1956, when the President asked again explicitly for elimination of the program, he was rebuffed. The Housing subcommittee of the House Banking and Currency Committee added to the President's omnibus housing bill a renewal of the farm housing program, plus an authorization for $500 million in loans over a five-year period, and the bill passed with a Congressional mandate to use the funds. They were used thereafter at a rate of about $75 million a year.

On March 16, 1961, President Kennedy produced a "radically different" farm program in a special message to Congress. For the first time in the history of price supports, the bill called for surplus control through quotas placed on bushels, tons, or other units, rather than on acreage. An acreage allotment allows the farmer to produce as much as he can on the reduced acreage in cultivation. For example, in the first ten years or so of acreage control, acreage under cultivation dropped by about four per cent while actual production rose by fifteen per cent.

The Kennedy proposal called for national committees of farmers to be elected to work out the actual program. This more stringent type of control was eliminated from the omnibus bill in the Agriculture Committees of both chambers and there were no attempts to restore them during floor debate. Last-minute efforts by Secretary Orville L. Freeman to up the ante, offering to raise wheat supports from $1.79 to $2.00, were useless. Persistence by the administration led eventually to rejection by wheat farmers in 1963 of all high price supports and acreage controls.

The politics of this rejected referendum is of general significance. Despite all the blandishments and inducements of the administration, the farmer had his way. The local price-support committees usually campaign in these referendums for the Department of Agriculture, but this time they did not. And thousands of small farmers, eligible to vote for the first time, joined with the local leadership to help defeat the referendum. It is not so odd that wheat farmers would reject a proposal that aims to regulate them more strictly than before. What is odd is that only wheat farmers are allowed to decide the matter. It seems that in agriculture, as in many other fields, the regulators are powerless without the consent of the regulated.

Agriculture is the field where the distinction between public and private has been almost completely eliminated, not by public expropriation of private domain but by private expropriation of public domain. For more than a generation, Americans have succeeded in expanding the public sphere without giving thought to the essential democratic question of how each expansion is to be effected. The creation of private governments has profoundly limited the capacity of the public government to govern responsibly and flexibly.

The techniques employed by interest groups are many and varied depending on the nature of the group and its objectives. But private interest groups are not the only ones who lobby when important public policy is at stake. In the following selection we see that not only a private interest group, the natural gas pipeline industry, but also administrative agencies and consumer groups were involved in the passage of the Natural Gas Pipeline Safety Act of 1968.

25

THE EFFECTS OF LOBBYING ON THE NATURAL GAS PIPELINE SAFETY ACT

The Natural Gas Pipeline Safety Act bill (S 1166 — PL 90-481) signed Aug. 12 [1968] by the President carried the marks and scars of three years of legislative lobbying battles. The final version of S 1166 was in some ways stronger than the gas pipeline industry — or at least a segment of the industry — wanted and in many ways weaker than supporters of strong safety legislation wanted. But generally the measure was one the industry "can live with."

S 1166 authorized the Secretary of Transportation to set up interim standards, and then continuing standards, for 760,000 miles of transmission and distribution lines and for a small mileage of gathering lines in residential and commercial areas. It permitted states to supervise the standards for facilities within their borders and provided penalties for violations and authorization of funds for the cost of the program.

The bill started out March 17, 1965, as S 1553, a one-sentence amendment to the Natural Gas Act giving the Federal Power Commission (FPC) authority to set standards for the safe transmission of natural gas. Between the time the proposal was introduced as a bill of less than 50 words giving the FPC authority to issue safety regulations for pipelines and the time it emerged as a detailed federal-state arrangement for administration of pipeline safety, the measure underwent wholesale changes and was the subject of legislative and lobbying fights.

BACKGROUND

The year 1938, when the Natural Gas Act became law, can be considered the beginning of federal involvement in the safety aspects of transmission of natural gas. That law gave the Federal Power Commission (FPC) authority to regulate natural gas rates and to certify construction of new interstate pipeline facilities.

Through the certification authority, the FPC began "to enhance

From the *Congressional Quarterly, Weekly Report* (August 16, 1968), pp. 2221–24. Copyrighted and reprinted by permission of Congressional Quarterly, Inc. The title is the editor's.

pipeline safety within the narrow limits of its existing powers." However, the FPC did not have "any express mandate for safety," and the agency's attempts to get Congress to give it a mandate failed. "Within narrow limits" the FPC required accident reports, made investigations of accidents, advised companies of questionable safety practices, prohibited operation at unsafe pressures and checked new pipeline plans for safe standards.

On balance however, so far as legislation and administrative regulations were concerned, safety had been a low priority item through most of the 30 years since the Natural Gas Act was passed. The major controversy was the FPC's authority to regulate the sale of natural gas. This was a producers-versus-consumers fight, and safety did not figure in it.

In 1951, as the use of natural gas increased following World War II, Rep. John W. Heselton (R Mass. 1945–59) introduced a bill authorizing the FPC to issue safety regulations for natural gas companies. The 81st Congress did not act on the bill, and he reintroduced it in the 82nd and 83rd Congresses. In 1954, however, it was not acted on, at Heselton's request. He told the House Interstate and Foreign Commerce Committee that industry spokesmen had told him they were working on updating the industry's safety code. Heselton said he wanted to give the industry time to act before asking for action on his legislation.

Congress in 1954, however, did pass legislation exempting from FPC control any gas company whose operations were entirely within one state, even though the company might get its gas from another state. Thus, safety regulations for intrastate companies were put under the control of state regulatory agencies.

Through the rest of the 1950s and into the 1960s, rate regulation continued to be the dominant issue in natural gas regulation. As the industry grew, the issue became more controversial and more intense. In 1956, two lobbyists and the Superior Oil Co. were fined for violating federal lobbying laws in a case involving gas rate regulation.

On March 4, 1965, a high pressure transmission line near Natchitoches, La., exploded. The blast killed 17 people, and the heat cremated everything combustible in a 13-acre area. There had been other pipeline accidents, but the Louisiana explosion focused Congress' attention on pipeline safety.

At that time, there was no federal legislation on gas line safety, and 22 states had no legislation.

Sen. Warren G. Magnuson (D Wash.), chairman of the Senate Commerce Committee, introduced a bill (S 1553) on March 17, 1965, adding a section to the Natural Gas Act which said:

"The Commission is authorized to prescribe such standards, rules, regulations, restrictions, conditions, or orders with respect to the construction, extension, operation and maintenance of pipeline transportation facilities of natural gas companies as, in its opinion, are necessary for the promotion of safety."

On July 8, Magnuson wrote to FPC Chairman Joseph C. Swidler and asked for a report with the details of accidents on major pipelines, to be used in conjunction with hearings on the bill, S 1553.

Hearings were held in 1966, but no action was taken. The Department of Transportation was created in 1966, however, with the task of overseeing all transportation functions; and on Feb. 16, 1967, President Johnson asked for pipeline safety regulation in his consumer safety message to Congress.

"With the creation of the Department of Transportation," Mr. Johnson said, "one agency now has responsibility for federal safety regulations of air, water and land transportation, and oil pipelines. It is time to complete this comprehensive system of safety by giving the Secretary of Transportation authority to prescribe minimum safety standards for the movement of natural gas by pipeline."

S 1166, a bill embodying the President's request, was passed by the Senate Nov. 9, 1967. The House passed its version July 2, 1968. The conference report (H Rept 1795) on the bill was adopted by the House July 26 and the Senate July 31.

State Regulation. The basis for state action was a pressure piping code known as the United States of America Standards Institute (USASI) B31.8. USASI is an organization of various trade, technical, and professional organizations, with separate committees to develop standards for specific industries.

In 1925 one of the professional organizations in USASI, the American Society of Mechanical Engineers, suggested that a pressure piping code be developed. It took 10 years for the first code to be issued. In 1942 it was expanded; and in 1950, when the great post-World War II increase in transmission of natural gas to cities was well underway, another revision was begun. A revamped code was issued in 1955, and it was updated in 1958, 1961, 1963 and 1967.

By 1966, 26 states had adopted safety codes. Of these, 25 used the USASI standards, or some modification of them. And, as federal legislation appeared more and more likely, additional states adopted the code or regulated pipeline safety until there were 47 states with pipeline safety regulations by early 1968.

However, testimony showed that there was considerable variation among the states in attitudes toward the code, in standards, and in exercising authority to enforce standards.

While crediting the industry with a good safety record, Secretary of Transportation Alan S. Boyd told the House Commerce Committee there were 10 major deficiencies in the code. One of the most important deficiencies frequently cited by advocates of the legislation was the absence of any requirements concerning evaluation of old pipe.

Pros and Cons

Industry. The gas pipeline industry had views on safety legislation as it might affect the entire industry. And the segments of the industry, each with its own characteristics, had views on the legislation as it might affect their segment.

Those segments were:

Gathering lines, small, low pressure lines, usually in rural areas, bringing natural gas from the wells to facilities that transfer it to the transmission lines. There are about 63,000 miles of gathering lines.

Transmission lines, the big, high-pressure lines that move gas from collecting points in the production areas to cities all across the country. There are about 224,000 miles of transmission lines.

Distribution lines, the low-pressure lines under towns and cities that carry gas to homes, factories, schools, hospitals, office buildings and wherever it is finally used. There are about 536,000 miles of distribution lines.

The gas line industry view was that it was as safety conscious as any other industry in America dealing with a dangerous product, and when its accident rate was compared with other industries, the pipeline business had as good a record as it should. The industry also cited the words of President Johnson, who said, in his consumer message of 1967, "The natural gas industry is among the most safety conscious in the nation."

The industry did not believe safety legislation was needed and wanted to be left under the jurisdiction of the state regulatory agencies.

Administration. Mr. Johnson, in his 1967 consumer message, outlined his reasons for calling for pipeline safety legislation, and the focus was on the weakness of state enforcement authority over pipeline safety.

"As pipelines age and as more and more of the system lies under areas of high population density, the hazards of pipeline failures — and explosions — increase," Mr. Johnson said. "Yet, 22 states have no safety regulations. Many of the remaining 28 states have weak or outmoded provisions. Although the gas industry had developed safety standards, they are not binding, and in some instances not adequate. There is no federal jurisdiction whatsoever over 80 percent of the nation's gas pipeline mileage and no clear authority to set minimum standards for the remaining 20 per cent."

Mr. Johnson referred to the 1965 gas explosion near Natchitoches, La.

LOBBYING ACTIVITY

By 1967, it appeared that Congress eventually would pass some type of gas pipeline safety legislation, despite the industry's belief that the status quo — regulation by the states — should be maintained. If the status quo could not be maintained, the industry wanted the state regulatory agencies to have as big a role as possible in setting standards and enforcing them.

It wanted the industry's code to be adopted as the federal standards. It wanted existing pipe excluded from the standards. It wanted to have a dominant voice on any pipeline standards committee and wanted the committee to have strong powers.

It did not want criminal penalties included in the legislation, and it did not want large civil penalties. It wanted a grace period, giving it time to correct a deficiency before a penalty could be ordered. It did not want to have to deal with both federal and state regulations.

The transmission lines wanted the federal government to pre-empt regulatory authority if there was to be federal regulation. The gathering lines wanted to be excluded from coverage under the bill. The basis for their bid for exclusion was that less than 2,000 miles of about 63,000 miles of gathering lines were in urban areas.

The distribution companies also faced a special problem — they were in the retail business, selling an energy fuel in competition with oil and electricity. They did not want Congress to pass legislation singling out their product as dangerous, because it could hurt them in the marketplace. The distribution companies were divided into two groups, investor-owned and municipal-owned. The municipal owned distribution companies wanted provisions in the law exempting them from coverage because of the nature of their ownership by cities.

The National Assn. of Regulatory and Utilities Commissioners (NARUC) opposed legislation which would dilute its members' authority over pipeline safety and enhance federal authority.

During Senate consideration of S 1166, the interests involved — the industry and its segments, the Government agencies, the consumer spokesmen — followed the usual lobbying practices. They testified before the appropriate committees and appealed for help from certain Members of Congress. But after the Senate passed the bill in November 1967, the fight intensified.

Industry pressure to change the bill more to the industry's liking was concentrated on the House Interstate and Foreign Commerce

Committee's Communications and Power Subcommittee. The major lobbying groups seeking changes in the bill were:

The American Gas Assn. (AGA), an organization of about 350 distribution companies, located in many of the towns and cities of America.

The Independent Natural Gas Assn. of America (INGAA), an association of interstate pipeline companies.

The American Petroleum Institute's Natural Gas Committee (API), joined by the Independent Petroleum Assn. of America, Mid-Continent Oil and Gas Assn. and Western Oil and Gas Assn.; API, with about 8,000 individual and 250 corporate members, was concerned mainly with gathering line facilities.

The American Public Gas Assn. (APGA), an association of about 175 municipally owned distribution companies.

The Natural Gas Processors Assn. (NGPA), an association of firms that use gathering lines and processing facilities.

The National Assn. of Regulatory and Utility Commissioners (NARUC), an association of state regulatory commissioners.

The AFL-CIO and various individual labor unions.

Also seeking changes in the bill was the Department of Transportation, individual Representatives and several gas companies, including the Columbia Gas System Service Corp., New York; Union Gas Co., Brooklyn, N.Y.; Pacific Gas and Electric Co., San Francisco, Calif.

Among those working to preserve the Committee bill was former Rep. Walter Rodgers (D Texas 1951–66), a Washington attorney who was on the Commerce Committee and who represented INGAA as a lobbyist.

The Subcommittee held hearings for five days, and then went to work rewriting a bill. There reportedly was bitter fighting within the subcommittee, with its chairman, Torbert H. Macdonald (D Mass.), trying unsuccessfully to preserve the consumer-oriented aspects of the Senate-passed bill against strong moves by a majority of subcommittee members to make some of the changes the industry wanted.

Efforts in the full Committee to reverse the work of the Subcommittee failed; and when the bill was reported out May 15, it showed the effectiveness of the industry's lobbying. (*Weekly Report p. 1189.*)

The major items the industry wanted and got were:

A change in the Senate language regarding hazards in existing pipe. That change required the Secretary of Transportation to find that a "particular" facility was hazardous before he could order the particular facility replaced. Under Senate language, if the Secretary found that a type of facility was potentially hazardous, he could order all of that type of facility replaced.

A change in the federal-state relationship regarding the standards and their enforcement. Under the Senate language, the Secretary was authorized to work out agreements with those states which adopt federal standards, allowing the states to enforce the standards. The House Committee bill allowed the states to certify their compliance and put the burden on the Secretary to prove a state was not in compliance as a prerequisite to rescinding its certification.

A change in the provision concerning the technical safety standards committee to require the committee's recommendations to be made effective unless the Secretary rejected them and published his reasons for rejecting them. Since the technical committee was industry oriented to start with, this gave the industry additional power to write standards to suit itself.

Lower civil penalties — a reduction from $1,000 to $500 a day for a single offense and a reduction from $400,000 to $100,000 in maximum penalties. The Committee did not approve criminal penalties.

The Committee also cut its authorization for appropriations to enforce the provisions of the bill sharply, reducing the fiscal 1970 appropriation from $13 million to $2 million and the 1971 appropriation from $15 million to $3 million.

Four members of the Committee, all of whom signed a minority report opposing the changes, wrote a letter to *The New York Times* May 3 saying, "In our opinion the bill was essentially gutted at the behest of the gas pipeline lobbies, most of whose proposals were adopted verbatim." The four were Reps. Richard L. Ottinger (D N.Y.), John E. Moss (D Calif.), John D. Dingell (D Mich.) and Brock Adams (D Wash.).

Rep. Joseph P. Vigorito (D Pa.), an early supporter of pipeline safety, used the words "industry sell-out" to describe his feelings about the bill, and said "the House version is so weak and so industry oriented that it would be better to have no bill at all than to sign this one into law." In a May 16 statement, he said "Lobbyists for the natural gas industry succeeded in rewriting the bill so as to weaken it in several important respects."

A legislative assistant said lobbyists for the industry "were in the office day after day, with copies of the amendments they wanted."

An aide to another Representative showed Congressional Quarterly a copy of remarks made by Transportation Secretary Boyd, at a meeting totally unrelated to pipeline safety, which lobbyists were sending around purporting to be Boyd's views on pipeline safety. The Boyd comments being used by the lobbyists said:

"Our job is not to usurp or improperly interfere with the transportation activities of our states, our urban areas, our private businesses. Our job is to look at these activities within the perspective of the public interest and the national purpose — and to do all we can to assist and encourage our states and localities and businesses to advance that interest and encourage that purpose."

Lobbyists also frequently stressed the need to reduce appropriations, in line with the surcharge tax bill, as a reason for lowering the authorization for enforcing the bill.

Boyd did not publicly criticize the lobbying efforts, but he called the House bill "worse than an empty gesture. It is a dangerous deception." President Johnson June 26 urged the House to restore the bill to the Senate standards.

When the House took up the bill July 2, supporters of the Committee bill easily beat back all attempts to amend it to the Senate version, and the bill passed by a 351-14 roll-call vote.

The industry also did well in the House-Senate conference.

The conference allowed the certification provision to remain in effect but added a provision making "it clear that when the Secretary moves to reject a certification the burden of proof is on the state agency to show that it is in compliance." The conference also agreed that as a condition of certification, the state must have injunctive powers in pipeline violation cases and civil penalties.

On penalties, the conferees agreed on the Senate maximum fine of $1,000 a day but set the total maximum at $200,000, closer to the House's $100,000 than the Senate's $400,000. The conferees also added a provision exempting facilities in existence on the day of enactment from civil penalties for a year after that date. And the provision requiring a grace period giving companies time to correct violations before being fined stayed in.

The conferees exempted gathering lines and authorized appropriations for enforcement much closer to the House figures than the Senate's — $2 million for 1970 (same as the House) and $4 million for 1971 (a million more than the House).

After the conference report was accepted by both bodies, Boyd said, "I believe the bill . . . is a workable instrument for protecting the safety of millions of Americans."

William H. Davidson Jr., a Trans-Continental Gas Co. official and INGAA spokesman, said he believed the public was protected, the industry could operate under the bill and that no excessive lobbying had taken place. "Certainly it isn't altogether what we'd like if we'd sat down and written the bill ourselves," he said, but he added that the House changes "improved" the bill.

Paul Rodgers, spokesman for NARUC, was more disturbed about the effects of the bill, because of the removal of authority from the states to the Transportation Department. "It went a lot further than what we hoped it would do," he said. "The political forces for the bill were very powerful. We came out well, under the circumstances, but I'm very concerned about our state role."

Part IV

NATIONAL GOVERNMENTAL STRUCTURES

CHAPTER SIX

The Presidency

The American Presidency is the only unique political institution that the United States has contributed to the world. It developed first in this country and later was imitated, usually unsuccessfully, in many nations. In no country and at no time has the institution of the Presidency achieved the status and power that it possesses in the United States. This chapter will analyze the basis, nature, and implications of the power of this great American institution.

Constitutional Background

The change that has taken place in the Presidency since the office was established in 1789 is dramatic and significant. The framers of the Constitution were primarily concerned with the control of the arbitrary exercise of power by the legislature; thus they were willing to give the President broad power since he was not to be popularly elected and would be constantly under attack by the coordinate legislative branch. Although the framers were not afraid of establishing a vigorous Presidency, there was a great deal of opposition to a potentially strong executive at the time the Constitution was drafted. In the *Federalist 70* Alexander Hamilton attempts to persuade the people of the desirability of a strong presidential office, and while persuading, he sets forth the essential constitutional basis of the office.

26   ALEXANDER HAMILTON

FEDERALIST 70

There is an idea, which is not without its advocates, that a vigorous executive is inconsistent with the genius of republican government. The enlightened well-wishers to this species of government must at least hope that the supposition is destitute of foundation; since they can never admit its truth, without, at the same time, admitting the condemnation of their own principles. Energy in the executive is a leading character in the definition of good government. It is essential to the protection of the community against foreign attacks; it is not less essential to the steady administration of the laws, to the protection of property against those irregular and high-handed combinations, which sometimes interrupt the ordinary course of justice, to the security of liberty against the enterprises and assaults of ambition, of faction, and of anarchy. Every man, the least conversant in Roman story, knows how often that republic was obliged to take refuge in the absolute power of a single man, under the formidable title of dictator, as well as against the intrigues of ambitious individuals, who aspired to the tyranny, and the seditions of whole classes of the community, whose conduct threatened the existence of all government, as against the invasions of external enemies, who menaced the conquest and destruction of Rome.

There can be no need, however, to multiply arguments or examples on this head. A feeble executive implies a feeble execution of the government. A feeble execution is but another phrase for a bad execution; and a government ill executed, whatever it may be in theory, must be, in practice, a bad government.

Taking it for granted, therefore, that all men of sense will agree in the necessity of an energetic executive, it will only remain to inquire, what are the ingredients which constitute this energy? How far can they be combined with those other ingredients, which constitute safety in the republican sense? And how far does this combination characterize the plan which has been reported by the convention?

The ingredients which constitute energy in the executive are, unity; duration; an adequate provision for its support; competent powers.

The ingredients which constitute safety in the republican sense are, a due dependence on the people; a due responsibility.

Those politicians and statesmen, who have been the most celebrated for the soundness of their principles, and for the justness of their views, have declared in favor of a single executive, and a numerous legislature. They have, with great propriety, considered energy as the most necessary qualification of the former, and have regarded this as most applicable to power in a single hand; while they have, with equal propriety, considered the latter as best adapted to deliberation and wisdom, and best calculated to conciliate the confidence of the people, and to secure their privileges and interests.

That unity is conducive to energy will not be disputed. Decision, activity, secrecy, and dispatch, will generally characterize the proceedings of one man, in a much more eminent degree than the proceedings of any greater number; and in proportion as the number is increased, these qualities will be diminished.

This unity may be destroyed in two ways; either by vesting the power in two or more magistrates, of equal dignity and authority; or by vesting it ostensibly in one man, subject, in whole or in part, to the control and co-operation of others, in the capacity of counsellors to him. . . .

The experience of other nations will afford little instruction on this head. As far, however, as it teaches anything, it teaches us not to be enamoured of plurality in the executive. . . .

Wherever two or more persons are engaged in any common enterprise or pursuit, there is always danger of difference of opinion. If it be a public trust of office, in which they are clothed with equal dignity and authority, there is peculiar danger of personal emulation and even animosity. From either, and especially from all these causes, the most bitter dissentions are apt to spring. Whenever these happen, they lessen the respectability, weaken the authority, and distract the plans and operations of those whom they divide. If they should unfortunately assail the supreme executive magistracy of a country, consisting of a plurality of persons, they might impede or frustrate the most important measures of the government, in the most critical emergencies of the state. And what is still worse, they might split the community into violent and irreconcilable factions, adhering differently to the different individuals who composed the magistracy. . . .

Upon the principles of a free government, inconveniences form the source just mentioned, must necessarily be submitted to in the formation of the legislature; but it is unnecessary, and therefore unwise, to introduce them into the constitution of the executive. It is here, too, that they may be most pernicious. In the legislature, promptitude of decision is oftener an evil than a benefit. The differences of opinion, and the jarrings of parties in that department of the government, though they may sometimes obstruct salutary plans, yet often promote deliberation and circumspection; and serve to check excesses in the majority. When a resolution, too, is once taken, the opposition must be at an end. That resolution is a law, and resistance to it punishable. But no favorable circumstances palliate, or atone for the disadvantages of dissention in the executive department. Here they are pure and un-mixed. There is no point at which they cease to operate. They serve to embarrass and weaken the execution of the plan or measure to which they relate, from the first step to the final conclusion of it. They con-stantly counteract those qualities in the executive, which are the most necessary ingredients in its composition — vigor and expedition; and this without any counterbalancing good. In the conduct of war, in which the energy of the executive is the bulwark of the national secu-rity, everything would be to be apprehended from its plurality.

It must be confessed, that these observations apply with principal weight to the first case supposed, that is, to a plurality of magistrates of equal dignity and authority, a scheme, the advocates for which are not likely to form a numerous sect; but they apply, though not with equal, yet with considerable weight, to the project of a council, whose concur-rence is made constitutionally necessary to the operations of the osten-sible executive. An artful cabal in that council would be able to dis-tract and to enervate the whole system of administration. If no such cabal should exist, the mere diversity of views and opinions would alone be sufficient to tincture the exercise of the executive authority with the spirit of habitual feebleness and dilatoriness.

But one of the weightiest objections to a plurality in the executive, and which lies as much against the last as the first plan, is, that it tends to conceal faults, and destroy responsibility. . . . It often becomes im-possible, amidst mutual accusations, to determine on whom the blame or the punishment of a pernicious measure . . . ought really to fall. It is shifted from one to another with so much dexterity, and under such plausible appearances, that the public opinion is left in suspense about the real author. . . .

A little consideration will satisfy us, that the species of security sought for in the multiplication of the executive, is unattainable. Numbers must be so great as to render combination difficult; or they are rather a source of danger than of security. The united credit and influence of several individuals must be more formidable to liberty than the credit and influence of either of them separately. When power, therefore, is placed in the hands of so small a number of men, as to admit of their interests and views being easily combined in a com-mon enterprise, by an artful leader, it becomes more liable to abuse, and more dangerous when abused, than if it be lodged in the hands of one man; who, from the very circumstances of his being alone, will be more narrowly watched and more readily suspected, and who cannot unite so great a mass of influence as when he is associated with others. . . .

I will only add, that prior to the appearance of the constitution, I rarely met with an intelligent man from any of the states, who did not admit as the result of experience, that the unity of the executive of this state was one of the best of the distinguishing features of our constitution.

The Nature of the Presidency

What is the position of the presidential office today? There is little doubt that it has expanded far beyond the expectations of the framers of the Constitution. The Presidency is the only governmental branch with the necessary unity and energy to meet many of the most crucial problems of twentieth-century government in the United States; people have turned to the President in times of crisis to supply the central direction necessary for survival. In the next selection Clinton Rossiter, one of the leading American scholars of the Presidency, discusses the present-day role of the office.

27 CLINTON ROSSITER

THE PRESIDENCY — FOCUS OF LEADERSHIP

No American can contemplate the Presidency . . . without a feeling of solemnity and humility — solemnity in the face of a historically unique concentration of power and prestige, humility in the thought that he has had a part in the choice of a man to wield the power and enjoy the prestige.

Perhaps the most rewarding way to grasp the significance of this great office is to consider it as a focus of democratic leadership. Free men, too, have need of leaders. Indeed, it may well be argued that one of the decisive forces in the shaping of American democracy has been the extraordinary capacity of the Presidency for strong, able, popular leadership. If this has been true of our past, it will certainly be true of our future, and we should therefore do our best to grasp the quality of

From *The New York Times Magazine*, November 11, 1956. Reprinted by permission of *The New York Times* and the author.

this leadership. Let us do this by answering the essential question: For what men and groups does the President provide leadership?

First, the President is *leader of the Executive Branch*. To the extent that our Federal civil servants have need of common guidance, he alone is in a position to provide it. We cannot savor the fullness of the President's duties unless we recall that he is held primarily accountable for the ethics, loyalty, efficiency, frugality and responsiveness to the public's wishes of the two and one-third million Americans in the national administration.

Both the Constitution and Congress have recognized his power to guide the day-to-day activities of the Executive Branch, strained and restrained though his leadership may often be in practice. From the Constitution, explicitly or implicitly, he receives the twin powers of appointment and removal, as well as the primary duty, which no law or plan or circumstances can ever take away from him, to "take care that the laws be faithfully executed."

From Congress, through such legislative mandates as the Budget and Accounting Act of 1921 and the succession of Reorganization Acts, the President has received further acknowledgment of his administrative leadership. Although independent agencies such as the Interstate Commerce Commission and the National Labor Relations Board operate by design outside his immediate area of responsibility, most of the Government's administrative tasks are still carried on within the fuzzy-edged pyramid that has the President at its lonely peak; the laws that are executed daily in his name and under his general supervision are numbered in the hundreds.

Many observers, to be sure, have argued strenuously that we should not ask too much of the President as administrative leader, lest we burden him with impossible detail, or give too much to him, lest we inject political considerations too forcefully into the steady business of the civil service. Still, he cannot ignore the blunt mandate of the Constitution, and we should not forget the wisdom that lies behind it. The President has no more important tasks than to set a high personal example of integrity and industry for all who serve the nation, and to transmit a clear lead downward through his chief lieutenants to all who help shape the policies by which we live.

Next, the President is *leader of the forces of peace and war*. Although authority in the field of foreign relations is shared constitutionally among three organs — President, Congress, and, for two special purposes, the Senate — his position is paramount, if not indeed dominant. Constitution, laws, customs, the practice of other nations and the logic of history have combined to place the President in a dominant position. Secrecy, dispatch, unity, continuity and access to information — the ingredients of successful diplomacy — are properties of his office, and Congress, needless to add, possesses none of them. Leadership in foreign affairs flows today from the President — or it does not flow at all.

The Constitution designates him specifically as "Commander in Chief of the Army and Navy of the United States." In peace and war he is the supreme commander of the armed forces, the living guarantee of the American belief in "the supremacy of the civil over military authority."

In time of peace he raises, trains, supervises and deploys the forces that Congress is willing to maintain. With the aid of the Secretary of Defense, the Joint Chiefs of Staff and the National Security Council — all of whom are his personal choices — he looks constantly to the state of the nation's defenses. He is never for one day allowed to forget that he will be held accountable by the people, Congress and history for the nation's readiness to meet an enemy assault.

In time of war his power to command the forces swells out of all proportion to his other powers. All major decisions of strategy, and many of tactics as well, are his alone to make or to approve. Lincoln and Franklin Roosevelt, each in his own way and time, showed how far the power of military command can be driven by a President anxious to have his generals and admirals get on with the war.

But this, the power of command, is only a fraction of the vast responsibility the modern President draws from the Commander in Chief clause. We need only think back to three of Franklin D. Roosevelt's actions in World War II — the creation and staffing of a whole array of emergency boards and offices, the seizure and operation of more than sixty strike-bound or strike-threatened plants and industries and the forced evacuation of 70,000 American citizens of Japanese descent from the West Coast — to understand how deeply the President's authority can cut into the lives and liberties of the American people in time of war. We may well tremble in contemplation of the kind of leadership he would be forced to exert in a total war with the absolute weapon.

The President's duties are not all purely executive in nature. He is also intimately associated, by Constitution and custom, with the legislative process, and we may therefore consider him as *leader of Congress*. Congress has its full share of strong men, but the complexity of the problems it is asked to solve by a people who still assume that all problems are solvable has made external leadership a requisite of effective operation.

The President alone is in a political, constitutional and practical position to provide such leadership, and he is therefore expected, within the limits of propriety, to guide Congress in much of its law-making activity. Indeed, since Congress is no longer minded or organized to guide itself, the refusal or inability of the President to serve as a kind of prime minister results in weak and disorganized government. His tasks as leader of Congress are difficult and delicate, yet he must bend to them steadily or be judged a failure. The President who will not give his best thoughts to leading Congress, more so the President who is temperamentally or politically unfitted to "get along with Congress," is now rightly considered a national liability.

The lives of Jackson, Lincoln, Wilson and the two Roosevelts should be enough to remind us that the President draws much of his real power from his position as *leader of his party*. By playing the grand politician with unashamed zest, the first of these men gave his epic administration a unique sense of cohesion, the second rallied doubting Republican leaders and their followings to the cause of the Union, and the other three achieved genuine triumphs as catalysts of Congressional action. That gifted amateur, Dwight D. Eisenhower, has also played the role for every drop of drama and power in it. He has demonstrated repeatedly what close observers of the Presidency know well: that its incumbent must devote an hour or two of every working day to the profession of Chief Democrat or Chief Republican.

It troubles many good people, not entirely without reason, to watch the President dabbling in politics, distributing loaves and fishes, smiling on party hacks, and endorsing candidates he knows to be unfit for anything but immediate delivery to the county jail. Yet if he is to persuade Congress, if he is to achieve a loyal and cohesive administration, if he is to be elected in the first place (and re-elected in the second), he must put his hand firmly to the plow of politics. The President is inevitably the nation's No. 1 political boss.

Yet he is, at the same time, if not in the same breath, *leader of public opinion*. While he acts as political chieftain of some, he serves as moral spokesman for all. It took the line of Presidents some time to sense the nation's need for a clear voice, but since the day when Andrew Jackson thundered against the Nullifiers of South Carolina, no effective President has doubted his prerogative to speak the people's mind on the great issues of his time, to serve, in Wilson's words, as "the spokesman for the real sentiment and purpose of the country."

Sometimes, of course, it is no easy thing, even for the most sensitive and large-minded Presidents, to know the real sentiment of the people or to be bold enough to state it in defiance of loudly voiced contrary opinion. Yet the President who senses the popular mood and spots new tides even before they start to run, who practices shrewd economy in his appearances as spokesman for the nation, who is conscious of his unique power to compel discussion on his own terms and who talks the language of Christian morality and the American tradition, can shout down any other voice or chorus of voices in the land. The President is the American people's one authentic trumpet, and he has no higher duty than to give a clear and certain sound.

The President is easily the most influential leader of opinion in this country principally because he is, among all his other jobs, our Chief of State. He is, that is to say, the ceremonial head of the Government of the United States, the *leader of the rituals of American democracy*. The long catalogue of public duties that the Queen discharges in England and the Governor General in Canada is the President's responsibility in this country, and the catalogue is even longer because he is not a king, or even the agent of one, and is therefore expected to go through some rather undignified paces by a people who think of him as a combination of scoutmaster, Delphic oracle, hero of the silver screen and father of the multitudes.

The role of Chief of State may often seem trivial, yet it cannot be neglected by a President who proposes to stay in favor and, more to the point, in touch with the people, the ultimate support of all his claims to leadership. And whether or not he enjoys this role, no President can fail to realize that his many powers are invigorated, indeed are given a new dimension of authority, because he is the symbol of our sovereignty, continuity and grandeur as a people.

When he asks a Senator to lunch in order to enlist his support for a pet project, when he thumps his desk and reminds the antagonists in a labor dispute of the larger interests of the American people, when he orders a general to cease caviling or else be removed from his command, the Senator and the disputants and the general are well aware — especially if the scene is laid in the White House — that they are dealing with no ordinary head of Government. The framers of the Constitution took a momentous step when they fused the dignity of a king and the power of a Prime Minister in one elective office — when they made the President a national leader in the mystical as well as the practical sense.

Finally, the President has been endowed — whether we or our friends abroad like it or not — with a global role as *a leader of the free nations*. His leadership in this area is not that of a dominant executive. The power he exercises is in a way comparable to that which he holds as a leader of Congress. Senators and Congressmen can, if they choose, ignore the President's leadership with relative impunity. So, too, can our friends abroad; the action of Britain and France in the Middle East is a case in point. But so long as the United States remains the richest and most powerful member of any coalition it may enter, then its President's words and deeds will have a direct bearing on the freedom and stability of a great many other countries.

Having engaged in this piecemeal analysis of the categories of Presidential leadership, we must now fit the pieces back together into a seamless unity. For that, after all, is what the Presidency is, and I hope this exercise in political taxonomy has not obscured the paramount fact that this focus of democratic leadership is a single office filled by a single man.

The President is not one kind of leader one part of the day, another kind in another part — leader of the bureaucracy in the morning, of the armed forces at lunch, of Congress in the afternoon, of the people in the evening. He exerts every kind of leadership every moment of the day, and every kind feeds upon and into all the others. He is a more exalted leader of ritual because he can guide opinion, a more forceful leader in diplomacy because he commands the armed forces personally, a more effective leader of Congress because he sits at the top of his party. The conflicting demands of these categories of leadership give him trouble at times, but in the end all unite to make him a leader without any equal in the history of democracy.

I think it important to note the qualification: "the history of democracy." For what I have been talking about here is not the Fuehrerprinzip of Hitler or the "cult of personality," but the leadership of free men. The Presidency, like every other instrument of power we have created for our use, operates within a grand and durable pattern of private liberty and public morality, which means that the President can lead successfully only when he honors the pattern — by working toward ends to which a "persistent and undoubted" majority of the people has given support, and by selecting means that are fair, dignified and familiar.

The President, that is to say, can lead us only in the direction we are accustomed to travel. He cannot lead the gentlemen of Congress to abdicate their functions; he cannot order our civil servants to be corrupt and slothful; he cannot even command our generals to bring off a *coup d'état*. And surely he cannot lead public opinion in a direction for which public opinion is not prepared — a truth to which our strongest Presidents would make the most convincing witnesses. The leadership of free men must honor their freedom. The power of the Presidency can move as a mighty host only with the grain of liberty and morality.

The President, then, must provide a steady focus of leadership — of administrators, Ambassadors, generals, Congressmen, party chieftains, people and men of good will everywhere. In a constitutional system compounded of diversity and antagonism, the Presidency looms up as the countervailing force of unity and harmony. In a society ridden by centrifugal forces, it is the only point of reference we all have in common. The relentless progress of this continental republic has made the Presidency our one truly national political institution.

There are those, to be sure, who would reserve this role to Congress, but, as the least aggressive of our Presidents, Calvin Coolidge, once testified, "It is because in their hours of timidity the Congress becomes subservient to the importunities of organized minorities that the President comes more and more to stand as the champion of the rights of the whole country." The more Congress becomes, in Burke's phrase, "a confused and scuffling bustle of local agency" the more the Presidency must become a clear beacon of national purpose.

It has been such a beacon at most great moments in our history. In this great moment, too, we may be confident it will burn brightly.

> The constitutional and statutory *authority* of the President is indeed extraordinary. Before discussing the way in which the Supreme Court has interpreted this authority, however, it is important to point out that the actual power of the President depends upon his political abilities. The President must act within the framework of a complex and diversified political constituency. He can use the authority of his office to buttress his strength, but this alone is not sufficient. Somehow he must be able to persuade those with whom he deals to follow him; otherwise, he will be weak and ineffective.

28   RICHARD E. NEUSTADT

PRESIDENTIAL POWER

In the United States we like to "rate" a President. We measure him as "weak" or "strong" and call what we are measuring his "leadership." We do not wait until a man is dead; we rate him from the moment he takes office. We are quite right to do so. His office has become the focal point of politics and policy in our political system. Our commentators and our politicians make a specialty of taking the man's measurements. The rest of us join in when we feel "government" impinging on our private lives. In the third quarter of the twentieth century millions of us have that feeling often.

. . . Although we all make judgments about presidential leadership, we often base our judgments upon images of office that are far removed from the reality. We also use those images when we tell one another whom to choose as President. But it is risky to appraise a man in office or to choose a man for office on false premises about the nature of his job. When the job is the Presidency of the United States the risk becomes excessive. . . .

We deal here with the President himself and with his influence on governmental action. In institutional terms the Presidency now includes 2000 men and women. The President is only one of them. But *his* performance scarcely can be measured without focusing on *him*. In terms of party, or of country, or the West, so-called, his leadership involves far more than governmental action. But the sharpening of spirit and of values and of purposes is not done in a vacuum. Although governmental action may not be the whole of leadership, all else is nurtured by it and gains meaning from it. Yet if we treat the Presidency as the President, we cannot measure him as though he were the government. Not action as an outcome but his impact on the outcome is the measure of the man. His strength or weakness, then, turns on his personal capacity to influence the conduct of the men who make up government. His influence becomes the mark of leadership. To rate a President according to these rules, one looks into the man's own capabilities as seeker and as wielder of effective influence upon the other men involved in governing the country. . . .

"Presidential" . . . means nothing but the President. "Power" means *his* influence. It helps to have these meanings settled at the start.

There are two ways to study "presidential power." One way is to focus on the tactics, so to speak, of influencing certain men in given situations: how to get a bill through Congress, how to settle strikes, how to quiet Cabinet feuds, or how to stop a Suez. The other way is to step back from tactics on those "givens" and to deal with influence in more strategic terms: what is its nature and what are its sources? What can *this* man accomplish to improve the prospect that he will have influence when he wants it? Strategically, the question is not how he masters Congress in a peculiar instance, but what he does to boost his chance for mastery in any instance, looking toward tomorrow from today. The second of these two ways has been chosen for this [selection]. . . .

In form all Presidents are leaders, nowadays. In fact this guarantees no more than that they will be clerks. Everybody now expects the man inside the White House to do something about everything. Laws and customs now reflect acceptance of him as the Great Initiator, an acceptance quite as widespread at the Capitol as at his end of Pennsylvania Avenue. But such acceptance does not signify that all the rest of government is at his feet. It merely signifies that other men have found it practically impossible to do *their* jobs without assurance of initiatives from him. Service for themselves, not power for the President, has brought them to accept his leadership in form. They find his actions useful in their business. The transformation of his routine obligations testifies to their dependence on an active White House. A President, these days, is an invaluable clerk. His services are in demand all over Washington. His influence, however, is a very different matter. Laws and customs tell us little about leadership in fact.

Why have our Presidents been honored with this clerkship? The answer is that no one else's services suffice. Our Constitution, our traditions, and our politics provide no better source for the initiatives a President can take. Executive officials need decisions, and political protection, and a referee for fights. Where are these to come from but the White House? Congressmen need an agenda from outside, something with high status to respond to or react against. What provides it better than the program of the President? Party politicians need a record to defend in the next national campaign. How can it be made except by "their" Administration? Private persons with a public axe to grind may need a helping hand or they may need a grinding stone. In either case who gives more satisfaction than a President? And outside the United States, in every country where our policies and postures influence home politics, there will be people needing just the "right" thing said and done or just the "wrong" thing stopped *in Washington*. What symbolizes Washington more nearly than the White House?

A modern President is bound to face demands for aid and service from five more or less distinguishable sources: from Executive officialdom, from Congress, from his partisans, from citizens at large, and from abroad. The Presidency's clerkship is expressive of these pressures. In effect they are constituency pressures and each President has five sets of constituents. The five are not distinguished by their membership; membership is obviously an overlapping matter. And taken one by one they do not match the man's electorate; one of them, indeed, is outside his electorate. They are distinguished, rather, by their different claims upon him. Initiatives are what they want, for five distinctive reasons. Since government and politics have offered no alternative, our laws and customs turn those wants into his obligations.

Why, then, is the President not guaranteed an influence commensurate with services performed? Constituent relations are relations of dependence. Everyone with any share in governing this country will belong to one (or two, or three) of his "constituencies." Since everyone depends on him why is he not assured of everyone's support? The answer is that no one else sits where he sits, or sees quite as he sees; no one else feels the full weight of his obligations. Those obligations are a tribute to his unique place in our political system. But just because it is unique they fall on him alone. *The same conditions that promote his leadership in form preclude a guarantee of leadership in fact.* No man or group at either end of Pennsylvania Avenue shares his peculiar status in our government and politics. That is why his services are in demand. By the same token, though, the obligations of all other men are different from his own. His Cabinet officers have departmental duties and constituents. His legislative leaders head *congressional* parties, one in either House. His national party organization stands apart from his official family. His political allies in the States need not face Washington, or one another. The private groups that seek him out are not compelled to govern. And friends abroad are not compelled to run in our elections. Lacking his position and prerogatives, these men cannot regard his obligations as their own. They have their jobs to do; none is the same as his. As they perceive their duty they may find it right to follow him, in fact, or they may not. Whether they will feel obliged *on their responsibility* to do what he wants done remains an open question. . . .

There is reason to suppose that in the years immediately ahead the power problems of a President will remain what they have been in the decades just behind us. If so there will be equal need for presidential expertise of the peculiar sort . . . that has [been] stressed [i.e., political skill]. Indeed, the need is likely to be greater. The President himself and with him the whole government are likely to be more than ever at the mercy of his personal approach.

What may the Sixties do to politics and policy and to the place of Presidents in our political system? The Sixties may destroy them as we know them; that goes without saying. But barring deep depression or unlimited war, a total transformation is the least of likelihoods. Without catastrophes of those dimensions nothing in our past experience suggests that we shall see either consensus of the sort available to F.D.R. in 1933 and 1942, or popular demand for institutional adjustments likely to assist a President. Lacking popular demand, the natural conservatism of established institutions will keep Congress and the party organizations quite resistant to reforms that could give him a clear advantage over them. Four-year terms for congressmen and senators might do it, if the new terms ran with his. What will occasion a demand for that? As for crisis consensus it is probably beyond the reach of the next President. We may have priced ourselves out of the market for "productive" crises on the pattern Roosevelt knew — productive in the sense of strengthening his chances for sustained support *within* the system. Judging from the Fifties, neither limited war nor limited depression is productive in those terms. Anything unlimited will probably break the system.

In the absence of productive crises, and assuming that we manage to avoid destructive ones, nothing now foreseeable suggests that our next President will have assured support from any quarter. There is no use expecting it from the bureaucracy unless it is displayed on Capitol Hill. Assured support will not be found in Congress unless contemplation of their own electorates keeps a majority of members constantly aligned with him. In the Sixties it is to be doubted . . . that pressure from electorates will move the same majority of men in either House toward consistent backing for the President. Instead the chances are that he will gain majorities, when and if he does so, by *ad hoc* coalition-building, issue after issue. In that respect the Sixties will be reminiscent of the Fifties; indeed, a closer parallel may well be the late Forties. As for "party discipline" in English terms — the favorite cure-all of political scientists since Woodrow Wilson was a youth — the first preliminary is a party link between the White House and the leadership on both sides of the Capitol. But even this preliminary has been lacking in eight of the fifteen years since the Second World War. If ballot-splitting should continue through the Sixties it will soon be "un-American" for President and Congress to belong to the same party.

Even if the trend were now reversed, there is no short-run prospect that behind each party label we would find assembled a sufficiently like-minded bloc of voters, similarly aligned in states and districts all across the country, to negate the massive barriers our institutions and traditions have erected against "discipline" on anything like the British scale. This does not mean that a reversal of the ballot-splitting trend would be without significance. If the White House and the legislative leadership were linked by party ties again, a real advantage would accrue to both. Their opportunities for mutually productive bargaining would be enhanced. The policy results might surprise critics of our system. Bargaining "within the family" has a rather different quality than bargaining with members of the rival clan. But we would still be a long way from "party government." Bargaining, not "discipline," would still remain the key to congressional action on a President's behalf. The critical distinctions between presidential party and congressional party are not likely to be lost in the term of the next President.

The President and His Cabinet

The Cabinet may enhance or detract from presidential power. Previous selections have pointed out the multiple responsibilities of the President, which require leadership of the public, his party, Congress, and the bureaucracy. As Richard F. Fenno suggests below, the Cabinet may affect the leadership capacities of the President in these various areas in many ways.

29   RICHARD F. FENNO, JR.

THE CABINET AND POLITICS

Face-to-face contact between the President and his Cabinet is occasional and limited. Both parties make their greatest expenditure of time and energy in activities beyond the immediate President-Cabinet nexus. For the Chief Executive, there are the multiple tasks of leadership — formal and informal, legal or extra-legal. For the Cabinet member, there are a host of involvements arising out of his departmental, constituency, partisan, and legislative relationships. What is the effect of these extensive extra-Cabinet activities on the President-Cabinet relationship? Do they help to account for the group behavior we have observed in the Cabinet meeting? Will the individual member's other involvements affect his position as adviser and "chief lieutenant" to the President? The answer to these questions must be sought by moving beyond the immediate President-Cabinet nexus and into the political system as a whole.

The President, it is commonly said, is "many men." He plays at least four distinguishable yet overlapping and frequently conflicting roles — as Chief Representative of the Nation, Chief of his Party, Chief Legislator, and Chief Executive. His leadership, like all leadership, can be understood in terms of the interrelation of personal and situational phenomena. In playing his variety of roles, singly or in juxtaposition, the President will be required to demonstrate many different personal abilities, involving intelligence, skill, and temperament. He will be required, also, to function in different contexts, with regard for the limitations imposed upon him, the social constituencies to which he speaks, the degree of support he wishes to get, the goals he seeks to achieve. In performing his tasks, the President needs assistance that is definable in terms of personal traits and assistance that is related to particular situations. The Cabinet member is a source of both of these types. Most Presidents display an awareness of their needs during the appointment process. If they should not, however, the search for diverse kinds of assistance will be pressed upon them by the necessities of survival.

The Cabinet member has built-in features which recommend him to the President as an extra-Cabinet-meeting source of assistance, for he, too, must be "many men." He, too, is cast in a diversity of roles, which require a corresponding diversity of personal talents and capabilities. The locus of his activities within the political system is similar to that of the Chief Executive. The Cabinet member, too, acts as the representative spokesman for the interests of large segments of the population. He, too, must reach out into a constituency to win and consolidate group support. As a member of a political party more or less committed to certain actions in the realm of policy or patronage, he is rarely free from the obligations and pressures of that relationship. Every Cabinet official is a chief executive in his own right — the head of a great administrative establishment. He is, next to the President, a top-level executive of the national government. In the conduct of the business of his department and in advocating its policies he is thrown into constant contact with the legislature. His usefulness to the President must be judged not just by what he does in the Cabinet meeting, but by his performance elsewhere in the political system. The ultimate question is, of course, how well suited the variety of Cabinet-member relationships is to the variety of presidential needs.

For the purposes of examination, the extra-Cabinet relationships of the Cabinet member have been divided into categories of public prestige, party, Congress, and departmental administration. They are designed to correspond roughly to the four presidential leadership roles mentioned earlier. The inclusion of a section on departmental administration under the rubric of "politics" is largely a matter of convenience, but it does indicate that it is the politics of administration with which that section is mainly concerned, and that no support is given here to a dichotomous view of politics and administration.

President, Cabinet, and Public Prestige

The President as Chief Representative. As Chief Representative of the Nation the President plays the most general of all his leadership roles. It transcends his position as leader of a party or as a legislative leader, involving as it does more than the task of mobilizing electoral and congressional majorities. As Chief Representative, the President speaks for the entire nation whenever a single voice is required, be it a time of crisis or of national ceremony. The Presidency in its unity can symbolize the nation as a whole; and as a human being, the President personalizes that symbol. He cannot avoid the role of preeminence in the public mind, though some individuals will make much more of it than others. Whenever he speaks or acts he commands nationwide attention. He can fix national goals, alter national morale, and raise national standards. In representing the nation the President finds his broadest basis of support in the population. He represents the most fundamental and most widely shared ideals of the community. He becomes a political leader in the highest sense of the term.

If the President's function as Chief Representative be construed in its purest sense, the Cabinet can be of little help. It is no match for the President, in terms of public relations. At the Republican National Convention of 1956, the members of the Eisenhower Cabinet were scheduled to make an unprecedented appearance before that body and before the American public via television. They were going to take turns reading the party platform. But scarcely had the first man opened his mouth when all television coverage abruptly switched to the San Francisco airport in anticipation of the President's forthcoming arrival. And while the members of the Cabinet spoke to the convention on the crucial policies of the Eisenhower administration, millions of Americans followed the presidential plane Columbine as it flew around in circles over the airfield. By the time the viewer was returned to the convention hall, the Cabinet members had long since disappeared in the crowd. The lesson, which the communications media understood, is obvious. There is only one President, and the gap in prestige between him and his closest subordinate is unbridgeable in the public eye. Even though, as in this case, it is the President's intention to publicize his Cabinet, he can, almost by moving a muscle, defeat that purpose.

His role as Chief Representative, however, is not exhausted by a single act performed at a moment when only he commands attention. He can fulfill the role only on the basis of the confidence he inspires and the prestige he commands in the nation as a whole. Confidence and prestige are intangible assets, accumulated over a period of time and amassed by actions in many areas of activity. Here, perhaps, the Cabinet member can be of assistance. By virtue of his performance in certain areas, he may bring to the administration as a whole an increment of prestige which can be banked or traded upon by the President. The net result may increase the President's success as Chief Representative of the Nation.

> *Cabinet and Prestige: Possibilities and Limitations.* Taken as a group, the Cabinet may add to or subtract from the public's estimation of the President. "I should not fear to predict the result of your administration," wrote James Buchanan to Franklin Pierce, "as soon as I learn who are members of your Cabinet." The selection of the Cabinet is a symbolic act for the interested public, and they hasten to judge the extent to which the appointments as a whole will bring him overall public support. The Cabinet is the show window of the administration, and a favorable reception for the group will be an asset which the President can use to augment his own public prestige.

Group prestige is, however, a highly perishable commodity. It may give the President a lift in the early days of his administration, while the concept of "the team" is uppermost in the public mind. There is usually a Cabinet honeymoon period while a partly-sympathetic and partly-apprehensive public waits for the Secretaries to act in their respective fields. The first Cabinet meeting is usually publicized with pictures and front page coverage. Quickly, however, "the team" and the Cabinet meeting vanish from sight. Departmental policies are the subject of attention. Praise and blame are allocated individually. Some members are constantly in the public eye and others hardly at all. The Cabinet group which had looked so "balanced" in the newspapers becomes less balanced in action. . . . Although the Cabinet group is periodically resurrected for public display, it rarely receives consideration as a whole.

If the Cabinet as a group, therefore, provides only minimal assistance by way of accumulating public prestige and confidence for the President, can the individual member do any more? The answer is probably yes — subject, however, to some very severe limitations of the political system in which the President-Cabinet relationship is placed. The appointment of a nationally known figure with an established reputation of his own can undoubtedly be of assistance to the Chief Executive. . . .

Cabinet and Party: Possibilities and Limitations. The Cabinet as a group has no institutionalized relationship with the political party. A few traditions have grown up by which it is made susceptible to party influences, but in no sense do they make it a party organ. Cabinet members are usually taken from the same party as the President, and customarily one or more members are party managers dealing with such partisan matters as the distribution of patronage. Otherwise, the party impact on the Cabinet and the Cabinet's effect on the party are not regularized. The President's actions will be influential in settling the nature and extent of party-cabinet relationships, if and when he tries to turn the Cabinet to some advantage in performing his functions as Party Chief.

The appointment of the Cabinet may symbolize some of the President's own notions about party leadership, and it may provoke some kind of response among the interested public. He could alienate large numbers of his party followers by its composition, and thus with one stroke undermine his party position. Ordinarily no President does this, however, and while each of his appointments does not please everyone, taken as a whole they do not threaten his leadership. On the other hand, his selection may do something by way of consolidating the party behind him. He may try to consolidate his party-in-the-electorate by bringing into the Cabinet representatives of those groups in the country which helped form his majority coalition — as when Roosevelt appointed independent Republican Harold Ickes and Eisenhower selected southerner Oveta Culp Hobby. He may choose to accentuate his own leadership within the party by selecting for representation only such individuals or factions as supported his original nomination — as Roosevelt did. He may, in an extreme case, wish to symbolize his independence of both his "parties" with a bipartisan selection — such as that of Martin Durkin.

The best known of all the types of Cabinet-party relationships is produced by the attempt to weld together the various factions within the party-in-the-government by bringing them into the President's advisory group. Such a move will be taken as a definite bid for party unity, looking toward harmonious relationships between its leader, the President, and the rest of the party. The President may seek out the leaders of the various factions or merely seek representatives of each. The most radical experiment of this sort on record was made by Lincoln, who invited and obtained for his Cabinet all of his major rivals for the Presidency. Warren Harding tried to get his two major opponents and failed, but he then selected representatives of various factions. . . . Eisenhower solicited suggestions from his major rival, Senator Taft, and selected at least one and possibly two of them. One cannot say, however, that the future role which the President will assume vis-à-vis the party is forecast by his quest for harmony. He may be, in effect, abdicating his leadership of the party-in-the-government as Harding was; he may be able to harness the group under his own leadership as Lincoln was; or he may be feeling his way along in a new situation as Eisenhower was, caught between the desire to be above party and the fear of isolating himself from it.

The symbolic appeal for party unity may, in itself, be a helpful gesture in keeping the party intact. Probably the best it can do, as in the case of the Cabinet's group prestige, is to postpone party splits long enough to get the new administration off on the right foot. Its net effect upon the party will be distinctly minor. Depending upon the condition of the party and the President's own self-confidence, however, it is a move which many Presidents cannot afford not to make. . . .

President, Cabinet, and Congress

The Cabinet Member in the Legislative-Executive Context. The executive and legislative branches of the government interact within a constitutional framework, which provides for independent bases of power but a sharing of decision-making authority. The President is given the constitutional authority to send messages to Congress, to "recommend to their consideration such measures as he shall judge necessary and expedient," to call special sessions, to exercise a veto power over legislation, and to control certain aspects of our foreign relations. The Congress, on the other hand, has the legal authority to set up executive departments and agencies, to appropriate money for the executive branch, and to confirm presidential appointments, to conduct investigations in the executive branch, and to share with the President the control and the conduct of foreign relations. This is by no means a complete catalogue of the points of formal contact, but it is sufficient to show the basis of the President's role as Chief Legislator and the basis of congressional control over the executive branch.

Threaded through and around the formal legal structure are a whole set of informal, less visible relationships which help to shape the character of the President's legislative relations. The subtle threat to a veto, a well-timed distribution of patronage, personal confidence or hostility — all these may be decisive in the making of a legislative decision favorable to the Chief Legislator. Interpersonal contact between the President and legislative leaders or between members of the executive branch and Congressmen may be most effective in winning cooperation. Nor is the continual interplay of the legislature and the executive branch through interest groups recorded in formal documents. The President needs help in both formal and informal legislative activities, and since the Cabinet member is constantly involved in both, he has the opportunity to furnish it.

The Cabinet member's position in the context of executive-legislative relations is by no means a consistent one. He will find himself playing two roles at once when he faces Congress — he is a presidential adviser, but he is also a department head. In the first role, he is bound tightly by the power-responsibility relationship to the Chief Executive. According to the hierarchical or vertical conception of authority, he acts as the agent of the President helping him to carry out his ultimate responsibility. But as a department head, the lines of responsibility are not quite so distinct. His department is subject to *both* presidential direction and legislative control — to both vertical and horizontal lines of responsibility. This conception of the Cabinet member's activity is not an internally harmonious one, and opportunities to help the President may also be opportunities to harm. . . .

Theoretical ambiguities become reinforced by ambiguities in the realm of informal power relationships, and the upshot is that the President-Cabinet member, power-responsibility relationship will not suffice as an explanation of the extra-Cabinet activity of the Cabinet member. The legislative branch is found to be competing with the President for control over the department head's activities. The clientele publics from which the Cabinet member draws so much of his support may have easy access to the legislature and may work through it to establish a proprietary relationship with the department. The department head, for his part, knows that from the President alone he cannot get all of the power that he needs to operate his department as he wishes. He frequently responds favorably to legislative control in return for the power which he draws from it. It may be of mutual benefit to the Cabinet member and "the legislature," i.e., a committee or a Congressman, to develop horizontal relationships. In formally institutionalized ways, in informal contact, or in combinations of both, department head–legislative-interest group relations develop and become counterweights to presidential control.

Depending on the circumstances, the Cabinet member will probably have alternatives of action when he confronts Congress. He may play his role as presidential adviser and department head in such a way that they mutually reinforce one another — in which case he may not only help the President but himself as well. Or, at the other extreme, he may be able to divorce one role from the other. If he appears as the President's man, he may aid his superior and may or may not (probably not) improve his own departmental position. If he operates independently of the President, he may aid his own future and may or may not (probably not) help the President. Between these extremes lie the intermediary positions most often taken — positions which accommodate, with shifting emphasis, one role to the other. The context in which this accommodation goes on is filled with sources of difficulty, as well as help, for the Chief Legislator. . . .

President, Cabinet, and Departmental Administration

The President as Chief Executive. "The executive power shall be vested in a President of the United States," who shall "take care that the laws are faithfully executed," and who "shall nominate, and by and with the consent of the Senate shall appoint" thousands of public officials. Such are the broad, vague lines of the President's mandate to function as the nation's Chief Executive. By following them, and by assuming responsibility for the effective management of the executive branch of the government, he performs his role as *Chief Executive-Administrator.* In 1848, President James K. Polk entered a pair of comments in his diary which may stand as one high-water mark in the performance of this leadership role:

> I have not had my full Cabinet together in council since the adjournment of Congress on the 14th of August last. I have conducted the government without their aid. Indeed, I have become so familiar with the duties and workings of the government, not only upon general principles, but in most of its minute details, that I find but little difficulty in doing this. I have made myself acquainted with the duties

of my subordinate officers, and have probably given more attention to details than any of my predecessors.

No president who performs his duty faithfully and conscientiously can have any leisure. If he entrusts the details and smaller matters to subordinates, constant errors will occur. I prefer to supervise the whole operations of the government myself than entrust the public business to subordinates, and this makes my duties very great.

The first comment that comes to mind *apropos* of such a feverish expenditure of energy is this: Polk died a few months later, surviving his tenure of office by only one month. But the essential point to be made involves the extraordinary primitiveness of Polk's prescription for presidential administration of governmental activity. In the twentieth century, no President can treat his department heads as superfluous.

The trenchant statement of the President's Committee on Administrative Management that "the President needs help" is well enough known. Quite apart from the specific context in which it was written, the sentiment has always been a valid one. It was George Washington who first recognized "the impossibility that one man should be able to perform all the great business of the state," and who found the solution to his problem by "instituting the great departments." From that day to this, the executive departments of the national government have been, formally speaking, "the major organizational and crucial elements in the administrative structure of the executive branch below the presidency." The department head becomes an "outpost of the President in an assigned field of administrative activities." He helps to implement the broad policy views of the President within his department, provides a responsible line of communication between the department and the President, and functions in general as a link in the hierarchical chain of command running from top to bottom within the executive branch. In addition to his functions as a presidential lieutenant, the department head is a chief executive in his own right, "the administrative leader of the agency to which he is assigned." He has an immense organization whose activities he must direct, coordinate, and keep on an even keel. He is positioned at the peak of one distinct pyramid of authority, concerned with the particular interests and problems of those groups of people subordinate to him. Administratively, then, the department head is cast in two interrelated yet distinguishable roles — one President-oriented, the other department-oriented. His formal responsibilities extend both upward toward the President and downward toward his own department.

In the frictionless world of organization-chart hierarchies, this double-jointed job presents no analytical problem. The department head takes his marching orders from the President and transmits them to his organization. He accepts political responsibility for day-to-day administration according to the standards established by his superior. Thus does he help the administrator-in-chief increase his own effectiveness. The political universe inhabited by the department head is, however, not so simply understood. Just as his possibilities of helping the Chief Legislator in Congress are complicated by the impingement of non-presidential forces upon him, so too are his possibilities of helping the Chief Executive-Administrator in the departments. There is, to begin with, the personality factor, the set of attitudes and abilities which the department head brings to his job. Furthermore, within his department he operates according to formal organizational prescription and under the influence of less formalized group interests, all of which set limits on his activity. As for the environment outside of his department, it is one of conflicting responsibilities and institutional rivalries, certain to involve him in problems of role conflict. . . .

The Cabinet and Politics: Some Conclusions

The investigations which we have made into Cabinet-member activity in the areas of public prestige, party, Congress, and departmental administration lead to a few conclusions about the Cabinet and the political system in which it operates. One striking circumstance is the extent to which the Cabinet concept breaks down in the course of the members' activities outside the Cabinet meeting. In matters of prestige, partisan politics, and legislative relations alike, the Cabinet as a collectivity has only a symbolic value, a value which readily disappears when the need for action supersedes the need for a show window. In the day-to-day work of the Cabinet member, each man fends for himself without much consideration for Cabinet unity. His survival, his support, and his success do not depend on his fellow members. His performance is judged separately from theirs. This condition is but another result of the combination of the centrifugal tendencies in our political system with the low degree of institutionalization which characterizes the Cabinet.

The political help which the President receives comes not from the group but from individual Cabinet members, who can and do augment the President's effectiveness in his leadership roles. It would be a serious mistake not to emphasize the possibilities for crucial assistance by individuals. But probably most striking is the fact that the possibilities for such assistance are very frequently negated by the number of limitations which surround them. There are pervasive limitations of a personal or a situational nature, and there are limitations inherent in the political system — all of which make it neither easy for a Cabinet member to help the President nor axiomatic that he should do so. In the final reckoning, the President receives much less assistance of a positive, non-preventive type from his individual Cabinet members than one might expect. This fact serves to accent the high degree of success which is represented by preventive assistance. It also helps to underline the tremendous gap which separates the presidential level of responsibility from that of his subordinates. It demonstrates, too, the extent to which the two levels are subject to the pulls of different political forces.

The President-Cabinet power-responsibility relationship is, according to the analysis of this chapter, inadequate as a total explanation for the extra-Cabinet performance of the individual member. As a group the Cabinet draws its life breath from the President, but as individuals the Cabinet members are by no means so dependent on him. In many instances, we are presented with the paradox that in order for the Cabinet member to be of real help to the President in one of his leadership roles, the member must have non-presidential "public" prestige, party following, legislative support, or roots of influence in his department. And in any case, the problems of his own success and survival will encourage him to consolidate his own nexus of power and will compel him to operate with some degree of independence from the President. For his part, the President's influence over the Cabinet member becomes splintered and eroded as the member responds to political forces not presidential in origin or direction. From the beginnings of his involvement in the appointment process, the President's power is subject to the pervasive limitations of the pluralistic system in which he seeks to furnish political leadership.

One final conclusion takes the form of a restatement of the pluralism of American politics. In every area we have noted the diffusion, the decentralization, and the volatility of political power. The same kaleidoscopic variety which characterized the factors influential in the appointment process is evident in the political processes which engulf the Cabinet member. Each member interacts with a great variety of political units, interest groups, party groups, and legislative groups, and each has his own pattern of action and his own constellation of power. The feudal analogy is an apt one. It frequently makes more sense to describe the Cabinet member as part of a "feudal pattern of fiefs, baronies, and dukedoms than . . . an orderly and symmetrical pyramid of authority."

Here, then, is an underlying explanation for Cabinet-meeting behavior. Departmentalism is a condition whose roots are grounded in the basic diversity of forces which play upon the individual member. By the same token, this pluralism generates centrifugal influences which help to keep the Cabinet in its relatively non-institutionalized state. The greatest problems for Cabinet and President, like the greatest problems in American politics, are those which center around the persistent dilemmas of unity and diversity.

The President and Congress

James M. Burns, in discussing the important factors affecting the interaction between the President and Congress, sets forth his view of the probable nature of presidential-congressional relations in the future. Do you feel that the viewpoint of Professor Burns has been borne out in light of recent circumstances?

30   JAMES M. BURNS

THE PRESIDENCY AND CONGRESS

. . . [T]he Presidency has absorbed the Cabinet, the executive departments, the Vice-Presidency. It has taken over the national party apparatus. Through consistently liberal appointments over the years it has a powerful influence on the doctrine of the Supreme Court. It has transformed the federal system. What about its impact on Congress, historically and constitutionally the great counterforce to the presidential office?

Here the change may be the most profound of all, at least in the long run. Our speculations need not be overly influenced by short-run developments, such as President Johnson's great success with Congress in his first two years in office. This success, coming on the heels of the congressional deadlock over many of Kennedy's major proposals, was largely due to some special circumstances: Johnson's standing on Capitol Hill, his particular legislative experience, the consolidation of presidential support after the rout of the Goldwater forces, and a congressional and popular urge to honor the late President's memory by supporting some of his major proposals. We must consider more basic and continuing forces that shape the relations of Congress and President as institutions.

One such force is reapportionment. The granting of greater representation in the House (and in state legislatures) to urban and suburban areas will bring the presidential and congressional constituencies into closer approximation and hence diminish some of the structural forces making for divergent policy. This shift may take longer than some expect, because it is the one-party district rather than the malap-

From James M. Burns, *Presidential Government: The Crucible of Leadership* (Houghton Mifflin Company, 1966), pp. 319–23. Reprinted by permission of the publisher and the author.

portioned district that lies at the heart of congressional party power on Capitol Hill. But in the long run reapportionment, along with the spread of heterogeneous urban and suburban population into presently rural districts, will diversify one-party areas and stimulate competitive two-party politics.

Another tendency that may bring Congress more into the presidential orbit is continuing congressional reform. Some of this might consist of formal change in organization and procedures, such as the strengthening of the Speaker early in 1965. Other changes will be less obvious, embracing the distribution of prestige and informal influence in the structure of both houses. The elected party leadership in Congress tends to support a President of the same party, as in the case of Senator Robert Taft lining up behind Eisenhower (just as the elected congressional leadership tends to diverge from the presidential party when the Presidency is in opposition hands). As the elected leadership continues to gain strength in Congress as compared to the committee chairmen — as in the long run I believe it will — the President will gain added influence over the legislature.

The most powerful force for unifying President and Congress will be the continuing and probably increasing consensus over freedom and equality. As long as the nation was deeply and closely divided over these goals, Congress with its bias toward conservatism was bound to be at odds with a President biased toward liberalism, except in times of crisis. Without a broad consensus it was impossible to mobilize steady congressional majorities behind presidential proposals for social welfare and other egalitarian measures. Congress has been slow to act when only a bare popular majority seemed to support Fair Deal or New Frontier programs, as suggested by the fate of major presidential proposals in Congress following the close popular majorities won by Truman in 1948 and Kennedy in 1960. Kennedy liked to quote Jefferson's remark that "great innovations should not be forced on slender majorities." They have not been, in Congress. Often a three-fifths or two-thirds majority of the electorate supporting liberal programs has been necessary to produce a dependable straight majority behind those programs in Congress, because of the distortions in congressional representation. But judging from polls, election data, and other indices, about three-fifths or two-thirds of the American voters have come to uphold in a general way federal welfare and regulatory measures at home and policies designed to support freedom and equality abroad. This consensus is bound to show in Congress.

This is not to predict joyous harmony between President and Congress. Relations will continue to be marked by misunderstanding, jealousies over status and protocol, and differences over policy. Oscillations between presidential and congressional power will continue, though probably with the balance of power continuing to shift toward the executive over the long run. Conflict will probably be especially acute in the fiscal sector, for the conservative grip on the spending and taxing committees and machinery of Congress will not soon be relaxed. But it is precisely in the fiscal sector of policy that the President will be under the greatest pressure to meet the claims of freedom and equality. The question will be whether the President has enough power to channel funds into federal programs for health, education, urban development, housing, and the like; whether he has the funds to staff effectively promotional, regulatory, and control agencies in civil rights and related fields. If congressional conservatives could not thwart passage of social legislation, they still might try to starve or cripple its implementation.

But even here the big guns seem to be on the President's side. The same consensus over freedom and equality that now pervades Congress as a whole should affect its fiscal policy making too in the long run. If in the short run fiscal conservatives in Congress are able to stymie presidential programs, the White House can retaliate by mobilizing interests that favor spending, dramatizing the social and economic ills that need to be attacked, returning to Congress for deficiency and emergency appropriations, using discretionary funds of the President, and other devices. The President has already been granted significant latitude in the use of funds to influence policy; the most notable example is the Civil Rights Act of 1964, which granted him power to withhold federal funds from any program or activity receiving direct or indirect federal assistance, in which racial discrimination was found to exist. President Kennedy asked Congress for presidential authority to change tax ratios within certain limits, in order to strengthen the arsenal of anti-recession weapons; Congress balked at granting this power, but may well change its mind in the future, especially in the face of a deepening economic recession. The actual coming of a recession would precipitate an even speedier and more drastic shift of fiscal authority to the White House, for no President today can afford to bear the political burden of a slump. In March 1933 Roosevelt warned that unless Congress acted in the economic emergency, "I shall ask the Congress for the one remaining instrument to meet the crisis — broad Executive power to wage a war against the emergency, as great as the power that would be given to me if we were in fact invaded by a foreign foe." No President could ask for less than this in a future crisis; he probably would ask for more. And no modern Congress could resist him, for part of the nation's consensus over freedom and equality is a commitment to federal action against depression and poverty. And because that commitment first and foremost binds the President and will do so indefinitely, it is part of the edifice of presidential government.

Presidential Style

When all is said and done presidential decision making often depends upon the style of the occupant of the White House. Perhaps positions of such great leadership should not depend so completely upon the personal characteristics of one man. But in the case of the American Presidency it is unavoidable. In our political system candidates for the Presidency are sifted by the political parties and the electorate very carefully. Presidents often reflect the times in which they live. Times of crisis have in the past tended to produce strong presidential leadership, whereas those of calm have supported less vigorous Presidents. The nature of presidential responsibilities today requires strong leadership.

31 SIDNEY WARREN

HOW TO PICK A PRESIDENT

Is there any way for the American people to determine whether a potential President will provide effective leadership? What standards should be applied in selecting a candidate for the highest office in the land? When a business organization seeks a man for a top job, the applicant's background, training, and experience are major factors in evaluating his competence. But how useful are these criteria for judging the future head of state?

In his incisive commentary on American political institutions published toward the end of the nineteenth century, *The American Commonwealth,* James Bryce entitled one of his chapters "Why Great Men Are Not Chosen President." With some notable exceptions, the Presidents during the era he was discussing were a mediocre lot selected for reasons that had nothing to do with their capacity to fill the office with distinction. During the bitter controversy over slavery, for example, both parties sought innocuous candidates who could be depended upon to dodge the issue. In 1840 the Whigs turned away from men of towering stature like Henry Clay and Daniel Webster in favor of a nonentity like William Henry Harrison, who, having been unable to earn a living as a farmer, turned to running a whiskey distillery and then became a clerk of a county court.

From the *Saturday Review,* July 4, 1964. Reprinted by permission of the author and the publisher. Copyright 1964, Saturday Review, Inc.

About fifty years later, when the nation was racked by agrarian discontent and the social consequences of urbanization and industrialization, the political parties still selected their candidates in what was sometimes the most haphazard manner. An indifferent Republican convention in 1888 gave the nomination to Benjamin Harrison, a man whose only distinction was a brief service in the Senate, who had been defeated for re-election and frankly described himself as "a dead duck," because James G. Blaine, too ill to run, cabled from Scotland, "Take Harrison." A contemporary observer, commenting on the political conventions of the time, declared that they functioned like "the exquisite economy of Nature, which ever strives to get into each place the smallest man that can fill it."

Nevertheless, feeble as the leadership frequently was, the Republic prospered — the nation could afford the luxury of mediocrity. In our era, however, when the President plays so strategic a role in promoting the nation's welfare at home and safeguarding its position of world leadership abroad, a Grant or Harding in the White House would be an unmitigated disaster. Today his preparation must be such as to fully prepare him to cope with the unprecedented problems not only at home but throughout the world.

Yet no school exists to prepare an aspirant for the unique and complex roles the Chief Executive is required to fill. Years spent in public service, whether in Congress, administration, or a governorship, may be helpful but do not necessarily prepare a man for greatness, or even for competence. If the Presidential office were merely administrative, involving technical proficiency in details and procedure, the requisite skills could be acquired. But as Franklin D. Roosevelt once said, the Presidency is pre-eminently a place of moral leadership. It therefore requires the ability to adapt the national purpose to the continually changing requirements of a dynamic society, to preserve and transmit to posterity the nation's heritage of humane and liberal values.

An impressive record of administrative competency may be misleading when assessing the potential of a candidate, as William Howard Taft sadly illustrates. Taft's distinguished career as judge, Governor-General of the Philippine Islands, and Secretary of War greatly impressed the party leaders. The judicial mind, however, is likely to hobble rather than encourage vigorous executive leadership. In a crisis, the President must often rely on his instincts and intuition. If he stops too long to prepare an opinion by chewing over evidence and consulting precedents, the race may be finished before he enters the lists. Moreover, emphasis on the machinery of government and official routine can thwart the kind of initiative that thrusts a country forward. Franklin D. Roosevelt, who lacked both interest in or talent for administration, injected vitality and dynamism into the councils of government.

A professional career in politics or a record of achievement in Congress is not necessarily a factor in the preparation of a President. Abraham Lincoln's experience was confined to a single term as a member of the House of Representatives a dozen years before his election. Woodrow Wilson spent a lifetime as an academician and had only two years as governor of New Jersey before entering the White House, yet he exercised a vigorous, commanding leadership of Congress, scoring triumphs that seasoned politicians could envy. Even before the electorate had digested the significance of Wilson's "New Freedom," with its tariff reform act, Federal Reserve Law, and Clayton antitrust legislation, it concluded that the scholar-turned-politician had proved a consummate master in the great game of politics. The failure that climaxed Wilson's administration was not caused by his lack of political experience but was the result of a tragic flaw of personality.

By contrast, Calvin Coolidge was hardly an amateur in politics. He reached the heights of political power after serving as city councilman, a member of both houses of the state legislature, mayor, lieutenant-governor, governor, and Vice President. Yet during his six years in the White House all he offered the American people was a steady stream of platitudes and banalities, encouraging a perilous blindness to the stirrings at home and abroad that were portents of debacle. As his biographer said, Coolidge believed his task "was to keep the Ship of State on an even keel before a favoring wind — not to reconstruct the hull or install motive power or alter the course. . . . He won no battles, challenged no traditions, instituted few reforms." Coolidge was completely inept as a party leader and a legislative leader. His bills were defeated and his vetoes overriden by Congress.

Whether a President will have the capacity to meet the demands made upon him by crises cannot be predicted solely on the basis of past achievement and service. If judged in terms of his background, James Buchanan should have been ideally suited for effective Presidential leadership. Few men came to office with a longer official training — forty years in the legislative, executive, and diplomatic service. Yet at a critical juncture in the nation's history, with the Union on a disaster course toward dissolution, he was tragically indecisive when the imperatives of the hour called for vigor and resolution.

Although Harry S. Truman had been in political life for a fairly substantial period, his nomination for the Vice Presidency in 1944 was agreed to by Democratic party leaders mainly because he was an ideal compromise candidate — he was acceptable to both North and South, to organized labor, and to the machine bosses. No premature termination of Roosevelt's leadership was anticipated, and when it occurred the nation as a whole was appalled that its fate during such a precarious period was in the hands of this unassuming man. One journalist characterized the new President as "a sedative in a double-breasted suit," and most informed observers were prepared to write off his administration. Truman had not been a member of the inner war council or made privy to the negotiations at the various wartime conferences, or been informed about the progress of atomic development. But the years that followed were decision-packed, with Truman demonstrating a creative and imaginative approach to foreign relations as striking as the feeling in the spring of 1943 that the man was not suited for his prodigious tasks.

To a great extent the Cabinet or parliamentary form of government in Great Britain solves the problem of unpredictability. The Prime Minister is the product of the House of Commons, steeped in its traditions, habituated to its ways, and is required to have been the leader of his party in that body before he can be chosen the Queen's First Minister. From leader of the loyal opposition to Prime Minister may involve a transition in power, but not a transition in leadership. As head of his party, he has been displaying leadership for years in the law-making body of a kind that the electorate has endorsed. There are no "Johnny-come-latelys" or dark horses. By contrast, the President's preparation is largely a random affair. Still, ours is a Presidential system, and, that being so, what are the criteria that ultimately determine Presidential success if the traditional yardsticks are largely irrelevant? Is there a common pattern displayed by "strong" Presidents that might provide clues to whether a candidate is adequately prepared?

Perhaps most important is a broad, expansive view of the office that would permit the occupant of the White House to extend the potentialities of executive prerogative to its outermost limits whenever the public necessity requires it. Theodore Roosevelt was better prepared for leadership by virtue of his approach to the Presidency than he was by the years he spent as police commissioner of New York, member of the federal Civil Service Commission, Assistant Secretary of the Navy, governor of New York, or even Vice President. As he once said:

> The most important factor in getting the right spirit in my administration was my insistence upon the theory that the executive power was limited only by specific restrictions and prohibitions appearing in the Constitution or imposed by Congress under its constitutional power.... I declined to adopt the view that what was imperatively necessary for the nation could not be done by the President unless he could find some specific authorization to do it.

John Fitzgerald Kennedy regarded the Presidency as the repository of political and moral leadership, believing that the occupant of the office must be willing to use the powerful tools available to him. The choice, he felt, was either to emulate Roosevelt and Wilson or Taft and Harding. In an address before the National Press Club a year before his inauguration he left no room for doubt as to which of the previous Presidents he would use as models. "Whatever the political affiliation of our next President," he said, "whatever his views may be on all the issues and problems that rush in upon us, he must above all be the Chief Executive in every sense of the word. He must be prepared to exercise the fullest powers of his office, all that are specified and some that are not. He must master complex problems as well as receive one-page memoranda. He must originate action as well as study groups. He must reopen the channels of communication between the world of thought and the seat of power."

It is no coincidence that throughout our history the Presidents who have been most ineffectual were those like Taylor, Taft, Harding, and Coolidge who were firmly committed to the concept that the Chief Executive could exercise only that authority specifically granted him by the Constitution. Taft could be considered their spokesman with his declaration that "the President can exercise no power which cannot be fairly and reasonably traced to some specific grant of power or justly implied and included within such express grant as proper and necessary to its exercise."

However rich and varied the aspirant's career, he comes ill-prepared to discharge the duties and responsibilities of the Presidential office if his theoretical position would inhibit rather than encourage bold, assertive leadership. In less tempestuous and complex times this element in the preparation of a President was of no great significance. As a matter of fact, the relatively untroubled periods in our history produced the textbook image of the Presidency as an equal and coordinate branch operating strictly within its own sphere and never trespassing beyond certain specified boundary lines. Today, however, it must encompass party and legislative leadership, providing direction in economic matters and initiative in world affairs.

Significantly, with the exception of George Washington, all the Presidents who made a lasting impact on the nation were men who eagerly sought the office and were avid for leadership in public affairs. To reach the White House would be the ultimate fulfilment of their profoundest ambitions. Once in office, they approached their tasks with driving zest and enthusiasm. Theodore Roosevelt, who was elevated to the Presidency through an accident of fate, probably would have achieved it eventually on his own. He reveled in the opportunity to occupy the seat of power. For him the Presidency was a glorious adventure and he enjoyed every minute of it; for his successor, whom he had hand-picked, it was an ordeal that he endured with outward stoicism but inward wretchedness. William Howard Taft was persuaded to take a job he never wanted and for which, realistically, he felt ill-suited. "Politics, when I am in it, makes me sick," he once said. His private letters offer pathetic evidence of his lack of self-confidence. Several months after his inauguration he wrote to Roosevelt:

> If I followed my impulse, I should still say "My dear Mr. President." I cannot overcome the habit. When I am addressed as "Mr. President," I turn to see whether you are not at my elbow. . . .
>
> I want you to know that I do nothing in the Executive Office without considering what you would do under the circumstances and without having in a sense a mental talk with you over the pros and cons of the situation. I have not the facility for educating the public as you had. . . .

The Presidency is a lonely place — that "splendid misery" as Thomas Jefferson once called it — especially in times of crisis when the occupant of the office must repeatedly make vital decisions for which he and he alone is responsible. No one can share the burden with him, and only a man who has confidence in his own judgment is adequately prepared for White House leadership. Harry S. Truman's initial response to the news of President Roosevelt's sudden death was certainly understandable. "I don't know whether you fellows ever had a load of hay or a bull fall on you," he told reporters, "but last night the stars and all the planets fell on me. . . . I've got the most terribly responsible job any man ever had." But Truman's inner core was sound and firm. Within weeks he began to demonstrate the inner security that enabled him to deal with the many grave problems that beset the nation.

Woodrow Wilson's self-confidence was of another caliber. Lacking humility, tinged with mysticism, this trait was to prove his undoing. "God ordained that I should be the next President of the United States," he announced as he was about to enter the White House. On another occasion he said, "I am sorry for those who disagree with me because I know I am right." While the President must be firmly convinced that the course he has chosen *is* the right one, he must at the same time be flexible enough to bend when circumstances require resilient behavior.

A significant element in a President's preparation is that he have a plan that embodies his view of the country's future. It should reflect his talent for creative innovation and demonstrate a sense of the direction in which the times are moving, diagnose contemporary maladies, and offer possible means for their solution. Today that plan must embrace Ghana and Ceylon as well as Georgia and Oregon. In Franklin D. Roosevelt's campaign speeches in 1932, he presented a plan for the economic future of the nation that was as bold in outline as it was imaginative. Although containing no specific blueprint, it articulated goals that were the basis for the "New Deal" program.

While campaign rhetoric and political oratory can be discounted to a large extent, they provide some means for discerning the quality of a candidate. What could have been expected from Warren G. Harding on the basis of the hackneyed speeches delivered from the front porch of his home? As William G. McAdoo colorfully put it, his addresses "leave the impression of an army of pompous phrases moving over the landscape in search of an idea; sometimes these meandering words would actually capture a straggling thought and bear it triumphantly, a prisoner in their midst, until it died of servitude and overwork!" The nation at the time was not aware of the machinations that gave Harding the nomination, but Americans recklessly voted for a man whose only claim to the highest office in the land was that he *looked* like a President.

A leading contemporary journal in all seriousness declared that whatever might be the defects of the nominee as a world statesman, Harding was "an exceedingly courteous gentleman." If he were elected, "good nature, both to political friends and to political enemies," would once again prevail in the White House. "The Senator's speeches may be properly criticized for their vagueness, for their lack of original thought, for their occasionally conflicting character . . . but they are certainly not lacking in the decencies of political controversy. And this is another case where style is the man."

Style is indeed the man. The last sentence, which succinctly and accurately summed up the matter, was a portent. The character of the nation is influenced by the "style" of its chosen head. With "normalcy" enthroned in the White House, the nation drifted, devitalized, without standards and without goals.

Leadership in our democratic society performs a strategic role above and beyond the functions mapped out by our constitutional system. An essential component is the President's capacity and will to influence public opinion so that necessary programs are carried out. Those men who were strong Presidents had both an intellectual and intuitive comprehension of this ingredient. As Theodore Roosevelt put it, "Our prime necessity is that public opinion should be properly educated." And again, "I do not desire to act unless I can get the bulk of our people to understand the situation and to back up the action; and to do that I have to get the facts vividly before them. The ineffectual Presidents were either indifferent about shaping public opinion or believed, with Calvin Coolidge, that "the people have their own affairs to look after and cannot give much attention to what Congress is doing."

The preparation of a President, then, is compounded of many intangibles. Attributes for which there is no specific training — character, convictions, and style — appear to be more basic for successful leadership than background, training, and experience. Political skill taken for granted, the effective leader captures the public imagination because he possesses moral and physical stamina, because he has a humanitarian outlook and the determination to alleviate the ills that plague our society, and because when he speaks and acts he does so not only for the moment but for the age. He has the capacity to inspire the people, to elevate them above the commonplace, to set a tone for the nation so that the vision of the future becomes the objective for the present. Such a President is a total President, both a politician and a statesman.

Presidential Transition

As the Presidency assumes greater importance, the problem of presidential transition becomes more critical. Although the Presidency is an institution, it is at the same time highly personal in many significant respects. The flavor of a presidential administration is often transferred to the bureaucracy and sometimes remains long after the new President has assumed office. In order for a new President to carry out his programs, he must have a high degree of cooperation from many parts of the administrative branch. He must be informed about the current problems of foreign and domestic policy even before he assumes office. Transition is more easily brought about when there is no change in the party of the President. A change in administration from one party to another can create many difficulties. When Eisenhower came into office in 1952, he confronted a bureaucracy that was largely dedicated to the New Deal and Fair Deal of the prior Democratic administrations. His selection of new Cabinet officers took place in an atmosphere of entrenched bureaucratic hostility. The following selection discusses the problem of presidential transition generally, with special emphasis upon the Eisenhower-Kennedy changeover in 1960–1961.

32   LAURIN L. HENRY

THE PROBLEM OF PRESIDENTIAL TRANSITION

In a sense, it is misleading to speak, as we sometimes carelessly do, of "transferring the Presidency." *Presidential responsibility* is essentially transferred on inauguration day, although even this may not be as simple as it appears. But the *Presidency,* except in its most

From Paul T. David (ed.), *The Presidential Election and Transition 1960–1961,* pp. 235, 260–67. Reprinted by permission of The Brookings Institution. Copyright 1961, The Brookings Institution.

formal aspects, is not a tangible thing that can be passed along intact from one man to another. Each new President must re-create the Presidency in unique form — starting with the materials at hand, but guided by his own concepts and limited by what events and his own skills permit him to make of the formal office. In the same sense, he may inherit a bureaucracy, but he cannot inherit an administration. He must build his own.

The *presidential transition,* then, consists of those critical decisions, acts, or events by which the new Presidency and new administration are given their characteristic shape, style, and content. Presidencies and administrations are, of course, ever-evolving, and it is impossible to say — at least not until they are over — at precisely what moment the outlines began to be stable. Usually, different aspects stabilize at different times. But certainly the first three months, or the first 100 days, to use the period of measure favored by journalists, are the most critical; by the end of the first six months the essential characteristics of style and approach, if not of continuing substantive policies, are likely to be apparent. . . .

The 1960–1961 transition can be identified as the one in which the "transition problem" came of age and received appropriate recognition. The unsatisfactory experience of 1952–1953 was remembered, and during 1960 scholars, journalists, and conscientious public servants called attention to the lessons of history and the facts of the current situation. In the resulting climate of public concern, political leaders responded with efforts to guard the public interest during the change of leadership made mandatory by the Twenty-second Amendment. The transfer of responsibility from Eisenhower to Kennedy, although by no means flawlessly executed, was the smoothest such transition in recent times. The gubernatorial transitions being carried out at the same time also benefited, for almost the first time, from specific attention to problems of transition at the state level.

AN IMPROVING RECORD

The "Presidential common law" covering such events was confirmed and further developed by the Eisenhower-Kennedy transition. Both the incoming and outgoing administrations recognized the obligation to make suitable preparations and to cooperate with each other in achieving a smooth transition. The necessity of starting some of these preparations before the election was accepted, although, unlike 1952, pre-election preparations were more prominent in the out-party than the in-party. However, Eisenhower followed unquestioningly the precedent of giving intelligence briefings to the candidates and, against his own political instincts, permitted some of the most essential staff preparations to go on within the administration. He was probably unduly sensitive on this point; in the future there should be a sufficient public understanding of the problem to permit overt preparations and pre-election communication between the administration and the candidates to the extent necessary.

The designation of Clifford and Persons as top-level liaison officers between the incoming and outgoing administrations was an innovation that proved useful and is likely to be used again. The need for such formalization presumably depends in part on the personalities involved and the circumstances. It might become less necessary if the President-elect is ready for early designation of key members of his administration.

Relations between Eisenhower and Kennedy were conducted at a level of dignity and responsibility that their successors will do well to emulate. Eisenhower's offers of assistance to Kennedy were up to the norm for an outgoing President. Kennedy's consideration for Eisenhower, which was especially noteworthy in an incoming President, set an example for other incoming officials and proved its utility soon after inauguration when he was able to consult Eisenhower in the Cuban crisis. Taking their cues from Kennedy, other members of the incoming administration overcame much of the suspicion usually shown by men in their positions and took advantage of the advance information and aid offered by their predecessors.

This transition was notable for the quick assertion of policy leadership, Kennedy took early action to prepare himself, and he and his associates made skillful use of the resources at hand, both inside and outside of the government. The bureaucracy was regarded not as an obstacle but as an instrument through which the new administration could achieve its purposes.

Some Continuing Problems

Despite these and other advances, the transition experience of 1960–1961 revealed the survival of old problems, some of which took on new or more acute forms. One was the problem of recruiting political executives on short notice and in a party system that does not clearly designate a cadre from which top appointees will be selected when the party next achieves power. In this case, Kennedy's creative cabinet-making achieved a result that might be envied in any parliamentary system, and the early "talent search" for lesser appointees was unusually effective for such an operation. The success of the Kennedy approach, in fact, suggests the desirability of continuing a high-level recruiting operation, on a smaller scale, in the White House. Nevertheless, the Kennedy staffing was done with a degree of haste that occasionally appalled even those most intimately involved. There were some costly mistakes and serious delays in filling several of the most important posts; and the work of completing the administration's personnel began to drag soon after inauguration.

This raises the question, which is not new, of pre-election staff work on personnel for presidential candidates. It is probably both impractical and undesirable for a candidate to attempt to reach firm decisions on cabinet and subcabinet appointments before he is elected. But would not a preliminary search for potential appointees of high caliber, and an assembly of dossiers on the obvious prospects, put the personnel operation that much ahead and permit faster and more rational decisions after election?

The obstacle usually cited is that such an operation, if it is to be useful, must be conducted by people in whom the candidate has special confidence, and such people cannot be spared from campaign assignments. This argument has great force. Yet, much of the preliminary spadework in the Kennedy talent search was done by individuals who had been given only minor roles in the campaign, and it appears in retrospect that this would have been a good investment of the time of even one or two who were relatively close to Kennedy during the campaign. Despite the difficulties and the danger of wasted effort, a greater realization of the stakes and the potential benefits may well bring future presidential candidates to the point of authorizing pre-election search for and investigation of potential appointees. A more organized approach to the appointment problems of a future administration might even prove helpful in relation to the problems of campaign strategy.

The scale of the Kennedy post-election preparations magnified what had hitherto been a problem of minor proportions: financing the activities of the President-elect and his staff, including consultants and persons designated for office in the executive agencies. Since it is clearly in the public interest to have the next administration ready to operate as completely as possible on inauguration day, the essential expenses of preparatory work after the election should be covered by a regular appropriation for that purpose. Establishing a proper amount and appropriate limitations on what can be considered reimbursable expenses would be debatable but not insoluble problems.

Although no grave difficulties arose in this turnover, the problem of reconciling policy control and career continuity along the upper edge of the civil service structure is still far from solved. Civil service Schedule C, which has evolved in a way probably unforeseen by either its original founders or critics, seems to have done part of the job of institutionalizing a zone of flexibility in which career and noncareer appointees mingle and in which adjustments can be made at the pleasure of the administration as situations change. Fortunately, the Democrats tended to regard Schedule C as a list of positions in which they could make changes and put in their own appointees if necessary but did not feel compelled to clear out all the incumbents who bore Schedule C labels. Thus many career men who had in one way or another got into Schedule C jobs were retained — at the pleasure of the Secretary, as before. Whether there should be more or less positions in Schedule C is a debatable issue, but it is more than a transition problem.

The important problem yet remaining is that there is no established system or practice giving protection to career men, either in Schedule C or regular civil service positions, who become casualties of policy or leadership changes. In this transition most such displaced persons were picked up and used elsewhere, partly through the efforts of the career executive placement service operated by the Civil Service Commission. However, most such reassignments resulted from personal arrangements and were possible because of the low level of partisan feeling that characterized the period. This might not be possible in a new administration that was reducing the total level of government activities amid suspicions of the bureaucracy in general. Despite the rejection of the Second Hoover Commission's proposal for a Senior Civil Service with rank-in-the-person, we may yet see some arrangement by which high ranking career men can be temporarily assigned to some central pool or reassigned without immediate loss of pay or status.

Shortly before he left the White House, President Eisenhower characterized as "silly" the present requirement that the outgoing President submit a State of the Union message, economic report, and budget to the new Congress. He suggested that these presentations be made the responsibility of the new President in years of presidential change, and that the date of inauguration be advanced to give the incoming President time to prepare them. Embedded in a "package" of reforms proposed by Senator Mansfield is a provision seeking to accomplish this objective. The Mansfield proposals . . . would abolish the electoral college and elect the President by direct popular vote, provide for federally financed and supervised presidential preference primaries in the states, provide federal financial assistance to the campaigns of major party candidates *if nominated after September 1,* and (making no change in the present election date) change presidential inauguration day to December 1.

Such proposals raise questions that go far beyond the scope of this chapter, but three brief comments from the viewpoint of transition problems are in order.

First, the present assignment of responsibility for the messages, although anomalous in form, raises no overwhelming difficulties in practice. New messages and appropriate budgetary revisions were prepared and presented in timely fashion by the new President in both 1953 and 1961. The existing arrangement burdens the outgoing administration with work that may be unnecessary but it may be better than a schedule that would give the incoming President full responsibility for the budget but insufficient time to take charge of preparing it. The present untidiness about the budget could be modified either by advancing inauguration day or by delaying the budget submission deadline. But in either course, small changes will not do. A new President should have at least 60 days, and preferably more, before having to assume responsibility for presenting the complete annual budget, for the budget has to be more or less built up from the bottom on the basis of given policies or assumptions.

Second, a strong case can be made for some shortening of the election-inauguration interval because of the inevitable uncertainties of leadership and paralysis of high level policy making in such periods. The relative obligations of the President and President-elect have been greatly clarified since the days when Hoover and Roosevelt engaged in futile maneuvering over the 1932–1933 depression crisis. But, as we have seen in the case of Eisenhower and Kennedy, there are stubborn ambiguities in the relationship that are dangerous under present-day requirements for quick decisions.

Third, there is a limit to how much the election-inauguration interval can be shortened without running the equal danger of having a new administration legally installed and responsible but actually disorganized and unready to function. Those who have participated in the process of organizing a new administration under the present schedule shudder at the thought of having to do it any faster. Any advance in inauguration day will require corresponding intensification of pre-election preparations by the candidates, in the realms both of personnel and of policy. There is room for some progress in this direction, but how much room is not clear, especially if, as in the Mansfield proposal, the campaign period itself is to be shortened. Shortening the election-inauguration interval will also require a strengthening and more effective use of the career service, and perhaps a change from the present custom of simultaneous replacement of so large a number of important executive officers on inauguration day. Even under the most optimistic assumptions about earlier preparations by candidates and improvement in relationships between incoming and outgoing administrations, a preparatory period of 30 to 45 days after election seems essential.

In summary, the Eisenhower-Kennedy transition was, from the viewpoint of the public interest, a considerable improvement over other party turnovers of recent times. It established some useful precedents and suggested some lines of improvement for the future. It also suggested some of the inherent limitations on ability to achieve smooth transitions within the framework of the present constitutional and party system. Fundamental constitutional changes from the presidential system seem out of the question, but there is some possibility of useful adjustments in scheduling along lines indicated by the Mansfield proposals. Reforms in the party system tending toward more doctrinal coherence and leadership stability, should they occur, would make a significant contribution to minimizing transitional difficulties. But in the transitions of the foreseeable future we shall be greatly dependent, as in the past, on the quality of the political leadership of the moment, plus an element of sheer luck in regard to the circumstances of the times.

CHAPTER SEVEN

Congress

The United States Congress, exercising supreme legislative power, was at the beginning of the nineteenth century the most powerful political institution in the national government. It was feared by the framers of the Constitution, who felt that unless it was closely guarded and limited it would easily dominate both the Presidency and the Supreme Court. Its powers were carefully enumerated, and it was made a bicameral body. This latter provision was not only to secure representation of different interests but also to limit the power of the legislature, which could not act as swiftly and with such force when hobbled by two houses often working against each other. Although still important, the power and prestige of Congress have suffered a decline relative to the powers of the President and the Supreme Court, not to mention the increasing power of the vast governmental bureaucracy. This chapter discusses the basis and nature of congressional power, and the factors influencing the current position of Congress vis á vis coordinate government departments.

Constitutional Background

Article I, Section 1 of the Constitution states that "all legislative powers herein granted shall be vested in a Congress of the United States, which shall consist of a Senate and House of Representatives." Section 8 specifically enumerates congressional powers, and provides that Congress shall have power "to make all laws which shall be necessary and proper for carrying into execution the foregoing powers, and all other powers vested by this Constitution in the government of the United States, or in any department or officer thereof."

Apart from delineating the powers of Congress Article I provides that the House shall represent the people, and the Senate the states through appointment of members by the state legislatures. The representative function of Congress is written into the Constitution, and at the time of the framing of the Constitution a great deal of discussion was centered upon the nature of representation and what constitutes adequate representation in a national legislative body. Further, relating in part to the question of representation, the framers of the Constitution had to determine what constitutes appropriate tasks for each branch of the legislature, and to what extent certain legislative activities should be within the exclusive or initial jurisdiction of the House or the Senate. All these questions depended to some extent upon the conceptualization the framers had of the House as representative of popular interests on a short-term basis, and the Senate as a reflection of conservative interests on a long-term basis. The following selection from *The Federalist* indicates the thinking of the framers about the nature and functions of the House of Representatives and the Senate.

33   HAMILTON OR MADISON

FEDERALIST 53

. . . No man can be a competent legislator who does not add to an upright intention and a sound judgment a certain degree of knowledge of the subjects on which he is to legislate. A part of this knowledge may be acquired by means of information, which lie within the compass of men in private, as well as public stations. Another part can only be attained, or at least thoroughly attained, by actual experience in the station which requires the use of it. The period of service ought, therefore, in all such cases, to bear some proportion to the extent of practical knowledge requisite to the due performance of the service. . . .

In a single state the requisite knowledge relates to the existing laws, which are uniform throughout the state, and with which all the citizens are more or less conversant. . . . The great theatre of the United States presents a very different scene. The laws are so far from being uniform that they vary in every state; whilst the public affairs of the union are spread throughout a very extensive region, and are extremely diversified by the local affairs connected with them, and can with difficulty be correctly learnt in any other place than in the central councils, to which a knowledge of them will be brought by the representatives of every part of the empire. Yet some knowledge of the affairs, and even of the laws of all the states, ought to be possessed by the members from each of the states. . . .

A branch of knowledge which belongs to the acquirements of a federal representative, and which has not been mentioned, is that of foreign affairs. In regulating our own commerce he ought to be not only acquainted with the treaties between the United States and other nations, but also with the commercial policy and laws of other nations. He ought not to be altogether ignorant of the law of nations; for that, as far as it is a proper object of municipal legislation, is submitted to the federal government. And although the House of Representatives is not immediately to participate in foreign negotiations and arrangements, yet from the necessary connection between the several branches of public affairs, those particular subjects will frequently deserve attention in the ordinary course of legislation, and will sometimes demand particular legislative sanction and co-operation. Some portion of this knowledge may, no doubt, be acquired in a man's closet; but some of it also can only be acquired to best effect, by a practical attention to the subject, during the period of actual service in the legislature. . . .

FEDERALIST 56

The . . . charge against the House of Representatives is, that it will be too small to possess a due knowledge of the interests of its constituents.

As this objection evidently proceeds from a comparison of the proposed number of representatives, with the great extent of the United States, the number of their inhabitants, and the diversity of their interests, without taking into view, at the same time, the circumstances which will distinguish the Congress from other legislative bodies, the best answer that can be given to it, will be a brief explanation of these peculiarities.

It is a sound and important principle that the representative ought to be acquainted with the interests and circumstances of his constituents. But this principle can extend no farther than to those circumstances and interests to which the authority and care of the representative relate. An ignorance of a variety of minute and particular objects, which do not lie within the compass of legislation, is consistent with every attribute necessary to a due performance of the legislative trust. In determining the extent of information required in the exercise of a particular authority, recourse then must be had to the objects within the purview of that authority.

What are to be the objects of federal legislation? Those which are of most importance, and which seem most to require knowledge, are commerce, taxation, and the militia.

A proper regulation of commerce requires much information, as has been elsewhere remarked; but as far as this information relates to the laws, and local situation of each individual state, a very few representatives would be sufficient vehicles of it to the federal councils.

Taxation will consist, in great measure, of duties which will be involved in the regulation of commerce. So far the preceding remark is applicable to this object. As far as it may consist of internal collections, a more diffusive knowledge of the circumstances of the state may be necessary. But will not this also be possessed in sufficient degree by a very few intelligent men, diffusively elected within the state? . . .

With regard to the regulation of the militia there are scarcely any circumstances in reference to which local knowledge can be said to be necessary. . . . The art of war teaches general principles of organization, movement, and discipline, which apply universally.

The attentive reader will discern that the reasoning here used, to prove the sufficiency of a moderate number of representatives, does not, in any respect, contradict what was urged on another occasion, with regard to the extensive information which the representatives ought to possess, and the time that might be necessary for acquiring it. . . .

FEDERALIST 57

. . . The House of Representatives is so constituted as to support in the members an habitual recollection of their dependence on the people. Before the sentiments impressed on their minds by the mode of their elevation, can be effaced by the exercise of power, they will be compelled to anticipate the moment when their power is to cease, when their exercise of it is to be reviewed, and when they must descend to the level from which they were raised; there for ever to remain unless a faithful discharge of their trust shall have established their title to a renewal of it.

I will add, as a . . . circumstance in the situation of the House of Representatives, restraining them from oppressive measures, that they can make no law which will not have its full operation on themselves and their friends, as well as on the great mass of the society. This has always been deemed one of the strongest bonds by which human policy can connect the rulers and the people together. It creates between them that communion of interest, and sympathy of sentiments, of which few governments have furnished examples; but without which every government degenerates into tyranny. If it be asked, what is to restrain the House of Representatives from making legal discriminations in favor of themselves, and a particular class of the society? I answer, the genius of the whole system; the nature of just and constitutional laws; and, above all, the vigilant and manly spirit which actuates the people of America; a spirit which nourishes freedom, and in return is nourished by it.

If this spirit shall ever be so far debased as to tolerate a law not obligatory on the legislature, as well as on the people, the people will be prepared to tolerate anything but liberty.

Such will be the relation between the House of Representatives and their constituents. Duty, gratitude, interest, ambition itself, are the cords by which they will be bound to fidelity and sympathy with the great mass of the people. It is possible that these may all be insufficient to control the caprice and wickedness of men. But are they not all that government will admit, and that human prudence can devise? Are they not the genuine, and the characteristic means, by which republican government provides for the liberty and happiness of the people? . . .

FEDERALIST 58

. . . In this review of the constitution of the House of Representatives . . . one observation . . . I must be permitted to add . . . as claiming, in my judgment, a very serious attention. It is, that in all legislative assemblies, the greater the number composing them may be, the fewer will be the men who will in fact direct their proceedings. In the first place, the more numerous any assembly may be, of whatever characters composed, the greater is known to be the ascendancy of passion over reason. In the next place, the larger the number, the greater will be the proportion of members of limited information and of weak capacities. Now it is precisely on characters of this description that the eloquence and address of the few are known to act with all their force. In the ancient republics, where the whole body of the people assembled in person, a single orator, or an artful statesman, was generally seen to rule with as complete a sway as if a sceptre had been placed in his single hands. On the same principle, the more multitudinous a representative assembly may be rendered, the more it will partake of the infirmities incident to collective meetings of the people. Ignorance will be the dupe of cunning; and passion the slave of sophistry and dec- lamation. The people can never err more than in supposing, that by multiplying their representatives beyond a certain list, they strengthen the barrier against the government of a few. Experience will for ever admonish them, that, on the contrary, after securing a sufficient num- ber for the purposes of safety, of local information, and of diffusive sympathy with the whole society, they will counteract their own views by every addition to their representatives. The countenance of the gov- ernment may become more democratic; but the soul that animates it will be more oligarchic. The machine will be enlarged, but the fewer, and often the more secret, will be the springs by which its motions are directed. . . .

FEDERALIST 62

Having examined the constitution of the House of Repre- sentatives . . . I enter next on the examination of the Senate.

The heads under which this member of the government may be con- sidered are — I. The qualifications of senators; II. The appointment of them by the state legislatures; III. The equality of representation in the Senate; IV. The number of senators, and the term for which they are to be elected; V. The powers vested in the Senate.

I. The qualifications proposed for senators, as distinguished from those of representatives, consist in a more advanced age and a longer period of citizenship. A senator must be thirty years of age at least; as a representative must be twenty-five. And the former must have been a citizen nine years; as seven years are required for the latter. The pro- priety of these distinctions is explained by the nature of the senatorial trust; which, requiring greater extent of information and stability of character, requires at the same time, that the senator should have reached a period of life most likely to supply these advantages. . . .

II. It is equally unnecessary to dilate on the appointment of sena- tors by the state legislators. Among the various modes which might have been devised for constituting this branch of the government, that which has been proposed by the convention is probably the most con- genial with the public opinion. It is recommended by the double ad- vantage of favoring a select appointment, and of giving to the state governments such an agency in the formation of the federal govern- ment, as must secure the authority of the former, and may form a con- venient link between the two systems.

III. The equality of representation in the Senate is another point, which, being evidently the result of compromise between the opposite pretensions of the large and the small states, does not call for much discussion. If indeed it be right, that among a people thoroughly incorporated into one nation, every district ought to have a *proportional* share in the government: and that among independent and sovereign states bound together by a simple league, the parties, however unequal in size, ought to have an *equal* share in the common councils, it does not appear to be without some reason, that in a compound republic, partaking both of the national and federal character, the government ought to be founded on a mixture of the principles of proportional [as found in the House of Representatives] and equal representation [in the Senate]. . . .

. . . [T]he equal vote allowed to each state, is at once a constitutional recognition of the portion of sovereignty remaining in the individual states, and an instrument for preserving that residuary sovereignty. So far the equality ought to be no less acceptable to the large than to the small states; since they are not less solicitous to guard by every possible expedient against an improper consolidation of the states into one simple republic.

Another advantage accruing from this ingredient in the constitution of the Senate is, the additional impediment it must prove against improper acts of legislation. No law or resolution can now be passed without the concurrence, first, of a majority of the people, and then, of a majority of the states. It must be acknowledged that this complicated check on legislation may, in some instances, be injurious as well as beneficial; and that the peculiar defense which it involves in favor of the smaller states, would be more rational, if any interests common to them, and distinct from those of the other states, would otherwise be exposed to peculiar danger. But as the larger states will always be able, by their power over the supplies, to defeat unreasonable exertions of this prerogative of the lesser states; and as the facility and excess of law-making seem to be the diseases to which our governments are most liable, it is not impossible, that this part of the constitution may be more convenient in practice than it appears to many in contemplation.

IV. The number of senators, and the duration of their appointment, come next to be considered. In order to form an accurate judgment on both these points, it will be proper to inquire into the purposes which are to be answered by the Senate; and, in order to ascertain these, it will be necessary to review the inconveniences which a republic must suffer from the want of such an institution.

First. It is a misfortune incident to republican government, though in a less degree than to other governments, that those who administer it may forget their obligations to their constituents, and prove unfaithful to their important trust. In this point of view, a senate, as a second branch of the legislative assembly, distinct from, and dividing the power with, a first, must be in all cases a salutary check on the government. It doubles the security to the people by requiring the concurrence of two distinct bodies in schemes of usurpation or perfidy, where the ambition or corruption of one would otherwise be sufficient. . . . [A]s the improbability of sinister combinations will be in proportion to the dissimilarity in the genius of the two bodies, it must be politic to distinguish them from each other by every circumstance which will consist with a due harmony in all proper measures, and with the genuine principles of republican government.

Second. The necessity of a senate is not less indicated by the propensity of all single and numerous assemblies, to yield to the impulse of sudden and violent passions, and to be seduced by factious leaders into intemperate and pernicious resolutions. Examples on this subject might be cited without number; and from proceedings within the United States, as well as from the history of other nations. But a position that will not be contradicted need not be proved. All that need be remarked is, that a body which is to correct this infirmity ought itself to be free from it, and consequently ought to be less numerous. It ought, moreover, to possess great firmness, and consequently ought to hold its authority by a tenure of considerable duration.

Third. Another defect to be supplied by a senate lies in a want of due acquaintance with the objects and principles of legislation. It is not possible that an assembly of men, called, for the most part, from pursuits of a private nature, continued in appointments for a short time, and led by no permanent motive to devote the intervals of public occupation to a study of the laws, the affairs, and the comprehensive interests of their country, should, if left wholly to themselves, escape a variety of important errors in the exercise of their legislative trust. . . .

Fourth. The mutability in the public councils, arising from a rapid succession of new members, however qualified they may be, points out, in the strongest manner, the necessity of some stable institution in the government. Every new election in the states is found to change one-half of the representatives. From this change of men must proceed a change of opinions; and from a change of opinions, a change of measures. But a continual change even of good measures is inconsistent with every rule of prudence, and every prospect of success. . . .

FEDERALIST 63

A *fifth* desideratum, illustrating the utility of a senate, the want of a due sense of national character. Without a select and stable member of the government, the esteem of foreign powers will no only be forfeited by an unenlightened and variable policy . . . ; but the national councils will not possess that sensibility to the opinion of the world, which is perhaps not less necessary in order to merit, than it is to obtain, its respect and confidence. . . .

I add, as a *sixth* defect, the want in some important cases of a due responsibility in the government to the people, arising from that frequency of elections, which in other cases produces this responsibility. . . .

Responsibility, in order to be reasonable, must be limited to objects within the power of the responsible party, and in order to be effectual, must relate to operations of that power, of which a ready and proper judgment can be formed by the constituents. The objects of government may be divided into two general classes; the one depending on measures, which have singly an immediate and sensible operation; the other depending on a succession of well chosen and well connected measures, which have a gradual and perhaps unobserved operation. The importance of the latter description to the collective and permanent welfare of every country, needs no explanation. And yet it is evident that an assembly elected for so short a term as to be unable to provide more than one or two links in a chain of measures, on which the general welfare may essentially depend, ought not to be answerable for the final result, any more than a steward or tenant, engaged for one year, could be justly made to answer for plans or improvements, which could not be accomplished in less than half a dozen years. Nor is it possible for the people to estimate the *share* of influence, which their annual assemblies may respectively have on events resulting from the mixed transactions of several years. It is sufficiently difficult, at any rate, to preserve a personal responsibility in the members of a *numerous* body, for such acts of the body as have an immediate, detached, and palpable operation on its constituents.

The proper remedy for this defect must be an additional body in the legislative department, which, having sufficient permanency to provide for such objects as require a continued attention, and a train of measures, may be justly and effectually answerable for the attainment of those objects.

Thus far I have considered the circumstances, which point out the necessity of a well constructed senate, only as they relate to the representatives of the people. To a people as little blinded by prejudice, or corrupted by flattery, as those whom I address, I shall not scruple to add, that such an institution may be sometimes necessary, as a defense to the people against their own temporary errors and delusions. As the cool and deliberate sense of the community ought, in all governments, and actually will, in all free governments, ultimately prevail over the views of its rulers; so there are particular moments in public affairs, when the people, stimulated by some irregular passion, or some illicit advantage, or misled by the artful misrepresentations of interested men, may call for measures which they themselves will afterwards be the most ready to lament and condemn. In these critical moments, how salutary will be the interference of some temperate and respectable body of citizens, in order to check the misguided career, and to suspend the blow meditated by the people against themselves, until reason, justice and truth can regain their authority over the public mind? What bitter anguish would not the people of Athens have often avoided, if their government had contained so provident a safeguard against the tyranny of their own passions? Popular liberty might then have escaped the indelible reproach of decreeing to the same citizens the hemlock on one day, and statues on the next.

It may be suggested that a people spread over an extensive region cannot, like the crowded inhabitants of a small district, be subject to the infection of violent passions; or to the danger of combining in the pursuit of unjust measures. I am far from denying that this is a distinction of peculiar importance. I have, on the contrary, endeavored in a former paper to show that it is one of the principal recommendations of a confederated republic. At the same time this advantage ought not to be considered as superseding the use of auxiliary precautions. It may even be remarked that the same extended situation, which will exempt the people of America from some of the dangers incident to lesser republics, will expose them to the inconveniency of remaining for a longer time under the influence of those misrepresentations which the combined industry of interested men may succeed in distributing among them. . . .

The Environment of
Congressional Decision Making

In *Federalist 51* Madison noted, "A dependence on the people is, no doubt, the primary control on the government." Congress was to respond to local interests in the House of Representatives and to a broader state-based constituency in the Senate. Congress was to be the primary law-making body. Presumably the views of constituents concerning matters of public policy were to be transmitted through the electoral process to members of Congress. These were to be taken into account by legislators, who would be held responsible at the polls. Congress was to legislate in an environment that would balance the interests of the community. The two-year term of office for members of the House in combination with election by the people was to make them directly and continuously responsive to popular wishes. The passage of the Seventeenth Amendment brought the Senate into this arena of popular control, although its six-year term of office makes it less responsive than the House.

Does Congress today fulfill its constitutional purpose? Is it a deliberative and responsive law-making body? The operation of Congress depends on the forces acting upon it. The environment of congressional decision making and in particular the relationship between congressmen and their constituents are discussed in the next two selections.

34 CLARENCE D. LONG

OBSERVATIONS OF A FRESHMAN CONGRESSMAN

A letter from PRAY (Paul Revere Association, Yeomen, Inc.) predicts that the nuclear test ban will end up with "the Russians and Zionists ruling the world, all Christianity wiped out, and all wives, mothers, and daughters in the brothels of Asia, China and India."

George W. ("Wake Up Humanity") Adams demands that I "banish organized religion damned quick lest organized religion banish the world a hell of a lot quicker."

A neighbor wants to know "What are you clowns doing in Washington?" A 13-year-old boy asks me if I have ever taken a bribe. A tired-looking woman timidly seeks help in getting veterans' benefits, since she just learned that her husband, who years ago abandoned her with 10 children, had recently died after living with another woman in Brazil.

This is a tiny sample of the requests, problems and comments that have come to me since January when, after a quarter of a century as a professor, I found myself a freshman again — in the United States Congress.

I was no stranger to Washington. The center of my Maryland seat — Baltimore, Carroll and Hartford Counties — is only one hour from the Capitol City. While professor of economics at the Johns Hopkins University in Baltimore, I had served in advisory capacities in the

From *The New York Times Magazine*, December 1, 1963. © 1963 by The New York Times Company. Reprinted by permission of *The New York Times* and the author.

Administrations of three Presidents and testified before numerous Congressional committees. I had read — and written — books on the operation of government.

Judging Congress

Now, taking inventory, I am impressed at how much I had to learn and what a gap in attitude and experience separates the "Hill" from the rest of Washington. Nowhere is this gap greater than between the attitudes I once had, and now have, concerning the effectiveness of Congress.

Is Congress doing its job? What is its job? How are we to judge its performance? These questions are especially pertinent as a new Administration takes over.

Surely the job of Congress is not just to pass a lot of laws. Many acts suppressing freedom of speech and religion, or giving fat pensions to all over 55, would not entitle Congress to praise for accomplishing a lot. Nor would a law limiting civilian control of the military — passed without hearing or debate — entitle it to credit for getting things done quickly.

Whether Congress is effective depends really on how well it does its job — how many witnesses it hears, how carefully it questions them and listens to them, how responsibly it debates the issues and how wisely it makes up its mind and votes.

On this question of quality there will necessarily be many verdicts. The fact is, there is plenty of everything in the record: brashness, ponderous emptiness, cheapness, stale humor, twisted logic.

But you can also find the classical oratory of George Mahon, the calm judgment of Wilbur Mills, the verbal time-bombs of Wayne Hays, and the good-humored sagacity of the gently powerful Carl Vinson, chairman of my Armed Services Committee.

In the late afternoon, when the quorum calls have brought the members together, and when minds are alerted by parliamentary maneuvering and the approaching vote, the House of Representatives is at its most impressive. Its occasional flashes of wit, of homely erudition, of adroitness, of eloquence to penetrate the mind and move the heart, I have seldom heard surpassed.

But the Congress should be judged neither by its best nor by its worst; it would be a poor service to the truth to maintain that it is as effective as it could be. Few observers, including members, would dispute that Congress could be doing a better job. Why doesn't it?

Rules Held Secondary

Many explanations are offered. Criticism has been directed at the seniority and staffing systems of the committees, at the parliamentary rules and procedures on the floor, at the appropriations process, at conflicts of interest, nepotism, and junketing, at disproportionate representation, campaign financing, and the poll tax.

My own feeling now is that procedures are secondary. If Americans value good Congressmen they can get them under any election procedures. If Congressmen are competent and well-intentioned, they can be effective with any set of rules.

My short stay in Congress has impressed me with three closely related factors that may hamper Congressmen from doing a better job:

The two-year term of House members, which forces them to campaign continually for re-election;

The vast amount of time Congressmen and their staffs must spend on service for their districts;

The modest net salary of Congressmen, which forces many of them to practice law or run businesses on the side, in order to support dual residences and educate their children.

The two-year term of Representatives is one of the briefest in American politics. The Constitutional Convention made it brief deliberately to keep it responsive to the people, and it has certainly had that effect. But has it not overshot its mark?

It was instituted at a time when the average Congressman represented only a few thousand instead of hundreds of thousands of constituents; when Congress met a month or two instead of nearly all year; and when the Federal Government confined its activities to national defense, the excise tax, and a few internal improvements, instead of pervading every aspect of personal and business life and spending a quarter to a third of all the income of the economy.

Considering and voting on laws was in those early days a very part-time job. It is now a very full-time job — actually too big for the most brilliant and well-informed legislator — even if he had full time to devote to it. Yet the two-year term requires that most Congressmen campaign, not just every other year, but literally all the time. The essence of campaigning is personal contact in the home district.

7 Days a Week

My "rubber-chicken" calendar for a not untypical week included the following: Addressed students of three high schools visiting the House floor, veterans groups in two counties, officers club in Army Chemical Center, and civil-defense officials of seven states; attended meeting of 13th District Community Council, and various meetings on urban renewal, alcoholism, and relocation of a post office; attended a bar mitzvah, two bull roasts, and dedication of a school; went to a Democratic club dinner, a political cocktail party and dinner for a visiting Indian industrialist.

This routine — on top of legislative and administrative work — goes on seven days and five nights a week, except in July and August. Holidays are busiest. On July 4, I marched in four parades, smiled at 200,000 people, spoke to 5,000 more in the evening, attended a party, drove 100 miles.

I have discovered — or think I have! — that a Congressman is judged by the overwhelming mass of his constituents on the personal service he gives the home folks and the contracts he brings to his area.

IMMIGRATION TROUBLE

Four times a young constituent tried to enlist in the Army and had been turned down for high blood pressure; yet the Selective Service Board would not reclassify him, and no employer would hire him while he was subject to draft. I arranged for one more physical exam — by this time his blood pressure was *really* high! — and got his classification changed. He just wrote to tell me that he is employed and happy.

A Naval officer fell in love with a girl in South Africa and, having been informed he could bring his fiance to the United States, paid her way to Niagara Falls, Canada. There she was given the sad news that it was all a mistake, no admittance. At my request the State Department cut the red tape and let her in. Shortly afterward I received their wedding announcement.

An elderly woman, ill and living on $25 a week, was pressed for $1,000 arrears in income taxes. I convinced the Internal Revenue Service that squeezing blood out of a turnip was a cinch compared to getting $1,000 from a sick old lady existing on a pittance. Now she can live, if not in luxury, at least at peace.

Not all cases are desperate. A constituent complains that post office trucks wake the neighborhood at 4:30 every morning. A lady begs me to investigate why her young son in Vietnam could get "plenty of whisky but no soap."

And not long ago a 7-year-old girl asked for some dirt from the White House lawn. I sent an assistant across town, instructing him not to knock on the front door — that the President was busy with Alabama! — but to reach through the back fence and dig some dirt into an envelope.

Many requests are important to more than one person, for most Congressmen run for office on an implied pledge to get business and jobs. Although my counties are in sound health, certain key firms in space, electronics and shipbuilding have lost employment. Small firms there, as everywhere, complain of increasing difficulties.

During recent months I have toured plants and offices and talked extensively with management, workers and union leaders. I visited the

Government procurement agencies, including Defense, General Services, Space, and Small Business.

These explorations led me in June to set up a Business Desk, to serve as a center of information on defense business and how to obtain it and to put firms and individuals in touch with Government agencies. Major accomplishments have included getting a contract for radiosondes against the opposition of the entire Pennsylvania delegation and successfully upholding the low bidder on a contract for paper butter dishes.

Salary Called Low

This service has brought an enthusiastic response from firms, as well as from workers who benefit from the fuller employment. But this service — and time spent listening to pleas for personal help — is what takes up half of my own energies and two-thirds of those of my excellent staff.

The salary of a Congressman is $22,500 [now $30,000] a year. This will seem ample to many readers; yet I am less well off than I was as a professor.

To begin with, my election left me with bills I had not even known about. (An Alabama Congressman told me his entire first year's salary went to debts from his campaign.) In addition, my salary, before being available to pay those bills, feed my family, and keep two children in college, must first cover a myriad of expenses, partly political and partly Congressional.

There is a durable myth that a Congressman is reimbursed for trips from Washington to home. In actual fact, he is paid for one round trip a year, at 20 cents a mile, and under a law just passed, two additional round trips, at actual expenses, up to 12 cents a mile.

In my case, the total reimbursement amounts to $53 for the year. Since I commute daily my annual expense for car, trains and taxis is a very considerable item.

Expenses Mount

Even Congressmen from distant states commute weekly by train or plane to their districts. A Congressman from Michigan confided that he spent $3,000 for trips last year. Within my district, I drove 3,000 miles a month at my own expense.

A Congressman is allowed $2,400 a year for stationery and supplies. For two offices and ten persons, this covers writing paper, desk supplies, radio tapes, flags donated to schools and patriotic organizations, the telephone in the Congressman's district office, and most expensive, his newsletter.

This year is not over; yet I have spent my entire year's allowance and am in debt to the stationers by $800. As I expand my newsletter circulation — one of the best ways to keep in touch with my large constituency — I shall have to dip further into my own pocket.

Most Congressmen maintain residences in Washington, as well as at home. For this, they get no allowance — only an income tax deduction on what they spend up to $3,000.

A Congressman is under daily pressure to spend on miscellaneous items: luncheons for visitors; chances on "baskets-of-cheer," space in program books of clubs and churches, tickets to dances, dinners and barbecues.

OUTSIDE JOBS

Balanced against all these expenses are a few fringe benefits: haircuts at $1.00 including tip, free parking, and a free footlocker valued officially at $21.57 but worth perhaps $12 in downtown Washington stores. Total value, under $200.

As a result of this financial strain, most Congressmen — used to a far higher living standard than I, a former professor — keep a hand in their law practices and businesses. This time and energy they spend on these activities can only be at the expense of what they should be spending on the complicated issues that face them in committee or on the floor. These other commitments account for the substantial membership in the Tuesday–Thursday Club — Congressmen who get to Washington on Tuesday morning and leave Thursday night.

Higher salaries would possibly attract better men to Congress — although I know of nobody who has resigned because of salary. They would certainly reduce moonlighting and give the voter a higher degree of full-time representation. They would also enable us more effectively to eliminate conflict of interest.

If these are some of the rules of practical politics which keep legislators too busy to legislate, what are the prospects of changing them?

So far as the two-year term is concerned; the main obstacle may not be the public — which seems startlingly sympathetic to a longer term — but Congress itself. Between 1789 and 1960 about 120 resolutions introduced in Congress proposed a term longer than two years. Only two of these were reported out of committee; only one was debated on the floor of the House where it was defeated during the 59th Congress — over half a century ago. And if the longer term ever survived the House it would probably lose in the Senate for the very practical reason that Senators would prefer to retain the present system under which a House member can never run for the Senate without losing his job!

As for cutting down on the service function of Congressmen, a farreaching proposal to delegate service chores has been made by the alert and fertile-minded Rep. Henry Reuss of Wisconsin, who believes Congress should adapt the Scandinavian institution of the *ombudsman*. This special administrator is appointed by the legislature to handle constituent complaints concerning the executive branch. Germany took up the idea in 1957 as a channel for complaints by members of the armed forces and Great Britain has considered its establishment.

Would this system work in the United States? I somehow doubt it.

Power of a Vote

First, Congressmen would scarcely abandon the one function which has been demonstrated to be the most effective means of getting re-elected.

Second, the main reason a Congressman can get things done is that he has a vote. The Defense Department will listen to me when I ask for justice for an enlisted man or an access road for Aberdeen Proving Ground, because my vote may someday be critical on a $2-billion military construction bill or a $1-billion pay raise. I can't picture an appointed bureaucrat getting that kind of attention.

Third, what might work for a small, closely knit nation will scarcely fit the needs of a continent of 200 million, composed of widely diverse economic, geographic and ethnic interests. People write their Congressmen because they want special attention to their peculiar needs which a huge, complex, indifferent bureaucracy never seems to give.

A Congressman can do a lot for the ordinary fellow because he is a Congressman. Separate the service from the office and I suspect it won't get done.

Lips vs. Heart

What are the prospects for raising salaries high enough to sustain full-time legislating? Congress can set its pay scales at anything it likes, subject to Presidential veto. Yet, currently, the President, the American Bar Association, and many others are urging Congress to raise its pay by at least $10,000 to $32,500; a bill to accomplish this is in the hands of the House Rules Committee, but still Congress drags its feet!

Every Congressman I have talked to wants the raise — some desperately. But many will hesitate to vote for it, and some are committed to vote against it. As one Congressman told the President when the subject came up: "My lips say 'No, No,' but my heart says 'Yes, Yes'!"

Most such Congressmen have rural constituencies unacquainted with the dis-economies of large-city living in general and of Washington in particular. And every Congressman hears from letter-writers who hold firmly to the philosophy that the only good Congressman is a broke one.

Function of Congress

This Congressman, it is plain, sees no real prospect of lasting mitigation of the working conditions that may reduce the effectiveness of Congress.

But do they have such a deleterious effect?

The answer to this depends on your view as to what is the function of a Congressman. On this there are two extreme views. One view — mine in my days of innocence! — is that it is to pass good laws. The other view — held by the old-time politician — is that it is to survive, by representing constituents, giving them what they want, and staying out of trouble.

Both views are unsound. The first is naive, the second cynical. Neither would require very special skill. If our problem were to pass a logically consistent legislative program without reference to popular consent, it would be easy to assemble half a thousand experts many times as learned as any Congress ever elected. But this would be the Platonian rule of "philosopher-kings," not a democracy which rules with public consent.

Role of Congressman

In an oligarchy of experts, wisdom is ultimately corrupted by power. On the other hand, in a crude democracy, power is dispersed, to the endless frustration of the expert.

Here seems to be the ideal role of the Congressman: To represent his constituency, by knowing its needs and aspirations — at the same time inspiring it to something better. Both functions — to represent and to lead — are indispensable if a democracy of ordinary humans is to survive scientific revolutions every decade.

The one requires the Congressman to keep close to his constituency. The other requires him to know what goes on, in economics, in science, and in law. No Congressman is capable of all this, but a surprising number attempt it and a few come amazingly close.

This small band could be enlarged if the public would support better working conditions for Congressmen. Since it is not likely to do this very soon or very materially, Congress will continue to be less than fully effective as a purely legislative body.

In adding up the score, however, let us put some of the blame on the public which makes the rules of practical politics, not entirely on the Congressman who has to live with them. And why shouldn't the critics of Congress-as-an-institution add the vital service function of Congress to its legislative one in deciding whether it gets a passing mark?

Clarence D. Long discussed the extent to which congressmen must involve themselves in activities that do not relate directly to law making. In fact, the alleviation of individual grievances of constituents is one of the most important functions of Congress today. Re-election does not depend so much upon the legislative activities of the congressman but upon his actions in behalf of constituents. In the legislative field the question remains: To what extent do constituents influence congressmen in the legislative process? The findings of an empirical study dealing with this question are presented below.

35   WARREN E. MILLER AND DONALD E. STOKES

CONSTITUENCY INFLUENCE IN CONGRESS

Substantial constituency influence over the lower house of Congress is commonly thought to be both a normative principle and a factual truth of American government. From their draft constitution we may assume the Founding Fathers expected it, and many political scientists feel, regretfully, that the Framers' wish has come all too true. Nevertheless, much of the evidence of constituency control rests on inference. The fact that our House of Representatives, especially by comparison with the House of Commons, has irregular party voting does not of itself indicate that Congressmen deviate from party in response to local pressure. And even more, the fact that many Congressmen *feel* pressure from home does not of itself establish that the local constituency is performing any of the acts that a reasonable definition of control would imply.

I. CONSTITUENCY CONTROL IN THE NORMATIVE THEORY OF REPRESENTATION

Control by the local constituency is at one pole of *both* the great normative controversies about representation that have arisen in modern times. It is generally recognized that constituency control is opposite to the conception of representation associated with

From *The American Political Science Review* (March 1963). Reprinted by permission of The American Political Science Association and the authors.

Edmund Burke. Burke wanted the representative to serve the constituency's *interest* but not its *will,* and the extent to which the representative should be compelled by electoral sanctions to follow the "mandate" of his constituents has been at the heart of the ensuing controversy as it has continued for a century and a half.

Constituency control also is opposite to the conception of government by responsible national parties. This is widely seen, yet the point is rarely connected with normative discussions of representation. Indeed, it is remarkable how little attention has been given to the model of representation implicit in the doctrine of a "responsible two-party system." When the subject of representation is broached among political scientists the classical argument between Burke and his opponents is likely to come at once to mind. So great is Burke's influence that the antithesis he proposed still provides the categories of thought used in contemporary treatments of representation despite the fact that many students of politics today would advocate a relationship between representative and constituency that fits *neither* position of the mandate-independence controversy.

The conception of representation implicit in the doctrine of responsible parties shares the idea of popular control with the instructed-delegate model. Both are versions of popular sovereignty. But "the people" of the responsible two-party system are conceived in terms of a national rather than a local constituency. Candidates for legislative office appeal to the electorate in terms of a *national* party program and leadership, to which, if elected, they will be committed. Expressions of policy preference by the local district are reduced to endorsements of one or another of these programs, and the local district retains only the arithmetical significance that whichever party can rally to its program the greater number of supporters in the district will control its legislative seat.

No one tradition of representation has entirely dominated American practice. Elements of the Burkean, instructed-delegate, and responsible party models can all be found in our political life. Yet if the American system has elements of all three, a good deal depends on how they are combined. Especially critical is the question whether different models of representation apply to different public issues. Is the saliency of legislative action to the public so different in quality and degree on different issues that the legislator is subject to very different constraints from his constituency? Does the legislator have a single generalized mode of response to his constituency that is rooted in a normative belief about the representative's role or does the same legislator respond to his constituency differently on different issues? More evidence is needed on matters so fundamental to our system.

II. An Empirical Study of Representation

To extend what we know of representation in the American Congress the Survey Research Center of The University of Michigan interviewed the incumbent Congressman, his nonincumbent opponent (if any), and a sample of constituents in each of 116 congressional districts, which were themselves a probability sample of all districts. These interviews, conducted immediately after the congressional election of 1958, explored a wide range of attitudes and perceptions held by the individuals who play the reciprocal roles of the representative relation in national government. The distinguishing feature of this research is, of course, that it sought direct information from both constituent and legislator (actual and aspiring). To this fund of comparative interview data has been added information about the roll call votes of our sample of Congressmen and the political and social characteristics of the districts they represent.

Many students of politics, with excellent reason, have been sensitive to possible ties between representative and constituent that have little to do with issues of public policy. For example, ethnic identifications may cement a legislator in the affections of his district, whatever (within limits) his stands on issues. And many Congressmen keep their tenure of office secure by skillful provision of district benefits ranging from free literature to major federal projects. In the full study of which this analysis is part we have explored several bases of constituency support that have little to do with policy issues. Nevertheless, the question how the representative should make up his mind on legislative issues is what the classical arguments over representation are all about, and we have given a central place to a comparison of the policy preferences of constituents and Representatives and to a causal analysis of the relation between the two.

In view of the electorate's scanty information about government it was not at all clear in advance that such a comparison could be made. Some of the more buoyant advocates of popular sovereignty have regarded the citizen as a kind of kibitzer who looks over the shoulder of his representative at the legislative game. Kibitzer and player may disagree as to which card should be played, but they were at least thought to share a common understanding of what the alternatives are.

No one familiar with the findings of research on mass electorates could accept this view of the citizen. Far from looking over the shoulder of their Congressmen at the legislative game, most Americans are almost totally uninformed about legislative issues in Washington. At best the average citizen may be said to have some general ideas about how the country should be run, which he is able to use in responding to particular questions about what the government ought to do. For example, survey studies have shown that most people have a general (though differing) conception of how far government should go to achieve social and economic welfare objectives and that these convictions fix their response to various particular questions about actions government might take.

What makes it possible to compare the policy preferences of constituents and Representatives despite the public's low awareness of legislative affairs is the fact that Congressmen themselves respond to many issues in terms of fairly broad evaluative dimensions. Undoubtedly policy alternatives are judged in the executive agencies and the specialized committees of the Congress by criteria that are relatively complex and specific to the policies at issue. But a good deal of evidence goes to show that when proposals come before the House as a whole they are judged on the basis of more general evaluative dimensions. For example, most Congressmen, too, seem to have a general conception of how far government should go in the area of domestic social and economic welfare, and these general positions apparently orient their roll call votes on a number of particular social welfare issues.

It follows that such a broad evaluative dimension can be used to compare the policy preferences of constituents and Representatives despite the low state of the public's information about politics. In this study three such dimensions have been drawn from our voter interviews and from congressional interviews and roll call records. As suggested above, one of these has to do with approval of government action in the social welfare field, the primary domestic issue of the New Deal-Fair Deal (and New Frontier) eras. A second dimension has to do with support for American involvement in foreign affairs, a latter-day version of the isolationist-internationalist continuum. A third dimension has to do with approval of federal action to protect the civil rights of Negroes.

Because our research focused on these three dimensions, our analysis of constituency influence is limited to these areas of policy. No point has been more energetically or usefully made by those who have sought to clarify the concepts of power and influence than the necessity of specifying the acts *with respect to which* one actor has power or influence or control over another. Therefore, the scope or range of influence for our analysis is the collection of legislative issues falling within our three policy domains. We are not able to say how much control the local constituency may or may not have over *all* actions of its Representative, and there may well be pork-barrel issues or other matters of peculiar relevance to the district on which the relation of Congressman to constituency is quite distinctive. However, few observers of contemporary politics would regard the issues of government provision of social and economic welfare, of American involvement in world affairs, and of federal action in behalf of the Negro as constituting a trivial range of action. Indeed, these domains together include most of the great issues that have come before Congress in recent years. . . .

III. The Conditions of Constituency Influence

Broadly speaking, the constituency can control the policy actions of the Representative in two alternative ways. The first of these is for the district to choose a Representative who so shares its views that in following his own convictions he does his constituents' will. In this case district opinion and the Congressman's actions are connected through the Representative's own policy attitudes. The second means of constituency control is for the Congressman to follow his (at least tolerably accurate) perceptions of district attitude in order to win re-election. In this case constituency opinion and the Congressman's actions are connected through his perception of what the district wants.

These two paths of constituency control are presented schematically in Figure 1. As the figure suggests, each path has two steps, one con-

FIGURE ONE

Connections Between a Constituency's Attitude and
Its Representative's Roll Call Behavior

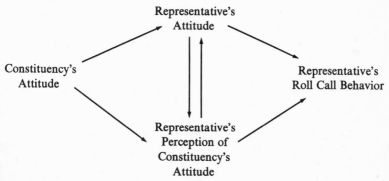

necting the constituency's attitude with an "intervening" attitude or perception, the other connecting this attitude or perception with the Representative's roll call behavior. Out of respect for the processes by which the human actor achieves cognitive congruence we have also drawn arrows between the two intervening factors, since the Congressman probably tends to see his district as having the same opinion as his own and also tends, over time, to bring his own opinion into line with the district's. The inclusion of these arrows calls attention to two other possible influence paths, each consisting of *three* steps, although these additional paths will turn out to be of relatively slight importance empirically.

Neither of the main influence paths of Figure 1 will connect the final roll call vote to the constituency's views if either of its steps is blocked. From this, two necessary conditions of constituency influence can be stated: *first,* the Representative's votes in the House must agree substantially with his own policy views or his perceptions of the district's views, and not be determined entirely by other influences to which the Congressman is exposed; and, *second,* the attitudes or perceptions governing the Representative's acts must correspond, at least imperfectly, to the district's actual opinions. It would be difficult to describe the relation of constituency to Representative as one of control unless these conditions are met.

Yet these two requirements are not sufficient to assure control. A *third* condition must also be satisfied: the constituency must in some measure take the policy views of candidates into account in choosing a Representative. If it does not, agreement between district and Congressman may arise for reasons that cannot rationally be brought within the idea of control. For example, such agreement may simply reflect the fact that a Representative drawn from a given area is likely, by pure statistical probability, to share its dominant values, without his acceptance or rejection of these ever having been a matter of consequence to his electors.

IV. Evidence of Control:
Congressional Attitudes and Perceptions

How well are these conditions met in the relation of American Congressmen to their constituents? There is little question that the first is substantially satisfied; the evidence of our research indicates that members of the House do in fact vote both their own policy views and their perceptions of their constituents' views, at least on issues of social welfare, foreign involvement, and civil rights. . . .

The connections of congressional attitudes and perceptions with actual constituency opinion are weaker. If policy agreement between district and Representative is moderate and variable across the policy domains, as it is, this is to be explained much more in terms of the second condition of constituency control that the first. The Representative's attitudes and perceptions most nearly match true opinion in his district on the issues of Negro rights [see Table 1]. . . .

V. Evidence of Control: Electoral Behavior

Of the three conditions of constituency influence, the requirement that the electorate take account of the policy positions of

TABLE ONE

Correlations of Constituency Attitudes

| | Correlation of constituency attitude with | |
Policy domain	Representative's perception of constituency attitude	Representative's own attitude
Social welfare	.17	.21
Foreign involvement	.19	.06
Civil rights	.63	.39

the candidates is the hardest to match with empirical evidence. Indeed, given the limited information the average voter carries to the polls, the public might be thought incompetent to perform any task of appraisal. Of constituents living in congressional districts where there was a contest between a Republican and a Democrat in 1958, less than one in five said they had read or heard something about both candidates, and well over half conceded they had read or heard nothing about either. And these proportions are not much better when they are based only on the part of the sample, not much more than half, that reported voting for Congress in 1958. The extent of awareness of the candidates among voters is indicated in Table II. As the table shows, even of the portion of the public that was sufficiently interested to vote, almost half had read or heard nothing about either candidate.

Just how low a hurdle our respondents had to clear in saying they had read or heard something about a candidate is indicated by detailed qualitative analysis of the information constituents *were* able to associate with congressional candidates. Except in rare cases, what the voters "knew" was confined to diffuse evaluative judgments about the candidate: "he's a good man," "he understands the problems," and so forth. Of detailed information about policy stands not more than a chemical trace was found. Among the comments about the candidates given in response to an extended series of free-answer questions, less than two percent had to do with stands in our three policy domains; indeed, only about three comments in every hundred had to do with legislative issues of *any* description.

This evidence that the behavior of the electorate is largely unaffected by knowledge of the policy positions of the candidates is complemented by evidence about the forces that *do* shape the voters' choices among congressional candidates. The primary basis of voting in American congressional elections is identification with party. In 1958 only one vote in twenty was cast by persons without any sort of

Awareness of Congressional Candidates among Voters, 1958

		Read or heard something about incumbent [a]		
		Yes	*No*	
Read or heard something about non-incumbent	*Yes*	24	5	29
	No	25	46	71
		49	51	100%

[a] In order to include all districts where the House seat was contested in 1958 this table retains ten constituencies in which the incumbent Congressman did not seek re-election. Candidates of the retiring incumbent's party in these districts are treated here as if they were incumbents. Were these figures to be calculated only for constituencies in which an incumbent sought re-election, no entry in this four-fold table would differ from that given by more than two percent.

party loyalty. And among those who did have a party identification, only one in ten voted against their party. As a result, something like 84 percent of the vote that year was cast by party identifiers voting their usual party line. What is more, traditional party voting is seldom connected with current legislative issues. As the party loyalists in a nationwide sample of voters told us what they liked and disliked about the parties in 1958, only a small fraction of the comments (about 15 per cent) dealt with current issues of public policy.

Yet the idea of reward or punishment at the polls for legislative stands is familiar to members of Congress, who feel that they and their records are quite visible to their constituents. Of our sample of Congressmen who were opposed for re-election in 1958, more than four-fifths said the outcome in their districts had been strongly influenced by the electorate's response to their records and personal standing. Indeed, this belief is clear enough to present a notable contradiction: Congressmen feel that their individual legislative actions may have considerable impact on the electorate, yet some simple facts about the Representative's salience to his constituents imply that this could hardly be true.

In some measure this contradiction is to be explained by the tendency of Congressmen to overestimate their visibility to the local public, a tendency that reflects the difficulties of the Representative in forming a correct judgment of constituent opinion. The communication most Congressmen have with their districts inevitably puts them in touch with organized groups and with individuals who are relatively well informed about politics. The Representative knows his constituents mostly from dealing with people who *do* write letters, who *will* attend meetings, who *have* an interest in his legislative stands. As a result, his sample of contacts with a constituency of several hundred thousand people is heavily biased: even the contacts he apparently makes at random are likely to be with people who grossly overrepresent the degree of political information and interest in the constituency as a whole.

But the contradiction is also to be explained by several aspects of the Representative's electoral situation that are of great importance to the question of constituency influence. The first of these is implicit in what has already been said. Because of the pervasive effects of party loyalties, no candidate for Congress starts from scratch in putting together an electoral majority. The Congressman is a dealer in increments and margins. He starts with a stratum of hardened party voters, and if the stratum is broad enough he can have a measurable influence on his chance of survival simply by attracting a small additional element of the electorate — or by not losing a larger one. Therefore, his record may have a very real bearing on his electoral success or failure without most of his constituents ever knowing what that record is.

Second, the relation of Congressman to voter is not a simple bilateral one but is complicated by the presence of all manner of intermediaries: the local party, economic interests, the news media, racial and nationality organizations, and so forth. Such is the lore of American politics, as it is known to any political scientist. Very often the Representative reaches the mass public through these mediating agencies, and the information about himself and his record may be considerably transformed as it diffuses out to the electorate in two or more stages. As a result, the public — or parts of it — may get simple positive or negative cues about the Congressman which were provoked by his legislative actions but which no longer have a recognizable issue content.

Third, for most Congressmen most of the time the electorate's sanctions are potential rather than actual. Particularly the Representative from a safe district may feel his proper legislative strategy is to avoid giving opponents in his own party or outside of it material they can use against him. As the Congressmen pursues this strategy he may write a legislative record that never becomes very well known to his constituents; if it doesn't win votes, neither will it lose any. This is clearly the situation of most southern Congressmen in dealing with the issue of Negro rights. By voting correctly on this issue they are unlikely to increase their visibility to constituents. Nevertheless, the fact of constituency influence, backed by potential sanctions at the polls, is real enough.

That these potential sanctions are all too real is best illustrated in the election of 1958 by the reprisal against Representative Brooks Hays in Arkansas' Fifth District. Although the perception of Congressman Hays as too moderate on civil rights resulted more from his service as intermediary between the White House and Governor Faubus in the Little Rock school crisis than from his record in the House, the victory of Dale Alford as a write-in candidate was a striking reminder of what can happen to a Congressman who gives his foes a powerful issue to use against him. The extraordinary involvement of the public in this race can be seen by comparing how well the candidates were known in this constituency with the awareness of the candidates shown by Table II above for the country as a whole. As Table III indicates, not a single voter in our sample of Arkansas' Fifth District was unaware of either candidate. What is more, these interviews show that Hays was regarded both by his supporters and his opponents as more moderate than Alford on civil rights and that this perception brought his defeat. In some measure, what happened in Little Rock in 1958 can happen anywhere, and our Congressmen ought not to be entirely disbelieved in what they say about their impact at the polls. Indeed, they may be under genuine pressure from the voters even while they are the forgotten men of national elections.

TABLE THREE

Awareness of Congressional Candidates among Voters in Arkansas Fifth District, 1958

		Read or heard something about Hays		
		Yes	No	
Read or heard something about Alford	Yes	100	0	100
	No	0	0	0
		100	0	100%

VI. CONCLUSION

Therefore, although the conditions of constituency influence are not equally satisfied, they are met well enough to give the local constituency a measure of control over the actions of its Representatives. Best satisfied is the requirement about motivational influences on the Congressman: our evidence shows that the Representative's roll call behavior is strongly influenced by his own policy preferences and by his perception of preferences held by the constituency.

However, the conditions of influence that presuppose effective communication between Congressman and district are much less well met. The Representative has very imperfect information about the issue preferences of his constituency, and the constituency's awareness of the policy stands of the Representative ordinarily is slight.

The findings of this analysis heavily underscore the fact that no single tradition of representation fully accords with the realities of American legislative politics. The American system *is* a mixture, to which the Burkean, instructed-delegate, and responsible-party models all can be said to have contributed elements. Moreover, variations in the representative relation are most likely to occur as we move from one policy domain to another. No single, generalized configuration of attitudes and perceptions links Representative with constituency but rather several distinct patterns, and which of them is invoked depends very much on the issue involved.

The issue domain in which the relation of Congressman to constituency most nearly conforms to the instructed-delegate model is that of civil rights. This conclusion is supported by the importance of the influence-path passing through the Representative's perception of district opinion, although even in this domain the sense in which the constituency may be said to take the position of the candidate into account in reaching its electoral judgment should be carefully qualified.

The representative relation conforms most closely to the responsible-party model in the domain of social welfare. In this issue area, the arena of partisan conflict for a generation, the party symbol helps both constituency and Representative in the difficult process of communication between them. On the one hand, because Republican and Democrat voters tend to differ in what they would have governments do, the Representative has some guide to district opinion simply by looking at the partisan division of the vote. On the other hand, because the two parties tend to recruit candidates who differ on the social welfare role of government, the constituency can infer the candidates' position with more than random accuracy from their party affiliation, even though what the constituency has learned directly about these stands is almost nothing. How faithful the representation of social welfare views is to the responsible-party model should not be exaggerated. Even in this policy domain, American practice departs widely from an ideal conception of party government. But in this domain, more than any other, political conflict has become a conflict of national parties in which constituency and Representative are known to each other primarily by their party association.

It would be too pat to say that the domain of foreign involvement conforms to the third model of representation, the conception promoted by Edmund Burke. Clearly it does in the sense that the Congressman looks elsewhere than to his district in making up his mind on foreign issues. However, the reliance he puts on the President and the Administration suggests that the calculation of where the public interest lies is often passed to the Executive on matters of foreign policy. Ironically, legislative initiative in foreign affairs has fallen victim to the very difficulties of gathering and appraising information that led Burke to argue that Parliament rather than the public ought to hold the power of decision. The background information and predictive skills that Burke thought the people lacked are held primarily by the modern Executive. As a result, the present role of the legislature in foreign affairs bears some resemblance to the role that Burke had in mind for the elitist, highly restricted *electorate* of his own day.

Congress and the Committee System

In 1885 Woodrow Wilson was able to state categorically in his famous work *Congressional Government,*

"The leaders of the House are the chairmen of the principal Standing Committees. Indeed, to be exactly accurate, the House has as many leaders as there are subjects of legislation; for there are as many Standing Committees as there are leading classes of legislation, and in the consideration of every topic of business the House is guided by a special leader in the person of the chairman of the Standing Committee, charged with the superintendence of measures of the particular class to which that topic belongs. It is this multiplicity of leaders, this many-headed leadership, which makes the organization of the House too complex to afford uninformed people and unskilled observers any easy clue to its methods of rule. For the chairmen of the Standing Committees do not constitute a cooperative body like a ministry. They do not consult and concur in the adoption of homogeneous and mutually helpful measures; there is no thought of acting in concert. Each Committee goes its own way at its own pace. It is impossible to discover any unity or method in the disconnected and therefore unsystematic, confused, and desultory action of the House, or any common purpose in the measures which its Committees from time to time recommend."

With regard to the Senate he noted,

"It has those same radical defects of organization which weaken the House. Its functions also, like those of the House, are segregated in the prerogatives of numerous Standing Committees. In this regard Congress is all of a piece. There is in the Senate no more opportunity than exists in the House for gaining such recognized party leadership as would be likely to enlarge a man by giving him a sense of power, and to steady and sober him by filling him with a grave sense of responsibility. So far as its organization controls it, the Senate . . . proceedings bear most of the characteristic features of committee rule."

The Legislative Reorganization Act of 1946 was designed to streamline congressional committee structure and provide committees and individual congressmen with increased expert staff; however, although the number of standing committees was reduced, subcommittees have increased so that the net numerical reduction is not as great as was originally intended. Further, because Congress still conducts its business through committees: (1) the senior members of the party with the majority in Congress dominate the formulation of public policy through the seniority rule; (2) policy formulation is fragmented with each committee maintaining relative dominance over policy areas within its jurisdiction; (3) stemming from this fragmentation party control is weakened, especially when the President attempts to assume legislative dominance.

In the selection by Charles L. Clapp the perspectives of congressmen themselves, expressed at a round-table conference conducted under the auspices of the Brookings Institution in Washington, reveal the nature of the committee system in Congress.

36 CHARLES L. CLAPP

THE CONGRESSMAN: HIS WORK AS HE SEES IT

"No one will be able to understand Congress unless he understands the committee system and how it functions," said one congressman at the opening session of the Brookings round table conference. The House and Senate must, of course, work their will on legislative proposals that are cleared by committees, but it is in the committee rooms that the real work is done. There, choices are made between alternative proposals and decisions are reached to pigeonhole or kill outright other bills. The latter actions virtually eliminate the possibility of further consideration by the House or Senate; the former involve determinations that generally govern the reception of the measure in the parent body. By weighting a measure with unpalatable items

From Charles L. Clapp, *The Congressman: His Work as He Sees It,* pp. 213–16, 308–12. Reprinted by permission of The Brookings Institution. Copyright © 1963, The Brookings Institution.

though reporting it, a committee can hasten its demise. By amending a bill so as to weaken the opposition it can almost guarantee success. By endorsing a measure strongly, a committee increases significantly the likelihood that it will be accepted. Close House and Senate adherence to committee recommendations is the practice although recommended legislation in controversial fields, such as agricultural policy, may face defeat on the floor. Normally, few substantive changes are made during floor debate. The volume and complexity of legislative proposals, the strong tradition of deferring to the "specialist," the search for ways to reconcile often conflicting pressures on congressmen, the very size of Congress — all conspire to enhance the authority of committee action. According to a congressional committee study, 90 percent of all the work of the Congress on legislative matters is carried out in committee.

The influence of committees in the legislative process is bolstered by the practice, particularly prevalent in the Appropriations Committee, of confining efforts to defeat or modify a proposal to activities within the committee itself. Once the battle has been fought and resolved there, those in the committee minority often do not press their case on the House floor. If they do intend to press it, they are careful, at the time of the committee vote, to "reserve" the right to do so. But the emphasis is on closing ranks and presenting a united front.

Committee pre-eminence and the difficulties involved in setting aside measures receiving committee endorsement have led party leaders on occasion to ignore seniority in making assignments to committees handling crucial or controversial legislation, as has been illustrated in Chapter 5. They also have led the Executive and the interest groups to concern themselves with the assignment process.

The central role of committees in the legislative process has also underscored the importance of strategic referral of bills to committee: by careful attention to the wording, a congressman may have his bill sent to a committee more favorably disposed to it than the one to which it might otherwise have been referred.

POWERS AND PROCEDURES

Committees are virtually autonomous bodies, hiring their own staffs, establishing their own rules of procedure, proceeding at their own pace for the most part, and resisting on occasion the urgings of the party. Chairmen may openly and successfully flaunt the party leadership, or they may have such stature that they are seldom requested to follow specific courses of action. And the reports of committees or their subcommittees may become as binding on executive departments as if they were law.

Committees differ tremendously in composition and method of operation, and may change significantly from one year to the next. As one congressman said, "Each committee tends to be unique in its unwritten rules — an organism in itself. The character changes with different chairmen and with different congresses." Some rely heavily on staff, interest groups, or the executive; others are relatively free from all such influences. Some are characterized by a lack of partisanship and generally report measures to the House floor by unanimous or nearly unanimous vote; strong partisanship is typical of others. In view of the central role of committees in the legislative process, an understanding of the working relationships that exist within the various committees is very helpful — often indispensable — to those who desire to influence legislation.

Just as different personalities alter procedures, the impact of a committee on the outlook of its members may be perceptible also. For example, service on the Appropriations Committee seems to make members more conservative. This is true in part because the membership is recruited carefully from the ranks of representatives likely to be susceptible to the socialization process. Although their attitudes toward issues vary, they are considered "reasonable" and "responsible," capable of adjusting easily to committee procedures and committee thinking. The fact that there is little turnover in committee membership tends to promote a group identity that is unusual and that aids in the assimilation of new members. Explained one liberal who sits on the committee:

> The Appropriations Committee develops a strange sort of breed. As soon as you get on the committee somehow you become more responsible as a member of Congress. You find you have to justify expenditures and you cannot pass over any situation very lightly. As a result you become more conservative. I think it is fair to say that on the whole the members of the Appropriations Committee are more conservative than most members of Congress. Committee members pause long before they support various programs. They are always thinking of what additional taxes are necessary to carry these programs out. Most congressmen, on the other hand, are just thinking how worthwhile the program would be, neglecting the point of how much additional taxes would be required.

The important work of committees takes place in closed rather than open sessions. It has been estimated that in recent years from 30 percent to 40 percent of committee meetings have been held in executive session. While House committees dealing with money matters and unusually technical or sensitive legislation, such as the Appropriations, Ways and Means, and Foreign Affairs committees are concerned with, are more disposed to meet in private than most other groups, nearly every committee makes fairly extensive use of this procedure.

Closed sessions facilitate compromise, promote candor and serious discussion, and eliminate the temptation to "play to the spectators," which occasionally overcomes members of Congress. Party representatives may have met together prior to a "mark-up" session in order to determine strategy and the party stand on a bill. But partisan stances are often sublimated and an atmosphere conducive to thoughtful consideration of legislation is more likely to prevail. Here representatives whose names the general public would not recognize may develop reputations among their colleagues based on their insights and their capacity for hard work. Despite the obvious advantages of holding executive sessions on many kinds of problems, there are persistent complaints, particularly from the press, that too many committee sessions are conducted behind closed doors. Far from promoting better legislation, these critics assert, closed sessions are often detrimental since, there, decisions are reached that would not be tolerated were the proceedings conducted in public. . . .

The Rules Committee. The Rules Committee possesses important powers, and its actions can go far to determine the nature of the legislation passed by the House. Thus control of the committee is eagerly sought by legislative leaders, and its resistance to suggestions of the Speaker and his allies inevitably leads to demands for reform of the group.

A center of controversy in recent years because of its occasional defiance of the wishes of the majority leadership, the Rules Committee was once a central element in the centralization of party responsibility in the House. It represented an important source of the Speaker's power; it was, in effect, *his* committee. He chaired it, determined its membership, and it bent to his will. Curtailment in 1910 of the Speaker's power of appointment has made the committee more independent of the leadership, despite the fact that in recent years the majority party has maintained a two to one edge in its membership. Since 1937 occasional coalitions of its Republican and conservative Southern Democratic members have functioned to thwart certain programs of the Democratic leadership when that party has controlled the House.

Most bills of any importance that are reported out of the legislative committees reach the House floor by means of a "rule" presented to the House by the Rules Committee. This resolution establishes the condition of debate on the bill: it specifies the time allocated for discussion and may stipulate the number and kind of amendments that can be offered. A rule from the committee does not guarantee House consideration of a measure — the leadership occasionally fails to schedule measures so reported — but it makes consideration likely. Committee refusal to grant a rule, on the other hand, usually means the bill will not be considered at all. The power of the committee to determine when to report out a bill is not an inconsiderable one either: timing is an important element of legislative strategy and delaying or expediting a bill can do much to affect its fate.

Measures are reported from the Rules Committee under an "open" rule, which places no limitation on the number or kind of amendments permitted during floor debate, or a "closed" rule. The latter is used less frequently and either permits no amendment or specifies those that are permissible. Closed rules are confined largely to complicated, technical measures, generally fiscal in nature, which come from the Appropriations or the Ways and Means Committee. Proponents of a bill may seek a closed rule to prevent the possibility that crippling amendments will be added; when they can get one, they gain an important initial advantage. Additionally, the committee may provide for waivers against points of order which could normally be raised against inclusion of non-privileged matters in privileged bills, such as legislation in an appropriations bill.

Generally, the Rules Committee cooperates with the legislative committees and the House leadership both in scheduling hearings on bills and in reporting them to the floor for House action. Seldom will a rule be granted for a measure opposed by the leadership, for example. But a bill it supports may occasionally either not be reported out or will be given a rule not favorable to the position of the majority party. In other instances, bills may be delayed in the Rules Committee until agreement is reached with the legislative committee regarding the nature of its activity on the floor: the Rules unit may elicit a promise to seek to amend the bill to conform more closely to Rules Committee preferences, or it may demand assurances that the committee will oppose amendments designed to disturb certain features of the bill. If the legislative committee declines to make the desired commitment, the bill may languish in the Rules Committee.

Few rules reported to the House are defeated. When they are rejected, the reason is more often opposition to the bill itself than a belief that the rule is unsatisfactory or unfair. The special orders under which measures proceed from the Rules Committee to the floor require only a majority vote; in effect they constitute suspension of the House rules, an action that ordinarily requires a two-thirds vote. Thus Rules Committee support eases the way of a measure.

Defenders of the Rules Committee maintain that while the committee has not always been responsive to the entreaties of the leadership, it has almost always been an accurate reflector of House opinion. Where it has clashed with the leadership, it has often expressed the judgment of the House. To charges that the committee flouts the will of the House, it is said that no committee that flagrantly ignored House opinion could maintain its power for long. And, it is asserted, the committee renders a valuable service to congressmen by refusing to act on bills on which the House does not wish to be recorded or in drafting rules so as to protect colleagues from difficult votes. The committee, it is said, often serves as a convenient whipping boy for the leadership or even the rank and file when in fact the latter groups privately applaud the actions taken. Stated one representative:

> There are many House members who spend time excoriating institutions like the Rules Committee, yet in their heart they thank Providence that the Rules Committee exists. They can't wait to get back home to make the Rules Committee a scapegoat. We could have done this or that, they say, if the reactionary Rules Committee hadn't bottled things up and prevented us from working our will. These people are secretly pleased that organizations like the committee exist to slow down the process and prevent bad legislation from developing. In a sense the Rules Committee takes them off the hook.

Explained another congressman, "Members are always going around to the Rules Committee and asking them to let a bill die there. Then they turn around and berate the committee for not reporting the bill out."

Although the values of the committee are appreciated, there is recognition that with respect to certain legislative proposals deemed important, if not crucial, to the program of the House leadership the Rules Committee has proved uncooperative and obstinate. It is often charged that the committee exceeds its "traffic manager" functions to perform a policy-making role rather than leaving determination of policy to the House itself. Undeniably the committee leaves its imprint on major legislation. As its chairman, Howard Smith, says: "My people did not elect me to Congress to be a traffic cop." One Democrat is particularly outraged that in certain circumstances a rule must be obtained to send a bill to conference. Said he: "After a bill has passed both houses, to let a half dozen men prevent the will of the majority of each house from being carried out is just outrageous."

While critics assert that the committee has denied the House the opportunity to vote on good legislation, friends of the Rules Committee unit retort that if a majority of the House desire action on a measure, there are sufficient means available to get it before the House despite lack of cooperation by the committee. Stated one House leader, "The Rules Committee which is nothing more than a committee on agenda has been unfairly used as a whipping boy. It never has had the power to bottle up legislation the majority really wanted." The main ways in which the Rules Committee can be circumvented are by (1) unanimous consent; (2) suspension of the rules; (3) Calendar Wednesday;

and (4) discharge. All of them are difficult ways by which to attain enactment of major legislation.[1]

The occasional reluctance of the Rules Committee to respond to leadership requests and its assumption of policy-making roles, combined with the difficulties inherent in seeking to bypass the committee by resorting to any of the procedures mentioned above, have led proponents of party responsibility to seek to return the committee to its earlier status as an instrument of the majority party. Failing that, they have sought to provide a more satisfactory means of circumventing the committee.

In recent years, critics of the committee have been successful on two occasions in imposing restrictions on the independence of the group. In 1949 they secured adoption of the "21 day rule." This provided that the chairman of a legislative committee could bring directly to the House floor any bill reported out of his committee for which the Rules Committee had failed to grant a rule within twenty-one calendar days of a request for action. The twenty-one day rule lasted only two years, falling victim to reduced majority party strength in the succeeding Congress. In 1961, the Democratic House majority sought to make the committee more responsive to its leadership by enlarging the membership of the committee from twelve to fifteen, maintaining the two to one party division. Explained one Democrat closely allied with the leadership: "The Rules Committee is a bit too powerful. If what we really want is to have a representative body and to have the majority will prevail, then it is clear something should be done to modify the Rules Committee."

And some Democrats who felt the need for an effective party policy committee believed the Rules Committee might be reconstituted to meet that need: "We need some kind of effective party instrument such

---

[1] A single objection can prevent consideration of a bill by unanimous consent, making it unlikely that controversial measures can be disposed of in that manner. Under suspension procedures the Speaker may, on the first and third Mondays of each month, recognize a member to move suspension of the rules and immediate consideration of a bill. But the Speaker has absolute power of recognition and may entertain or refuse to entertain such a motion. And, even if the Speaker is cooperative, suspension requires a two-thirds vote, which may be difficult to obtain. Calendar Wednesday provides that on Wednesdays the Speaker may call on committee chairmen (in alphabetical order by committee) who may call up for a vote any bill that has previously been reported out of their committee. But the measure must be disposed of in the same legislative day, and dilatory tactics may make this difficult. Further, hostile chairmen heading committees further up the list may prevent consideration of the bill in question by bringing up a bill from their own committee. The discharge petition is a difficult procedure since a majority of the membership must sign the petition to bring about action, and many legislators refuse to sign any discharge petition as a matter of policy.

as the policy committee. The Rules Committee might perform this function provided it is increased to make it more representative of the party point of view. As it stands now, it is not an effective instrument of Democratic party policy."

Although the 1961 changes did not make the committee a potential policy committee, they clearly made it more responsive to majority party leadership, for the time being at least. Even so, despite the increased majority, the leadership was not able to dislodge from the committee some measures in which it was interested. In 1963, the House voted to make permanent the larger committee size. The importance of the committee in the legislative process soon was emphasized by the intra-party struggle which developed when it was announced that a member of the committee from Texas could leave Congress to accept a judgeship. A tentative agreement between the Speaker and the Texas delegation as to a successor was quickly challenged by liberal Democrats, who feared the views of the designee would lead him to be less cooperative with the leadership than the congressman leaving the committee. Whether the move by the liberals was designed to substitute another congressman as the successor to the seat or merely to wrest concessions from the member designated was not immediately apparent.

> The committee system helps Congress in many ways. It allows congress to do business in an orderly fashion in the absence of a disciplined party system. It helps Congress to develop specialized knowledge in an age in which lawmaking is generally highly technical. One of the most vital functions fulfilled by the committee system is that of representation, as illustrated in the article about the House Agriculture Committee below.

37   CHARLES O. JONES

REPRESENTATION IN CONGRESS: THE CASE OF THE HOUSE AGRICULTURE COMMITTEE

Students of American politics are told that our political system is fundamentally a *representative* democracy. Concepts of

From *The American Political Science Review* (June 1961). Reprinted by permission of The American Political Science Association and the author.

representation, since Burke, have commonly employed his distinction between action taken in response to instructions from constituents and action based on an independent appraisal of the national interest. A very recent analysis has offered a refinement of this, by distinguishing three types: "delegate," "trustee" and "politico." Theory and history alike tell us, however, that a representative does not invariably act in only one of these roles. There have been a number of empirical studies on representatives, few of which concentrate on specific policy fields; and studies also of the play of interests in the enactment of specific legislation, but without a systematic account of the legislative committee members involved, acting in their representative capacities as they saw them. How then can we tell when to expect a representative to view his role in one way rather than another? The aim of this article is to shed a little light on some aspects of this broad question by means of a case study.

The subjects of the study were the members of the House Agriculture Committee and their action on the omnibus farm legislation (H. R. 12954 ans S. 4071) in 1958 (85th Congress, second session). . . .

For analytical purposes the most useful concept I developed, to account for the behavior of a representative, was one I shall call his "policy constituency." This may be defined as those interests within his geographical or legal constituency which he perceives to be affected by the policy under consideration. When he regards these interests as actively and homogeneously concerned, they are ordinarily sufficient to determine his public stand. When he sees them as weak, indifferent or divided, other factors come into play. But he is affected too by the nature of the committee institution within which the policy is being formed.

The House Agriculture Committee and Its Work

Organization. In 1958 a Republican President was again faced with a Democratic Congress in a congressional campaign year. The margin of control for Democrats in the House Agriculture Committee was a less-than-comfortable four votes; the split was 19 to 15. The margin in subcommittees was one vote in most cases. . . .

The principal work units in the House Agriculture Committee are the subcommittees. In 1958 there were 18 subcommittees of two kinds — ten commodity subcommittees and eight special-action subcommittees. The former are more important since they consider legislation designed to solve the many crises for specific commodities. Usually a member is assigned to at least one commodity subcommittee of his choice. The chairman consults the ranking minority leader but has the last word on appointments. Actually few decisions have to be made, since most commodity subcommittees are permanent and their membership is continuing; only the new members need assignments. The size of subcommittees varies considerably (from 12 for tobacco to five for rice), giving the chairman some flexibility in case several members are interested in one commodity. . . .

Representing Agriculture. As might be expected, congressmen from constituencies with significant interests in farm policy make up the membership of the House Agriculture Committee. In 1958 there was but one exception to this rule — Victor Anfuso, Democrat from Brooklyn. Thirteen of the 19 Democrats came from areas where tobacco, cotton, peanuts, and rice are the principal commodities. Republican Committee members came from areas producing corn, hogs, small grain, wheat, and areas where the farming is diversified.

Committee members may be classified by commodities of greatest interest to their constituencies, as in Table [I]. Commodities receiving price supports are grown in the constituencies of members of all six groups there listed. The *basic* commodities, so labeled by the Agricultural Adjustment Act of 1938, are corn, cotton, tobacco, rice, wheat, and peanuts; price supports have been mandatory for them. An increasing number of *non-basics* have also received price supports, *e.g.,* milk and wool. The "diversified" (mainly non-basics) group often find their interests conflicting with those of representatives in the other groups. They complain that their farmers are at a disadvantage since their non-basics either do not receive price supports or receive less support than the basics; the price supports for the few basics grown do not make up for the deprivation of profits attributable to acreage and marketing controls (the complaint of California cotton farmers); and they must pay higher prices for the basics as well as pay higher taxes.

Almost without exception the six groups show an alignment between commodity interests and party allegiance. The corn and livestock group has five Republicans and one Democrat; the cotton and rice group, seven Democrats; the dairy, livestock, small grains group, two Democrats and three Republicans; the diversified group, four Republicans and two Democrats; the tobacco group, seven Democrats; and the wheat group, three or four Republicans. Consequently, different commodities will ordinarily be favored when different parties are in control. For example, cotton, rice, and tobacco usually receive more attention when the Democrats are a majority in the Committee.

Committee organization has been strongly influenced by the commodity problems in agriculture. First, subcommittees are established to deal with currently critical commodity problems. Second, members are assigned to commodity subcommittees on the basis of their constituency interests. Table [II] shows the high correlation prevailing. Only one Democrat (Anfuso) was assigned to no commodity subcommittee representing producers in his constituency and he has no agricultural production at all in his Brooklyn district, though the poultry trade is important there. Two Republicans (Harrison and Dixon) found themselves on subcommittees of little or no concern to their constituencies. Significantly both of these members were identified by other members as being supporters of Secretary Benson's recommendations.

Party considerations dictate that some members must be on subcommittees of no concern to their constituencies: there must be Republicans on the cotton subcommittee and Democrats on the wheat subcommittee. For the most part, members who have little interest in the proceedings are expected either to remain silent during hearings or not to attend. . . . [Here the author discusses the legislation introduced in 1958 and the modifications made to secure its passage.]

TABLE [ONE]

Committee Members and Their
Constituencies' Commodities[a]

---

1. *Corn and Livestock*
   Harrison (R-Nebraska)
   Harvey (R-Indiana)
   Hill (R-Colorado)[b]
   Hoeven (R-Iowa)
   Polk (D-Ohio)
   Simpson (R-Illinois)[b]
2. *Cotton and Rice*
   Abernethy (D-Mississippi)
   Albert (D-Oklahoma)
   Gathings (D-Arkansas)
   Grant (D-Alabama)
   Jones (D-Missouri)
   Poage (D-Texas)
   Thompson (D-Texas)
3. *Dairy, Livestock, Small Grains*
   Johnson (D-Wisconsin)
   Knutson (D-Minnesota)
   Quie (R-Minnesota)
   Tewes (R-Wisconsin)
   Williams (R-New York)[b]

4. *Diversified* (non-basics)
   Anfuso (D-New York)
   Dague (R-Pennsylvania)
   Dixon (R-Utah)
   Hagen (D-California)
   McIntire (R-Maine)
   Teague (R-California)
5. *Tobacco*
   Abbitt (D-Virginia)
   Bass (D-Tennessee)
   Cooley (D-North Carolina)
   Jennings (D-Virginia)
   McMillan (D-South Carolina)
   Matthews (D-Florida)
   Watts (D-Kentucky)
6. *Wheat*
   Belcher (R-Oklahoma)
   Krueger (R-North Dakota)[b]
   Smith (R-Kansas)

---

[a] Members were classified on the basis of their constituencies' principal commodities, as listed in the *Census of Agriculture*, Vol. I, 1956, and interviews with the members.

[b] These members were not interviewed. Simpson, Williams and Krueger clearly belonged to the groups to which they have been assigned. Hill might also have been included in the wheat group.

TABLE [TWO]

Constituency Interests and Commodity Subcommittee Assignments[a]

Member[b]	Major agricultural interests in constituency	Commodity subcommittees
Democrats		
Poage	Cotton, Livestock, Peanuts	Cotton; Livestock & Feed Grains (C)
Grant	Cotton, Peanuts, Wood Products	Forests (C); Peanuts
Gathings	Cotton, Rice, Soybeans	Cotton (C); Rice; Soybeans-Oilseeds
McMillan	Cotton, Tobacco, Peanuts	Forests; Peanuts (C); Tobacco
Abernethy	Cotton	Cotton; Dairy Products (C); Soybeans-Oilseeds
Albert	Cotton, Livestock	Livestock and Feed Grains; Peanuts; Wheat (C)
Abbitt	Tobacco, Peanuts	Tobacco (C); Peanuts
Polk	Feed Grains, Livestock, Dairy	Dairy Products; Tobacco
Thompson	Rice, Cotton, Peanuts	Rice (C); Poultry-Eggs
Jones	Cotton, Livestock, Soybeans	Rice; Soybeans-Oilseeds (C); Wheat
Watts	Tobacco, Feed Grains, Seeds	Tobacco; Wheat
Hagen	Cotton, Alfalfa Seed, Potatoes, Fruit	Cotton; Soybeans-Oilseeds
Johnson	Dairy, Forests, Livestock	Dairy Products; Forests; Poultry-Eggs
Anfuso	None	Poultry-Eggs
Bass	Tobacco, Cotton	Tobacco; Wheat
Knutson	Wheat, Dairy, Feed Grains	Dairy Products
Jennings	Tobacco, Livestock	Livestock and Feed Grains; Tobacco; Wheat
Matthews	Tobacco, Peanuts, Vegetables	Livestock and Feed Grains; Tobacco
Republicans		
Hoeven	Feed Grains, Livestock	Livestock and Feed Grains; Soybeans-Oilseeds
Simpson	Feed Grains, Livestock	Cotton; Livestock and Feed Grains; Soybeans-Oilseeds; Tobacco
Dague	Tobacco, Truck Farming, Poultry, Dairy	Tobacco; Wheat
Harvey	Feed Grains, Livestock	Livestock and Feed Grains; Soybeans-Oilseeds

TABLE TWO (*cont.*)

Constituency Interests and Commodity
Subcommittee Assignments

Member[b]	Major agricultural interests in constituency	Commodity subcommittees
Belcher	Wheat	Cotton; Peanuts; Wheat
McIntire	Forests, Poultry, Potatoes	Forests; Poultry-Eggs; Tobacco
Williams	Dairy, Truck Farming	Dairy Products; Rice
Harrison	Feed Grains, Livestock	Peanuts; Poultry-Eggs
Dixon	Wheat, Potatoes, Small Grain, Sugar Beets	Forests; Poultry-Eggs
Smith	Wheat	Peanuts; Wheat
Krueger	Wheat, Small Grains	Rice; Wheat
Teague	Vegetables, Fruit, Small Grains, Cotton	Cotton; Forests
Tewes	Dairy, Tobacco, Livestock	Dairy Products; Tobacco
Quie	Dairy, Feed Grains, Livestock	Dairy Products; Tobacco

[a] The major interests were deduced from the *Census of Agriculture, 1954,* Vol. 1, 1956, and from interviews with members.

[b] Members listed according to committee rank. Chairman Cooley, whose principal interests were tobacco, cotton and poultry, and William Hill, whose principal interests were wheat, feed grains, and sugar beets, were *ex officio* members of all the committees by virtue of their positions as chairman and ranking minority member, respectively.

CONCLUSIONS

The conclusions suggested by this case study can be set forth . . . as follows:

1. If a policy measure is seen to affect substantial interests in a representative's legal constituency, then he will rely on his perception of the interests affected (his "policy constituency") when he acts at the working level (usually the subcommittee) in regard to this measure.

   A. Institutional arrangements affect his ability to represent his policy constituency. The House Agriculture Committee is organized to allow a maximum of constituency-oriented representation.

   B. The representative has a "sense" of constituency interests drawn from first-hand experience in the "legal" constituency and this "sense" influences his perception of a policy constituency.

   C. Party allegiance is an important modifying factor.

      (1) The legislative majority party may demand a vote in support of its policies. The legislative minority party may de-

mand a vote in opposition to the majority's policies. The Administration may press for support for its stands.

(2) Representatives, whether or not affected by the legislation, tend to support their party's position more as the action moves beyond the basic working level, and most at the final vote.

2. If a measure is seen to have little or no direct effect on interests in a representative's legal constituency, then he will tend more readily to look to his political party for a cue when he acts in regard to this measure.

A. The representative will tend the more to suggest that he relies on "independent judgment," the less his constituency's interests are seen to be directly or positively affected by a policy.

B. He will vote in support of his political party but will not actively support the policy in other ways if his constituency interests are not perceived to be affected. . . .

An adequate concept of representation should account for a total action pattern, not merely a final vote. The representative on the House Agriculture Committee can view his composite role retrospectively as one in which he has taken several separate actions to make up a total pattern in regard to the omnibus farm legislation. He also can recognize that on different occasions he felt differing demands upon him in his several capacities, as a member of a party, a representative of a constituency, a member of a committee, of a Congress, of interest groups, etc. He was able to reconcile, compromise or avoid some of the inherent conflicts in these demands, at least in part, because of the multiple action points. Examples of such reconciliations in this case study justify a final hypothesis which merits separate study:

3. If a representative has a multiplicity of conflicting demands upon him in any series of actions on policy, he can satisfy many of them, over a period of time, because of the multiplicity of action points at successive stages in the legislative process.

The Senate: Folkways and Folk Wisdom

Reading *The Federalist,* students can see that the framers of the Constitution expected the Senate to be the most important conservative force in our government. To some extent the Seventeenth Amendment, which provided for the popular election of Senators, modified conservative expectations, but the long term of office, one of the most important provisions designed to ensure conservativism in this branch of the government, remains. Proportionately, of course, the less populous states are better represented in the Senate than in the House. This fact, combined with the seniority system, reliance upon committees, and southern solidarity renders the Senate, in the words of one commentator, an "old southern home." Its essential conservatism remains, and it is still an institution in which state and regional influence is dominant. The conservatism of the Senate is reflected in what Donald R. Matthews calls "the folkways of the Senate," informal patterns of behavior resulting from a lack of party organization and formal structure. These "folkways" help to minimize conflict and make the Senate a viable decision-making body.

38   DONALD R. MATTHEWS

THE FOLKWAYS OF THE SENATE

The Senate of the United States, just as any other group of human beings, has its unwritten rules of the game, its norms of conduct, its approved manner of behavior. Some things are just not done; others are met with widespread approval. "There is great pressure for conformity in the Senate," one of its influential members said. "It's just like living in a small town."

What are the standards to which the senators are expected to conform? What, specifically, do these unwritten rules of behavior say? Why do they exist? In what ways do they influence the senators? How, concretely, are they enforced? What kinds of senators obey the folkways? Which ones do not, and why?

These are difficult questions for an outsider to analyze. Only those who have served in the Senate, and perhaps not even all of them, are likely to grasp its folkways in all their complexity. Yet, if we are to understand why senators behave as they do, we must try to understand them.

APPRENTICESHIP

The first rule of Senate behavior, and the one most widely recognized off the Hill, is that new members are expected to serve a proper apprenticeship.

The freshman senator's subordinate status is impressed upon him in many ways. He receives the committee assignments the other senators

From Donald R. Matthews, *U.S. Senators and Their World,* Chap. 5, pp. 92–103, 116–17 in the Vintage Edition. Copyright © 1960, University of North Carolina Press. Reprinted by permission of the publisher.

do not want. The same is true of his office suite and his seat in the chamber. In committee rooms he is assigned to the end of the table. He is expected to do more than his share of the thankless and boring tasks of the Senate, such as presiding over the floor debate or serving on his party's Calendar Committee. According to the folkways of the Senate, the freshman is expected to accept such treatment as a matter of course.

Moreover, the new senator is expected to keep his mouth shut, not to take the lead in floor fights, to listen and to learn. "Like children," one freshman said, "we should be seen and not heard." Just how long this often painful silence must be maintained is not clear, but it is certainly wiser for a freshman to postpone his maiden efforts on the floor too long than to appear overly aggressive. Perhaps, ideally, he should wait until pushed reluctantly to the fore. "I attended the floor debates and voted for a year without giving a single speech" a senior senator said with pride.

> Finally, one day, a matter came up with which I had had considerable experience in the House. My part in it had gotten some publicity. ———— leaned over to me and said, "————, are you going to speak on this?" I said, "No." "You know a great deal about this," he replied. "I think you should speak." I answered that I had not prepared a speech and that I would rather not speak on the bill. "Look," he said, "I am going to get up on the floor and ask you a question about this bill. Then you will *have* to speak!" And that's how I made my first speech in the Senate.

Freshmen are also expected to show respect for their elders ("You may think you are smarter than the older fellows, but after a time you find that this is not true") and to seek their advice (" 'Keep on asking for advice, boy,' the committee chairman told me. 'That's the way to get ahead around here' "). They are encouraged to concentrate on developing an acquaintanceship in the Senate. ("Young senators should make a point of getting to know the other senators. This isn't very hard: there are only ninety-nine of them. And if the other senators know and like you, it increases your effectiveness.")

The freshman who does not accept his lot as a temporary but very real second-class senator is met with thinly veiled hostility. For instance, one old-timer tells this story: "When I came to the Senate, I sat next to Senator Borah. A few months later, he had a birthday. A number of the older men got up and made brief, laudatory speeches about it. Borah was pleased. Then a freshman senator — one who had only been in the chamber three or four months — got to his feet and started on a similar eulogy. He was an excellent speaker. But between each of his laudatory references to Borah, Borah loudly whispered, 'That son-of-a-bitch, that son-of-a-bitch.' He didn't dislike the speaker, personally. He just didn't feel that he should speak so soon."

Even so, the veterans in the Senate remark, rather wistfully, that the practice of serving an apprenticeship is on the way out, and, to some extent, they are undoubtedly correct. The practice seems to have begun well before the popular election of senators and the exigencies of the popularly elected official have placed it under considerable strain. As one very senior senator, whose service extends back almost to the days before popular election, ruefully explained: "A new senator today represents millions of people. He feels that he has to *do* something to make a record from the start."

This judgment is also colored by the tendency in any group for the old-timers to feel that the younger generation is going to hell in a handbasket. To the present-day freshmen in the Senate, the period of apprenticeship is very real and very confining. As one of them put it, "It reminds me a little of Hell Week in college." Indeed, the nostalgic talk of the older senators regarding the unhappy lot of the freshman in the good old days is one way the senior senators keep the younger men in their place. One freshman Democrat, for example, after completing a floor speech found himself sitting next to Senator George, then the dean of the Senate. Thinking that he should make polite conversation, the freshman asked the Georgia patriarch what major changes had taken place in the Senate during his long service. Senator George replied, "Freshmen didn't use to talk so much."

Legislative Work

"There are two kinds of Congressmen — show horses and work horses. If you want to get your name in the papers, be a show horse. If you want to gain the respect of your colleagues, keep quiet and be a work horse." Senator Carl Hayden of Arizona remembers being told this when he first came to the Congress many years ago. It is still true.

The great bulk of the Senate's work is highly detailed, dull, and politically unrewarding. According to the folkways of the Senate, it is to those tasks that a senator *ought* to devote a major share of his time, energy, and thought. Those who follow this rule are the senators most respected by their colleagues. Those who do not carry their share of the legislative burden or who appear to subordinate this responsibility to a quest for publicity and personal advancement are held in disdain.

This results, at first, in a puzzling disparity between the prestige of senators inside and outside the Senate. Some of the men most highly respected by their colleagues are quite unknown except on the Hill and in their own states; others whose names are household words are thought to be second-raters and slackers. The words used to describe those senators who seem to slight their legislative duties are harsh — "grandstanders," "demagogues," "headline hunters," "publicity seekers," "messiahs." They are said to do nothing but "play to the galleries," to suffer from "laziness" and "verbal diarrhea," and not to be "team players." It is even occasionally hinted that they are mentally or emotionally deranged.

But this does not mean that all publicity is undesirable. It takes publicity to get, and stay, elected. This publicity, as long as it does not interfere with the performance of legislative duties, is considered necessary and desirable. Nor is there any objection to publicity calculated to further the cause of a program or policy or to publicity which flows from a senator's position or performance. But the Senate folkways do prescribe that a senator give first priority to being a legislator. Everything else, including his understandable desire for personal and political publicity, must be secondary to this aspect of his job.

SPECIALIZATION

According to the folkways of the Senate, a senator should not try to know something about every bill that comes before the chamber nor try to be active on a wide variety of measures. Rather, he ought to specialize, to focus his energy and attention on the relatively few matters that come before his committees or that directly and immediately affect his state. "When you come to the Senate," one administrative assistant said, "you have to decide which street corner you are going to fight on."

In part, at least, senators ought to specialize because they must: "Thousands of bills come before the Senate each Congress. If some senator knows the fine details of more than half a dozen of them, I've never heard of him." Even when a senator restricts his attention to his committee work, the job is more than one man can do. "I belong to twelve or thirteen committees and subcommittees," a leading senator says. "It's physically impossible to give them all the attention I should. So I have picked out two or three subcommittees in which I am especially interested and have concentrated on them. I believe that this is the usual practice around here."

The relatively few senators who have refused to specialize agree. One of these, a relatively young man of awesome energy, says, "I'll be perfectly frank with you. Being active on as wide a range of issues as I have been is a man-killing job. In a few years I suspect that I will be active on many fewer issues. I came down here a young man and I'm gradually petering out." The limit of human endurance is not, however, the only reason for a senator to specialize. By restricting his attention to matters concerning his committee work and his home state, the senator is concentrating on the two things he should know best. Only through specialization can he know more about a subject than his colleagues and thus make a positive contribution to the operation of the chamber.

Moreover, speaking too much tends to decrease a senator's legislative impact. "Look at ————," one of them said. "He came in here with his mouth open and he hasn't closed it yet. After a while, people stop listening." Furthermore, a senator who is too active outside his specialty may destroy his influence within his area of special competence. "When ————, one of my best friends in the Senate, came here he was known as an expert on ————, and they used to listen to him as such. But then he began talking on many other issues as well. As a result, he lost some of his effectiveness on ———— matters as well as on the other issues to which he addressed himself."

Almost all the senators are agreed that: "The really effective senators are those who speak only on the subjects they have been dealing with at close quarters, not those who are on their feet on almost every subject all the time." Why this pressure for specialization? Why does this folkway exist? There would seem to be a number of reasons.

The formal rules of the Senate provide for what amounts to unlimited debate. Even with the folkways limiting the activity of freshmen, discouraging "playing to the galleries," and encouraging specialization, the Senate moves with glacial speed. If many more senators took full advantage of their opportunities for debate and discussion, the tempo of action would be further slowed. The specialization folkway helps make it possible for the Senate to devote less time to talking and more to action.

Moreover, modern legislation is complex and technical, and it comes before the Senate in a crushing quantity. The committee system and specialization — in a word, a division of labor within the chamber — increase skill and decrease the average senator's work load to something approaching manageable proportions. When a senator refuses to "go along" with specialization, he not only challenges the existing power structure but also decreases the expert attention which legislative measures receive.

Courtesy

The Senate of the United States exists to solve problems, to grapple with conflicts. Sooner or later, the hot, emotion-laden issues of our time come before it. Senators as a group are ambitious and egocentric men, chosen through an electoral battle in which a talent for invective, righteous indignation, "mud-slinging," and "engaging in personalities" are often assets. Under these circumstances, one might reasonably expect a great deal of manifest conflict and competition in the Senate. Such conflict does exist, but its sharp edges are blunted by the felt need — expressed in the Senate folkways — for courtesy.

A cardinal rule of Senate behavior is that political disagreements should not influence personal feelings. This is not an easy task; for, as one senator said, "It's hard not to call a man a liar when you know that he is one."

Fortunately, a number of the chamber's formal rules and conventions make it possible for him to approximate this ideal — at least so far as overt behavior is concerned. The selection of committee members and chairmen on the basis of their seniority neatly by-passes a potential cause of grave dissention in the Senate. The rules prohibit the questioning of a colleague's motives or the criticism of another state. All remarks made on the floor are, technically, addressed to the presiding officer, and this formality serves as a psychological barrier between antagonists. Senators are expected to address each other not by name but by title — Earle C. Clements does not disagree with Irving M. Ives, but rather the Senior Senator from Kentucky disagrees with the Senior Senator from New York.

Sometimes the senators' efforts to achieve verbal impersonality become ludicrous in their stilted formality. For example:

> MR. JOHNSON of Texas. The Senator from Texas does not have any objection, and the Senator from Texas wishes the Senator from California to know that the Senator from Texas knew the Senator from California did not criticise him. . . .[1]

Few opportunities to praise publicly a colleague are missed in the Senate. Senators habitually refer to each other as "The distinguished Senator from ———" or "The able Senator from ———." Birthdays, anniversaries, re-election or retirement from the Senate, and the approach of adjournment are seized as opportunities for the swapping of praise. Sometimes, on these occasions, the sentiment is as thick as Senate bean soup. For example, the following recently took place on the Senate floor and was duly printed in the *Record:*

> MR. JOHNSON of Texas. Mr. President, if the Senate will indulge me, I should like the attention of members of both sides of the aisle for a bipartisan announcement of considerable importance. It involves the minority leader, the distinguished Senator from California (MR. KNOWLAND).
>
> For many years, I have been closely associated with the Senator from California. Like every member of this chamber — on either side of the aisle — I have found him to be able, patriotic, courteous, and thoughtful.

[1] *Congressional Record* (Daily Edition), April 24, 1956, p. 6148.

But I wonder how many of my colleagues know that he is also a five-time winner in the contest for the proudest granddaddy in the Senate?

His fifth victory was chalked up last Monday when Harold Jewett II discovered America. Anybody who has found buttons lying on the floor in front of the minority leader's desk in the past few days can know now that they popped right off BILL KNOWLAND's shirt.[2]

This kind of behavior — avoiding personal attacks on colleagues, striving for impersonality by divorcing the self from the office, "buttering-up" the opposition by extending unsolicited compliments — is thought by the senators to pay off in legislative results. Personal attacks, unnecessary unpleasantness, and pursuing a line of thought or action that might embarrass a colleague needlessly are all thought to be self-defeating — "After all, your enemies on one issue may be your friends on the next." Similar considerations also suggest the undesirability of excessive partisanship. "I want to be able to pick up votes from the other side of the aisle," one Republican said. "I hope that a majority of the Republicans will vote for anything I sponsor. But always some of them are going to have special problems that impel them to vote against the party." They also suggest, despite partisan differences, that one senator should hesitate to campaign against another. "The fellows who go around the country demagoguing and calling their fellow senators names are likely to be ineffective senators. It's just human nature that the other senators will not cooperate with them unless they have to."

In private, senators are frequently cynical regarding this courtesy. They say that "it doesn't mean a thing," that it is "every man for himself in the Senate," that some of their colleagues "no more should be senators than I should be Pope," that it is "just custom." Senator Barkley's advice to the freshman senator — if you think a colleague stupid, refer to him as "the able, learned and distinguished senator," but if you *know* he is stupid, refer to him as "the *very* able, learned and distinguished senator" — is often quoted. Despite its blatant hypocrisy, the practice persists, and after serving in the Senate for a period of years most senators grow to appreciate it. "You discover that political self-preservation dictates at least a semblance of friendship. And then before you know it, you really *are* friends. It is rather like the friendships that might develop within a band of outlaws. You all hang together or you will hang separately."

Courtesy, far from being a meaningless custom as some senators seem to think it is, permits competitors to cooperate. The chaos which ensues when this folkway is ignored testifies to its vital function.

[2] *Congressional Record* (Daily Edition), June 13, 1956, pp. 9147–48.

Reciprocity

Every senator, at one time or another, is in a position to help out a colleague. The folkways of the Senate hold that a senator should provide this assistance and that he be repaid in kind. The most important aspect of this pattern of reciprocity is, no doubt, the trading of votes. Occasionally this is done quite openly in the course of public debate. The following exchange, for example, took place during the 1956 debate on acreage allotments for burley tobacco:

> MR. LANGER [North Dakota]. We don't raise any tobacco in North Dakota, but we are interested in the tobacco situation in Kentucky, and I hope the Senator will support us in securing assistance for the wheat growers in our State.
> MR. CLEMENTS [Kentucky]. I think the Senator will find that my support will be 100 per cent.
> MR. BARKLEY [Kentucky]. Mr. President, will my colleague from Kentucky yield?
> MR. CLEMENTS. I yield.
> MR. BARKLEY. The colloquy just had confirms and justifies the Woodrow Wilsonian doctrine of open covenants openly arrived at. (Laughter.)[3]

Usually, however, this kind of bargain is either made by implication or in private. Senator Douglas of Illinois, who tried unsuccessfully to combat this system, has analyzed the way in which a public works appropriation bill is passed.

> . . . This bill is built up out of a whole system of mutual accommodations in which the favors are widely distributed, with the implicit promise that no one will kick over the applecart; that if Senators do not object to the bill as a whole, they will "get theirs." It is a process, if I may use an inelegant expression, of mutual backscratching and mutual logrolling.
> Any member who tries to buck the system is only confronted with an impossible amount of work in trying to ascertain the relative merits of a given project; and any member who does ascertain them, and who feels convinced that he is correct, is unable to get an individual project turned down because the senators from the State in which the project is located, and thus is benefiting, naturally will oppose any objection to the project; and the other members of the Senate will feel that they must support the Senators in question, because if they do not do so, similar appropriations for their own States at some time likely will be called into question.[4]

[3] *Congressional Record* (Daily Edition), February 16, 1956, pp. 2300–2301.
[4] *Ibid.*, June 13, 1956, p. 9153.

Of course, *all* bills are not passed as the result of such implicit or explicit "deals."

On the other hand, this kind of bargaining (or "logrolling" or "backscratching" or "trading off," phrases whose invidious connotations indicate the public's attitude toward these practices) is not confined just to the trading of votes. Indeed, it is not an exaggeration to say that reciprocity is a way of life in the Senate. "My boss," one highly experienced administrative assistant says, "will — if it doesn't mean anything to him — do a favor for any other Senator. It doesn't matter *who* he is. It's not a matter of friendship, it's just a matter of I won't be an S.O.B. if you won't be one."

It is this implicit bargaining that explains much of the behavior of senators. Each of them has vast power under the chamber's rules. A single senator, for example, can slow the Senate almost to a halt by systematically objecting to all unanimous consent requests. A few, by exercising their right to filibuster, can block the passage of all bills. Or a single senator could sneak almost any piece of legislation through the chamber by acting when floor attendance is sparse and by taking advantage of the looseness of the chamber rules. While these and other similar powers always exist as a potential threat, the amazing thing is that they are rarely utilized. The spirit of reciprocity results in much, if not most, of the senators' actual power not being exercised. If a senator *does* push his formal powers to the limit, he has broken the implicit bargain and can expect, not cooperation from his colleagues, but only retaliation in kind. "A man in the Senate," one senator says, "has just as much power as he has the sense to use. For this very reason he has to be careful to use it properly or else he will incur the wrath of his colleagues."

To play this game properly and effectively requires tolerance and an understanding of the often unique problems and divergent views of the other senators. "No man," one highly placed staff assistant says, "can really be successful in the Senate until he has adopted a *national* point of view. Learning what the other senators' problems are and working within this framework to pass legislation give him this outlook. If he assumes that everyone thinks and feels the same way he and his constituents do, he will be an ineffective legislator." It demands, too, an ability to calculate how much "credit" a senator builds up with a colleague by doing him a favor or "going along." If a senator expects too little in return, he has sold himself and his constituents short. If he expects too much, he will soon find that to ask the impossible is fruitless and that "there are some things a senator just can't do in return for help from you." Finally, this mode of procedure requires that a senator live up to his end of the bargain, no matter how implicit the bargain may have been. "You don't *have* to make these commitments," one senator said, "and if you keep your mouth shut you are often better off, but if you *do* make them, you had better live up to them."

These are subtle skills. Some men do not have them in sufficient quantity to be successful at this sort of bargaining. A few take the view that these practices are immoral and refuse, with some display of righteous indignation, to play the game that way. But these men are the exceptions, the nonconformists to the Senate folkways.

INSTITUTIONAL PATRIOTISM

Most institutions demand an emotional investment from their members. The Senate of the United States is no exception. Senators are expected to believe that they belong to the greatest legislative and deliberative body in the world. They are expected to be a bit suspicious of the President and the bureaucrats and just a little disdainful of the House. They are expected to revere the Senate's personnel, organization, and folkways and to champion them to the outside world.

Most of them do. "The most remarkable group that I have ever met anywhere," "the most able and intelligent body of men that it [has] been my fortune to meet," "the best men in political life today"; thus do senators typically describe their colleagues. The Senate as an institution is usually described in similar superlatives.

A senator whose emotional commitment to Senate ways appears to be less than total is suspect. One who brings the Senate as an institution or senators as a class into public disrepute invites his own destruction as an effective legislator. One who seems to be using the Senate for the purposes of self-advertisement and advancement obviously does not belong. Senators are, as a group, fiercely protective of, and highly patriotic in regard to, the Senate.

This, after all, is not a great deal different from the school spirit of P.S. 34, or the morale of a military outfit, or the "fight" of a football team. But, as we shall see, its political consequences are substantial, for some senators are in a better position than others to develop this emotional attachment.

INFLUENCES ON CONFORMITY

We have seen that normative rules of conduct — called here folkways — exist in the Senate. Moreover, we have seen that they perform important functions. They provide motivation for the performance of legislative duties that, perhaps, would not otherwise be performed. They discourage long-windedness in a chamber of one hundred highly verbal men who are dependent upon publicity and unrestrained by any formal limitations on debate. They encourage the development of expertism and division of labor and discourage those who would challenge it. They soften the inevitable personal conflict of a legislative body so that adversaries and competitors can meet (at the very least) in an atmosphere of antagonistic cooperation or (at best) in an atmosphere of friendship and mutual respect. They encourage senators to become "compromisers" and "bargainers" and to use their substantial powers with caution and restraint. Without these folkways the Senate could hardly operate in anything like its present form. . . .

There are unwritten rules of behavior, which we have called folkways, in the Senate. These rules are normative, that is, they define how a senator ought to behave. Nonconformity is met with moral condemnation, while senators who conform to the folkways are rewarded with high esteem by their colleagues. Partly because of this fact, they tend to be the most influential and effective members of the Senate.

These folkways, we have suggested, are highly functional to the Senate social system since they provide motivation for the performance of vital duties and essential modes of behavior which, otherwise, would go unrewarded. They discourage frequent and lengthy speech-making in a chamber without any other effective limitation on debate, encourage the development of expertness and a division of labor in a group of overworked laymen facing unbelievably complex problems, soften the inevitable personal conflicts of a problem-solving body, and encourage bargaining and the cautious use of awesome formal powers. Without these folkways, the Senate could hardly operate with its present organization and rules.

Nonetheless, the folkways are no more perfectly obeyed than the nation's traffic laws. Men who come to the Senate relatively late in life, toward the close of a distinguished career either in or out of politics, have a more difficult time fitting in than the others. So do those elected to the Senate with little prior political experience. The senators who aspire to the presidency find it hard to reconcile the expectations of their Senate colleagues with their desire to build a national following. Finally, all senators belong to, or identify with, many other groups beside the Senate, and the expectations and demands of these groups sometimes conflict with the folkways. This seems to happen most often with the liberals from large, urban two-party states. When confronted with such a conflict situation, a senator must choose between conforming to the folkways, and thus appearing to "sell out," or gaining popularity back home at the expense of good will, esteem, and effectiveness in the Senate, a course which diminishes his long-run ability to achieve what his followers demand. For this reason, conflicts between the demands of constituents and legislative peers are by no means automatically resolved in favor of constituents.

It would be a mistake to assume that the folkways of the Senate are unchangeable. Their origins are obscure, but sparse evidence scattered throughout senatorial memoirs suggests that they have changed very little since the nineteenth century. Certainly the chamber's small membership and gradual turnover are conducive to the transmission of such rules virtually unchanged from one generation to the next. Yet the trend in American politics seems to be toward more competitive two-party politics; a greater political role for the mass media of communications and those skilled in their political use; larger, more urban constituencies. All these are factors which presently encourage departure from the norms of Senate behavior. In all likelihood, therefore, nonconformity to the folkways will increase in the future if the folkways remain as they are today. Moreover, the major forces which presently push senators toward nonconformity tend to converge upon a relatively small group of senators. Certainly, this is a more unstable situation than the random distribution of such influences — and, hence, of nonconforming behavior — among the entire membership of the Senate.

In 1963 Senators Clark and Douglas charged openly in the Senate that it was run by the "Establishment," a small minority dominated by southern conservative Democrats and conservative Republicans from other parts of the country. The influence of the "Senate Establishment" is gradually breaking down. The passage of the Civil Rights Bill of 1964 illustrates a declining influence of the South in both the House and Senate. Although there may be an eventual demise of this inner group in the Senate, it will continue to exercise significant power for many years to come. For this reason the following selection by a former senator is highly pertinent to the contemporary political scene.

39   JOSEPH S. CLARK AND OTHERS

THE SENATE ESTABLISHMENT

Mr. CLARK. Mr. President, I desire to address the Senate on the subject of the Senate establishment and how it operates. Perhaps the first thing to do is to state what I mean by "the Senate establishment." Senators may recall that last May, Richard Rovere, the very able reporter who writes for magazines such as the New Yorker and Esquire . . . wrote an article on the establishment of the United States; and in the article he compared those who he thought ran America —

From *The Congressional Record*, February 19, 20, 21, and 25, 1963.

although I suspect that to some extent he had his tongue in his cheek — with the British establishment, which is headed by the royal family, and includes the peers, whether hereditary or only for life, and most of the aristocracy, if not the plutocracy, of Great Britain and northern Ireland. . . .

I believe that the concept of an establishment in America is something which all of us who try to understand the sometimes almost inexplicable ways in which we in this country act would do well to contemplate. Just as Great Britain has its establishment and the United States of America perhaps has its establishment, so, as I pointed out last year, the U.S. Senate has its establishment. I wish to discuss today what that establishment is, how it operates, and why in my opinion the present establishment is not operating in the interests of the future of the United States, or the future of the U.S. Senate, and certainly is not operating to the benefit of the future of the Democratic Party.

The Senate establishment, as I see it, after a relatively brief sojourn here — I am now in my seventh year — is almost the antithesis of democracy. It is not selected by any democratic process. It appears to be quite unresponsive to the caucuses of the two parties, be they Republican or Democratic. It is what might be called a self-perpetuating oligarchy with mild, but only mild, overtones of plutocracy. The way it operates is something like this:

There are a number of States, most of them Democratic, but one or two of them Republican, which inevitably and always return to the U.S. Senate members of one party, and under a custom which has grown up over the years of following the rule of seniority in making committee assignments, and in connection with the distribution of other perquisites of Senate tenure, the result has been that those who have been here longest have become chairmen of committees, and as such chairmen, have exercised virtual control over the distribution of favors, including committee assignments and other perquisites of office in the Senate, and largely — although not always, and not entirely, because there are exceptions — determine who shall be selected to posts of leadership in this body. . . .

As I see it, the Senate establishment pretty well controls the assignment of Members to committees. How is that done? I think it is interesting to note that it is not only the present Senate establishment which does that. From time to time, going back at least to the early days of the present century, the same system prevailed. There have always been those who fought against the establishment, who thought that the Democratic caucus and the Republican caucus should determine who would select the members of committees and the other perquisites of office. . . .

It was true then, as it is now, that the establishment was bipartisan.

The senior ranking members of the minority party are a part of the establishment; and they, in conference — usually informal, always friendly — with their colleagues on the other side of the aisle pretty well decide who is going to do what to whom.

That is what is happening in the Senate today. That is what has happened in the Senate many times before. But it does not always happen in the Senate, and it need not happen in the Senate much longer. Whenever it does happen in the Senate, in a constantly shrinking world, in which change is inevitable, I suggest that the existence of that kind of oligarchical rule is a detriment to the national interest.

There was a very famous occasion when the rank and file of the Senate membership overturned the establishment and in a couple of years passed legislation — which had long been bottled up in previous Senates — and important to the welfare of the country as almost any other program in the long sweep of history.

I shall relate what happened in 1913, after Woodrow Wilson was elected President of the United States on a party platform which pledged to bring into legislative form the New Freedom — the program on which he defeated both William Howard Taft, seeking reelection to the Presidency, and Theodore Roosevelt, running on the Bull Moose ticket.

In 1913 the Democrats captured control of the Senate for the first time in 16 years. A majority of the Democratic Senators were progressive and espoused the progressive principles of the Baltimore platform, but the committee chairmanships and the important committee posts were to go to the conservative Democrats under the old seniority system in the Senate.

Note the striking analogy. A large majority of the Democratic Senators in the 88th Congress are also progressive. A majority of them support the Democratic platform adopted in Los Angeles in 1960. On that platform President Kennedy was swept into office by a very narrow majority.

We now stand at the beginning of the third session of what might be called a Kennedy Congress, but actually it is not a Kennedy Congress, and it seems to me that it is not going to be a Kennedy Congress. The principal reason why it is not going to be a Kennedy Congress, so far as the Senate is concerned, is, in my opinion, that we are operating under archaic, obsolete rules, customs, manners, procedures, and traditions — and because the operation under those obsolete and archaic setups is controlled by this oligarchical Senate establishment, a majority of the Members of which, by and large, are opposed to the program of the President.

I do not wish to overstate the case. There are able and effective Members of the establishment who will support the program of the

President in many areas. There are a few Members of the establishment who will support the program of the President in some areas. But, by and large, the two-thirds majority of the Democratic Senators who are Kennedy men, and therefore liberals, and therefore want to get the country moving again, and therefore believe in the inevitability of change, are represented sparsely, if at all, in the Senate establishment.

I return now to a consideration of the situation of 1913. At that time, I point out again, the committee chairmanships and the important committee positions would have gone to conservative Democrats under the old seniority system in the Senate. The progressive Democrats, however united to insure the passage of their progressive legislation and modified the Senate rules to aid in the translation of the Baltimore platform into legislation.

At that time there were 51 Democratic Senators, 44 Republicans, and 1 Progressive. Forty of the Democrats, 10 of the Republicans, and 1 Progressive — a total of 51 — could be safely labeled as in sympathy with the important planks of the Baltimore platform and of the policy of President Woodrow Wilson. I refer to the currency, tariff, civil service reform, pure food, and health planks.

In all, the progressives of the three parties had a very slim majority in the Senate of 1913, but that majority was sufficient, and it enabled the Democratic Senators, with the aid of their Progressive colleague and of their friends in the Republican Party, to set aside the seniority system in the Senate, to displace senior committee chairmen, to replace the senior committee chairmen with young men, some of whom had not served in the Senate for more than 2 years; and, as a result of quiet meetings during different evenings in Washington they took over the Senate, reconstituted the membership of all committees, got rid of all the senior chairmen, and put their own men in. . . .

The end results of the revolution of 1913 in the Senate of the United States were: First, emasculation of the old Senate seniority system; second, committee domination by the progressives, which meant the Wilson men; third, the Senate being democratized in terms of its rules and procedures; and fourth, the planks of the Baltimore platform being enacted into legislation.

I plead with my colleagues to do the same thing now — if not now, then next year — if not next year, then the year after — but let us get it done, while President Kennedy is still at the White House, if we want to preserve the Democratic Party for progressive principles, if we want to get the help of a number of our progressive friends on the Republican side — if we want to move this country forward and not be blocked by the hand of the past.

MR. DOUGLAS. Mr. President, will the Senator yield?

MR. CLARK. I yield to the Senator from Illinois.

MR. DOUGLAS. Is it not likely that, if it had not been for this successful revolution, in all probability the Federal Reserve System would not have been brought into being?

MR. CLARK. The Senator is quite correct. The establishment in those days had been opposed to the Federal Reserve System.

MR. DOUGLAS. Is it not likely that the Underwood tariff, which greatly reduced previous tariffs, would not have been put into effect?

MR. CLARK. I think that is quite correct.

MR. DOUGLAS. Is it not also likely that the Federal Trade Act would not have been passed?

MR. CLARK. The Senator is entirely correct.

MR. DOUGLAS. Is it not also true that, in all probability the other companion measure, dealing with unfair competitive practices, would not have been passed?

MR. CLARK. I believe that was the Clayton Act, which amended the Sherman Antitrust Act and put teeth into it.

MR. DOUGLAS. That is correct.

MR. CLARK. The Senator is correct.

MR. DOUGLAS. Is it not true that, in all probability, the Agricultural Credit Act would not have been passed?

MR. CLARK. I am confident the Senator is correct.

MR. DOUGLAS. In other words, the great domestic achievements of the Wilson administration from 1913 to 1915, before the war diverted the attention of the country from domestic reforms, would not have been possible had it not been for the procedural changes in the designation of committees by the rank and file of the Senators of the Democratic Party?

MR. CLARK. They were dependent upon modernization of the Senate procedures for committee makeup. I thank the Senator for the interjection. . . .

To return to my subject, in 1961, and again this year, the Democratic conference approved a statement of the majority leader to the effect that the composition of the Democratic steering committee should reflect both the geographical distribution and the ideological views of Democratic Members of the Senate. . . .

MR. DOUGLAS. Mr. President, will the Senator yield?

MR. CLARK. I am glad to yield to my friend from Illinois.

MR. DOUGLAS. Is it not true that prior to the establishment of the present steering committee, and prior to the death of Senator Chavez, of the 15 members on the steering committee only 1 was from any of the 12 States which lie between the Alleghenies and the Rockies and can be described as the East and West Central States?

MR. CLARK. The Senator is correct. . . . [T]here are now on the com-

JOSEPH S. CLARK AND OTHERS   363

mittee 7 out of 15 members from the South, including both Senators
from Florida.

Therefore, 47 percent of the total membership of the steering committee comes from those 13 States [including Oklahoma].

If we were to be guided solely on the basis of geography, this section
of the country would be entitled to five seats. I point out that without
exception these able, charming, friendly Senators from the South, all
of whom are good friends of mine, belong to the conservative wing of
the Senate Democratic Party. There are three Senators from the North-
east, all members of the liberal wing of the Democratic Party. There
are three Senators from the Pacific and Mountain States out of 17 western Senators representing 12 of the 13 Western States. Two of these
three Senators, I believe they would agree, are proud members of the
conservative wing of the Democratic Party. The other member, the
distinguished and able majority leader, is a follower of the President of
the United States and of the liberal wing of our party.

As a result of the succession of the Senator from Illinois [Mr. Doug-
las] to the committee, there are now two Senators from the Midwest,
both of them liberals, Senators who support our President, almost always — Senators Humphrey and Douglas — out of 15 Senators representing 9 of the 12 Middle Western States.

Mr. DOUGLAS. Mr. President, will the Senator yield further?

Mr. CLARK. I am happy to yield to my friend from Illinois.

Mr. DOUGLAS. When I first came to the Senate, in 1949, there was
only 1 Democrat from those 12 States, Senator Lucas, of Illinois. We
have gained 14 seats since then, so there are now, I believe, 15 Democratic Senators from these States. Indeed, the great gains which the
Democratic Party has made since the election of 1946 have been
largely and almost exclusively from what is roughly known as the Mississippi Valley, from the territory drained by the Mississippi River and
its tributaries. And yet up until a few days ago we had but one representative on the steering committee.

Mr. CLARK. If the Senator will permit me to make an interjection at
this point, the Senator from Ilinois is correct. There are 15 from the
Middle West.

Mr. DOUGLAS. I appreciate that comment. Prior to the last selection,
which I must admit came as a great surprise to me, there was only one
representative on the steering committee from the Middle West,
which on a geographical basis within our party was the most underrepresented area in the Nation. It is still underrepresented.

Mr. CLARK. The Senator is correct.

Turning from geography to ideology, and to recapitulate, of the 15
members on the committee, there are 9 whom, I am confident, any objective observer would classify as conservative: Senators Smathers,

Bible, Ellender, Hayden, Holland, Johnston, McClellan, Robertson, and Russell. . . .

According to my count — and some may differ one way or the other — there are at most 27 conservative Democrats out of 67 Democrats in the entire Senate; so 9 out of 15 Senators who are members of the vital committee which selects committee members are from the conservative ranks of our party, and only 6 from the liberal wing . . . the modern wing, which numbers, at a minimum, 40 — and I should say more nearly 45 — of the 67 Democratic Members of the Senate. Those six are Senators Mansfield, Humphrey, Dodd, Douglas, Williams of New Jersey, and Clark. . . .

I suggest in all candor that . . . the present membership of the steering committee accordingly does not fairly represent either the geography or the ideology of the Democratic Members of the Senate. . . .

Whom does the steering committee of the Democratic Party represent? It represents the Democratic side of the establishment. It represents those who hold the positions of committee chairmen. Senator Mansfield has recently resigned as chairman of the Committee on Rules and Administration. His resignation was effective a few days ago.

Senator Bible is chairman of the Committee on the District of Columbia. Senator Ellender is chairman of the Committee on Agriculture and Forestry. Senator Hayden is chairman of the Committee on Appropriations. Senator Johnston is chairman of the Committee on Post Office and Civil Service. Senator McClellan is chairman of the Committee on Government Operations. Senator Robertson is chairman of the Committee on Banking and Currency. Senator Russell is chairman of the Committee on Armed Services. . . .

. . . [T]his control of the establishment over the Senate requires the support of a dwindling group of Republican conservatives headed by the able and distinguished minority leader, and that as a result of what has happened since the election of 1958, when 18 forward-looking, modern Senators joined this body, and the election of 1960, when the Senator from Rhode Island and several other Senators joined this body, and now because of the election of 1962, when a substantial group of splendid forward-looking liberal Senators joined this body, and now because of the election of 1962, when a substantial group of splendid forward-looking liberal Senators joined the Senate, the attrition on the establishment has been very substantial indeed.

Let me point out that since 1958 the establishment has lost control of the Banking and Currency Committee, the Commerce Committee, the Committee on Government Operations, the Interior Committee, and, as of Monday believe it or not, the Judicial Committee. They never had control of the Committee on Labor and Public Welfare. They have lost control of the Public Works Committee.

Therefore time is on our side. Unless catastrophe overtakes the liberals of both parties in the election of 1964, I predict that we are within striking distance of obtaining control of the committee system of the Senate for the liberal and forward-looking elements on both sides of the aisle.

... [T] he majority leader ... asked me to comment on whether the actions of the steering committee had revealed a constant pattern or bias in favor of junior senators who had voted against cloture [and thus supporting the position of the Southern Senate Establishment] and to overlook the claim of Senators, frequently of greater seniority, who had voted for cloture. . . .

... I have had prepared a table [p. 366] which shows the names of Senators on the Democratic side who sought [new] committee assignments, what their first, second, and third choices were, and the position they took either for or against a change in rule XXII, and therefore, almost automatically, the position they took on cloture. . . .

CONCLUSIONS

1. Eight nonfreshmen Senators (Bartlett, Byrd, Cannon, Hayden, Jordan, McGee, Smathers, Thurmond) who opposed rules change submitted eligible bids for new committee assignments. Seven of them (88 percent) got new assignments. Six (75 percent) got the assignments which represented their first choice (only Thurmond was disappointed.)

2. Fourteen nonfreshmen Senators who favored rules change applied for new committee assignments. Five (36 percent) got new assignments (Mansfield, Hart, Pell, Young, and Clark); only one Senator (7 percent) of the group — Senator Mansfield — got the committee which was his first choice.

MR. PROXMIRE. Mr. President . . . this is a startling analysis. . . . The Senator says that eight nonfreshmen Senators who opposed a rules change and supported the South submitted eligible bids for new committee assignments, and that seven of those eight got new assignments, and that six out of the eight, or three-fourths, got their first choice. . . . Then the Senator says that 14 nonfreshmen Senators who favored a rules change applied for new committee assignments, and that in sharp contrast whereas among those who voted with the South on rules change 88 percent, or 7 out of 8 had gotten an assignment they sought. Of those who voted against the South only 5, or nearly 36 percent, or 1 out of 3, got any new assignment. . . . Only one of those Senators, or 1

| Name | New committee assignments received | Choice | Position on rule XXII | |
			For change	Against change
Bartlett	Appropriations	1st		X
Burdick	None		X	
Byrd (West Virginia)	Rules	No. 1		X
Cannon	Commerce (applied for Commerce and Finance)			X
Clark	Rules	No. 2	X	
Engle	None		X	
Hart	Commerce	No. 3	X	
Hayden	Interior	No. 1		X
Jordan	Public Works	No. 1		X
Lausche	None		X	
Long (Missouri)	None		X	
McGee	Post Office and Civil Service	No. 1		X
Moss	None		X	
Mansfield	Appropriations	No. 1	X	
Muskie	None		X	
Neuberger	None		X	
Pell	Government Operations	No. 2	X	
Proxmire	None		X	
Smathers	Foreign Relations	No. 1		X
Thurmond	None			X
Yarborough	None		X	
Young (Ohio)	Armed Services	No. 2	X	

out of 14, got the committee which was his first choice, and that was the majority leader. . . .

In other words, of all the Senators applying for a committee assignment in the entire Senate who opposed the South, only the majority leader out of the 14 got his first choice. In other words, all the others were turned down, whereas of the Senators who had voted with the South, six out of eight got their first choice. . . . Then there was another elimination, which reinforces the objectivity of this analysis, and that is that the freshman Senators were eliminated from consideration in this particular analysis.

MR. CLARK. I should like now to continue my theme that the South is overrepresented in the committee structure of the Senate in terms of geography and also in terms of the ideological convictions of Members on the Democratic side of the Senate. The overrepresentation has resulted from the strict carrying out of that rule of seniority which the steering committee so frequently violated — on nine committees to be exact — in the course of making committee assignments for the present session of Congress.

I ask unanimous consent that a brief statement showing the overrepresentation may be printed in the Record at this point as a part of my remarks.

There being no objection, the statement was ordered to be printed in the Record, as follows:

Southern Control of Key Senate Committees. There are 23 Democratic Senators from the South, including the 11 States of the Confederacy and Oklahoma and Arkansas. The southern Senators make up 34 percent of the 67-man Democratic block in the Senate at present. The 23 Senators from the South have far more than 34 percent of the seats on the 4 most important standing committees of the Senate, however, and more than their share of the seats of the Democratic leadership committees.

Committee	*Southern seats*	*Entitled*	*Overrepresentation*
Appropriations	9 (50 percent) out of 18	6	3
Armed Services	5 (42 percent) out of 12	4	1
Finance	6 (55 percent) out of 11	4	2
Foreign Relations	5 (42 percent) out of 12	4	1
Policy	3 (33 percent) out of 9	3	0
Steering	7 (47 percent) out of 15	5	2

MR. CLARK. It will be noted that 50 percent of the members of the Democratic representation on the Appropriations Committee are southern Senators; 42 percent are on the Committee on Armed Services; 55 percent are on the Committee on Finance; 42 percent are on the Committee on Foreign Relations; 47 percent are on the steering committee.

I make the comment, not in criticism of any southern Senator, for surely they are entitled to press their own claims for membership on important committees. I make the comment only to show the extent to which the Senate establishment, led by Senators from the South, but very ably abetted by northern Senators of the Republican Party, led by the intrepid minority leader, has a stranglehold on the four most important legislative committees — Appropriations, Armed Services, Finance, and Foreign Relations — and on the very important Democratic steering committee. It is my contention that if we are to advance the program of the President and do justice to the fair claims of Senators from other sections of the country or of a different ideology, the stranglehold of the bipartisan Senate establishment must eventually be broken; and I believe it will eventually be.

MR. DOUGLAS. Mr. President, while I have been listening to the Senator from Pennsylvania [Mr. Clark] for the past 3 days, and have been studying his remarks in the Congressional Record each morning closely, I have been debating with myself whether I should seek recognition from the Presiding Officer to discuss the points which he has brought out.

I am well aware that to speak on this subject is not popular; that it does not advance one in the assignment of positions; and that it tends to be resented by many who occupy influential positions in the Senate and in the country.

Nevertheless, I felt that it was my duty to indicate that the Senator from Pennsylvania did not stand alone in what he said, and that some indication should be given, through the Congressional Record, that there are some — and I believe many — of us who believe in the basic positions which he has been advancing.

Let me say at the very beginning that I have no personal complaints to make so far as my own treatment is concerned. I am a member of two important committees, the Banking and Currency Committee, of which I have been a member ever since I first came to the Senate more than 14 years ago, and the Finance Committee, which I tried to get on for a number of years and had some difficulty in making, but to which I was finally assigned. I am also a member of the Joint Economic Committee.

So I want to make it clear that I have absolutely no complaint about the way I have been assigned to committees, nor have I any complaint whatsoever about the way I have been treated by those who hold different opinions from mine on public policy. Furthermore, I have no animus toward those who are in control of the party senatorial policy. I do not question their motives. I think they are conscientious, according to their lights, and that they have in many ways estimable qualities which deserve recognition.

Nevertheless, the Senator from Pennsylvania has put his finger on one of the weaknesses of our party and one of the weaknesses of the Senate.

The Democratic Party wins its presidential elections by the votes of the great industrial States. It wins those elections on platforms which are believed in by the voters and which pledge to carry out legislative programs which will be in the interest of the great masses of the American people; namely, the wage earners, the small farmers, the white-collar workers, the small businessmen, the housewives, and the consumers. That is how we win our presidential elections. Then the Congress convenes, and we are not able to pass any considerable portion of the program upon which we have gone to the country, and we find that the machinery of the Senate, and I think largely of the House, is in the hands of those who fundamentally do not believe in the program by which the presidential election was won and for which the great mass of voters in the country cast their ballots.

We all know this to be a fact. No one can be around this body for 2 or 3 years — indeed, less than that — without knowing it to be the case. No one can be around here for any space of time without knowing that the combination against such a program operates from both sides of the aisle; that what we have is really a bipartisan alliance, a coalition which is basically opposed to the platform of the Democratic Party.

Many of us have been reading the book "The Deadlock of Democracy" by James Burns, in which I think he correctly states that there are four parties. Even though I think his classification is not precisely accurate, there are four parties. There are the liberal and progressive Democrats, the conservative Democrats, the conservative Republicans, and the liberal Republicans — a small but gallant band. The two center groups, conservative Democrats and conservative Republicans, work in very close alliance with each other, dominate the major committees, control the procedures of the Senate, and in the main stymie the legislation for which the presidential candidate of the Democratic Party has gone to the country.

There is no use, to my mind, in denying these facts, but apparently it is regarded as bad form to call attention to them. I am reminded of the story in Hans Christian Andersen's "Fairy Tales," about the emperor who had a suit of clothes supposedly woven for him which was in reality nonexistent. He paraded in this suit of clothes. Others were expected to admire the suit of clothes. Finally, a very naive boy said, "The emperor has no clothes." Then the illusion was punctured and the people saw the king in his full nakedness. The reluctance of some to discuss the facts of the organization of the Senate is similar to the reluctance to admit that the emperor had no clothes.

Consider the committee chairmanships. Of 14 major chairmen, 10 come from the Southern States, 2 from the Southwestern States, and 2 from States in other parts of the country.

I refer to the bipartisan coalition — I suppose the Senator from Pennsylvania would call it the senatorial establishment — and its followers. I suppose the author of "The Citadel" would call it the club. They mean the same thing and largely refer to the same persons. They control the Senate.

I personally believe the result of permitting the coalition's dominance to continue has been that we have not moved forward in the field of legislation as rapidly as we should have done. I also feel, as a Democrat, that it is of increasing disadvantage to the party in making an appeal to the country, because people are properly saying, "You campaign on these platforms, but you do not or cannot put them into effect when we elect you."

Therefore, the bipartisan alliance, which really carries out the Republican platform, operates against Democratic senatorial and congressional candidates from the North and the West, operates against our presidential candidate, and is indeed an albatross around the neck of the Democratic Party.

Yet we are not supposed to talk about it because we might offend someone or might indicate that matters are decided in a different way from the way they are discussed in public. In short, we should not call attention to the nakedness of the emperor.

However, I happen to be one who believes that the truth in these matters is extremely important and that to recognize the facts is the first step toward cure. We all know it is so in the field of medicine. Diagnosis comes first; cure comes second. As long as one denies he is ill, as long as he believes everything is fine, he will not take steps to cure the situation. Not until evidence piles up, crippling symptoms appear, and real sickness develops are corrective measures adopted. . . .

Mr. President, I think the party and the Senate need a few people who will say, "The emperor has no clothes on," and who will state the truth.

It is not popular to do that. The Senator from Pennsylvania [Mr. Clark] took great risks by making the speech he made. He can always be accused of "sour grapes," and can be told, "The legislation you favor will not go through. The dam your constituents want will not be built. The river improvements your constituents want will not be made." But the Senator from Pennsylvania felt that he must speak out, and I think he has performed a very valuable service.

He did not speak to a crowded Senate; and I am not speaking to a crowded Senate, either, exactly. Very few of the lords of the press are now in the Press Gallery. But our words will appear in the Congressional Record, which some people read; and voices in this country are not entirely muffled.

Mr. President, I wish to say, in all kindness, that the Democratic Party is not served by putting the Congressional structure of the Party in opposition to its platform. The Democratic Party is not served by attempting to deny the existence of palpable truths. The Democratic Party is not served when Senators such as the Senator from Utah [Mr. Moss], the Senator from North Dakota [Mr. Burdick], the Senator from Wisconsin [Mr. Proxmire], the Senator from Michigan [Mr. Hart], the Senator from Ohio [Mr. Young], and the Senator from California [Mr. Engle] are discriminated against; nor is the Democratic Party served when Senators who go along with the bipartisan coalition are rewarded. . . .

Unless we put more vitality into the congressional work of our party, it will be very hard to go before the voters in 1964 and urge them to vote for the party. The tragedy is that in 1964, of the 24 now sitting Democratic Senators who then will be running for reelection, 21 come from the North and from the West, and, in the main, represent the progressive wing or the liberal wing of the party; they may pay with their political lives for the sins of others.

Sometimes, Mr. President, in my sardonic moments, I wonder whether this is also a part of the plan — to discredit the party, to defeat the Senators from the North and the Senators from the West who otherwise might threaten the supremacy of the bipartisan alliance, and then to emerge with an even tighter control over the Senate than before, with the bipartisan coalition swollen in numbers and the liberal opposition diminished. . . .

MR. MANSFIELD. What I believe those who complain of an "establishment" are, in the final analysis, complaining against is the ever-present fact of frustration, the frustration of working in this body, the frustration of half a loaf, the frustration of compromise that of necessity is always with us. Who among us does not feel this heavy cloak of dissatisfaction? Less than absolute power to achieve one's will is the essence of frustration. Yet less than absolute power to achieve one's will is also an essential of democracy. The practice of democracy is therefore frustrating, and let us be sure that when it ceases to be so for any group or faction, at that same time there will also have ceased to be a democracy. That same principle pervades all we do here, and we should thank God it does.

Now let us begin the substantive debates of the 88th Congress. I urge the Senate to get off the business of the Senate and get on with the business of the Nation.

CHAPTER EIGHT

The Judiciary

The establishment and maintenance of an independent judicial system is an important part of constitutional government. On this basis the United States Supreme Court was created, and its members were given life tenure and guaranteed compensation; however, Congress was given power to structure the entire subordinate judicial system, including control over the appellate jurisdiction of the Supreme Court. Regardless of any initial lack of power and various attempts made by and through Congress to curb its power, the Supreme Court today occupies a predominant position in the governmental system. This chapter will analyze the evolution of the Court, and indicate the nature and implications of its present powers.

Constitutional Background

The Supreme Court and the judicial system play an important part in the intricate separation of powers scheme. Through judicial review both legislative and executive decisions may be overruled by the courts for a number of reasons. To some extent, then, the judiciary acts as a check upon arbitrary action by governmental departments and agents. The intent of the framers of the Constitution regarding the role of the judiciary, particularly the Supreme Court, in our governmental system is examined in *Federalist 78*.

40 ALEXANDER HAMILTON

FEDERALIST 78

We proceed now to an examination of the judiciary department of the proposed government.

In unfolding the defects of the existing confederation, the utility and necessity of a federal judicature have been clearly pointed out. It is the less necessary to recapitulate the considerations there urged; as the propriety of the institution in the abstract is not disputed; the only questions which have been raised being relative to the manner of constituting it, and to its extent. To these points, therefore, our observations shall be confined.

The manner of constituting it seems to embrace these several objects: 1st. The mode of appointing the judges; 2nd. the tenure by which they are to hold their places; 3rd. The partition of the judiciary authority between different courts, and their relations to each other.

First. As to the mode of appointing the judges: This is the same with that of appointing the officers of the union in general, and has been so fully discussed . . . that nothing can be said here which would not be useless repetition.

Second. As to the tenure by which the judges are to hold their places: This chiefly concerns their duration in office; the provisions for their support; the precautions for their responsibility.

According to the plan of the convention, all the judges who may be appointed by the United States are to hold their offices *during good behavior;* which is conformable to the most approved of the state constitutions. . . . The standard of good behavior for the continuance in office of the judicial magistracy is certainly one of the most valuable of the modern improvements in the practice of government. In a monarchy, it is an excellent barrier to the despotism of the prince; in a republic, it is a no less excellent barrier to the encroachments and oppressions of the representative body. And it is the best expedient which can be devised in any government, to secure a steady, upright, and impartial administration of the laws.

Whoever attentively considers the different departments of power must perceive, that, in a government in which they are separated from each other, the judiciary, from the nature of its functions, will always be the least dangerous to the political rights of the constitution; because it will be least in a capacity to annoy or injure them. The executive not only dispenses the honors, but holds the sword of the community. The legislature not only commands the purse, but prescribes the rules by which the duties and rights of every citizen are to be regulated. The judiciary, on the contrary, has no influence over either the sword or the purse; no direction either of the strength or of the wealth of the society; and can take no active resolution whatever. It may truly be said to have neither FORCE NOR WILL, but merely judgment; and must ultimately depend upon the aid of the executive arm for the efficacious exercise even of this faculty.

This simple view of the matter suggests several important consequences: It proves incontestably, that the judiciary is beyond comparison, the weakest of the three departments of power, that it can never attack with success either of the other two; and that all possible care is requisite to enable it to defend itself against their attacks. It equally proves, that, though individual oppression may now and then proceed from the courts of justice, the general liberty of the people can never be endangered from that quarter; I mean so long as the judiciary remains truly distinct from both the legislature and executive. For I agree, that "there is no liberty, if the power of judging be not separated from the legislative and executive powers." It proves, in the last place, that as liberty can have nothing to fear from the judiciary alone, but would have everything to fear from its union with either of the other departments; that, as all the effects of such an union must ensue from a dependence of the former on the latter, notwithstanding a nominal and apparent separation; that as, from the natural feebleness of the judiciary, it is in continual jeopardy of being overpowered, awed or influenced by its co-ordinate branches; that, as nothing can contribute so much to its firmness and independence as PERMANENCY IN OFFICE, this quality may therefore be justly regarded as an indispensable ingredient in its constitution; and, in a great measure, as the CITADEL of the public justice and the public security.

The complete independence of the courts of justice is peculiarly essential in a limited constitution. By a limited constitution, I understand one which contains certain specified exceptions to the legislative no *ex post facto* laws, and the like. Limitations of this kind can be preserved in practice no other way than through the medium of the courts of justice, whose duty it must be to declare all acts contrary to the manifest tenor of the constitution void. Without this, all the reservations of particular rights or privileges would amount to nothing.

Some perplexity respecting the right of the courts to pronounce legislative acts void, because contrary to the constitution, has arisen from an imagination that the doctrine would imply a superiority of the judiciary to the legislative power. It is urged that the authority which can declare the acts of another void, must necessarily be superior to the one whose acts may be declared void. As this doctrine is of great importance in all the American constitutions, a brief discussion of the grounds on which it rests cannot be unacceptable.

There is no position which depends on clearer principles than that every act of a delegated authority, contrary to the tenor of the commission under which it is exercised, is void. No legislative act, therefore, contrary to the constitution, can be valid. To deny this would be to affirm, that the deputy is greater than his principal; that the servant is above his master; that the representatives of the people are superior to the people themselves; that men, acting by virtue of powers, may do not only what their powers do not authorize, but what they forbid.

If it be said that the legislative body are themselves the constitutional judges of their own powers, and that the construction they put upon them is conclusive upon the other departments, it may be answered, that this cannot be the natural presumption, where it is not to be collected from any particular provisions in the constitution. It is not otherwise to be supposed that the constitution could intend to enable the representatives of the people to substitute their *will* to that of their constituents. It is far more rational to suppose that the courts were designed to be an intermediate body between the people and the legislature, in order, among other things, to keep the latter within the limits assigned to their authority. The interpretation of the laws is the proper and peculiar province of the courts. A constitution is, in fact, and must be, regarded by the judges as a fundamental law. It must therefore belong to them to ascertain its meaning, as well as the meaning of any particular act proceeding from the legislative body. If there should happen to be an irreconcilable variance between the two, that which has the superior obligation and validity ought, of course, to be preferred; in other words, the constitution ought to be preferred to the statute, the intention of the people to the intention of their agents.

Nor does his conclusion by any means suppose a superiority of the judicial to the legislative power. It only supposes that the power of the people is superior to both; and that where the will of the legislature declared in its statutes, stands in opposition to that of the people declared in the constitution, the judges ought to be governed by the latter, rather than the former. They ought to regulate their decisions by the fundamental laws, rather than by those which are not fundamental. . . .

It can be of no weight to say, that the courts, on the pretense of a repugnancy, may substitute their own pleasure to the constitutional intentions of the legislature. This might as well happen in the case of two contradictory statutes; or it might as well happen in every adjudication upon any single statute. The courts must declare the sense of the law; and if they should be disposed to exercise WILL instead of JUDGMENT, the consequence would equally be the substitution of their pleasure to that of the legislative body. The observation, if it proved anything, would prove that there ought to be no judges distinct from the body.

If then the courts of justice are to be considered as the bulwarks of a limited constitution, against legislative encroachments, this consideration will afford a strong argument for the permanent tenure of judicial officers, since nothing will contribute so much as this to that independence spirit in the judges, which must be essential to the faithful performance of so arduous a duty.

This independence of the judges is equally requisite to guard the constitution and the rights of individuals, from the effects of those ill-humors which the arts of designing men, or the influence of particular conjunctures, sometimes disseminate among the people themselves, and which, though they speedily give place to better information, and more deliberate reflection, have a tendency, in the meantime, to occasion dangerous innovations in the government, and serious oppressions of the minor party in the community. . . . Until the people have, by some solemn and authoritative act, annulled or changed the established form, it is binding upon themselves collectively, as well as individually; and no presumption, or even knowledge of their sentiments, can warrant their representatives in a departure from it, prior to such an act. But it is easy to see, that it would require an uncommon portion of fortitude in the judges to do their duty as faithful guardians of the constitution, where legislative invasions of it had been instigated by the major voice of the community.

But it is not with a view to infractions of the constitution only, that the independence of the judges may be an essential safeguard against the effects of occasional ill-humors in the society. These sometimes extend no farther than to the injury of the private rights of particular classes of citizens, by unjust and partial laws. Here also the firmness of the judicial magistracy is of vast importance in mitigating the severity, and confining the operation of such laws. It not only serves to moderate the immediate mischiefs of those which may have been passed, but it operates as a check upon the legislative body in passing them; who, perceiving that obstacles to the success of an iniquitous intention are to be expected from the scruples of the courts, are in a manner compelled by the very motives of the injustice they meditate, to qualify their attempts. . . .

That inflexible and uniform adherence to the rights of the constitution, and of individuals, which we perceive to be indispensable in the courts of justice, can certainly not be expected from judges who hold their offices by a temporary commission. Periodical appointments, however regulated, or by whomsoever made, would, in some way or other, be fatal to their necessary independence. If the power of making them was committed either to the executive or legislature, there would be danger of an improper compliance to the branch which possessed it; if to both, there would be an unwillingness to hazard the displeasure of either; if to the people, or to persons chosen by them for the special purpose, there would be too great a disposition to consult popularity, to justify a reliance that nothing would be consulted but the constitution and the laws.

There is yet a further and a weighty reason for the permanency of judicial offices, which is deducible from the nature of the qualifications they require. It has been frequently remarked, with great propriety, that a voluminous code of laws is one of the inconveniences necessarily connected with the advantages of a free government. To avoid an arbitrary discretion in the courts, it is indispensable that they should be bound down by strict rules and precedents, which serve to define and point out their duty in every particular case that comes before them; and it will readily be conceived, from the variety of controversies which grow out of the folly and wickedness of mankind, that the records of those precedents must unavoidably swell to a very considerable bulk, and must demand long and laborious study to acquire a competent knowledge of them. Hence it is, that there can be but few men in the society, who will have sufficient skill in the laws to qualify them for the stations of judges. And making the proper deductions for the ordinary depravity of human nature, the number must be still smaller, of those who unite the requisite integrity with the requisite knowledge....

From *Federalist 78* students can observe that the intent of the framers of the Constitution, at least as expressed and represented by Hamilton, was to give to the courts the power of judicial review, i.e., the power to declare legislative or executive acts unconstitutional. Students should note that this concept was not explicitly written into the Constitution. Although the reason for this omission is not known, it is reasonable to assume that the framers felt that the nature of judicial power implied judicial review. Further, it is possible that the framers did not expressly mention judicial review because they had to rely on the states for adoption of the Constitution; judicial power would extend to the states as well as to the coordinate departments of the national government.

The power of the Supreme Court to invalidate an act of Congress was stated by John Marshall in *Marbury* v. *Madison*, 1 Cranch 137 (1803). At issue was a provision in the Judiciary Act of 1789 which extended the *original jurisdiction* of the Supreme Court by authorizing it to issue writs of mandamus in cases involving public officers of the United States and private persons, a power not conferred upon the Court in the Constitution. Marbury had been appointed a justice of the peace by President Adams under the Judiciary Act of 1801, which was passed by the Federalists after Jefferson and the Republican party won the elections in the fall of 1800, so that President Adams could fill various newly created judicial posts with Federalists before he left office in March, 1801. Marbury was scheduled to receive one of these commissions, but when Jefferson took office on March 4, with Madison as his Secretary of State, it had not been delivered. Marbury filed a suit with the Supreme Court requesting it to exercise its original jurisdiction and issue a writ of mandamus (a writ to compel an administrative officer to perform his duty) to compel Madison to deliver the commission, which both Jefferson and Madison were opposed to doing. In his decision, Marshall, a prominent Federalist, stated that although Marbury had a legal right to his commission, and although mandamus was the proper remedy, the Supreme Court could not extend its original jurisdiction beyond the limits specified in the Constitution; therefore, that section of the Judiciary Act of 1789 permitting the court to issue such writs to public officers was unconstitutional. Incidentally, the Republicans were so outraged at the last-minute appointments of Adams that there were threats that Marshall would be impeached if he issued a writ of mandamus directing Madison to deliver the commission. This is not to suggest that Marshall let such considerations influence him; however, from a political point of view his decision was thought to be a masterpiece of reconciling his position as a Federalist with the political tenor of the times.

41

MARBURY v. MADISON

1 Cranch 137 (1803)

Mr. Chief Justice Marshall delivered the opinion of the Court, saying in part:

. . . The authority, therefore, given to the Supreme Court, by the [Judiciary Act of 1789] . . . establishing the judicial courts of the United States, to issue writs of mandamus to public officers, appears not to be warranted by the Constitution [because it adds to the original jurisdiction of the Court delineated by the framers of the Constitution in Article III; had they wished this power to be conferred upon the Court it would be so stated, in the same manner that the other parts of the Court's original jurisdiction are stated]; . . . it becomes necessary to inquire whether a jurisdiction so conferred can be exercised.

The question whether an act repugnant to the Constitution can become the law of the land, is a question deeply interesting to the United States; but, happily, not of an intricacy proportioned to its interest. It seems only necessary to recognize certain principles supposed to have been long and well established, to decide it.

That the people have an original right to establish, for their future government, such principles as, in their opinion, shall most conduce to their own happiness, is the basis on which the whole American fabric has been erected. The exercise of this original right is a very great exertion; nor can it nor ought it to be frequently repeated. The principles, therefore, so established, are deemed fundamental. And as the authority from which they proceed is supreme, and can seldom act, they are designed to be permanent.

This original and supreme will organizes the government, and assigns to different departments their respective powers. It may either stop here, or establish certain limits not to be transcended by those departments.

The government of the United States is of the latter description. The powers of the legislature are defined and limited; and that those limits may not be mistaken, or forgotten, the Constitution is written. To what purpose are powers limited, and to what purpose is that limitation committed to writing, if these limits may, at any time, be passed by those intended to be restrained? The distinction between a government with limited and unlimited powers is abolished, if those limits do not confine the persons on whom they are imposed, and if acts prohibited and acts allowed, are of equal obligation. It is a proposition too plain to be contested, that the Constitution controls any legislative act repugnant to it; or, that the legislature may alter the Constitution by an ordinary act.

Between these alternatives there is no middle ground. The Constitution is either a superior paramount law, unchangeable by ordinary means, or it is on a level with ordinary legislative acts, and, like other acts, is alterable when the legislature shall please to alter it.

If the former part of the alternative be true, then a legislative act contrary to the Constitution, is not law; if the latter part be true, then written constitutions are absurd attempts, on the part of the people, to limit a power in its own nature illimitable.

Certainly all those who have framed written constitutions contemplate them as forming the fundamental and paramount law of the nation, and, consequently, the theory of every such government must be, that an act of the legislature, repugnant to the constitution, is void.

This theory is essentially attached to a written constitution, and is consequently to be considered, by this court, as one of the fundamental principles of our society. It is not, therefore, to be lost sight of in the further consideration of this subject.

If an act of the legislature, repugnant to the Constitution, is void, does it, notwithstanding its invalidity, bind the courts, and oblige them to give it effect? Or, in other words, though it be not law, does it constitute a rule as operative as if it was a law? This would be to overthrow in fact what was established in theory; and would seem, at first view, an absurdity too gross to be insisted on. It shall, however, receive a more attentive consideration.

It is emphatically the province and duty of the judicial department to say what the law is. Those who apply the rule to particular cases, must of necessity expound and interpret that rule. If two laws conflict with each other, the courts must decide on the operation of each.

So if the law be in opposition to the Constitution; if both the law and the Constitution apply to a particular case, so that the court must either decide that case conformably to the law, disregarding the Constitution, or conformably to the Constitution, disregarding the law, the court must determine which of these conflicting rules governs the case. This is of the very essence of judicial duty.

If, then, the courts are to regard the Constitution, and the Constitution is superior to any ordinary act of the legislature, the Constitution, and not such ordinary act, must govern the case to which they both apply.

Those, then, who controvert the principle that the Constitution is to be considered, in court, as a paramount law, are reduced to the necessity of maintaining that courts must close their eyes on the Constitution, and see only the law.

This doctrine would subvert the very foundation of all written constitutions. It would declare that an act which, according to the principles and theory of our government, is entirely void, is yet, in practice, completely obligatory. It would declare that if the legislature shall do what is expressly forbidden, such act, notwithstanding the express prohibition, is in reality effectual. It would be giving to the legislature a practical and real omnipotence, with the same breath which professes to restrict their powers within narrow limits. It is prescribing limits, and declaring that those limits may be passed at pleasure.

That it thus reduces to nothing what we have deemed the greatest improvement on political institutions, a written constitution, would of itself be sufficient, in America, where written constitutions have been viewed with so much reverence, for rejecting the construction.

But the peculiar expressions of the Constitution of the United States furnish additional arguments in favor of its rejection.

The judicial power of the United States is extended to all cases arising under the Constitution.

Could it be the intention of those who gave this power, to say that in using it the Constitution should not be looked into? That a case arising under the Constitution should be decided without examining the instrument under which it arises?

This is too extravagant to be maintained.

In some cases, then, the Constitution must be looked into by the judges. And if they can open it at all, what part of it are they forbidden to read or to obey?

There are many other parts of the Constitution which serve to illustrate this subject.

It is declared that "no tax or duty shall be laid on articles exported from any State." Suppose a duty on the export of cotton, of tobacco, or of flour; and a suit instituted to recover it. Ought judgment to be rendered in such a case? Ought the judges to close their eyes on the Constitution, and only see the law?

The Constitution declares "that no bill of attainder or *ex post facto* law shall be passed."

If, however, such a bill should be passed, and a person should be prosecuted under it, must the court condemn to death those victims whom the Constitution endeavors to preserve?

"No person," says the Constitution, "shall be convicted of treason unless on the testimony of two witnesses to the same overt act, or on confession in open court."

Here the language of the Constitution is addressed especially to the courts. It prescribes, directly for them, a rule of evidence not to be departed from. If the legislature should change that rule, and declare one witness, or a confession out of court, sufficient for conviction, must the constitutional principle yield to the legislative act?

From these, and many other selections which might be made, it is apparent that the framers of the Constitution contemplated that instrument as a rule for the government of courts, as well as of the legislature.

Why otherwise does it direct the judges to take an oath to support it? This oath certainly applies in an especial manner to their conduct in their official character. How immoral to impose it on them, if they were to be used as the instruments, and the knowing instruments, for violating what they swear to support!

The oath of office, too, imposed by the legislature, is completely demonstrative of the legislative opinion on this subject. It is in these words: "I do solemnly swear that I will administer justice without respect to persons, and do equal right to the poor and to the rich; and that I will faithfully and impartially discharge all the duties incumbent on me as ——, according to the best of my abilities and understanding, agreeably to the Constitution and laws of the United States."

Why does a judge swear to discharge his duties agreeably to the Constitution of the United States, if that Constitution forms no rule for his government — if it is closed upon him, and cannot be inspected by him?

If such be the real state of things, this is worse than solemn mockery. To prescribe, or to take this oath, becomes equally a crime.

It is also not entirely unworthy of observation, that in declaring what shall be the supreme law of the land, the Constitution itself is first mentioned; and not the laws of the United States generally, but those only which shall be made in pursuance of the Constitution, have that rank.

Thus, the particular phraseology of the Constitution of the United States confirms and strengthens the principle, supposed to be essential to all written constitutions, that a law repugnant to the Constitution is void; and that courts, as well as other departments, are bound by that instrument.

The rule must be discharged.

Powers and Limitations of the Supreme Court

Paul A. Freund, in his book entitled *On Understanding the Supreme Court* (1949), notes that the Supreme Court has a definite political role. He asks:

"Is the law of the Supreme Court a reflection of the notions of 'policy' held by its members? The question recalls the controversy over whether judges 'make' or 'find' the law. A generation or two ago it was thought rather daring to insist that judges make law. Old Jeremiah Smith, who began the teaching of law at Harvard after a career on the New Hampshire Supreme Court, properly deflated the issue. 'Do judges make law?' he repeated. 'Course they do. Made some myself.' Of course Supreme Court Justices decide cases on the basis of their ideas of policy."

To emphasize this point today is to repeat the familiar. The Court makes policy. It would be difficult to conceive how a Court having the power to interpret the Constitution could fail to make policy, i.e., could fail to make rulings that have *general* impact upon the community as a whole. The essential distinction between policy making and adjudication is that the former has a general effect while the latter touches only a specifically designated person or group.

If the Supreme Court has this power of constitutional interpretation, how is it controlled by the other governmental departments and the community? Is it, as some have claimed, completely arbitrary in rendering many of its decisions? Is it potentially a dictatorial body? The late Justice Robert H. Jackson answered some of these questions in the following selection.

42   ROBERT H. JACKSON

THE SUPREME COURT
AS A UNIT OF GOVERNMENT

We ought first to inquire what kind of institution the Supreme Court really is, the degree of its independence, the nature of its power, and the limitations on its capacity and effectiveness. . . .

The Supreme Court of the United States was created in a different manner from most high courts. In Europe, most judiciaries evolved as subordinates to the King, who delegated to them some of his functions. For example, while the English judges have developed a remarkably independent status, they still retain the formal status of Crown servants. But here, the Supreme Court and the other branches of the Federal Government came into existence at the same time and by the same act of creation. "We the People of the United States" deemed an independent Court equally as essential as a Congress or an Executive, especially, I suppose, to "establish Justice, insure domestic Tranquility," and to "secure the Blessings of Liberty to ourselves and to our Posterity." The status of the Court as a unit of the Government, not as an institution subordinate to it, no doubt has given it prestige, for the people do not regard the Justices as employees of the Government of the day or as civil servants, as in continental Europe. Also, federal judges enjoy two bulwarks of independence — life tenure (except for impeachable misbehavior) and irreducible salaries (except by taxation and inflation).

Nonetheless, the Constitution-makers left the Court in vital respects a dependent body. The political branches nominate and confirm the Justices, a control of the Court's composition which results in a some-

From Robert H. Jackson, *The Supreme Court in the American System of Government*, pp. 9–14, 21–27. Copyright © 1955, by William Eldred Jackson and G. Bowdoin Craighill, Jr., Executors. Reprinted by permission of the executors and the publishers, Harvard University Press.

what lagging political influence over its trend of decision, and any party that prevails in the Federal Government through several presidential terms will gradually tend to impress its political philosophy on the Court. The political branches also from time to time may alter the number of Justices, and that power was used to influence the course of decision several times before it was again proposed by President Roosevelt.

The Court also is dependent on the political branches for its powers in other vital respects. Its only irrevocable jurisdiction is original, and that reaches only cases affecting Ambassadors, public Ministers, or Consuls, or cases in which a state is a party. In all other cases it has appellate jurisdiction, but "with such exceptions and under such regulations as Congress shall make." One Congress, fearing a decision unfavorable to its post-Civil War enactments, ousted the court of jurisdiction in a case that had already been argued, and the Court submitted. The Court also is dependent upon the political branches for the execution of its mandates, for it has no physical force at its command. The story is traditional that President Jackson once withheld enforcement, saying, "John Marshall has made his decision: — *now let him enforce it!*" Also, the Court, of course, depends upon Congress for the appropriation of funds with which to operate. These all add up to a fairly formidable political power over the Supreme Court, if there were a disposition to exert it.

But perhaps the most significant and least comprehended limitation upon the judicial power is that this power extends only to cases and controversies. We know that this restriction was deliberate, for it was proposed in the Convention that the Supreme Court be made part of a Council of Revision with a kind of veto power, and this was rejected.

The result of the limitation is that the Court's only power is to decide lawsuits between adversary litigants with real interests at stake, and its only method of proceeding is by the conventional judicial, as distinguished from legislative or administrative, process. This precludes the rendering of advisory opinions even at the request of the nation's President and every form of pronouncement on abstract, contingent, or hypothetical issues. It prevents acceptance for judicial settlement of issues in which the interests and questions involved are political in character. It also precludes imposition on federal constitutional courts of nonjudicial duties. Recent trends to empower judges to grant or deny wiretapping rights to a prosecutor or to approve a waiver or prosecution in order to force a witness to give self-incriminating testimony raise interesting and dubious questions. A federal court can perform but one function — that of deciding litigations — and can proceed in no manner except by the judicial process. . . .

While the President or the Congress can take up any subject at any time, a court in our Anglo-American system is a substantially passive instrument, to be moved only by the initiative of litigants. The Supreme Court cannot take most cases until at least one and generally two courts below have heard and decided them, which, with the present congestion of calendars, may be very long indeed. Also, as an appellate court, it properly can act only on the state of facts revealed by the record made in the court below, supplemented sometimes by general information of which it may take judicial notice. Hence a claim of right may be prejudiced by the incompetence, carelessness, or collusion of attorneys, as where they fail to make an adequate record to support the question sought to be raised. The decision of a case also may depend on its peculiarities of fact, for it is still true that hard cases make bad law. And when it is all over, the judicial decree, however broadly worded, actually binds, in most instances, only the parties to the case. As to others, it is merely a weather vane showing which way the judicial wind is blowing — a precedent that the Court in a similar case is likely to follow. Its real weight in subsequent cases, however, will depend on many factors, such as the quality of the prevailing opinion, the strength of any dissent, the acceptance or criticism by the profession, and the experience in application of the rule. Thus, the process of the courts is adapted to the intensive examination of particular legal grievances.

No conclusion as to what can be expected of the Court is valid which overlooks the measure of its incapacity to entertain and decide cases under its traditional working methods. With few exceptions, Congress has found it necessary to make review in the Supreme Court not the right of a litigant but a discretionary matter with the Court itself, in order to keep the volume of its business within its capacity. Last term, review was sought by appeal and certiorari in 1,452 cases, only 119 of which were allowed. It is not necessary to detail the considerations which move the Court to grant review beyond saying that the grant is not intended merely to give a litigant another chance, nor does it depend on the dollars involved or the private interests affected, but upon the importance of the case to a uniform and just system of federal law. . . .

From what I have said it might almost be assumed that the Supreme Court could be ignored in the power equation of the American Government. But in living history this institution has profoundly influenced, for better or for worse, the course of the nation. Not only has it been the center of bitter debate itself, but its decisions have played some part in nearly every great political issue that has vexed our people.

What authority does the Court possess which generates this influence? The answer is its power to hold unconstitutional and judicially unenforceable an act of the President, of Congress, or a constituent state of the Federation. That power is not expressly granted or hinted at in the Article defining judicial power, but rests on logical implication. It is an incident of jurisdiction to determine what really is the law governing a particular case or controversy. In the hierarchy of legal values, if the higher law of the Constitution prohibits what the lower law of the legislature attempts, the latter is a nullity; otherwise, the Constitution would exist only at the option of Congress. Thus it comes about that in a private litigation the Court may decide a question of power that will be of great moment to the nation or to a state.

The assertion of this power over the enactments of the states met with strong resistance, and its application to laws of Congress provoked bitter and persistent opposition. It is needless to trace the evolution of the power as now exercised. The Rooseveltian struggle with the Court did not impair the power, which is as positively asserted today as in pre-Roosevelt days. But neither did that struggle end the controversy over the proper use of the power, a controversy which lies just beneath the surface and is likely to break forth from time to time as long as the Republic shall last.

Public opinion, however, seems always to sustain the power of the Court, even against attack by popular executives and even though the public more than once has repudiated particular decisions. It is inescapable in our form of government that authority exist somewhere to interpret an instrument which sets up our whole structure and defines the powers of the Federal Government in about 4,000 words, to which a century and a half have added only about half as many amendatory words. The people have seemed to feel that the Supreme Court, whatever its defects, is still the most detached, dispassionate, and trustworthy custodian that our system affords for the translation of abstract into concrete constitutional commands.

The Constitution has gone through several cycles of interpretation, each of which is related to the political and economic condition of the period. Federal powers were consolidated and invigorated under Marshall. A reaction marked by conflict over the very nature and binding force of the compact embittered the time of Taney. There followed a period when attention turned to nationalism and to railroad building and industrial growth stimulated by a long period of almost uninterrupted peace. That came to an end in 1914, and we entered the period of international violence which now burdens and vexes us and puts our internal liberties under new strains.

That the Sureme Court, in some instances, can interpose judicial authority between political forces and those whose liberty they would override is a great distinction from those governments abroad which have been subverted by dictatorship. But I have tried to point out that while our judiciary is an effective instrument for applying to the case of an individual the just laws enacted by representatives of a freedom-respecting society, it has grave jurisdictional, procedural, and political shortcomings. These counsel against leaving the protection of liberty wholly to the judiciary, while heedlessly allowing the elected branches of the Government to be constituted without regard to their members' attitudes toward liberty.

Let us take the factor of delay. Since the Court may pronounce a judgment of unconstitutionality only in deciding a case or controversy, obviously it cannot take the initiative in checking what the Justices may know to be constitutional violations. It has no self-starting capacity and must await the action of some litigant so aggrieved as to have a justiciable case. Also, its pronouncement must await the decision in the lower courts. Often it is years after a statute is put on the books and begins to take effect before a decision on a constitutional question can be heard by the Supreme Court. The Smith Act of 1940 was held constitutional for the first time in 1951, and the Alien Registration Act, also of 1940, was passed on in 1952. The run of constitutional litigation, like that of all litigations, is slow and costly.

Such delays often mean that the damage is done before the remedy for invasion of civil liberties is available. For example: In 1951 the Court cast serious doubt upon the legality of the Attorney General's list of subversive organizations promulgated in 1947. But the list had long been widely circulated and accepted, and despite the Court's views it has never ceased to be used in the press, in the executive department, by and before congressional committees, and even in courts to prejudice individuals in their liberty, position, and good name.

Then, too, many of the most vital acts of government cannot be challenged at all by the case and controversy route, because the questions are political or involve the spending power, foreign affairs, or the war power. The Supreme Court is a tribunal of limited jurisdiction, narrow processes, and small capacity for handling mass litigation; it has no force to coerce obedience, and is subject to being stripped of jurisdiction or smothered with additional Justices any time such a disposition exists and is supported strongly enough by public opinion. I think the Court can never quite escape consciousness of its own infirmities, a psychology which may explain its apparent yielding to expediency, especially during war time.

If I may borrow a summation from my former self, I will repeat to you the conclusion of a lecture to the lawyers of the Ministry of Justice of France, delivered at their invitation in April 1946, when they were in the throes of writing a new constitution for France. After discussing the judicial vis-a-vis the political power in our system, I said:

> Opinion, of course, will differ as to the advantages and disadvantages of this constitutional and judicial system. The United States on the whole has been a prosperous country, with varied resources, making a

favorable background for any experiment in government. Its inhabitants have not faced the strains that beset some less-favored nations. Even so, our history has not been free of sanguinary internal conflicts. It would not be realistic to contend that judicial power always has been used wisely. The Court has been sharply attacked by Presidents Jefferson, Jackson, Lincoln, and both Roosevelts. Yet no substantial sentiment exists for any curtailment of the Court's powers. Even President Roosevelt in the bitterest conflict with judicial power in our history suggested only change in the Court's composition, none in its constitutional prerogatives. The real strength of the position of the Court is probably in its indispensability to government under a written Constitution. It is difficult to see how the provision of a 150-year-old written document can have much vitality if there is not some permanent institution to translate them into current commands and to see to their contemporary application. Courts will differ from time to time in the emphasis they will place on one or another of the Constitution's provisions, in part no doubt responsive to the atmosphere of the changes in public opinion. Interpretations will change from one generation to another, precedents will sometimes be overruled, innovations will be made that will not always be predictable. This always has been the history of the Supreme Court.

The legal profession in all countries knows that there are only two real choices of government open to a people. It may be governed by law or it may be governed by the will of one or of a group of men. Law, as the expression of the ultimate will and wisdom of a people, has so far proven the safest guardian of liberty yet devised. I think our constitutional and judicial system has made a valuable and enduring contribution to the science of government under law. We commend it to your notice, not because we think it is perfect, but because it is an earnest effort to fulfill those aspirations for freedom and the general welfare which are a common heritage of your people and of mine.

The Supreme Court as well as the lower courts are not only controlled by external factors. They may exercise judicial self-restraint in certain cases to avoid difficult and controversial issues and to avoid outside pressure to limit the powers of the judiciary. The discussion by John P. Roche deals with the background, the nature, and the implications of judicial doctrines of self-restraint.

43 JOHN P. ROCHE

JUDICIAL SELF-RESTRAINT

Every society, sociological research suggests, has its set of myths which incorporate and symbolize its political, economic, and social aspirations. Thus, as medieval society had the Quest for the Holy Grail and the cult of numerology, we, in our enlightened epoch, have as significant manifestations of our collective hopes the dream of impartial decision-making and the cult of "behavioral science." While in my view these latter two are but different facets of the same fundamental drive, namely, the age-old effort to exorcise human variables from human action, our concern here is with the first of them, the pervasive tendency in the American political and constitutional tradition directed toward taking the politics out of politics, and substituting some set of Platonic guardians for fallible politicians.

While this dream of objectivizing political Truth is in no sense a unique American phenomenon, it is surely true to say that in no other democratic nation has the effort been carried so far and with such persistance. Everywhere one turns in the United States, he finds institutionalized attempts to narrow the political sector and to substitute allegedly "independent" and "impartial" bodies for elected decision-makers. The so-called "independent regulatory commissions" are a classic example of this tendency in the area of administration, but unquestionably the greatest hopes for injecting pure Truth-serum into the body politic have been traditionally reserved for the federal judiciary, and particularly for the Supreme Court. The rationale for this viewpoint is simple: "The people must be protected from themselves, and no institution is better fitted for the role of chaperone than the federal judiciary, dedicated as it is to the supremacy of the rule of law."

Patently central to this function of social chaperonage is the right of the judiciary to review legislative and executive actions and nullify those measures which derogate from eternal principles of truth and justice as incarnated in the Constitution. Some authorities, enraged at what the Supreme Court has found the Constitution to mean, have essayed to demonstrate that the Framers did not intend the Court to exercise this function, to have, as they put it, "the last word." I find no merit in this contention; indeed, it seems to me undeniable not only

Quoted with permission from *The American Political Science Review,* Vol. 49 (September 1955).

that the authors of the Constitution intended to create a federal government, but also that they assumed *sub silentio* that the Supreme Court would have the power to review both national and state legislation.

However, since the intention of the Framers is essentially irrelevant except to antiquarians and polemicists, it is unnecessary to examine further the matter of origins. The fact is that the United States Supreme Court, and the inferior federal courts under the oversight of the high Court, have enormous policy-making functions. Unlike their British and French counterparts, federal judges are not merely technicians who live in the shadow of a supreme legislature, but are fully equipped to intervene in the process of political decision-making. In theory, they are limited by the Constitution and the jurisdiction it confers, but, in practice, it would be a clumsy judge indeed who could not, by a little skillful exegesis, adapt the Constitution to a necessary end. This statement is in no sense intended as a condemnation; on the contrary, it has been this perpetual reinvigoration by reinterpretation, in which the legislature and the executive as well as the courts play a part, that has given the Constitution its survival power. Applying a Constitution which contains at key points inspired ambiguity, the courts have been able to pour the new wine in the old bottle. Note that the point at issue is not the legitimacy or wisdom of judicial legislation; it is simply the enormous scope that this prerogative gives to judges to substitute their views for those of past generations, or, more controversially, for those of a contemporary Congress and President.

Thus it is naive to assert that the Supreme Court is limited by the Constitution, and we must turn elsewhere for the sources of judicial restraint. The great power exercised by the Court has carried with it great risks, so it is not surprising that American political history has been sprinkled with demands that the judiciary be emasculated. The really startling thing is that, with the notable exception of the McCardle incident in 1869, the Supreme Court has emerged intact from each of these encounters. Despite the plenary power that Congress, under Article III of the Constitution, can exercise over the appellate jurisdiction of the high Court, the national legislature has never taken sustained and effective action against its House of Lords. It is beyond the purview of this analysis to examine the reasons for congressional inaction; suffice it here to say that the most significant form of judicial limitation has remained self-limitation. This is not to suggest that such a development as statutory codification has not cut down the area of interpretive discretion, for it obviously has. It is rather to maintain that when the justices have held back from assaults on legislative or executive actions, they have done so on the basis of self-established rationalizations. . . .

The remainder of this paper is therefore concerned with two aspects of this auto-limitation: first, the techniques by which it is put into practice; and, second, the conditions under which it is exercised. . . .

TECHNIQUES OF JUDICIAL SELF-RESTRAINT

The major techniques of judicial self-restraint appear to fall under the two familiar rubrics: procedural and substantive. Under the former fall the various techniques by which the Court can avoid coming to grips with substantive issues, while under the latter would fall those methods by which the Court, in a substantive holding, finds that the matter at issue in the litigation is not properly one for judicial settlement. Let us examine these two categories in some detail.

Procedural Self-Restraint. Since the passage of the Judiciary Act of 1925, the Supreme Court has had almost complete control over its business. United States Supreme Court *Rule 38,* which governs the certiorari policy, states, (§5) that discretionary review will be granted only "where there are special and important reasons therefor." Professor Fowler Harper has suggested in a series of detailed and persuasive articles on the application of this discretion [*University of Penna. Law Review,* vols. 99–101; 103] that the Court has used it in such a fashion as to duck certain significant but controversial problems. While one must be extremely careful about generalizing in this area, since the reasons for denying certiorari are many and complex, Harper's evidence does suggest that the Court in the period since 1949 has refused to review cases involving important civil liberties problems which on their merits appeared to warrant adjudication. As he states at one point: "It is disconcerting when the Court will review a controversy over a patent on a pin ball machine while one man is deprived of his citizenship and another of his liberty without Supreme Court review of a plausible challenge to the validity of government action." . . .

Furthermore, the Supreme Court can issue certiorari on its own terms. Thus in *Dennis* v. *United States,* appealing the Smith Act convictions of the American Communist leadership, the Court accepted the evidential findings of the Second Circuit as final and limited its review to two narrow constitutional issues. This, in effect, burked the basic problem: whether the evidence was sufficient to demonstrate that the Communist party, U.S.A., was *in fact* a clear and present danger to the security of the nation, or whether the Communists were merely shouting "Fire!" in an empty theater.

Other related procedural techniques are applicable in some situations. Simple delay can be employed, perhaps in the spirit of the Croatian proverb that "delay is the handmaiden of justice." . . . However, the technique of procedural self-restraint is founded on the essentially simple gadget of refusing jurisdiction, or of procrastinating the acceptance of jurisdiction, and need not concern us further here.

Substantive Self-Restraint. Once a case has come before the Court on its merits, the justices are forced to give some explanation for whatever action they may take. Here self-restraint can take many forms, notably, the doctrine of political questions, the operation of judicial parsimony, and — particularly with respect to the actions of administrative officers of agencies — the theory of judicial inexpertise.

The doctrine of political questions is too familiar to require much elaboration here. Suffice it to say that if the Court feels that a question before it, *e.g.,* the legitimacy of a state government, the validity of a legislative apportionment, or the correctness of executive action in the field of foreign relations, is one that is not properly amenable to judicial settlement, it will refer the plaintiff to the "political" organs of government for any possible relief. The extent to which this doctrine is applied seems to be a direct coefficient of judicial egotism, for the definition of a political question can be expanded or contracted in accordian-like fashion to meet the exigencies of the times. A juridical definition of the term is impossible, for at root the logic that supports it is circular: political questions are matters not soluble by the judicial process; matters not soluble by the judicial process are political questions. As an early dictionary explained, violins are small cellos, and cellos are large violins.

Nor do examples help much in definition. While it is certainly true that the Court cannot mandamus a legislature to apportion a state in equitable fashion, it seems equally true that the Court is without the authority to force state legislators to implement unsegregated public education. Yet in the former instance the Court genuflected to the "political" organs and took no action, while in the latter it struck down segregation as violative of the Constitution.

Judicial parsimony is another major technique of substantive self-restraint. In what is essentially a legal application of Occam's razor, the Court has held that it will not apply any more principles to the settlement of a case than are absolutely necessary, *e.g.,* it will not discuss the constitutionality of a law if it can settle the instant case by statutory construction. Furthermore, if an action is found to rest on erroneous statutory construction, the review terminates at that point: the Court will not go on to discuss whether the statute, properly construed, would be constitutional. A variant form of this doctrine, and a most important one, employs the "case or controversy" approach, to wit, the Court, admitting the importance of the issue, inquires as to whether the litigant actually has standing to bring the matter up. . . .

A classic use of parsimony to escape from a dangerous situation occurred in connection with the evacuation of the Nisei from the West Coast in 1942. Gordon Hirabayashi, in an attempt to test the validity of the regulations clamped on the American-Japanese by the military, violated the curfew and refused to report to an evacuation center. He was convicted on both counts by the district court and sentenced to three months for each offense, the sentences to run *concurrently*. When the case came before the Supreme Court, the justices sustained his conviction for violating the *curfew,* but refused to examine the validity of the evacuation order on the ground that it would not make any difference to Hirabayashi anyway; he was in for ninety days no matter what the Court did with evacuation.

A third method of utilizing substantive self-restraint is particularly useful in connection with the activities of executive departments or regulatory agencies, both state and federal. I have entitled it the doctrine of judicial *inexpertise,* for it is founded on the unwillingness of the Court to revise the findings of experts. The earmarks of this form of restraint are great deference to the holdings of the expert agency usually coupled with such a statement as "It is not for the federal courts to supplant the [Texas Railroad] Commission's judgment even in the face of convincing proof that a different result would have been better." In this tradition, the Court has refused to question *some* exercises of discretion by the National Labor Relations Board, the Federal Trade Commission, and other federal and state agencies. But the emphasis on *some* gives the point away: in other cases, apparently on all fours with those in which it pleads its technical *inexpertise,* the Court feels free to assess evidence *de novo* and reach independent judgment on the technical issues involved. . . .

In short, with respect to expert agencies, the Court is equipped with both offensive and defensive gambits. If it chooses to intervene, one set of precedents is brought out, while if it decides to hold back, another set of equal validity is invoked. Perhaps the best summary of this point was made by Justice Harlan in 1910, when he stated bluntly that "the Courts have rarely, if ever, felt themselves so restrained by technical rules that they could not find some remedy, consistent with the law, for acts . . . that violated natural justice or were hostile to the fundamental principles devised for the protection of the essential rights of property."

This does not pretend to be an exhaustive analysis of the techniques of judicial self-restraint; on the contrary, others will probably find many which are not given adequate discussion here. The remainder of this paper, however, is devoted to the second area of concern: the conditions under which the Court refrains from acting.

The Conditions of Judicial Self-Restraint

The conditions which lead the Supreme Court to exercise auto-limitation are many and varied. In the great bulk of cases, this restraint is an outgrowth of sound and quasi-automatic legal maxims which defy teleological interpretation. It would take a master of the conspiracy theory of history to assign meaning, for example, to the great majority of certiorari denials; the simple fact is that these cases do not merit review. However, in a small proportion of cases, purpose does appear to enter the picture, sometimes with a vengeance. It is perhaps unjust to the Court to center our attention on this small proportion, but it should be said in extenuation that these cases often involve extremely significant political and social issues. In the broad picture, the refusal to grant certiorari in 1943 to the Minneapolis Trotskyites convicted under the Smith Act is far more meaningful than the similar refusal to grant five hundred petitions to prison "lawyers" who have suddenly discovered the writ of habeas corpus. Likewise, the holding that the legality of congressional apportionment is a "political question" vitally affects the operation of the whole democratic process.

What we must therefore seek are the conditions under which the Court holds back *in this designated category of cases.* Furthermore, it is important to realize that there are positive consequences of negative action: as Charles Warren has implied, the post-Civil War Court's emphasis on self-restraint was a judicial concomitant of the resurgence of states' rights. Thus self-restraint may, as in wartime, be an outgrowth of judicial caution, or it may be part of a purposeful pattern of abdicating national power to the states.

Ever since the first political scientist discovered Mr. Dooley, the changes have been rung on the aphorism that the Supreme Court "follows the election returns," and I see no particular point in ringing my variation on this theme through again. Therefore, referring those who would like a more detailed explanation to earlier analyses, the discussion here will be confined to the bare bones of my hypothesis.

The power of the Supreme Court to invade the decision-making arena, I submit, is a consequence of that fragmentation of political power which is normal in the United States. No cohesive majority, such as normally exists in Britain, would permit a politically irresponsible judiciary to usurp decision-making functions, but, for complex social and institutional reasons, there are few issues in the United States on which cohesive majorities exist. The guerrilla warfare which usually rages between Congress and the President, as well as the internal civil wars which are endemic in both the legislature and the administration, give the judiciary considerable room for maneuver. If, for example, the Court strikes down a controversial decision of the Federal Power Commission, it will be supported by a substantial bloc of congressmen; if it supports the FPC's decision, it will also receive considerable congressional support. But the important point is that *either* way it decides the case, there is no possibility that Congress will exact any vengeance on the Court for its action. A disciplined majority would be necessary to clip the judicial wings, and such a majority does not exist on this issue.

On the other hand, when monolithic majorities do exist on issues, the Court is likely to resort to judicial self-restraint. A good case here is the current tidal wave of anti-Communist legislation and administrative action, the latter particularly with regard to aliens, which the Court has treated most gingerly. About the only issues on which there can be found cohesive majorities are those relating to national defense, and the Court has, as Clinton Rossiter demonstrated in an incisive analysis [*The Supreme Court and the Commander-in-Chief,* Ithaca, 1951], traditionally avoided problems arising in this area irrespective of their constitutional merits. Like the slave who accompanied a Roman consul on his triumph whispering "You too are mortal," the shade of Thad Stevens haunts the Supreme Court chamber to remind the justices what an angry Congress can do.

To state the proposition in this brief compass is to oversimplify it considerably. I have, for instance, ignored the crucial question of how the Court knows when a majority *does* exist, and I recognize that certain aspects of judicial behavior cannot be jammed into my hypothesis without creating essentially spurious epicycles. However, I am not trying to establish a monistic theory of judicial action; group action, like that of individuals, is motivated by many factors, some often contradictory, and my objective is to elucidate what seems to be one tradition of judicial motivation. In short, judicial self-restraint and judicial power seem to be opposite sides of the same coin: it has been by judicious application of the former that the latter has been maintained. A tradition beginning with Marshall's *coup* in *Marbury* v. *Madison* and running through *Mississippi* v. *Johnson* and *Ex Parte Vallandigham* to *Dennis* v. *United States* suggests that the Court's power has been maintained by a wise refusal to employ it in unequal combat.

The Process of Judicial Decision Making

> The preceding selection should dissuade students from accepting the common assumption that judicial decision making is quasi-scientific, based upon legal principles and precedent, with the judges set apart from the political process. The interpretation of law, whether constitutional or statutory, involves a large amount of discretion. The majority of the Court can always read its opinion into law if it so chooses.
>
> Justice William J. Brennan, a current member of the Supreme Court, discusses below the general role of the Court and the procedures it follows in decision making.

44 WILLIAM J. BRENNAN, JR.

HOW THE SUPREME COURT COMES TO ARRIVE AT DECISIONS

Throughout its history the Supreme Court has been called upon to face many of the dominant social, political, economic and even philosophical issues that confront the nation. But Solicitor General Cox only recently reminded us that this does not mean that the Court is charged with making social, political, economic or philosophical decisions.

Quite the contrary. The Court is not a council of Platonic guardians for deciding our most difficult and emotional questions according to the Justices' own notions of what is just or wise or politic. To the extent that this is a government function at all, it is the function of the people's elected representatives.

The Justices are charged with deciding according to law. Because the issues arise in the framework of concrete litigation they must be decided on facts embalmed in a record made by some lower court or administrative agency. And while the Justices may and do consult history and the other disciplines as aids to constitutional decision, the text of the Constitution and relevant precedents dealing with that text are their primary tools.

It is indeed true, as Judge Learned Hand once said, that the judge's authority

> depends upon the assumption that he speaks with the mouth of others: the momentum of his utterances must be greater than any which his personal reputation and character can command; if it is to do the work assigned to it — if it is to stand against the passionate resentments arising out of the interests he must frustrate — he must preserve his authority by cloaking himself in the majesty of an over-shadowing past, but he must discover some composition with the dominant trends of his times.

ANSWERS UNCLEAR

However, we must keep in mind that, while the words of the Constitution are binding, their application to specific problems is

From *The New York Times Magazine*, October 12, 1963. © 1963, by The New York Times Company. Reprinted by permission of the author and *The New York Times*.

not often easy. The Founding Fathers knew better than to pin down their descendants too closely.

Enduring principles rather than petty details were what they sought.

Thus the Constitution does not take the form of a litany of specifics. There are, therefore, very few cases where the constitutional answers are clear, all one way or all the other, and this is also true of the current cases raising conflicts between the individual and governmental power — an area increasingly requiring the Court's attention.

Ultimately, of course, the Court must resolve the conflicts of competing interests in these cases, but all Americans should keep in mind how intense and troubling these conflicts can be.

Where one man claims a right to speak and the other man claims the right to be protected from abusive or dangerously provocative remarks the conflict is inescapable.

Where the police have ample external evidence of a man's guilt, but to be sure of their case put into evidence a confession obtained through coercion, the conflict arises between his right to a fair prosecution and society's right to protection against his depravity.

Where the orthodox Jew wishes to open his shop and do business on the day which non-Jews have chosen, and the Legislature has sanctioned, as a day of rest, the Court cannot escape a difficult problem of reconciling opposed interests.

Finally, the claims of the Negro citizen, to borrow Solicitor General Cox's words, present a "conflict between the ideal of liberty and equality expressed in the Declaration of Independence, on the one hand, and, on the other hand, a way of life rooted in the customs of many of our people."

Society Is Disturbed

If all segments of our society can be made to appreciate that there are such conflicts, and that cases which involve constitutional rights often require difficult choices, if this alone is accomplished, we will have immeasurably enriched our common understanding of the meaning and significance of our freedoms. And we will have a better appreciation of the Court's function and its difficulties.

How conflicts such as these ought to be resolved constantly troubles our whole society. There should be no surprise, then, that how properly to resolve them often produces sharp division within the Court itself. When problems are so fundamental, the claims of the competing interests are often nicely balanced, and close divisions are almost inevitable.

Supreme Court cases are usually one of three kinds: the "original" action brought directly in the Court by one state against another state or states, or between a state or states and the Federal Government.

Only a handful of such cases arise each year, but they are an important handful.

A recent example was the contest between Arizona and California over the waters of the lower basin of the Colorado River. Another was the contest between the Federal Government and the newest state of Hawaii over the ownership of lands in Hawaii.

The second kind of case seeks review of the decisions of a Federal Court of Appeals — there are 11 such courts — or of a decision of a Federal District Court — there is a Federal District Court in each of the 50 states.

The third kind of case comes from a state court — the Court may review a state court judgment by the highest court of any of the 50 states, if the judgment rests on the decision of a Federal question.

When I came to the Court seven years ago the aggregate of the cases in the three classes was 1,600. In the term just completed there were 2,800, an increase of 75 per cent in seven years. Obviously, the volume will have doubled before I complete 10 years of service.

How is it possible to manage such a huge volume of cases? The answer is that we have the authority to screen them and select for argument and decision only those which, in our judgment, guided by pertinent criteria, raise the most important and far-reaching questions. By that device we select annually around 6 per cent — between 150 and 170 cases — for decision.

PETITION AND RESPONSE

That screening process works like this: When nine Justices sit, it takes five to decide a case on the merits. But it takes only the votes of four of the nine to put a case on the argument calendar for argument and decision. Those four votes are hard to come by — only an exceptional case raising a significant Federal question commands them.

Each application for review is usually in the form of a short petition, attached to which are any opinions of the lower courts in the case. The adversary may file a response — also, in practice usually short. Both the petition and response identify the Federal questions allegedly involved, argue their substantiality, and whether they were properly raised in the lower courts.

Each Justice receives copies of the petition and response and such parts of the record as the parties may submit. Each Justice then, without any consultation at this stage with the others, reaches his own tentative conclusion whether the application should be granted or denied.

The first consultation about the case comes at the Court conference at which the case is listed on the agenda for discussion. We sit in con-

ference almost every Friday during the term. Conferences begin at 10
in the morning and often continue until 6, except for a half-hour recess
for lunch.

Only the Justices are present. There are no law clerks, no stenographers, no secretaries, no pages — just the nine of us. The junior Justice
acts as guardian of the door, receiving and delivering any messages
that come in or go from the conference.

ORDER OF SEATING

The conference room is a beautifully oak-paneled cham-
ber with one side lined with books from floor to ceiling. Over the man-
tel of the exquisite marble fireplace at one end hangs the only adorn-
ment in the chamber — a portrait of Chief Justice John Marshall. In
the middle of the room stands a rectangular table, not too large but
large enough for the nine of us confortably to gather around it.

The Chief Justice sits at the south end and Mr. Justice Black, the
senior Associate Justice, at the north end. Along the side to the left of
the Chief Justice sit Justices Stewart, Goldberg, White and Harlan.
On the right side sit Justice Clark, myself and Justice Douglas in that
order.

We are summoned to conference by a buzzer which rings in our several chambers five minutes before the hour. Upon entering the conference room each of us shakes hands with his colleagues. The handshake
tradition originated when Chief Justice Fuller presided many decades
ago. It is a symbol that harmony of aims if not of views is the Court's
guiding principle.

Each of us has his copy of the agenda of the day's cases before him.
The agenda lists the cases applying for review. Each of us before coming to the conference has noted on his copy his tentative view whether
or not review should be granted in each case.

The Chief Justice begins the discussion of each case. He then yields
to the senior Associate Justice and discussion proceeds down the line
in order of seniority until each Justice has spoken.

Voting goes the other way. The junor Justice votes first and voting
then proceeds up the line to the Chief Justice, who votes last.

Each of us has a docket containing a sheet for each case with appropriate places for recording the votes. When any case receives four
votes for review, that case is transferred to the oral argument list. Applications in which none of us sees merit may be passed over without
discussion.

Now how do we process the decisions we agree to review?

There are rare occasions when the question is so clearly controlled
by an earlier decision of the Court that a reversal of the lower court

judgment is inevitable. In these rare instances we may summarily reverse without oral argument.

EACH SIDE GETS HOUR

The case must very clearly justify summary disposition, however, because our ordinary practice is not to reverse a decision without oral argument. Indeed, oral argument of cases taken for review, whether from the state or Federal courts, is the usual practice. We rarely accept submissions of cases on briefs.

Oral argument ordinarily occurs about four months after the application for review is granted. Each party is usually allowed one hour, but in recent years we have limited oral argument to a half-hour in cases thought to involve issues not requiring longer argument.

Counsel submit their briefs and record in sufficient time for the distribution of one set to each Justice two or three weeks before the oral argument. Most of the members of the present Court follow the practice of reading the briefs before the argument. Some of us often have a bench memorandum prepared before the argument. This memorandum digests the facts and the arguments of both sides, highlighting the matters about which we may want to question counsel at the argument.

Often I have independent research done in advance of argument and incorporate the results in the bench memorandum.

We follow a schedule of two weeks of argument from Monday through Thursday, followed by two weeks of recess for opinion writing and the study of petitions for review. The argued cases are listed on the conference agenda on the Friday following argument. Conference discussion follows the same procedure I have described for the discussions of certiorari petitions.

OPINION ASSIGNED

Of course, it is much more extended. Not infrequently discussion of particular cases may be spread over two or more conferences.

Not until the discussion is completed and a vote taken is the opinion assigned. The assignment is not made at the conference but formally in writing some few days after the conference.

The Chief Justice assigns the opinions in those cases in which he has voted with the majority. The senior Associate Justice voting with the majority assigns the opinions in the other cases. The dissenters agree among themselves who shall write the dissenting opinion. Of course, each Justice is free to write his own opinion, concurring or dissenting.

The writing of an opinion always takes weeks and sometimes months. The most painstaking research and care are involved.

Research, of course, concentrates on relevant legal materials — precedents particularly. But Supreme Court cases often require some familiarity with history, economics, the social and other sciences, and authorities in these areas, too, are consulted when necessary.

When the author of an opinion feels he has an unanswerable document he sends it to a print shop, which we maintain in our building. The printed draft may be revised several times before his proposed opinion is circulated among the other Justices. Copies are sent to each member of the Court, those in the dissent as well as those in the majority.

Some Change Minds

Now the author often discovers that his work has only begun. He receives a return, ordinarily in writing, from each Justice who voted with him and sometimes also from the Justices who voted the other way. He learns who will write the dissent if one is to be written. But his particular concern is whether those who voted with him are still of his view and what they have to say about his proposed opinion.

Often some who voted with him at conference will advise that they reserve final judgment pending the circulation of the dissent. It is a common experience that dissents change votes, even enough votes to become the majority.

I have had to convert more than one of my proposed majority opinions into a dissent before the final decision was announced. I have also, however, had the more satisfying experience of rewriting a dissent as a majority opinion for the Court.

Before everyone has finally made up his mind a constant interchange by memoranda, by telephone, at the lunch table continues while we hammer out the final form of the opinion. I had one case during the past term in which I circulated 10 printed drafts before one was approved as the Court opinion.

Uniform Rule

The point of this procedure is that each Justice, unless he disqualifies himself in a particular case, passes on every piece of business coming to the Court. The Court does not function by means of committees or panels. Each Justice passes on each petition, each time, no matter how drawn, in long hand, by typewriter, or on a press. Our Constitution vests the judicial power in only one Supreme Court. This does not permit Supreme Court action by committees, panels, or sections.

The method that the Justices use in meeting an enormous caseload varies. There is one uniform rule: Judging is not delegated. Each Justice studies each case in sufficient detail to resolve the question for himself. In a very real sense, each decision is an individual decision of every Justice.

The process can be a lonely, troubling experience for fallible human beings conscious that their best may not be adequate to the challenge.

"We are not unaware," the late Justice Jackson said, "that we are not final because we are infallible; we know that we are infallible only because we are final."

One does not forget how much may depend on his decision. He knows that usually more than the litigants may be affected, that the course of vital social, economic and political currents may be directed.

This then is the decisional process in the Supreme Court. It is not without its tensions, of course — indeed, quite agonizing tensions at times.

I would particularly emphasize that, unlike the case of a Congressional or White House decision, Americans demand of their Supreme Court judges that they produce a written opinion, the collective expression of the judges subscribing to it, setting forth the reason which led them to the decision.

These opinions are the exposition, not just to lawyers, legal scholars and other judges, but to our whole society, of the bases upon which a particular result rests — why a problem, looked at as disinterestedly and dispassionately as nine human beings trained in a tradition of the disinterested and dispassionate approach can look at it, is answered as it is.

It is inevitable, however, that Supreme Court decisions — and the Justices themselves — should be caught up in public debate and be the subjects of bitter controversy.

FREUND'S VIEW

An editorial in The Washington Post did not miss the mark by much in saying that this was so because

> one of the primary functions of the Supreme Court is to keep the people of the country from doing what they would like to do — at times when what they would like to do runs counter to the Constitution. . . . The function of the Supreme Court is not to count constituents; it is to interpret a fundamental charter which imposes restraints on constituents. Independence and integrity, not popularity, must be its standards.

Certainly controversy over its work has attended the Court throughout its history. As Professor Paul A. Freund of Harvard remarked, this has been true almost since the Court's first decision:

> When the Court held, in 1793, that the State of Georgia could be sued on a contract in the Federal courts, the outraged Assembly of that state

passed a bill declaring that any Federal marshal who should try to collect the judgment would be guilty of a felony and would suffer death, without benefit of clergy, by being hanged. When the Court decided that state criminal convictions could be reviewed in the Supreme Court, Chief Justice Roane of Virginia exploded, calling it a "most monstrous and unexampled decision. It can only be accounted for by that love of power which history informs us infects and corrupts all who possess it, and from which even the eminent and upright judges are not exempt."

But public understanding has not always been lacking in the past. Perhaps it exists today. But surely a more informed knowledge of the decisional process should aid a better understanding.

It is not agreement with the Court's decisions that I urge. Our law is the richer and the wiser because academic and informed lay criticism is part of the stream of development.

Consensus Needed

It is only a greater awareness of the nature and limits of the Supreme Court's function that I seek.

The ultimate resolution of questions fundamental to the whole community must be based on a common consensus of understanding of the unique responsibility assigned to the Supreme Court in our society.

The lack of that understanding led Mr. Justice Holmes to say 50 years ago:

We are very quiet there, but it is the quiet of a storm center, as we all know. Science has taught the world skepticism and has made it legitimate to put everything to the test of proof. Many beautiful and noble reverences are impaired, but in these days no one can complain if any institution, system, or belief is called on to justify its continuance in life. Of course we are not excepted and have not escaped.

Painful Accusation

Doubts are expressed that go to our very being. Not only are we told that when Marshall pronounced an Act of Congress unconstitutional he usurped a power that the Constitution did not give, but we are told that we are the representatives of a class — a tool of the money power.

I get letters, not always anonymous, intimating that we are corrupt. Well, gentlemen, I admit that it makes my heart ache. It is very painful, when one spends all the energies of one's soul in trying to do good work, with no thought but that of solving a problem according to the rules by which one is bound, to know that many see sinister motives and would be glad of evidence that one was consciously bad.

But we must take such things philosophically and try to see what we can learn from hatred and distrust and whether behind them there may not be a germ of inarticulate truth.

The attacks upon the Court are merely an expression of the unrest that seems to wonder vaguely whether law and order pay. When the ignorant are taught to doubt they do not know what they safely may believe. And it seems to me that at this time we need education in the obvious more than investigation of the obscure.

Groups more often than individuals are involved in court cases and controversies. Litigation is a time-consuming and expensive process, requiring financial resources and endurance for survival. It is a rare individual who has the capacity and motivation to use the judicial process. For this reason individual interest in court cases is often represented by pressure groups. Other aspects of our political system also lead to extensive group rather than individual participation before courts, which becomes clear in the following selection.

45   CLEMENT E. VOSE

LITIGATION AS A FORM OF PRESSURE GROUP ACTIVITY

The conventional judicial process is distinguished from legislative and administrative processes by features which forbid, conceal, or control the participation of organized pressure groups. Justice Robert H. Jackson warned that "perhaps the most significant and least comprehended limitation upon the judicial power is that this power extends only to cases and controversies." This limitation has meant that the Supreme Court of the United States refuses to provide advisory opinions and avoids what judges are fond of calling "political questions." It cannot be overstressed that the Supreme Court's only power is to decide lawsuits between adversaries with real interests at stake. Under the case system that marks American jurisprudence, a court is a "substantially passive instrument, to be moved only by the initiative of litigants." This contrasts with the power of the President and the Congress to deal with any subject as desired.

Despite this limiting prerequisite, the Supreme Court does possess considerable control over the particular cases to be decided. The Judiciary Act of 1925 gave the Court almost complete discretionary control

From Clement E. Vose, "Litigation as a Form of Pressure Group Activity," *Annals of the American Academy of Political and Social Science,* Vol. 319 (September 1958). Reprinted by permission of the publishers.

of its appellate business through grant or denial of the writ of certiorari. This statute settled the modern principle that the Supreme Court's function was: "not to see justice done in every case, but to decide the more important policy issues presented within the frame of a 'case' or 'controversy,' concerning the federal balance, the relations of the branches of the federal government, or the fundamental rights of the individual in relation to government." [From James Willard Hurst, *The Growth of American Law*, Boston, 1950.] Elaborating upon the function of deciding important policy issues, Chief Justice Fred M. Vinson, in 1949, told the bar that the Supreme Court is interested only in "those cases which present questions whose resolution will have immediate importance beyond the particular facts and parties involved." Vinson added that "what the Court is interested in is the actual practical effect of the disputed decision — its consequences for other litigants and in other situations." This meant that lawyers whose petitions for certiorari were granted by the Supreme Court were representing not only their clients, "but tremendously important principles, upon which are based the plans, hopes and aspirations of a great many people throughout the country."

It is the thesis of this article that organizations — identifiable by letterhead — often link broad interests in society to individual parties of interest in Supreme Court cases. Since the American judicial system is built upon specific cases with specific facts, it is assumed that study of the role of specific organizations is relevant to understanding.

REASONS ORGANIZATIONS GO TO COURT

Organizations support legal action because individuals lack the necessary time, money, and skill. With no delays a case takes an average of four years to pass through two lower courts to the Supreme Court of the United States. A series of cases on related questions affecting the permanent interest of a group may extend over two decades or more. The constant attention that litigation demands, especially when new arguments are being advanced, makes the employment of regular counsel economical. This may be supplemented by a legal staff of some size and by volunteer lawyers of distinction. Parties also pay court costs and meet the expense of printing and briefs. Organizations are better able to provide the continuity demanded in litigation than individuals. Some individuals do maintain responsibility for their own cases even at the Supreme Court level, but this is difficult under modern conditions.

The form of group participation in court cases is set by such factors as the type of proceeding, standing of the parties, legal or constitutional issues in dispute, the characteristics of the organization, and its interest in the outcome. . . . The cases have sometimes placed organizations as parties, but more often the organization supports a member or an officer in litigation. One example must suffice.

The constitutional concept of religious freedom has been broadened in recent years by the Supreme Court decisions in cases involving members of the sect known as Jehovah's Witnesses. Most of the cases began when a Jehovah's Witness violated a local ordinance or state statute. Since 1938, the Witnesses, incorporated as the Watchtower Bible and Tract Society and represented by its counsel, Hayden Cooper Covington, have won forty-four of fifty-five cases in the United States Supreme Court. As a result Jehovah's Witnesses now enjoy: "the rights to solicit from house to house, to preach in the streets without a license, to canvass apartment buildings regardless of the tenants' or owners' wishes, to be recognized as ministers of an accredited religion and thus be exempt from the draft, to decline to serve on juries, and to refuse to salute or pledge allegiance to the flag."

The NAACP

Since 1909 the National Association for the Advancement of Colored People has improved the legal status of Negroes immeasurably by the victories it has won in more than fifty Supreme Court cases. During its early years, the NAACP relied upon prominent volunteer lawyers like Moorfield Storey, Louis Marshall, and Clarence Darrow to represent Negroes in the courts. Limited success coupled with its failure to win gains from Congress led the NAACP in the 1930's to make court litigation fundamental to its program. A separate organization, the NAACP Legal Defense and Educational Fund, was incorporated for this purpose. The goal of the NAACP was to make Negroes "an integral part of the nation, with the same rights and guarantees that are accorded to other citizens, and on the same terms." This ambition meant that beginning in 1938 Thurgood Marshall as special counsel for the NAACP Legal Defense and Educational Fund held what was "probably the most demanding legal post in the country." . . .

By presenting test cases to the Supreme Court, the NAACP has won successive gains protecting the right of Negroes in voting, housing, transportation, education, and service on juries. Each effort has followed the development of new theories of legal interpretation and required the preparation of specific actions in the courts to challenge existing precedent. The NAACP Legal Defense Fund has accomplished these two tasks through the co-operation of associated and allied groups. First, as many as fifty Negro lawyers practicing in all parts of the country have been counsel in significant civil rights cases in the lower courts. . . . Second, the NAACP has long benefited from its official advisory group, the National Legal Committee composed of leading Negro and white lawyers. . . . Third, other organizations with no direct connection with the Legal Defense Fund have sponsored a few cases. State and local chapters of the NAACP have often aided Negroes who were parties in cases, especially in the lower courts. The St. Louis Association of Real Estate Brokers was the chief sponsor of the important restrictive covenant case of *Shelley* v. *Kraemer*. A Negro national college fraternity, Alpha Phi Alpha, sponsored quite completely the successful attack on discrimination in interstate railway dining cars. . . .

THE AMERICAN LIBERTY LEAGUE

The experience of the American Liberty League, organized in 1934 by conservative businessmen to oppose the New Deal, provides another variation on the theme of organizations in litigation. When the League proved unable to prevent enactment of economic regulation by Congress, a National Lawyers' Committee was formed to question the constitutionality of the legislation. . . .

Members of the National Lawyers' Committee of the American Liberty League, but not the organization itself, participated in litigation. The committee's first public announcement had stated that "it will also contribute its services in test cases involving fundamental constitutional questions." Although the intention was to offer free legal services to citizens without funds to defend their constitutional rights, members of the National Lawyers' Committee actually represented major corporations which challenged the constitutionality of New Deal legislation in the Supreme Court. . . .

AIDING THE GOVERNMENT DEFENSE

Judicial review in the United States constitutes an invitation for groups whose lobbying fails to defeat legislation to continue opposition by litigation. The NAACP has taken advantage of this in questioning state segregation laws, and, especially before 1937, business groups of various sizes — the American Liberty League, trade associations, and corporations — contested the constitutionality of state and federal regulatory legislation. This exploitation of judicial review has been balanced by the practice of victorious groups in legislation continuing to support administrative agencies in charge of enforcement. When statutes are challenged, organizations often support the Justice Department in Washington or a state Attorney General in defending them. This is to say that when losers in legislation have brought test cases in the courts, the legislative winners have aided the official legal defense.

THE NATIONAL CONSUMERS' LEAGUE

The efforts of the National Consumers' League to defend the validity of protective labor legislation affords an example of this private organizational aid to the public defense of legislation. Organized by society women in 1899 to improve the lot of women and children in industry, the National Consumers' League sought first to boycott goods produced under substandard conditions and then to persuade state legislatures to control factory practices through legislation. When employers in the hotel and laundry business organized to defeat legislation in the courts, the National Consumers' League, in 1908, organized a Committee on Legislation and Legal Defense of Labor Laws to "assist in the defense of the laws by supplying additional legal counsel and other assistance."

The leaders of the National Consumers' League . . . learned to prod state Attorneys General in order to gain adequate defense for statutes under fire in the courts. . . .

ORGANIZATIONS AS "FRIENDS OF THE COURT"

The appearance of organizations as *amici curiae* has been the most noticed form of group representation in Supreme Court cases. This does not concern the technical office of *amicus curiae* for which an attorney is appointed to assist the court in deciding complex and technical problems. Today, the Supreme Court does sometimes, as in formulating its decree in the School Segregation Cases issue a special invitation to the Solicitor General or to state Attorneys General to act as *amici curiae*. Of interest here is the rule under which individuals, organizations, and government attorneys have been permitted to file briefs and/or to make oral argument in the Supreme Court. During the last decade *amici curiae* have submitted an average of sixty-six briefs and seven oral arguments in an average total of forty cases a term.

The frequent entrance of organizations into Supreme Court cases by means of the *amicus curiae* device has often given litigation the distinct flavor of group combat. This may be illustrated by the group representation in quite different cases. In 1943, when a member of the Jehovah's Witnesss challenged the constitutionality of a compulsory flag salute in the schools, his defense by counsel for the Watchtower Bible and Tract Society was supported by separate *amici curiae*, the American Civil Liberties Union and the Committee on the Bill of Rights of the American Bar Association. The appellate state board of education was supported by an *amicus curiae* brief filed by the American Legion. In 1951, in a case testing state resale price maintenance, the United States was an *amicus* against a Louisiana statute while the Commonwealth of Pennsylvania, the Louisiana State Pharmaceutical Association, American Booksellers, Inc., and the National Association of Retail Druggists entered *amici curiae* briefs in support of the statute.

Many *amici curiae* briefs are workmanlike and provide the Court with helpful legal argument and material. Yet writers who favor their use by organizations and recognize that "the *amicus curiae* has had a long and respected role in our own legal system and before that, in the Roman law," believe that many briefs in recent years display a "time-wasting character." Another authority has said that after 1947 there were multiplying signs "that the brief *amicus curiae* has become essentially an instrumentality designed to exert extrajudicial pressure on judicial decisions." Concern over this by the Members of the Supreme Court was shown in 1946 when Justice Robert H. Jackson, in a dissenting opinion, criticized an *amicus curiae* brief by the American Newspaper Publishers Association:

> Of course, it does not cite a single authority not available to counsel for the publisher involved, and does not tell us a single new fact except this one: "This membership embraces more than 700 newspaper publishers whose publications represent in excess of eighty per cent of the total daily and Sunday circulation of newspapers published in this country. The Association is vitally interested in the issue presented in this case, namely, the right of newspapers to publish news stories and editorials pending in the courts."

Justice Jackson told his colleagues, "This might be a good occasion to demonstrate the fortitude of the judiciary." [*Craig* v. *Harney*, 331 U.S. 367, 397 (1946).]

REGULATION OF ORGANIZATIONS IN THE COURTS

Judges, lawyers, legislators, and citizens have reacted to appearances that organizational activity in court cases touches the integrity of the judicial process. A number of limitations have resulted. But in protecting the legal system against these dangers, regulations may be too harsh on organizations and interfere unduly with the freedom of association their functioning represents. . . .

Picketing of Federal Courthouses. During the trial of the leaders of the Communist party under the Smith Act in the Federal District Court for the Eastern District of New York located at Foley Square in New York City, picketing and parading outside the court were a daily occurrence. When the Senate Judiciary Committee was considering bills to limit this practice, it received many statements like the following: "Assuming under our form of representative government pressure groups must be tolerated in our legislative and executive branches, I feel there is no good reason why our courts should be subjected to such pressures." In accord with this view, Congress, in 1959, enacted legislation prohibiting any person from parading, picketing, or demonstrating in or near a federal courthouse with the intent of "interfering with, obstructing, or impeding" the administration of justice or of "influencing any judge, juror, witness, or court officer" in the discharge of his duty.

Mass Petitions to the Supreme Court. In 1953, the National Committee to Secure Justice in the Rosenberg Case addressed a petition claimed to have the support of 50,000 persons to the Supreme Court. Among many condemnations of this was one urging that "the Court must consult its own collective conscience on such matters without reference to the number of persons who are willing to sign a petition." No rule prevents groups from such indecorous action but Justice Hugo Black has expressed the intense disapproval of the Supreme Court. In 1951, when granting a stay of execution to Willie McGhee, a Negro under the death penalty in Mississippi, Justice Black lamented the "growing practice of sending telegrams to judges in order to have cases decided by pressure." Declaring that he would not read them, he said that "the courts of the United States are not the kind of instruments of justice that can be influenced by such pressures." Justice Black gave an implied warning to the bar by noting that "counsel in this case have assured me they were not responsible for these telegrams." . . .

Conclusion

There is a logical relationship of organizational interest in litigation and the importance of courts in forming public policy. Although courts act only in cases between parties with concrete interests at stake, organizations concerned with the impact of the outcome may become quite active participants. Organizations may do this by sponsoring a "test case" brought in the name of a private party, they may aid the government attorney in a case, or they may file a brief as an *amicus curiae.* Considering the importance of the issues resolved by American courts, the entrance of organizations in these ways seems in order. Indeed the essential right of organizations to pursue litigation would appear to follow from the generous attitude of American society toward the freedom of individuals to form associations for the purpose of achieving common goals. Of course, traditional judicial procedures should be followed and the attorneys for organizations, as well as for individuals, must address their arguments to reason. If these standards of conduct are followed there is no incompatibility between the activity of organizations in litigation and the integrity or independence of the judiciary.

CHAPTER NINE

The Bureaucracy

American bureaucracy today is an important fourth branch of the government. Too frequently the administrative branch is lumped under the heading of the "Executive" and is considered to be subordinate to the President. But the following selections will reveal that the bureaucracy is often autonomous, acting outside of the control of Congress, the President, and even the Judiciary. This fact raises an important problem for our constitutional democracy: How can the bureaucracy be kept responsible if it does not fit into the constitutional framework that was designed to guarantee limited and responsible government?

46   PETER WOLL

THE NATURE OF THE BUREAUCRACY

The administrative branch today stands at the very center of our governmental process; it is the keystone of the structure. And administrative agencies exercise legislative and judicial as well as executive functions — a fact that is often overlooked. . . .

How should we view American bureaucracy? Ultimately, the power of government comes to rest in the administrative branch. Agencies are given the responsibility of making concrete decisions carrying out vague policy initiated in Congress or by the President. The agencies can offer expert advice, closely attuned to the most interested pressure groups, and they often not only determine the policies that the legislature and executive recommend in the first place, but also decisively affect the policy-making process. Usually it is felt that the bureaucracy is

From Peter Woll (ed.), *Public Administration and Policy* (Harper Torchbooks, 1966), pp. 1–14. Reprinted by permission of the publisher.

politically "neutral," completely under the domination of the President, Congress, or the courts. We will see that this is not entirely the case, and that the President and Congress have only sporadic control over the administrative process.

The bureaucracy is a semi-autonomous branch of the government, often dominating Congress, exercising strong influence on the President, and only infrequently subject to review by the courts. If our constitutional democracy is to be fully analyzed, we must focus attention upon the administrative branch. What is the nature of public administration? How are administration and politics intertwined? How are administrative constituencies determined? What is the relationship between agencies and their constituencies? What role should the President assume in relation to the administrative branch? How far should Congress go in controlling agencies which in fact tend to dominate the legislative process? Should judicial review be expanded? What are the conditions of judicial review? How do administrative agencies perform judicial functions, and how do these activities affect the ability of courts to oversee their actions? These questions confront us with what is called the problem of administrative responsibility: that is, how can we control the activities of the administrative branch? In order to approach an understanding of this difficult problem, it is necessary to appreciate the nature of the administrative process and how it interacts with other branches of the government and with the general public. It is also important to understand the nature of our constitutional system, and the political context within which agencies function.

CONSTITUTIONAL DEMOCRACY AND BUREAUCRATIC POWER

We operate within the framework of a constitutional democracy. This means, first, that the government is to be limited by the separation of powers and Bill of Rights. Another component of the system, federalism, is designed in theory to provide states with a certain amount of authority when it is not implied at the national level. Our separation of powers, the system of checks and balances, and the federal system, help to explain some of the differences between administrative organization here and in other countries. But the Constitution does not explicitly provide for the administrative branch, which has become a new fourth branch of government. This raises the question of how to control the bureaucracy when there are no clear constitutional limits upon it. The second aspect of our system, democracy, is of course implied in the Constitution itself, but has expanded greatly since it was adopted. We are confronted, very broadly speaking, first with the problem of constitutional limitation, and secondly with the problem of democratic participation in the activities of the bureaucracy. The bureaucracy must be accommodated within the framework of our system of constitutional democracy. This is the crux of the problem of administrative responsibility.

Even though the Constitution does not explicitly provide for the bureaucracy, it has had a profound impact upon the structure, functions, and general place that the bureaucracy occupies in government. The administrative process was incorporated into the constitutional system under the heading of "The Executive Branch." But the concept of "administration" at the time of the adoption of the Constitution was a very simple one, involving the "mere execution" of "executive details," to use the phrases of Hamilton in *The Federalist*. The idea, at that time, was simply that the President as Chief Executive would be able to control the executive branch in carrying out the mandates of Congress. In *Federalist 72*, after defining administration in this very narrow way, Hamilton stated:

> ... The persons, therefore, to whose immediate management the different administrative matters are committed ought to be considered as Assistants or Deputies of the Chief Magistrate, and on this account, they ought to derive their offices from his appointment, at least from his nomination, and ought to be subject to his superintendence.

It was clear that Hamilton felt the President would be responsible for administrative action as long as he was in office. This fact later turned up in what can be called the "presidential supremacy" school of thought, which held and still holds that the President is *constitutionally* responsible for the administrative branch, and that Congress should delegate to him all necessary authority for this purpose. Nevertheless, whatever the framers of the Constitution might have planned if they could have foreseen the nature of bureaucratic development, the fact is that the system they constructed in many ways supported bureaucratic organization and functions independent of the President. The role they assigned to Congress in relation to administration assured this result, as did the general position of Congress in the governmental system as a check or balance to the power of the President. Congress has a great deal of authority over the administrative process.

If we compare the powers of Congress and the President over the bureaucracy it becomes clear that they both have important constitutional responsibility. Congress retains primary control over the organization of the bureaucracy. It alone creates and destroys agencies, and determines whether they are to be located within the executive branch or outside it. This has enabled Congress to create a large number of *independent* agencies beyond presidential control. Congress has the authority to control appropriations and may thus exercise a great deal of power over the administrative arm, although increasingly the Bureau of the Budget and the President have the initial, and more often than not the final say over the budget. Congress also has the authority to define the jurisdiction of agencies. Finally, the Constitution gives to the legislature the power to interfere in high level presidential appointments, which must be "by and with the advice and consent of the Senate."

Congress may extend the sharing of the appointive power when it sets up new agencies. It may delegate to the President pervasive authority to control the bureaucracy. But one of the most important elements of the separation of powers is the electoral system, which gives to Congress a constituency which is different from and even conflicting with that of the President. This means that Congress often decides to set up agencies beyond presidential purview. Only rarely will it grant the President any kind of final authority to structure the bureaucracy. During World War II, on the basis of the War Powers Act, the President had the authority to reorganize the administrative branch. Today he has the same authority, provided that Congress does not veto presidential proposals within a certain time limit. In refusing to give the President permanent reorganization authority, Congress is jealously guarding one of its important prerogatives.

Turning to the constitutional authority of the President over the bureaucracy, it is somewhat puzzling to see that it gives him a relatively small role. He appoints certain officials by and with the advice and consent of the Senate. He has directive power over agencies that are placed within his jurisdiction by Congress. His control over patronage, once so important, has diminished sharply under the merit system. The President is Commander-in-Chief of all military forces, which puts him in a controlling position over the Defense Department and Agencies involved in military matters. In the area of international relations, the President is by constitutional authority the "Chief Diplomat," to use Rossiter's phrase. This means that he appoints Ambassadors (by and with the advice and consent of the Senate), and generally directs national activities in the international arena — a crucially important executive function. But regardless of the apparent intentions of some of the framers of the Constitution as expressed by Hamilton in *The Federalist*, and in spite of the predominance of the Presidency in military and foreign affairs, the fact remains that we seek in vain for explicit constitutional authorization for the President to be "Chief Administrator."

This is not to say that the President does not have an important responsibility to act as Chief of the bureaucracy, merely that there is no constitutional mandate for this. As our system evolved, the President was given more and more responsibility until he became, in practice, Chief Administrator. At the same time the constitutional system has often impeded progress in this direction. The President's Committee on Administrative Management in 1937, and later the Hoover Commissions of 1949 and 1955, called upon Congress to initiate a series of reforms increasing presidential authority over the administrative branch. It was felt that this was necessary to make democracy work. The President is the only official elected nationally, and if the administration is to be held democratically accountable, he alone can stand as its representative. But meaningful control from the White House requires that the President have a comprehensive program which encompasses the activities of the bureaucracy. He must be informed as to what they are doing, and be able to control them. He must understand the complex responsibilities of the bureaucracy. Moreover, he must be able to call on sufficient political support to balance the support which the agencies draw from private clientele groups and congressional committees. This has frequently proven a difficult and often impossible task for the President. He may have the *authority* to control the bureaucracy in many areas, but not enough *power*.

On the basis of the Constitution, Congress feels it quite proper that when it delegates legislative authority to administrative agencies it can relatively often place these groups outside the control of the President. For example, in the case of the Interstate Commerce Commission . . . Congress has delegated final authority to that agency to control railroad mergers and other aspects of transportation activity, without giving the President the right to veto. The President may feel that a particular merger is undesirable because it is in violation of the anti-trust laws, but the Interstate Commerce Commission is likely to feel differently. In such a situation, the President can do nothing because he does not have the *legal authority* to take any action. If he could muster enough political support to exercise influence over the ICC, he would be able to control it, but the absence of legal authority is an important factor in such cases and diminishes presidential power. Moreover, the ICC draws strong support from the railroad industry, which has been able to counter-balance the political support possessed by the President and other groups that have wished to control it. Analogous situations exist with respect to other regulatory agencies.

Besides the problem of congressional and presidential control over the bureaucracy, there is the question of judicial review of administrative decisions. The rule of law is a central element in our Constitution. The rule of law means that decisions judicial in nature should be handled by common law courts, because of their expertise in rendering due process of law. When administrative agencies engage in adjudication their decisions should be subject to judicial review — at least, they should if one supports the idea of the supremacy of law. Judicial decisions are supposed to be rendered on an independent and impartial basis, through the use of tested procedures, in order to arrive at the accurate determination of the truth. Administrative adjudication should not be subject to presidential or congressional control, which would mean political determination of decisions that should be rendered in an objective manner. The idea of the rule of law, derived from the common law and adopted within the framework of our constitutional system, in theory limits legislative and executive control over the bureaucracy.

The nature of our constitutional system poses very serious difficulties to the development of a system of administrative responsibility. The Constitution postulates that the functions of government must be separated into different branches with differing constituencies and separate authority. The idea is that the departments should oppose each other, thereby preventing the arbitrary exercise of political power. Any combination of functions was considered to lead inevitably to arbitrary government. This is a debatable point, but the result of the Constitution is quite clear. The administrative process, on the other hand, often combines various functions of government in the same hands. Attempts are made, of course, to separate those who exercise judicial functions from these in the prosecuting arms of the agencies. But the fact remains that there is a far greater combination of functions in the administrative process than can be accommodated by strict adherence to the Constitution.

It has often been proposed, as a means of alleviating what may be considered the bad effects of combined powers in administrative agencies, to draw a line of control from the original branches of the government to those parts of the bureaucracy exercising similar functions. Congress would control the legislative activities of the agencies, the President the executive aspects, and the courts the judicial functions. This would maintain the symmetry of the constitutional system. But this solution is not feasible, because other parts of the Constitution, giving different authority to these three branches make symmetrical control of this kind almost impossible. The three branches of the government are not willing to give up whatever powers they may have over administrative agencies. For example, Congress is not willing to give the President complete control over all executive functions, nor to give the courts the authority to review all the decisions of the agencies. At present, judicial review takes place only if Congress authorizes it, except in those rare instances where constitutional issues are involved.

Another aspect of the problem of control is reflected in the apparent paradox that the three branches do not always use to the fullest extent their authority to regulate the bureaucracy, even though they wish to retain their power to do so. The courts, for example, have exercised considerable self-restraint in their review of administrative decisions.

They are not willing to use all their power over the bureaucracy. Similarly, both Congress and the President will often limit their dealings with the administrative branch for political and practical reasons.

In the final analysis, we are left with a bureaucratic system that has been fragmented by the Constitution, and in which administrative discretion is inevitable. The bureaucracy reflects the general fragmentation of our political system. It is often the battleground for the three branches of government, and for outside pressure groups which seek to control it for their own purposes.

The Rise of the Administrative Process

What has caused the development of this large administrative branch which exercises all the functions of government, usually within the same agency? The reasons for the rise of the bureaucracy can be largely explained by observing how the transfer of legislative, executive, and judicial functions has occurred from the primary branches of the government.

Administrative agencies exercise legislative power because Congress and the President are unable and unwilling to cope with all the legislative problems of the nation. The President is "Chief Legislator." Congress is supposed to exercise the primary legislative function. But clearly, given the scope of modern government, it would be impossible for the President and Congress to deal on a continuous basis with the myriad legislative concerns that arise. The President's "program" is necessarily incomplete. It deals with major legislative problems which happen to be of interest to him and of concern to the nation at a particular time. Much of the President's program is formulated by the bureaucracy. In any event, it ultimately has to be carried out by administrative agencies, provided Congress approves.

For the most part Congress is concerned with formulating policy in very broad terms. It has neither the technical information nor the time to cope with the intricate phases of modern legislation. Moreover, it is often unwilling to deal with difficult political questions, for this would necessitate taking sides and alienating various segments of the public. It frequently passes on to the bureaucracy the burden of reconciling group conflict. The bureaucracy receives the unresolved disputes that come both to Congress and to the President, making it one of the most important political arms of the government. The concept of the bureaucracy as neutral is actually contrary to the facts.

Turning to the judicial arena, the development of administrative law has taken place because of the need for a more flexible mechanism for resolving cases and controversies arising under new welfare and regulatory statutes. The idea that the functions of government can be divided into legislative, executive, and judicial categories, and segregated into three separate branches of the government, is outdated because of the growth of a complex and interdependent economy requiring government regulation. Effective regulatory power often requires a combination of legislative and judicial functions.

Examples of the Development of Administrative Agencies. At the beginning of the republic, our bureaucracy was very small. It was quite capable of domination by the President, and at that time the President was the Chief Administrator in fact as well as in theory. No one then could conceive of the growth of a complex bureaucracy such as we know today, and it was only proper to feel that the activities of the executive branch would be, for the most part, politically neutral under the control of the President and Congress. The fact that the President was supposed to be politically neutral gave the concept of a neutral bureaucracy real meaning.

The original bureaucracy consisted of the War, Navy, State, and Treasury Departments, along with the office of Attorney General (the Department of Justice was created in 1870). These departments were extraordinarily small, and although distance and the difficulty of communications may have created some barriers to presidential domination over an agency such as the State Department, most agencies were easily subject to scrutiny by both Congress and the White House. This was the only time in American history when it was accurate to picture the administrative branch as a hierarchical structure with the President at the apex.

The development of administrative agencies after the Civil War resulted from public pressure which in turn reflected changing economic, social, and political conditions. For the most part agencies were created to deal with specific problems. The growth of the major departments reflected the expansion of government generally. The *laissez faire* ideal of a government remote from the community began to prove inadequate at the end of the nineteenth century. At this time, expanded powers were given to the Justice Department under the Sherman Act of 1890. This was necessary, it was felt, to deal with the rising restraints of trade and the growth of monopolies. In the regulatory area, the Interstate Commerce Commission was created in 1887 as the first national regulatory agency to supervise the railroad industry. The general expansion of the government was reflected in the establishment of the Justice Department in 1870, the Post Office Department in 1882, and the Department of Agriculture in 1889, succeeding the Commissioner of Agriculture, an office established in 1862. Present day bureaucracy has its roots in the latter part of the nineteenth century. But even then the administrative branch was fairly small and relatively powerless.

In examining the characteristics of nineteenth century bureaucracy, it can be seen that although the ideal of *laissez faire* had begun to tarnish, nevertheless it was still powerful and was reflected in the domination of big business interests within the governmental process. Although the frontier had receded significantly, it was still an important factor in absorbing excess energy and alleviating at least some of the grievances caused by economic interdependence. National communications were not highly developed. The integrative force of a strong Presidency was just beginning to be felt. The concept of the welfare state, which led to the vast expansion of the bureaucracy during the New Deal period, was unknown. Both theoretical and practical considerations militated against the creation at that time of a significant and pervasive administrative process. There was, it is true, a great deal of agitation and demand for government action to curb economic abuses. This was quite evident, for example, in the strong agitation of agricultural interests leading to the creation of the ICC. However, these protests were largely ineffective.

The real growth of the administrative process came in the twentieth century, when added powers were given to agencies which were already established, and new agencies were developed to expand government influence.

Expansion of the Bureaucracy in the Twentieth Century. The twentieth century saw the growth of a welfare philosophy of government, an enlargement of the problems created by the interdependence of economic groups, and the development of the country into a national community where the impact of activity in one area was felt in many others. There was increased political pressure for more government action which in turn required an expanded administrative process. Neither Congress, the Presidency, nor the judiciary could cope with the tremendous increase in the workload of government. Nor could they meet all the needs for innovation in the governmental process. Where a new type of adjudication was required to handle an increasing number of complex cases, the common law framework as well as the Constitution prevented the judiciary from embarking upon necessary programs and new procedures. Congress continued to work in modern times much as it had in the past, dealing with problems through a rather cumbersome hearing process.

It would be very difficult for Congress radically to change the legislative process because of constitutional as well as political limitations. These create obstacles to unity and continuity in the legislature. The courts too are constrained by the system. To take an example: suppose the judiciary decided to change the "case and controversy" rule, which requires that they adjudicate only cases properly brought before them involving concrete controversies. This would clearly violate Article 3 of the Constitution, and would be very difficult to bring about without a constitutional Amendment. These are the kinds of factors that led increasingly to the growth of bureaucracy. New forms of government were needed, and the administrative branch, which was not hampered by constitutional restrictions to the same degree as the original three branches, was able to fill this need.

Turning to some examples of agencies created in the twentieth century: the Federal Reserve Board, established in 1913 to stand at the head of a Federal Reserve system, was necessitated by changes in the banking industry which had resulted in a need for some kind of national control and standards. The Federal Trade Commission, created in 1914, was designed to expand the control of the national government over restraints of trade and deceptive business practices. The FTC reflects the need for a separate administrative agency with authority distinct from that of the courts and the Justice Department. This need indicated in part the failure of the Sherman Act of 1890 as it had been administered by the Justice Department through an unsympathetic judiciary. By 1920, the Federal Power Commission had been created, and in 1927 initial steps were taken to regulate the communications industry with the establishment of a Federal Radio Commission, which in 1934 was transformed into the Federal Communications Commission.

The proliferation of agencies during the New Deal can be seen in the Securities and Exchange Commission of 1933, the National Labor Relations Board of 1935, the Civil Aeronautics Board and Civil Aeronautics Administration (now the Federal Aviation Agency) created in 1937, reorganized in 1958, and now the central core of the Department of Transportation. New regulatory bureaus were created in the Department of Agriculture and other executive departments. Many New Deal agencies were created on the basis of presidential support rather than on the demands of private interests. This contrasted with the Interstate Commerce Commission which was created primarily because of strong agrarian demands for government control. The New Deal period was a time when President Roosevelt acted as a focal point for the expansion of the bureaucracy, and it was his ingenuity and power that often provided the balance of political support necessary for this purpose.

Since the New Deal period, there has been a notable expansion of bureaucratic power in the Defense Department, which has been put on a permanent basis since World War II and has strong political support from the armaments industry. Also an agency such as NASA reflects changing technology and subsequent innovations in governmental policy. NASA has now become one of our most important agencies, employing a large number of people and receiving huge appropriations.

CHARACTERISTICS OF ADMINISTRATIVE AGENCIES

Administrative agencies are generally characterized by their size, the complexity of the decisions that they must make, specialization, and the combination of several governmental functions. Another characteristic of primary importance is the fact that no agency can exist without strong political support. All agencies have constituencies to which they are responsible. Their constituencies include congressional committees with which they negotiate appropriations and policy changes; the White House; the courts, which will review certain of their decisions provided the conditions of judicial review are met; and private groups. Administrative agencies operate within a highly charged political environment and this fact immediately distinguishes government bureaucracy from private business. The administrative process in government cannot be considered similar to that in business, except in a very limited range of activities. And insofar as their activities are not political, they are not particularly significant for the study of government.

THE PROBLEM OF ADMINISTRATIVE RESPONSIBILITY

How do the agencies perform the tasks that have been assigned to them? Are they acting responsibly within the framework of our constitutional democracy? These questions involve an analysis of administrative procedure and accountability. The bureaucracy must be viewed as a political decision-making arena, and the appropriateness of particular decisions must be analyzed in terms of the goals that have been set for society and for government. Are agencies making the best decisions possible? Are they fair when they render adjudicative decisions? Are their activities sufficiently coordinated to assure a certain minimum level of efficiency? Does the President have the kind of controls that he needs over the bureaucracy? Should Congress become more or less involved in administrative activities? Is it feasible to expand judicial review, given the nature and characteristics of the administrative process? These and other questions must be analyzed in order to understand the proper role of the bureaucracy in our governmental process.

Because the bureaucracy is only sporadically controlled by the President, Congress, and the Judiciary, it is necessary to devise new techniques to insure administrative responsibility. In "Bureaucracy and Constitutionalism" Norton E. Long emphasizes the inevitability of administrative discretion and the need to

strengthen the *internal* democratic character of the bureaucracy to insure constitutional responsibility. He points out that
although our ideological and constitutional context suggests
the desirability of a neutral administrative branch, it is only
because administrators are not politically neutral but dedicated
to the ideals of our political system that we are saved from a
totally arbitrary bureaucracy.

47   NORTON E. LONG

BUREAUCRACY AND CONSTITUTIONALISM

There is an old aphorism that fire is a good servant but a
bad master. Something like this aphorism is frequently applied to the
appropriate role of the bureaucracy in government. Because bureaucracy is often viewed as tainted with an ineradicable lust for power, it
is alleged that, like fire, it needs constant control to prevent its erupt-
ing from beneficent servitude into dangerous and tyrannical mastery.

The folklore of constitutional theory relegates the bureaucracy to
somewhat the same low but necessary estate as Plato does the appe-
titive element of the soul. In the conventional dichotomy between
policy and administration, administration is the Aristotelian slave,
properly an instrument of action for the will of another, capable of
receiving the commands of reason but incapable of reasoning. The
amoral concept of administrative neutrality is the natural complement
of the concept of bureaucracy as instrument; for according to this
view the seat of reason and conscience resides in the legislature, whatever grudging concession may be made to the claims of the political
executive, and a major, if not the major, task of constitutionalism is
the maintenance of the supremacy of the legislature over the bureaucracy. The latter's sole constitutional role is one of neutral docility to
the wishes of the day's legislative majority.

The source of this doctrine is found in part in a reading of English
constitutional history and in part in the political metaphysics of John
Locke. The drama of English constitutional development may be seen
as first the concentration of power in the Norman kings, with the
suppression of feudal anarchy, and then the gradual attainment of parliamentary supremacy. Because the bureaucracy was created by the

From Norton E. Long, "Bureaucracy and Constitutionalism," *American Political
Science Review*, Vol. 46 (September 1952), pp. 808–18. Reprinted by permission of
The American Political Science Association and the author.

kings as an instrument of national unification, it became identified with them and was envisaged as a monarchical rather than a popular element, and one which required control. At a later date the class monopoly of the upper hierarchy of the civil service reinforced liberal suspicions of the bureaucracy, and it seemed especially clear that the most bureaucratic part of the bureaucracy, the military, had to be placed firmly under civilian, i.e., legislative, control.

John Locke, writing the apologia for the Glorious Revolution and its accompanying shift in political power, held that "there can be but one supreme power, which is the legislative, to which all the rest are and must be subordinate. . . ."[1] To be sure, Locke conceived of the legislature only as the fiduciary of the people, from whom all legitimate power ultimately stemmed. But since the legislature was considered the authentic voice of the people changeable only by revolution, this limitation could be forgotten in practice. Despite Locke's qualifications, the latter-day exponents of his views have given currency to what Jackson called the "absurd doctrine that the legislature is the people." Professor Charles Hyneman, accepting the majority will metaphysics of Willmoore Kendall, has ably expounded the consequence of that point of view in his . . . *Bureaucracy in a Democracy*. It is his position that in a democracy the people should get what they want, and that what the legislature wants is the best approximation of what the people want; ergo, we should fashion our institutions for legislative supremacy, at least with respect to the bureaucracy.[2] Hyneman's position is extreme but not substantially different from others who argue that Congress is our board of directors. Even Paul Appleby reflects at times the conventional bureaucratic homage to Congress, though his central position rejects the claim of any single organ to monopolize the democratic process.[3] Acceptance of the principle of legislative supremacy by practicing administrators is, of course, more a counsel of expediency than an article of faith. It pays for the administrator to call Congress our board of directors, whatever his private conviction may be.

Unfortunately for the simplicity of the theory that democracy means giving the people what they want and that this means giving the legislature what it wants, the legislature is divided into two branches and

[1] John Locke, *The Second Treatise of Civil Government and A Letter concerning Toleration* (Oxford: Blackwell [Basil] & Mott, Ltd., 1947), Ch. 8, p. 87.

[2] See Part 1 of *Bureaucracy in a Democracy* (New York: Harper and Brothers, 1950). For a penetrating but sympathetic criticism of Hyneman's view, see Chester I. Bernard's review of the book in *American Political Science Review*, 44 (December, 1950), 990–1004.

[3] For Appleby's central position, see Ch. 16 of his *Big Democracy* (New York: Alfred A. Knopf, Inc., 1945) and p. 164 of his *Policy and Administration* (University: University of Alabama Press, 1949).

the President is an independently elected official. In case of conflict between any or all of these, who should be supreme as the authentic representative of what the people want? Professor Hyneman has his uneasy moments between President and legislature. Realism compels some doubts as to the validity of the voice of congressional committees, and closer examination bogs the theory down in exceptions and qualifications.

The will of the people, like sovereignty, is regarded as a metaphysical first principle, supplying an absolute from which certain consequences can be deduced. Yet to possess meaning in political analysis, the concept must be defined in operational terms. How do you discover what the people want? The mode of consultation can make a world of difference. At various times President, Senate, House, Supreme Court, Dr. Gallup, and a host of other agents and agencies have claimed a special ability to express the people's will. The Achilles heel of Rousseau's *volonté generale* was that it had to find a voice, and his solutions ranged from enlightened dictatorship to counting the votes. The will of the people in Professor Elliott's sense is the democratic myth, and in Mosca's the political formula. It serves as a symbol to legitimatize the acts of any group that can successfully identify itself with it in the public mind. Properly understood, it probably should be treated as a value symbol of our political culture, an object for investigation involving a political process — and not a principle from which we can logically excogitate the appropriate role of bureaucracy.

Dissatisfaction with the view of bureaucracy as instrument and Caliban has grown among students of government as first-hand experience in government and historical research have undermined accepted dogma. Professor C. J. Friedrich has pointed to the beneficent role of bureaucracy as the core of modern government.[4] Fritz Morstein Marx has described the vital role of the Prussian bureaucracy in developing the *Rechtsstaat*.[5] The studies of Pendleton Herring, John M. Gaus and Leon O. Wolcott, Arthur W. MacMahon and John D. Millett have illustrated the genuinely representative part played by the bureaucracy in American government.[6] And in a widely used text Professor J. A. Corry has not hesitated to refer to administration as the main-

[4] *Constitutional Government and Democracy*, rev. ed. (Boston: Ginn and Company, 1950), Ch. 2.

[5] "Civil Service in Germany," in Leonard D. White, *et al., Civil Service Abroad* (New York, McGraw-Hill Book Company, Inc., 1935).

[6] Pendleton Herring, *Public Administration and the Public Interest* (New York: McGraw-Hill Book Company, Inc., 1936); J. M. Gaus and L. O. Wolcott, *Public Administration and the United States Department of Agriculture* (Chicago: Public Administration Service, 1940); A. W. MacMahon and J. D. Millett, *Federal Administrators, A Biographical Approach to the Problem of Departmental Management* (New York: Columbia University Press, 1939).

spring of government and to the administrative, as distinguished from the political, executive as a fourth branch of government. An assessment of the vital role of bureaucracy in the working American constitution seems to be overdue.

The most ardent advocate of legislative supremacy can no longer blink the fact of administrative discretion and even administrative legislation. Nor does any one seriously suppose that the clock can be turned back. Improvement there may be in the capacity and willingness of the legislature to exercise general policy superintendence, but anything approaching the conditions necessary to achieve a separation of policy from administration is highly doubtful. The bureaucracy is in policy, and major policy, to stay; in fact, barring the unlikely development of strong majority party legislative leadership, the bureaucracy is likely, day in and day out, to be our main source of policy initiative. The role of the legislature and of the political executive may come to consist largely of encouraging, discouraging and passing on policy which wells up from the agencies of administration. All of this is because the bureaucracy is not just an instrument to carry out a will formed by the elected Congress and President. It is itself a medium for registering the diverse wills that make up the people's will and for transmuting them into responsibility proposals for public policy.

Growth in the power of the bureaucracy is looked upon as a menace to constitutionalism. By some it is seen as a dangerous enhancement of the power of the President, by others as an alarming accretion of power to a non-elective part of the government. The logic of *either-or* sees a cumulative process in which the supremacy of the elected legislative is replaced by the supremacy of an appointed bureaucracy. Given the alternative, the choice of the supremacy of an elected legislature would be clear, but that choice is an unreal bogy. To meet our needs, we have worked out a complex system in which the bureaucracy and legislature perform complementary and interlocking functions. Both are necessary, and the supremacy of either would be a constitutional misfortune. We sometimes forget that the authors of the *Federalist* and Jefferson alike were aware of the danger of legislative tyranny.

Professor Friedrich and others have argued that the essence of constitutionalism is the division of power in such a way as to provide a system of effective regularized restraints upon governmental action. The purpose of this division of power is not to create some mechanical equipoise among the organs of government but so to represent the diversity of the community that its own pluralism is reflected in a pluralism within the government. As Mosca has well said, "the only demand that is important, and possible, to make of a political system is that all social values shall have a part in it, and that it shall find a place for all who possess any of the qualities which determine what prestige and what influence an individual, or a class, is to have."[7] Now it is extremely clear that our Congress fails to do this and that the bureaucracy in considerable measure compensates for its deficiency. Important and vital interests in the United States are unrepresented, underrepresented, or malrepresented in Congress. These interests receive more effective and more responsible representation through administrative channels than through the legislature.

In considerable part this is due to the nature of the presidency and its constituency. Responsible behavior in the sense of sensitivity to long-range and broad considerations, the totality of interests affected, and the utilization of expert knowledge by procedures that ensure a systematic collection and analysis of relevant facts, is more characteristic of the executive than of Congress. Despite the exceptions, and there are many, this kind of responsible behavior is more expected, more politically feasible, and more frequently practiced in the administrative branch. The bureaucracy headed by the presidency is both compelled and encouraged to respond to, and even to assist in the development of broad publics . . . , but broad publics seldom emanate from the organization and the geographic concentration necessary for effectiveness in the congressional committee process. The public's conception of the President as national leader creates an expectation as to his role that differs markedly from any stereotype of Congress or Congressman. This general conception of the presidency not only imposes itself on the incumbent of the office, enforcing a degree of responsibility for playing a national part, but also provides the political means for its performance by organizing a nationwide public. As one President has remarked, the presidency is the best pulpit in the land. It has a nation for its congregation. But what is important here is the expectation that the President should offer a national and party program which provides a degree of synthesis for the agencies of administration. Imperfectly effective as are the organs of coordination — Cabinet, Bureau of the Budget, National Security Council, inter-Departmental committees, and the rest — they are far more effective at ensuring integration than is even the well-disciplined House Appropriations Committee, with its stubbornly fragmented procedures.

In addition to the broader constituency represented by the presidency and the national concern imposed by this office on the subordinate agencies of administration, there is another factor to account for the vital role of these agencies in supplementing congressional representation. It is simply that the shield of presidential power permits the

[7] Gaetano Mosca, *The Ruling Class,* trans. by Hannah D. Kahn, ed. by Arthur Livingston (New York: McGraw-Hill Book Company, Inc., 1939), p. 258.

development of the agencies of administration into institutions to mediate between the narrow and the broad interest at work in the subject matter of their concern. The presidency provides a balancing power that permits and sustains a perspective which the overwhelming concentration of narrow interests in the congressional subject matter committee makes difficult in the legislative process. Representation of consumer interests in the Bureau of Agricultural Economics, for example, depends upon presidential protection. Under this same shelter, agencies may develop organizational codes stereotyped in public expectations, that permit the continuance of broader representation and encourage responsibility in the range and manner in which problems are considered and solutions sought.

To the modern student of government, Aristotle's characterization of an election as an oligarchical device always comes somewhat as a shock. Nonetheless, its implications for representative democracy are significant. If one were to set forth in law the facts of life of the American Congress, it would appear that, to be eligible, overwhelmingly a candidate had first to be in the upper upper-income bracket or second, either personally or through his associates, to be able to command substantial sums of money. Expressed as custom, such conditions are passed over save for the carping criticism of Marxists; yet if they were expressed in law, they would clearly characterize our constitution as oligarchic.

While the Jacksonian conception of the civil service as a domain for the common man was not expressly designed as a balance to the inevitably oligarchical aspects of an elected legislature, it has been influential in that direction. Accustomed as we are to the identification of election with both representation and democracy, it seems strange at first to consider that the nonelected civil service may be both more representative of the country and more democratic in its composition than the Congress.

As it operates in the civil service, the recruitment process brings into federal employment and positions of national power, persons whose previous affiliations, training, and background cause them to conceive of themselves as representing constituencies that are relatively uninfluential in Congress. These constituencies, like that of the presidency, are in the aggregate numerically very large; and in speaking for them as self-appointed, or frequently actually appointed, representatives, the bureaucrats fill in the deficiencies of the process of representation in the legislature. The importance of this representation lies not only in offsetting such defects as rural overrepresentation, the self-contained district, and other vagaries of our system of nominations that leave many without a voice, but in the qualitative representation of science, the professions, the institutions of learning, and the conscience of society as it is expressed in churches, civil liberties groups, and a host of others.

The democratic character of the civil service stems from its origin, income level, and associations. The process of selection of the civil service, its contacts, milieu, and income level after induction make the civil service as a body a better sample of the mass of the people than Congress. Lacking a caste system to wall them off from their fellows, the members of this sample are likely to be more responsive to the desires and needs of the broad public than a highly selected slice whose responsiveness is enforced by a mechanism of elections that frequently places more power in the hands of campaign-backers than voters. Furthermore, it is unlikely that any overhauling of our system of representation in Congress will remove the need for supplementary representation through the bureaucracy. The working interaction of President, Congress, courts, and the administrative branch makes the constitutional system a going concern — not the legal supremacy of any one of them.

Given the seemingly inevitable growth in the power of the bureaucracy through administrative discretion and administrative law, it is of critical importance that the bureaucracy be both representative and democratic in composition and ethos. Its internal structuring may be as important for constitutional functioning as any theoretical or practicable legislative supremacy. That wonder of modern times, the standing army possessed of a near-monopoly of force yet tamely obedient to the civil power, is a prime example of the efficacy of a balance of social forces as a means to neutralization as a political force. A similar representation of the pluralism of our society in the vitals of the bureaucracy insures its constitutional behavior and political equilibrium.

It is not by any means sure that the people think that what they want is the same as what Congress wants. In fact, there is considerable evidence that the ordinary man views Congressmen, if not Congress as an institution, with considerable skepticism. The retort that the people elected the Congress falls somewhat wide of the mark. Given the system of parties and primaries, rural overrepresentation, seniority rule, interest-dominated committees, and all the devices that give potent minorities a disproportionate say, it should occasion no surprise if Congress' claim exclusively to voice what the people want be taken with reservations.[8] Skepticism of the exclusiveness of the claim, how-

---

[8] Cf. Barnard, *op. cit.* (above, n. 2), p. 1004, and James MacGregor Burns, *Congress on Trial* (New York: Harper and Brothers, 1949). Hyneman is aware of these misgivings: "If there is widespread and serious doubt that Congress can make the major decisions — including the decision as to what authority the President shall have — in a way that the American people as a whole will find acceptable, then we had better get

ever, is no warrant for denying the vital contribution of the representative legislature to the maintenance of constitutionalism. Without it bureaucratic absolutism would be well-nigh unavoidable.

If one rejects the view that election is the *sine qua non* of representation, the bureaucracy now has a very real claim to be considered much more representative of the American people in its composition than the Congress. This is not merely the case with respect to the class structure of the country but, equally significantly, with respect to the learned groups, skills, economic interests, races, nationalities, and religions. The rich diversity that makes up the United States is better represented in its civil service than anywhere else.

While it has distressed those who see in the bureaucracy merely an efficient instrument for executing policy framed elsewhere, its persistent refusal to block the path of the common man by educational qualifications beyond the reach of the poor has made the civil service a democratic *carrière ouverte aux talents.* Like Napoleon's soldiers, the humble clerk carries a marshal's baton in his knapsack. And the open avenue of opportunity in the government has meant much in providing substance to the forms of democracy. At a time when administration has become a towering fact, the significance of our recruitment process for a democratic and representative bureaucracy over-shadows an academic preoccupation with the objective of a merely technical proficiency. One has only to consider seriously the role of bureaucracy as formulator of the bulk of the policy alternatives for legislature and political executive alike — as rule-maker-in-chief — to recognize that representativeness must be a prime consideration in the recruitment process.

It can hardly be denied that, despite the attempt to achieve it by the recruitment process, representativeness in the agencies of government is seriously inadequate. The capture of commissions such as the I.C.C. by the regulated interests has often been charged, not without persuasive evidence. In his pioneering work *Public Administration and the Public Interest,* Pendleton Herring has documented the problem. Yet however crassly one-sided an agency of government may become, few indeed will be found so completely under the dominance of a single interest as the subject matter committees of Congress. And those that are so dominated have a bad conscience not shared by their brethren on the Hill.

---

busy with the improvement of our political organization, our electoral system, and the organization of Congress so that the grounds for such doubt will be removed" (*op. cit.,* p. 217). Burns and others have pointed out the road blocks in the way of such reform. Compensation for congressional deficiencies through the presidency and bureaucracy seems the normal course of our development. Had Professor Hyneman considered the possibilities of moral restraints, as Barnard suggests, this road might not have seemed so perilous.

The Department of Agriculture is probably as clearly a clientele department as any in the United States government. Nevertheless, it compares most favorably with the Senate and House Agricultural Committees in the breadth of its conception of the public interest. (In point of fact, the luckless Bureau of Agriculture Economics incurred congressional wrath for daring to act on the assumption that it had a responsibility to the consumer.) As mediator, moderator, and synthesizer of the raw demands of the agricultural pressure groups, the Department works to attain a feasible national farm policy in a context of political and group demands. The structure of the Department in itself insures some consideration of the many aspects of the nation's agriculture in the formation and formulation of policy alternatives. Agronomists, soil chemists, nutritionists, economists, market analysts, and a host of others organized in bureaus and divisions bring together and into focus the elements necessary for responsible decisions. The point of view of personnel trained to think of a national economy and to utilize a scientific outlook is a needed counterpoise to the immediacy of political demands and the narrowness of pressure group perspective. In addition, the very permanence of the Department and the comparative permanence of many of its personnel provide a range of vision that at least partially transcends the headlines of the moment. Of course, it is true that sometimes, as in the Forest Service, the interest of the Department seems to be a bureaucratic contemplation of its own navel. Still the Department institutionalizes, however inadequately in its bad moments, the long view and the broad look on the nation's agricultural problems. While occasional Congressmen and occasional pressure groups also may take the long view, in the main such behavior is exceptional and little reliance can be placed on it.

Responsibility is a product of responsible institutions; and with all their deficiencies — which are many indeed — the departments of administration come closer than any other organs of government to achieving responsible behavior by virtue of the breadth and depth of their consideration of the relevant facts and because of the representative character of their personnel. As continuing organizations, they can learn from their mistakes. They can even make their mistakes meaningful. That is, they can make explicit to themselves the hypotheses on which they act and so make failure itself a source of knowledge. In however limited a form, these agencies are organized to make self-corrective behavior possible.

The difficulties of arriving at self-corrective behavior in the disorganized and heatedly partisan atmosphere of Congress are all too apparent. Legislatures such as the British Parliament have at times developed wisdom and perpetuated it in a sound tradition workably related to the problems confronting the nation. But in the absence of a disciplined party system with reasonable continuity of leadership, conditions are too anarchical in our Congress to permit that body to try to organize its experience for the production of knowledge. The conditions of political success do not encourage the cooperative corporate endeavor that characterizes our successful disciplines dedicated to the discovery of fact and the testing of hypotheses. One must hasten to admit that few agency heads willingly admit failure and search for its causes. The extraordinary but explicable overestimate of the magnitude of reconversion unemployment by the O.W.M.R. after World War II was regarded less as an opportunity and a first-rate challenge to reëxamine some fundamental economic thinking than as a botch to be dealt with by the palliative arts of propaganda. Even the eminently sane strategic bombing survey was frequently imperiled by an expediential urge to color the facts. Nonetheless, for the Air Force to undertake a strategic bombing survey at all is an encouraging instance of the recognition of the need of self-corrective behavior. Similarly, the State Department may undertake a review of China policy not simply to provide a brief for the defense but to examine the causes of past failure and to extract the lessons that may lead to future success. Given the current situation, such a review is beyond the capacity of Congress to undertake. In addition to the anarchic conditions already noted, a major reason for this lies in a phenomenon pointed out by Roland Young: the members of Congress, majority as well as minority, do not identify themselves with administration. Law in action is administration — and it is the work of the bureaucrats from whom and from whose works Congressmen instinctively dissociate themselves. Policy in practice thus is never the responsibility of Congress. The "foul up" is always the fault of the Administration, and Congress is well-nigh in the position of the British King who can do no wrong. Yet the penalty for the failure to accept responsibility for the test of legislation in administration is blindness to the possible lessons of experience. It may be that if government is ever to learn from its experience, the learning process will in large measure depend on the functioning of the bureaucracy.

Through the breadth of the interests represented in its composition, the bureaucracy provides a significant constitutionalizing element of pluralism in our government. Through its structure, permanence, and processes, it provides a medium in which the conditions requisite for the national interpretation of experience can develop. Thus it has a substantial part to play in the working constitution as representative organ and as source of rationality.

Returning now to Aristotle's suggestive analysis of the real components of a constitution, it is interesting to consider the ethical constitution of the bureaucracy. What is the prevailing ethos of the leading elements in the bureaucracy and how does it compare with those of the other branches of government, notably that of Congress? A detailed analysis of working attitudes towards the rule of law, civil liberties, and due process would be illuminating. A powerful case might well be made that in practice the bureaucracy shows far more concern and respect for each of these constitutional fundamentals than does the Congress. Certainly no agency shows such blatant disregard for due process as is customary with congressional committees, while the entire body's acquiescence in the abuse of congressional immunity bespeaks a disregard for constitutional safeguards that goes beyond committee excesses.

It was the bureaucracy, acting through the Department of Justice, that drafted Truman's unsuccessful veto of the McCarran Act, despite the potentially great power with the administration of this act could place in the hands of reputedly power-hungry bureaucrats. And if the executive branch has a sorry record on a loyalty program whose procedures give less opportunity to the accused than to a common felon, the explanation lies in a pusillanimous attitude to Congress rather than in a lack of scruples. One may search the records of Congress for a wigging administered to the F. B. I. similar to that frequently administered to the Home Office by the British Parliament. It is the nation's good fortune in having a man of the character of J. Edgar Hoover heading the F. B. I. rather than careful congressional scrutiny that has thus far secured us from the danger inherent in a national police.

Clearly the difference in ethos in the congressional and administrative branches of the government is not due to any mysterious vice in the one or virtue in the other. The difference must relate to the backgrounds and education of the personnel recruited for each and the seemingly wide difference in what constitutes successful practice in each as well as to the forces that bear upon them. Both branches are products of the effective political sentiments bearing upon them; they are rivals in political competence, varying according to their respective patterns of representativeness and responsibility. (For example, criticism of law schools and law reviews wrings the withers of no Congressman; it does have effect upon the bureaucracy and the courts.) Altogether, the climate of influential opinion is different, and the working of the group structure through the relevant institutions of selection and election produces a different result.

Given the views and composition of Congress, it is a fortunate fact of our working constitution that it is complemented by a bureaucracy indoctrinated with the fundamental ideals of constitutionalism. This varied group, rooted in the diversity of the country, can be counted on to provide important representation for its pluralism. In a real and important sense, it provides a constitutional check on both legislature and executive.

It is no neutral instrument like the German bureaucracy, available to Nazi and democrat alike, pleading its orders from *"Die höhe Tiere"* as an excuse for criminal acts. Be it noted that this plea of duty to carry out orders neutrally met short shrift at Nuremberg. Facing the facts should lead to some interesting changes in the theory of the desirability of administrative neutrality. It is the balance of social forces in the bureaucracy that enables it both to perform an important part in the process of representation and to serve as a needed addition to a functioning division of power in government. Were the administrative branch ever to become a neutral instrument, it would, as a compact and homogeneous power group, either set up shop on its own account or provide the weapon for some other group bent on subverting the constitution.

A candid review of the causes leading to the overthrow of constitutional governments in recent years will show few, if any, examples where prime responsibility can be placed on the bureaucracy. With the exception of the military in Spain and South America, one must look elsewhere. Indeed, the very weakness of bureaucracies incapable of maintaining order has been a major chink in the constitutional armor; but anarchical legislatures incompetent to govern, accompanied by the rise of totalitarian political parties, have been the political causes of the debacle of constitutionalism. It is high time that the administrative branch is recognized as an actual and potentially great addition to the forces of constitutionalism. The advice of the devotees of Locke would make it a neutral instrument, a gun for hire by any party. Fortunately, such advice cannot be taken. Far better would be to recognize that, by appropriate recruitment, structure, and processes, the bureaucracy can be made a vital part of a functioning constitutional democracy, filling out the deficiencies of the Congress and the political executive. The theory of our constitution needs to recognize and understand the working and the potential of our great fourth branch of government, taking a rightful place beside President, Congress, and Courts.

PART V

GOVERNMENT AND POLICY: SOME OUTPUTS OF THE POLITICAL SYSTEM

CHAPTER TEN

Civil Liberties and Civil Rights

Civil liberties and civil rights cover a very broad area. Among the most fundamental civil liberties are those governing the extent to which individuals can speak, write, and read what they choose. The democratic process requires the free exchange of ideas. Constitutional government requires the protection of minority rights and above all of the right to dissent.

Freedom of Speech and Press

There are many reasons to support freedom of speech and press. One of these is the impossibility of proving the existence of an Absolute Truth. No person nor group of men can be infallible. The "best" decisions are those that are made on the basis of the most widespread information available pertaining to the subject at hand. Freedom of information is an integral part of the democratic process. In the following selection, from John Stuart Mill's famous essay *On Liberty,* published in 1859, the justifications for permitting liberty of speech and press are discussed.

48 JOHN STUART MILL

LIBERTY OF THOUGHT AND DISCUSSION

The time, it is to be hoped, is gone by when any defence would be necessary of the "liberty of the press" as one of the securities against corrupt or tyrannical government. No argument, we may suppose, can now be needed, against permitting a legislature or an executive, not identified in interest with the people, to prescribe opinions to them, and determine what doctrines or what arguments they shall be allowed to hear. This aspect of the question, besides, has been so often and so triumphantly enforced by preceding writers, that it needs not be specially insisted on in this place. Though the law of England, on the subject of the press, is as servile to this day as it was in the time of the Tudors, there is little danger of its being actually put in force against political discussion, except during some temporary panic, when fear of insurrection drives ministers and judges from their propriety; and, speaking generally, it is not, in constitutional countries, to be apprehended, that the government, whether completely responsible to the people or not, will often attempt to control the expression of opinion, except when in doing so it makes itself the organ of the general intolerance of the public. Let us suppose, therefore, that the government is entirely at one with the people, and never thinks of exerting any power of coercion unless in agreement with what it conceives to be their voice. But I deny the right of the people to exercise such coercion, either by themselves or by their government. The power itself is illegitimate. The best government has no more title to it than the worst. It is as noxious, or more noxious, when exerted in accordance with public opinion, than when in opposition to it. If all mankind minus one, were of one opinion, and only one person were of the contrary opinion, mankind would be no more justified in silencing that one person, than he, if he had the power, would be justified in silencing mankind. Were an opinion a personal possession of no value except to the owner; if to be obstructed in the enjoyment of it were simply a private injury, it would make some difference whether the injury was inflicted only on a few persons or on many. But the peculiar evil of silencing the expression of an opinion is, that it is robbing the human race; posterity as well as the existing generation; those who dissent from the opinion, still more than those who hold it. If the opinion is right, they are deprived of the opportunity of exchanging error for truth: if wrong, they lose, what is almost as great a benefit, the clearer perception and livelier impression of truth, produced by its collision with error.

It is necessary to consider separately these two hypotheses, each of which has a distinct branch of the argument corresponding to it. We can never be sure that the opinion we are endeavoring to stifle is a false opinion; and if we were sure, stifling it would be an evil still.

First: the opinion which it is attempted to suppress by authority may possibly be true. Those who desire to suppress it, of course deny its truth; but they are not infallible. They have no authority to decide the question for all mankind, and exclude every other person from the means of judging. To refuse a hearing to an opinion, because they are sure that it is false, is to assume that *their* certainty is the same thing as *absolute* certainty. All silencing of discussion is an assumption of infallibility. Its condemnation may be allowed to rest on this common argument, not the worse for being common.

Unfortunately for the good sense of mankind, the fact of their fallibility is far from carrying the weight in their practical judgment, which is always allowed to it in theory; for while every one well knows himself to be fallible, few think it necessary to take any precautions against their own fallibility, or admit the supposition that any opinion, of which they feel very certain, may be one of the examples of the error to which they acknowledge themselves to be liable. Absolute princes, or others who are accustomed to unlimited deference, usually feel this complete confidence in their own opinions on nearly all subjects. People more happily situated, who sometimes hear their opinions disputed, and are not wholly unused to be set right when they are wrong, place the same unbounded reliance only on such of their opinions as are shared by all who surround them, or to whom they habitually defer: for in proportion to a man's want of confidence in his own solitary judgment, does he usually repose, with implicit trust, on the infallibility of "the world" in general. And the world, to each individual, means the part of it with which he comes in contact; his party, his sect, his church, his class of society: the man may be called, by comparison, almost liberal and large-minded to whom it means anything so comprehensive as his own country or his own age. Nor is his faith in this collective authority at all shaken by his being aware that other ages, countries, sects, churches, classes, and parties have thought, and even now think, the exact reverse. He devolves upon his own world the responsibility of being in the right against the dissentient worlds of other people; and it never troubles him that mere accident has decided which of these numerous worlds is the object of his reliance, and that the same causes which make him a Churchman in London, would have made him a Buddhist or a Confucian in Peking. Yet it is as evident in itself, as any amount of argument can make it, that ages are no more infallible than individuals; every age having held many opinions which subsequent ages have deemed not only false but absurd; and it is as certain that many opinions, now general, will be rejected by future ages, as it is that many, once general, are rejected by the present.

The objection likely to be made to this argument, would probably take some such form as the following. There is no greater assumption of infallibility in forbidding the propagation of error, than in any other thing which is done by public authority on its own judgment and responsibility. Judgment is given to men that they may use it. Because it may be used erroneously, are men to be told that they ought not to use it at all? To prohibit what they think pernicious, is not claiming exemption from error, but fulfilling the duty incumbent on them, although fallible, of acting on their conscientious conviction. If we were never to act on our opinions, because those opinions may be wrong, we should leave all our interests uncared for, and all our duties unperformed. An objection which applies to all conduct, can be no valid objection to any conduct in particular. It is the duty of governments, and of individuals, to form the truest opinions they can; to form them carefully, and never impose them upon others unless they are quite sure of being right. But when they are sure (such reasoners may say), it is not conscientiousness but cowardice to shrink from acting on their opinions, and allow doctrines which they honestly think dangerous to the welfare of mankind, either in this life or in another, to be scattered abroad without restraint, because other people, in less enlightened times, have persecuted opinions now believed to be true. Let us take care, it may be said, not to make the same mistake: but governments and nations have made mistakes in other things, which are not denied to be fit subjects for the exercise of authority: they have laid on bad taxes, made unjust wars. Ought we therefore to lay on no taxes, and, under whatever provocation, make no wars? Men, and governments, must act to the best of their ability. There is no such thing as absolute certainty, but there is assurance sufficient for the purposes of human life. We may, and must, assume our opinion to be true for the guidance of our own conduct: and it is assuming no more when we forbid bad men to pervert society by the propagation of opinions which we regard as false and pernicious.

I answer, that it is assuming very much more. There is the greatest difference between presuming an opinion to be true, because, with every opportunity for contesting it, it has not been refuted, and assuming its truth for the purpose of not permitting its refutation. Complete liberty of contradicting and disproving our opinion, is the very condition which justifies us in assuming its truth for purposes of action; and on no other terms can a being with human faculties have any rational assurance of being right.

When we consider either the history of opinion, or the ordinary conduct of human life, to what is it to be ascribed that the one and the other are no worse than they are? Not certainly to the inherent force of the human understanding; for, on any matter not self-evident, there are ninety-nine persons totally incapable of judging of it, for one who is capable; and the capacity of the hundredth person is only comparative; for the majority of the eminent men of every past generation held many opinions now known to be erroneous, and did or approved numerous things which no one will now justify. Why is it, then, that there is on the whole a preponderance among mankind of rational opinions and rational conduct? If there really is this preponderance — which there must be, unless human affairs are, and have always been, in an almost desperate state — it is owing to a quality of the human mind, the source of everything respectable in man either as an intellectual or as a moral being, namely, that his errors are corrigible. He is capable of rectifying his mistakes, by discussion and experience. Not by experience alone. There must be discussion, to show how experience is to be interpreted. Wrong opinions and practices gradually yield to fact and argument: but facts and arguments, to produce any effect on the mind, must be brought before it. Very few facts are able to tell their own story, without comments to bring out their meaning. The whole strength and value, then, of human judgment, depending on the one property, that it can be set right when it is wrong, reliance can be placed on it only when the means of setting it right are kept constantly at hand. In the case of any person whose judgment is really deserving of confidence, how has it become so? Because he has kept his mind open to criticism of his opinions and conduct. Because it has been his practice to listen to all that could be said against him; to profit by as much of it as was just, and expound to himself, and upon occasion to others, the fallacy of what was fallacious. Because he has felt, that the only way in which a human being can make some approach to knowing the whole of a subject, is by hearing what can be said about it by persons of every variety of opinion, and studying all modes in which it can be looked at by every character of mind. No wise man ever acquired his wisdom in any mode but this; nor is it in the nature of human intellect to become wise in any other manner. The steady habit of correcting and completing his own opinion by collating it with those of others, so far from causing doubt and hesitation in carrying it into practice, is the only stable foundation for a just reliance on it: for, being cognizant of all that can, at least obviously, be said against him, and having taken up his position against all gainsayers — knowing that he has sought for objections and difficulties, instead of avoiding them, and has shut out no light which can be thrown upon the subject from any quarter — he has a right to think his judgment better than that of any person, or any multitude, who have not gone through a similar process.

It is not too much to require that what the wisest of mankind, those who are best entitled to trust their own judgment, find necessary to warrant their relying on it, should be submitted to by that miscellaneous collection of a few wise and many foolish individuals, called the public. The most intolerant of churches, the Roman Catholic Church, even at the canonization of a saint, admits, and listens patiently to, a "devil's advocate." The holiest of men, it appears, cannot be admitted to posthumous honors, until all that the devil could say against him is known and weighed. If even the Newtonian philosophy were not permitted to be questioned, mankind could not feel as complete assurance of its truth as they now do. The beliefs which we have most warrant for, have no safeguard to rest on, but a standing invitation to the whole world to prove them unfounded. . . .

We have now recognized the necessity to the mental well-being of mankind (on which all their other well-being depends) of freedom of opinion, and freedom of the expression of opinion, on four distinct grounds; which we will now briefly recapitulate.

First, if any opinion is compelled to silence, that opinion may, for aught we can certainly know, be true. To deny this is to assume our own infallibility.

Secondly, though the silenced opinion be an error, it may, and very commonly does, contain a portion of truth; and since the general or prevailing opinion on any subject is rarely or never the whole truth, it is only by the collision of adverse opinions that the remainder of the truth has any chance of being supplied.

Thirdly, even if the received opinion be not only true, but the whole truth; unless it is suffered to be, and actually is, vigorously and earnestly contested, it will, by most of those who receive it, be held in the manner of a prejudice, with little comprehension or feeling of its rational grounds. And not only this, but, fourthly, the meaning of the doctrine itself will be in danger of being lost, or enfeebled, and deprived of its vital effect on the character and conduct: the dogma becoming a mere formal profession, inefficacious for good, but cumbering the ground, and preventing the growth of any real and heartfelt conviction from reason or personal experience.

Before quitting the subject of freedom of opinion, it is fit to take some notice of those who say, that the free expression of all opinions should be permitted, on condition that the manner be temperate, and do not pass the bounds of fair discussion. Much might be said on the impossibility of fixing where these supposed bounds are to be placed; for if the test be offence to those whose opinion is attacked, I think experience testifies that this offence is given whenever the attack is telling and powerful, and that every opponent who pushes them hard, and whom they find it difficult to answer, appears to them, if he shows any strong feeling on the subject, an intemperate opponent. But this, though an important consideration in a practical point of view, merges in a more fundamental objection. Undoubtedly the manner of asserting an opinion, even though it be a true one, may be very objectionable, and may justly incur severe censure. But the principal offences of the kind are such as it is mostly impossible, unless by accidental self-betrayal, to bring home to conviction. The gravest of them is, to argue sophistically, to suppress facts or arguments, to misstate the elements of the case, or misrepresent the opposite opinion. But all this,

even to the most aggravated degree, is so continually done in perfect
good faith, by persons who are not considered, and in many other respects may not deserve to be considered, ignorant or incompetent, that
it is rarely possible on adequate grounds conscientiously to stamp the
misrepresentation as morally culpable; and still less could law pre-
sume to interfere with this kind of controversial misconduct. With regard to what is commonly meant by intemperate discussion, namely,
invective, sarcasm, personality, and the like, the denunciation of these
weapons would deserve more sympathy if it were ever proposed to in-
terdict them equally to both sides; but it is only desired to restrain the
employment of them against the prevailing opinion: against the un-
prevailing they may not only be used without general disapproval, but
will be likely to obtain for him who uses them the praise of honest zeal
and righteous indignation. Yet whatever mischief arises from their use,
is greatest when they are employed against the comparatively defence-
less; and whatever unfair advantage can be derived by any opinion
from this mode of asserting it, accrues almost exclusively to received
opinions. The worst offence of this kind which can be committed by a
polemic, is to stigmatize those who hold the contrary opinion as bad
and immoral men. To calumny of this sort, those who hold any unpopular opinion are peculiarly exposed, because they are in general few
and uninfluential, and nobody but themselves feels much interest in
seeing justice done them; but this weapon is, from the nature of the
case, denied to those who attack a prevailing opinion: they can neither
use it with safety to themselves, nor, if they could, would it do anything but recoil on their own cause. In general, opinions contrary to
those commonly received can only obtain a hearing by studied moder-
ation of language, and the most cautious avoidance of unnecessary offence, from which they hardly ever deviate even in a slight degree without losing ground: while unmeasured vituperation employed on the
side of the prevailing opinion, really does deter people from professing
contrary opinions, and from listening to those who profess them. For
the interest, therefore, of truth and justice, it is far more important to
restrain this employment of vituperative language than the other;
and, for example, if it were necessary to choose, there would be much
more need to discourage offensive attacks on infidelity, than on religion. It is, however, obvious that law and authority have no business
with restraining either, while opinion ought, in every instance, to determine its verdict by the circumstances of the individual case; con-
demning every one, on whichever side of the argument he places himself, in whose mode of advocacy either want of candor, or malignity, big-
otry, or intolerance of feeling manifest themselves; but not inferring
these vices from the side which a person takes, though it be the contrary side of the question to our own: and giving merited honor to

every one, whatever opinion he may hold, who has calmness to see and honesty to state what his opponents and their opinions really are, exaggerating nothing to their discredit, keeping nothing back which tells, or can be supposed to tell, in their favor. This is the real morality of public discussion; and if often violated, I am happy to think that there are many controversialists who to a great extent observe it, and a still greater number who conscientiously strive towards it.

Mill does not justify absolute liberty of speech and press but implies that there are boundaries — although difficult to determine — to public debate. Democratic governments have always been faced with this dilemma: At what point can freedom of speech and press be curtailed? The Supreme Court has had difficulty in making decisions in areas involving censorship and loyalty and security. Freedom of speech and press cannot be used to destroy the very government that protects these liberties.

Justice Holmes, in *Schenck* v. *United States,* 249 U.S. 47 (1919), stated his famous "clear and present danger" test, which subsequently was applied at both the national and state levels, for deciding whether or not Congress could abridge freedom of speech under the First Amendment:

"The most stringent protection of free speech would not protect a man in falsely shouting fire in a theatre and causing a panic. It does not protect a man from an injunction against uttering words that may have all the effects of force. . . . The question in every case is whether the words used are used in such circumstances and are of such a nature as to create a clear and present danger that they will bring about the substantive evils that Congress has a right to prevent. It is a question of proximity and degree. When a nation is at war many things that might be said in time of peace are such a hindrance to its efforts that their utterance will not be endured so long as men fight and that no Court could regard them as protected by any constitutional right."

In 1940 Congress passed the Smith Act, Section 2 of which made it unlawful for any person:

"(1) to knowingly or willfully advocate, abet, advise, or teach the duty, necessity, desirability, or propriety of overthrowing or destroying any government in the United States by force or violence . . . ; (2) with intent to cause the overthrow or destruction of any government in the United States, to print, publish, edit, issue, circulate, sell, distribute, or publicly display any written or printed matter advocating, advising, or teaching the duty, necessity, desirability, or propriety of overthrowing or destroying any government in the United States by force or violence; (3) to organize or help to organize any society, group, or assembly of persons who teach, advocate, or encourage the overthrow or destruction of any government in the United States by force or violence; or to be or become a member of, or affiliate with, any such society . . . , knowing the purposes thereof."

The constitutionality of this act was tested in *Dennis* v. *United States,* 341 U.S. 494 (1951), which contained five opinions. Vinson spoke for the Court, with Frankfurter and Jackson concurring; Black and Douglas dissented.

49

DENNIS v. UNITED STATES

341 U.S. 494 (1951)

Mr. Chief Justice Vinson announced the judgment of the Court, saying in part:

Petitioners were indicted in July, 1948, for violation of the conspiracy provisions of the Smith Act. . . . A verdict of guilty as to all the petitioners was returned by the jury on October 14, 1949. The Court of Appeals affirmed the convictions. . . . We granted certiorari. . . .

. . . Our limited grant of the writ of certiorari has removed from our consideration any question as to the sufficiency of the evidence to support the jury's determination that petitioners are guilty of the offense charged. Whether on this record petitioners did in fact advocate the overthrow of the Government by force and violence is not before us, and we must base any discussion of this point upon the conclusions stated in the opinion of the Court of Appeals, which treated the issue in great detail. That court held that the record in this case amply supports the necessary finding of the jury that petitioners, the leaders of the Communist Party in this country, were unwilling to work within our framework of democracy, but intended to initiate a violent revolution whenever the propitious occasion appeared. . . .

I

It will be helpful in clarifying the issues to treat next the contention that the trial judge improperly interpreted the statute by charging that the statute required an unlawful intent before the jury could convict. More specifically, he charged that the jury could not find the petitioners guilty under the indictment unless they found that petitioners had the intent to "overthrow . . . the Government of the United States by force and violence as speedily as circumstances would permit."

. . . The structure and purpose of the statute demand the inclusion of intent as an element of the crime. Congress was concerned with those who advocate and organize for the overthrow of the Government. Certainly those who recruit and combine for the purpose of advocating overthrow intend to bring about that overthrow. We hold that the statute requires as an essential element of the crime proof of the intent of those who are charged with its violation to overthrow the Government by force and violence. . . .

II

The obvious purpose of the statute is to protect existing Government, not from change by peaceable, lawful and constitutional means, but from change by violence, revolution and terrorism. That it is within the *power* of the Congress to protect the Government of the United States from armed rebellion is a proposition which requires little discussion. Whatever theoretical merit there may be to the argument that there is a "right" to rebellion against dictatorial governments is without force where the existing structure of the government provides for peaceful and orderly change. We reject any principle of governmental helplessness in the face of preparation for revolution, which principle, carried to its logical conclusion, must lead to anarchy. No one could conceive that it is within the power of Congress to prohibit acts intended to overthrow the Government by force and violence. The question with which we are concerned here is not whether Congress has such *power,* but whether the *means* that it has employed conflict with the First and Fifth Amendments to the Constitution.

One of the bases for the contention that the means which Congress has employed are invalid takes the form of an attack on the face of the statute on the grounds that by its terms it prohibits academic discussion of the merits of Marxism-Leninism, that it stifles ideas and is contrary to all concepts of a free speech and a free press. Although we do not agree that the language itself has that significance, we must bear in mind that it is the duty of the federal courts to interpret federal legislation in a manner not inconsistent with the demands of the Constitution. . . . This is a federal statute which we must interpret as well as judge. . . .

The very language of the Smith Act negates the interpretation which petitioners would have us impose on that Act. It is directed at advocacy, not discussion. Thus, the trial judge properly charged the jury that they could not convict if they found that petitioners did "no more than pursue peaceful studies and discussions or teaching and advocacy in the realm of ideas." He further charged that it was not unlawful "to conduct in an American college or university a course explaining the philosophical theories set forth in the books which have been placed in evidence." Such a charge is in strict accord with the statutory language, and illustrates the meaning to be placed on those words. Congress did not intend to eradicate the free discussion of political theories, to destroy the traditional rights of Americans to discuss and evaluate ideas without fear of governmental sanction. Rather Congress was concerned with the very kind of activity in which the evidence showed these petitioners engaged.

III

But although the statute is not directed at the hypothetical cases which petitioners have conjured, its application in this case has resulted in convictions for the teaching and advocacy of the overthrow of the Government by force and violence, which, even though coupled with the intent to accomplish that overthrow, contains an element of speech. For this reason, we must pay special heed to the demands of the First Amendment marking out the boundaries of speech.

We pointed out in *Douds, supra,* that the basis of the First Amendment is the hypothesis that speech can rebut speech, propaganda will answer propaganda, free debate of ideas will result in the wisest governmental policies. It is for this reason that this Court has recognized the inherent value of free discourse. An analysis of the leading cases in this Court which have involved direct limitations on speech, however, will demonstrate that both the majority of the Court and the dissenters in particular cases have recognized that this is not an unlimited, unqualified right, but that the societal value of speech must, on occasion, be subordinated to other values and considerations. . . .

The rule we deduce from these cases [*Schenck* and others] is that where an offense is specified by a statute in nonspeech or nonpress terms, a conviction relying upon speech or press as evidence of violation may be sustained only when the speech or publication created a "clear and present danger" of attempting or accomplishing the prohibited crime, e.g. interference with enlistment. The dissents . . . in emphasizing the value of speech, were addressed to the argument of the sufficiency of the evidence. . . .

In this case we are squarely presented with the application of the "clear and present danger" test, and must decide what that phrase imports. We first note that many of the cases in which this Court has reversed convictions by use of this or similar tests have been based on the fact that the interest which the State was attempting to protect was itself too insubstantial to warrant restriction of speech. . . . Overthrow of the Government by force and violence is certainly a substantial enough interest for the Government to limit speech. Indeed, this is the ultimate value of any society, for if a society cannot protect its structure from armed internal attack, it must follow that no subordinate value can be protected. If, then, this interest may be protected, the literal problem which is presented is what has been meant by the use of the phrase "clear and present danger" of the utterances bringing about the evil within the power of Congress to punish.

Obviously, the words cannot mean that before the Government may act, it must wait until the *putsch* is about to be executed, the plans have been laid and the signal is awaited. If Government is aware that a group aiming at its overthrow is attempting to indoctrinate its members and to commit them to a course whereby they will strike when the leaders feel the circumstances permit, action by the Government is required. The argument that there is no need for Government to concern itself, for Government is strong, it possesses ample powers to put down a rebellion, it may defeat the revolution with ease needs no answer. For that is not the question. Certainly an attempt to overthrow the Government by force, even though doomed from the outset because of inadequate numbers or power of the revolutionists, is a sufficient evil for Congress to prevent. The damage which such attempts create both physically and politically to a nation makes it impossible to measure the validity in terms of the probability of success, or the immediacy of a successful attempt. In the instant case the trial judge charged the jury that they could not convict unless they found that petitioners intended to overthrow the Government "as speedily as circumstances would permit." This does not mean, and could not properly mean, that they would not strike until there was certainty of success. What was meant was that the revolutionists would strike when they thought the time was ripe. We must therefore reject the contention that success or probability of success is the criterion.

The situation with which Justices Holmes and Brandeis were concerned in *Gitlow* was a comparatively isolated event [involving a conviction for criminal anarchy in New York of one Gitlow for circulating Communist literature], bearing little relation in their minds to any substantial threat to the safety of the community. . . . They were not confronted with any situation comparable to the instant one — the development of an apparatus designed and dedicated to the overthrow of the Government, in the context of world crisis after crisis.

Chief Justice Learned Hand, writing for the majority below, interpreted the phrase as follows: "In each case [courts] must ask whether the gravity of the 'evil,' discounted by its improbability, justifies such invasion of free speech as is necessary to avoid the danger." 183 F. 2d at 212. We adopt this statement of the rule. . . .

Likewise, we are in accord with the court below, which affirmed the trial court's finding that the requisite danger existed. The mere fact that from the period 1945 to 1948 petitioners' activities did not result in an attempt to overthrow the Government by force and violence is of course no answer to the fact that there was a group that was ready to make the attempt. The formation by petitioners of such a highly organized conspiracy, with rigidly disciplined members subject to call when the leaders, these petitioners, felt that the time had come for action, coupled with the inflammable nature of world conditions, similar uprisings in other countries, and the touch-and-go nature of our relations with countries with whom petitioners were in the very least ideologically attuned, convince us that their convictions were justified on this score. And this analysis disposes of the contention that a conspiracy to advocate, as distinguished from the advocacy itself, cannot be constitutionally restrained, because it comprises only the preparation. It is the existence of the conspiracy which creates the danger. . . . If the ingredients of the reaction are present, we cannot bind the Government to wait until the catalyst is added. . . .

We hold that §§2(a) (1), 2(a) (2) and (3) of the Smith Act, do not inherently, or as construed or applied in the instant case, violate the First Amendment and other provisions of the Bill of Rights, or the First and Fifth Amendments because of indefiniteness. Petitioners intended to overthrow the Government of the United States as speedily as the circumstances would permit. Their conspiracy to organize the Communist Party and to teach and advocate the overthrow of the Government of the United States by force and violence created a "clear and present danger" of an attempt to overthrow the Government by force and violence. They were properly and constitutionally convicted for violation of the Smith Act. The judgments of conviction are affirmed. . . .

Mr. Justice Black, dissenting, said in part:

. . . At the outset I want to emphasize what the crime involved in this case is, and what it is not. These petitioners were not charged with an attempt to overthrow the Government. They were not charged with overt acts of any kind designed to overthrow the Government. They were not even charged with saying anything or writing anything designed to overthrow the Government. The charge was that they agreed to assemble and to talk and publish certain ideas at a later date: The indictment is that they conspired to organize the Communist Party and to use speech or newspapers and other publications in the future to teach and advocate the forcible overthrow of the Government. No matter how it is worded, this is a virulent form of prior censorship of speech and press, which I believe the First Amendment forbids. . . .

But let us assume, contrary to all constitutional ideas of fair criminal procedure, that petitioners although not indicted for the crime of actual advocacy, may be punished for it. Even on this radical assumption, the other opinions in this case show that the only way to affirm these convictions is to repudiate directly or indirectly the established "clear and present danger" rule. This the Court does in a way which greatly restricts the protections afforded by the First Amendment. The opinions for affirmance indicate that the chief reason for jettisoning the rule is the expressed fear that advocacy of Communist doctrine endangers the safety of the Republic. Undoubtedly, a governmental policy of unfettered communication of ideas does entail dangers. To the Founders of this Nation, however, the benefits derived from free expression were worth the risk. They embodied this philosophy in the First Amendment's command that "Congress shall make no law . . . abridging the freedom of speech, or of the press. . . ." I have always believed that the First Amendment is the keystone of our Government, that the freedoms it guarantees provide the best insurance against destruction of all freedom. At least as to speech in the realm of public matters, I believe that the "clear and present danger" test does not "mark the furthermost constitutional boundaries of protected expression" but does "no more than recognize a minimum compulsion of the Bill of Rights." . . .

So long as this Court exercises the power of judicial review of legislation, I cannot agree that the First Amendment permits us to sustain laws suppressing freedom of speech and press on the basis of Congress' or our own notions of mere "reasonableness." Such a doctrine waters down the First Amendment so that it amounts to little more than an admonition to Congress. The Amendment as so construed is not likely to protect any but those "safe" or orthodox views which rarely need its protection. I must also express my objection to the holding because, as Mr. Justice Douglas' dissent shows, it sanctions the determination of a crucial issue of fact by the judge rather than by the jury. Nor can I let this opportunity pass without expressing my objection to the severely limited grant of certiorari in this case which precluded consideration here of at least two other reasons for reversing these convictions: (1) the record shows a discriminatory selection of the jury panel which prevented trial before a representative cross-section of the community; (2) the record shows that one member of the trial jury was violently hostile to petitioners before and during the trial.

Public opinion being what it now is, few will protest the conviction of these Communist petitioners. There is hope, however, that in calmer times, when present pressures, passions and fears subside, this or some later Court will restore the First Amendment liberties to the high preferred place where they belong in a free society.

Mr. Justice Douglas, dissenting, said in part:
. . . [N]ever until today has anyone seriously thought that the an-

cient law of conspiracy could constitutionally be used to turn speech into seditious conduct. Yet that is precisely what is suggested. I repeat that we deal here with speech alone, not with speech *plus* acts of sabotage or unlawful conduct. Not a single seditious act is charged in the indictment. . . .

Free speech has occupied an exalted position because of the high service it has given our society. Its protection is essential to the very existence of a democracy. The airing of ideas releases pressures which otherwise might become destructive. When ideas compete in the market for acceptance, full and free discussion exposes the false and they gain few adherents. Full and free discussion even of ideas we hate encourages the testing of our own prejudices and preconceptions. Full and free discussion keeps a society from becoming stagnant and unprepared for the stresses and strains that work to tear all civilizations apart.

Full and free discussion has indeed been the first article of our faith. We have founded our political system on it. It has been the safeguard of every religious, political, philosophical, economic, and racial group amongst us. We have counted on it to keep us from embracing what is cheap and false; we have trusted the common sense of our people to choose the doctrine true to our genius and to reject the rest. This has been the one single outstanding tenet that has made our institutions the symbol of freedom and equality. We have deemed it more costly to liberty to suppress a despised minority than to let them vent their spleen. We have above all else feared the political censor. We have wanted a land where our people can be exposed to all the diverse creeds and cultures of the world.

There comes a time when even speech loses its constitutional immunity. Speech innocuous one year may at another time fan such destructive flames that it must be halted in the interest of the safety of the Republic. That is the meaning of the clear and present danger test. When conditions are so critical that there will be no time to avoid the evil that the speech threatens, it is time to call a halt. Otherwise, free speech which is the strength of the Nation will be the cause of its destruction.

Yet free speech is the rule, not the exception. The restraint to be constitutional must be based on more than fear, on more than passionate opposition against the speech, on more than a revolted dislike for its contents. There must be some immediate injury to society that is likely if speech is allowed. . . .

. . . This record . . . contains no evidence whatsoever showing that the acts charged, viz., the teaching of the Soviet theory of revolution with the hope that it will be realized, have created any clear and present danger to the Nation. The Court, however, rules to the contrary. . . .

The political impotence of the Communists in this country does not, of course, dispose of the problem. Their numbers; their positions in industry and government; the extent to which they have in fact infiltrated the police, the armed services, transportation, stevedoring, power plants, munitions works, and other critical places — these facts all bear on the likelihood that their advocacy of the Soviet theory of revolution will endanger the Republic. But the record is silent on these facts. If we are to proceed on the basis of judicial notice, it is impossible for me to say that the Communists in this country are so potent or so strategically deployed that they must be suppressed for their speech. I could not so hold unless I were willing to conclude that the activities in recent years of committees of Congress, of the Attorney General, of labor unions, of state legislatures, and of Loyalty Boards were so futile as to leave the country on the edge of grave peril. To believe that petitioners and their following are placed in such critical positions as to endanger the Nation is to believe the incredible. It is safe to say that the followers of the creed of Soviet Communism are known to the F.B.I.; that in case of war with Russia they will be picked up overnight as were all prospective saboteurs at the commencement of World War II; that the invisible army of petitioners is the best known, the most beset, and the least thriving of any fifth column in history. Only those held by fear and panic could think otherwise. . . .

. . . The political censor has no place in our public debates. Unless and until extreme and necessitous circumstances are shown, our aim should be to keep speech unfettered and to allow the processes of law to be invoked only when the provocateurs among us move from speech to action.

Vishinsky wrote in 1938 in the Law of the Soviet State, "In our state, naturally, there is and can be no place for freedom of speech, press, and so on for the foes of socialism."

Our concern should be that we accept no such standard for the United States. Our faith should be that our people will never give support to these advocates of revolution, so long as we remain loyal to the purposes for which our Nation was founded.

Freedom of Religion

The Establishment Clause of the First Amendment states: "Congress shall make no law respecting an establishment of religion, or prohibiting the free exercise thereof." How does this affect the rights of the individual? First, every person is free to worship in his own way. In line with this meaning, the establishment of religion cannot be curtailed by government; that is, government cannot take action that would prevent religious groups from operating in accordance with their beliefs. There are, however, exceptions, and the meaning of the protection of religion in the First Amendment has varied from one case to another. In this area as in all others involving civil liberties and civil rights the Supreme Court has had to try to balance the needs of the state with the rights of the individual. Religious freedom is not absolute.

The Supreme Court has long held that there must be a wall of separation between church and state, which means that government cannot discriminate among religious creeds. At the present time there is a controversy over federal aid to parochial schools. It has been virtually impossible for Congress to reach an agreement upon the extent to which private schools with religious affiliations should receive federal aid. It is questionable how much aid can be given without jeopardizing the separation of church and state.

At the state and local level separation between church and state has raised many questions. Should bus transportation be given to private school students as well as those attending the public schools? Should released time be given for religious exercises in the public schools? And, perhaps the most controversial of all, should public schools have officially sanctioned prayers?

In the case of *Everson* v. *Board of Education*, 330 U.S. 1 (1947), the Supreme Court had to face the issue of how far local government could go in aiding Catholic parochial schools. New Jersey had authorized local boards of education to reimburse parents for money they spent on bus transportation without regard to the nature of the school attended. Both those going to public and private schools could receive reimbursement. When this statute was challenged as a violation of the wall of separation doctrine, the Supreme Court upheld it. In its opinion the Court pointed out that secular education serves a public purpose, and therefore tax money can be spent on private nonprofit schools as well as on public education. Although reimbursement for bus transportation to parochial schools constituted a degree of aid to religion, it was not in this case considered sufficient to justify a holding that it violated the First Amendment. The state was not acting as an agent of any religion, but remained neutral. It was providing a public service for all school children, in much the same way as it provides policemen and traffic control to assist children in reaching school safely.

Another issue that has developed concerning freedom of religion is whether the public schools may institute a "released time" program to permit religious instruction during the school day. In *McCollum* v. *Board of Education*, 333 U.S. 203

(1948), the Court held that a board of education could not use tax-supported property for religious instruction. An Illinois program had been providing for released time for students while they received religious instruction on school property. In *Zorach* v. *Clauson,* 343 U.S. 306 (1952), the Court retreated slightly from its decision in *McCollum* when it upheld a New York program that permitted students to go to religious centers beyond school property for religious instruction during the school day.

The status of the wall of separation doctrine today is ambiguous. The Supreme Court has held that a religious oath for office requiring an expressed belief in God is unconstitutional. (See *Torcaso* v. *Watkins,* 367 U.S. 488 [1961].) But Sunday closing laws are not unconstitutional, for even though they may once have had a religious motivation, today they achieve secular goals. (See *McGowan* v. *Maryland,* 366 U.S. 420 [1961].) The most controversial decision of all made by the Supreme Court regarding the Establishment Clause was that in *Engel* v. *Vitale,* the famous school prayer case of 1962.

50

ENGEL v. VITALE

370 U.S. 421 (1962)

Mr. Justice Black delivered the opinion of the Court, saying in part:

The respondent Board of Education of Union Free School District No. 9, New Hyde Park, New York, acting in its official capacity under state law, directed the School District's principal to cause the following prayer to be said aloud by each class in the presence of a teacher at the beginning of each school day:

> Almighty God, we acknowledge our dependence upon Thee, and we beg Thy blessings upon us, our parents, our teachers and our country.

This daily procedure was adopted on the recommendation of the State Board of Regents, a governmental agency created by the State Constitution to which the New York Legislature has granted broad supervisory, executive, and legislative powers over the State's public school system. These state officials composed the prayer which they recommended and published as a part of their "Statement on Moral and Spiritual Training in the Schools," saying: "We believe that this

Statement will be subscribed to by all men and women of good will, and we call upon all of them to aid in giving life to our program."

Shortly after the practice of reciting the Regents' prayer was adopted by the School District, the parents of ten pupils brought this action in a New York State Court insisting that use of this official prayer in the public schools was contrary to the beliefs, religions, or religious practices of both themselves and their children. Among other things, these parents challenged the constitutionality of both the state law authorizing the School District to direct the use of prayer in public schools and the School District's regulation ordering the recitation of this particular prayer on the ground that these actions of official governmental agencies violate that part of the First Amendment of the Federal Constitution which commands that "Congress shall make no law respecting an establishment of religion" — a command which was "made applicable to the State of New York by the Fourteenth Amendment of the said Constitution." The New York Court of Appeals, over the dissents of Judges Dye and Fuld, sustained an order of the lower state courts which had upheld the power of New York to use the Regents' prayer as a part of the daily procedures of its public schools so long as the schools did not compel any pupil to join in the prayer over his or his parents' objection. We granted certiorari to review this important decision involving rights protected by the First and Fourteenth Amendments.

We think that by using its public school system to encourage recitation of the Regents' prayer, the State of New York has adopted a practice wholly inconsistent with the Establishment Clause. There can, of course, be no doubt that New York's program of daily classroom invocation of God's blessings as prescribed in the Regents' prayer is a religious activity. It is a solemn avowal of divine faith and supplication for the blessings of the Almighty. The nature of such a prayer has always been religious, none of the respondents has denied this and the trial court expressly so found. . . .

The petitioners contend among other things that the state laws requiring or permitting use of the Regents' prayer must be struck down as a violation of the Establishment Clause because that prayer was composed by governmental officials as a part of a governmental program to further religious beliefs. For this reason, petitioners argue, the State's use of the Regents' prayer in its public school system breaches the constitutional wall of separation between Church and State. We agree with that contention since we think that the constitutional prohibition against laws respecting an establishment of religion must at least mean that in this country it is no part of the business of government to compose official prayers for any group of the American people to recite as a part of a religious program carried on by government.

It is a matter of history that this very practice of establishing governmentally composed prayers for religious services was one of the reasons which caused many of our early colonists to leave England and seek religious freedom in America. The Book of Common Prayer, which was created under governmental direction and which was approved by Acts of Parliament in 1548 and 1549, set out in minute detail the accepted form and content of prayer and other religious ceremonies to be used in the established, tax-supported Church of England. The controversies over the Book and what should be its content repeatedly threatened to disrupt the peace of that country as the accepted forms of prayer in the established church changed with the views of the particular ruler that happened to be in control at the time. Powerful groups representing some of the varying religious views of the people struggled among themselves to impress their particular views upon the Government and obtain amendments of the Book more suitable to their respective notions of how religious services should be conducted in order that the official religious establishment would advance their particular religious beliefs. Other groups, lacking the necessary political power to influence the Government on the matter, decided to leave England and its established church and seek freedom in America from England's governmentally ordained and supported religion.

It is an unfortunate fact of history that when some of the very groups which had most strenuously opposed the established Church of England found themselves sufficiently in control of colonial governments in this country to write their own prayers into law, they passed laws making their own religion the official religion of their respective colonies. Indeed, as late as the time of the Revolutionary War, there were established churches in at least eight of the thirteen former colonies and established religions in at least four of the other five. But the successful Revolution against English political domination was shortly followed by intense opposition to the practice of establishing religion by law. . . .

By the time of the adoption of the Constitution, our history shows that there was a widespread awareness among many Americans of the dangers of a union of Church and State. . . . The First Amendment was added to the Constitution to stand as a guarantee that neither the power nor the prestige of the Federal Government would be used to control, support or influence the kinds of prayer the American people can say — that the people's religions must not be subjected to the pressures of government for change each time a new political administration is elected to office. Under that amendment's prohibition against governmental establishment of religion, as reinforced by the provisions of the Fourteenth Amendment, government in this country, be it state or federal, is without power to prescribe by law any particular form of prayer which is to be used as an official prayer in carrying on any program of governmentally sponsored religious activity.

There can be no doubt that New York's state prayer program officially establishes the religious beliefs embodied in the Regents' prayer. The respondents' argument to the contrary, which is largely based upon the contention that the Regents' prayer is "non-denominational" and the fact that the program, as modified and approved by state courts, does not require all pupils to recite the prayer but permits those who wish to do so to remain silent or be excused from the room, ignores the essential nature of the program's constitutional defects. Neither the fact that the prayer may be denominationally neutral, nor the fact that its observance on the part of the students is voluntary can serve to free it from the limitations of the Establishment Clause, as it might from the Free Exercise Clause, of the First Amendment, both of which are operative against the States by virtue of the Fourteenth Amendment. Although these two clauses may in certain instances overlap, they forbid two quite different kinds of governmental encroachment upon religious freedom. The Establishment Clause, unlike the Free Exercise Clause, does not depend upon any showing of direct governmental compulsion and is violated by the enactment of laws which establish an official religion whether those laws operate directly to coerce nonobserving individuals or not. This is not to say, of course, that laws officially prescribing a particular form of religious worship do not involve coercion of such individuals. When the power, prestige and financial support of government is placed behind a particular religious belief, the indirect coercive pressure upon religious minorities to conform to the prevailing officially approved religion is plain. But the purposes underlying the Establishment Clause go much further than that. Its first and most immediate purpose rested on the belief that a union of government and religion tends to destroy government and to degrade religion. The history of governmentally established religion, both in England and in this country, showed that whenever government had allied itself with one particular form of religion, the inevitable result has been that it had incurred the hatred, disrespect and even contempt of those who held contrary beliefs. That same history showed that many people had lost their respect for any religion that had relied upon the support of government to spread its faith. The Establishment Clause thus stands as an expression of principle on the part of the Founders of our Constitution that religion is too personal, too sacred, too holy, to permit its "unhallowed perversion" by a civil magistrate. Another purpose of the Establishment Clause rested upon an awareness of the historical fact that governmentally established religions and religious persecutions go hand in hand. The Founders knew that only a few years after the Book of Common Prayer became the only accepted form of religious services in the established Church of England, an Act of Uniformity was passed to compel all Englishmen to attend those services and to make it a criminal offense to conduct or attend religious gatherings of any other kind — a law which was consistently flouted by dissenting religious groups in England and which contributed to widespread persecutions of people like John Bunyan who persisted in holding "unlawful [religious] meetings . . . to the great disturbance and distraction of the good subjects of this kingdom. . . ." And they knew that similar persecutions had received the sanction of law in several of the colonies in this country soon after the establishment of official religions in those colonies. It was in large part to get completely away from this sort of systematic religious persecution that the Founders brought into being our Nation, our Constitution, and our Bill of Rights with its prohibition against any governmental establishment of religion. The New York laws officially prescribng the Regents' prayer are inconsistent with both the purposes of the Establishment Clause and with the Establishment Clause itself.

It has been argued that to apply the Constitution in such a way as to prohibit state laws respecting an establishment of religious services in public schools is to indicate a hostility toward religion or toward prayer. Nothing, of course, could be more wrong. The history of man is inseparable from the history of religion. And perhaps it is not too much to say that since the beginning of that history many people have devoutly believed that "More things are wrought by prayer than this world dreams of." It was doubtless largely due to men who believed this that there grew up a sentiment that caused men to leave the cross-currents of officially established state religions and religious persecution in Europe and come to this country filled with the hope that they could find a place in which they could pray when they pleased to the God of their faith in the language they chose. And there were men of this same faith in the power of prayer who led the fight for adoption of our Constitution and also for our Bill of Rights with the very guarantees of religious freedom that forbid the sort of governmental activity which New York has attempted here. These men knew that the First Amendment, which tried to put an end to governmental control of religion and of prayer, was not written to destroy either. They knew rather that it was written to quiet well-justified fears which nearly all of them felt arising out of an awareness that governments of the past had shackled men's tongues to make them speak only the religious thoughts that government wanted them to speak and to pray only to the God that government wanted them to pray to. It is neither sacrilegious nor antireligious to say that each separate government in this country should stay out of the business of writing or sanctioning official prayers and leave that purely religious function to the people themselves and to those the people choose to look to for religious guidance.

It is true that New York's establishment of its Regents' prayer as an officially approved religious doctrine of that State does not amount to a total establishment of one particular religious sect to the exclusion of all others — that, indeed, the governmental endorsement of that prayer seems relatively insignificant when compared to the governmental encroachments upon religion which were commonplace 200 years ago. To those who may subscribe to the view that because the Regents' official prayer is so brief and general there can be no danger to religious freedom in its governmental establishment, however, it may be appropriate to say in the words of James Madison, the author of the First Amendment:

> [I]t is proper to take alarm at the first experiment on our liberties. . . . Who does not see that the same authority which can establish Christianity, in exclusion of all other Religions, may establish with the same ease any particular sect of Christians, in exclusion of all other Sects? That the same authority which can force a citizen to contribute three pence only of his property for the support of any one establishment, may force him to conform to any other establishment in all cases whatsoever?

The judgment of the Court of Appeals of New York is reversed and the cause remanded for further proceedings not inconsistent with this opinion.

Reversed and remanded.

Mr. Justice Frankfurter took no part in the decision of this case.

Mr. Justice White took no part in the consideration or decision of this case.

Mr. Justice Douglas concurred in a separate opinion.

Mr. Justice Stewart, dissenting.

A local school board in New York has provided that those pupils who wish to do so may join in a brief prayer at the beginning of each school day, acknowledging their dependence upon God and asking His blessing upon them and upon their parents, their teachers, and their country. The court today decides that in permitting this brief nondenominational prayer the school board has violated the Constitution of the United States. I think this decision is wrong.

The Court does not hold, nor could it, that New York has interfered with the free exercise of anybody's religion. For the state courts have made clear that those who object to reciting the prayer must be entirely free of any compulsion to do so, including any "embarrassments and pressure." Cf. *West Virginia State Board of Education* v. *Barnette,* 319 US 624. But the Court says that in permitting school children to say this simple prayer, the New York authorities have established "an official religion."

With all respect, I think the Court has misapplied a great constitutional principle. I cannot see how an "official religion" is established by letting those who want to say a prayer say it. On the contrary, I think that to deny the wish of these school children to join in reciting this prayer is to deny them the opportunity of sharing in the spiritual heritage of our Nation.

The Court's historical review of the quarrels over the Book of Common Prayer in England throws no light for me on the issue before us in this case. England had then and has now an established church. Equally unenlightening, I think, is the history of the early establishment and later rejection of an official church in our own States. For we deal here not with the establishment of a state church, which would, of course, be constitutionally impermissible, but with whether school children who want to begin their day by joining in prayer must be prohibited from doing so. Moreover, I think that the Court's task, in this as in all areas of constitutional adjudication, is not responsibly aided by the uncritical invocation of metaphors like the "wall of separation," a phrase nowhere to be found in the Constitution. What is relevant to the issue here is not the history of an established church in sixteenth century England or in eighteenth century America, but the history of the religious traditions of our people, reflected in countless practices of the institutions and officials of our government.

At the opening of each day's Session of this Court we stand, while one of our officials invokes the protection of God. Since the days of John Marshall our Crier has said, "God save the United States and this Honorable Court." Both the Senate and the House of Representatives open their daily Sessions with prayer. Each of our Presidents, from George Washington to John F. Kennedy, has upon assuming his office asked the protection and help of God.

The Court today says that the state and federal governments are without constitutional power to prescribe any particular form of words to be recited by any group of the American people on any subject touching religion. The third stanza of "The Star-Spangled Banner," made our National Anthem by Act of Congress in 1931, contains these verses:

> Blest with victory and peace, may the heav'n rescued land
> Praise the Pow'r that hath made and preserved us a nation!
> Then conquer we must, when our cause it is just,
> And this be our motto "In God is our Trust."

In 1954 Congress added a phrase to the Pledge of Allegiance to the Flag so that it now contains the words "one Nation *under God* indivisible, with liberty and justice for all." In 1952 Congress enacted legislation calling upon the President each year to proclaim a National Day of Prayer. Since 1865 the words "IN GOD WE TRUST" have been impressed on our coins.

Countless similar examples could be listed, but there is no need to belabor the obvious. It was all summed up by this Court just ten years ago in a single sentence: "We are a religious people whose institutions presuppose a Supreme Being." *Zorach* v. *Clauson,* 343 US 306, 313.

I do not believe that this Court, or the Congress, or the President has by the actions and practices I have mentioned established an "official religion" in violation of the Constitution. And I do not believe the State of New York has done so in this case. What each has done has been to recognize and to follow the deeply entrenched and highly cherished spiritual traditions of our Nation — traditions which come down to us from those who almost two hundred years ago avowed their "firm reliance on the Protection of Divine Providence" when they proclaimed the freedom and independence of this brave new world.

I dissent.

A storm of controversy arose over the Supreme Court's decision in *Engel* v. *Vitale.* Misunderstanding the intention of the Supreme Court, which was clearly to *increase* religious freedom rather than restrict it, opponents of the school prayer decision succeeded in introducing a proposed constitutional amendment in Congress. Known as the Becker Amendment, it had the support of extremist groups throughout the country as well as many well-intentioned citizens who felt that the Court's decision unduly restricted their religious freedom and indeed implied a bias against religion. The proposed amendment, which had virtually no chance of passing the first congressional hurdle, clearly overruled decisions of the Supreme Court that had prevented the use of public school facilities for religious exercises, as well as its opinion in the school prayer case.

51

THE BECKER AMENDMENT

ARTICLE —

SECTION 1. Nothing in this Constitution shall be deemed to prohibit the offering, reading from, or listening to prayers or biblical scriptures, if participation therein is on a voluntary basis, in any governmental or public school, institution, or place.

SECTION 2. Nothing in this Constitution shall be deemed to prohibit making reference to belief in, reliance upon, or invoking the aid of God or a Supreme Being in any governmental or public document, proceeding, activity, ceremony, school, institution, or place, or upon any coinage, currency, or obligation of the United States.

SECTION 3. Nothing in this article shall constitute an establishment of religion.

SECTION 4. This article shall be inoperative unless it shall have been ratified as an amendment to the Constitution by the legislatures of three-fourths of the several States within seven years from the date of its submission to the States by the Congress.

Equal Protection of the Laws

By now most students are thoroughly familiar with the evolution of the "separate but equal" doctrine first enunciated by the Supreme Court in *Plessy* v. *Ferguson,* 163 U.S. 537 (1896). Students should note that what is involved in cases in this area is legal interpretation of the provision in the Fourteenth Amendment that no state may deny "to any person within its jurisdiction the equal protection of the laws." The *Plessy* case stated that separate but equal accommodations, required by state law to be established on railroads in Louisiana, did not violate the equal protection of the laws clause of the Fourteenth Amendment. The Court went on to say that the object of the Fourteenth Amendment

"was undoubtedly to enforce the absolute equality of the two races before the law, but in the nature of things it could not have been intended to abolish distinctions based upon color, or to enforce social, as distinguished from political, equality, or a commingling of the two races upon terms unsatisfactory to either. Laws permitting, and even requiring, their separation in places where they are liable to be brought into contact do not necessarily imply the inferiority of either race to the other, and have been generally, if not universally, recognized as within the competency of the state legislatures in the exercise of their police power. The most common instance of this is connected with the establishment of separate schools for white and colored children, which has been held to be a valid exercise of the legislative power even by courts of States where the political rights of the colored race have been longest and most earnestly enforced."

Both the police power and education are within the reserved powers of the states; they are reserved, however, only insofar as they do not conflict with provisions of the Constitution. The Supreme Court, in *Brown* v. *Board of Education,* 347 U.S. 483 (1954), finally crystallized its interpretation of the equal protection of the laws clause in a way that resulted in a significant decrease in state power in an area traditionally reserved to states, viz., education. In addition, a general principle was established which extended far beyond the field of education.

52

BROWN v. BOARD OF EDUCATION OF TOPEKA

347 U.S. 483 (1954)

Mr. Chief Justice Warren delivered the opinion of the Court, saying in part:

These cases come to us from the States of Kansas, South Carolina, Virginia, and Delaware. They are premised on different facts and different local conditions, but a common legal question justifies their consideration together in this consolidated opinion.

In each of the cases, minors of the Negro race, through their legal representatives, seek the aid of the courts in obtaining admission to the public schools of their community on a nonsegregated basis. In each instance, they had been denied admission to schools attended by white children under laws requiring or permitting segregation according to race. This segregation was alleged to deprive the plaintiffs of the equal protection of the laws under the Fourteenth Amendment. In each of the cases other than the Delaware case, a three-judge federal district court denied relief to the plaintiffs on the so-called "separate but equal" doctrine announced by this Court in *Plessy* v. *Ferguson*. . . .

The plaintiffs contend that segregated public schools are not "equal" and cannot be made "equal," and that hence they are deprived of the equal protection of the laws. Because of the obvious importance of the question presented, the Court took jurisdiction. . . .

In the first cases in this Court construing the Fourteenth Amendment, decided shortly after its adoption, the Court interpreted it as proscribing all state-imposed discriminations against the Negro race. The doctrine of "separate but equal" did not make its appearance in this Court until 1896 in the case of *Plessy* v. *Ferguson, supra,* involving not education but transportation. American courts have since labored with the doctrine for over half a century. In this Court, there have been six cases involving the "separate but equal" doctrine in the field of public education. . . . In more recent cases, all on the graduate school level, inequality was found in that specific benefits enjoyed by white students were denied to Negro students of the same educational qualifications. . . . In none of these cases was it necessary to re-examine the doctrine to grant relief to the Negro plaintiff. And in *Sweatt* v. *Painter* [339 U.S. 629 (1950)], the Court expressly reserved decision on the question whether *Plessy* v. *Ferguson* should be held inapplicable to public education.

In the instant cases, that question is directly presented. Here, unlike *Sweatt* v. *Painter,* there are findings below that the Negro and white schools involved have been equalized, or are being equalized, with respect to buildings, curricula, qualifications and salaries of teachers, and other "tangible" factors. Our decision, therefore, cannot turn on merely a comparison of these tangible factors in the Negro and white schools involved in each of the cases. We must look instead to the effect of segregation itself on public education.

In approaching this problem, we cannot turn the clock back to 1868 when the Amendment was adopted, or even to 1896 when *Plessy* v. *Ferguson* was written. We must consider public education in the light of its full development and its present place in American life throughout the Nation. Only in this way can it be determined if segregation in public schools deprives these plaintiffs of the equal protection of the laws.

Today, education is perhaps the most important function of state and local governments. Compulsory school attendance laws and the great expenditures for education both demonstrate our recognition of the importance of education to our democratic society. It is required in the performance of our most basic public responsibilities, even service in the armed forces. It is the very foundation of good citizenship. Today it is a principal instrument in awakening the child to cultural values, in preparing him for later professional training, and in helping him to adjust normally to his environment. In these days, it is doubtful that any child may reasonably be expected to succeed in life if he is denied the opportunity of an education. Such an opportunity, where the state has undertaken to provide it, is a right which must be made available to all on equal terms.

We come then to the question presented: Does segregation of children in public schools solely on the basis of race, even though the physical facilities and other "tangible" factors may be equal, deprive the children of the minority group of equal educational opportunities? We believe that it does.

In *Sweatt* v. *Painter, supra,* in finding that a segregated law school for Negroes could not provide them equal educational opportunities, this Court relied in large part on "those qualities which are incapable of objective measurement but which make for greatness in a law school." In *McLaurin* v. *Oklahoma State Regents, supra* [339 U.S. 637 (1950)], the Court, in requiring that a Negro admitted to a white graduate school be treated like all other students, again resorted to intangible considerations: "his ability to study, to engage in discussions and exchange views with other students, and, in general, to learn his profession." Such considerations apply with added force to children in grade and high schools. To separate them from others of similar age and qualifications solely because of their race generates a feeling of inferiority as to their status in the community that may affect their hearts and minds in a way unlikely ever to be undone. The effect of this separation of their educational opportunities was well stated by a finding in the Kansas case by a court which nevertheless felt compelled to rule against the Negro plaintiffs:

> Segregation of white and colored children in public schools has a detrimental effect upon the colored children. The impact is greater when it has the sanction of the law; for the policy of separating the races is usually interpreted as denoting the inferiority of the Negro group. A sense of inferiority affects the motivation of a child to learn. Segregation with the sanction of law, therefore, has a tendency to retard the educational and mental development of Negro children and to deprive them of some of the benefits they would receive in a racially integrated school system.

Whatever may have been the extent of psychological knowledge at the time of *Plessy* v. *Ferguson,* this finding is amply supported by modern authority. Any language in *Plessy* v. *Ferguson* contrary to this finding is rejected.

We conclude that in the field of public education the doctrine of "separate but equal" has no place. Separate educational facilities are inherently unequal. Therefore, we hold that the plaintiffs and others similarly situated for whom the actions have been brought are by reason of the segregation complained of, deprived of the equal protection of the laws guaranteed by the Fourteenth Amendment. This disposition makes unnecessary any discussion whether such segregation also violates the Due Process Clause of the Fourteenth Amendment.

Because these are class actions, because of the wide applicability of this decision, and because of the great variety of local conditions, the formulation of decrees in these cases presents problems of considerable complexity. On re-argument, the consideration of appropriate relief was necessarily subordinated to the primary question — the constitutionality of segregation in public education. We have now announced that such segregation is a denial of the equal protection of the laws. In order that we may have the full assistance of the parties in formulating decrees, the cases will be restored to the docket, and the parties are requested to present further argument on Questions 4 and 5 previously propounded by the Court for the re-argument this Term [which deal with the implementation of desegregation]. The Attorney General of the United States is again invited to participate. The Attorneys General of the states requiring or permitting segregation in public education will also be permitted to appear as *amici curiae* upon request to do so by September 15, 1954, and submission of briefs by October 1, 1954.

It is so ordered.

On the same day the decision was announced in the *Brown* case (1954), the Court held that segregation in the District of Columbia was unconstitutional on the basis of the due process clause of the Fifth Amendment. (See *Bolling* v. *Sharpe,* 347 U.S. 497 [1954].) This situation reversed the normal one in that a protection explicitly afforded citizens of states was not expressly applicable against the national government, and could be made so only through interpreting it into the concept of due process of law.

After hearing the views of all interested parties in the *Brown* case the Court, on May 31, 1955, announced its decision concerning the implementation of desegregation in public schools.

53

BROWN v. BOARD OF
EDUCATION OF TOPEKA

349 U.S. 294 (1955)

Mr. Chief Justice Warren delivered the opinion of the Court, saying in part:

These cases were decided on May 17, 1954. The opinions of that date, declaring the fundamental principle that racial discrimination in public education is unconstitutional, are incorporated herein by reference. All provisions of federal, state, or local law requiring or permitting such discrimination must yield to this principle. There remains for consideration the manner in which relief is to be accorded.

Because these cases arose under different local conditions and their disposition will involve a variety of local problems, we requested further argument on the question of relief. . . . The parties, the United States, and the States of Florida, North Carolina, Arkansas, Oklahoma, Maryland, and Texas filed briefs and participated in the oral argument.

These presentations were informative and helpful to the Court in its consideration of the complexities arising from the transition to a system of public education freed of racial discrimination. The presentations also demonstrated that substantial steps to eliminate racial discrimination in public schools have already been taken, not only in some of the communities in which these cases arose, but in some of the states appearing as *amici curiae,* and in other states as well. Substantial progress has been made in the District of Columbia and in the communities in Kansas and Delaware involved in this litigation. The defendants in the cases coming to us from South Carolina and Virginia are awaiting the decision of this Court concerning relief.

Full implementation of these constitutional principles may require solution of varied local school problems. School authorities have the primary responsibility for elucidating, assessing, and solving these problems; courts will have to consider whether the action of school authorities constitutes good faith implementation of the governing constitutional principles. Because of their proximity to local conditions and the possible need for further hearings, the courts which originally heard these cases can best perform this judicial appraisal. Accordingly, we believe it appropriate to remand the cases to those courts.

In fashioning and effectuating the decrees, the courts will be guided by equitable principles. Traditionally, equity has been characterized by a practical flexibility in shaping its remedies and by a facility for adjusting and reconciling public and private needs. These cases call for the exercise of these traditional attributes of equity power. At stake is the personal interest of the plaintiffs in admission to public schools as soon as practicable on a nondiscriminatory basis. To effectuate this interest may call for elimination of a variety of obstacles in making the transition to school systems operated in accordance with the constitutional principles set forth in our May 17, 1954, decision. Courts of equity may properly take into account the public interest in the elimination of such obstacles in a systematic and effective manner. But it should go without saying that the vitality of these constitutional principles cannot be allowed to yield simply because of disagreement with them.

While giving weight to these public and private considerations, the courts will require that the defendants make a prompt and reasonable start toward full compliance with our May 17, 1954, ruling. Once such a start has been made, the courts may find that additional time is necessary to carry out the ruling in an effective manner. The burden rests upon the defendants to establish such time is necessary in the public interest and is consistent with good faith compliance at the earliest practicable date. To that end, the courts may consider problems related to administration, arising from the physical condition of the school plant, the school transportation system, personnel, revision of school districts and attendance areas into compact units to achieve a system of determining admission to the public schools on a nonracial basis, and revision of local laws and regulations which may be necessary in solving the foregoing problems. They will also consider the adequacy of any plans the defendants may propose to meet these problems and to effectuate a transition to a racially nondiscriminatory school system. During this period of transition, the courts will retain jurisdiction of these cases.

The judgments below, except that in the Delaware case, are accordingly reversed and the cases are remanded to the District Courts to take such proceedings and enter such orders and decrees consistent with this opinion as are necessary and proper to admit to public schools on a racially nondiscriminatory basis with all deliberate speed the parties to these cases. The judgment in the Delaware case — ordering the immediate admission of the plaintiffs to schools previously attended only by white children — is affirmed on the basis of the principles stated in our May 17, 1954, opinion, but the case is remanded to the Supreme Court of Delaware for such further proceedings as that Court may deem necessary in the light of this opinion.

It is so ordered.

After the second decision of the Supreme Court in *Brown* v.
Board of Education in 1955, it soon became clear that many
southern states would proceed with deliberate speed not to
implement the desegregation of public schools but to obstruct
the intent of the Supreme Court. The Southern Manifesto, an
excerpt from which is reprinted below, clearly indicated the
line that would be taken by many southern congressmen to
justify defiance of the Supreme Court. The gist of the Manifesto
was simply that the Supreme Court did not have the constitutional authority to interfere in an area such as education, which
falls within the reserved powers of the states. The difficulty of
changing the fabric of society by judicial decisions is illustrated
in the area of desegregation of public schools. Ten years after
the initial opinion of the Court less than 10 per cent of the
Negro students in the seventeen southern states, including the
border states and the District of Columbia, were attending
integrated classrooms. Legal decisions alone cannot determine
the course of events.

54

THE SOUTHERN MANIFESTO

The unwarranted decision of the Supreme Court in the
public school cases is now bearing the fruit always produced when
men substitute naked power for established law.

The Founding Fathers gave us a Constitution of checks and balances because they realized the inescapable lesson of history that no
man or group of men can be safely entrusted with unlimited power.
They framed this Constitution with its provision for change by
amendment in order to secure the fundamentals of government
against the dangers of temporary popular passion or the personal pre-
dilections of public officeholders.

We regard the decision of the Supreme Court in the school cases as a
clear abuse of judicial power. It climaxes a trend in the Federal Judiciary undertaking to legislate, in derogation of the authority of Con-

From "The Southern Manifesto," a document signed by 101 congressmen from
eleven southern states and presented to Congress on March 12, 1956.

gress, and to encroach upon the reserved rights of the States and the people.

The original Constitution does not mention education. Neither does the 14th amendment nor any other amendment. The debates preceding the submission of the 14th amendment clearly show that there was no intent that it should affect the system of education maintained by the States.

55   HARRY S. ASHMORE

THE DESEGREGATION DECISION: TEN YEARS AFTER

On the morning of May 17, 1954, the laws of seventeen of the United States, and the federal statutes governing the District of Columbia, required racial segregation in public education. By noon this legal vestige of slavery was invalid, the Supreme Court having proclaimed that the public schools of the vast region must be opened to Negroes.

Predictions were freely made on the day outraged Southern politicians promptly labeled Black Monday, and they ranged from roseate to dire. Perhaps the only prophecy that has stood the test of ten troubled years is that of a judicial expert who forecast that the *Brown* decision would launch a generation of litigation.

Cases before local, state and federal courts turning on the *Brown* precedent now number in the thousands, and the tide is still rising. The reason, of course, is that the landmark decision was far more than a directive to desegregate five local school districts. It was, as the nine justices in a rare display of unanimity clearly intended, the enunciation of a public policy intended to rid the nation of every manifestation of overt racial discrimination.

The structure of law erected upon the *Brown* precedent is largely judge-made. The Congress, hamstrung by Southern intransigence and a sharp national division of public opinion, only this year has seriously addressed itself to fundamental civil rights legislation. Still the cumulative reach of the court decisions is enormous, going far beyond the

Reprinted by permission of Willis Kingsley Wing. Copyright © 1964, by Saturday Review, Inc. This article originally appeared in the *Saturday Review*, May 16, 1964.

Mr. Ashmore and the *Arkansas Gazette* were awarded double Pulitzer Prizes in 1958 for distinguished reporting of the Little Rock integration controversy.

issue of segregation in education, which still remains central and unresolved.

In striking down the variety of legal devices by which Southern
states have attempted to maintain their segregated schools, the Supreme Court has employed the Fourteenth Amendment as its constitutional instrument. In the process it has abrogated states rights to impose federal standards not only upon the organization of the schools
but upon the conduct of a wide variety of public functions. Time after
time the Court has affirmed the federal government's obligation to uphold the Bill of Rights, no matter where its guarantees are being violated, or by whom. In practice this has meant that the reluctant executive branch has had to exercise police powers in a fashion virtually un-
heard of before 1954. In three states the Justice Department has been
pushed to the extreme of taking over law enforcement from local officials with a massive show of arms.

At the end of the decade the implications of these developments
loom far larger than the actual results. The citadels of segregation still
stand across much of the South. But they are under constant attack
now by an increasingly militant Negro leadership, solidly supported by
the Negro rank and file. And the Rights Movement itself is the direct
product of the *Brown* precedent. Negroes everywhere read the 1954
school decision as a declaration that the essential neutrality of the federal government in racial matters had come to an end. The law of the
land now did not merely permit but affirmatively supported the minority's crusade for equality, and in Arkansas, Mississippi, and Alabama Negroes would see the federal presence literally standing between them and the resistant white majority.

Even before the leading edge of the Negro crusade impatiently departed the courtroom in favor of the sidewalk, events were forcing the
Supreme Court away from its initial narrow application of the antidis-
crimination precedent to official institutions and actions. The end of
legal segregation did not mean the end of *de facto* segregation, and
here the pattern in the nation at large differed little from that in the
South. Below the thin crust of the Negro middle class, the Negro mass
was walled off from the white community as effectively, and in some
ways more inhumanely, in the ghettoes of New York, Chicago, and
San Francisco as it was in the "niggertowns" of Richmond, Atlanta,
and Memphis.

It was in the private sector that the embattled Southern states proposed to erect their final defense against integrated education. The
threatened last resort would be the total abandonment of the public
system, with white children presumably attending white schools supported wholly by private funds. The obvious practical difficulties of
the scheme have confined it largely to the oratorical level, but in

Prince Edward County, Virginia, the attempt actually has been made. In its current session the Supreme Court will decide whether the Constitution can be read to require a once-sovereign state to provide a free education for all of its children, whether or not a majority of white voters wants to tax itself for the purpose.

The great sit-in campaign, aimed at forcing Negro admission to accommodations called public although privately owned, also has forced the Supreme Court to take a new look at one of the most revered of all American institutions, private property. The issue here is whether an entrepreneur who makes a general offer of goods or services, whether he is operating Mrs. Murphy's boardinghouse or Harry Truman's haberdashery, can arbitrarily choose his customers. If the Court holds that he cannot, it will write a significant new definition of private ownership, with implications that go well beyond the immediate issue of race.

It is quite clear that some of the Supreme Court Justices have not been easy in their own minds about the great expansion of federal authority inherent in this progression. The unanimous vote in *Brown* has dwindled to five-to-four in some recent applications of the precedent, and it is by no means improbable that the anti-discrimination majority may actually become a minority in the key public accommodations cases presently looming large on the docket.

If the Court should decide that it has, for the time being at least, reached the outer limits of the law, the *Brown* precedent will still stand as the great constitutional monument of our time. The Rights Movement, which it served as catalyst, is well past the point where it can be turned back by an adverse Supreme Court ruling. Indeed, it is being argued in a nervous Congress that the need for civil rights legislation is not to advance the Negro cause, but to control and contain it.

Underlying the surface tensions is a stern reality. The *Brown* precedent provides for, and the minority is avidly demanding, new relationships between whites and Negroes that are unacceptable under prevailing white attitudes. This is a national, not a uniquely Southern condition. Moreover the collision has come at a time when, in vital employment areas affecting most Negroes, the economic growth that could ameliorate the most immediate grievances has virtually come to a standstill.

Ten years ago, when the *Brown* decision came down, the shortage of manpower was such that the automobile manufacturers were sending teams south from Detroit to recruit Negro workers. This meant that an ambitious colored man at one stroke could escape the overt oppression of his Southern homeland, vastly improve his income and living standards and, perhaps most important of all, find a place in a skilled labor group where his status was equal to that of whites. This year the industry, harvesting the fruits of automation, will produce 25 per cent more automobiles with 80 per cent of the 1954 work force, and Detroit, with a restless mass of unemployed Negroes, is one of the tinderboxes of racial unrest.

Experience with the theoretically open school systems of non-Southern cities also has compounded Negro frustrations. With most child-bearing white families safely ensconced in solidly white neighborhoods, the effort to redistribute children to obtain an effective pattern of integration has required such drastic, essentially artificial devices as bussing children of both races long distances across crowded cities. Even where these experiments have been conscientiously supported by school and municipal officials, success has been limited and white dissatisfaction widespread. In enlightened New York, state court decisions handed down in Brooklyn and Malverne have sustained white parents protesting against having their children arbitrarily transferred across neighborhood boundaries to predominantly Negro schools. In these cases the anti-discrimination precedent has been held to mean that a white child cannot be denied the school of his choice on racial grounds, and this irony also is on its way to the Supreme Court.

Integrated neighborhoods would, of course, produce integrated schools, but the black and white patterns of housing have remained largely inviolate. The small Negro middle-class has gained significant new mobility even in suburbia, but the great majority of colored Americans remains ghetto-bound, and its efforts to break out are encountering retrograde action.

All of this is commonly cited as evidence of a widespread backlash of white public opinion brought on by the excesses of the Negro rights demonstrations. Rather, it seems to me, it is simply a belated revelation of prejudicial white attitudes that have always existed and can no longer be cloaked beneath Fourth-of-July pieties. Sensitive white Americans are discovering, with shock and dismay, what Negroes have long since learned by experience — that white tolerance dissipates rapidly when the abstractions of racial equality are translated into practices that threaten the established system of caste. At the extreme we see Northern communities reacting in the traditional pattern of the south, where fear is often translated into anger, and danger into brutal repression.

On the other side, we are nearing the end of the time when the Negro cause could advance from goal to clearly defined goal, making a record of steady, measurable progress that would sustain the tactical demands of the leadership for discipline and restraint. Principles of equality of treatment have been established, and written into law, but only in peripheral areas has practice been brought into conformity. Negroes have been guaranteed the right of admission to an integrated community, but nowhere in this fair land does an integrated community yet exist — and so the demands for freedom now echo a general frustration that often renders them as incoherent as they are passionate.

It is possible to read these manifestations as the harbingers of revolution, and it is fashionable to do so. In each of the past ten springs the approach of warm weather has brought forth predictions of massive racial violence, first in the South and now in the great cities outside the region. Certainly no one could deny that in the present state of tension a major race riot with widespread bloodshed is possible and may even be inevitable. But there remains the remarkable fact that we haven't had one yet, and with it the salient question: If the situation does get out of hand in a given city, or cities, what happens next?

No Negro leader can doubt that any outbreak of violence, whether spontaneous or organized, would be summarily put down by overwhelming white force. Thus the Negro revolution, if there is to be one, is practically denied the revolutionary's usual weapons — sustained campaigns of terror, sabotage, and guerrilla warfare. Nor does subversion offer any hope for the Negro revolutionary. While there is significant sympathy for his cause in the white power structure, nowhere is there any effective body of radical opinion that could be counted on to support the drastic remedies proposed by Black Muslims on the right, or the Freedom Now Party on the left.

We have, in fact, already had a reverse demonstration of the radical dilemma. In the South white activists have attempted to head off the Negro movement by mob violence, as in Little Rock and Oxford; by terror, as in the assassination of Medgar Evers; and by sabotage, as in the recurrent dynamiting of property owned by Negroes and sympathetic whites. Organized efforts on any significant scale have brought down the full weight of the federal government, in the person of armed U.S. troops. And so far at least those who have transgressed the red line of violence and have been caught have found themselves largely abandoned by respectable segregationists.

Finally, it seems to me the Negro movement is inherently devoid of true revolutionary character simply because its members do not seek to remake the community, only to join it. Social scientists, probing happily in the rich new territory of the Negro subconscious, turn up abundant evidence of alienation. Still the drive seems to be to obtain only what has been denied — a secure place in the larger commonalty whose standards, shabby though a moralist might find them, are those set by the white majority.

If I am correct in my view that a revolutionary resolution of the American racial issue is as unlikely as a sudden healing outburst of brotherly love, the prospect is for a protracted, wearing war of nerves.

Most whites feel that they must give up something of value if Negroes are to gain their ordained place in society. I do not believe that this is so, but so long as it remains the conviction of the white community the drive for Negro rights will have the character of an adversary proceeding in which progress is possible but agreement in principle is not. This condition, inescapable now even for the white refugee in the most thoroughly restricted suburb, is ultimately intolerable and has its own force.

The ten abrasive years since *Brown* ought at least to have shucked us of the more debilitating of our national illusions. Chief among these was the happy notion that if we officially declared the Negro equal he automatically would become so — or at least would be able to stride briskly down the path that has led to effective accommodation of other racial minorities. It must be apparent by now that, morally and practically, the Negro's problem is special. If he is to get his just due he will need something more than the collected works of Horatio Alger and the support of a benevolent interracial committee.

Once we wear out the usual arguments over state and local responsibility, the primary burden is going to fall, inescapably, upon the central government. The immediate palliative must be more welfare services, already a federal preserve, and more jobs, which only the most addicted consumers of NAM propaganda now believe can be provided by the private sector in the range and quantity required by Negroes dispossessed by automation — three out of every five, according to the Urban League.

These unhappy facts belatedly have been noted in Washington. War on Poverty has become a slogan and inexorably will become a program. I do not know whether in the vagaries of a campaign year we can expect any more than warmed-over New Deal panaceas. But as Sargent Shriver's Poor Corps marches forth to battle, its intelligence reports clearly indicate that the mission is only incidentally to relieve resident and displaced white Appalachians. The primary attack must be upon the squalid Negro slums that stretch from sea to shining sea.

For the future, we still must look to the law to fulfill its historic role of preceptor.

In the ten years since *Brown* the courts have offered us much valuable instruction. The first lesson is that racial justice can no longer wait for a glacial change in the hearts and minds of men. The second is that the practice of racial equality can alter attitudes when argument and moral suasion cannot, a lesson to be read in the eyes of the rising generation of white and Negro children as they gaze with wonder upon their elders' seizures of racial prejudice.

So we will come back finally to the public schools, that battered, bureau-ridden, harassed, dispirited system of universal education that was once our national pride and remains our national hope. They did it once before, the red brick PS on the city street and the red schoolhouse on the village green. They made room for the frightened children with broken accents, peculiar religions, undernourished lunch boxes, and lice in their hair; contained the cruel curiosity of earlier settlers; taught the lessons of democracy and saw that they were put into practice.

It is a flaccid, morally disoriented society that now dumps a similar, even heavier burden upon our ill-prepared teachers. We ask them somehow to create a new melting pot in a dispersed educational system that operates without a national policy, leaving its professional practitioners exposed to meddling politicians and sustained only by the ministrations of local board members who often look upon education as a well-intentioned hobby.

Ten years after *Brown* the American race problem cannot be neatly defined as a moral, an economic, a social, or an educational issue. It is all of these at once, and it cannot be resolved by a society that no longer pays much attention to its preachers; is content with prosperity at the top even though the lower levels of its social and economic structure are in disarray; and cannot muster the will to put aside the petty religious, professional, and regional interests that stand in the way of an effective public school system.

By frightening a sometimes complacent citizenry, and always prodding an atrophied national conscience, marching Negroes may be offering a great gift to the society that has rejected them. The ugly manifestations of racial bitterness are an injunction to get back to the hard job to which we once professed dedication, the creation of one nation, under God.

Electoral Reapportionment

A development of profound significance to the political process has been the entrance of the federal judiciary into the sphere of legislative reapportionment. The Court has always attempted to avoid "political questions" that are highly controversial. Judicial intervention into the arena of electoral reapportionment was accompanied by a shift on the Supreme Court from a majority emphasizing self-restraint in such matters to one desiring positive judicial action.

What does the Constitution say about electoral apportionment? There is no explicit provision pertaining to representation in *state* legislatures, and regarding congressional districts, Article I provides only that each state shall have a number of representatives in proportion to its population and that every ten years this number may be changed in accordance with whatever directives Congress makes. Thus the matter of congressional districting seemed to be solely within the jurisdiction of Congress, and by implication the apportionment of state legislative districts would be the exclusive concern of state governments.

Gradually it became evident that leaving the redistricting up to Congress and state legislatures would not bring about equality of representation. In *Colgrove* v. *Green,* 328 U.S. 549 (1946), a strong appeal was made to the Supreme Court to change congressional districting in Illinois that had resulted in giving a very unfair advantage to rural interests. For example, a congressional district in Chicago with a population of close to a million voters had the same representation in the House of Representatives as a southern Illinois rural district with a population of only about 100,000 voters. Regardless of such disparities, the Supreme Court ruled that the issue of equal representation was not a matter of judicial concern. It was a political question that should be left up to Congress to resolve. After holding in the *Colegrove* case that congressional districting was beyond judicial scrutiny, the Court later refused to intervene in the districting for elections to state legislatures. (See *South* v. *Peters,* 339 U.S. 276 [1950].)

In 1962 the judicial doctrine of self-restraint in the field of legislative reapportionment changed completely in the historic case of *Baker* v. *Carr,* 369 U.S. 186 (1962). A civil action had been brought against the state of Tennessee to prohibit it from holding further elections under the provisions of a 1901 apportioning statute that based apportionment upon a census taken in the year 1900. All efforts to change the method of apportionment as the population of the state grew and shifted failed, resulting in what the Court called a "crazy-quilt" of representation. For example, a relatively urban county with a population of approximately 37,000 voters had only twice as much representation as a rural county with a population of less than 3,000. There seemed to be no logic whatsoever in the patterns of representation from county to county. Counties with almost exactly the same number of voters had substantially different numbers of representatives in the state legislature. When the *Baker* case was initially brought before the Federal District Court of Tennessee, the action was dismissed for lack of jurisdiction on the basis of the *Colegrove* doctrine. The appellants had claimed that their rights under the Fourteenth Amendment, Equal Protection of the Laws Clause had been violated by the lack of equal representation in the state. In the opinion printed below the Supreme Court overruled the District Court decision, holding that apportionment of the Tennessee State Legislature was a proper matter for judicial concern.

56

BAKER v. CARR

369 U.S. 186 (1962)

Mr. Justice Brennan delivered the opinion of the Court, saying in part:

This civil action was brought under 42 USC §§ 1983 and 1988 to redress the alleged deprivation of federal constitutional rights. The complaint, alleging that by means of a 1901 statute of Tennessee apportioning the members of the General Assembly among the State's 95 counties, "these plaintiffs and others similarly situated, are denied the equal protection of the laws accorded them by the Fourteenth Amendment to the Constitution of the United States by virtue of the debasement of their votes," was dismissed by a three-judge court. . . . The court held that it lacked jurisdiction of the subject matter and also that no claim was stated upon which relief could be granted. . . . We hold that the dismissal was in error, and remand the cause to the District Court for trial and further proceedings consistent with this opinion.

The General Assembly of Tennessee consists of the Senate with 33 members and the House of Representatives with 99 members. . . .

. . . Tennessee's standard for allocating legislative representation among her counties is the total number of qualified voters resident in the respective counties, subject only to minor qualifications. Decennial reapportionment in compliance with the constitutional scheme was effected by the General Assembly each decade from 1871 to 1901. . . . In 1901 the General Assembly abandoned separate enumeration in favor of reliance upon the Federal Census and passed the Apportionment Act here in controversy. In the more than 60 years since that action, all proposals in both Houses of the General Assembly for reapportionment have failed to pass.

Between 1901 and 1961, Tennessee has experienced substantial growth and redistribution of her population. In 1901 the population was 2,020,616, of whom 487,380 were eligible to vote. The 1960 Federal Census reports the State's population at 3,567,089, of whom 2,092,891 are eligible to vote. The relative standings of the counties in terms of qualified voters have changed significantly. It is primarily the continued application of the 1901 Apportionment Act to this shifted and enlarged voting population which gives rise to the present controversy.

Indeed, the complaint alleges that the 1901 statute, even as of the time of its passage, "made no apportionment of Representatives and Senators in accordance with the constitutional formula . . . , but instead arbitrarily and capriciously apportioned representatives in the Senate and House without reference . . . to any logical or reasonable formula whatever." It is further alleged that "because of the population changes since 1900, and the failure of the legislature to reapportion itself since 1901," the 1901 statute became "unconstitutional and obsolete." Appellants also argue that, because of the composition of the legislature effected by the 1901 apportionment act, redress in the form of a state constitutional amendment to change the entire mechanism for reapportioning, or any other change short of that, is difficult or impossible. The complaint concludes that "these plaintiffs and others similarly situated, are denied the equal protection of the laws accorded them by the Fourteenth Amendment to the Constitution of the United States by virtue of the debasement of their votes." They seek a declaration that the 1901 statute is unconstitutional and an injunction restraining the appellees from acting to conduct any further elections under it. They also pray that unless and until the General Assembly enacts a valid reapportionment, the District Court should either decree a reapportionment by mathematical application of the Tennessee constitutional formulae to the most recent Federal Census figures, or direct the appellees to conduct legislative elections, primary and general, at large. They also pray for such other and further relief as may be appropriate.

1. THE DISTRICT COURT'S OPINION AND ORDER OF DISMISSAL

Because we deal with this case on appeal from an order of dismissal granted on appellees' motions, precise identification of the issues presently confronting us demands clear exposition of the grounds upon which the District Court rested in dismissing the case. The dismissal order recited that the court sustained the appellees' grounds "(1) that the Court lacks jurisdiction of the subject matter, and (2) that the complaint fails to state a claim upon which relief can be granted. . . ."

The court proceeded to explain its action as turning on the case's presenting a "question of the distribution of political strength for legislative purposes." For, "from a review of [numerous Supreme Court] . . . decisions there can be no doubt that the federal rule, as enunciated and applied by the Supreme Court, is that the federal courts, whether from a lack of jurisdiction or from the inappropriateness of the subject matter for judicial consideration, will not intervene in cases of this type to compel legislative reapportionment."

The court went on to express doubts as to the feasibility of the various possible remedies sought by the plaintiffs. Then it made clear that its dismissal reflected a view not of doubt that violation of constitutional rights was alleged, but of a court's impotence to correct that violation:

> With the plaintiff's argument that the legislature of Tennessee is guilty of a clear violation of the state constitution and of the rights of the plaintiffs the Court entirely agrees. It also agrees that the evil is a serious one which should be corrected without further delay. But even so the remedy in this situation clearly does not lie with the courts. It has long been recognized and is accepted doctrine that there are indeed some rights guaranteed by the Constitution for the violation of which the courts cannot give redress.

In light of the District Court's treatment of the case, we hold today only (a) that the court possessed jurisdiction of the subject matter; (b) that a justiciable cause of actions is stated upon which appellants would be entitled to appropriate relief; and (c) because appellees raise the issue before this Court, that the appellants have standing to challenge the Tennessee apportionment statutes. Beyond noting that we have no cause at this stage to doubt the District Court will be able to fashion relief if violations of constitutional rights are found, it is improper now to consider what remedy would be most appropriate if appellants prevail at the trial.

II. JURISDICTION OF THE SUBJECT MATTER

. . . Our conclusion, . . . that this cause presents no nonjusticiable "political question" settles the only possible doubt that it is a case or controversy [under Article 3].

Article 3 § 2 of the Federal Constitution provides that "the judicial Power shall extend to all Cases, in Law and Equity, arising under this Constitution, the Laws of the United States, and Treaties made, or which shall be made, under their Authority; . . ." It is clear that the cause of action is one which "arises under" the Federal Constitution. The complaint alleges that the 1901 statute effects an apportionment that deprives the appellants of the equal protection of the laws in violation of the Fourteenth Amendment. Dismissal of the complaint upon the ground of lack of jurisdiction of the subject matter would, therefore, be justified only if that claim were "so attenuated and unsubstantial as to be absolutely devoid of merit." . . . Since the District Court obviously and correctly did not deem the asserted federal constitutional claim unsubstantial and frivolous, it should not have dismissed the complaint for want of jurisdiction of the subject matter. And of course no further consideration of the merits of the claim is relevant to a determination of the court's jurisdiction of the subject matter.

An unbroken line of our precedents sustains the federal courts' jurisdiction of the subject matter of federal constitutional claims of this nature. . . .

The appellees refer to *Colegrove* v. *Green,* 328 US 549, as authority that the District Court lacked jurisdiction of the subject matter. Appellees misconceive the holding of that case. The holding was precisely contrary to their reading of it. Seven members of the Court participated in the decision. Unlike many other cases in this field which have assumed without discussion that there was jurisdiction, all three opinions filed in Colgrove discussed the question. Two of the opinions expressing the views of four of the Justices, a majority, flatly held that there was jurisdiction of the subject matter. . . .

We hold that the District Court has jurisdiction of the subject matter of the federal constitutional claim asserted in the complaint.

III. STANDING

A federal court cannot "pronounce any statute, either of a State or of the United States, void, because irreconcilable with the Constitution, except as it is called upon to adjudge the legal rights of litigants in actual controversies." Have the appellants alleged such a personal stake in the outcome of the controversy as to assure that concrete adverseness which sharpens the presentation of issues upon which the court so largely depends for illumination of difficult constitutional questions? This is the gist of the question of standing. . . .

We hold that the appellants do have standing to maintain this suit. . . .

These appellants seek relief in order to protect or vindicate an interest of their own, and of those similarly situated. Their constitutional claim is, in substance, that the 1901 statute constitutes arbitrary and capricious state action, offensive to the Fourteenth Amendment in its irrational disregard of the standard of apportionment prescribed by the State's Constitution or of any standard, effecting a gross disproportion of representation to voting population. The injury which appellants assert is that this classification disfavors the voters in the counties in which they reside, placing them in a position of constitutionally unjustifiable inequality vis-à-vis voters in irrationally favored counties. A citizen's right to a vote free of arbitrary impairment by state action has been judicially recognized as a right secured by the Constitution, when such impairment resulted from dilution by a false tally, or by a refusal to count votes from arbitrarily selected precincts, or by a stuffing of the ballot box.

It would not be necessary to decide whether appellants' allegations of impairment of their votes by the 1901 apportionment will, ultimately, entitle them to any relief, in order to hold that they have standing to seek it. If such impairment does produce a legally cognizable injury, they are among those who have sustained it. They are entitled to a hearing and to the District Court's decision on their claims. "The very essence of civil liberty certainly consists in the right of every individual to claim the protection of the laws, whenever he receives an injury."

IV. Justiciability

In holding that the subject matter of this suit was not justiciable, the District Court relied on *Colegrove* v. *Green,* and subsequent per curiam cases. The court stated: "From a review of these decisions there can be no doubt that the federal rule . . . is that the federal courts . . . will not intervene in cases of this type to compel legislative reapportionment." We understand the District Court to have read the cited cases as compelling the conclusion that since the appellants sought to have a legislative apportionment held unconstitutional, their suit presented a "political question" and was therefore nonjusticiable. We hold that this challenge to an apportionment presents no nonjusticiable "political question." The cited cases do not hold the contrary.

Of course the mere fact that the suit seeks protection of a political right does not mean it presents a political question. Such an objection "is little more than a play upon words." Rather, it is argued that apportionment cases, whatever the actual wording of the complaint, can involve no federal constitutional right except one resting on the guaranty of a republican form of government, and that complaints based on that clause have been held to present political questions which are nonjusticiable.

We hold that the claim pleaded here neither rests upon nor implicates the Guaranty Clause and that its justiciability is therefore not foreclosed by our decisions of cases involving that clause. The District Court misinterpreted *Colegrove* v. *Green* and other decisions of this Court on which it relied. Appellants' claim that they are being denied equal protection is justiciable, and if "discrimination is sufficiently shown, the right to relief under the equal protection clause is not diminished by the fact that the discrimination relates to political rights." To show why we reject the argument based on the Guaranty Clause, we must examine the authorities under it. But because there appears to be some uncertainty as to why those cases did present political questions, and specifically as to whether this apportionment case is like those cases, we deem it necessary first to consider the contours of the "political question" doctrine.

Our discussion, even at the price of extending this opinion, requires review of a number of political question cases, in order to expose the attributes of the doctrine — attributes which, in various settings, diverge, combine, appear, and disappear in seeming disorderliness. Since that review is undertaken solely to demonstrate that neither singly nor collectively do these cases support a conclusion that this apportionment case is nonjusticiable, we of course do not explore their implications in other contexts. That review reveals that in the Guaranty Clause cases and in the other "political question" cases, it is the relationship between the judiciary and the coordinate branches of the Federal Government, and not the federal judiciary's relationship to the States, which gives rise to the "political question."

We have said that "in determining whether a question falls within [the political question] category, the appropriateness under our system of government of attributing finality to the action of the political departments and also the lack of satisfactory criteria for a judicial determination are dominant considerations." The nonjusticiability of a political question is primarily a function of the separation of powers. Much confusion results from the capacity of the "political question" label to obscure the need for case-by-case inquiry. Deciding whether a matter has in any measure been committed by the Constitution to another branch of government, or whether the action of that branch exceeds whatever authority has been committed, is itself a delicate exercise in constitutional interpretation, and is a responsibility of this Court as ultimate interpreter of the Constitution. To demonstrate this requires no less than to analyze representative cases and to infer from them the analytical threads that make up the political question doctrine. We shall then show that none of those threads catches this case. . . .

We come, finally to the ultimate inquiry whether our precedents as to what constitutes a nonjusticiable "political question" bring the case before us under the umbrella of that doctrine. A natural beginning is to note whether any of the common characteristics which we have been able to identify and label descriptively are present. We find none: The question here is the consistency of state action with the Federal Constitution. We have no question decided, or to be decided, by a political branch of government coequal with this Court. Nor do we risk embarrassment of our government abroad, or grave disturbance at home if we take issue with Tennessee as to the constitutionality of her action here challenged. Nor need the appellants, in order to succeed in this action, ask the Court to enter upon policy determinations for which judicially manageable standards are lacking. Judicial standards under the Equal Protection Clause are well developed and familiar, and it has been open to courts since the enactment of the Fourteenth Amendment to determine, if on the particular facts they must, that a discrimination reflects *no* policy, but simply arbitrary and capricious action. . . .

484

We conclude that the complaint's allegations of a denial of equal protection present a justiciable constitutional cause of action upon which appellants are entitled to a trial and a decision. The right asserted is within the reach of judicial protection under the Fourteenth Amendment.

The judgment of the District Court is reversed and the cause is remanded for further proceedings consistent with this opinion.

Reversed and remanded.

Mr. Justice Whittaker did not participate in the decision of this case.

Mr. Justice Douglas, concurring.

While I join the opinion of the Court and, like the Court, do not reach the merits, a word of explanation is necessary. I put to one side the problems of "political" questions involving the distribution of power between this Court, the Congress, and the Chief Executive. We have here a phase of the recurring problem of the relation of the federal courts to state agencies. More particularly, the question is the extent to which a State may weight one person's vote more heavily than it does another's. . . .

It is . . . clear that by reason of the commands of the Constitution there are several qualifications that a State may not require.

Race, color, or previous condition of servitude are impermissible standards by reason of the Fifteenth Amendment. . . .

Sex is another impermissible standard by reason of the Nineteenth Amendment.

There is a third barrier to a State's freedom in prescribing qualifications of voters and that is the Equal Protection Clause of the Fourteenth Amendment, the provision invoked here. And so the question is, may a State weight the vote of one county or one district more heavily than it weights the vote in another?

The traditional test under the Equal Protection Clause has been whether a State has made "an invidious discrimination," as it does when it selects "a particular race or nationality for oppressive treatment."

I agree with my Brother Clark that if the allegations in the complaint can be sustained a case for relief is established. We are told that a single vote in Moore County, Tennessee, is worth 19 votes in Hamilton County, that one vote in Stewart or in Chester County is worth nearly eight times a single vote in Shelby or Knox County. The opportunity to prove that an "invidious discrimination" exists should therefore be given the appellants. . . .

With the exceptions of *Colegrove* v. *Green,* 328 US 549, *MacDougall* v. *Green,* 335 US 281, *South* v. *Peters,* 339 US 276, and the decisions they spawned, the Court has never thought that protection of voting rights was beyond judicial cognizance. Today's treatment of those cases removes the only impediment to judicial cognizance of the claims stated in the present complaint.

The justiciability of the present claims being established, any relief accorded can be fashioned in the light of well-known principles of equity.

Mr. Justice Clark, concurring.

One emerging from the rash of opinions with their accompanying clashing of views may well find himself suffering a mental blindness. The Court holds that the appellants have alleged a cause of action. However, it refuses to award relief here — although the facts are undisputed — and fails to give the District Court any guidance whatever. One dissenting opinion, bursting with words that go through so much and conclude with so little, condemns the majority action as "a massive repudiation of the experience of our whole past." Another describes the complaint as merely asserting conclusory allegations that Tennessee's apportionment is "incorrect," "arbitrary," "obsolete," and "unconstitutional." I believe it can be shown that this case is distinguishable from earlier cases dealing with the distribution of political power by a State, that a patent violation of the Equal Protection Clause of the United States Constitution has been shown, and that an appropriate remedy may be formulated. . . .

Although I find the Tennessee apportionment statute offends the Equal Protection Clause, I would not consider intervention by this Court into so delicate a field if there were any other relief available to the people of Tennessee. But the majority of the people of Tennessee have no "practical opportunities for exerting their political weight at the polls" to correct the existing "invidious discrimination." Tennessee has no initiative and referendum. I have searched diligently for other "practical opportunities" present under the law. I find none other than through the federal courts. The majority of the voters have been caught up in a legislative strait jacket. Tennessee has an "informed, civically militant electorate" and "an aroused popular conscience," but it does not sear "the conscience of the people's representatives." This is because the legislative policy has riveted the present seats in the Assembly to their respective constituencies, and by the votes of their incumbents a reapportionment of any kind is prevented. The people have been rebuffed at the hands of the Assembly; they have tried the constitutional convention route, but since the call must originate in the Assembly it, too, has been fruitless. They have tried Tennessee courts with the same result, and Governors have fought the tide only to flounder. It is said that there is recourse in Congress and perhaps that may be, but from a practical standpoint this is without substance. To date Congress has never undertaken such a task in any State. We therefore must conclude that the people of Tennessee are stymied and without judicial intervention will be saddled with the present discrimination in the affairs of their state government.

Finally, we must consider if there are any appropriate modes of effective judicial relief. The federal courts are, of course, not forums for political debate, nor should they resolve themselves into state constitutional conventions or legislative assemblies. Nor should their jurisdiction be exercised in the hope that such a declaration, as is made today, may have the direct effect of bringing on legislative action and relieving the courts of the problem of fashioning relief. To my mind this would be nothing less than blackjacking the Assembly into reapportioning the State. If judicial competence were lacking to fashion an effective decree, I would dismiss this appeal. However, like the Solicitor General of the United States, I see no such difficulty in the position of this case. One plan might be to start with the existing assembly districts, consolidate some of them, and award the seats thus released to those counties suffering the most egregious discrimination. Other possibilities are present and might be more effective. But the plan here suggested would at least release the strangle hold now on the Assembly and permit it to redistrict itself. . . .

In view of the detailed study that the Court has given this problem, it is unfortunate that a decision is not reached on the merits. The majority appears to hold, at least sub silentio, that an invidious discrimination is present, but it remands to the three-judge court for it to make what is certain to be that formal determination. It is true that Tennessee has not filed a formal answer. However, it has filed voluminous papers and made extended arguments supporting its position. At no time has it been able to contradict the appellants' factual claims; it has offered no rational explanation for the present apportionment; indeed, it has indicated that there are none known to it. As I have emphasized, the case proceeded to the point before the three-judge court that it was able to find an invidious discrimination factually present, and the State has not contested that holding here. In view of all this background I doubt if anything more can be offered or will be gained by the State on remand, other than time. Nevertheless, not being able to muster a court to dispose of the case on the merits, I concur in the opinion of the majority and acquiesce in the decision to remand. However, in fairness I do think that Tennessee is entitled to have my idea of what it faces on the record before us and the trial court some light as to how it might proceed.

As John Rutledge (later Chief Justice) said 175 years ago in the course of the Constitutional Convention, a chief function of the Court is to secure the national rights. Its decision today supports the proposition for which our forebears fought and many died, namely that "to be fully conformable to the principle of right, the form of government must be representative." That is the keystone upon which our government was founded and lacking which no republic can survive. It is well for this Court to practice self-restraint and discipline in constitutional adjudication, but never in its history have those principles received sanction where the national rights of so many have been so clearly infringed for so long a time. National respect for the courts is more enhanced through the forthright enforcement of those rights rather than by rendering them nugatory through the interposition of subterfuges. In my view the ultimate decision today is in the greatest tradition of this Court.

Mr. Justice Frankfurter, whom Mr. Justice Harlan joins, dissenting. The Court today reverses a uniform course of decision established by a dozen cases, including one by which the very claim now sustained was unanimously rejected only five years ago. The impressive body of rulings thus cast aside reflected the equally uniform course of our political history regarding the relationship between population and legislative representation — a wholly different matter from denial of the franchise to individuals because of race, color, religion or sex. Such a massive repudiation of the experience of our whole past in asserting destructively novel judicial power demands a detailed analysis of the role of this Court in our constitutional scheme. Disregard of inherent limits in the effective exercise of the Court's "judicial Power" not only presages the futility of judicial intervention in the essentially political conflict of forces by which the relation between population and representation has time out of mind been and now is determined. It may well impair the Court's position as the ultimate organ of "the supreme Law of the Land" in that vast range of legal problems, often strongly entangled in popular feeling, on which this Court must pronounce. The Court's authority — possessed neither of the purse nor the sword — ultimately rests on sustained public confidence in its moral sanction. Such feeling must be nourished by the Court's complete detachment, in fact and in appearance, from political entanglements and by abstention from injecting itself into the clash of political forces in political settlements.

A hypothetical claim resting on abstract assumptions is now for the first time made the basis for affording illusory relief for a particular evil even though it foreshadows deeper and more pervasive difficulties in consequence. The claim is hypothetical and the assumptions are abstract because the Court does not vouchsafe the lower courts — state and federal — guide-lines for formulating specific, definite, wholly unprecedented remedies for the inevitable litigations that today's unbrageous disposition is bound to stimulate in connection with politically motivated reapportionments in so many States. In such a setting, to promulgate jurisdiction in the abstract is meaningless. It is devoid of reality as "a brooding omnipresence in the sky" for it conveys no intimation what relief, if any, a District Court is capable of affording that would not invite legislatures to play ducks and drakes with the judiciary. For this Court to direct the District Court to enforce a claim to which the Court has over the years consistently found itself required to deny legal enforcement and at the same time to find it necessary to withhold any guidance to the lower court how to enforce this turnabout, new legal claim, manifests an odd — indeed an esoteric — conception of judicial propriety. One of the Court's supporting opinions, as elucidated by commentary, unwittingly affords a disheartening preview of the mathematical quagmire (apart from divers judicially inappropriate and elusive determinants), into which this Court today catapults the lower courts of the country without so much as adumbrating the basis for a legal calculus as a means of extrication. Even assuming the indispensable intellectual disinterestedness on the part of judges in such matters, they do not have accepted legal standards or criteria or even reliable analogies to draw upon for making judicial judgments. To charge courts with the task of accommodating the incommensurable factors of policy that underlie these mathematical puzzles is to attribute, however flatteringly, omnicompetence to judges. The Framers of the Constitution persistently rejected a proposal that embodied this assumption and Thomas Jefferson never entertained it.

Recent legislation, creating a district appropriately described as "an atrocity of ingenuity," is not unique. Considering the gross inequality among legislative electoral units within almost every State, the Court naturally shrinks from asserting that in districting at least substantial equality is a constitutional requirement enforceable by courts. Room continues to be allowed for weighting. This of course implies that geography, economics, urban-rural conflict, and all the other nonlegal factors which have throughout our history entered into political districting are to some extent not to be ruled out in the undefined vista now opened up by review in the federal courts of state reapportionments. To some extent — aye, there's the rub. In effect, today's decision empowers the courts of the country to devise what should constitute the proper composition of the legislatures of the fifty States. If state courts should for one reason or another find themselves unable to discharge this task, the duty of doing so is put on the federal courts or on this Court, if State views do not satisfy this Court's notion of what is proper districting.

We were soothingly told at the bar of this Court that we need not worry about the kind of remedy a court could effectively fashion once the abstract constitutional right to have courts pass on a state-wide system of electoral districting is recognized as a matter of judicial rhetoric, because legislatures would heed the Court's admonition. This is not only an euphoric hope. It implies a sorry confession of judicial impotence in place of a frank acknowledgment that there is not under our Constitution a judicial remedy for every political mischief, for every undesirable exercise of legislative power. The Framers carefully and with deliberate forethought refused so to enthrone the judiciary. In this situation, as in others of like nature, appeal for relief does not belong here. Appeal must be to an informed, civically militant electorate. In a democratic society like ours, relief must come through an aroused popular conscience that sears the conscience of the people's representatives. In any event there is nothing judicially more unseemly nor more self-defeating than for this Court to make in terrorem pronouncements, to indulge in merely empty rhetoric, sounding a word of promise to the ear, sure to be disappointing to the hope. . . .

Dissenting opinion of Mr. Justice Harlan, whom Mr. Justice Frankfurter joins.

The dissenting opinion of Mr. Justice Frankfurter, in which I join, demonstrates the abrupt departure the majority makes from judicial history by putting the federal courts into this area of state concerns — an area which, in this instance, the Tennessee state courts themselves have refused to enter.

It does not detract from his opinion to say that the panorama of judicial history it unfolds, though evincing a steadfast underlying principle of keeping the federal courts out of these domains, has a tendency, because of variants in expression, to becloud analysis in a given case. With due respect to the majority, I think that has happened here.

Once one cuts through the thicket of discussion devoted to "jurisdiction," "standing," "justiciability" and "political question," there emerges a straightforward issue which, in my view, is determinative of this case. Does the complaint disclose a violation of a federal constitutional right, in other words, a claim over which a United States District Court would have jurisdiction . . . ? The majority opinion does not actually discuss this basic question, but, as one concurring Justice observes, seems to decide it "sub silentio." However, in my opinion, appellants' allegations, accepting all of them as true, do not, parsed down or as a whole, show an infringement by Tennessee of any rights assured by the Fourteenth Amendment. Accordingly, I believe the complaint should have been dismissed for "failure to state a claim upon which relief can be granted."

It is at once essential to recognize this case for what it is. The issue here relates not to a method of state electoral apportionment by which seats in the *federal* House of Representatives are allocated, but solely to the right of a State to fix the basis of representation in its *own* legislature. Until it is first decided to what extent that right is limited by the Federal Constitution, and whether what Tennessee has done or failed to do in this instance runs afoul of any such limitation, we need not reach the issues of "justiciability" or "political question" or any of the other considerations which in such cases as *Colegrove* v. *Green,* 328 US 549, led the Court to decline to adjudicate a challenge to a state apportionment affecting seats in the federal House of Representatives, in the absence of a controlling Act of Congress.

The appellants' claim in this case ultimately rests entirely on the Equal Protection Clause of the Fourteenth Amendment. It is asserted that Tennessee has violated the Equal Protection Clause by maintaining in effect a system of apportionment that grossly favors in legislative representation the rural sections of the State as against its urban communities. . . .

I can find nothing in the Equal Protection Clause or elsewhere in the Federal Constitution which expressly or impliedly supports the view that state legislatures must be so structured as to reflect with approximate equality the voice of every voter. Not only is that proposition refuted by history, as shown by my Brother Frankfurter, but it strikes deep into the heart of our federal system. Its acceptance would require us to turn our backs on the regard which this Court has always shown for the judgment of state legislatures and courts on matters of basically local concern.

In the last analysis, what lies at the core of this controversy is a difference of opinion as to the function of representative government. It is surely beyond argument that those who have the responsibility for devising a system of representation may permissibly consider that factors other than bare numbers should be taken into account. The existence of the United States Senate is proof enough of that. To consider that we may ignore the Tennessee Legislature's judgment in this instance because that body was the product of an asymmetrical electoral apportionment would in effect be to assume the very conclusion here disputed. Hence we must accept the present form of the Tennessee Legislature as the embodiment of the State's choice, or, more realistically, its compromise, between competing political philosophies. The federal courts have not been empowered by the Equal Protection Clause to judge whether this resolution of the State's internal political conflict is desirable or undesirable, wise or unwise. . . .

. . . [R]educed to its essentials, the charge of arbitrariness and capriciousness rests entirely on the consistent refusal of the Tennessee Legislature over the past 60 years to alter a pattern of apportionment that was reasonable when conceived.

A Federal District Court is asked to say that the passage of time has rendered the 1901 apportionment obsolete to the point where its continuance becomes vulnerable under the Fourteenth Amendment. But is not this matter one that involves a classic legislative judgment? Surely it lies within the province of a state legislature to conclude that an existing allocation of senators and representatives constitutes a desirable balance of geographical and demographical representation, or that in the interest of stability of government it would be best to defer for some further time the redistribution of seats in the state legislature.

Indeed, I would hardly think it unconstitutional if a state legislature's expressed reason for establishing or maintaining an electoral imbalance between its rural and urban population were to protect the State's agricultural interests from the sheer weight of numbers of those residing in its cities. . . .

In conclusion, it is appropriate to say that one need not agree, as a citizen, with what Tennessee has done or failed to do, in order to deprecate, as a judge, what the majority is doing today. Those observers of the Court who see it primarily as the last refuge for the correction of all inequality or injustice, no matter what its nature or source, will no doubt applaud this decision and its break with the past. Those who consider that continuing national respect for the Court's authority depends in large measure upon its wise exercise of self-restraint and discipline in constitutional adjudication, will view the decision with deep concern.

I would affirm.

> After the *Baker* decision the Supreme Court on February 17, 1964 rendered additional decisions affecting congressional apportionment. In *Wesberry* v. *Sanders*, 376 U.S. 1 (1964), the Court relied on Article I, Section 2 of the Constitution, which provides that congressmen must be chosen "by the people of the several states," as a basis for holding that congressional districts must be as nearly as possible equal in population. The *Baker* case was used as precedent.

57

WESBERRY v. SANDERS

376 U.S. 1 (1964)

Mr. Justice Black delivered the opinion of the Court, saying in part:

Appellants are citizens and qualified voters of Fulton County, Georgia, and as such are entitled to vote in congressional elections in Georgia's Fifth Congressional District. That district, one of ten created by a 1931 Georgia statute, includes Fulton, DeKalb, and Rockdale Counties and has a population according to the 1960 census of 823,680. The average population of the ten districts is 394,312, less than half that of the Fifth. One district, the Ninth, has only 272,154 people, less than one-third as many as the Fifth. Since there is only one Congressman for each district, this inequality of population means that the Fifth District's Congressman has to represent from two to three times as many people as do Congressmen from some of the other Georgia districts.

Claiming that these population disparities deprived them and voters similarly situated of a right under the Federal Constitution to have their votes for Congressmen given the same weight as the votes of other Georgians, the appellants brought this action . . . asking that the Georgia statute be declared invalid and that the appellees, the Governor and Secretary of the State of Georgia, be enjoined from conducting elections under it. The complaint alleged that appellants were deprived of the full benefit of their right to vote, in violation of (1) Art. I, § 2 of the Constitution of the United States, which provides that "The House of Representatives shall be composed of Members chosen every second year by the People of the several States . . ."; (2) the Due Process, Equal Protection, and Privileges and Immunities Clauses of the Fourteenth Amendment; and (3) that part of Section 2 of the Fourteenth Amendment which provides that "Representatives shall be apportioned among the several States according to their respective numbers. . . ."

The case was heard by a three-judge District Court, which found unanimously, from facts not disputed, that:

> It is clear by any standard . . . that the population of the Fifth District is grossly out of balance with that of the other nine congressional districts of Georgia and in fact, so much so that the removal of DeKalb and

Rockdale Counties from the District, leaving only Fulton with a population of 556,326, would leave it exceeding the average by slightly more
than forty per cent.

Notwithstanding these findings, a majority of the court dismissed
the complaint, citing as their guide Mr. Justice Frankfurter's minority
opinion in *Colegrove* v. *Green,* an opinion stating that challenges to
apportionment of congressional districts raised only "political" questions, which were not justiciable. Although the majority below said
that the dismissal here was based on "want of equity" and not on justiciability, they relied on no circumstances which were peculiar to the
present case; instead, they adopted the language and reasoning of Mr.
Justice Frankfurter's Colegrove opinion in concluding that the appellants had presented a wholly "political" question. Judge Tuttle, dis-
agreeing with the court's reliance on that opinion, dissented from the
dismissal, though he would have denied an injunction at that time in
order to give the Georgia Legislature ample opportunity to correct the
"abuses" in the apportionment. He relied on *Baker* v. *Carr,* which,
after full discussion of Colegrove and all the opinions in it, held that
allegations of disparities of population in state legislative districts
raise justiciable claims on which courts may grant relief. We noted
probably jurisdiction. 374 US 802. We agree with Judge Tuttle that in
debasing the weight of appellants' votes the State has abridged the
right to vote for members of Congress guaranteed them by the United
States Constitution, that the District Court, should have entered a declaratory judgment to that effect, and that it was therefore error to dismiss this suit. The question of what relief should be given we leave for
further consideration and decision by the District Court in light of existing circumstances. . . .

This statement in Baker, which referred to our past decisions holding congressional apportionment cases to be justiciable, we believe was
wholly correct and we adhere to it. Mr. Justice Frankfurter's Colegrove
opinion contended that Art. I, § 4, of the Constitution had given Congress "exclusive authority" to protect the right of citizens to vote for
Congressmen, but we made it clear in Baker that nothing in the language of that article gives support to a construction that would immu-
nize state congressional apportionment laws which debase a citizen's
right to vote from the power of courts to protect the constitutional
rights of individuals from legislative destruction. . . . The right to vote
is too important in our free society to be stripped of judicial protection
by such an interpretation of Article I. This dismissal can no more be
justified on the ground of "want of equity" than on the ground of
"nonjusticiability." We therefore hold that the District Court erred in
dismissing the complaint.

This brings us to the merits. We agree with the District Court that the 1931 Georgia apportionment grossly discriminates against voters in the Fifth Congressional District. A single Congressman represents from two to three times as many Fifth District voters as are represented by each of the Congressmen from the other Georgia congressional districts. The apportionment statute thus contracts the value of some votes and expands that of others. If the Federal Constitution intends that when qualified voters elect members of Congress each vote be given as much weight as any other vote, then this statute cannot stand.

We hold that, construed in its historical context, the command of Art. I, § 2, that Representatives be chosen "by the People of the several States" means that as nearly as is practicable one man's vote in a congressional election is to be worth as much as another's. This rule is followed automatically, of course, when Representatives are chosen as a group on a statewide basis, as was a widespread practice in the first 50 years of our Nation's history. It would be extraordinary to suggest that in such statewide elections the votes of inhabitants of some parts of a State, for example, Georgia's thinly populated Ninth District, could be weighed at two or three times the value of the votes of people living in more populous parts of the State, for example, the Fifth District around Atlanta. We do not believe that the Framers of the Constitution intended to permit the same vote-diluting discrimination to be accomplished through the device of districts containing widely varied numbers of inhabitants. To say that a vote is worth more in one district than in another would not only run counter to our fundamental ideas of democratic government, it would cast aside the principle of a House of Representatives elected "by the People," a principle tenaciously fought for and established at the Constitutional Convention. The history of the Constitution, particularly that part of it relating to the adoption of Art. I, § 2, reveals that those who framed the Constitution meant that, no matter what the mechanics of an election, whether statewide or by districts, it was population which was to be the basis of the House of Representatives. . . .

The debates at the Convention make at least one fact abundantly clear: that when the delegates agreed that the House should represent "people" they intended that in allocating Congressmen the number assigned to each State should be determined solely by the number of the State's inhabitants. The Constitution embodied Edmund Randolph's proposal for a periodic census to ensure "fair representation of the people," an idea endorsed by Mason as assuring that "numbers of inhabitants" should always be the measure of representation in the House of Representatives. The Convention also overwhelmingly agreed to a resolution offered by Randolph to base future apportionment squarely on numbers and to delete any reference to wealth. And the delegates defeated a motion made by Elbridge Gerry to limit the number of Representatives from newer Western States so that it would never exceed the number from the original States.

It would defeat the principle solemnly embodied in the Great Compromise — equal representation in the House of equal numbers of people — for us to hold that, within the States, legislatures may draw the lines of congressional districts in such a way as to give some voters a greater voice in choosing a Congressman than others. The House of Representatives, the Convention agreed, was to represent the people as individuals, and on a basis of complete equality for each voter. The delegates were quite aware of what Madison called the "vicious representation" in Great Britain whereby "rotten boroughs" with few inhabitants were represented in Parliament on or almost on a par with cities of greater population. Wilson urged that people must be represented as individuals, so that America would escape the evils of the English system under which one man could send two members to Parliament to represent the borough of Old Sarum while London's million people sent but four. The delegates referred to rotten borough apportionments in some of the state legislatures as the kind of objectionable governmental action that the Constitution should not tolerate in the election of congressional representatives. . . .

It is in the light of such history that we must construe Art. I, § 2, of the Constitution, which, carrying out the ideas of Madison and those of like views, provides that Representatives shall be chosen "by the People of the several States" and shall be "apportioned among the several States . . . according to their respective numbers." It is not surprising that our Court has held that this Article gives persons qualified to vote a constitutional right to vote and to have their votes counted. *United States* v. *Mosley,* 238 US 383; *Ex parte Yarbrough,* 110 US 651. Not only can this right to vote not be denied outright, it cannot, consistently with Article I, be destroyed by alteration of ballots, see *United States* v. *Classic,* 313 US 299, or diluted by stuffing of the ballot box, see *United States* v. *Saylor,* 322 US 385. No right is more precious in a free country than that of having a voice in the election of those who make the laws under which, as good citizens, we must live. Other rights, even the most basic, are illusory if the right to vote is undermined. Our Constitution leaves no room for classification of people in a way that unnecessarily abridges this right. In urging the people to adopt the Constitution, Madison said in No. 57 of *The Federalist:*

> Who are to be the electors of the Federal Representatives? Not the rich more than the poor; not the learned more than the ignorant; not the haughty heirs of distinguished names, more than the humble sons

of obscure and unpropitious fortune. The electors are to be the great
body of the people of the United States. . . .

Readers surely could have fairly taken this to mean, "one person,
one vote."

While it may not be possible to draw congressional districts with
mathematical precision, that is no excuse for ignoring our Constitution's plain objective of making equal representation for equal numbers of people the fundamental goal for the House of Representatives.
That is the high standard of justice and common sense which the
Founders set for us.

Reversed and remanded.

Mr. Justice Clark wrote a separate opinion, concurring in part and
dissenting in part;

Mr. Justice Harlan dissented, saying in part:
I had not expected to witness the day when the Supreme Court of
the United States would render a decision which cast grave doubt on
the constitutionality of the composition of the House of Representatives. It is not an exaggeration to say that such is the effect of today's
decision. The Court's holding that the Constitution requires States to
select Representatives either by elections at large or by elections in districts composed "as nearly as is practicable" of equal population places
in jeopardy the seats of almost all the members of the present House of
Representatives.

In the last congressional election, in 1962, Representatives from 42
States were elected from congressional districts. In all but five of those
States, the difference between the populations of the largest and smallest districts exceeded 100,000 persons. A difference of this magnitude
in the size of districts the average population of which in each State is
less than 500,000 is presumably not equality among districts "as nearly
as is practicable," although the Court does not reveal its definition of
that phrase. Thus, today's decision impugns the validity of the election of 398 Representatives from 37 States, leaving a "constitutional"
House of 37 members now sitting.

Only a demonstration which could not be avoided would justify this
Court in rendering a decision the effect of which, inescapably as I see
it, is to declare constitutionally defective the very composition of a
coordinate branch of the Federal Government. The Court's opinion
not only fails to make such a demonstration. It is unsound logically on
its face and demonstrably unsound historically. . . .

. . . [T]he language of Art. I, §§ 2 and 4, the surrounding text, and
the relevant history are all in strong and consistent direct contradic-

tion of the Court's holding. The constitutional scheme vests in the States plenary power to regulate the conduct of elections for Representatives, and, in order to protect the Federal Government, provides for congressional supervision of the States' exercise of their power. Within this scheme, the appellants do not have the right which they assert, in the absence of provision for equal districts by the Georgia Legislature or the Congress. The constitutional right which the Court creates is manufactured out of whole cloth.

The unstated premise of the Court's conclusion quite obviously is that the Congress has not dealt, and the Court believes it will not deal, with the problem of congressional apportionment in accordance with what the Court believes to be sound political principles. Laying aside for the moment the validity of such a consideration as a factor in constitutional interpretation, it becomes relevant to examine the history of congressional action under Art. I, § 4. This history reveals that the Court is not simply undertaking to exercise a power which the Constitution reserves to the Congress; it is also overruling congressional judgment. . . .

Today's decision has portents for our society and the Court itself which should be recognized. This is not a case in which the Court vindicates the kind of individual rights that are assured by the Due Process Clause of the Fourteenth Amendment, whose "vague contours," *Rochin* v. *California,* 342 US 165, of course leave much room for constitutional developments necessitated by changing conditions in a dynamic society. Nor is this a case in which an emergent set of facts requires the Court to frame new principles to protect recognized constitutional rights. The claim for judicial relief in this case strikes at one of the fundamental doctrines of our system of government, the separation of powers. In upholding that claim, the Court attempts to effect reforms in a field which the Constitution, as plainly as can be, has committed exclusively to the political process.

This Court, no less than all other branches of the Government, is bound by the Constitution. The Constitution does not confer on the Court blanket authority to step into every situation where the political branch may be thought to have fallen short. The stability of this institution ultimately depends not only upon its being alert to keep the other branches of government within constitutional bounds but equally upon recognition of the limitations on the Court's own functions in the constitutional system.

What is done today saps the political process. The promise of judicial intervention in matters of this sort cannot but encourage popular inertia in efforts for political reform through the political process, with the inevitable result that the process is itself weakened. By yielding to the demand for a judicial remedy in this instance, the Court in my view does a disservice both to itself and to the broader values of our system of government.

Believing that the complaint fails to disclose a constitutional claim, I would affirm the judgment below dismissing the complaint.

Mr. Justice Stewart.

I think it is established that "this Court has power to afford relief in a case of this type as against the objection that the issues are not justiciable," and I cannot subscribe to any possible implication to the contrary which may lurk in Mr. Justice Harlan's dissenting opinion. With this single qualification I join the dissent because I think Mr. Justice Harlan has unanswerably demonstrated that Art. I, § 2, of the Constitution gives no mandate to this Court or to any court to ordain that congressional districts within each State must be equal in population.

Appendix[a]

State and number of representatives[b]	Largest district	Smallest district	Difference between largest and smallest districts
Alabama (8)	. . . . . .	. . . . . .	. . . . . .
Alaska (1)	. . . . . .	. . . . . .	. . . . . .
Arizona (3)	663,510	198,236	465,274
Arkansas (4)	575,385	332,844	242,541
California (38)	588,933	301,872	287,061
Colorado (4)	653,954	195,551	458,403
Connecticut (6)	689,555	318,942	370,613
Delaware (1)	. . . . . .	. . . . . .	. . . . . .
Florida (12)	660,345	237,235	423,110
Georgia (10)	823,680	272,154	551,526
Hawaii (2)	. . . . . .	. . . . . .	. . . . . .
Idaho (2)	409,949	257,242	152,707
Illinois (24)	552,582	278,703	273,879
Indiana (11)	697,567	290,596	406,971
Iowa (7)	442,406	353,156	89,250
Kansas (5)	539,592	373,583	166,009
Kentucky (7)	610,947	350,839	260,108
Louisiana (8)	536,029	263,850	272,179
Maine (2)	505,465	463,800	41,665
Maryland (8)	711,045	243,570	467,475
Massachusetts (12)	478,962	376,336	102,626
Michigan (19)	802,994	177,431	625,563
Minnesota (8)	482,872	375,475	107,397

Appendix[a] (cont.)

State and number of representatives[b]	Largest district	Smallest district	Difference between largest and smallest districts
Mississippi (5)	608,441	295,072	313,369
Missouri (10)	506,854	378,499	128,355
Montana (2)	400,573	274,194	126,379
Nebraska (3)	530,507	404,695	125,812
Nevada (1)	......	......	......
New Hampshire (2)	331,818	275,103	56,715
New Jersey (15)	585,586	255,165	330,421
New Mexico (2)	......	......	......
New York (41)	471,001	350,186	120,815
North Carolina (11)	491,461	277,861	213,600
North Dakota (2)	333,290	299,156	34,134
Ohio (24)	726,156	236,288	489,868
Oklahoma (6)	552,863	227,692	325,171
Oregon (4)	522,813	265,164	257,649
Pennsylvania (27)	553,154	303,026	250,128
Rhode Island (2)	459,706	399,782	59,924
South Carolina (6)	531,555	302,235	229,320
South Dakota (2)	497,669	182,845	314,824
Tennessee (9)	627,019	223,387	403,632
Texas (23)	951,527	216,371	735,156
Utah (2)	572,654	317,973	254,681
Vermont (1)	......	......	......
Virginia (10)	539,618	312,890	226,728
Washington (7)	510,512	342,540	167,972
West Virginia (5)	422,046	303,098	118,948
Wisconsin (10)	530,316	236,870	293,446
Wyoming (1)	......	......	......

[a] The populations of the districts are based on the 1960 Census. The districts are those used in the election of the current 88th Congress. The populations of the districts are available in the biographical section of the Congressional Directory, 88th Cong., 2nd Sess.

[b] 435 in all.

After the *Wesberry* decision the Supreme Court held, in a series of decisions in June, 1964, that the Equal Protection Clause of the Fourteenth Amendment required the equal apportionment of *both* houses of state legislatures. Obviously such a decision could not be made regarding Congress because of constitutional specifications requiring that the Senate represent states as units, with two senators for each state, regardless of population. The precedent-setting decision in June, 1964 was *Reynolds* v. *Sims*. In holding that both houses of bicameral state legislatures must now be apportioned on a population basis, the Court nevertheless provided that some deviations might be permissible. In what can only be described as a mystical statement the Court held, "So long as the divergencies from a strict population standard are based on legitimate considerations incident to the effectuation of a rational state policy, some deviations from the equal-population principle are constitutionally permissible with respect to the apportionment of seats in either or both of the two houses of a bicameral state legislature." Thus political subdivisions of a state may be given some representation that is not directly related to population. But the Court made it abundantly clear that the states would not be permitted to stray very far from the equal-population principle.

In April, 1968 the Supreme Court extended its reapportionment doctrine by holding that a County Commissioner's Court in Texas, which was elected from single-member districts that were substantially unequal in population, violated the equal protection clause of the Fourteenth Amendment. The Court held that since the County Commissioner's Court was a unit of local government with jurisdiction over the entire geographic area of the county, it was subject to the "one man–one vote" rule.

As a result of the *Baker* and *Reynolds* decisions substantial changes are being made throughout the country on the basis of representation in state legislatures. Already Federal District Courts have required the reapportionment of many state legislatures. There is little doubt that the Supreme Court's decisions affecting state legislatures as well as the requirement for equal population in congressional districts will have a profound effect upon the pattern of American politics. The long-felt power of the rural sections of the country will begin to fade. If the present trend toward the increment of *suburban* populations continues, these areas may begin to exercise important political power. In the final analysis the suburbs may be the biggest beneficiaries of equal apportionment. Therefore, although the reapportioned state legislatures may be more sympathetic to urban problems than their predecessors, there is no guarantee that urban issues will be emphasized unless a community of interest develops between the suburbs and the urban centers. Thus reapportionment will not necessarily bring about the renewed interest in the problems of the city that those who feel urban interests have been submerged in the face of rural legislatures have hoped for.

Are there any arguments that can be advanced against equal apportionment? Certainly it is important for any political system to take into account varied interests. The representation of equal numbers of people in different electoral districts may not by itself bring about this equality. As the suburbs grow in population it is entirely possible that with the advent of equal apportionment both the center city and the rural areas of the country will be underrepresented in relation to their importance. Public policy formulated by officials elected from constituencies whose boundaries are determined solely on the basis of equal population may not balance the interests of all sections of the country.

The following selection attempts to analyze systematically the effects of malapportionment in state legislatures upon different areas of public policy.

58   THOMAS R. DYE

MALAPPORTIONMENT AND PUBLIC POLICY IN THE STATES

Commentators on state policy have often implied that malapportionment seriously affects the policy choices of state legislatures. In the literature on state politics it is frequently argued that there are important policy differences between urban and rural constituencies and that malapportionment, by over-representing rural interests, grants them a real advantage in policy-making. It is also frequently predicted that reapportionment on a population basis will bring about noticeable shifts in many state policies.

Malapportionment of state legislatures has been successfully challenged on the grounds that it denies to the citizens equal protection of the laws.[1] This challenge was essentially a normative one, stemming from deeply held values about political equality. The merits of this type of challenge do not lend themselves to empirical verification. However, statements about the effect of malapportionment on public policy, and predictions about the policy consequences of reapportionment, can be tested empirically. Such tests, of course, in no way reflect upon the moral quality of the proposition "as nearly as practicable one man's vote should be equal to another's."[2] But they can help us

From Thomas R. Dye, "Malapportionment and Public Policy in the States," *The Journal of Politics*, Vol. 27, No. 3 (August 1965). Reprinted by permission of the author and the publisher.

[1] *Baker* v. *Carr*, 369 U.S. 186 (1962); *Reynolds* v. *Sims*, 84 S.Ct. 1362 (1964).

[2] *Wesberry* v. *Sanders*, 84 S.Ct. 526 (1964), p. 530.

to know what to expect in the way of policy changes in the wake of reapportionment. In the past, proponents of reapportionment have been very enthusiastic about its expected consequences. Having attributed a lack of party competition, unfair distributions of state funds, conservative tax schemes, unprogressive education policies, and penny-pinching welfare programs to rural over-representation, they naturally expect to see these conditions changed by reapportionment. Court-ordered reapportionment is viewed as a source of strength for state legislatures rather than an infringement of a heretofore exclusive prerogative of these bodies. Reapportionment, it is said, will help states come to grips with important domestic problems in the nation and reassume their rightful place in our federal system.

In contrast, a few scholars have sounded a note of caution regarding the expected consequences of reapportionment. On the basis of roll call analyses in the Missouri and Illinois legislatures, David Derge concluded that metropolitan and non-metropolitan legislators seldom opposed each other in unified voting blocs.[3] It is difficult to see how reapportioning legislatures to reduce rural over-representation would have much effect on policy-making, if we accept Derge's conclusions that only infrequently do rural-urban divisions influence legislative decisions anyway. Duane Lockard also entered a caveat about the consequences of malapportionment. With specific references to conditions in Massachusetts and Connecticut he asked: "Do states with fair apportionment respond to urban appeals more readily? If anyone has made a systematic study of this, I am unaware of it, but limited evidence does not seem to indicate that the states with fair apportionment are any more considerate of urban problems than states with malapportionment."[4] Herbert Jacob was equally skeptical of the consequences of malapportionment. He computed rank-order correlation coefficients for the relationship between malapportionment and party competition, highway fund distributions, and certain welfare expenditures for the fifty states.[5] On the basis of low coefficients, he concluded,

---

[3] David Derge, "Metropolitan and Outstate Alignments in the Illinois and Missouri Legislative Delegations," *American Political Science Review*, Vol. 53 (December, 1958), pp. 1051-1065.

[4] Duane Lockard, *The Politics of State and Local Government* (New York: Macmillan, 1963), p. 319.

[5] The correlation coefficient is a measure of the strength of the relationship between variables. If two variables are perfectly related — if it is always possible to predict one variable from the other — and if the value of one variable always increases (or decreases) when the other variable increases (or decreases), the correlation coefficient will be +1.0. If two variables are perfectly related but when one variable increases the other decreases, the correlation coefficient will be −1.0. A zero correlation indicates the absence of a relationship. The closer the correlation coefficient approximates +1.0 or −1.0, the stronger the relationship. The square of the correlation coefficient provides a measure of the amount of variation in one variable explained by the other. [Ed.]

"it is improbable that it (reapportionment) will substantially invigorate state governments or dissolve the stalemates which sap public confidence in them."[6]

The purpose of the study reported here was to examine systematically the impact of malapportionment on party competition and public policy in all fifty states. If the policy choices of malapportioned legislatures are noticeably different from the policy choices of well-apportioned legislatures, and these differences in policies can be traced to malapportionment rather than some other condition, then reapportionment can be expected to have a significant impact on state policies. However, if the policy choices of well-apportioned and malapportioned legislatures do not differ significantly, or if differences which do occur are the product of some condition other than malapportionment, then more caution is warranted regarding the policy changes that reapportionment may bring. The same test applies to expectations about the impact of reapportionment on party competition. Only if there is significantly more party competition in well-apportioned legislatures than in malapportioned ones, and this increased competition is attributable to apportionment rather than some other condition, is one safe in predicting that reapportionment will bring about greater party competition.

Measuring Malapportionment

Several measures of the malapportionment of state legislatures are available. Perhaps the most common measure is the theoretical minimum percentage of a state's population that can elect a majority of each house.[7] The two minimum percentages for each chamber can be added to provide an index of malapportionment for the legislature as a whole. Percentages are additive in this case because the real denominator is the power of each house to influence policy and this is assumed to be real. In 1960 this index ranged from a low of 37 for Nevada with the least representative legislature to a high of 96 for Oregon with the most representative legislature. Hereafter this measure is referred to as the "index of representativeness."

Another index was devised by David and Eisenberg to focus on urban under-representation in state legislatures.[8] Because urban areas are most likely to be the subject of discrimination, the authors felt that urban under-representation should be a specific object of measurement, in addition to theoretical measures of representativeness. In

[6] Herbert Jacob, "The Consequences of Malapportionment: A Note of Caution," *Social Forces*, Vol. 43 (December, 1964), pp. 256–261.

[7] Manning J. Dauer and Robert G. Kelsay, "Unrepresentative States," *National Municipal Review*, Vol. 44 (December, 1955), pp. 571–575.

[8] Paul T. David and Ralph Eisenberg, *Devaluation of the Urban and Suburban Vote*, Bureau of Public Administration, University of Virginia, 1961.

order to determine the degree of discrimination against urban areas, David and Eisenberg computed the "value" of a vote cast in the largest urban counties of each state. First they computed the average population of a single member district in each state. Actual constituencies were then compared to these average constituencies: the "value" of a vote was represented by the ratio of an actual constituency to the average constituency in each state. For example, in a district with twice the population of the state's average district, the value of a vote would be .50. The "value" of a vote in the largest category of county in each state was computed for each house and then the measures for both houses were averaged to provide an "index of urban representation" for each legislature. In 1960 this index ranged from a low of .12 for Georgia, where the largest counties were most discriminated against in apportionment, to a high of 1.05 in Louisiana, where the largest counties were granted the greatest legislative representation.

A third measure of malapportionment is the technically sophisticated "apportionment score" proposed by Glendon Schubert and Charles Press.[9] The apportionment score combines inverted coefficients of variation for each state (divide the population of the average district by the standard deviation of all districts and subtract the quotient from 1.0) with statistical measures of skewness and kurtosis in the distribution of districts by size of population. The result is an index that measures the combination of variance, skewness, and kurtosis in the populations of legislative districts in each state. According to this scale, in 1962 Massachusetts, with the highest apportionment score, was technically the best apportioned legislature in the nation and Indiana, with the lowest score, was the worst.

All three of these measures — the index of representativeness, the index of urban under-representation, and the apportionment score — are used in this study. Each measure depicts a slightly different aspect of malapportionment; each results in a slightly different ranking of states. The first measure focuses on the theoretical minimum proportion of a state's population that can control the legislature, the second measure focuses on urban under-representation, and the third measure focuses on the degree to which a state's apportionment scheme approaches the statistical concept of normality. In the analysis to follow we shall evaluate the political relevance of each of these measures.

Measuring Public Policy

Measuring state policy choices is an even more difficult task than measuring malapportionment. In the 1960–61 legislative-

---

[9] Glendon Schubert and Charles Press, "Measuring Malapportionment," *American Political Science Review*, Vol. 58 (June, 1964), pp. 302–327; and corrections published December, 1964, pp. 966–970.

biennium, more than 104,000 bills were introduced in the state legislatures throughout the nation. Each bill rejected or enacted represents a separate policy choice. What policies are to be selected in order to assess the impact of malapportionment? It was decided to select 30 measures of state policy in three of the most important subject matters of state politics — education, welfare, and taxation. Education is the largest category of state spending. In fact, with the exception of national defense, education is the nation's largest public undertaking. The responsibility for this undertaking rests with the fifty state governments. Twelve variables reflecting important attributes of state educational systems were selected for analysis:

Public School Expenditures Per Pupil in Average Daily Attendance, 1960–61

Average Annual Salary Per Member of Instructional Staff, 1961–62

Male School Teachers as a Percent of Total, 1961–62

Pupil-Teacher Ratio: Enrollment Per Member of Instructional Staff, 1961–62

Percent of Elementary Teachers with B.A. Degree, 1962

Percent of Secondary Teachers with M.A. Degree, 1962

Drop-out Rate: High School Grads in 1963 as Percent of 9th Graders in 1959

Percent of Selective Service Examinees Disqualified for Failing Mental Test, 1962

Average Size of School District in Pupils, 1961–62

State Participation: School Revenues from State as Percent of Total School Revenue, 1961–62

Federal Participation: School Revenues from Federal Sources as Percent of Total School Revenues, 1961–62

Per Capita State Expenditures for Higher Education, 1961

Welfare expenditures are the second largest category of state expenditures. Although many state welfare efforts are federally assisted, responsibility for welfare programs and benefits rests with the fifty state governments. Ten welfare variables were selected for analysis:

Average Weekly Payment Per Recipient Unemployment Compensation, 1961

Average Monthly Payment, Old Age Assistance, 1961

Average Monthly Payment Per Family, Aid to Dependent Children, 1961

Average Monthly Payment, Aid to Blind, 1961

Average Monthly Assistance, Medical Assistance for Aged (Kerr-Mills), 1961

Per Capita State and Local Expenditures for Welfare, 1960

Per Capita State and Local Expenditures for Health and Hospitals, 1960

State Participation: Percent State Expenditures of Total Expenditures for Welfare, 1960

State Participation: Percent State Expenditures of Total Expenditures for Health and Hospitals, 1960

Federal Participation: Per Capita Federal Grants to the State for Health, Welfare and Related Purposes, 1960
•

Eight measures of tax burden and revenue structure in the states were also selected:

Total State and Local Tax Revenues Per Capita, 1960

State Revenues Per Capita, 1960

State Revenues as a Percent of Total State and Local Revenues, 1960

Percent of Total State and Local Revenues from Federal Sources, 1960

Income Tax Revenues as a Percent of Total Tax Revenues, 1961

Sales Tax Revenues as a Percent of Total Tax Revenues, 1961

Alcohol and Tobacco Tax Revenues as a Percent of Total Tax Revenues, 1961

Motor Fuel and Vehicle Tax Revenues as a Percent of Total Tax Revenues, 1961

All 30 variables were obtained for each of the fifty states.

MEASURING THE IMPACT OF
MALAPPORTIONMENT ON PUBLIC POLICY

The method chosen to assess the impact of malapportionment on party competition as well as state education, welfare, and tax policies was that of linear regression analysis. First, simple correlation coefficients were computed for the relationships between the several measures of malapportionment and the selected measures of state policy.[10] These simple coefficients show the extent to which differences in policies among the fifty states are associated with malapportionment, but they do not deal with the possibility that some other intervening variables and not malapportionment, might account for these differences. For example, if it is shown that, in general, wealthy states are better apportioned than poor states, it might be that differences in the policies of well-apportioned and malapportioned states are really a product of the fact that the former are wealthy while the latter are poor. If this were the case, policy differences between the states might be attributed to wealth rather than malapportionment. Other inter-

[10] See n. 5 for an explanation of correlation coefficients. [Ed.]

vening variables might be urbanization, industrialization, or the educational level of the state's population. Several studies have shown these socio-economic variables, all of them interrelated, to be associated with variations in state policies. In order to isolate the effect of malapportionment on state policies from the possible effects of socio-economic variables, it is necessary to control for these latter variables. This required that partial correlation coefficients be computed which would show the relationship between malapportionment and the several measures of state policies while controlling for the effect of urbanization, industrialization, income, and education. If relationships between malapportionment and state policies which appear in simple correlation coefficients disappear when socio-economic variables are controlled, then we may conclude that there is no independent relationship between malapportionment and public policy. On the other hand, if the correlation coefficients between malapportionment and state policies remain significant, even after the effects of socio-economic variables are controlled, then we may more readily conclude that malapportionment does have an independent effect on public policy.

In interpreting correlation coefficients in this study, it was decided to dismiss as insignificant those coefficients which might easily have occurred by chance. An analysis of variance test for the significance of r identifies those coefficients which could occur by chance more than 5 out of 100 times in the correlation of any set of random digits.[11] All calculations are made on the basis of observations about all 50 states (except with regard to party competition for which Nebraska and Minnesota are dropped from analysis because of their non-partisan character). Given a constant number of observations in all correlations, it is possible to state that only simple coefficients above .30 and partial coefficients above .35 are significant at the .05 level, and that all other coefficients can be dismissed as likely to be a product of chance.

MALAPPORTIONMENT AND PARTY COMPETITION

Before turning to a discussion of malapportionment and public policy, let us briefly consider the impact of malapportionment on party competition in state legislatures. Party competition in state legislatures is measured here by the percentage of total seats in each house of the legislature between 1954 and 1964 which were held by the

[11] The analysis of variance test determines the possibility that any coefficient might have been obtained by correlating sets of 50 random numbers from an imaginary infinite universe of states. It does not matter that the fifty states are a universe rather than a sample. The allusion to sampling in tests of significance is a hypothetical one. It helps us to determine whether the correlations which are obtained might have been obtained by correlating various columns of 50 digits found in a table of random numbers. See Hubert M. Blalock, *Social Statistics* (New York: McGraw-Hill, 1960), pp. 302–305.

majority party. Percentages are then inverted so that the competition scores in the house and senate of Alabama, Arkansas, Louisiana, Mississippi, and South Carolina, where the minority party did not hold a single seat during those years, are set at 0 and all other scores range upward. If it is true that malapportionment adversely affects party competition, then malapportioned legislatures should be less competitive than well-apportioned legislatures, and these differences in competition should be attributable to malapportionment rather than some other social or economic condition.

TABLE ONE

The Relationship between Malapportionment and Party Competition in State Legislatures, Controlling for the Effect of Four Socio-economic Variables

| Party competition 1954–1964 | Malapportionment | | | | | |
| | Index of representation | | Urban under-representation | | Apportionment score | |
	Simple	Partial	Simple	Partial	Simple	Partial
Lower Houses	.13	.28	.44	.35	.39	.27
Upper Houses	.06	.30	.50	.38	.43	.29

Note: Figures at the left under each heading are simple correlation coefficients for 48 states; figures at the right are fourth-order partial coefficients which control for the effect of urbanization, industrialization, income, and education.

The simple correlation coefficients in Table 1 indicate a significant relationship between the index of urban under-representation and party competition in both upper and lower chambers. Discrimination against urban areas in representation is associated with decreases in party competition. However, this relationship noticeably weakens when the effects of urbanization, industrialization, income, and education are controlled. The apportionment score also appears related to party competition in simple correlations, but this relationship falls well below accepted significance levels once socio-economic variables are controlled.

Coefficients obtained with the index of urban under-representation are higher than those obtained with either the index of representativeness or the apportionment score. Both of these latter two indices measure malapportionment in an abstract sense and not its discrimination against a particular interest. We might conclude that malapportionment itself does not affect party competition except when it operates to discriminate against urban areas. However, none of the coefficients in Table 1 are very high. Urban under-representation at best can explain less than 25 per cent of the variation among the several states in party competition. Factors other than urban under-representation must be looked to in order to account for 75 per cent of the total variation in party competition among the states.

MALAPPORTIONMENT AND PUBLIC POLICY

Table 2 shows the relationship between malapportionment and 30 separate measures of education, welfare, and tax policies in the fifty states. Simple correlation coefficients are shown at the left under each measure of malapportionment, while partial coefficients — controlling for the combined effect of urbanization, industrialization, income, and education in the states — are shown at the right. Perhaps the most striking feature of Table 2 is that none of the coefficients are very high. For the most part, variations in public policy among the states can *not* be explained by malapportionment.

In the field of education, it might be hypothesized that malapportionment results in lower per pupil expenditures, lower teachers' salaries, and higher pupil-teacher ratios, which in turn produce lower teacher qualifications, higher drop-out rates, and more selective service mental failures. The signs of the coefficients in Table 2 tend to bear out these relationships, but few of the coefficients obtain at a level of significance that would merit much confidence in these hypotheses. None of the coefficients under the index of representativeness or the apportionment score are statistically significant. This helps confirm our suspicion that malapportionment in its technical aspects has no policy relevance. Only six of the twelve simple coefficients under the index of urban under-representation are above the level of significance and only four of these hold up well once socio-economic variables are controlled. Urban under-representation is slightly related to higher pupil-teacher ratios, higher drop-out rates, and increased state and federal participation in public school finance. Yet these relationships are not so close to warrant predictions about changes in these policies once urban areas are given better representation. Per-pupil school expenditures decline with increases in malapportionment, yet this relationship is clearly a product of the fact that pupil expenditures are greater in the rural, less wealthy, agricultural states; once socio-economic variables are controlled, the relationship between pupil expenditures and malapportionment disappears. Likewise the realtionship between low teachers' salaries and malapportionment also disappears once socio-economic variables are controlled.

Few policy variables in the welfare field appear related to malapportionment. The closest relationship is between urban under-representation and state participation in the provision of health and

TABLE TWO

The Relationship between Malapportionment and State Education, Welfare and Tax Policies Controlling for the Effect of Four Socio-economic Variables

State policy measures	Index of representation		Malapportionment Urban under-representation		Apportionment score	
	Simple	Partial	Simple	Partial	Simple	Partial
Education						
Per Pupil Expenditures	.12	.06	.36	.12	.09	.01
Average Teachers' Salaries	.28	.20	.30	−.17	.01	.27
Teachers with B.A.	.24	.18	.13	.29	.12	.24
Teachers with M.A.	.07	.10	.14	.07	.09	.04
Male Teachers	.22	−.01	.15	.01	.01	−.10
Pupil-Teacher Ratio	−.11	−.23	−.31	−.40	−.15	−.21
Drop-out Rate	.06	.29	.37	.53	.15	.29
Mental Failures	−.09	−.27	−.15	−.26	−.16	−.14
Size of School Districts	−.24	−.31	−.10	−.20	−.14	−.15
State Participation	−.25	−.34	−.32	−.42	−.23	−.28
Federal Participation	−.06	−.13	−.33	−.38	−.07	−.18
Higher Education Expenditures	−.07	−.07	−.15	−.07	−.16	−.20

Welfare						
Unemployment Benefits	.17	.20	.29	.09	.13	.03
Old Age Benefits	−.01	.07	.37	.04	.01	.06
ADC Benefits	.12	.11	.49	.06	.14	.09
Blind Benefits	−.08	.16	.32	.09	.01	.02
Kerr-Mills Benefits	.13	.18	.34	.27	.05	.05
Welfare Expenditures, per Capita	.04	.05	.09	.01	−.17	.02
Health Expenditures, per Capita	−.21	.03	−.01	.01	−.08	.05
State Participation, Welfare	−.12	−.17	−.26	−.11	−.08	−.05
State Participation, Health	.10	.06	.34	.31	.17	.18
Federal Participation	.01	−.08	−.31	−.18	−.28	−.29
Taxation						
Total Taxes per Capita	.15	.05	.26	.17	.01	.09
State Revenue per Capita	−.16	−.07	−.18	−.17	−.10	−.09
State Percent of Total Revenue	−.01	−.06	−.30	−.20	−.13	−.10
Federal Percent of Total Revenue	−.03	−.09	−.36	−.23	−.04	−.08
Income Taxes	.12	.07	.14	.01	.02	.05
Sales Taxes	−.14	−.15	−.20	−.20	−.14	−.09
Alcohol & Tobacco Taxes	.14	.04	.13	−.01	.02	.07
Motor Fuel Taxes	.22	.08	.01	.04	−.19	.14

Note: Figures at the left under each heading are simple correlation coefficients for 50 states; figures at the right are fourth-order partial coefficients which control for the effect of urbanization, industrialization, income, and education.

hospital services. Yet urban under-representation accounts for only 11 percent of the total variation among the states in the extent of their participation in the health field. The level of payments to recipients of unemployment compensation, old age assistance, aid to dependent children, and aid to the medically indigent aged under Kerr-Mills laws, appears to be slightly related to urban under-representation on the basis of simple coefficients. Most of these coefficients disappear, however, once socio-economic variables are controlled. In short, the relationship between urban representation and welfare policies among the fifty states is a product of intervening socio-economic variables. There is no evidence that reapportionment will bring any noticeable liberalization of welfare policies.

Not one of the relationships between malapportionment and the eight selected tax policies are statistically significant. It is doubtful, for example, that reapportionment will bring higher tax levies. Neither total state and local taxes per capita nor total state revenues per capita are significantly related to apportionment. While federal grants constitute a larger share of the revenue of malapportioned states, this is merely a product of the fact that these states tend to be less wealthy; the relationship between federal support and malapportionment disappears when socio-economic variables are controlled. State revenues are a larger share of total revenues in malapportioned states, but this relationship also appears as a product of socio-economic variables rather than malapportionment itself. It was hypothesized that well-apportioned states would place greater reliance in their tax structure on progressive income taxation, while malapportioned states would rely more on regressive sales taxation. The signs of the coefficients in Table 2 tend to confirm this hypothesis, but the coefficients are so low, the relationships so slight, that they might easily have occurred by chance. Certainly there is no evidence that reapportionment will bring about any substantial changes in state tax structures.

It is interesting to note that the few significant policy correlations obtained in this study, were obtained with David and Eisenburg's index of urban under-representation. This index measures the degree to which a particular political interest is affected by malapportionment rather than the existence of malapportionment in the technical sense. The failure to obtain any significant policy correlates with the index of representativeness suggests that the theoretical minimum population which *could* control a legislature is not a relevant political variable. Nor does the extent to which the populations of legislative districts approach a normal statistical curve, as measured by the Schubert and Press apportionment score, appear to be a politically relevant variable. Schubert and Press rebuked earlier scholars for their technically unsophisticated measures of malapportionment. . . . Yet it turns out that David and Eisenburg with their less sophisticated measure came closer to identifying the relevant political aspect of malapportionment than Schubert and Press. For malapportionment becomes relevant when it operates to discriminate against specific political interests in a state.

CONCLUSION

On the whole, the policy choices of malapportioned legislatures are not noticeably different from the policy choices of well-apportioned legislatures. Most of the policy differences which do occur turn out to be a product of socio-economic differences among the states rather than a direct product of apportionment practices. Relationships that appear between malapportionment and public policy are so slight that reapportionment is not likely to bring about any significant policy changes. Of course, these conclusions are predicted on results obtained from analyzing 30 selected measures of public policy in three separate fields — education, welfare, and taxation. Conceivably malapportionment could have a more direct effect on some area of policy-making that was not investigated. However, expenditures for welfare and education, the liberality of welfare benefits, teachers' qualifications and salaries, the quality of public education, the tax burden, the revenue structure, and the extent of state participation in education, health, and welfare, are certainly among the most important issues in state politics. And apportionment practices seem to have little impact on the outcome of these issues.

At this point it seems appropriate to enter a caveat regarding the conclusions that can be drawn from these operations. All that has been shown is that reapportionment is not likely to have a direct impact on party competition or on certain policy outcomes. This is *not* to say that reapportionment will have no effect on state political systems or processes. Quantification necessitates a simplification of what may be a very complex question. The consequences of reapportionment may be so subtle and diverse that they defy quantitative measurement. Perhaps the consequences in each state will vary so much that direct interstate comparisons are inappropriate. Certainly we need more refined analyses of the impact of apportionment systems on state political processes and policy outcomes; we especially need more "before and after" studies of reapportionment. But these operations do succeed in challenging the easy assumptions and simple generalizations about the effects of malapportionment on public policy, and they caution us not to expect major policy changes in the wake of reapportionment.

How can we account for the bitter political battles fought over reapportionment in many states if malapportionment really has little effect on public policy? Perhaps the explanation lies in the distinction between the potential for power and the exercise of power. Certainly mal-apportionment overweights rural representation in legislatures. Mal-apportionment may give rural legislators a potential for power over their urban counterparts, *but* if they do not vote together with a high degree of unity to oppose urban interests on actual questions of public policy, their "power" may be more hypothetical than real. Legislative control can change hands and still leave policies unchanged if there are few policy differences between those placed in power and those dispossessed. Suburban voters, for example, may be just as conservative as the rural voters whose voice they may replace. In addition, divisions other than rural-versus-urban may characterize much of the legislative process: divisions between the parties, between a Governor's supporters and his opponents, between economic interests and organized groups, between liberals and conservatives, between labor and management, between regions of a state, and so forth. Reapportionment could change the distribution of power between rural and urban constituencies and yet have so subtle an effect on these other divisions that few policy changes would result. In short, even rural-urban divisions are affected by reapportionment, these divisions are only one of many types of legislative divisions.

These conclusions need not moderate enthusiasm for reapportionment. The moral case for equality of representation is as compelling as it ever was. The impact on reapportionment of public policy, however, may be somewhat less sweeping than many expect.

Civil Rights Today

The varied problems of civil rights and equal protection of the laws are illustrated in the Report of the United States Commission on Civil Rights (1963). The *Brown* decisions dealt only with the problem of segregation in public education. Other significant problem areas include voting, the administration of justice, housing, employment, and generally the extent to which the Negro and members of other minority groups are treated equally in whatever endeavors they undertake. After a great deal of debate and a lengthy Senate filibuster, the Civil Rights Act of 1964 was passed. This was the first major civil rights bill since Reconstruction days. The 1964 Act strengthened those of 1957 and 1960 by extending voting rights. Moreover, it barred discrimination on grounds of race, color, religion, or national origin in public accommodations, if the discrimination was supported by state laws or action, if the lodgings were provided to transient guests or interstate travelers, or if the firm involved was engaged in interstate commerce. Under this public accommodations section (Title II), restaurants, motion picture houses, theaters, hotels, and numerous other "public" establishments had to provide equal facilities. The 1964 law also contained provisions strengthening the Civil Rights Commission, giving the Attorney General new authority to initiate suits to bring about desegregation, and provided for equal employment opportunity. The scope of the Act is extensive. Its passage illustrates the reluctance of civil rights groups to rely solely upon judicial doctrine to bring about desegregation. However, enforcement of the Civil Rights Bill is to take place primarily through the courts. This can be a slow and expensive process. *Potentially* the Act can remedy many of the deprivations of equal rights found throughout the United States.

On August 6, 1965 President Lyndon Johnson signed the 1965 Voting Rights Act into law. This bill provided that the Attorney General could initiate suits to suspend literacy tests and other devices used to discriminate in federal, state, or local elections or primary elections, if less than 50 per cent of the eligible Negroes were registered in any state or political subdivision. The 50 per cent minimum was set to guarantee that discrimination clearly existed before the federal government could take action. If such discrimination could be demonstrated, federal examiners could be assigned under the terms of the act to conduct the registration of the voters. The 1965 law strengthened the potential authority of the federal government to protect voting rights. The conditions that led to both the 1964 and 1965 laws, as well as the complexities of the problem of protecting civil rights, are discussed next.

59

REPORT OF THE UNITED STATES COMMISSION ON CIVIL RIGHTS

VOTING

For most citizens of the United States, the exercise of the right to vote is the only personal participation they have in political self-government. Yet, for almost 100 years, this fundamental right has been denied to many Americans on the wholly arbitrary and irrelevant ground of race.

When Congress established the Commission on Civil Rights in 1957, it directed the Commission to investigate formal allegations that citizens were being denied the right to vote by reason of their color, race, religion, or national origin. In the 6 years since 1957, the Commission has conducted hearings, investigations, surveys, and related research. Its findings reveal clearly that the promise of the 14th and 15th amendments to the Constitution remains unfulfilled.

In its 1959 Report, the Commission noted the lack of vigorous enforcement of Federal laws designed to eliminate racial restrictions on voting. The Department of Justice since 1960, has initiated and sustained a determined attack on voter discrimination. The President, in public pronouncements, has made clear the immorality of denying the ballot to American citizens simply because of color. Yet, while few persons have sought to justify such discrimination on either moral or legal grounds, the right to vote is still denied many Americans solely because of their race.

After 5 years of Federal litigation, it is fair to conclude that case-by-case proceedings, helpful as they have been in isolated localities, have not provided a prompt or adequate remedy for widespread discriminatory denials of the right to vote. Two recent cases, as yet undecided, are aimed at discriminatory practices in the entire State of Mississippi and a large portion of Louisiana. If decided in favor of the Government, they will represent a major step forward. Even then, however, enforcement and registration will have to proceed on a county-by-county basis with many of the same difficulties manifested in the more limited suits.

In 1957, Congress enacted the first Civil Rights Act since 1875. One salient provision authorized the Federal Government to bring civil suits to end discriminatory voting practices. The Civil Rights Act of 1960 strengthened the earlier act by providing that States, as well as registrars, could be sued. It also required the preservation of voting records for 22 months and permitted the appointment of Federal referees to register voters. To implement the referee provisions, a judicial finding of a "pattern or practice" of discrimination by registration or election officials is required. Even where a "pattern or practice" is found, the court still has full discretion to leave the registration process in the hands of the officials who have discriminated in the past. If the court does appoint a referee, the local registrar would not be displaced, since the referee can only register applicants who have applied to the registrar and been rejected.

In 1961, this Commission found that substantial numbers of Negro citizens had been denied the right to vote in 100 counties of 8 Southern States. However, it was too early at that time to make a meaningful evaluation of what the new laws could accomplish in those counties.

That evaluation is the subject of this chapter of the 1963 Commission report. In 1956, the last year before the passage of legislation to secure the right to vote, about 5 percent of the voting-age Negroes in the 100 counties were registered to vote. Despite the subsequent passage of two civil rights acts, the institution of 36 voting rights suits by the Department of Justice, and the operation of several private registration drives, Negro registration in these counties has risen only to 8.3 percent. The most recent reliable statistics indicate that only 55,711 of the 668,082 voting-age Negroes in the 100 counties have access to the ballot.

The reasons for the low rate of increase in Negro registration appear to include the high cost of litigation, the slowness of the judicial process on both the trial and appellate level, the inherent complexity of supervising the enforcement of decrees, intimidation and reprisals against Negroes who seek to vote, and the employment of diverse techniques by State and local officials to subvert the Constitution of the United States.

The 100 counties in which the Commission found voting denials in 1961 amounted to but 9 percent of the total number of counties in the 11 States of the former Confederacy. However, these 100 counties contained nearly a third of all Negroes of voting age in the 11 States. In view of the present evidence, the Commission was overly conservative in finding denials in only these areas. Eleven of the 40 counties in which the Department of Justice has filed suits alleging discrimination or intimidation by individual defendants are not within the 100. In addition, the broad-gage litigation in Louisiana and Mississippi challenges the application of certain State laws and regulations in all 82 counties in Mississippi and in 21 of Louisiana's 64 parishes. Proposed legislation authorizing the appointment of Federal voting referees where less than 15 percent of the Negro voting-age population is registered would cover 900,000 potential voters in over 250 counties.

Techniques of Discrimination. The practices used by voter registrars today to prevent Negro enfranchisement are the same as those described in the *1961 Voting Report.* An examination of voting complaints filed with the Commission during 1962 and 1963 demonstrates this, as do Justice Department voting suits filed during the intervening period.

Several methods were cited in 1961. One was the discriminatory application of legal qualifications, such as literacy tests, constitutional interpretation tests, calculation of age to the exact day, and requirements of good moral character. Others involved the use of plainly arbitrary procedures. These included requirement of vouchers or some other unduly technical method of identification, rejection for insignificant errors in filling out forms, failure to notify applicants of rejection, imposition of delaying tactics, and discrimination in giving assistance to applicants.

The Commission pointedly warned of a third possible form of discrimination. This has occurred in areas where virtually all the voting-age whites have been registered regardless of qualifications while Negroes have been systematically rejected. If litigation or a change in policy should result in the adopting or strict standards and procedures which would be equally applied to all applicants, the results of past discrimination would be perpetuated by virtue of the fact that the burden of the new requirements would fall on Negro applicants.

During 1962 and the first 7 months of 1963, the Commission received 104 voting complaints. No novel techniques of discrimination were involved. All of those cited in the *1961 Voting Report* were included except the requirement of calculating age to the precise day. The most common were the discriminatory application of legal standards, especially interpretations of "good moral character," and arbitrary procedures such as delay and refusing to notify applicants of their success or failure. Several complaints involved reprisals or intimidation by private citizens and public officials.

During 1962 and 1963, the Justice Department filed 22 voting suits. Of these, eight were directed at reprisals or intimidation. The remaining 14 were based on practices described in the *1961 Voting Report*. One challenged the registration laws as being inherently discriminatory in nature. The others alleged unequal application of standards to whites and Negroes and in some cases resort to delaying tactics.

The danger foreseen by the Commission that prior discrimination might be perpetuated where extremely strict standards are adopted has materialized. To counteract this "freezing" of the rolls, the Department has asked in every appropriate suit for decrees which would require registrars to apply the same standards to future Negro applicants that they had applied to whites in the past. Encountering a reluctance on the part of the district courts to issue such orders, the Department has appealed adverse rulings in three States to the Fifth Circuit Court of Appeals.

The constitutional argument for refusing to allow past discrimination to be permanently frozen into the rolls has been articulated by the Fifth Circuit Court of Appeals:

> Obviously a blanket requirement that all persons who have never paid the poll tax before, that being a relatively small percentage of white people and all Negroes, who now desire to pay their poll tax for the first time must see the Sheriff personally operates unequally and discriminatorily against Negroes. . . . Sheriff Dogan's new instructions by necessary result re-create and perpetuate the very discrimination which prevailed under his former instructions and practices.[1]

[1] *United States* v. *Dogan*, 314 F 2d 767, 772–73 (5th Cir. 1963).

EDUCATION

Nearly 10 years after the Supreme Court decision in the *School Segregation Cases,* Negro schoolchildren still attend segregated schools in all parts of the Nation.

In the South, most schools continue to be segregated by official policy, notwithstanding the Supreme Court's finding that segregation on the basis of race cannot constitutionally be enforced. But in the North and West, school segregation is widespread because of existing segregated housing patterns and the practice of assigning pupils to neighborhood schools. Whether this northern-style segregation is unconstitutional has yet to be considered by the Supreme Court, but the contention that it runs counter to the equal protection clause is being vigorously asserted.

Protests in the North and West. In the North and West, Negro protests until recently took the form of petition and personal appearance before school boards. However, segregated schools have now become targets of public demonstrations. The metropolitan area of New York City, which includes northern New Jersey, has been the center of demonstrations, picketing, sit-ins, and school boycotts since the summer of 1961. Englewood, N.J., has had periodic rallies featuring Negro celebrities, sit-ins in the school superintendent's office, picketing of the Governor's office in Trenton, school boycotts, and sit-ins in a white school by Negro children assigned to a nearby Negro school. Negroes have picketed in suburban Philadelphia and in Boston, Chicago, and St. Louis. In Boston, some 3,000 junior and senior high school students stayed out of school for a day and attended workshops in neighborhood churches and social centers where they were instructed in Negro history, U.S. Government and civil rights, and the principles of nonviolence. In St. Louis, 30 parents and ministers blocked the departure from a West End school of 12 buses containing about 500 children who were being transported to under-utilized white-schools miles away, where they would attend all-Negro classes. Two weeks later, 2,000 Negroes marched on the board of education headquarters carrying signs saying "Freedom Now" and "Don't Teach Segregation."

The increase in the nonwhite population in the cities of the North and West since 1950 has had a severe impact on the public school systems. Besides a higher birth rate and the white exodus to the suburbs where housing is not generally available to Negroes, the factors creating school segregation include the arrival of nonwhite newcomers who tend to settle in those parts of the city where nonwhites already live. This is due partly to low economic status, partly to a desire to be near friends or relatives, and partly to their inability to find housing else-where. An additional factor in some places is the large and dispropor-tionately white enrollment in private and parochial schools. All these factors make it difficult to achieve racial heterogeneity in the public schools even when a school board desires to do so.

In the 16 school systems in the North and West on which the Com-mission assembled data, the percentage of nonwhite pupils greatly ex-ceeded the proportion of nonwhites in the total population. On the whole, the percentage of minority-group children in the public ele-mentary schools is about double the percentage of nonwhites in the total population.

The proportionate size of the minority group enrollment does not entirely determine the percentage of segregated schools. At the ele-mentary level, Chicago, with the same proportional minority group enrollment as New York, has over 60 percent more segregated schools. Chicago has tenaciously confined its Negro pupils to neighborhood schools, refused to rezone attendance areas on the fringes of the con-centrated Negro residential areas, and declined to relax its rules for-bidding transfers from area of residence. In contrast, New York City has made strenuous efforts to limit segregation in its schools. Its open enrollment program enables Negro and Puerto Rican pupils to trans-fer out of schools in which they are enrolled in excessive proportions to predominantly white schools. It also provides transportation for those electing to do so. . . .

   Desegregation in the South. While housing patterns cre-ate segregation in the North and West, most schools in the South con-tinue to be segregated by official policy. Even in ostensibly desegre-gated school districts, most schools are still segregated.

There are 6,196 school districts in the 17 Southern and Border States. Of these, 3,052 have both Negro and white students. A total of 979 or 32.1 percent of these biracial districts have policies or practices permitting the admission of Negroes to formerly all-white schools. Yet only 8 percent of the Negro pupils in the South attend schools with white children.

In the fall of 1962, 52 districts were desegregated for the first time. There were 31 in the previous year. Thirteen of the newly desegre-gated districts acted under court order, although, in many of the oth-ers, legal action was pending or threatened.

The Border States (Delaware, Kentucky, Maryland, Missouri, Okla-homa, and West Virginia) and the District of Columbia account for the bulk of desegregation to date. Of the 979 desegregated school dis-tricts, 702 lie in the border areas. Similarly, over 251,000 (94.7 percent) of the approximately 265,000 Negro students who attend school with whites in the South do so in the border areas. South Carolina, Alabama, and Mississippi, by contrast, have no Negroes attending school with white students below the college level.

Progress continues to be slow in the South. The Supreme Court's warning that a pace found acceptable for desegregation 9 years ago will not necessarily satisfy the Court today soon may be reflected in lower court rulings. Similar changes may flow from the Court's declaration of June 1963 that "no official transfer plan or provision of which racial segregation is the inevitable consequence may stand under the Fourteenth Amendment."

JUSTICE

The rights of citizens to speak freely, to assemble peaceably, and to petition government for the redress of grievances are guaranteed by the first amendment to the Constitution. These rights are protected against State encroachment by the 14th amendment. Official actions taken to stop recent civil rights protest demonstrations in the name of peace and order often have infringed upon these protected rights.

To determine the extent of these infringements, and to study the dilemma often caused by the need to guarantee private rights while maintaining public order the Commission focused its administration of justice study on five cities where protest demonstrations have taken place. They are Birmingham, Ala.; Cairo, Ill.; Baton Rouge, La.; Jackson, Miss.; and Memphis, Tenn. In its study, the Commission found that existing legal remedies for blocking official interference with legitimate demonstrations are insufficient and that protests against civil rights deprivations are being frustrated. The study also demonstrated that effective legal remedies must be fashioned if unwarranted official interference is not to result in the total suppression of constitutional rights to protest.

During its current term, the Commission also investigated the participation of Negroes in the administration of justice. The Commission found that in many places, Negroes have been discriminated against as lawyers; as law enforcement, court, and prison employees; and as prisoners. The results of this study also are presented in this chapter.

Civil Rights Protests and State Action. On February 1, 1960, four college students in Greensboro, North Carolina, entered a variety store, made several purchases, sat down at the lunch counter, ordered coffee, and were refused service because they were Negroes. They remained in their seats until the store closed. In the spring and summer of 1960, young people, both white and Negro, participated in similar protests against segregation and discrimination wherever it was to be found. They sat in white libraries, waded at white beaches, and slept in the lobbies of white hotels. Many were arrested for trespassing, disturbing the peace, and disobeying police officers who ordered them off the premises. Thus began the sweeping protest movement against entrenched practices of segregation.

Since the equal protection clause of the 14th amendment prohibits State-enforced segregation, it is clear that convictions under a statute or ordinance requiring segregation cannot be sustained. In general, officials who acted to suppress demonstrations in the cities studied did not attempt to apply such laws directly. But any arrest, even without a conviction, operates as a sanction, since the imprisoned protester still must stay in jail or post bail, retain counsel, and defend himself.

The Supreme Court, following the *School Segregation Cases,* has consistently held that State and local governments may not segregate publicly owned or operated facilities. It has recently held that a municipality may not arrest and prosecute Negroes for peaceably seeking the use of city-owned and -operated facilities. But in both Jackson and Memphis, police arrested protesters seeking desegregated use of public facilities. The charge in most of these cases was breach of the peace or disorderly conduct. In finding the protesters guilty, a city judge in Jackson found that, while they had been orderly, their conduct could have provoked a breach of the peace by others. However, the mere "possibility of disorder by others cannot justify exclusion of persons from a place if they otherwise have a constitutional right (founded upon the Equal Protection Clause) to be present." The exercise of the first amendment freedoms of speech and assembly cannot be abridged "unless shown likely to produce a clear and present danger of a serious substantive evil that rises far above public inconvenience, annoyance, or unrest."

The right to use vehicles and terminal facilities in interstate commerce on a nonsegregated basis is another right that has been established by Federal court decisions and specific orders of the Interstate Commerce Commission. In Baton Rouge, Memphis, Jackson, and Birmingham, when protesters sought to use such facilities, they were arrested. They were charged, not with violation of segregation laws, but with breach of the peace. In Jackson, more than 300 demonstrators were arrested during the 1961 Freedom Rides. Local authorities claimed that they committed a breach of the peace by refusing to obey police commands to leave the interstate bus terminal's segregated waiting rooms. The riders claimed their Federal rights peaceably to seek and obtain unsegregated service as did protesters in the other cities. An early application to the Supreme Court for an injunction to stay the State criminal prosecutions in Jackson was denied. The lengthy route through the Mississippi courts is still being pursued some two and a half years later.

The constitutionality of arrests and prosecutions of those who seek desegregated service at privately owned facilities open to the public has also been questioned. These protests have included lunch counter sit-ins, which have occurred throughout the country and in four of the five cities studied by the Commission. While this type of demonstration has formed only a part of the total civil rights protest movement, it has presented one of the most difficult constitutional problems arising from protest activities. The question these cases raise is whether the arrest and conviction of protesters peacefully seeking such desegregated service represents unlawful "State action" under the 14th amendment.

Having disposed of the first sit-in cases on other grounds, the Supreme Court in May 1963 approached the question in a series of sit-in cases from Greenville, S.C.; New Orleans, Birmingham, and Durham. The protesters had been convicted, not for breach of the peace, but for trespass on the private property of those who operated restaurants and lunch counters. Confronted with an apparent conflict between the proprietors' property rights and the protesters' right to be free from State-enforced segregation, the Court found that State action was involved and reversed the convictions.

The Greenville and Birmingham cases involved ordinances requiring operators of eating places to segregate. Although not directly invoked, these ordinances were found to have left such operators no choice but to segregate. The Court held that the use of the State's criminal processes to arrest and convict the protesters had the effect of enforcing the segregation ordinances and was consequently prohibited State action in violation of the equal protection clause of the 14th amendment. In New Orleans, where there was no law requiring segregation in eating places, the Court ruled that city officials' public statements that attempts to secure desegregated service would not be permitted had the same effect as segregation ordinances.

These decisions have removed virtually all doubt about the validity of trespass convictions in situations such as Birmingham, where there are laws requiring segregated eating facilities. Moreover, the principle of the New Orleans case apparently applies to situations such as the Commission found in Baton Rouge and Jackson, where city officials were publicly committed to using State criminal processes to maintain segregation. But the applicability of the 1963 sit-in decisions to situations such as Cairo is not clear. Here, the voice of the State has clearly spoken for desegregation. The Mayor of Cairo has personally urged proprietors to obey the Illinois law prohibiting discrimination in places of public accommodation. Yet students were arrested for trespass when they sought service at a private restaurant.

Many cities either do not have or have repealed segregation ordinances. Many officials either have never made or have stopped making public statements committing the State to maintenance of segregation. This has brought to the Court the broad question of whether the State has any right to arrest and prosecute protesters for seeking equal access to places of public accommodation.

In these situations, the protesters acted to secure immediate desegregated use of a facility. But different problems may be presented when protesters engage in street demonstrations against discrimination in general. One such incident occurred in March 1961, when 187 Negro students marched on the South Carolina State House to make their grievances known to the public and the legislature, which was then in session. Refusing to disperse, they were arrested and convicted for breach of the peace. Their appeals were decided by the Supreme Court in February 1963. The Court found that the protesters had been orderly, that they had not obstructed pedestrian or vehicular traffic, and that there had been no clear and present threat of violence by bystanders which the police were unable to control. Reversing the convictions, the Court held that "in arresting, convicting, and punishing the petitioners under the circumstances disclosed by this record, South Carolina infringed the petitioners' constitutionally protected rights of free speech, free assembly, and freedom to petition for redress of grievances."

Application of this Supreme Court decision to events in the five cities is difficult because the material facts differ in each case. On many occasions Memphis and Cairo officials did not interfere with mass demonstrations on public streets. Cairo police arrested protesters under an ordinance requiring parade permits which was enacted after the demonstrations started. The Illinois attorney general joined in an NAACP suit challenging the constitutionality of the ordinance. State and local officials and protest leaders later consented to dismissal of the suit on the understanding that the charges against the arrested protesters would be dismissed and the ordinance would not again be invoked against peaceful street demonstrations. Baton Rouge officials did not interfere with mass street demonstrations during the 1960 protests. In 1961, official policy changed. Conduct that had been permitted in 1960 resulted in arrests.

The official policy in both Jackson and Birmingham, throughout the period covered by the Commission's study, was one of suppressing street demonstrations. While police action in each arrest may not have been improper, the total pattern of official action, as indicated by the public statements of city officials, was to maintain segregation and to suppress protests. The police followed that policy and they were usually supported by local prosecutors and courts.

Discrimination in Processes of Justice. Denials of equal protection may arise not only from attempts by officials to enforce segregation but also in the processes of justice when an official treats a person differently because of his color, race, religion, or national origin.

In civil rights demonstrations, the role of the policeman has been significant; his actions often speak for the community. When a policeman acts to deprive a person of his constitutional rights, he violates Federal law. Moreover, police inaction which results in a failure to provide adequate protection to persons asserting their constitutional rights may also constitute a violation of Federal law. When Montgomery police failed to provide protection for the Freedom Riders in 1961, a Federal district judge declared, "The failure of the defendant law enforcement officers to enforce the law in this case clearly amounts to unlawful State action in violation of the Equal Protection Clause of the Fourteenth Amendment."

Testimony at the Commission's Memphis hearings disclosed that none of the protesters there was subjected to physical mistreatment by the police. Nor were there any allegations of lack of police protection for demonstrators. On one occasion in Cairo, protesters complained of police beatings and the use of tear gas. They also charged that State police and sheriff's deputies failed in another instance to protect demonstrators against a crowd of violent whites. Commission investigations found some evidence to support these allegations; however, such instances were not part of a pattern of action by law enforcement officials in those cities.

There have been few complaints of police mistreatment of protesters in Baton Rouge. In fact, a leader of the 1960 protests praised the police for their conduct. But in 1961, students complained of police misconduct in dispersing a protest assembly and of mistreatment of arrested demonstrators by jail guards.

The situation was different in Jackson and Birmingham. There, the Commission found a pattern of police abuse of civil rights protesters. In Jackson, there were continuing police efforts to disperse by force many forms of demonstrations and there was evidence of mistreatment of students, both in the county jail and State penitentiary.

Evidence also showed there was continuing abuse of protesters by Birmingham police. In 1963, dogs, clubs, and firehoses were used to disperse mass demonstrations. Violent reaction by Negroes followed. The reaction was directed not against white bystanders, but against the city police.

Prosecutors claimed that Negro students received the same treatment in the criminal process as anyone else. But in October 1962 the district attorney in Baton Rouge told Commission investigators:

> I'm going to make it just as hard on these outside agitators as I can. And I don't know a judge or official [in Baton Rouge] who doesn't agree with me.

His statement was addressed primarily to the fixing of bail requirements for arrested demonstrators. Discriminatory use of bail requirements raises a question of denial of equal protection.

In neither Memphis nor Birmingham did bail requirements present
a serious problem, although the aggregate bond cost was high when
mass arrests were made. In Cairo, most students were released on their
own recognizance. The 1961 mass arrests of Freedom Riders in Jackson presented a serious bail problem. Surety bonds were required, and
exhaustive efforts by protest leaders were unsuccessful in finding a
company anywhere in the country to write the bonds. The result was
that most of the riders spent extended periods in the county jail and
State penitentiary. . . .

Participation in Agencies of Justice. Participation by
Negroes in the agencies of justice as police officers, prosecutors, judges,
jurors, and other officials and employees has often been prohibited or
limited. This exclusion raises equal protection issues; so does segregation of Negroes in justice facilities such as police stations, court houses,
jails, and prisons. Such segregation has been widely practiced in many
parts of the country. Concerning such practices, the Commission
pointed out in its *1961 Report:* "This can hardly contribute to impar-
tiality in the administration of justice or to respect for the agencies of
law on the part of those who are excluded."

The Negro protest movement also has highlighted the inequalities
suffered by Negro lawyers in the administration of justice. Thousands
of demonstrators have required the services of legal counsel. The
greatest burden of providing these services has fallen upon local Negro
lawyers.

In order to determine whether counsel was available to civil rights
protesters and whether their counsel suffered any special difficulties
because of involvement in civil rights litigation, the Commission conducted a study based upon a questionnaire survey of 17 Southern and
Border States and upon field investigations in the five cities where
large-scale protest demonstrations had occurred. Questionnaires were
sent to 3,555 lawyers, of whom about one-eighth were Negroes. There
were 242 responses from Negro lawyers and 1,081 responses from
whites, constituting a total return of 37.2 percent. Among the respondents, only 14 percent (184 lawyers) answered that they had represented Negro clients in civil rights cases within the preceding 8 years.
One-third of this group reported having suffered threats of physical
violence, loss of clients, or social ostracism as a result.

The Commission's study shows that Negro lawyers have played an
active role far out of proportion to their numbers in handling civil
rights cases in the South in recent years. Many have suffered reprisals
as a result.

In those same States, Negro lawyers have faced difficulty in gaining admission to law schools, impediments to admission to the bar, and severe limitations on their professional association and contacts.

In the five cities where the Commission conducted field investigations, protesters who were arrested and prosecuted were in most cases represented by Negro lawyers. The Commission's survey disclosed that, among the respondents who had taken civil rights cases, 86 percent were Negroes.

Between 1940 and 1960, the number of Negro lawyers in the Southern and Border States increased by 75 percent. Yet, in proportion to the total Negro population, the number is still very small. Several factors appear to contribute to this situation. Until World War II, nearly all of these States not only excluded Negroes from publicly supported law schools, but also failed to establish segregated institutions. They provided funds for a limited number of qualified Negroes to receive their legal education elsewhere, mainly in the North.

Twenty-seven percent of the questionnaire responses from Negro lawyers claimed that "occasionally" or "infrequently" Negroes were excluded from admission to the bar on racial grounds. Most complaints referred to the discriminatory screening of bar examination applicants or to examination grading based upon a racial quota. However, only 6 percent of the white respondents indicated that racial discrimination has been a factor in limiting Negro admissions to the bar. Most of these answers cited inadequate educational and economic backgrounds as the underlying factor.

Most of the Negro lawyers are almost entirely dependent on Negro clientele. The economic position of the rural Negro is such that it is often impossible for a Negro lawyer to subsist professionally in smaller southern towns. Added to this is the problem, related by many of the Negro respondents, that Negro clients often seek out white lawyers because they feel them to be more capable, or because they feel that Negro lawyers are at a disadvantage against a white adversary and before a white judge and jury.

The opportunities for professional contacts and continuing legal education that attend bar association membership appear to be severely limited for Negro lawyers. Except where State bar association membership is a prerequisite to practice, exclusion of Negroes from State and local associations seems to be common throughout the Southern and Border States. Even where Negroes are admitted to membership, they are usually excluded or discouraged from participation in social and educational programs sponsored by the associations.

Negro Employment by Agencies of Justice. To determine the extent of Negro employment in agencies of justice, the Commission sent questionnaires to the chief justice of the State's highest court, to the attorney general, to the superintendent of State police and to the administrators of the State's prison and parole agencies in every State in the Nation. Questionnaires were sent to the court of original criminal jurisdiction, the prosecutor, and the sheriff in each county in the United States with a Negro population of over 5,000. Questionnaires also were sent to police departments in all cities with a Negro population of over 5,000.

Police departments of 124 Southern and Border State cities responded, as did 106 departments in Northern and Western States. The responses show that, on the basis of population proportion, relatively few Negroes are employed in northern and western departments. In southern and border departments, their participation is generally token.

In its study of Negro employment by the county sheriffs' departments the Commission received questionnaire responses from 170 departments in Southern and Border States and from 102 departments in the North and West. The questionnaires disclosed a common practice in the South of assigning Negro sheriff's deputies, as was the case with Negro police officers, to law enforcement duties in segregated areas. Many departments also place limitations on the Negro deputy's authority to apprehend white suspects. Such limitations were found to be almost nonexistent in the North and West.

State police and highway patrols employed almost no Negroes. One Negro officer was reported in the 12 Southern and Border States which responded. There were 33 Negro officers found in 19 Northern and Western States.

The Commission's survey disclosed that Negro employment in county prosecutors' offices throughout the country was extremely limited. In 289 counties in Southern and Border States, only 7 Negro lawyers, 3 investigators, and 2 stenographers were reported. Among the Northern and Western States, 103 prosecutors responded. Their offices employed 35 Negro investigators and 88 secretaries. Twenty-seven counties employed Negro lawyers. Many with substantial Negro populations employed no Negroes in any professional or administrative capacity.

The Department of Justice serves the Federal Government as prosecuting agency. There are U.S. attorneys' offices in each Federal judicial district. Three Negroes were serving as U.S. attorneys. At the close of 1962, 35 of 778 assistant U.S. attorneys were Negroes. Other offices in the Department employed 1,372 attorneys, of whom 34 were Negro. While Negro participation is low, it has increased substantially since 1960.

Negro employment in State courts was rare in the Southern and Border States. No Negro judges or court clerks were reported. Among the positions of jury commissioner, bailiff, and secretary, Negroes occupied 3 percent or fewer of the jobs. For probation officers, the percentage was slightly higher.

In the North and West, Negro employment in State courts was considerably higher. This was especially so in California, Indiana, Iowa, Minnesota, and New Mexico. In probation positions, Negro representation was particularly high.

The Commission also surveyed Negro employment in Federal courts. The Administrative Office of the United States Courts advised that "each court has its own employment practices." In all Federal courts responding from Southern and Border States, no Negro judges or Negro court employees were found with the exceptions of one probation officer in the Southern District of West Virginia and a few court criers. In courts in the District of Columbia, Negroes served as judges, clerks, secretaries and clerical workers, bailiffs, and probation officers. However, among Federal courts reporting from the North and West, little Negro employment was found.

At State adult correctional institutions in Southern and Border States, Negro employment was rare. Two-thirds of the small number reported served in Maryland. In Arkansas, Alabama, Georgia, Kentucky, Louisiana, Mississippi, Oklahoma, and Tennessee, no Negroes were found in administrative, professional, or clerical positions or as correctional officers. At juvenile institutions — where separate facilities are more often established for each race — Negro employment was considerably higher. Among adult institutions reporting from Northern and Western States, about one-thirtieth of the administrative, professional, clerical, and correctional officer positions were filled by Negroes. Negro employment at juvenile institutions accounted for about 12 percent of the positions tabulated.

Token employment of Negroes also was found at Federal correctional institutions in Southern and Border States. The Commission received data from 15 facilities with 2,390 employees, of whom only 70 were Negro. At 18 Federal institutions in the North and West, Negro employment was slightly lower. Only at the facilities operated by the Bureau of Prisons, the Department of Correction, and the Department of Public Welfare in the District of Columbia was there substantial Negro employment.

Segregation in Facilities. While discrimination exists in employment, segregation occurs in the facilities of justice. Criminal suspects are usually first detained in police department jails or lockups. Of 114 departments in Southern and Border States responding to the Commission survey, 83 percent reported racial segregation in these facilities. In contrast to this were the responses of 105 northern and western departments, 95 percent of which reported no segregation.

Comparable figures were received on segregation in county jails, which are customarily used for the detention of persons awaiting trial or serving short sentences. Of 152 responses from Southern and Border States, 87 percent reported segregated facilities; 83 percent of the respondents in the North and West (99 counties) reported no segregation.

Responses also were received from State adult and juvenile correctional institutions throughout the country. These included reception and assignment centers, prisons, work farms and camps, reformatories and training schools. A total of 145 institutions reported from Southern and Border States. Of these, 93 were completely segregated. Forty-one institutions maintained partial segregation in housing and in one or more other areas such as dining facilities and work details. Only 13 institutions reported no segregation. All of these are in the States of Delaware, Kentucky, Maryland, Missouri, Virginia, and West Virginia. Of 236 institutions reporting from Northern and Western States, 220 were totally desegregated. The remainder segregated living quarters.

As late as 1954, inmates were segregated throughout the Federal correctional system, particularly in the use of living quarters, dining areas, and auditoriums. Today, all Federal institutions are completely desegregated with the exception of a single cell block at the U.S. Penitentiary in Atlanta, where desegregation is underway. Administrators of Federal facilities in the South reported that very few problems attended desegregation and that the process has assisted in rehabilitation.

Clerks of criminal courts of original jurisdiction in the counties surveyed reported on racial segregation in courthouse facilities. In Southern and Border States, courtroom segregation was reported in 17 percent of the returns, waiting room segregation in 14 percent, segregation in jury boxes in 5 percent, and segregation of rest rooms in 63 percent. In responses from counties in the North and West, no racial segregation in any courthouse facilities was reported.

In April 1963, the Supreme Court reversed the conviction of a Negro found guilty of contempt in a Richmond, Va., traffic court for refusing to sit on the side of the courtroom reserved for Negroes. The Court said:

> Such a conviction cannot stand, for it is no longer open to question that a State may not constitutionally require segregation of public facilities. . . . State-compelled segregation in a court of justice is a manifest violation of the State's duty to deny no one the equal protection of its laws.

CHAPTER ELEVEN

Economic and Social Policy

The federal government has always had an important economic role to play. The nature of this role has varied during different periods of history, but the political and economic realms have never been completely separate.

The Economic Role of Government

There are many facets to the relationship between government and the economy. The government acts both as promoter and regulator of economic interests. Economic interdependence has resulted throughout our history from demands being made upon the government to act as an umpire for conflicting interests. Regulation has not been established by unilateral government decree but by governmental response to pressure of various kinds from the community.

60 MICHAEL D. REAGAN

THE EXPANDING ECONOMIC ROLE OF GOVERNMENT

. . . [T]he economic role of government has been enlarged many times over in our day. The ubiquity of this development in all economically advanced or advancing nations is sufficient proof against the unenlightened conservative's easy explanation that it is all the fault of "that man in the White House," whether Roosevelt, Tru-

From Michael D. Reagan, "The Expanding Economic Role of Government," *The Managed Economy*. Copyright © 1963, by Oxford University Press, Inc. Reprinted by permission of the publisher.

man, Eisenhower, or Kennedy. And . . . the limits of essential intervention have not yet been reached. This will become clearer as we turn
now to brief description of the traditional, the more recent, and the
just-emerging roles of government (particularly the national government) that arise from the necessity for social control of economic life.

Traditional Economic Roles

The role of government which is least often acknowledged by businessmen, although it is the most hoary and traditional of
all, is as promoter and, especially since the 1930's, customer of private
enterprise. . . . Protective tariffs, land grants to railroads, and Alexander Hamilton's funding of the Revolutionary War debt, exemplify
earlier American contributions of government to business growth, as
does the Supreme Court's reading laissez faire into the Constitution in
the period from 1880 to 1937.

In the twentieth century, business promotion has been the direct
goal of many measures usually thought of as "regulatory." The Transportation Act of 1920, the subsidies of the Civil Aeronautics Act, and
the aid to railroads given in the 1958 legislation, for example, fall into
this category, as do the "hot oil" compact, by which crude oil production is limited to a rate estimated as appropriate to expected demand,
and sugar legislation which allocates markets among domestic producers, importers, and foreign producers. Each of these measures, while ostensibly protecting or enhancing the public's interests, has the effect of
protecting and enhancing the financial interests of producers.

Outright subsidy, without a regulatory aim, is also a time-honored
characteristic of the American political economy. A few of numerous
examples are the Reconstruction Finance Corporation — begun
under President Hoover but only terminated under Eisenhower —
which primed business for a generation; the Small Business Administration, which has supplemented private banking capital in more recent years; and the lead-zinc stabilization program of 1961, which will
subsidize small producers at least through 1965.

Promotion through tax incentives has made "depletion allowance"
and "rapid amortization" every-day terms. A whole generation of business firms owes its power as much to war-time rapid amortization as to
competitive acumen.

The most important of all promotional developments have been
by-products of governmental growth in providing collective services
generally: roads, schools, and, in particular, defense. Since governments themselves engage in little direct goods-production, the vast rise
in public budgets has meant a corresponding increase in public payments to private producers, as government "contracts out" its hardware and service programs.

As the technology has become more complex, governmental promotion of business has also added a new dimension: the stimulation of productivity through research and development expenditures. . . .

Although most spokesmen for the Establishment, whether on the government or the industry side, deny vehemently that our economy requires tremendous defense expenditures to stay afloat, it is an indisputable fact that such expenditures are a sizable portion of total demand. And it is equally clear that the least diminution in the distribution of this largesse will be met with screams of anguish from governors and senators, labor union officials and local merchants, as well as corporate managers, in whatever areas defense contracts may be cut back. In the aerospace industry, leading manufacturers of airplanes in the 'forties and early 'fifties, and of missiles and rockets in the 'sixties, have been dependent on government orders for from 50 to 100 per cent of their gross business. And the conditions under which contracts have been let have added frosting to the cake. Negotiated, guaranteed-profit arrangements, not competitive bidding, have been the rule. . . .

With the passage of the Sherman Antitrust Act in 1890, the national government took on the role of protector of competition. While this has become a traditional task, it remains a highly controversial one. . . .

Verbally, business spokesmen accept this logic and pay formal obeisance to the Sherman and Clayton Acts. Operationally, however, their support often turns into opposition — always, if one's own business is the subject of antitrust litigation. . . .

A politics of competition has thus developed in which almost all pay homage to the logic of antitrust in the abstract while seeking to avoid its concrete application. When a President has an Assistant Attorney General who pushes antitrust vigorously, as Bicks did under Eisenhower, his Administration is invariably charged with being "anti-business," for the business community rarely admits that the health of business generally may require action against specific business behavior. . . .

NEWER AND EMERGING ROLES

With the Great Depression, realization finally came to the United States that income protection programs were an inescapable responsibility of the national government. When one-fourth of the labor force was unemployed and state and local governments had exhausted their resources the choice became federal action or starvation. Relief funds — the dole — were the immediate response, but the modern sense of values finds this approach repulsive, so Old Age and Survivors Insurance, minimum wage and maximum hour legislation, and unemployment compensation were adopted in the 'thirties as "automatic stabilizers." . . . The federal personal income tax, made possible by the Sixteenth Amendment in 1913, for some years also redistributed incomes, though more from top to middle than from top to bottom; but now the effect seems to be negligible. Taxes have, of course, always had an impact on the distribution of income and thus on the social structure of a society. What is relatively new, however, is our consciousness of this and our ability (improved though not perfect) to measure the incidence of this impact.

Together, the automatic stabilizers, federal welfare payments, and income taxes constitute a substantial array of government economic programs. To these we may add the agricultural price-support programs, whose particular form may be all wrong, but whose essential justification is valid: that the farm economy cannot of itself protect the incomes of its participants because the farmer has to take the price that is given for his product, while he must pay the price that is demanded for his purchases from the industrial sector. . . .

Income-protection programs and those designed to lessen the unequal distribution of income under unrestricted capitalism are important not only in themselves but, perhaps more, as contributions to government's role in maintaining a balance of power among social groups. . . .

When it comes to the matter of allocating the nation's resources to meet its social needs, there are two main approaches. One is the market mechanism, in which individual dollar "votes" are cast for one product or service as against another among those offered. Consumer sovereignty and producer freedom to offer any product the producer desires are the rubrics used by advocates. The other approach is collective or public allocation, in which the mechanism is representative government: voters choose representatives and political leaders who then, partly as followers of apparent constituency demands, partly as leaders independently assessing community needs, determine the scope of public services.

The issue of resource allocation goes to the heart of the current division of opinion over the role of government in the economy. Free enterprise ideologists contend that the market mechanism can satisfy all wants, except defense, education, and the maintenance of order. They believe that market allocation is the "democratic" way, and that every dollar taxed by government to pay for a collective service is a dollar less that the consumer is free to allocate as he wishes. Thus, in their minds, public allocation is "arbitrary" and "undemocratic," because the citizen pays the tax to supply a particular service, whether he wishes to or not.

In contrast, socialists and liberals though they differ on such matters as democratization of economic power and public ownership, believe that many public needs are better met by government than by private action and that public allocation does not involve a net loss of freedom or democracy so long as the political process is open, free, and democratic. Liberals tend more often to look upon government as a popular instrument to be employed freely to do what individual action cannot or does not adequately accomplish unaided, while conservatives — as least as defined in the American business community — tend to see government as something apart from the people and its decisions as unrelated to popular wants. They are, of course, quite inconsistent on this point, for they will speak of a new public service program as an arbitrary imposition by government upon the people and in the same breath speak slightingly of political pandering to public opinion.

Probably more nonsense is spoken about the relationship of public and private allocation to freedom and democracy than about any other question of political economy. Several points can be made on this subject. First, it is incorrect to assert that consumer freedom is invariably diminished in exact proportion to the level of taxation. This represents an overstatement of the valid point that every dollar taxed means a dollar less that can be freely spent on privately supplied goods. But if people desire better roads, better schools, more public housing, or increased foreign aid, then freedom of choice can only be exercised through public allocation, that is, through taxes. These wants cannot be purchased privately and individually. Therefore people's freedom would be restricted, not enlarged, if public allocation were not available.

Second, even if a person disapproves of one or another of the public programs which his tax dollar goes to support, he is still subject to the doctrine of majority rule, which provides a legitimate political basis for compelling him to contribute. The only feasible alternative would be minority rule, which only a few extremists on the right and the left would prefer. Defenders of free enterprise are in a poor position to contest the argument of majority rule, it might be added, in as much as it is a rare corporation today that does not require the employee, as a condition of employment, to contribute to retirement, life insurance, and health insurance plans — without any vote at all.

Third, income inequalities mean unequal "votes" in the market place. The assumption of those who believe in the sovereignty of the consumer is that goods will be distributed according to composite social preferences if only each individual is free to buy the goods he wants. The validity of this rests on a further assumption, however, that each bidder for goods has the same number of dollars. And this assumption is manifestly not valid. The merest whims of a man who makes $20,000 per year may be gratified, while a man making only $2000 may not be able to provide for even his physical necessities. As long as extreme inequalities of personal wealth exist in this country, there will have to be public allocation of goods and services to mitigate the effects of this maldistribution.

While opponents of collective services continue to win occasional battles, like the one in 1962 over medical care for the aged, theirs is essentially a rearguard action which can cause frustrating delays in meeting public needs but cannot permanently stop such measures. The solidity of the social security system instituted in 1935 attests to this fact. As society in general becomes more affluent and the income of more and more of the population moves above the subsistence level, the demand for public services will increase, and this demand will be met out of a growing national income without cutting the private standard of living. Moreover, the growth of industrialism and urbanism continually increases the range of public services required.

Furthermore, as we become more aware of the inequities of a system of welfare programs through private collectives (corporations) which vary widely in coverage and adequacy, and as we come to see more clearly that proper public services are an important component of a high standard of living, the positive virtues of public as opposed to private programs will increase the political pressure for improved balance between the two sectors. The pace may be agonizingly slow, but the secular trend is surely toward increased public sector services.

As the self-sustaining, self-stimulating, and self-regulating forces of the private economy become more manifestly inadequate, the economic roles of government become more and more important. When opponents of government action charge that we are moving toward a planned or managed economy, they are quite right. Their error is in supposing that this is an arbitrary development rather than, a necessary response to modern economic structure, technological forces, and humanistic values. They are also wrong in assuming that the managerial role of the national government will produce a trend toward dictatorship or at least a less democratic system.

The fact is that only through public planning and management of the basic directions of the economy can we have any freedom and democratic control over economic development. For it is only over government that we have institutionalized popular control. Since there is no such mechanism for popular control of corporate decisions, and since the choice is not control or no control, but public or private control, we either have democratic public control or elitist, undemocratic private control. Thus we have to ask the following pertinent questions about the economic role of government:

First, does government intervene enough? Or does it leave to private, uncontrolled decision matters that we cannot afford to handle in that way, e.g., investment, price, and wage decisions having widespread public impact?

Second, how can the *ad hoc,* incomplete plans that have been developed for one problem after another over a period of many generations be fused into a mutually reinforcing, coherent, integrated set of goals and programs to ensure that first things come first and that one program does not undercut another?

Government and Urban Problems

One major dilemma confronting the federal government today is ambiguously described as the "urban problem." Federal policies governing urban areas have been far from successful; one reason is that the nature of urban problems has not been clearly defined. James Q. Wilson pinpoints some major dilemmas confronting policy makers in their attempts to solve the "urban problem," and proposes some solutions.

61   JAMES Q. WILSON

THE WAR ON CITIES

President Johnson's special message to Congress on improving the nation's cities was a notable document, both for what it said and what it did not. It was, in many respects, the sanest and most thoughtful presidential statement on "the urban problem" ever issued. It avoided most of those rhetorical absurdities which link the future of Western civilization with the maintenance of the downtown business district; it stressed the primacy of human and social problems over purely physical ones; and it conceded with great candor the dilemmas, contradictions, and inadequacies of past and present federal programs. . . .

I

The fundamental problem afflicting federal policy in this area . . . is that *we do not know what we are trying to accomplish.* We have neither concrete goals nor clear priorities; as a result, not only are federal programs productive of dilemmas, the dilemmas are each year

From James Q. Wilson, "The War on Cities," *The Public Interest,* No. 3 (Spring 1966), pp. 27–44. Copyright © 1966 by National Affairs, Inc. Reprinted by permission of the author and publisher.

becoming more expensive and more obvious. Do we seek to raise standards of living, maximize housing choices, revitalize the commercial centers of our cities, end suburban sprawl, eliminate discrimination, reduce traffic congestion, improve the quality of urban design, check crime and delinquency, strengthen the effectiveness of local planning, increase citizen participation in local government? All these objectives sound attractive — in part, because they are rather vague — but unfortunately they are in many cases incompatible.

Improving urban design is made harder by efforts to find housing for the poor, for well-designed housing almost always costs more than the poor can afford. A "revitalized" downtown business district not only implies, *it requires* traffic congestion — an "uncongested" Broadway or State Street would be no Broadway or State Street at all. Effective local planning requires *less*, not more citizen participation — the more views represented, the less the possibility of agreement on any single (especially any single comprehensive) view. Maximum housing choices, unconstrained by discriminatory practices, and reinforced by higher incomes, will give more people the opportunity to join the movement to the suburbs.

American political life has a proven and oft-remarked genius for surviving and even prospering on dilemmas and contradictions. Government maintains the support of potentially hostile groups by letting different federal agencies serve incompatible goals and by encouraging local communities to follow competing policies at federal expense. The new Department of Housing and Urban Development (HUD) stands squarely in this tradition. Under its previous name (the Housing and Home Finance Agency) it subsidized the flight to the suburbs with FHA mortgage insurance, while trying to lure suburbanites back to the central city with subsidies provided by the Urban Renewal Administration. The Public Housing Administration built low-rent units for the poor while urban renewal was tearing them down. Furthermore, the goals for most programs — especially urban renewal — were determined at the local level. This meant that urban renewal, in itself simply a tool, was used for very different purposes in different cities — in some places to get Negroes out of white neighborhoods, in others to bring middle-class people closer to downtown department stores, in still other places to build dramatic civic monuments, and in a few places to rehabilitate declining neighborhoods and add to the supply of moderately priced housing. Throughout its life, HHFA could have the best of both worlds — in Washington, its leaders could make broad policy statements which were intended to satisfy whatever critics of the program the administration was most sensitive to; meanwhile, in the hundreds of communities where the actual purposes of our housing programs were determined by the decisions of local gov-

erning bodies, many objectives which bore only the loosest relationship to federal policy statements were being pursued.

One can admire a system which so neatly accommodates the tensions
of political reality without approving of all its consequences. And
these consequences stem, in my view, from the fact that, in thinking
about solutions to the "urban problem," we have committed ourselves
to certain means before we have made a commitment to any goals. The
means have been federally subsidized alterations in the housing stock
and in certain other physical equipment (mass transportation, community facilities, and the like). The *a priori* commitment to these techniques has the result that alternative tactics to reach certain goals are
not systematically considered, or are considered only as afterthoughts.
Surely few would ever have disagreed that the two greatest causes of inadequate housing have been the fact that some people have not been
able to afford good housing and that some have, because of race, been
denied an opportunity to bid freely for such housing as exists. Yet it
was not until last year that HHFA requested of Congress a program
that would improve the purchasing power of poor families by direct
income subsidies; and it was not until this year that legislation was
proposed by the President to bar discrimination in the sale or rental of
housing (an executive order by President Kennedy had previously
barred discrimination in federally assisted housing, which is about
one-fifth of the total).

In the meantime — and continuing right down to the present —
local communities are allowed great latitude in deciding how federal
funds will be spent on the bread-and-butter programs: urban renewal
and public housing. If the Main Street merchants are in power, they
can use renewal funds to tear down low-cost housing and put up luxury apartments near the department stores — in effect redistributing
income from the poor to the well-to-do while reducing the stock of
low-cost housing. If more generous souls are in power, the worst housing is torn down to make room for middle or lower-middle-income
housing; the income transfer from poor to not-so-poor is much less, but
it is still in the wrong direction. And if the mayor simply is seeking
funds with which to run his city in the face of a declining tax base, he
discovers that he must join with those who want one of these urban renewal programs because that is about the only way he can get large-
scale federal money into his city. He discovers, in short, that he has to
hurt his poorest and weakest citizens in order to provide for the general welfare; his only option is to try to do it as humanely as possible.
Under any or all of these conditions, urban renewal may or may not
produce attractive, well-designed new structures; that is a separate
issue. The point is that for almost any legitimate community objective — improving the supply of housing, strengthening the tax base,

etc. — urban renewal has in most cases proved to be an unwieldy and costly tool. . . .

II

What, indeed, is the "urban problem"? The language of crisis with which this subject is normally discussed — "sick cities," "the urban crisis," "spreading blight" — is singularly unilluminating. I doubt that most residents of most American cities would recognize in such terms a fair description of the conditions in their communities. Since such words are usually uttered or printed in Washington, D.C., or New York City, perhaps the most we can infer is that life is tough in these two places — though the staggering expense the authors of such words are willing to incur in order to live in the very center of these cities suggests that the "crisis" is at least bearable.

Viewed in historical perspective, and taking American cities as a whole, the conditions of urban life have, by most measures, been getting steadily better, not worse. . . .

American cities have fully participated in the prosperity of the country — indeed, they have participated more than the rural areas; and this no doubt accounts for the fact that, whatever problems the cities have, people are moving to the cities in very large numbers. But it would be a mistake to try to be unreservedly optimistic about these aggregate trends. Certain classes of people within cities continue to confront problems, and these problems vary with the size and kind of the city in question. Three of these problems are especially noteworthy.

High Expectations. First, there is what might be called the "psychological urban problem" — i.e., our expectations are increasing faster than our achievements. As more affluent suburbs spring up, with neat lawns and good schools, the apparent gap between the quality of life in the central city and at the periphery increases. The suburbanites, adjusting rapidly to residential comfort, become more discontented with the conditions that surround the places where they work in the central city, even though these conditions are also (on the average) improving. Those city dwellers who cannot, for reasons of income or race, move to the suburbs, grow increasingly envious of those who can; the prizes of worldly success are held up before their eyes but out of their reach.

Because whites are gaining, in income and housing, faster than Negroes (though they are gaining also), the gap between the two groups is widening. (The full-employment economy of World War II narrowed the gap because of the need to fill manpower shortages; the under-employment prosperity of the 'fifties widened the gap; a continued Vietnamese war and the re-emergence of labor shortages may once again reduce the gap.) Moreover, within the Negro community itself, greater progress is being made in schooling than in income. The fact of Negro life is that a high school diploma is worth less to a Negro than to a white person, and the disparity is most obvious precisely where educational progress has been the greatest — in the cities.

In addition, the central city has remained the place where important members of the commercial and intellectual elite live. This is the group which, more than any other, sets the tone and provides the rhetoric of public discussion on "urban problems." By habit and tradition, it prizes the cultural amenities of the large central city and it tends to resent the spread of lower-class people into areas where these cultural and commercial institutions are established — even though that spread has been caused by the very increases in freedom and prosperity which the elite itself values. In the resulting distress, we see the conflict between the two major functions of the central city — on the one hand, the maintenance of a highly urbane style of life and of a concentrated and diverse market for the exchange of wealth and ideas; on the other hand, the provision of a place in which the lower classes, especially the immigrant lower classes, are housed, employed, educated, and by slow degrees assimilated to the standards of civility of American society. It is no longer possible to keep these two functions geographically separate within the central city, because it is no longer possible to confine the lower classes to high-density ghettoes — they have moved out into low-density ghettoes, thereby consuming much more land area than before, including land around or near the city's universities, hospitals, museums, and theaters.

The psychological urban problem cannot be solved, it can only be coped with. Indeed, it has been caused precisely because so many other problems *have* been coped with, if not solved. Efforts to lessen the gap between expectations and achievements will, in the short run, only make the discontent produced by that gap more acute. That is one of the inevitable tensions in a society committed to self-improvement.

Technical Problems, Political Solutions. The second kind of urban problem might be called the "technical" problem. By this I mean both that the problems are created because people are living in highly interdependent, dense settlements in an industrial society and that the solutions to these problems are technically feasible. If the problems are not solved, it is not for lack of knowledge. It might be more meaningful, indeed, to call them "political" problems, inasmuch as the obstacles to their solution are largely political. . . .

There is no reason in principle why these problems cannot be solved or significantly alleviated. We know, or can discover, techniques for stopping pollution; the crucial task is devising an appropriate combination of legal sanctions, tax policies, and incentives that will make these techniques effective. Open space and other unique natural resources can be conserved by public purchase, by easements, and by tax policies. Those persons who are determined to produce ugliness in parts of the city where ugliness is out of place (and this is not everywhere; every city, like every home, ought to have some place — the equivalent of Fibber McGee's closet — where we can store necessary ugliness) can be restrained by fines, taxes, and laws from carrying on those activities, or can be induced by subsidies to hide the ugliness by appropriate devices. There is nothing very difficult about hiding or getting rid of junked automobiles — provided that the people who are pleased by the absence of junk are willing to share the necessary cost of achieving the result. Even the design of private buildings can be improved by rewarding builders who leave open spaces around their buildings and who hire good architects and artists. The fiscal imbalance between public needs and public resources in the central city can be corrected by using a combination of transfer payments and user charges to insure that the suburbanite who uses the central city pays his fair share of the cost of that use and that everyone, regardless of whether he uses the facilities, pays his fair share of the cost of supplying essential common services such as education, police protection, and the like. . . .

The Negroes in the City. The third sense in which there is an urban problem is the most important. It results from the fact that the large central cities are where the immigrant lower classes congregate.

Today, with Negroes constituting the most important part of the urban lower class, the challenge to the central city is greater than ever before, because the Negroes create a unique set of problems. Unlike most previous migrants, they are marked by color. Furthermore, the Negro came originally from a slave culture in which he had no opportunity to acquire a complete range of political, economic, and social skills, and in which his family was subjected to systematic disruption and abuse. Unlike other immigrants — even other colored immigrants, such as the Chinese and Japanese — the Negro began his migration to the central city lacking the relevant skills and experience, and with a weakened family structure. Urbanization, of course, places further strains on community and family ties. The result is a central-city population with little money, few skills, a weakened capacity to cope with large bureaucratic institutions, and high rates of social disorder — crime, broken homes, alcoholism, narcotics addiction, illegitimacy, delinquency, and unemployment.

The argument over the details of the Moynihan Report on the Negro family has to some extent obscured its most important implication, which I cannot believe anyone will reject: if all Negroes were turned white tomorrow, they would still have serious problems. Whether these problems are more the result of a weak family structure, or of the impact of urbanization, or of the past history of discrimination, or of a depressed economic position, is very hard to say. But I suspect that whatever the cause, there are few aspects of this problem which will not be cured — or will not cure themselves — in time.

In time. In how much time? And what does one do in the meantime? I incline to the view that in the long run the acculturational problem of the Negro — i.e., the problem of being unable, as an individual or a family, and as compared with previous migrants to the cities, to cope with the fact of poverty — will be reduced by improvements in income and education; habits will change as class changes, though more slowly. Perhaps I say this because it is easier to think of changing class position than cultural values, though altering the former is hard enough. Perhaps I say it because of the great and obvious differences between middle-class and lower-class Negroes, differences much greater than those between middle-class and lower-class whites. And perhaps I am wrong.

But whatever the strategic factor is, we cannot as yet say we have discovered it. The best that can be said in our favor is that we are perhaps the only free society which has ever tried to change a large racial minority by massively upgrading its condition. The debate about what the goal of "equality" means — whether a random distribution of Negroes throughout the city and the social structure, or a distinctive Negro enclave with guaranteed rights of entry and departure, or some combination of the two — is less interesting to me than the fact that, wherever we want to go, we don't know how to get there. And for the present, the urban Negro is, in a fundamental sense, *the* "urban problem." . . .

III

Federal policies have moved only by halting steps in a direction that acknowledges that the "urban problem" is not primarily, or even significantly, a housing problem. The rent supplement program is a recognition of the need to deal directly with the cause of slum housing — i.e., the fact that there are people who cannot afford non-slum housing. The call for legislation to bar discrimination in the housing market is a recognition of the need to reduce the inflated prices of Negro housing by giving Negroes access to the entire housing market. (Although the principle is sound, not much is likely to happen as a result of such a statute; open occupancy laws already on the books in many states and cities have not broken up the Negro enclaves, partly because housing outside such enclaves sometimes costs more than housing inside them.) But for the present, these and other modifications are largely frosting on a tasteless cake. The major thrust of federal policy is now, and always has been, a commitment to maintain and enhance the physical shells of existing American cities — adding, where appropriate, a few new towns to handle the overflow. The desire to make all American cities "livable" not only exaggerates the extent to which cities are now "unlivable," but it thoughtlessly lumps together all cities — whether or not they continue to serve any functions, whether or not there is any rational grounds for conserving them at public expense, and even whether or not the local leadership conceives of urban conservation as driving the poor across the city line into somebody else's city. . . .

There is an alternative policy which could direct federal activities. It would require, not the scrapping of existing federal programs, but only their redirection. Such a policy would begin with a recognition of the different kinds of "urban problems" — some of which, like poverty, are as much rural as urban problems, and others of which, like the gap between expectations and achievements, are not problems that government can do anything about. Such a policy would, I suggest, contain the following elements:

First, the federal government would assume responsibility for placing a floor under the capacity of Americans to acquire a minimally satisfactory level of personal and family amenities — housing, food, clothing, medical care. Where possible, guaranteeing such resources to every family would be done by combining aggregate fiscal policies which produce full employment with direct income transfers — in the form, say, of a negative income tax, family allowances, or rent subsidies — such that each family has maximum free choice as to the type and location of its housing. . . .

Second, public power and public funds would be used to provide those common benefits (or, as the economists say, collective goods) which are enjoyed, and thus must be paid for, by everybody. Fresh air, pure water, open spaces, park land, and police protection are the most common examples of indivisible benefits, to achieve which public powers must be exercised. Ironically, it is in this area (where even in the days of Adam Smith it was agreed that public intervention was required) that federal action has been the slowest in developing. The reason, of course, is understandable enough; most collective goods require control over those aspects of community life — the education of the young, the policing of the city, and the use of land — which Americans have long insisted be kept in local hands. So long as most of us lived and worked in the same place — i.e., the central city — purely local control of these matters may have made sense. What services we used as we travelled to and from work we also paid for through taxes.

Upper-middle-class citizens with a strong interest in (and a healthy capacity to pay for) common benefits, such as parks and the like, lived in — and often governed — the central city. With the exodus to the suburbs, and our self-segregation into radically different kinds of communities on the periphery, differences in preferences and income which used to co-exist within a single taxing authority now are separated by political boundaries. If the incidence of costs and benefits of various collective goods is to be equalized throughout the metropolitan area, some higher taxing authority must assume responsibility for transfer payments. There are only two such authorities — the state and the federal government.

Third, where possible, central cities facing a fiscal crisis ought to receive block grants from state or federal governments in order to help defray the cost of servicing the poor, providing decent education and police protection, etc. At the present time, cities must commit themselves to a whole range of federally conceived programs in order to get money they urgently need, even though many of these programs may be either irrelevant or harmful to the interests of parts of the city's population. . . .

Fourth, the federal government ought to encourage, through special incentives, cities to experiment with various user charges as a way of making certain that non-residents pay their fair share of the services they use in the cities where they work or shop, and that residents have a more precise and personal way than voting for or against the mayor to indicate how much of a particular local service they really desire for themselves. At the present time, large groups of people get something for nothing — non-residents who park on the city's streets, for example, or residents who, owning no taxable property, enthusiastically vote for more and more free public facilities. The whole burden is thrown on the property-tax payer, and he cannot sustain it.

Fifth, urban renewal and other land clearance programs can be used as a tool to aid in providing common benefits (by assembling land and financing good design for public buildings, schools, and the like) and as a way of eliminating hazardous or unsalvageable structures. . . .

IV

It is possible to conceive of a rational policy for dealing with so-called "urban" problems, once one begins to realize that the word "urban" is less relevant than the word "human." . . .

For almost two decades we have been "attacking" the problems of the city — almost literally — by mounting successive assaults against various real and imagined difficulties. Each assault force has had its own leadership and ideology and the weaknesses of each have been the signal for a new assault, under different leadership and with a new ideology. First came public housing, then urban redevelopment, then urban renewal, and now the demonstration program. The old assaults of course never vanished, they just moved over a bit (not without complaints) to let the newcomers in. The common objective is to capture and hold central-city real estate; the differences in tactics concern the number of fronts on which the fighting is to proceed. In general, each successive assault has had broader objectives — the current President's message calls for a change in the "total environment." The motto is, "more is better." Perhaps it will all work out, if humane weapons are used and we evacuate the wounded. But I suspect that in the confusion the real enemies — poverty, ignorance, despair — may slip away, to live and strike again in another place.

CHAPTER TWELVE

Government and Foreign Policy

Are the requirements for foreign policy decision making different from those of domestic policy? The framers of the Constitution recognized that in many important respects foreign policy needs are unique. For example, under the terms of the Constitution, the President was given more authority and greater discretion in foreign than in domestic policy making; the needs of unity and dispatch in the execution of foreign policy were understood at that time.

Today the President stands at the center of the foreign policy making process. His primacy in foreign affairs is recognized by the Supreme Court, which has held on several occasions that the President can be given greater discretionary authority to make crucial foreign policy decisions than would be constitutionally permissible in the domestic arena.

The unique position of the President in foreign affairs raises the critical question of democratic control over the foreign policy process. On the one hand, he may not always be effectively checked under our system of separation of powers; on the other hand, he is the only national official elected by the entire nation. At first, his broad electoral constituency would seem to imply important public control over his actions in formulating foreign policy. Indeed, this possibility has even worried some who feel that the President should not be hamstrung by the often irrational demands of the populace on this subject. A close examination of the nature of the foreign policy process as well as of political behavior reveals that "public opinion" has a very limited effect upon presidential actions. The following selection discusses the nature of the foreign policy process, with particular reference to the role of the Presidency and public opinion.

62   KENNETH N. WALTZ

OPINION AND CRISES IN AMERICAN FOREIGN POLICY

The fear of public opinion impressing itself upon foreign policy is necessarily great if elections go far toward determining policy and if the outcome of elections is determined by the inclinations of ill-informed voters. The fears become greater still if the dread voice of public opinion is able to dictate policy between elections as well. On both counts Walter Lippmann has written democracy's indictment with a telling eloquence:

> The unhappy truth is that the prevailing public opinion has been destructively wrong at the critical junctures. The people have imposed a veto upon the judgments of informed and responsible officials. They have compelled the governments, which usually knew what would have been wiser, or was necessary, or was more expedient, to be too late with too little, or too long with too much, too pacifist in peace and too bellicose in war, too neutralist or appeasing in negotiation or too intransigent. Mass opinion has acquired mounting power in this century. It has shown itself to be a dangerous master of decisions when the stakes are life and death.[1]

All masters of decision are dangerous. Have the people been more dangerous than most of them? This question and many others are raised by Lippmann's statement. Does public opinion prevail in the Western democracies as Lippmann argues? If it does, has the mass voice in and between crises been simply wrong? If the great undifferentiated public, which he describes and assumes to be decisive, has indeed been wrong "at the critical junctures," have others — professors and pundits, political leaders and highly-placed officials — been more often and more nearly correct in their assessment of events and their estimate of policy requirements? If the democracies have erred consistently and disastrously as he says, have other types of modern government interpreted the world more reliably and acted more successfully upon their interpretations? . . .

From Kenneth N. Waltz, *Foreign Policy and Democratic Politics: The American and British Experience,* Chap. 10. Copyright © 1967, by Little, Brown and Company (Inc.). Reprinted by permission of the publisher.

[1] Lippmann, *The Public Philosophy* (Boston: Little, Brown, 1955), p. 20.

Three worries about the effect of democratic opinion on foreign policy are widespread. (1) Democracies will prefer the easy way. This is not to say that duties will always be shirked and dangers avoided. It is, for example, sometimes simpler to fight for a peace of "unconditional surrender" than to negotiate a limited settlement that is more likely to endure. (2) The public reaction to complicated international events is often unpredictable; feelings, whether of patriotism or fear, supplant reason and produce a response based on moods of the moment rather than on solid and sensible analyses. (3) The opinions of the many override the wisdom of the experienced; men of experience, by disguising their voices of wisdom when speaking to the untutored masses, compound the difficulty. Haunted by the memory of the democracies' failures to respond to the challenge of the totalitarian countries in the 1930's and dismayed by America's inability to adjust force to political purpose in and immediately after World War II, critics of democratic institutions found ample sustenance for a far-reaching pessimism. Although somewhat allayed by the rapidity and breadth of response to Soviet challenges in the period that began in 1947 and reached into the 1950's, pessimism reappeared in the Eisenhower years. Lippmann's critique, Emmet Hughes's description of the nation's plight as conveyed in the title of his book *America the Vincible*, the officially sponsored investigation by the Gaither Committee, and the unofficial but highly authoritative studies of the Rockefeller Brothers' Fund, all reflected the fear that the 1950's like the 1930's were years of the locusts.

Does the common citizen, one must wonder, have the fortitude to sustain costly military programs, the benefits of which are necessarily uncertain? Will the public permit the government the flexibility it requires in dealing with a dangerous and changing world? Whether or not the citizenry is dogged and sensible, how closely is foreign policy controlled by the opinions of its citizens?

POLITICAL LEADERSHIP AND THE PUBLIC SUPPORT OF PROGRAMS

Often the person discussing the relation of opinion to policy is in the undignified posture of a dog chasing his tail. When it is charged that the people have been unduly complacent, the remedy prescribed may well be that their leaders should arouse themselves. Robert C. Sprague, Co-chairman of the Gaither Committee, businessman, and self-styled conservative Republican, expressed his belief before Senator Jackson's Subcommittee that the nation faced a threat to its survival to which it had not yet awakened. Who could awaken the country? In the opinion of Sprague, there was one man alone "in the United States that can do this effectively, and that is the President."

The thought is perennial. It was Plato who said in effect: the people are sick; their rulers must be cured. The question of leadership lies beneath the problem of the people's willingness to sacrifice, and it directly affects the stability of their opinions as well. When Churchill sought to awaken his countrymen to mounting dangers in the 1930's, few of the leading men of any party followed him. Are the people at fault when Prime Minister, Foreign Secretary, military officials, and others who bear a national trust assure them that armaments are adequate and that military preparations are proceeding at the necessary pace? The correspondence of the people's opinion to the position taken by their governors is strikingly illustrated by the rapid reversal of opinion on the controversial introduction of conscription in 1939, the first time Britain had adopted such a measure in peacetime. Before conscription was adopted, 39 percent of the voters favored it, with 53 percent opposed and 8 percent doubtful. A week after the legislation was passed, 58 percent approved, 38 percent opposed, and 4 percent were uncertain.

The survival of the nation depends not only on fortitude in reacting to a threat that has at last become obvious but also upon the people's willingness to pay and to serve when danger is not immediately visible. George C. Marshall, reflecting four years later upon his judgment of 1945 that the military force levels projected at that time were unrealistically high, explained in terms of public opinion the conclusion he had reached:

> When it comes to [military] appropriations in piping times of peace, I don't think America will ever learn its lesson, because the political pressures are tremendous. In the next place, my associates haven't lived through the education I had had in the 1920's and the immediate problems I had inherited in 1938, 1939, and 1940, when our degree of poverty was very trying. I could well understand that. They just thought I underestimated public opinion in the United States.
>
> Well, I am a great respecter of public opinion, but, on the other hand, I am also a great respecter of the tremendous political influence of the budget and the fact that it almost gets beyond control when it relates to things that do not produce immediate results like good roads, agriculture matters, and such.

Were American citizens, as Marshall thought, less willing to serve than to pay and not sufficiently willing to do either?

Before and after Korea, the marked tendency of American defense policy was to substitute machines for men in the demanding task of containing the Russian and Chinese Communists. The Truman-Bradley "old look" had meant reliance on air power and atomic bombs, with an army of minimum size. The insufficiency of such an establishment was demonstrated by the invasion of the Republic of

Korea from the north. With the Korean War ended, military policy slipped back to the old basis with a "new look" label attached. The Army Vice Chief of Staff, General Bolté, along with many others, despairingly tried to drive home the lesson that events had failed to teach. "Recent history has shown — and logic will sustain it — that the only way to defeat ground forces is by ground forces. The lesson of Korea should ever be before us."

A strong inclination to keep defense costs low as measured in manpower is often said to be the military attitude of democracies. That democracy is alone the cause of the attitude is doubtful. The democracies that are thought to have this attitude are advanced industrial powers. For such countries to emphasize equipment more heavily than men may simply be an attempt to play from their strongest suit. In other fields, such a practice is accepted as mere common sense. . . .

It is no more unusual that America, Britain, and other industrial democracies should seek to substitute machines for men in their military establishments than that they do so in agriculture, in dam-building, or in any of a number of other endeavors. . . .

One may nevertheless fear that political economizing — in terms of votes — will complement economic rationality in such a way as to make the preference for the machine difficult to undo even when international conditions would indicate its folly. Public pressure for rapid demobilization in 1945 and 1946 was strong and apparently effective. The conclusion frequently drawn is that at the outset of the Cold War public opinion placed the American government at a grave disadvantage. Those who reach such a conclusion have failed to bear in mind that civil and military leaders did not themselves urge upon the public the importance of remaining militarily prepared. Nor have they made the important distinction between enthusiasm for "bringing the boys home" and willingness to support a sizable peacetime military establishment. The latter was not lacking. The American public, in addition to supporting measures for improving our defenses in general, strongly favored the adoption of Universal Military Training. In nine surveys taken between December, 1945, and January, 1956, public support for the program, expensive in manpower, ran upwards of 65 percent on eight occasions and only once fell as low as 60 percent. Opposition to the measure never exceeded 33 percent and only once rose above 25 percent. More generally, as Samuel P. Huntington has written and convincingly demonstrated, "Governmental policy and mass opinion on the level of military effort have frequently differed, but in every case the Administration has been in favor of less military effort and public opinion in favor of more."[2] The statement applies, with

[2] Citations from Huntington are taken from Samuel P. Huntington, *The Common Defense* (New York: Columbia University Press, 1961).

variations that do not change the picture of broad and constant support, to all segments of the population and all sections of the country; and the pattern has been constant from at least 1937 onward.

When pollsters have asked where budgetary savings should be made, only small numbers of respondents have cited defense spending. As Huntington notes, one cannot say that the American people have put lower taxes or welfare programs ahead of an adequate national defense. At the same time the public in general, unsophisticated in matters of weaponry and strategy, looks to the administration for a definition of adequacy. "If the critics vigorously and articulately attack the Administration for reducing military strength, the Administration eventually is forced to make a public defense of its policies. The public listens to the Administration, not the critics, and the reassurances of the Administration induce mass acquiescence in its policies." The attitude of support and the implicit willingness to build the basis for a mass army have provided policymakers with a broad range of choice.

ELECTORAL PUNISHMENT AND INTERNATIONAL CRISES

Democracies have often been thought defective not only in their ability to sustain costly military establishments in time of peace but also in their ability to move with speed and finesse in response to the shifting currents of international affairs. May one not say of the years since World War II that the close concern of the American people with problems of foreign policy has made it difficult for their government to conduct an international policy of feint and maneuver? Is it not likely that the more people care about foreign policy the more closely their opinions will limit the government? Such an effect has not been noticeable, partly because the concern of the public has outpaced its knowledge.

An international event ordinarily does not disturb the nation unless it has first obsessed the government. In the face of such an event, the people rally behind their chief executive, as one would expect them to do in any cohesive country. William Gladstone long ago commented in a letter to the Duke of Argyll that if the justification for the continuation of the Crimean War by England was that the people approved of the war and supported it, then such justification could be given for any war that England ever waged within eighteen months of its commencement. A comparable statement, adjusted for the speed with which events are now publicly registered, can be made of America's reaction to crises. Franklin Roosevelt's popularity fluctuated in accordance with the recurrence of crises in Europe. The outbreak of fighting in Korea gave a lift to President Truman's low standing with the public. In June of 1950, immediately before the attack, 37 percent of those polled approved of the way Truman was doing his job, while

45 percent did not. In July of 1950, the corresponding figures were 46 percent and 37 percent. The invasion of Egypt by Britain and France, coming late in the American electoral campaign of 1956, apparently added a little to Eisenhower's wide margin of victory. A year and a half later, in April of 1958, the deepening of an economic recession, following upon Russia's lofting her first Sputnik, drove Eisenhower's popularity down to 49 percent, which for him was a low point. The following summer, a *contretemps* in Lebanon, which led the President to send American troops, boosted him to his 1958 high of 58 percent. The Cuban missile crisis of October, 1962, worked similar wonders for Kennedy. In April of that year, 77 percent had approved of the way he was handling "his job as President." A gradual decline then set in, to 73 percent in May following April's crisis in steel, to 71 percent in June following a slump in the stock market, to 67 percent in September after federal troops were sent to Mississippi, and to 61 percent before the confrontation with Russia in October. In December, however, 74 percent expressed themselves as satisfied with the President's performance in office.

The first effect of an international crisis is to increase the President's popular standing. One may wonder if this is so only when the response of the President is firm or when he otherwise gives the impression of being able to deal with the situation effectively and without inconvenience to the public. It is in fact not necessary to add such qualifications to the statement that so far as the public is concerned the President in a moment of crisis has the widest freedom of action. President Kennedy, facing threats to Berlin, sent additional troops to Europe and in the summer of 1961 called up 150,000 reservists, an act usually thought to be politically dangerous. The political costs, on balance, were nil. Several months earlier, the United States had unofficially sponsored an invasion of Cuba at the Bay of Pigs. In the wake of the ill-fated attempt, President Kennedy's popular standing reached its highest point ever, 83 percent, as compared with an average of 70 percent during his thirty-four months in office.

At the moment of crisis, there is not time for dissension to develop. The public poses few problems for the President who acts deftly, or even clumsily, in a short and sharp encounter. If the crisis is prolonged and the blood of Americans is shed in carrying out the government's policy, should one not expect a different reaction? The experience of the Korean War seems to have led everyone to do so. In view of America's commitment of troops to combat on the mainland of Asia, questions debated since the early 1950's have once again become urgent.

America's military response in Korea had been prompt; it was also fairly effective. The North Korean and subsequently the Chinese invaders were met and thrown back; the line of the 38th Parallel was restored and improved upon slightly; the United States and the non-Communist world were stronger at the conclusion of the affair than they had been at its beginning. Still, as the war dragged on, public support dwindled. Polls taken by the American Institute of Public Opinion from June of 1950 to November of 1952 found anywhere from 81 to 35 percent supporting "President Truman's decision to send US troops to Korea," with 11 to 51 percent opposed. Polls of the National Opinion Research Center showed from 80 to 51 percent in support of the decision to send "American troops to stop the Communist invasion of South Korea," with from 13 to 40 percent opposed. Different emphases in the wording of the questions may account for the discrepant results. No matter what poll one may look at, the line graph of President Truman's popular standing moved parallel to and consistently below the steadily declining popular support of America's fighting in Korea. In July, October, and December of 1950, 46, 39, and 36 percent of those polled approved of the way the President was "handling his job." After 1950 and to the end of his term, approval fluctuated between 32 and 23 percent.

To take the full measure of the problem of executive leadership in a democracy, one must constantly bear in mind that a painful and costly policy may have to be long pursued, with the gains from the policy largely invisible. The rewards may be found mainly in preventing worse situations that might have arisen were the costly action not undertaken. It is clear that the decision to resist in Korea was widely approved and the execution of that decision over the next three years was not. If one dwells on the courage with which the decision was made to intervene in Korea, it becomes dismaying to notice that the party of the President who made it was punished in the subsequent national election. In the 1952 election, according to Key, "several million persons" voted against themselves "on domestic matters." On grounds of domestic policy, these millions would have preferred a Democratic Administration. They were impelled to vote for Eisenhower by confidence in him as a man who could make peace, which was matched by distaste for the Democrats as a party that had taken their country into a war that the administration was unable to bring to a conclusion.

In the 1948 election, a bipartisan truce on foreign-policy questions had for the most part prevailed, while economic and welfare questions were sharply debated. In the campaign of 1952, the Democrats played upon the people's interest in prosperity and, as ever, attached the depression label to the Republican Party. Republicans drew political advantage from the higher taxes and prices that the war had brought and from the drafting of American boys to fight and die in a war that was said to be useless. The loss of China to the Communists, the Soviet threat to Europe, and corruption in government were also prominent issues. According to University of Michigan surveys, foreign issues worked almost entirely in favor of the Republican Party. Twelve percent of self-declared Democrats criticized the handling of foreign affairs, especially the Korean War, by their own party, as opposed to 6 percent who had something good to say about the Democratic Administration in this field. Twenty-two percent of respondents mentioned being favorably impressed with Eisenhower's ability to handle foreign problems and particularly the Korean War, as compared with 9 percent who spoke favorably of his ability to manage domestic affairs. The corresponding figures for Stevenson were 2 percent and 7 percent. In party rather than personal terms, 43 percent referred favorably to the Democrats on domestic policies and issues, 33 percent to the Republicans. On matters of foreign policy, preferences were reversed: 13 percent expressed approval of the Republican Party, while only 3 percent had kind words for the Democrats. By a different measure, the Republicans led as the party more likely to keep the country out of war by a ratio of more than two to one in the spring of 1952, while the Democrats continued to find favor as the "party of prosperity."

Out of the military and political experience of Korea a conviction developed, widely shared by officials, commentators, and students of politics, that America ought not or could not fight another peripheral action, costly in manpower and without "victory" in sight. Charles Wilson, Eisenhower's first Secretary of Defense, once said, "We can't afford to fight limited wars. We can only afford to fight a big war, and if there is one that is the kind it will be." Either we should not fight at all, such reasoning runs, or, in fighting, we should take every advantage of the modern means of warfare available to us in order to strike for victory. Where Wilson thought that militarily the United States ought not to fight another "Korea," others concluded that politically America cannot. In 1951, following the Congressional hearings that were prompted by the relief of General MacArthur, a Republican minority report declared:

> We believe that a policy of victory must be announced to the American people in order to restore unity and confidence. It is too much to expect that our people will accept a limited war. Our policy must be to win. Our strategy must be devised to bring about decisive victory.

Herman Kahn, drawing an electoral lesson from Stevenson's defeat, concluded *"that if there is another unpopular Limited War followed by the loss of the ensuing national election by the party in power, the ability of the United States to fight Limited War will be sadly impaired."* For their Korean venture, it appeared that the Democrats were punished severely at home; Republicans as well as Democrats presumably learned the electoral lesson. Some commentators were therefore tempted to say dogmatically that no President would ever again be willing to take the nation into such a war. Irving Kristol, for example, carried Kahn's qualified conclusion to such an extreme when he wrote:

> The Korean War was unpopular to a degree that makes it inconceivable for any future Administration to contemplate that kind of limited, rigorously defensive military action. The scholars and the diplomats can continue to devise ingenious gradients of warfare, countering each enemy action with just so much (and no more) reaction. But they are indulging in a paper game. The American people cannot provide the kind of mercenary, professional soldiers such plans require.

Students of politics seconded the impressions of public officials and underscored the worries that military strategists and political pundits entertained. It will be sufficient to cite two of the weightiest. Some years after the event, Key advanced the opinion that "the failure of the Truman Administration to make plain the reasons for American involvement in the Korean episode — a novel sort of enterprise for the United States — may have made it impossible to drum up public support for American participation in brush wars and thereby restricted us to atomic wars. At any rate, the successful Republican exploitation of the issue in 1952 will give statesmen cause for the greatest reluctance to engage in comparable enterprises, no matter what the need or provocation."[3] Brzezinski and Huntington incline to a compatible conclusion: "The normal and generally healthy play of partisan politics continually restricts an Administration's freedom of action. In times of crisis, restrictions may be supplemented by mass demands for quick victories and simple solutions. For almost two years the Truman Administration found itself boxed into a position where it could neither win the Korean War nor extricate itself from the war."[4] . . .

It is useful to take up the problem in its most difficult terms. The novelty of the Korean crisis was excuse enough for the vacillations of the Truman Administration. One can hope to learn from experience, and yet in international relations it must be expected that each succeeding experience will be novel. It is impossible always to act wisely. Even wise actions may not preclude a grueling and costly fight, and under such circumstances the clear explanation of policies will not keep internal recriminations from growing. A President who does what the moment seems to require can then often expect that he and his party will have to pay the domestic political bill, however unjustly it may be drawn. Here again foreign policy is not so very different from

[3] Key, *Public Opinion and American Democracy*, p. 261 n.
[4] Zbigniew Brzezinski and Samuel P. Huntington, *Political Power:* USA/USSR (New York: Viking, 1964), p. 414.

domestic policy. The Republicans, in office when the market crashed in 1929, still bear some onus as the party of depression. It would, of course, only be just to say that the crash and the succeeding depression were bigger than any party and that had Al Smith been sitting in the White House backed by an overwhelming majority of Democrats in both Houses of Congress, he would not have been able to prevent these disasters, either. And so the Democrats, in office during the wars in which America has fought in this century, long remained in the public mind the party of war. While this is not surprising, it may be rather discouraging.

Actually, for several reasons it should not be. First, the election of 1952 was more a personal trubute to Eisenhower than a triumph for the Republican Party, less a repudiation of the Democratic Party than a conclusion electorally expressed that the Republicans had found a man who could see the country safely through a difficult international situation. . . .

The second reason for not being deeply concerned that fear of being labeled the "party of war" will dissuade a party in power from standing firm in the face of aggression is that the reputations of parties are more fairly won and more easily lived down than is sometimes supposed. Traditionally, the Republicans have been viewed as the party of peace and depression. A Republican President, one must note, did conclude an honorable peace in 1953, which the Democrats for three years had been unable to do, and did avoid becoming militarily involved in Indochina in the following year. Republicans, at the same time, have been less willing to run a deficit in order to combat unemployment and less warmly in favor of social-welfare programs. Democrats have long been viewed as the party of prosperity, but also as the party of war. For a decade, from 1951 to 1961, only 15 to 25 percent of the public had thought of the Democratic Party as the "best" party to keep the country out of war, while from 26 to 42 percent had, on this ground, preferred the Republicans. It is not true, however, that only the good fortune of having Barry Goldwater to oppose them in the election of 1964 enabled the Democrats to shed the unwanted reputation for bellicosity. In July of 1962, presumably because of Kennedy's performance in office, Democrats found as much public approval on the peace issue as did Republicans; and in February and May of 1963, Democrats were favored over their rivals by margins of 32 to 23 and 31 to 26 percent.

Finally, harsh criticism of the party that is trying to carry out a given action does not necessarily indicate unwillingness to support other parts of the President's foreign policy. It may not even imply a disavowal of the action criticized. A distinction must be drawn between critical attitudes, on the one hand, and the willingness of refusal to support policies, on the other. Republicans who in the 1950's criticized American policies in China, for example, were assigning blame for events that had already occurred. Their criticism did not indicate that they would withhold support from the President should he seek to undertake difficult international actions. Republicans in Congress did not deny the President the opportunity to carry out his policy. Indeed, because they had granted him the instruments he asked for, Republicans could more easily say that the ill-conceived policy of a Democratic President had opened the way for Communist conquest of China. Any party in opposition will try to lay the blame for national ills upon the party in power. It is then misleading to say that Truman erred in failing to associate the Republican Party with his Far Eastern policy, wrong also to argue that if he had woven a bipartisan net around his China policy as he did on European questions, his fall in popularity would have been cushioned. No intelligently led opposition party would have bought shares in an American enterprise in China that looked as though it could be saved from bankruptcy only at a price that almost no one was willing to pay. In the very years when much political sport was had with the Truman Administration's troubles in the Far East, a majority of Republican legislators supported such radically new and far-reaching programs as the Truman Doctrine, the Marshall Plan, the Atlantic Defense Treaty, and such difficult actions as the Berlin Airlift and even the military effort in Korea.

Governmental Freedom of Action

The chances that a President will be unable to carry out a controversial policy are slight, nor is it at all likely that he will be dissuaded from pursuing a difficult and possibly unpopular line of policy by the fear that he and his party will thereby be electorally punished. Parties and Presidents must care about losing a little of their popularity on one issue or another if democratic government is to be responsive to the wishes and worries of the people. At the same time, in politics as in all human affairs, there are situations in which one is damned if he does and damned if he does not. No man and no party can govern without accepting this truth. If the United States disengages in Southeast Asia and North Vietnam sweeps to the tip of the Camau peninsula, the President in power and the party that he leads will be found to be at fault. But they will also be found at fault if the scale of American involvement is increased in order to hold what remains of the peninsula or to regain lost ground. In the most difficult matters, and international crises are certainly among them, there is no single policy whose widespread popularity would survive the test of action. If the world is a mess and the United States must act in it, then Presidents will often be in a position of deciding which of several unpopular policies they will follow. They will have no chance to pick a policy that will lose them no votes at all. If timidity and quiescence were truly and clearly more popular than boldness and action, then one would rightly worry that democratic countries would always fall prey to the aggressive thrusts of others. If belligerence were always more admired, then one would live teetering on the brink of nuclear war. If either condition prevailed, Presidents would always experience pressure to act in one way whether or not it was appropriate to the situation at hand.

Brzezinski and Huntington suggested that a President steadily losing public support may find himself boxed in, as to a considerable extent Truman did. After months of costly and inconclusive fighting, withdrawal would have been humiliating, and to threaten the use of unlimited means in order to achieve a limited end, as Eisenhower and Dulles did later, would have failed of acceptance at home and lacked credibility abroad. The box, however, was not built by "mass demands for quick victories and simple solutions." As data previously cited make clear, no such demands were made. Nevertheless, as the war dragged on, impatience grew, and the country lost confidence in the competence of the government. Kristol, Kahn, and others thereupon concluded that the constraints of political competition severely limit America's contrivance and conduct of policy. Since World War II, foreign policy has usually been the most prominent of issues, but its electoral effect has nevertheless been diluted by juxtaposition with other problems and policies when voters made their decisions. One who bases his vote in part on performance in office must also ask himself how the competing candidate and party are likely to do. Numerous surveys have indicated that both parties are looked upon as competent to manage foreign policy. Furthermore, most people continue to vote in the present as they have voted in the past, whether or not the policies and programs of their preferred party have pleased them. When such countervailing factors are borne in mind, the fear that electoral punishment will dramatically affect foreign policy loses most of its force. International affairs have gone badly while Presidents of both parties were in power. Neither party has suffered any very deep political damage as a result. . . .

The American government had apparently decided before the event that it would not meet force with force in Korea. But it did. Numerous statements by Eisenhower, Dulles, and others indicated that in Indochina in the spring of 1954 the United States would fight or somehow retaliate if the Communists continued to drive forward. But this time, it did not do so. In neither case can it be said that fear of the people's opinion or of domestic political consequences noticeably affected the final decision. Nor had weariness with the war in Korea persuaded the public that giving way in other parts of the world would be preferable to fighting. Asked in May and September of 1953 and again in April of 1954 whether the American air force should be used if necessary to prevent the Communists from taking over all of Indochina, from 52 to 60 percent agreed that it should. In all three polls, a larger percentage still, that is from 59 to 65 percent, favored sending American troops, with always about a third of the sample opposed to either alternative. For the next decade, as economic and military commitments grew, American policies in Indochina were viewed with a mixture of mild disinterest, mature skepticism, and judicial calm, with never an inclination to force the government's hand. Following the naval incidents of Tonkin Bay early in August of 1964, President Johnson proposed and the Congress overwhelmingly accepted a resolution that practically gave the President a free hand in Southeast Asia (Public Law 88-408). In February of 1965, the American bombing of North Vietnam began. In March of that year, 27,000 American troops were serving in Vietnam; in June, 54,000; in September, 128,500; by May of 1966, more than 250,000. Against the background of these events and in the presence of continued political unrest in South Vietnam, Americans, in their answers to pollsters, revealed themselves as being reluctantly willing to fight, amenable to settlement, anxious to negotiate, and, though obviously wary, worried, and confused, willing to give the President wide latitude.

Such a pattern of opinion persisted, even as the scale of American involvement increased and the toll of American lives rose. In the late spring of 1964, for example, of the 74 percent who then knew of the fighting in Vietnam, 53 percent opposed and 28 percent favored "the United States getting out of the Viet Nam war completely." At the same time, 46 percent favored trying for some such "compromise agreement with Communist China" as "making all Viet Nam neutral," with 29 percent against doing so. In January of 1965, the respondents of the Gallup Poll affirmed by a margin of four to one their belief that the Vietcong were defeating the South Vietnamese, and by a margin of two to one their opinion that the latter would not be able to form a stable government. Still, by a margin of almost two to one they subscribed to the statement that the United States was right to have become militarily involved. At the same time, 81 percent expressed themselves in favor of President Johnson's calling an international conference with Chinese and Southeast Asian leaders to see if a peace agreement could be arranged, while only 11 percent dissented. In February and March of 1966, a group of behavioral scientists, most of them located at Stanford University, sponsored a survey to find what the deeper attitudes were. Though the questioning, conducted by the National Opinion Research Center, was more detailed, the attitudes uncovered were much the same as those previously reported. For example, 52 percent would favor "a new government in which the Vietcong took some part," 36 percent would not. Offered three choices, 49 percent said they would continue to do in Vietnam as their government was then doing, 23 percent would prefer to fight a major war, and 19 percent would simply withdraw. Some 60 percent would fight a major war if the only alternative to it were withdrawal of American troops. At the same time, 88 percent favored "negotiations with the Vietcong if they were willing to negotiate," while 8 percent opposed them. In general, President Johnson's actions in Vietnam were endorsed by 61 percent and disapproved of by 29 percent, while 10 percent expressed no opinion.

What thoughts lay behind the answers? Did the public perhaps entertain such notions as these — that delaying actions at low cost are worth mounting, that it is well to demonstrate that nothing is free for the taking, but that, all things considered, the time to leave had arrived if leaving could be gracefully arranged? While it is too much to attribute such intricacy, clarity, and precision of thought to the public mind, the state of the people's opinion permitted the President to fashion such an interpretation of America's position should he have wished to. It could not at any rate be said that public opinion constituted a pressing limit upon Presidential action, nor did the warning of the Korean experience lead the government to avoid military involvement. As difficulties in Vietnam multiply, criticism of the government will grow. Indeed, by the spring of 1966, disenchantment had begun to set in. In fairly steady progression, those approving of the way "Mr. Johnson is handling his job as President" declined from 69 percent of those asked in July of 1965 to 66 percent in early November and to 58 percent in March of 1966. If the public standing and moral authority of the administration should gravely weaken, it will be time for a change, whether or not blame has been justly accorded. Obviously President Johnson has been keenly aware of the domestic political risks he was running. To have changed policies because of electoral fears for the future would not have been honorable. Examination of public opinion in periods of crisis has led us to the conclusion that it would not have been practical either. In their foreign policies, governments of all types have sometimes been fainthearted. One need not fear that pusillanimity is especially encouraged by the pressures of public opinion as it operates in the American democracy.

The fears born of the military and electoral struggles of the Korean era have faded. In the 1950's, it was fashionable to affirm that the American democracy would not sustain distant and indecisive military engagements firmly or long enough. In the 1960's it has become more common to suppose that the American government is impervious to criticism and given too free a hand even during protracted periods of crisis. Both worries are important; each has in its day been exaggerated. Two dangers threaten especially. With multiplication internationally of the arenas of major contention, it will become more difficult to remember that American security interests require military engagement only where the adversary is of such strength that he is or may become a threat to the nation. Beyond that, though the margin of power that America enjoys over any other contender may be a source of comfort to her citizens, it may also worry the observer. Powerful nations have often abused their power to the detriment of themselves and of others. More than has been the case with any modern state, the restraint of the American nation must now be self-imposed. A nation as powerful as America may become impatient with the defensive pose it has struck and long maintained. Senator J. William Fulbright has detected in American foreign policy "signs of that fatal presumption, that overextension of power and mission, which brought ruin to ancient Athens, to Napoleonic France and to Nazi Germany." He has warned his country not to become "what it is not now and never has been, a seeker after unlimited power and empire." Is Senator Fulbright premature in his pessimism and unduly alarmed by the experience of war in Vietnam?

In the case of Vietnam, spokesmen for the administration have asserted the vital importance of showing that insurgencies are costly, damaging, and doomed to defeat; they have argued that China must be contained for a time as the Soviet Union was earlier. One may wonder if the assertion and the argument do not rest on an overestimation of Chinese capability, a failure to appreciate the penchant for independence of the Indochinese whatever the political orientation of their governments, and an overlooking of the possibility that any increase in Chinese strength would be more of a worry to the Soviet Union than to the United States. The questions involved are, however, difficult ones on which no light can be shed by demonstrations and little by public debates. Nonetheless, with international restraints pressing less closely, internal correctives become all the more important. The American government is well supplied with them. To critics such as Senators Mike Mansfield, J. William Fulbright, and Robert Kennedy, the administration pays the closest heed; for institutionally and politically their positions are strong. Fulbright's eloquent warnings are not misplaced. It is because of him and other powerful critics that the dangers of hubris are lessened.

One of the valuable qualities of the American political system is the persistence of effective criticism. Opposition to the President's foreign policy has most often since the war centered in the House of Representatives; on questions of foreign aid, for example, it lodged in the Appropriations Committee. In contrast, the Foreign Relations Committee, strong enough to influence the whole Senate, soon converted its members, even those once isolationist, to support of the country's new policies. That was the pattern until recently. In his first years of office, President Johnson showed an unusual ability to keep issues closed, to prevent arguments from occurring in publicly conspicuous places. From February of 1965 onward, from the time when American military forces were first committed to battle in Southeast Asia, however, Senator Fulbright reluctantly permitted his Committee to begin to oppose the President's policies — in Vietnam, with regard to China generally, and on matters of foreign aid. The function of opposing, like the task of providing leadership, sometimes migrates from one political institution to another.

Conclusion

There is no end to one's worries. One who is not busily worried about a possible absence of support for waging limited wars is liable instead to fear that the United States is politically prevented from acquiescing in defeat on those occasions when losing would be the least unhappy of all the unhappy choices. The American reaction to the Chinese Revolution after World War II supposedly illustrates one type of recurrent difficulty: an unwillingness to acquiesce in "necessary" defeats. Unwilling (and sometimes wisely so) to expend the manpower and materiel that a drive for victory would require, the government is also reluctant to say simply that the goal is not worth its price. One may then fear that the American people will be overly eager to fight, ever unwilling to compromise, and thus be able to press a government to rashly adventurous actions. Denis Brogan created a phrase that caught on when he attributed the McCarthyite hysteria of the early 1950's to America's "illusion of omnipotence," understandable in view of her history but unforgivable as the attitude of a country that stood as the leader of the "free world." Internal political criticism first focused on the "loss" of China, grew with Representative Nixon's dramatization of the charges against Alger Hiss, became still more widespread when McCarthy made his flamboyant charges in February of 1950 that there were 205 or 57 or whatever number of Communists in the State Department, and reached a crescendo in the years of the Korean struggle. The frenzied frustration and self-indulgent hysteria of the McCarthy-Korea years could be interpreted charitably as a momentary reaction, a relapse after the vigorous and wholly unaccustomed activities in international policies that the Truman Doctrine, the Marshall Plan, and the formation of NATO represented. They could also be seen as the awkward and erratic responses of a parvenu who did not know how to behave in the international arena. Finally, of course, they could be and sometimes were taken as demonstrations of the proposition that her political institutions and national character make America unfit for a leader's role in the world.

Are the American people hopelessly naïve and in their naïveté a danger to the world? Is America given to vacillation between the poles of international commitment and national withdrawal? Is the American political system incurable without institutional surgery? Taking America's policy toward China as a difficult last example will enable us to suggest answers to these questions and at the same time make summary comments on the present chapter.

Though opinion on the sensitive subject of China has often been contradictory, it has neither been rashly belligerent nor naïve about the causes of American difficulties. Early in 1954, for example, the Gallup Poll asked: "What, in your opinion, are the main reasons that China went Communist?" Seventy-three percent of those polled thought the reasons were to be found in the ignorance of the Chinese masses, the skill of the Communists, and the corruption of the Nationalist regime; 10 percent blamed American policy and traitorous action; 17 percent gave miscellaneous replies; and 23 percent did not know. Though multiple responses to the single question cloud the finding, it is nevertheless some evidence of maturity of political outlook that only 10 percent of the replies ascribed to American officials responsibility for events in China. Asked in April of 1955 whether we should "be friendly to Red China and try to win her away from Russia," or should "treat her as an enemy," 47 percent preferred the first alternative and 40 percent, the second. At the same time, 78 percent opposed China's admission to the United Nations and 65 percent were against trading with her. More recently, 53 percent of those who realize that China's government is Communist opposed her admission to the United Nations (31 percent were in favor); but 75 percent of the same sample would stay in the United Nations "if Communist China gets in," and only 5 percent would thereupon leave. While distaste for the Chinese Communist regime is deep and persistent, 62 percent oppose and only 10 percent favor "helping Nationalists to attack Communists."

If the American people in general are more sophisticated than is sometimes supposed, are they not still in their inclinations dangerously unsteady? Paul Ramsey has recently written that "perhaps because of the Calvinism gone to seed in the atmosphere, and the lack of any doctrine of the Two Realms in which a human destiny is played out, the American people are ill prepared for the self-discipline necessary for the limitation of warfare." His conclusion may once have been true, though not necessarily for the reasons he suggests. William C. Foster, a man of both business and political affairs, seems to have thought so. "We must," he once urged, "attempt to get away from the strange dichotomy with which we have traditionally viewed force, refusing to consider it except as a last resort, then approaching it in a crusading manner with a 'punish the bandit' view which has been prevalent in our recent conflicts." While the religious beliefs of the general public have not changed noticeably since the Cold War began, America's notions of the place of force in foreign policy have evolved as her expectations of an easy international life have dwindled. Samuel Lubell, who is not the most scientific of pollsters but who may be the most perceptive, has drawn a sharp distinction between the typical American reaction of 1952 and of 1962. He reports that in 1952 he found people saying, "I'm against this idea that we can go on trading hills in Korea indefinitely." In other words, they implied, it may be well to strike at the enemy with all the power at our command. Early in 1962, in contrast, he reported the prevalent fear as being that "if we throw a nuclear bomb at them we'll get it back in this country." With the feeling that "all-out war" has become "unthinkable," acceptance of the likelihood of small wars has grown, and so has the willingness to fight them. "It's just a little country," Lubell found some people saying, "but if we let the Reds walk off with it we will be lowered in the eyes of the world."

Ever since 1948, 80 percent or more of Americans polled have replied affirmatively to such questions about Berlin as this one: "Should we stay in Berlin even if doing so means war with Russia?" Should the audacity of the reply cause one to fear that the President may order shots to be fired so that by doing what the people seem to want he will look more like a leader? Or should one think of such responses as indicating a reluctant willingness to fight in situations of tremendous risk if the government should decide that other policies would be riskier still?

For several reasons, it is the latter question that merits an affirmative answer. (1) In an era of Cold War, the American people have not, despite what is frequently said, demanded either victory or withdrawal, though occasionally articulate minorities and a few highly placed public officials have done so. (2) Reluctance to retreat and willingness to fight in order to avoid having to do so are more the product of the international condition of bipolarity than of internally generated political pressures. People *and* Presidents, the public at large *and* the dominant elites have united in their belief that the United States must stand firm in the fact of aggression abroad. (3) One must ask what it means to "stand firm." The actions and words of the President, more than of anyone else, will define for the public this difficult term. To put it crudely: defeats will be described as unimportant and compromises, as triumphs, if it is at all possible to do so. The Cuban confrontation in October of 1962 was said to be an American victory over

Khrushchev — he removed the Russian missiles. But Castro remained in power and a number of the Soviet Union's technicians remained in the country. Khrushchev was able to retreat, which is said to demonstrate that dictators enjoy freedom from internal constraint. But the United States, it should also be noted, was able to settle for something less than the achievement of ends that had earlier been widely proclaimed.

The people react to what the President does, and some of them at least form an opinion of how well he does it. If a President says that we need not fight, as Eisenhower in effect did when the French were besieged at Dienbienphu, no spontaneous rush to the colors is likely. Willingness to fight should not be identified with eagerness to do so. Reluctance to give way should not be confused with a stubborn unwillingness to compromise. It would seem from the record that the mass of the American people have learned to live with danger, to tolerate ambiguity, to accept setbacks, and to understand that victory is sometimes impossible or that it can be gained only at a price the wise would refrain from paying.

Index

Numbers in boldface type indicate major authors and selections in the book.